THE LEO AMERY DIARIES
Volume 1: 1896–1929

THE
LEO AMERY
DIARIES

Volume 1: 1896–1929

Edited by John Barnes and David Nicholson

Introduction by Julian Amery

HUTCHINSON

London Melbourne Sydney Auckland Johannesburg

Hutchinson & Co. (Publishers) Ltd

An imprint of the Hutchinson Publishing Group

3 Fitzroy Square, London W I P 6 J D

Hutchinson Group (Australia) Pty Ltd
30–32 Cremorne Street, Richmond South, Victoria 3121
PO Box 151, Broadway, New South Wales 2007

Hutchinson Group (NZ) Ltd
32–34 View Road, PO Box 40–086, Glenfield, Auckland 10

Hutchinson Group (SA) (Pty) Ltd
PO Box 337, Bergvlei 2012, South Africa

First published 1980

© Julian Amery 1980

Set in Monotype Garamond

Printed in Great Britain by The Anchor Press Ltd
and bound by Wm Brendon & Son Ltd
both of Tiptree, Essex

British Library Cataloguing in Publication Data
Amery, Leopold Stennett
    The Leo Amery diaries.
    Vol. 1: 1896–1929
    1. Great Britain – Politics and government
    – 20th century
    2. Great Britain – Politics and government
    – 1837–1901
    I. Title   II. Barnes, John
    III. Nicholson, David
    941.082′092′4   DA566.7

ISBN 0 09 131910 2

To the memory of Mrs L. S. Amery

Contents

Preface

My father, Leo Amery, kept a diary, spasmodically in the years 1906–14 but then continuously, with only two breaks from 1917 until his death in 1955. It was his usual practice to dictate the entries daily before dealing with other correspondence, though pressure of business sometimes led him to record the experiences of three or four days together. Occasionally, especially in the earlier years, those of two or three weeks were written up from notes in his engagement book.

The diaries were not, of course, written for publication. I have, however, been advised that they constitute what is probably the fullest day-by-day record of the period compiled by any British public figure of the front rank. Accordingly I have thought it right to offer a selection from them and from Leo Amery's voluminous correspondence to the public.

My own political responsibilities have left me no time to undertake myself the task of selection and commentary. I have, however, been very fortunate in securing the co-operation in this task of Mr John Barnes and Mr David Nicholson. They have studied the diaries and correspondence in depth, made the appropriate selections and written the necessary linking passages. Both co-editors have professional academic commitments, both hold First Class degrees in History, and both are involved in politics.

John Barnes was elected to a Research Fellowship at Caius College, Cambridge, immediately on taking his degree, and subsequently became a lecturer in Government at the London School of Economics. He contested Walsall North in three parliamentary elections, was an Alderman on Greenwich Borough Council, and since 1973 has been a member of the Kent County Council. Co-author of *Baldwin, A Biography* (1969), he is also a member of the editorial board of the *History of the Conservative Party* and is contributing the fourth volume covering the period from 1940 to 1974. He is at work also on a biography of Harold Macmillan.

David Nicholson was at Christ Church, Oxford, and served in what is now the Department of Employment. He was for a time on the secretariat

PREFACE

of the Donovan Royal Commission on Trade Unions. He has also been
working on a thesis at the London School of Economics on the Empire
Trade and Protectionist lobby in the Conservative Party during the 1920s.
Since 1972 he has worked in the Research Department of the Conservative Party, at first in its Economic Section and since 1974 as Head of its
Political Section where he acted as a senior adviser to the Shadow Cabinet.
He was the author of several newspaper and periodical articles on the
centenary of Leo Amery's birth in 1973, and is also preparing the fourth
and final volume of *My Political Life* – my father's memoirs – which he left
uncompleted.

My personal contribution has been limited to the introduction which
follows and to giving such broad guidance as I could to the editors in the
light of my talks with my father over many years.

It is hoped to publish the second volume of these diaries in late 1980.
This will cover the period from 1929 to 1955 including the crisis of 1931,
the approach to the Second World War and my father's part in the formation and work of Churchill's wartime coalition in which he served as
Secretary of State for India.

JULIAN AMERY

Editors' Note

Amery's diaries, while spasmodic for the earlier years, almost wholly cover the years 1917, 1918 and 1919 and are again complete from March 1922 until almost the moment of death in 1955. Those from 1918 have been bound into annual volumes and annotated subsequently. Most annotations relate to the period at which he was writing his memoirs (1945–55), and they are not always accurate.

The period covered in this volume is largely accounted for by selections from the diary, but – usually where the diary is unavailable – it has been supplemented from Amery's letters to his mother and to his wife, which necessarily are often terse, and to others. Various letters to him have been included, especially in the pre-1914 period, when they seem relevant, but this volume and its successor are in no sense a collection of Amery's letters and papers.

Sadly, the available diaries and papers for the pre-1914 period have not cast much light on to such matters as the strife in the Conservative Party following Joseph Chamberlain's launching of Tariff Reform in May 1903, or Amery's clandestine activities in organising resistance in England and Northern Ireland to Home Rule in the 1912–14 period. As a result of deficiencies in the papers and the exigencies of space in this volume, the selection in the pre-1914 period necessarily appears somewhat disjointed. Our aim for this period has been to illustrate, so far as was possible, Amery's political beliefs, his personality, his ways of operating, and the beliefs and personalities of certain of his closest allies, like Joseph Chamberlain, Lord Milner, Henry Wilson and F. S. Oliver.

The diary itself was usually dictated to his secretary the morning following the event described, but there are periods when it represents an elaborated account of jottings made in a pocket book or takes the form of recollections made on the basis of an engagement diary. Clear indications have been left in the text to enable the reader to identify which are contemporary entries and which are written after a short delay. Only in 1925 are these entries written up after any great lapse of time, and to all intents and purposes therefore the diary is not influenced by hindsight.

We have been able to publish only a fraction of the original. The seven volumes from March 1922 alone contain more than three-quarters of a million words. The entries remaining are themselves only part of each day's entry, and while omissions in the passages quoted have been indicated by ellipses, the parts of the entry omitted at the beginning or end have not. The reader should realise therefore that Amery's practice was to indicate in each day his activities and whom he saw throughout the day. Many entries, however, do no more than this, merely indicating his visitors and lunch guests with little or no indication of what was discussed. Such lists, while of some interest to the specialist historian, contain nothing worth reprinting here and have been omitted.

What has been retained comprises a virtually complete reproduction of Amery's record of Cabinet business (he was not only a Cabinet minister from 1923 to 1929, but a secretary to the War Cabinet of 1917–18), all of them transactions which bear on the day-by-day ebb and flow of political life. Omitted is the great bulk of departmental business since the entries are so terse that they would have borne more annotation than text, accounts of his activities in the mountains or on the moors, and above all the great bulk of the more personal material.

We have also omitted virtually all accounts of Parliamentary debates except when it seems to provide a flavour missing from Hansard and from contemporary press accounts. Material bearing on Party deliberations, such as backbench meetings, has been retained in larger measure since it is harder to track down, and indeed in some cases, e.g. on Shadow Cabinet meetings in opposition and the origins of the Conservative Research Department, cannot be found elsewhere.

The diaries as presented here inevitably give a one-sided picture of the man, essentially that of a politician with what Vansittart called 'Alpinising energy', arguing with and persuading his colleagues. No doubt this was the Amery that most of them remembered, but the athlete and aesthete, the conversationalist and friend, the author of soundly based fantasies about the Trojan War and thoughtful works about politics and the constitution is now represented here, although we hope to have retained enough to prevent this from becoming a false picture of the man.

Finally, it should be noted that we have kept the original punctuation and spelling, except where Amery's secretary's errors render sense difficult.

Editors' Acknowledgements

First we wish to thank the Rt Hon. Julian Amery for entrusting us with this eminent and highly satisfying task, for putting all his father's diaries and papers at our disposal, and for his advice and encouragement while we have been working on this task.

Secondly, we thank Julian Watson, now with Cassells, publishers, for his work, advice and interest in preparing this volume for publication while he was at Hutchinson, Kevin McDermott for finalising that work, and Sue Major, who prepared the text for printing.

Thirdly, we thank all those who have helped in the immense task of typing even lengthier extracts than appear here: in particular Mrs Paula Dagama Pinto, Mrs Eleanor Barber and Miss Michele Busk, and also all those who have helped in moments of need, including Miranda Bradshaw, Susie Fairlie, Sarah Gurney, Mary Hennikor-Major, Selena Marks, Sue O'Brien, Alison Spicer and Laura Stirling-Aird.

Finally, both editors would like to express their lasting gratitude to Mary Barnes, the one for her lavish and frequent hospitality, and both for her infinite patience over the several years of domestic disruption involved in this volume's gestation.

List of abbreviations

A.J.B.	A. J. Balfour
Austen	Austen Chamberlain
B.	Brydde (Mrs L. S. Amery)
Billy	W. A. G. Ormsby-Gore
B.L., Bonar	Andrew Bonar Law
Bob	Lord Robert Cecil
BR Committee	Belligerent Rights Committee
BWL	British Workers' League
CID	Committee of Imperial Defence
CO	Colonial Office
David	J. C. C. Davidson
DO	Dominions Office
EIA	Empire Industries Association
EMB	Empire Marketing Board
EPA	Empire Parliamentary Association
F.E.	F. E. Smith
FO	Foreign Office
Hamar	Hamar Greenwood
H. of C.	House of Commons
HM	His Majesty, e.g. George V
H.W.	Sir Henry Wilson
IEC	Imperial Economic Committee
IFS	Irish Free State
IO	India Office
IWC	Imperial War Cabinet
Jix	Sir W. Joynson-Hicks
Joe, J. C.	Joseph Chamberlain
K. (of K.)	Lord Kitchener (of Khartoum)
L.G.	David Lloyd George
Lord M.	Lord Milner
L.S.A.	Leo Stennet Amery

LIST OF ABBREVIATIONS

Ned	Sir Edward Grigg
Neville	Neville Chamberlain
NUA	National Unionist Association
O.G.	W. A. G. Ormsby-Gore
OSC	Overseas Settlement Committee
OSO	Overseas Settlement Office
PC	Privy Council(lor)
Philip	Sir Philip Lloyd Greame (later Cunliffe Lister)
PM	Prime Minister
PR	Proportional Representation
PUS	Permanent Under Secretary
Robin	Geoffrey Robinson (later Dawson)
Sam	Sir Samuel Hoare
S.B.	Stanley Baldwin
S. of S.	Secretary of State
Squiff	H. H. Asquith
S.W.	Sir Samuel Wilson
SWC	Supreme War Council
TPC	Turkish Petroleum Company
TR, TRL	Tariff Reform, Tariff Reform League
TUC	Trade Union Committee
TUTR	Trade Union Tariff Reform (League)
Willie	W. C. Bridgeman or Lord Peel (see context)
Winston	W. S. Churchill
WO	War Office
Worthy	Sir L. Worthington Evans
Wullie, Wully	Sir W. Robertson

Introduction

Leo Amery embarked on adult life with no political connections and only limited means but with formidable personal qualities. He had been head of the school at Harrow, won a First in Greats at Balliol and was elected a History Fellow of All Souls. He had a working knowledge of fourteen languages and, before 1914, had travelled widely, not only in Europe, but also in the Middle East, Africa, North America and Australia – a more remarkable achievement for a young man then than it would become in the age of air travel. Though short in stature – he was only 5 ft 4 in. – he had a powerful physique, no small asset in politics, and made mountaineering and skiing his chief relaxations.

Soon after coming down from Oxford, Amery joined *The Times*, becoming their principal correspondent in the South African War and later a leader writer and commentator on military affairs. In politics, Amery at first gravitated to the Fabian Movement, reacting like many young men of his day against the social injustices of the *laissez-faire* system and its failure to mobilise national resources more efficiently. He saw much of the Webbs, Bernard Shaw, H. G. Wells and Halford McKinder and was for a short time private secretary to the radical elder statesman, Leonard Courtney.

With the Boer War he came under fresh influences. The greatest and most enduring was that of Alfred Milner, then Britain's proconsul in South Africa. Milner had developed a conception of how to organise the resources of the British Empire both to further national ends and to improve conditions of life. He was the theoretician of British Imperialism. Through Milner Amery became an honorary member of the 'Kindergarten' and a lifelong friend of such men as Bob Brand, Lionel Curtis, Geoffrey Robinson (Dawson), later editor of *The Times*, and John Buchan. Another powerful South African influence was Cecil Rhodes with his romantic view of the world mission of the English-speaking peoples and his practical belief in the contribution which capitalism could make to that mission's fufilment. The development of South Africa and the creation of Rhodesia afforded eloquent testimony to what capitalism could achieve in the way of material civilisation. The Oxford scholarships founded under Rhodes' will, and which he discussed with Amery before his death, suggested that money could serve even more transcendent purposes.

Amery returned from South Africa with a growing sense of mission. He would devote his life to helping to weld the self-governing colonies and colonial dependencies which made up the rather ramshackle Victorian Empire into an effective Imperial union; united for defence, for foreign affairs, and for trade, investment and migration. He saw in such a union not just a means of national power, individual prosperity or social reform. Here was a civilising mission to which the British peoples could dedicate themselves: one from which they would derive a sense of purpose and a source of pride.

This concept of Empire was much more than a political programme. It was an ideology that constituted a coherent system of thought to which every issue, political, economic, social, cultural and even moral could be related. More than that, it was a faith. This faith would sustain him throughout his life.

In the first phase (1899–1922) of his public career Amery acquired unusual influence as a 'backroom boy'. As a leader writer on *The Times* he soon became a powerful if anonymous advocate of Milner's work in South Africa. From the same pulpit he promoted the reform of the Army in the light of the bitter experience of the Boer War described in detail in the mammoth *Times History of the South African War* which he edited and largely wrote. After 1903 he preached ardent support for Joseph Chamberlain's campaign for tariff reform and Imperial preference. It was Chamberlain, indeed, who eventually in 1911 found Amery a winnable constituency in Birmingham. He was to hold it for thirty-five years.

In the House of Commons Amery took an active part in the controversies of the day but his major political contribution continued to be made behind the scenes. His press campaign for Army reform had made him a number of friends among the military. He thus became the natural link between the Conservative Opposition leaders and those officers, particularly Henry Wilson (then Director of Operations), who were opposed to Irish Home Rule, as was Amery himself. Their determination that the Army should not be used to coerce Ulster culminated in the Curragh Mutiny. Amery's connection with the military over Ireland also made him a natural channel through which the General Staff kept the Opposition leadership informed of the growing threat of German military power.

In the First World War he had little but contempt for Asquith's war leadership and spent most of 1915 and 1916 on active service in Belgium, the Balkans and on the Salonika front. But, when Lloyd George came to power in December 1916, he was, at Milner's instance, made an Assistant Secretary to the newly established War Cabinet. Secretaries though anonymous can wield great influence: Amery made the most of his role. He contributed actively to the formation of the Imperial War Cabinet which brought together the British and Dominion Prime Ministers and their principal colleagues. He played a significant part in the creation of the Supreme Allied War Council under Marshal Foch. He was also much involved in the formulation of British policy towards the territories conquered from the Ottoman Empire in the Middle East, among other things drafting the Balfour Declaration on Palestine. After the war he was given office as an Under Secretary at the Colonial Office where he proved an active lieutenant to Milner.

It was in the second phase (1922–32) of his career that Amery emerged as 'his own man'. As Parliamentary and Financial Secretary at the Admiralty, he found himself increasingly at odds with the Government: Ireland was one major source of difference; another the need to find a positive alternative to socialism. This he held to be tariff reform both as a means of serving the cause of Empire and of attracting trade union support. He accordingly took the lead in organising 'the revolt of the Under Secretaries' which led directly to the break-up of the Coalition and Lloyd George's downfall. A few months later, after the resignation of Bonar Law, he helped to secure the choice of Baldwin rather than Curzon as Prime Minister. Baldwin had long been a tariff reformer and he and Amery had become close friends.

In the Bonar Law–Baldwin Governments of 1922–3, Amery served as First Lord of the Admiralty. He was instrumental in securing the start of the Singapore naval base which he thought essential to offset the Japanese naval threat to Australia and New Zealand. He initiated a new naval building programme and played a constructive role in establishing the revised machinery for Imperial defence.

But his influence went well beyond the confines of his office. It was soon apparent that he rather than Austen or Neville was the real political heir of Joseph Chamberlain. He convinced Baldwin and his colleagues that tariff reform and Imperial preference offered the best and perhaps the only Conservative solution to Britain's economic problems. He accordingly proposed a campaign of some months' duration to prepare public opinion for the changes involved, particularly the increase in food prices. But Baldwin, fearful, with some reason, that Lloyd George might 'steal his clothes' by advocating the same solution, called an immediate general election in December 1923. The result was disastrous with a loss to the Conservatives of eighty-eight seats. The British democracy had rejected the long-debated policies of tariff reform and Imperial preference. The timing of the election might have been Baldwin's; but the policies were Amery's; and his influence suffered. Baldwin, moreover, lost his nerve over fiscal reform and a whole decade was added to the 'locust years'. Looking back in old age Amery would sometimes wonder whether he had been right to back Baldwin against Lloyd George.

In the Conservative Government of 1924–9 Amery became Secretary of State for the Dominions and Colonies, holding the office for longer than any previous incumbent since Joseph Chamberlain. He advocated a far-reaching scheme of Imperial development with Britain as the source of men and money and with the Dominions and Britain as mutually interdependent markets. Preference was to be the link. But he saw also that tariffs could help to solve Britain's heavy domestic unemployment. Anticipating later Keynesian theory he argued that the employment generated behind tariff barriers would spill over into increased demand and so create more jobs in other industries. In the 1920s, indeed, he was among the first active politicians to propose deliberately expansionist economic policies.

Among his more important reforms was the creation of the Dominions Office as a separate establishment from the Colonial Office. Thereafter the Dominions Office became a kind of political secretariat linking the British Government to the Dominion Governments by a continuous exchange of views – largely by telegram – on all important subjects. This did much to induce a common approach to international affairs on the part of the different Dominion Governments. The Dominions Office, indeed, became, with the Bank of England, the basic piece of machinery on which the British Commonwealth was articulated until in the second half of the century it ceased, by a process of dilution, to be in any real sense an effective political power group.

More fundamental to the future of the Commonwealth was the new definition of Dominion status which Amery hammered out with Balfour during the Imperial Conference of 1926. It proclaimed that Britain and the Dominions were 'autonomous communities within the British Empire, equal in status, in no way subordinate one to another in any aspect of their domestic or external affairs, though united by a common allegiance to the Crown and freely associated as members of the British Commonwealth of Nations'. A new phase in the story of the British peoples had begun.

Amery followed up the 1926 Conference by undertaking a tour of all the Dominions with the objects of explaining the new definition of Dominion status and of campaigning for a united Commonwealth based on a system of preferential tariffs. It was the first time a British Minister in office had ever visited all the self-governing Dominions.

Five years as Secretary of State for the Dominions and Colonies made

Amery the acknowledged leader of the Imperial movement. Yet for him these were frustrating years. His main objective of fiscal reform was blocked by Baldwin's pledge not to introduce tariffs or preferences without a fresh mandate from the electorate. Amery tried hard to secure safeguards for particular industries and with some success; but each battle brought him into prolonged conflict with Winston Churchill, then Chancellor of the Exechequer and a convinced free trader. The majority of Conservative Members of Parliament sided with Amery; but the Cabinet was unwilling to risk another appeal to the country on a full-blown programme of tariff reform. As a result, when time ran out, Baldwin called the general election on the uninspiring slogan of 'Safety First'. The Conservatives were duly defeated.

After the defeat Amery took a markedly independent line. He kept in close contact with Baldwin but was critical in public and private of his hesitations over fiscal policy. In this period he worked closely with Beaverbrook. But Baldwin was saved by the gong. The second Labour Government broke up in the financial crisis of 1931, to make way in August for a Coalition led by MacDonald and Baldwin. The new Government was pledged to maintain the gold standard and free trade; and Amery was excluded from it partly as an earnest that Baldwin would not press for fiscal reform. But events soon dictated an about-turn. In the autumn the Government abandoned the gold standard, replacing it with the Sterling Area, and at last adopted tariff reform and Imperial preference. An Imperial Conference followed at Ottawa. Amery was active behind the scenes but his intervention, directed to pushing British Ministers further than they wanted to go, was resented by Baldwin and Chamberlain and contributed to his continued exclusion from office. Ironically it was left to Churchill, the arch free trader, to remind the House of Commons that Amery had played a far more active part in bringing about the fiscal revolution than any of the Ministers who signed the Ottawa Agreements.

Those Agreements, coupled with the creation of the Sterling Area, did much to justify the hopes which Amery had set on tariff reform and Imperial preference. The seven years of peace that remained saw a very marked increase in inter-Empire trade. As a result, the British Commonwealth and Empire recovered more quickly from the Great Depression than any other country or group of countries. Even more significant was the habit of economic and financial co-operation engendered by the Agreements and the creation of Sterling. When war came the Dominions gave Britain unlimited credit. This made a vital contribution to British survival in the bitter early phase of the war (before the Lend-Lease Agreements) when every purchase from the United States and other countries had to be paid for in hard cash. It was to be the same in the scarcely less bitter aftermath of victory when Lend-Lease was cut off and before Marshall Aid was introduced.

In the third phase (1932–40) of his career Amery remained on the back benches of the House of Commons. He championed Eleanor Rathbone's proposal for family allowances. He also supported Samuel Hoare's Bill for constitutional advance in India against Churchill and the right wing of the Party. But increasingly after the abortive Disarmament Conference which met between 1932 and 1934 he grew concerned with the threat to peace in Europe. He had no confidence in the League of Nations and diagnosed that the key to preventing war in Europe was to keep Mussolini and Hitler apart. For this reason he was against the Government's decision to impose sanctions on Italy for invading Abyssinia. He argued that to do so would only drive Italy into Germany's arms. On this his was almost a lone voice in Parliament, though some of the keenest observers of the German threat, notably Vansittart, shared his view.

The pace of German rearmament and Hitler's claim for the return of the former German colonies caused Amery growing concern. The murder of Chancellor Dollfuss by the Nazis in 1934 finally convinced him of the full extent of the German danger and of the need for rearmament. Austrian independence was, as he saw it, the one bone of contention between Rome and Berlin. It must be the British and European interest to maintain it. His views on Austria gained support in the House of Commons but not enough to persuade the Chamberlain Government to stand up against the *Anschluss* of Nazi Germany and Austria. After the invasion of Austria, Amery saw no hope of saving the peace except in rapid rearmament and firm diplomacy. This brought him into increasingly bitter opposition to Neville Chamberlain's policy of appeasement. It also brought him to a closer understanding with Churchill, his old adversary over tariff reform and constitutional advance in India. Churchill was the most eloquent of the opponents of appeasement; but he was deeply mistrusted by the Conservative Party and virtually isolated within it. Thus it was Amery who became chairman of the backbench group of some forty Conservative Members opposed to Neville Chamberlain's policy. Eden joined the group after his resignation from the Government in February 1938. Amery sought to bring Churchill into it. But the bulk of its members, including Eden, were reluctant to agree.

With the outbreak of war in September 1939, Churchill and Eden returned to office. Amery remained excluded and thus became a focus for those Conservatives who felt that Chamberlain was incapable of waging war. Amery was convinced, from the beginning, that nothing but a broad-based National Government could save the country. He accordingly opened a negotiation first with Arthur Greenwood, the deputy leader of the Labour Party, and later with its leader, Attlee, to prepare the downfall of the Government. Britain's defeat in Norway provided the opportunity. In the ensuing debate Amery dealt Chamberlain the *coup de grâce*, closing his speech with Cromwell's words 'in the name of God, go'.

In the National Government that followed Amery had hoped to be given the economic overlordship of the Home Front. Churchill, however, had no intention of sharing power and offered Amery the India Office instead. To many this seemed a curious appointment since he and Churchill had differed sharply over the Government of India Act of 1935. Amery himself feared at the time that he had been sidetracked from the main direction of the war. But the office gave plenty of scope for his energies. India was an empire of its own closely connected with the Middle Eastern and later with the Far Eastern theatres of war. Amery's main task, working with two great Viceroys, Linlithgow and Wavell, was to mobilise the human and material resources of the subcontinent in support of the war. No less important, with the Japanese enemy at the gate, was the need to contain the efforts of Gandhi and the Congress Party to overthrow the Raj.

In these essential matters his Indian administration was eminently successful. His efforts, however, to find a constitutional settlement under which a united India might advance to full Dominion status foundered, like those of the subsequent Labour Government, on the rock of Hindu–Muslim rivalry. Amery came to the conclusion that Indian unity could only be preserved in independence on the basis of constitutional forms very different from the Westminster model and which would have ensured genuine power sharing between religious and racial minorities and the Hindu majority. But neither the Cabinet at home – especially its Labour members – nor the Congress leaders in India were ever prepared seriously to contemplate this.

India and those battle areas where Indian forces were engaged absorbed Amery's main energies throughout the war but as a member of the Cabinet he was naturally involved in other spheres as well. He fought a long battle in the discussions over post-war economic policies where he feared that American economic imperialism and 'anti-Colonialism' would threaten the very existence of the Commonwealth and Empire. He was also among the first to diagnose the threat of Soviet imperialism to Eastern Europe.

In the general election of 1945 Amery lost his Birmingham seat. He was then aged seventy-one and, despite a number of inquiries after a seat, never returned to the House of Commons. Nor would he accept a peerage. There were no life peerages then; and he feared that to go to the House of Lords must prejudice the political prospects of his son, myself. Even so, he did not retire from the political arena. In the last phase

17

(1945–55) of his life he reverted to the 'backroom' role of his youth. Working through the Empire Industries Association and a group of Conservative backbenchers he masterminded the Conservative campaign against the Washington Loan Agreements and those sections of the General Agreements on Tariffs and Trade which proscribed any extension of the system of Imperial preference. His views, expounded in speeches and books, found widespread support in the House of Commons. Resolutions promoted by him were carried at successive Conservative Party conferences.

The Conservatives returned to power in 1951 pledged to stay *in* the Suez Canal zone and to get *out* of GATT. In the event they reversed the prepositions deciding to stay *in* GATT and got *out* of Suez. American pressures and Commonwealth apathy had proved too strong for them. In 1954, for the first time since 1903, the Conservative leaders at the Annual Party Conference opposed a resolution in favour of Imperial preference. A vote was taken and the tariff reformers were beaten. Amery's defeat that day – he had spoken powerfully in the debate – marked the virtual end of the campaign launched at Birmingham by Joseph Chamberlain half a century before.

The retreat from Empire continued in other fields notably with Eden's decision, taken in the same year and against Churchill's better judgement, to withdraw from the base in the Suez Canal zone. A meeting called by Amery in his house contributed powerfully to the formation of the so-called 'Suez Group' of MPs and peers who decided to oppose the withdrawal from Suez.

Over Imperial preference and over Suez, Amery was fighting rearguard actions. But in another sphere he was among the pioneers. Already before the war he had given support to Coudenhove-Kalergi's movement for a united Europe. He had not envisaged, then, that this new Europe should comprise Britain but rather that the Commonwealth and the European continent should combine in close alliance. After the war, however, he recognised that Britain alone could no longer offer the Commonwealth all the investment, markets or migrants which it needed. Nor could Britain make the same contribution to Commonwealth defence as in the past. In a world where the standards of power were set by the United States and the Soviet Union there seemed to be only one way to renew British strength and meet the needs of an expanding Commonwealth. This was to bring about a junction between the nations of Western Europe. If Britain and those nations could be harnessed together they would form an industrial base strong enough to provide the markets and the investment for which the developing countries of the Commonwealth and the French Union were looking.

When, therefore, in 1946, Churchill called at Zürich for a united

Europe, Amery came out in full support and became an active vice-president of the United Kingdom Council of the European Movement. His belief that the cause of the Commonwealth and the cause of Europe were not only compatible but complementary reconciled many Conservatives to Churchill's European initiative. It helped to prevent what might otherwise have been a serious split in the Conservative Party.

Amery's concept of Europe was akin to General de Gaulle's 'Europe of States'. He never thought a European federation likely. His experience of the Commonwealth had taught him how strong were the national loyalties even of young countries speaking the same language. Europe, he judged, might need rather stronger institutional bonds than the Commonwealth, but he declined to be dogmatic about these, believing that Europe would develop constitutional forms of its own not yet perceived by the theorists.

What is Leo Amery's place in our political history? Disraeli was the patriarch of the Imperial movement; Froude, Seeley and Dilke its prophets. Joseph Chamberlain and Milner were, in their day, its unchallenged leaders. After their deaths the mantle fell on Amery. He was effective in debate and powerful on the platform though hardly Joseph Chamberlain's peer in political leadership. But he was at least Milner's peer in intellect and far more vigorous in pressing his policies. The combination of qualities was formidable. Others, of course, made their contribution: Neville Chamberlain by right of descent and Beaverbrook as the ablest publicist of them all. But from 1922 until his death Amery was the philosopher and leader of the Imperial movement.

His personal contributions were many and varied. Cabinet memoranda, speeches in the House, popular journalism and skilful pamphlets all served their turn; above all the ceaseless badgering of his colleagues. But there were also articles and books of more transcendent value and some of the ideas advocated in his *Thoughts on the Constitution* are still very much the subject of debate.

Among his miscellaneous achievements must be counted the securing in 1925 of the Mosul oilfields, then the greatest after the Persian, for the British protectorate of Iraq, the encouragement of a Jewish national home in Palestine and the creation of the Empire Marketing Board – Britain's first venture in overseas aid.

But his most original contribution was to the development of a new Commonwealth concept. Joseph Chamberlain and Milner had thought loosely of a federal Empire. Amery knew the Dominions too well ever to believe they would accept the loss of sovereignty involved in a federal system. They had travelled too far along the road to nationhood. At the same time he believed that, given an effective economic and financial framework, like-minded nations could be brought to work very closely together in foreign policy and defence, in trade and investment, in science, health, education and the arts. He saw this co-operation as primarily inter-governmental and organised through the Dominions Office and the Bank of England. But the action of governments would need to be buttressed and seconded by active groups such as the Commonwealth Parliamentary Association, the Royal Empire Society, Rhodes House, the Overseas League and the Commonwealth Press Association.

Amery regarded this concept of Commonwealth as a more advanced form of co-operation between states than the eighteenth- or nineteenth-century concepts of federation and confederation. He thought it better suited to an age of strong nationalist emotions and one marked by continued growth in the role of central governments. He would some-times illustrate the point by arguing that it was much easier for London and Canberra to adopt a common policy than for Washington to carry the support of the Eastern and Western seaboards of the United States. This was because the British and Australian Governments, once agreed on a policy, would know how to sell it in the terms best suited to their own public opinion. An American president by contrast could speak only with one voice when announcing his policy from Washington.

Amery regarded the Commonwealth concept as naturally suited to the British Empire with its common British heritage. But he went further, believing that the Commonwealth could well be extended to include like-minded foreign countries. He also held that the example of the Commonwealth might well prove relevant to the development of a united Europe.

As a coherent military, political and economic system the British Commonwealth declined rapidly after the withdrawal of the Suez expe-dition in 1956. The flames of Arab and African nationalism were already being fanned by Communist propaganda and in part, at least, by American policy. After 1956 the British and French Governments bowed to this new force. Within a decade of Amery's death little remained of the structure to which he had dedicated his life.

This does not mean that his life's work was a failure. Shakespeare was right when he made Mark Antony say of statesmen that 'the good is oft interred with their bones'. From the Boer War until the time of Amery's death the nations of the British Empire and Commonwealth together constituted a great power in world affairs. In two world wars, in the Great Depression between the wars, and in the aftermath of the Second World War they managed by their co-operation to defend the cause of freedom and to advance the prosperity of their peoples. Amery made a massive personal contribution to this process over an active career of more than sixty years: this was no small thing. Since then the vision of a united Commonwealth has faded. But something may yet rise from the ashes. If the nations of Europe are to join forces effectively enough to offer an alternative pole of attraction to the super-powers they will need to do so in voluntary association with some at least of the countries they once ruled.

What of the man himself? His culture and philosophy were rooted in the classics and his reading of history. He drew his strength and inspiration from the mountains. He was a scholar but he was also a mountaineer. The scholar in him and his training on *The Times* led him to pack too many points into his speeches, a defect which, with his lack of theatre, diminished his immediate oratorical impact even if it added strength to his argument. The mountaineer in him gave him a certain pugnacity. Like a good general he was careful to understand the strong points as well as the weaknesses of an adversary. But once he had made up his mind, he smote his opponents hip and thigh with a single-mindedness and disregard for their sensitivities which often startled and sometimes shocked. Though essentially a constructive thinker, he had, in fact, an unusual power to destroy. He may yet be best remembered for his part in bringing down the Lloyd George Coalition and the Neville Chamberlain Government.

For the most part his pugnacity was confined to political invective and polemic pamphleteering. But not exclusively; he was the last Privy Councillor to punch another Member who had impugned his honour and knock him down on the floor of the House of Commons!

When Amery died, Churchill said of him that 'he was above all a great patriot'. But there was nothing insular or chauvinistic about his patriotism. Perhaps because of his gift of tongues he seemed equally at ease in the capitals of Europe, the bazaars of the Middle East or the wide open spaces of the 'outer Empire'. He had no prejudices, social or racial, and though he set himself high standards he did not expect to find them in others.

The diary extracts published in this volume are almost wholly concerned with Amery's political activities. This is partly for reasons of space and partly because the more interesting or diverting incidents in his personal life have already been told in his two volumes of non-political memoirs – *Days of Fresh Air* and *In the Rain and the Sun*. In private life he had a wide circle of friends though few cronies. He was sociable with an abiding curiosity in new people and new ideas but not gregarious or 'clubbable'. He seemed equally happy alone or in a crowd. Young people were naturally drawn to him not because he cultivated them but because he treated them, as he treated everyone, as if they were his contemporaries and almost his colleagues. He enjoyed the good things of life when they came his way but with a marked indifference to their absence. Even in old age his energies seemed boundless and, when no more urgent theme occupied his mind, he would devote the time to classical or philosophical studies or even to the writing of poetry and fables.

He was exceptionally lucky in his marriage to my mother, Bryddie Greenwood. She was a Canadian of United Empire Loyalist stock and easily identified with his own strong Imperialist faith. But she was also the sister of Hamar Greenwood, a Liberal Member of Parliament and Minister in much of the period covered by this volume. This relationship helped to bridge the gulf of political partisanship and to keep personal relations with friends in the opposite camp in good repair.

Bryddie Amery played a full part in Amery's election campaigns and did more than her fair share in guarding his constituency base. She worked on Lord Milner to defend her husband's interests when he was overseas during the First World War and entertained for him on a generous scale both in and out of office. The diaries show, and my own recollection confirms, that in his years at the Colonial Office her receptions during 'the season' were attended by at least 150 guests every week, drawn partly from overseas and partly from British public life. She accompanied my father on their strenuous tour of the Dominions in 1927 and kept up a voluminous correspondence with friends and acquaintances throughout the Commonwealth. When my father returned to office as Secretary of State for India in the Second World War she became a very active chairman of the India Comforts Fund, a charity devoted to the welfare of Indian troops and prisoners of war. In addition, and despite the problems of rationing, she kept open house in London throughout the war largely with the help of food parcels received from friends they had made throughout the Commonwealth – an uncovenanted but no less welcome return on their work for the Imperial cause!

She bore my father two sons, my elder brother John and myself. We were still both schoolboys in the period covered by this volume and the story of John's tragedy belongs to later years.

To me Leo Amery was father, friend and teacher, and unfailing in each capacity. I can only hope his diaries will convey something not only of his ideas and actions but also of his personality to those who knew him less or not at all.

JULIAN AMERY

I

Balkans and South Africa
1896–1902

In the late 1890s, when Leo Amery graduated from Oxford, he was presented with a brief opportunity for travel which, as with most young men then, seemed likely to be his last. The Middle East, then ruled by Turkey, was still relatively inaccessible, but the Eastern Question had been in 1855 the cause of Britain's last continental war, and constantly threatened to plunge her into further hostilities during the 1870s and 1880s. Having been elected to a Fellowship of All Souls, Amery chose to pay a short visit to Constantinople in the Christmas vacation of 1896. With felicitous timing, he arrived there shortly after six thousand Christian Armenians – who formed much of the trading class in Turkey and were consequently regarded as a dangerous fifth column in the capital and Asiatic Turkey – had been massacred in the streets by groups of boatmen and ruffians. The immediate occasion for this foretaste of the more determined attempt at a 'final solution' by the Turks during the First World War was an abortive effort by a group of Armenian revolutionaries to blow up the Ottoman Bank.

L.S.A. to his mother, from the Pera Palace Hotel, Constantinople, 17 December 1896

The morning being fine I started out with Demosthenes my dragoman for a tour of sight seeing in Stamboul. . . . I talked a good deal with Demosthenes about political affairs. He knew of the Ottoman Bank affair a few hours before and took refuge on a French steamer. . . . I went to the *Hammam* [Turkish Bath] afterwards, a hot dark place where a grinning little Turkish lad scrubbed me with a rough glove and soaped me with a great square cake of soap. A very wretched looking Armenian helped me dress: the poor fellow has not yet got over the terror [in which] his brother and other relatives were killed and he himself was only saved by the compassion of his fellow Turks in the *Hammam*.

[*Added, 18 December 1896*] We drove together to the *Selamlik* [the

23

official parade to the Friday morning prayers] and a glorious sight it was. The appearance and bearing of the Turkish soldiers impressed me a great deal. I believe these are the only ones in the Empire that ever get paid. The Pashas I liked less: they were heavily decorated, largely I believe for brave acts of espionage. The great sight, of course, was the Padishah [Abdul Hamid II], the Shadow of God upon earth. . . . With him sat old Osman Ghazi, the Lion of Plevna,* a fine looking old warrior. It was very impressive to hear the great shout of salute with which the Sultan was greeted, still more impressive to think that almost all that vast assembly would be overwhelmed with joy if someone could but succeed to destroy him.

L.S.A. to his mother, 20 December 1896

Today . . . went for a row up the Golden Horn to Eyub. . . . Our boatman was a cheerful young ruffian and told us some things about the massacres of last August which though they did not surprise me brought the horror of the present tyranny very clearly to my mind. I asked him why they had massacred the Armenians and he replied because they had high orders to do so, that his brother, an officer, told him that it was the Sultan's command. And this jolly *caidji* of ours confessed to having cut the throats of twenty-seven Armenians with his own hands.†

L.S.A. to his mother, 29 December 1896

I have decided to remain where I am and not move into Stamboul‡ as the Pasha can find no family bold enough to take me in and face the dangers of being inflicted with spies and police supervision for ever afterwards. . . . I lunched at a Greek monastery belonging to the Patriarchate of Jerusalem and after lunch visited the Greek Orthodox Patriarch with whom I had a long and vigorous discussion in ancient Greek, which I found somewhat difficult to comprehend at times owing to the difference between modern Greek pronunciation and the pronunciation we are taught at school.

L.S.A. to his mother, 1 January 1897

I have made the acquaintance of Sir Howard Vincent, M.P., a nice old fellow but very ignorant and quite surprised that I should learn Turkish and get about among the native population and go to mosques, etc.

*He had held Plevna, now in Bulgaria, against the Russians in the war of 1877.
†This was undoubtedly the man who Amery, in his memoirs, recalls displaying a gold watch: ' "It was given to me by an Armenian gentleman," he said, with a horrible reminiscent leer' (*My Political Life* (Hutchinson, 1953), I, p. 69).
‡i.e. The old city: L.S.A. was staying in the Pera Palace Hotel in Beyoglu, the 'European' quarter, north of the Golden Horn.

On his return from this visit to Constantinople, Amery obtained from C. P. Scott, the editor of the *Manchester Guardian*, a free hand 'to write as many articles as I chose about anything and everything between Vienna and Constantinople' (*My Political Life*, I, p. 72). After various articles on Austro-Hungarian affairs, Amery moved into Serbia and Bulgaria (both then much smaller than at present) and European Turkey, which then covered much of modern southern Yugoslavia, Albania, and northern Greece. Extracts from his letters to his mother give a remarkable description of the atmosphere in these Turkish dominions, where the native Christians were in a state of latent revolt.

L.S.A. to his mother

From Uskub (modern Skopje), 19 January 1898:   At the frontier the Turks collared my revolver (at least one of them, the other being luckily in my pocket) and my cartridges. . . . However, I hope to get both ammo and revolver back through the Vali . . . I saw the Vali this morning and going to dine with him tomorrow. He is a Kurd and a fair rascal I have heard say.

From Prizrend, undated, January 1898:   All this country is Albanian but they are milder here and to some very slight extent under the control of the Government. Of course the Government dare not tax them as that would provoke a revolt. . . . Even in this lax country though the Vali thought fit to attach to my person two mounted cavaliers. . . . In addition the Vali has given me a permanent companion in the shape of his own private dragoman who follows me as a faithful Sancho Panza and dogs my steps wherever I go. Poor fellow, he is fairly well meaning but horribly afraid of my doing something too bold. The Vali has attached him to me to some slight extent as a compliment, mainly in order to spy upon my movements and prevent my sowing sedition or whatnot and also in order that the poor fellow who probably has not received pay for months may get a tip and set himself up in new clothes.

From Uskub, 30 January 1898:   I have just come back from my little excursion into the borders of Albania. Any chance I might have had of running into danger was prevented by the Turkish Government which absolutely refused to let me go anywhere. At Prizrend I had a regular row with the authorities and for a day or two the whole machinery of Government was thrown out of order because I announced my intention of going to Luma which is a district reputed very savage. The whole police of the *Sanjak* [Turkish administrative district] were called out to prevent my escaping. . . . I went to the Vali this evening to curse him but I could do very little against his confounded Turkish politeness.

3 February 1898: I am still in Uskub waiting for special permits to travel in the region where the oppression of the Bulgarians has been taking place. I am just sending off a letter to the *Manchester Guardian* describing some of the things I have myself witnessed.

From Uskub, early February 1898: It is not the natural attractions of Uskub or the claims of its muddy streets that detains me here so long. The fact is that the journey I intend making to investigate the recent barbarities in this neighbourhood is meeting with the greatest opposition here. The Vali who since I announced my intentions has treated me with the most studied insolence refuses to let me go and although I have wired Constantinople and already received an answer two days ago that the necessary orders had been given, he denies that he has received it.

    [*Later*] This afternoon two Bulgarians who came to see me in the hotel were dragged off by the police and a police commissary has been sitting in the hotel all the evening.

6 February 1898: All night the police have been marching up and down outside my house so now I have wired to be put provisionally under Austrian protection.

9 February 1898: On Sunday [6 February] three persons, a peasant, a woman and a schoolboy from the Bulgarian Gymnasium here, whose father, a priest, is in prison and was I believe badly tortured, were seized at the door of the hotel by the police. I was upstairs but as soon as I heard of it I ran after them and when I came up with them I asked their names so that I might be able to find out afterwards if they were imprisoned for any length of time, or merely examined and let go. While doing so I was seized by a commissaire of police who tried to drag me away. As the scoundrel had no right to touch me I broke my umbrella over his head (the only weapon I had on me). The *Zaptieh* [Turkish gendarme] and another man rushed for me: luckily the commissaire had enough sense to prevent the *Zaptieh* clubbing me with his rifle which he was just engaged in doing. . . . The Vali on his side is bringing up a trumpery criminal charge with false witnesses to condemn me on the charge of an unprovoked attack on the police and interference with the discharge of their duties. I was summoned this morning to present myself for trial today. . . . Through Mr Pisko [the Austrian consul] I politely but firmly declined to have anything to do with the Turkish courts. The Vali is doing all he can to avoid an investigation into the recent Bulgarian atrocities and get me away from Uskub. . . .

This afternoon I heard that M. Matoff, head of the Bulgarian Gymnasium here, and M. Maroff, head of the Bulgarian Girls' School, have been imprisoned for the crime of having been seen once or twice in my company and having sent some poor people to see me. Owing to want of room in the prison they have been confined, I am told, in a filthy cell which serves as a w c to the rest of the prison. Can you imagine anything more awful for two men of refinement and education. . . . I cannot very well leave Uskub until I am assured these two poor men are again at liberty. . . .

I forgot to tell you that the Vali accused me of being a paid agent of the Bulgarian secret revolutionary societies at Sofia.

[*Later, 11 February 1898*] Since writing the above I decided suddenly to go to Constantinople via Salonika and personally complain to Currie. When I got to Salonika late last night Heathcote, late of Balliol now Vice-Consul, met me and told me that twenty minutes after my departure from Uskub a telegram had come from Currie saying that Eliot, his second secretary, was coming tomorrow to investigate the whole affair and that I should return to Uskub at once. The Vali is already, I hear from Pisko, getting terribly frightened and if Eliot acts anything like a man, the worthy Hafiz Mehmed Pasha will have a bad time of it. Perhaps Eliot may even make a tour of inquiry through the troubled district with him which would be a very good thing. . . . About four gendarme spies went down to Salonika with me yesterday: of course they never calculated on my returning so suddenly and now they are kicking their heels feeling rather foolish. I find everyone in Uskub especially in the Bazaar takes such a tremendous interest in me since the affair with the police commissaire. The Bulgarians are as happy as if each one of them had dared to thrash an officer themselves and regard me with mixed admiration and awe. The Turks have spent the last week talking together about killing me or throwing me into the Vardar over the bridge, but they have not the least intention of doing so.

From Uskub, 13 February 1898: Since my last letter Mr Eliot from the Embassy has come and settled my affair with the Vali – at least in so far as the trial against me is to be promptly dropped and I am to be allowed to travel back to Sofia along the route of my own choosing, and lastly that the masters imprisoned on my account are to be released.

Amery later quoted a sequel to these developments as an example of how even the capacity of the press to exaggerate can be exceeded, because the written word is finite, by rumour spread by word of mouth. The following autumn, travelling in the neighbouring *Sanjak* of Novibazar, he was greeted by the story of the previous winter's Macedonian insurrection, the climax of which was the saving of the insurgents from extermination by an Englishman of gigantic stature – Amery was only five feet four inches tall – who, armed only with a club, had routed two Turkish battalions.

In the spring of 1898 Amery travelled with F. E. Smith, the later Lord Birkenhead, whom he had met briefly at a Harrow entrance scholarship examination; they were later contemporaries at Oxford, both becoming Fellows of All Souls. They proceeded to Venice, by sea to Athens and thence to Asia Minor but unfortunately no record of this journey survives in Amery's papers. That summer he toured the Dolomites, Croatia, Bosnia and Herzegovina, from where he sent articles to *The Times* on the Austro-Hungarian administration of the last two provinces. While in Cetinje, the capital of Montenegro, he was telegraphed by *The Times* to proceed to Crete, then torn by a successful revolt against Turkish rule.

C. F. Moberly Bell, the manager of *The Times* newspaper, asked Amery to assist Sir Valentine Chirol, its foreign editor, and he started regular work with the newspaper early in 1899. On 22 August he was despatched by Bell to South Africa to report on what was expected to be the peaceful settlement between the British and the Boers of the problem of the Uitlanders, who wished for more political rights and more economic development in the Boer republics. By the time he arrived on 11 September, the situation had deteriorated. After visiting both Sir Alfred Milner, the High Commissioner, and Cecil Rhodes, former Prime Minister of Cape Colony, he moved to Bloemfontein and Pretoria where he met the Boer chiefs, including Smuts – who was to become a life-long friend, ally, and correspondent.

Amery hoped to become *The Times* war correspondent on the Boer side in the coming war, and so he moved to their headquarters at Sandspruit on 6 October. The Boer ultimatum was sent to the British on the 9th and on the 11th General Joubert's Boers advanced on Ladysmith. Joubert, however, had to withdraw his permission to allow Amery to stay 'in order to prevent something uncivilised happening', and Amery was obliged to remove speedily to Cape Town, where he found himself in the position of chief of *The Times*' war correspondence service. Over the following months he regularly wrote to Chirol in London from Cape Town both privately and for publication in the newspaper.

For a month, Amery visited the front in Natal, and through over-sleeping missed being captured in the famous armoured train with Winston Churchill, who was then the *Morning Post*'s war correspondent. He had to return to Cape Town and thus missed the battles of Black Week (10–15 December), Lord Methuen's defeat at Magersfontein and Sir

Redvers Buller's defeat at Colenso. Mafeking, Kimberley, and Ladysmith remained invested, but once again the Boers were not strong or bold enough to push south into Cape Colony where they had a potential fifth column.

The British command of the seas ensured the despatch of massive reinforcements, and also of Lords Roberts and Kitchener who arrived in Cape Town on 10 January 1900 to take over as supreme commander and as chief of staff respectively. Roberts launched an attack in February; on the 15th, after a flank march, the British entered Kimberley; on the 27th Cronje, the Boer commander, was forced to surrender at Paardeberg. The relief of Ladysmith, and later of Mafeking, followed, although Boer guerrilla warfare continued for nearly two years.

Rt Hon. L. H. Courtney to Moberly Bell, 6 August 1898

I sent the said Amery to you last Christmas twelve months, since which he has become more famous. His adventures in Macedonia assumed the importance of an International episode, and his article in the current *Edinburgh* [*Review*] on the situation in Austria-Hungary shows at once the extent of his knowledge and the sobriety of his judgment. I think if you took him over, it would be very much to your advantage and I recommend it for your sake more than his. . . .

Though he was with me a working year I can't say I thoroughly indoctrinated him with my own sentiments. He has a certain stubborn quiet pugnacity.

L.S.A. to his mother, 10 October 1898

Just arrived at Athens after three days' voyage from Cattaro. The coasting along the Albanian shore was rather interesting – my desire to penetrate into that curious country is only increased.

L.S.A. to Sir Valentine Chirol, 4 October 1899

I am off to the Natal border today and I hope General Joubert will give me permission to correspond on his side. He would give no definite answer the other day on the ground that there was no war yet. Still I live in hope.

L.S.A. to his mother, from the Boer Camp, Sandspruit, 6 October 1899

Arrangements here are not very military from the point of view of drill and pipe clay, but there is a good deal of rough and ready efficiency, and if the war does come off, I dare say the Boers will give a good account of themselves. They are all very confident of victory, especially the real Boer, who I can picture to you best as a Swiss guide on horseback with a rifle over his shoulder instead of rope and axe.

L.S.A. to Chirol, 25 October 1899

The one thing vital is not to let the natives get out of hand and, if they do, suppress them ourselves before doing anything further to the Boers.

I have had talks with Milner as to future and he certainly is for nothing less than annexation of Transvaal, though he hesitates a little about [the Orange] Free State. Annexation of both seems to be the only thing. But there can be no talk of a *Dominion* for *years* and years after the annexation – not until you have a large English majority in Transvaal and a fair-sized English population in Rhodesia.

L.S.A. to Chirol, 25 November 1899

These letters have run two blockades, for after I had got them at Estcourt, Estcourt itself was cut off the South by the Boer forces and I had to ride through on a stormy night to get them down here for the mail. It was a most excellent adventure. I got a local farmer to go with me and he took me all over the country, up steep hills and through innumerable steep ravines and flooded rivers with absolute certainty in the inkiest of pouring nights, and finally led me right between two Boer camps not 400 yards apart. Within 300 yards of another camp we had to dismount and cut a barbed wire fence and had scarcely remounted before we saw a sentry. We were off at a hard gallop at once before he could even guess where the sound came from, and luckily were three-quarters of a mile away before my guide's horse came a cropper.

The incapacity, indecision and timidity displayed by our Commanding Officers is something awful. They are always on the defensive, always on the point of scuttling out of any position if twenty Boers can be seen about. At the present moment 6000 men at Estcourt and 5000 at Mooi River are both 'invested' by and in mortal terror before some 3000 Boers. The soldiers are tremendously overworked and get precious little sleep, all for nothing. They are continually marched 10 or 12 miles to look at a small party of Boers and then hastily retreated. Not half enough use is made of the knowledge of local people – only now are they beginning to organise a body of scouts. . . . Outside my window two Colonials are discussing the war and their contempt and bitterness in talking about our military authorities would surprise people in England if they could realise it.

Anyhow the facts of the military situation up to date have been: (1) that our soldiers are brave and their rifle shooting is as good as the Boers; (2) that we have not half enough mounted men and a very poor intelligence department; (3) that our artillery has been hopelessly outranged throughout and almost useless; (4) that our Commanding Officers are like babies, absolutely helpless, planless and undecided, at the same time very disdainful of any suggestions made by colonials. . . . I say all this in no factious spirit, but I really feel the thing is terribly serious. If we muddle along much longer there will be a general outcry all over South Africa: 'give us peace at any price and remove your damn censors and incompetent supercilious officers.'

L.S.A. to G.E. Buckle (undated)

The conduct of affairs here have been most feeble and inefficient. No proper scouting, even picketing insufficient – I rode slap into the middle of Estcourt some night ago from Frere and was never challenged. The panic and indecision of the Staff here on Tuesday when 200 Boers or so appeared 6 miles off was simply sickening. . . . All day long they telegraphed backwards and forwards . . . whether they should scuttle or not.

L.S.A. to Chirol, 11 December 1899

If this war settles the unity of South Africa (as did the American Civil War) and if it also breaks the back of the War Office, it would have conferred two incalculable benefits on the Empire. If the military people had not been so hoity-toity and self-sufficient we might have raised 20,000 mounted infantry in this country worth at least 50,000 of Tommy Atkins. As it is it is the local contingents and the naval guns that have saved us from utter catastrophe. Tommy is brave but painfully slow to move and difficult to feed sufficiently, without natural military instinct and a sheep without his officers. What we should have done if the Boer strategy had been as clever as their actual tactics heaven only knows. In every engagement we have been outgeneralled. . . .

. . . as I told you in my last letter expenses in this country are terribly heavy. I see no way out of it for you but to start a new encyclopaedia. Or shall I write you a history of the Transvaal War? A good solid standard work with lots of diplomatic and military information, largely embodying what has appeared in *The Times* throughout, backed by confabs with Milner and others – a work 'which we can recommend in half morocco'? The idea has only occurred to me this moment as a joke suggested by the encyclopaedia, but on second thoughts I am not sure there isn't something in it. One might lay hands on some good military men to write chapters – which could appear in *The Times* first. Or of course I could write it all myself which for me would be easier but perhaps less appropriate for *The Times* – unless it were anonymous, otherwise people might scoff at my military criticism.

L.S.A. to his mother, from Cape Town, 14 December 1899

For all I know I may not be back till April if this war lingers on as bad generalship in many cases, the vastness of the country, and the bravery of the Boers makes it seem quite likely. You see *The Times* must have some sort of manager and general director here to look after correspondents spread over half a Continent. I have a clear dozen correspondents under me in South Africa and a free hand to appoint or dismiss as I like. I have also to keep *The Times* politically informed. The only person they could send out to take my place is Chirol and I think it would be a mistake to change while the thing is halfway through. It is a great experience for me, and I meet any number of interesting men.

L.S.A. to Chirol, 17 December 1899

I heard a good story from George Peel tonight. After Modder River he went over the battlefield and amidst all the graves of our dead he saw one grave and on it the inscription written by some Tommy: 'One Boer'.

L.S.A. to Chirol, 19 December, 1899

Another awful mistake of ours is the way we let the existence of the railway completely paralyse our movements. The railway induces a mental paralysis on all our Generals: it is so simple and obvious to stick to it – to improvise other transport requires thinking out afresh as it was not in the original programme and so it is not done. . . . Our warfaring hitherto may be summed up as composed of periods of timid unintelligent inertia varied by blind rushes like those of a bull at a gate.

L.S.A. to Chirol, 9 January 1900

London* by the way avers that the only order Methuen ever gave at Modder River was the order to retreat which luckily miscarried, or else Pole-Carew and his men across the river would all have been left as prisoners. At Magersfontein there were no orders.

Our whole army system wants changing root and branch. Our army is rotten with favouritism and antiquated stupidity. Our drill and tactics want revolutionising.

*Perceval London was *The Times* correspondent with Lord Methuen, commander of the British force on the 'western front' in the Transvaal.

L.S.A. to Chirol, 23 January 1900

The new chiefs* have very quickly put a new life into everything. Under the thoroughly incompetent management of Forestier Walker,† the whole campaign was rapidly degenerating into a series of little border wars. . . . Walker had a big opportunity of making his name and hopelessly missed it – that, practically, is what Roberts said to me in a short interview I had with him last week. As for Kitchener, the shrug of the shoulders and the grunt he gave when I touched on the subject spoke volumes. . . . He is extremely obliging and genial to everybody, military and civilian. He is absolutely unafraid of responsibility which most of our officers fear far more than Mauser bullets, and contemptuous of red tape which most of them worship like a fetish. . . . Somebody asked him if he didn't intend reorganising the transport arrangements. 'No, I am going to organise them.'

All the same, Roberts is by no means a mere figurehead. All the important decisions are made by him.

Army reorganisation is going to be a tremendous question. It is not a mere matter of detail, of improved artillery and a few alterations at the War Office, but a complete revolution in the whole character of our Army. This means a social revolution – the Army must be democratised and, at the same time, made an expert Army; each private soldier should be a picked man capable of looking after himself and of understanding the meaning of a battle. The rank and file of our regular army will have to be of the class of superior mechanics – real experts. The whole of the regular Army must be just a cadre for filling up in times of stress with volunteers who know how to shoot straight, every half a dozen of them looked after by one of our experts. Our Regulars of course will have to be long service, anything up to 25 or 30 years. And there must be a complete change in the whole Army spirit. The whole caste system, the whole idea of the Army as a sort of puppet show where smartness, gilt braid and gallantry play the leading role must vanish and give place to something real, something business like.

Has Bell talked to you at all about my suggestion of a *Times* History of the Transvaal War based largely, but not exclusively, on the work of our special correspondents? If decided on it should be decided on soon to prevent all the correspondents writing huge books of their own.

L.S.A. to his mother, 1 March 1900

I had rotten bad luck with my up-country trip this time in that I missed

---

*Field Marshal Lord Roberts and General Lord Kitchener.
†General Sir F. W. Forestier Walker, Commander at the Cape.

the great battle of February 18 [the successful attack on the Boer positions south of the River Tugela] and only got to Paardeberg after Cronje was wounded. . . .

I camped close by the river and we used to sit at breakfast in the morning and watch the dead horses and cattle float by. At one time we had 15 caught in a projecting tree just under our camp and the smell of them was something terrible. Our drinking water was strongly flavoured with dead horse.

L.S.A. to his mother, 13 March 1900

I see a certain amount of the Kiplings with whom I usually sit at the same table and find Rudyard K. fairly amusing at times.

L.S.A. to Chirol, 26 March 1900

[Princess Radziwill] is a worshipper of Rhodes and conceives she has a great influence over him and hates Milner because she thinks Milner cold-shoulders Rhodes and tries to keep him in the background. As to her influence over Rhodes I don't know – but Rhodes told the Union Company before leaving last week that he would postpone his voyage if she took a berth on the steamer and so I believe the Company put her off on the pretext that every cabin was engaged. Nevertheless, Rhodes seems to confide a good many things to her – perhaps merely out of indiscretion. She also corresponds a good deal with [Lord] Salisbury (so she says).

L.S.A. to his mother, 1 April 1900

It is only perfectly natural that the pro-Transvaal people [in Britain] should be unpopular. In no other country would they ever even have been suffered to exist. Just imagine conciliation meetings in Germany while the 1870 war was on! And out here the so-called 'conciliation' people flaunt Transvaal badges openly.

L.S.A. to Chirol, 3 April 1900

The little reverse we have suffered just now near Bloemfontein will perhaps teach the good public at home that the British officer is still as great a fool as ever and that there are very few who you could trust alone with a thousand men if there were 50 Boers anywhere within 10 miles. . . .

I don't think people at home have sufficiently realised the stupidity of the army is not merely concentrated in the generals but is an all pervading atmosphere. . . .

I think the Mandarin system* is getting intolerable. The only thing to do is to withdraw all Imperial questions from the Commons. A radical alteration of the Lords might do something. Limit England to a fixed number of elected peers and create so many new ones as to swamp the territorial aristocracy in the voting, include all the Privy Council in the Lords, *ex officio*, and have peers for each colony. And then gradually create the constitutional practice that all matters of Imperial concern should be discussed first in the new Lords and be passed without too much questioning by the Commons, much as money Bills are passed by the present Lords. Then you would have an Imperial Parliament with the English Commons possessing a veto (gradually no doubt decreasing) over Imperial matters. You could also add Colonial men of importance to the Cabinet – the body has no constitutional existence and there is nothing therefore to say who shall or shall not be on it. And last of all you must have some Imperial contribution or Imperial tax, small to begin with but gradually increasing. Whilst you have that the House of Parliament which contains the Colonial Representatives will also have the power of the purse – as long as they have no power of the purse the Commons who have will assert themselves too much. The Commons once thoroughly weakened by the withdrawal of all the Imperial politicians to the other House, will split up quite comfortably and naturally on the Moderate and Progressive lines; viz. semi-socialistic, cheap education and cheap locomotion and housing Poor party versus the party who object to having taxes which fall on themselves – lines which exist already but are confused with Imperial and other questions. Once the Commons are thoroughly parochial Home Rule has lost all terrors.

But why should I bother you with vague talk in execrable handwriting?

L.S.A. to Moberly Bell, from Cape Town, 8 May 1900

I have come in freely for abuse, I see by the papers, for my suggesting that all is not for the best in the best of all possible armies. The *South African News* here calls me every term of abuse except pimp – a word it reserves for Rudyard Kipling.

L.S.A. to Chirol, 15 May 1900

Rhodes has gone off to Beira with a lot of pigs and fowls and bulls to stock his country [Rhodesia] with. He is going to offer the Bushmen a capitation grant to encourage them to stay and is also going to construct irrigation

---

**'Mandarin' was an expression favoured by Milner and his followers. It denoted not so much Civil Servants as dilettante and unimaginative statesmen.

THE LEO AMERY DIARIES

works. I have been allowed to look at a confidential letter of his to Milner on the whole subject of colonisation in which he urges it as the best form of military occupation and as the only means of curing racial feeling by bringing Dutch and English into actual contact. . . . In dealing with some details of the division of settler colonies into individual agricultural and common grazing land, he refers to Lycurgus' land distribution in ancient Sparta and chaffs Milner about helots in a playful vein which I had no idea existed in C.J.R.

L.S.A. to Chirol, 7 July 1900

We have done one good thing towards conciliating the Dutch: that is, we have shown our resolve not to let the natives get out of bounds. We enforce the pass laws, we repress looting. . . . My own idea of the settlement of the native difficulty is to encourage native self-government in local matters, and eventually even have a sort of House of Assembly, able to legislate on matters concerning natives, subject to a veto of the White House.

In Basutoland the natives practically have a sort of Parliamentary Government, and representative institutions work well amongst the Kaffir race everywhere – if they are left to themselves. But in a White Election they are a mistake. They are treated by both sides to turn a disputed election. But if they ever ventured to try and agitate for some measure benefiting their status as against the white man, the farce of political rights would soon be put an end to, just as in the Southern States [of the USA]. A white legislature would be much more tolerant and reasonable towards the just demands of a black assembly than a white electorate to Kaffir voters. . . .

The whole future of the native question will probably lead to a sort of caste system. In politics, business, education, etc. there will be a gradual equalisation and intercourse, but there will be no social intercourse and no marriage to any great extent except in towns where half-breeds will always be common. The right thing will be to keep the sexual and social part of this caste system as strict as possible and otherwise do everything towards greater equality. I mean there is no reason why someday a Kaffir of ability should not be a leading South African statesman respected and all that, but not invited to meet white ladies and still less to marry them. Just so in India many Rajahs even are low caste and however honoured in their own way would never defile a Brahmin mendicant's pot of rice by touching it. . . . No doubt as in India the racial distinctions of the castes will decrease. In five hundred years' time I expect the South African white man will contain a strong dark blend, and the end of all things may be a brown South African race, comparable to the Abyssinians or Somalis.

That doesn't matter, what does matter is that there should not be too quick a mixture now or for the next few centuries. South Africa must develop as a white man's country under the guidance of white men, and not as a bastard country like most of South America.

Amery's criticisms of the organisation of the British Army bore fruit in two respects: first, in the line he took, or encouraged others to take, in the mammoth *Times History of the South African War*, which he edited, and second but later, in constant pressure for army reform. The eventual *Times History* was published in six volumes in collaboration with various assistant editors and Amery later estimated that he gave '5 years of solid work out of the nine during which I was actively engaged on the task' (*My Political Life*, I, p. 158). Whatever the success of the exercise in educating Amery in military affairs and enabling him to press his case for army reform, it did not produce for Moberly Bell the financial sums he required. To a claim by Amery that a wounded officer had had the *History* read to him by his wife, Bell replied with a cutting recording the death of the same officer 'after long sufferings heroically endured'. On the other hand Lord Roberts wrote to Ian Hamilton that he had been reading Amery's chapter on the battle of Colenso: 'It is enough to make a dead man turn in his grave, and the worst of it is that every word of it is true.'

The war dragged on until, with the publication of Volume II of the *History* imminent, Amery departed in April 1902 for South Africa to act as *The Times'* correspondent for the peace negotiations and collect more material for the next volumes. He later reflected (*My Political Life*, I, p. 161) on how speedily the war in open country could have been ended had aircraft been employed. However, in 1901–02 the British had had to resort to lines of barbed wire and blockhouses in dealing with the few thousand mounted Boers remaining. These methods also involved the gathering together of the Boer fighters' families in what became notorious as the first so-called 'concentration camps'.

Peace was, in fact, signed at Pretoria on 31 May 1902. The terms included the annexation of the Boer Republics and the surrender of all Boers in arms, while those who took an oath of allegiance to the King were allowed to go free. On the other hand, £3 million was given to the Boers as compensation for the destruction of their farms, the Dutch language was allowed in the schools and courts, and Britain undertook to grant a civil administration.

L.S.A. to his mother, from Pretoria, 24 May 1902

The negotiations have been interesting but I have not been allowed to write anything at all. Kitchener keeps a very strict censorship on the press and lets nothing go through. I tried the other day with a long wire, but though I argued with him for some time it was no good. I rode out to Irene Concentration Camp the other day and was tremendously impressed by the arrangements made for the health and happiness of the people there. They are fed most liberally and everything possible is done to amuse and cheer them up. The schools in these camps are doing a wonderful work for the Boer children, who are eager to learn and progress wonderfully. I shouldn't wonder if the concentration camps won't have done more to reconcile the Dutch to England than anything else.

L.S.A. to Moberly Bell, from Pretoria, 19 June 1902

K[itchener] has departed in a perfect halo and Johannesburg which a month ago was grumbling at him, was completely captivated by his speech the other night. Do you know he is realising £9,000,000 by sales of blockhouses, barbed wire entanglements (the troops have been compelled to unravel these and roll them up), captured and other stock, old rations and God knows what. I have no doubt that if the war had gone on a year or two longer K. would have declared a dividend.

2

Army Reform and Tariff Reform

1902–05

Amery returned from South Africa in October 1902 and for the next two years was engaged on Volume III of *The Times History*. Volume II had ended with an account of 'Black Week', the succession of defeats in December 1899, and the new volume began with an analysis of the impressions and lessons provoked. In his memoirs Amery explained that he wrote these judgements confidently, not only because he had been in South Africa at the time and had 'steeped myself in my subject', but because 'my conception of my task was in essence propagandist – to secure the reform of our Army in preparation for coming dangers' (*My Political Life*, I, p. 192), and he cited Russia's aggressive plans in the Far East and the doubling of Germany's battle fleet.

Brodrick, the Secretary of State for War, had put forward a scheme for Army expansion in March 1901 which now faced criticism in Parliament, especially from a group of Conservative MPs known as the 'Hughligans' because their leader was Lord Hugh Cecil. They included Winston Churchill, elected for Oldham as a Conservative in 1900. In January 1903 Amery and Churchill dined and discussed a series of speeches Churchill was to deliver on Army reform. The two differed, however, on the economic future of the Empire. When in May 1903 Joseph Chamberlain raised the standard of tariff reform, Churchill left the Conservative Party for an initially profitable twenty-year exile in the Liberal Party. As Amery later wrote, 'his patriotism has always been for England . . . the other, newer conception, that of the Commonwealth as the object of a wider patriotism . . . has never seriously influenced his thinking, his eloquence or his actions' (*My Political Life*, I, p. 196).

Amery's *Times* articles that spring on Army reform were later republished under his own name in a book, *The Problem of the Army*. He had argued that what was needed for Britain's strategic commitments was a

Regular Army of high quality, highly trained and mobile, so that it could be despatched to any threatened point. There had to be a clear separation between it and the local defence forces of the United Kingdom. If a continental war appeared likely (this was the year before the Anglo-French *entente*), Amery insisted that such a war would entail the training of the nation's whole manhood.

A particular point that Amery took up at this time was the establishment of South Africa as a service station for the home-based Army – an idea indicated by climate, training space and nearness to both the Middle East and Germany's African colonies, the strategic danger points outside Europe. A weekly series of letters to Lord Milner in South Africa in February and March 1903 and another one of 24 May casts a fascinating light on his methods of lobbying for this, and his view of the need for a 'Prussian general staff' to run the Government and administer the Empire. He was ultimately unsuccessful because the Government had been paralysed by the tariff reform split.

At this time Amery came into contact with Lord Esher, a member of the Royal Commission inquiry into the South African war, who in November 1903 was appointed chairman of a committee of three to reorganise the War Office. Amery had given evidence to the Royal Commission on 24 March. 'We had the evidence of that clever little fellow – Amery – today. . . . He has seen a good deal and got a great amount of information from officers, but has often naturally been misled as to facts,' Esher wrote. 'He is full of intelligence.' The other members of the committee were Admiral Sir John (later Lord) Fisher, then Commander-in-Chief at Portsmouth, and Sir George Clarke who became the first secretary of the new Committee of Imperial Defence.

The Esher Committee's report (published February 1904) was an important landmark in British military history. It recommended a more formal organisation of the Committee of Imperial Defence (CID), the creation of an Army Council, the appointment of an Inspector-General of the Forces, the reorganisation of War Office Finance and a more decentralised system of territorial Army commands. Over the next ten years Esher rendered vital service as a permanent member of the CID and was chairman of many of its sub-committees.

Amery was only slightly involved at this time with the conflict over the control of the Indian Army between the two great imperial proconsuls, Curzon and Kitchener. Kitchener, as Commander-in-Chief, wanted to end civilian interference by abolishing the post of military member of the Viceroy's Council, while Curzon, the Viceroy, wished to play the military member off against the Commander-in-Chief. Both pulled strings at home. In fact *The Times* generally supported Curzon, and Amery received a ten-page letter from Kitchener protesting about this. After a compromise in

Kitchener's favour which simply gave the military member the title of Military Supply Member, and an attempt by Curzon to get his way by appointing an energetic general opposed to Kitchener, Curzon resigned in August 1905 when the appointment was refused by the Cabinet and the Secretary of State.

Well before the change of Government at the end of 1905 Amery had become less concerned with military organisation than with the problem of expanding the numbers of the armed forces, and in the summer of 1905 Milner, now returned from South Africa, persuaded Lord Roberts to initiate a campaign for universal military service. This led to the foundation of the National Service League. Amery did much speaking himself and also wrote many of the speeches Roberts delivered in the House of Lords and elsewhere.

For a year after the articles on Army reform Amery remained the military correspondent of *The Times*, but upon the outbreak of the Russo-Japanese war in February 1904 he obtained the services of Colonel Repington for writing the almost daily articles then required. At the start of 1905 Repington finally replaced him as *The Times'* military correspondent and from then on Amery began to expand his activities in other areas, notably in politics.

In the early months of 1903 the position of the Unionist Government seemed secure, while the Liberals were bitterly divided between the anti-Boer war majority under their leader Sir Henry Campbell-Bannerman, and the Imperialists led by Rosebery, Asquith, Grey and Haldane. Sidney and Beatrice Webb were encouraged by the hope that some, at least, of the latter might join with the more progressive Unionists to think that such a combination might assist in implementing their ideal of a welfare state. Thus originated the 'Coefficients', a dining club which the Webbs set up in November 1902. It initially included Haldane and Grey, who were Liberal Imperialists, W. A. S. Hewins, a Unionist and later Director of the London School of Economics, and Leo Maxse, editor of the *National Review*. Among its other members were such names as Bertrand Russell and H. G. Wells, who described the 'Coefficients' in his novel *The New Machiavelli*. The character Crupp, based on Amery, explained his credo: 'We have got to pick up the tradition of aristocracy, reorganise it and make it work.' To 'Crupp's' evident approval, a colleague remarked: 'The British empire is like some of those early vertebrated monsters – its backbone is bigger than its cranium. . . . Germany is beating England in every matter upon which competition is possible.' He and his colleagues were up against 'that old middle Victorian persuasion that whatever is inconvenient or disagreeable to the English mind could be annihilated by not thinking about it'.

Like his original, Crupp was intense and practical. 'We want to get hold of the handles, and to do that one must go where the power is, and give it as constructive a twist as one can. That's my Toryism.' Did his Party colleagues share this rather 'Prussian' Toryism? 'No, but theirs' is soft, and mine is hard – mine will wear theirs' out.'

This strange combination was however soon to be divided down the middle by the raising of an issue which, as Amery later wrote, was 'the summons to a new and glorious task in the world of politics'. Joseph Chamberlain had already as Colonial Secretary emphasised the need to develop the vast territories which Britain possessed and which she was colonising. Even in May 1902 he forecast the need for change in the existing fiscal system known as free trade (i.e. free interchange of commodities between nations without the intervention of import duties, quotas, or other restrictions) – both to protect British home industries and to give the colonies a preference on their imports. It was hoped that a gesture might be made by the preferential revision of the existing and exceptional revenue duty on colonial corn, and it was afterwards revealed that the Cabinet had later provisionally agreed to this. However, Ritchie, the Chancellor of the Exchequer, who was a Unionist free trader, abolished the corn duty altogether in his 1903 Budget. Chamberlain reacted with a speech in Birmingham on 15 May 1903, in which he suggested the desirability of extending preferences on colonial imports, and seeking to protect British industries against foreign competition.

Although dubbed 'protection', and its supporters 'protectionists', by Liberal and other free trade critics, the new creed involved much more than the defence of the vested interests of home manufacturers or even the jobs of industrial workers. By seeking to give Dominion agriculture preferential access to the British market, Chamberlain was proposing both the economic development of the various parts of the Empire and their drawing together in closer economic co-ordination. The parallel was drawn at the time with the German *Zollverein* of the early nineteenth century, which had without doubt hastened German political unity, and a modern parallel, though different in important respects, would be the European Economic Community. As Chamberlain told his Birmingham audience: 'It is an issue much greater in its consequences than any of our local disputes. . . . You have an opportunity; you will never have it again.'

Chamberlain's programme was known by its supporters as tariff reform. Its immediate effects were disastrous for the Unionist Party. A controversy was started which was to occupy Amery's energies for the years immediately following and again in the 1920s, and was not to be finally resolved – with the belated victory of tariff reform – until 1932. Chamberlain was its first victim: he resigned office on the grounds that he could best promote his case from outside the Cabinet, but unaware of his resignation various of the chief free traders simultaneously offered theirs.

The weakened Government never regained the initiative in face of the Liberals, reunited by the threat to their main ideological 'sacred cow'.

Amery kept no diary during this exciting period, and his surviving letters bearing on the subject are relatively few. Letters to his mother tell of a gathering of fellow tariff reformers to ensure that the wider, Imperial economic development side of the tariff reform drive was not overshadowed by the emphasis given by industrialists and their employees to its more insular aspect, industrial protection. This group became known as the 'Compatriots'. Strife in the party intensified. The more aggressive Chamberlainites organised pressure against free trade Unionists and succeeded in removing some of them as candidates for the next election.

Amery spoke for supporters of tariff reform at meetings all over the country. In February 1905 Chamberlain suggested his name to the Liberal Unionist Association* in East Wolverhampton, a sufficiently 'safe' Liberal seat for Sir Henry Fowler, the sitting member, to have had an unopposed return in the Unionist landslide of 1900, although it was not until April that Amery was summoned to be examined by a crowded meeting and selected. The issue was soon to be put to the test: on 4 December 1905 Balfour resigned after months of paralysed government and Campbell-Bannerman was able to form a government, despite Unionist hopes that Asquith, Grey and Haldane would refuse to serve. Led by Asquith, however, they took their places and the most disastrous general election for the Conservative and Unionist Party since 1831 ensued.

Winston Churchill to L.S.A., 24 January 1903

I have read with great pleasure and almost entire agreement your two most interesting articles in *The Times* [There follows a long list of detailed criticisms] ... I think the articles have created very favourable impressions and your attempts to be very nice to Brodrick and to prove that he is the greatest War Minister since Lord Cardwell are, on the whole, the most damaging part of the attack.

L.S.A. to his mother, 27 January 1903

Winston Churchill was here last night to discuss army reform questions with me. I was quite surprised to find how much he let me talk and how readily he listened to my suggestions on some points. It was only at rare intervals that he addressed me as if I were a public audience.

*The Liberal Unionist Party was composed of those who had broken with Gladstone over Home Rule for Ireland in 1886.

L.S.A. to his mother, 9 February 1903

Ian Hamilton sent me a letter of Kitchener's a few days ago (this is strictly private) in which K. said 'I have written to Brodrick about the Council of Defence which he wishes to reorganise, and told him that the important thing is to get a first rate secretary for it. I have suggested Amery of *The Times* for the job as I know no one better fitted for it' or words to that effect. I don't suppose Brodrick will offer me the post.

Churchill to L.S.A., 10 February 1903

I wish you would jot down on a slip of paper the gist of your arguments about the neglect of the War Office to have a number of our officers instructed in Japanese and familiarised with the Japanese troops. I think that this was such a good point, that it would come in very well in the House of Commons, if you will generously make me a present of it.*

L.S.A. to Lord Milner, 20 February 1903

Whether what I have done has had much effect I cannot tell yet but I heard from a friend in the House yesterday that the re-assembled members were discussing my article hard. The whole War Office have also been working like Trojans ever since the articles appeared on getting together a sort of counter-case. . . .

Besides writing I have also for some weeks been discussing with Beckett, Winston Churchill and other Army Reform MPs and bringing them round to this South African business which they were originally not very sound on . . . I almost wish I were an MP and had powerful lungs. I also made Ian Hamilton write to Kitchener five or six weeks ago to tell K. to write home to Brodrick that he would abate his demands for an increase of the white garrison in India if he could be assured that a large and well-equipped expeditionary force would be kept in South Africa and I believe that K. has done so or told Ian Hamilton that he would do so. . . . Balfour's declaration about the Committee of Defence sounds good as far as it goes and may yet become the beginning of great things. I see a dim vision of the Empire run as far as policy goes by a great council (not great in numbers) representing purely thinking and intelligence departments (commercial and diplomatic as well as military intelligence), in which as far as administration was concerned each part remains self-governing as before – the underlying principle of the Prussian general staff system being applied to the whole of Imperial policy.

*This was a year before the Russo–Japanese war.

Howbeit, at present Balfour's recognition is only one of principle. Six or eight gentlemen round a deal table cannot do much effective strategy unless they have got sufficient men behind them to work their subjects up for them.

Milner to L.S.A., from Johannesburg, 25 February 1903

I need hardly say I have read [your article in *The Times*] with the greatest possible agreement – enthusiastic agreement on the main points . . . but with an unshakable conviction that there is not the least chance of a change so radical or requiring so much imagination and contempt for 'practical difficulties' being carried out by the present lot or by any possible successors. The other side are quite too hopeless on all these subjects. They can only babble of 'peace', 'retrenchment' and hold up old maidenly hands to the ceiling 'the terrible growth of militarism' . . . 'Joe' could do it, but Joe is already over-burdened and his visit to S[outh] A[frica] has certainly *not rested him* . . . as for myself, *no thank you*. I much appreciate the compliment but I too am *weary*, to the point of weeping at my already existent work, let alone taking up another labour of Hercules.

Henry Wilson to L.S.A., 26 February 1903

By God's grace *you* have lit a fire (and not a candle) on which much nonsense and makebelieve will be burnt, and by the light of which the true path may be selected. Now don't let the matter drop. Serve 'em up 'ot and 'ot like potatoes or chestnuts!

L.S.A. to his mother, from All Souls College, 9 March 1903

I went to see Arthur Balfour yesterday morning to talk to him about my Army views. I came at 12.30 and talked an hour and then stayed to lunch. He wanted to go off and play golf, but I swore it would rain; he then wanted to go and hear Lord Raleigh lecture, but I got him into a chair and like the Ancient Mariner fixed him with my glittering eye, and talked at him till four o'clock. He was to go down to the Rothschilds that evening where he was going to meet Ian Hamilton and talk over army matters with him. He didn't know, poor fellow, that I.H. and I knew of this and had prepared a joint scheme of attack upon him.

L.S.A. to his mother, from London, 9 April 1903

I had only a very short talk with Joe on Monday (about troops in South Africa) as he had a Cabinet meeting but he told me he agreed with me on most of my Army views – had in fact come to nearly the same conclusions himself – and asked me to do some notes for him on the question of the advantages of S. Africa as a Station. Don't say anything about this as Joe wouldn't like it to get about that he has been consulting an outsider about these matters instead of listening only to Brodrick.

L.S.A. to Lord Milner, 24 May 1903

I believe the prospects of the South African Army are improving, in fact the thing is very likely to go through now. Joe tackled the subject soon after he came back and was met by Brodrick with a flat 'impossible' and with the statement that all the military experts were against it. Joe saw through this and asked leave to talk to Ian Hamilton. Hamilton played up well. After this first talk Hamilton and myself concocted a memorandum which he sent Joe and Joe showed to Cabinet. Result: Hamilton called up before a small council of Joe, Balfour, Ritchie, Brodrick and Roberts (I am not sure now if Selborne or Devonshire were there). From his account H[amilton] distinctly scored off Brodrick in the presence of the others. Next stage, Joe concocts a memo. About this time I see Joe (I should explain of course that my day to day confabulations with Hamilton over all this is unknown to anyone except ourselves and you when you get this) and Joe shows me his memo. It was excellent, none the less so because I recognised my own phrases here and there, though I really smiled when Joe explained a point to me with the help of the little arithmetical illustration that I had devised for Hamilton a few days before. Next stage Joe leaves me the memo to make notes on: I concoct some thirty pages of foolscap which Joe takes away for Easter holidays working out some of the financial points etc. Result second and final memo by Joe which has gone round Cabinet. It is highly secret, but Hamilton tells me it is excellent and covers all the ground. My latest advices are that Brodrick has practically given in and that only Roberts is still inclined to hold out. If it is really so I do not give Bobs more than three or four days against Joe's attack.

Diary, as reconstructed from pocket book in 1950

19 May 1903: Dined with Edward Grey at 22 Grosvenor Road. This was after Chamberlain's famous [Birmingham] speech and I remember making an impassioned appeal to Grey not to reject Chamberlain's ideas and finding him very sticky.

L.S.A. to Lord Milner, 20 June 1903

I am afraid the question of the Army in South Africa has been completely over-shadowed by the great issues raised by Mr C[hamberlain] and I doubt if we can now reckon on the same amount of support from him. Still the thing is under way. . . .

I am very annoyed with our Liberal Imperialist friends. Quite apart from the question of developing the Colonies by preferential trade, it seems to me impossible ever to get the Colonies really interested in our foreign policy and consequently ready to take their part in it or contribute towards the necessary armaments while that foreign policy is so largely directed by the peculiar economic interests of our free trade system. What I mean is that our system, which has néglected the market within the Empire, which has allowed itself to be shut out from Europe and America, depends for its continuance upon the limited open markets still left in countries like China, etc. So when in a very natural sort of way Russia spreads over into Manchuria, a really large section of such trade as we still have is threatened with extinction, and we have to threaten war to keep her out of a country we have no desire to control ourselves, a thoroughly unsatisfactory policy. We can only bluster or cave in for we have no power to keep the door open to us in Manchuria by the peaceful and friendly pressure of tariff retaliation.

The Australian or Canadian has no interest in this policy and he has no intellectual sympathy with it. He is not going to circumscribe his liberty of action or tax himself in order that we may carry this free-trade-by-force-of-arms policy out a bit more effectively. . . . It is no use at present telling the Australian to subscribe to the fleet in Eastern waters when he knows it is kept there not for his defence but to menace Russia and compel her to keep the open door for Lancashire cotton. . . . Not feeling quite strong enough to keep the door open in Europe by threat of force, [England] tries to do so elsewhere by forcibly retarding the expansion of other Powers. The policy has increased our armaments and our territory enormously in the last twenty years. I believe if we had gone in for Imperial Preference in the 'forties we should now be a second United States in many respects both as regards prosperity and as regards armaments, but we should not be holding Nigeria or Uganda.

How the Cabinet is going to split up nobody can say yet. Arnold Forster is throwing himself on J.C.'s side with tremendous vigour and enthusiasm. Lansdowne spoke excellently the other day. Others are mostly sitting on the fence. . . . Of the Press, *The Times* and the *Daily Telegraph* are going strong, the other Unionist papers rather wobbly or even veiledly hostile. *Spectator* almost as hysterical as the *Daily News*. Leo Maxse radiant with joy and hope, walking on air with visions of the temple of Mandarindom being broken into on every side.

Forgive me for inflicting so long a letter on you.

John Buchan to L.S.A., 25 July 1903

I see from Reuter that you have been writing to *The Times* to air heresies on the Tariff question. I don't think you are right, and I feel that this whole business complicates and confuses the question of Federation. My only hope is that when Joe is beaten in the Country, I may have leisure in Opposition to hammer out some coherent policy, and we may go back in two years' time with [Imperial] Federation as an intelligible Party Policy.

Lord Esher to L.S.A., 9 September 1903

I received this morning a telegram from the King at Balmoral, in which HM draws attention to the very interesting letter of 'Civilian' [a critic of the Esher–Amery proposals for Army reform] and then goes on to say 'any reply from you would be inadvisable and a great mistake, as it would involve you in a discussion which I think would be highly irregular in a member of a Royal Commission'.

As you are aware I myself had 'me doots' but after this expression of opinion, you will agree that I cannot write a reply in my own hand.

Now the question is what shall we do? Will you (in *The Times* leader) deal with the question? Or will you print the enclosed which I have concocted. . . . You will have to decide.

Meanwhile I want to tell you confidentially the King has returned from Germany *very keen* about the scheme, that he has seen Arthur Balfour, and he had got him to say that the Cabinet will take up the question at once. The King pointed out the impossibility of meeting Parliament again without a scheme for W[ar] O[ffice] reform. All this is good.

Rudyard Kipling to L.S.A., 11 November 1903

As regards Joseph [Chamberlain] it seems to me that he is doing remarkably well for himself in the fiscal line. The main point for the next year at least ought to be army reform, because when a man has not any food he can if properly trained be in a position to steal it, whereas if he is not trained to steal, his position becomes embarrassing if and when he cannot get any food.

Admiral Fisher to L.S.A., 2 December 1903

This afternoon I happened to remark to Lord Esher (who has been staying with me and not knowing that he knew you) how greatly I admired *The Problem of the Army* of which I have ventured to print a precis for private circulation and he seemed to think you might like to accompany him on his next visit to me on December 11.

Leo Maxse to L.S.A., 24 December 1903

I have just been able to squeeze a quite inadequate note to the *National Review* advising people to read your book. I really can speak very highly of it, because when dog tired last night about 3 a.m. it kept me awake. The chapters that I particularly fastened on, viz. the need for an Imperial Staff and the problems of the War Office, are extraordinary good. . . . I wonder when I read their speeches whether our public men ever give themselves any time either to read or to think.

L.S.A. to Arnold Forster, 15 January 1904

May I make one or two casual suggestions with regard to the war that looks like coming off in the Far East?

One is, that in addition to the ordinary military and naval attachés you should send out several officers with South African experience to start at once on the spot on getting together materials and opinions for a history of the Russo–Japanese war for the benefit of the British Army, bringing out its main lessons for us.

The second is that, as after all there is always a possibility, however remote, of our being dragged in ourselves, you should without delay get confidential agents at work in Finland, Poland, the Caucasus, Southern Russia, and perhaps Turkestan, to study the lie of the land and get in touch with the revolutionary elements, so that if the necessity should arise we might know where and how we could best help an outbreak.

The Caucasus is, to my mind, specially important. Any operations against India must for a long time to come be mainly based on Tiflis [capital of Georgia, in the Russian Caucasus], and a serious movement among the Armenians might paralyse all operations from that base for months.

L.S.A. to his mother, 31 January 1904

Our little political dinner the other night was a great success and I expect a league of enthusiastic [tariff] reformers will soon be set on foot. The company on Friday night were Maxse, Garvin (a remarkably able fellow who writes for the *Daily Telegraph*), Mackinder, Hewins, Arnold Ward, Gwynne (Reuter's chief correspondent in South Africa), Saxon Mills, a journalist, Sir T. Cuninghame, a soldier, and Gerard Craig Sellar.

L.S.A. to Milner (in South Africa), 26 February 1904

The last week or two has been giving us a splendid example of the impossibility of running the Empire by the British democracy in the

House of Commons. If you had not had a Government already very shaky, and an Opposition thirsting for the spoils and still more for new cries on which to get in, you would never have heard anything about the Chinese labour Ordinance. As it is, the thing has been worked with a vengeance. . . . I did think you had got Asquith straight on the point, but I am afraid the temptation, with office looming so near and wall paper for 10 Downing Street already selected by Mrs A., was too much for him, and his performance was as bad as anybody else's, if not worse. Haldane won't speak, because he says he is too suspect with his own party.

I have been engaged . . . lately in trying to get together a small League or Association of people who think constructively and Imperially and are prepared to defend their views in speech and print. . . . So far, though there has been plenty of revolt against laissez-faire and Little Englandism, there has been no coherent general intellectual output to put in its place. . . . At present, no doubt, we shall mainly think and worry about the economic side, but there are lots more in the background, from compulsory service and the demolition of the Treasury to the construction of an Imperial Council and the putting of the House of Commons into its proper place. If we get on at all, I hope you will join us when you come back. Our present numbers are about thirty, and we are limiting ourselves to fifty *pro tem.*, and may increase later.

Fossils, even if 'whole hog' Chamberlainites, protectionist manufacturers, Parliamentary place hunters, and all that clan, will be as far as possible kept out.

L.S.A. to A. J. Balfour, 27 October 1904

In view of the present trouble and what may come of it, if not this week at any rate in the next decade, has the Defence Committee at all considered the possibility of getting Sweden to join us in an attempt to rescue Finland from the Russians?

But regarding it as a purely military question, you will observe that, looking at the map, Finland is most extraordinarily defensible for any Power that holds the command of the sea. And of the actual land front with Russia, the only point against which the Russians can easily bring troops in any numbers is the narrow strip facing St Petersburg. . . . The merit of the scheme is of course that it strikes at the very heart of Russia, and, as long as a hostile army is at the gates of St Petersburg, India will be safe, and the Japanese will be able to do what they like in Manchuria. . . .

I do hope you will give the subject some consideration. It is really astonishing how weak the Russian military position on that side is.

A. J. Balfour to L.S.A., 3 November 1904

Your letter on the subject of Finland is profoundly interesting. I have not been able, as yet, to go over in detail with my military advisers the steps of your reasoning, but it is quite obvious that should hostilities break out (as I hope they will not) between us and Russia, your scheme is well worth consideration.

Kitchener to L.S.A., 21 September 1905

I have so seldom written to you that I need not apologise for inflicting you with such a letter, and I feel sure you will consider what I write as quite private and confidential. . . .

On receipt of nearly every mail I find it necessary greatly against my wish to put a contradiction in the local papers of some statement that has appeared in *The Times* and been republished by them. . . . Now I do not for a moment suppose *The Times* wishes to misrepresent my views or actions, but there is no doubt that *The Times* is being used by someone to start and ventilate those absurd rumours presumably with the object of discrediting my admiration of the Indian Army, and I think you will agree that with a native army and native press always ready to take the worst view of such utterances much harm is thus done. I feel sure I have only to mention this to you to stop its continuance in the future.

In the second place, I want to refer shortly to the unpleasant incidents out here, not that I wish in the very least for further publicity, but because from what I know of Curzon and his intentions I think it highly probable that he will on his return home make an unjustifiable attack on me and my administration of the Indian Army in revenge for his recent defeat, and forewarned is forearmed.

Amery had in April been adopted as candidate for Wolverhampton East; he appears now to have sought advice on the relative merits of *The Times* and Parliament.

G. E. Buckle to L.S.A., 28 June 1905

You seem to me to be exceptionally well qualified for almost all the higher departments of journalism; and though you may be equally adapted for success in politics and Parliament, that is hardly yet proved as your journalistic capacities are. Personally I have always considered that, if you remained with us, you would come to fill my chair. . . .

I have a strong feeling that political and Parliamentary life without an easy competence [i.e. private income] is beset with pitfalls and seldom really satisfactory in the long run. Whereas you may be sure that, if you stick by *The Times*, *The Times* will stick by you. It differs from all other journalistic institutions in its fidelity to, and consideration for, its tried and trusted servants.

I dare say you have weighed all these considerations; but I wished to let you know how anxious I am to keep you as a colleague.

3

In the Wilderness
1906–10

In the election of January 1906 the Unionists were routed. Their numbers in the Commons fell from 334 to 157 of whom 109 supported the Chamberlain tariff reform policy, 32 the Balfourian compromise (although Balfour himself lost his seat) and 11 were out-and-out free traders, as against 401 Liberals, 29 Labour and 83 Irish Nationalists. Amery was not elected.

The main issue to face the Opposition was the future of the Chamberlain policy, but this was linked with the issue of the leadership. Chamberlain, who was in July 1906 to be incapacitated by a stroke, told Lord Ridley, chairman of the Tariff Reform League, that he did not propose to challenge Balfour's leadership but publicly requested from Balfour a statement on fiscal policy. On 14 February Balfour wrote to Chamberlain that 'fiscal reform is and would always remain the first constructive work of the Unionist Party'. Chamberlain wrote back welcoming this, and the exchange became known as the 'Valentine Letters'.

Several of Amery's letters and diary entries in this and the following year referred to the need for Lord Milner, who had been censured by the Liberals for his administration in South Africa, to come forward as the champion of a constructive Unionist policy based on the Chamberlainite programme (see entries for 28 September, 17 and 18 December 1906). Amery managed to persuade him to give two addresses in December 1906 covering the whole field of social and Imperial policy. Nothing, however, would induce Milner to take up active politics: he was too shy and sincere to indulge in the theatrical appeal that is essential for political success. Amery also tried to persuade him to take on the chairmanship of the Tariff Reform League, and this he considered, but Austen Chamberlain, who with his father crippled was in effect the leader of the movement, did not like the idea and Lord Ridley remained chairman. Amery later regretted that the League was not able to play a more significant role.

During these two years Amery pursued his work at *The Times*, frequently writing the paper's leaders. He completed *The History of the*

South African War and delivered four addresses to the recently formed Compatriots' Club which were to be the basis of his small book on the protectionist case, *Fundamental Fallacies of Free Trade*. He also helped to form a Trade Unionist Tariff Reform League which he later wrote 'never secured from Conservative headquarters the attention or support which it deserved' (*My Political Life*, I, p. 298). This attempt to stimulate working-class Conservatives both to play a greater part in the Party, press for tariff reform and counter socialist propaganda which was now challenging the Liberal predominance over the working-class vote, will constantly be encountered in the years before 1918.

The greatest opportunity of these years to knit the Dominions closer was presented by the Imperial Conference of 1907. Alfred Lyttelton, Chamberlain's successor as Colonial Secretary from 1903 to 1906, had as early as April 1905 sent a circular to the Dominion Prime Ministers proposing an Imperial Council which might form a permanent body consisting of the Prime Ministers or their alternatives and a representative of India, and a permanent commission to follow up Council resolutions and prepare material in advance. The Governments of Australia, Cape Colony and Natal in South Africa welcomed this proposal and New Zealand, in the throes of an election campaign, was substantially in favour. But Laurier, the Prime Minister of Canada, viewed it with great disfavour, considering it a threat to the autonomy of the Dominions.

Amery followed up Lyttelton's initiative during 1906, meeting Dr Jameson (famous for the Raid of 1895) who as Prime Minister of Cape Colony was constantly in London during the autumn of 1906, Deakin, the Prime Minister of Australia, and Laurier himself, through his friend, the future Canadian premier Mackenzie King. Through articles in *The Times* Amery kept up the pressure during the Conference. Partly because of the lack of sympathy for any closer unity from Laurier and Botha ('the two foreigners') but mainly because of the hostility to concessions on either the constitutional or the preferential front from Asquith, as Chancellor of the Exchequer, and Churchill, as Colonial Secretary, there was no progress. The resolutions of the 1902 Conference urging the British Government to consider the introduction of preferential treatment of Dominion and colonial goods were simply reaffirmed, with the British Government alone dissenting.

Joseph Chamberlain to L.S.A., 19 January 1906

I hope that my warnings to you not to be too sanguine spared you some disappointment but I need not say I am most sincerely sorry that your splendid fight [at Wolverhampton East] was not better rewarded.

From the first I felt that it was a forlorn hope, but I still believe that it will bear good fruit in the future. . . .

You did not spare yourself and no one else could have done as well, and I always felt that the pecuniary expense of such a contest, especially if you are unsuccessful, ought not to fall wholly upon you, and I hope that you will without hesitation accept from the funds at my disposal the enclosed cheque for £500 towards the cost to which you have been put.

It is of course a personal matter as between yourself and me and does not therefore come into the Election accounts. I only wish I could have done more to assist a candidature in which I was very much interested.

A. J. Balfour to L.S.A., 30 July 1906

Many thanks for your book.*

You are one of the few people from whose writings on the great controversy I anticipate genuine pleasure.

Diary

24 September 1906: Ian Hamilton said the King was very keen that the Duke of Connaught [the King's brother] should succeed Kitchener in India, that Haldane [Secretary of State for War] is very anxious to keep Kitchener out there, as he doesn't know what to do with him if he comes back, but that John Morley [Secretary of State for India] wants him to come back as he doesn't know what to do with him out there. I suggest that he should be tempted to come back *via* the United States or Canada and given leave to investigate the strategic and railway conditions of that continent. The probability being that he would then chuck the army and go in for railway finance on a large scale.

Finished reading Life of Lord Randolph Churchill† in the evening. General impression left that Randolph was an impossible person, and that it was fortunate that he was snuffed out early.

28 September 1906: Lunched with Lord Milner. Hammered away hard at the necessity of his coming out into the open, and of attaching himself definitely to one party. He conceded the necessity, but was evidently very unwilling, and still thinks that he can be to some extent outside of the party machine and not too absolutely identified, though he realises that

---

*Fundamental Fallacies of Free Trade.

†Presumably that by Lord Rosebery, published in 1906. Winston Churchill's life of his father appeared the following year.

the Unionist party is the only one to which he could expound his views with any chance of their adoption. . . .

Wrote leader on Milner's speech about anti-nationalism in answer to the Cape address. My wireless telegraphy and labour and militarism leaders went in the same night, so all three leaders in the paper were mine.

2 October 1906: Dinner at Savoy. Jameson, Farrar, Maxse, Mackinder, Hewins, O'Connor, Holland (Jameson's secretary) and Harold [Amery]. Much interesting talk. Urged upon Jameson the necessity of getting something done at the next Colonial Conference, especially in the matter of permanent advisory council, under which the governing side of the Colonial Office might be put. Also suggested that it might make all the difference if he now wrote to Laurier and Deakin. A little flattery to the former, coming from a junior Prime Minister in the empire might to a world of good. Jameson very much taken with the idea and promised to do so.

Maxse in best Maxsean form; extra pessimistic. On O'Connor's suggesting that if a real crisis came English patriotism would show itself, he retorted, 'Yes, I know England will rise as one man, and be about as much use!'

24 October 1906: Went to Colonial Office to talk over Imperial Conference with Churchill. Churchill didn't turn up till nearly twelve but in return gave me nearly one and a half hour's talk while office business waited. Found him hopelessly anti-Imperial and his whole outlook strongly opposed to anything in the nature of an Imperial Council exercising any voice in our foreign policy, said we should never have secured the Japanese Alliance or the French *entente* if such control had existed. I didn't tell him that Grey had expressed himself strongly in favour of such a council but argued the thing on its merits. We both got rather warm. He flatly refused to consider the idea of preference in the Crown Colonies; and was very hostile to the notion of bringing colonials into the Colonial Office, etc., though he admitted that more could be done as regards the army and navy. His whole view was, that till the Colonies were a real military power whose 'alliance' was of any real use to us, there was no reason for giving them any voice in our affairs.

Winston wound up by saying that they would do everything to give the Prime Ministers a good time and butter them up, and that he would be glad of any further suggestions I could send him.

6 November 1906: Went . . . to another conspiracy at Mrs Jack Tennant's to see what can be done to organise the sound people in the Liberal party to keep the Government in order on Imperial questions. Lady Edward

Cecil and Maxse were there, extreme as usual, and we really did more practical business after they left.

17 November 1906 (in Oxford):   United Club dinner at Randolph. Bonar Law first rate. The carefulness of his preparation in striking contrast with F. E. Smith's vigorous but unfinished effort. To my surprise Smith wound up his speech by a strong proclamation in favour of sweeping Land Reform. A thing we had talked about before and had discussed launching later on.

30 November 1906:   Long talk with Brodrick. I remembered Miss Brooke-Hunt had told me she found B. going about the Natal battlefields with my history cursing me by all his gods, and taxed B. with it. He, on the contrary, declared that my volumes were his gospel, but that even the gospels nowadays were occasionally criticised. Also suggested that it was the material (i.e. weight of the volume) rather than the substance that caused him annoyance on long and hot days. He told me a great deal about the difficulty of his position with Roberts at one end saying the war was over and Hicks Beach at the other blazing up in a temper if he dared to approach him for more money. Poor B. very sorry for himself and full of his own past heroic actions.

15 December 1906:   Saw a young man called George Lloyd. A keen Tariff Reformer who wants to stand for Parliament, but before that to spend another nine months or so in the middle east, studying trade conditions there for the Board of Trade. Advised him to see Boraston but to go on with his Board of Trade work, as we badly wanted men with his special knowledge.

F. S. Oliver to L.S.A., 17 December 1906

Milner's speech was admirable. . . . If he will only keep on at it we shall have a leader to follow. . . . But I have a kind of doubt about Milner for this one reason – I read his speech very carefully word by word and it seemed to me that he must hate speech-making very much? Is that really so? He seemed to be forcing his thoughts painfully into a form which was thoroughly inconjurial to him. The order of his argument – the very order of the words – is the literary and not the oratorical order. He seems to be half conscious of this, but his struggle to get it right has rather the effect of a translation. Don't please misunderstand my meaning which is this – *stick to him and make him speak and keep on speaking till he gets the balance of the game.*

Diary

18 December 1906: Long talk after breakfast with Milner. He told me
nothing would induce him to become a party leader or to take office. He
was not fitted for it by nature. His health, which would allow him to do a
great deal of steady work, would not stand the racket of fussing about,
nor would his means allow him those conveniences which would make
that sort of life more tolerable. He seemed very determined and so it was
no use arguing the point then, but both then and later on in the train I
urged that he should get into correspondence with the Colonial Prime
Ministers about the Conference, and also prepare at leisure another speech
on the question of social reform.

A. Chamberlain to L.S.A., 23 January 1907

I would add that whilst fully appreciating the value of Milner's active
co-operation [with the Tariff Reform League] and the weight of his
name I think that in matters of organisation, and in popular touch and
sympathy, in 'instinct' if you like, he is inferior to Ridley. . . . I think him
a statesman of a high order but I do not think he is an organiser.

L.S.A. to Milner, 16 April 1907

Now for the Conference, Deakin, barring his talkativeness, is, I believe,
perfectly splendid. As for Laurier, Jameson's remarks about him cannot
be conveyed to you without shocking my secretary too deeply. His
mildest expression is that the damned music-master is likely to spoil the
whole show. To one thing, however, he is amenable, that is flattery, and
I hear on the first night, when the Premiers had their private conference,
Jameson and Deakin laid on the butter with a lavish towel, and pointed
out that he ought to be president of the conference unless C[ampbell
B[annerman, the British Prime Minister] were present. The worst of it
is, that when they have got him up to a certain point, he goes astray again
the very next day and has to be kept going constantly. He will want not
only flattery, however, but more forcible pressure as well, especially from
the Canadian end. I have done a good deal already myself. . . .

Botha is, on the whole, very good but, as Jameson says, he is already
picking up tricks from the music-master and it will be very difficult for
Jameson and Moor to keep him steady through the Conference. The
others are all very sound; in fact the danger is that it will be the English
members of the Conference against the two foreigners [Botha and Laurier]
and the pro-foreign Ministry [the Liberal Government].

In October 1907 Amery went to South Africa, initially for reasons of health and also to renew old contacts and his knowledge of the political situation there. While in Egypt, on his return journey, he heard the news of his mother's death. Between then and January 1909 when he takes up his diary for a period* there is no regular source of information in the Amery papers, and this regrettably applies to the dramatic by-election at Wolverhampton East, which took place in April 1908 as a result of Sir Henry Fowler, the sitting Liberal Member, taking a peerage. The political climate had greatly improved, and Winston Churchill had only recently been defeated by Sir William Joynson-Hicks in Manchester, while three other Unionist tariff reformers had been victorious in Mid-Devon, Hereford, and Worcester. But these three had normally been Unionist seats, whereas Wolverhampton East was 'safely' Liberal. After an extremely vigorous campaign dominated on Amery's side by the Chamberlainite policy, and culminating on the eve of poll with eleven meetings and a great rally of five thousand in the Drill Hall, he was beaten by only eight votes.†

1908 was marked by bad trade, rising unemployment and dearer food, which all contributed to a weakening of the free trade case and a strengthening of that for tariff reform. To fill both the political and financial vacua, the Liberals proposed taxation of land values which was introduced by the Lloyd George Budget of 1909. The House of Lords rejected the Budget and precipitated the political crisis which was to be sharpened by industrial militancy and the agitation of the suffragette movement and to merge into the Home Rule crisis, thus ensuring turbulent British politics up to the outbreak of war in 1914. Despite the difficulties of arguing the case for the Lords' apparent defence of their vested interests, Amery agreed with Milner and Chamberlain that an election fought on the fiscal issue could only do good. The disappointing result of the January 1910 election was partly the result of a revival in trade, but also that of the passions raised by the Lords' action. Thus the Unionists obtained only 272 seats against the Liberal total of 274 (the Liberals, however, had a net loss of 105), which was boosted by the alliance with 41 Labour MPs and 82 Irish Nationalists.

Amery who, while touring Canada between July and October 1909, had broken a leg riding in a paper-chase at Winnipeg conducted his campaign in Wolverhampton East on one leg. He now decided to abandon what Milner called 'that cursed seat' and tried to find a better one. After a short visit to South Africa we find him assessing a number of seats

*The only existing previous diary is for September to December 1906. The whole of 1909 and the first nine months of 1910 are covered.
†In 1906 he had been defeated for the seat by 5610 to 2745. In the by-election the figures were 4514 and 4506. In January 1910 the votes were 5276 and 4462.

during the spring and summer, while keeping in touch with the work of the 'Milner Kindergarten', and meeting Miss Bryddie Greenwood, whom he married on 16 November 1910 after a further tour of Canada between July and September. Her brother, Hamar Greenwood, a young lawyer from Canada, was already a Liberal MP.

Meanwhile in Parliament the Irish Nationalists allowed the 1909 Finance Bill (which they had been blocking in the Commons) to pass in return for a resolution at the end of March 1910 committing the Government to the introduction of a Parliament Bill to limit the powers of the House of Lords. They saw the existing veto of the Lords as a permanent obstacle to Home Rule and, of course, the Irish would only support the Government in general and the Parliament Bill in particular if they were assured that Home Rule would be conceded. So it is fortunate for the historian that Amery, a strong protagonist on both issues, but especially the latter, should have kept a fairly regular diary from 1911 to 1913.

In May 1910 King Edward VII had died and the general feeling that George V should not immediately have to face a constitutional crisis as a result of the Government's wish to reform the Lords, was put in a series of letters to *The Times* over the signature of 'Pacificus'. These were believed at the time to be by Lord Esher but were in fact by the engaging F. S. Oliver. On 17 June a small conference, composed of four representatives each of the Government and the Unionist Opposition, met to try and find a way out, but this broke up on 10 November without reaching any agreement. The real stumbling block, Amery wrote in his memoirs (*My Political Life*, I, p. 362), was over the category of issues which might be termed 'constitutional' by an impartial committee and where the Unionists insisted that there should be a referendum as an alternative to a dissolution. They 'could not acquiesce in any solution which opened the door to the permanent disruption of the United Kingdom by a temporary House of Commons majority' while Asquith and his colleagues could not consent to any proposal which would effectively deny Redmond, the Irish Nationalist leader, his objective of Home Rule.

There was no alternative open to the Government but a fresh election, with an assurance being extracted from the King that in the event of a Liberal victory he would if necessary overrule the Lords' veto by the creation of new peers. Amery was taking a short honeymoon in the New Forest but was suddenly invited to contest Bow and Bromley, which had in January been held by the Unionists with Liberal support against George Lansbury, who was regarded as one of the more extreme socialists. During the campaign Lloyd George, speaking at Mile End, made a personal appeal to the Bow and Bromley Liberals, who were not contesting in December, to 'support my friend Lansbury'. A Unionist majority of 740 was thus converted into one for Lansbury of 863. It was Amery's fourth defeat.

L.S.A. to Milner, from the Rand Club, Johannesburg, 11 November 1907

Added to the [economic] depression all the chief people here feel the soreness of being back once more under the Boer regime. Once more Johannesburg is treated as an alien, half hostile, element, once more all the billets are given without question to *onze Menze* ['our people']. . . . Botha means well in many ways, but his point of view is naturally very different from ours and he has to humour his followers. Smuts' point of view on political matters is probably nearer ours but on the other hand he is perhaps much more bitter than Botha. In either case they will do things that will not be pleasing.

All the same, granting all that, I am as optimistic as ever I was about the ultimate result. The British have got the voice and the vote in Parliament, and that is a tremendous lever. The Boers, or at least their leaders, are desperately afraid of effective criticism, whether in the Assembly or in the Press. The Progressives have stopped many things and modified others and will grow more effective. . . . Robin [Dawson] has given me several instances of cases where criticism in the [*Johannesburg*] *Star* has caused the composition of commissions to be altered. . . . The British population will grow again later on, even if it goes down for another year or so. Bad as the mines are, the country as a whole is really developing. It will be frightfully slow compared to what might have been, but the process will go on all the same. After all, Kruger, who deliberately tried to check the industry, and was absolutely indifferent to Uitlander criticisms, could not stop the growth. Revenue necessity was too much for him and revenue necessity . . . will operate still more on these people with their larger commitments. . . .

F. S. Oliver to L.S.A., 29 November 1907

I don't suppose the thought has ever suggested itself to your modest heart that you are missed? . . . Even Zollverein* misses you and he had become quite cross and ill-mannered. . . . The matron of Printing House Square misses you, her lawful spouse, and through your desertion and to the scandal of us all, has gone upon the street, like Lady Wishfort, in a rage of lecherous inclination. That the fogs are thicker and more frequent than usual must be set down to the same cause. . . .

After all much has been going right. The will of Jehovah is becoming

---

*Pseudonym of a *Times* correspondent with whom Amery had crossed swords.

more apparent day by day. Even A.J.B., regarding the wall through his pince-nez, has been able to read the writing that is upon it. Only the *Morning Post** is purblind and refuses to see that Arthur has seen – like a cackling guide who won't be satisfied unless you exclaim at the beauties of the temple.

. . . You will mingle your tears with ours when you hear that the largest and most maternal of our rabbits has died – 'of the potbelly', so Beatrix informs me: a strange disease! If it was fatal to humans the Treasury bench would be swept pretty clean, leaving nothing but Grey and Winston.

Asquith by the way has become a public scandal. Senile oscillation is going to be his undoing. Anxious nonconformists speak of him in hushed tones along with Dilke which is most unjust to Dilke.

Milner to L.S.A., 27 December 1907

I have done enough speaking to satisfy even you, and if I have achieved no positive good, I hope I have at least prevented some mischief. The Unionist Party, with *The Times*, I am sorry to say, at the head were all 'rushing violently down a steep place' into the bog of a purely Conservative narrow middle-class and negative policy. I think I have helped to spoil that rotten game and kept the constructive and Imperial ideas to the front.

Diary

11 January 1909: Having gone down to Belvoir meaning to get a chance of talking to A.J.B., naturally hardly got in a word there and very few on the way up. He is not really interested in politics except when in the House face to face with a speech from the other side. The idea of encouraging the young by familiar talk on politics is quite foreign to him: he could not create a 'kindergarten'.

14 January 1909: Hewins convinced the Government cannot find a Budget and will go to the country on any pretext as soon as Parliament meets. Says his office have been working away at a tariff for the last six months and that everything is perfectly ready for running it through on this year's Budget if required.

21 January 1909: Spent the afternoon in the Turkish bath trying to boil out my cold and reading Marx's *Kapital*. Found it very dreary reading

*A 'die-hard' newspaper critical of Balfour.

and insufferably long winded. . . . I had no idea that the case was presented by him in quite so crude a fashion as this. As a corrective to my contemptuous feelings about Marx I read a review of *Fundamental Fallacies* in the *Economist* in which the work was described as 'cleverish' but otherwise treated as too ridiculous for serious consideration.

Moberley Bell to L.S.A., 3 February 1909

We have decided to get out of the *History of the War* by publishing an Index which we will get made by our intelligence department and distributing it to the subscribers.

The matter has become such a public disgrace that we decline to be associated with it any longer – and if you can afford to ignore it, we cannot.*

I am very sorry that we are compelled to come to this decision but I think if you knew the sort of things that are said openly of you individually and of us as fathering the book you would recognise that we have treated you with culpable tolerance and sustained a damage which no conceivable profit could ever make good.

Because I have hitherto tried to treat the matter jocularly you have chosen to treat all our representations with contempt and absolutely to neglect fulfilling an engagement for which you have been very liberally paid.

Diary

6 February 1909: Dined with the Trade Union Tariff Reform Association and proposed the toast of the Association. Expressed the hope that they were but the beginning of a body which would gradually dispute the tyranny of the present official Labour representatives and that the time would come when at least 20 or 30 of them would sit on the Unionist side of the House of Commons.

15 February 1909: Dined with F.E. [Smith] and found there Ridley, Gilbert Parker, Goulding, Remnant, Harold Smith, Leslie Scott, Hewins, Ware, Garvin, Courthope, Hope [and other Conservative MPs and candidates]. After dinner formed a sort of committee to discuss T[ariff] R[eform] Amendment to the Address, etc. Gilbert Parker voted F.E. into the Chair, and somebody else suggested Goulding as Secretary. The whole thing rather pre-arranged, and its main object to give F.E. the

---

*L.S.A. was criticised for his delays in producing the *History*.

chance of leading the TR amendment and posing as the leader of the younger men. Hence by no means anxious that the TR Amendment should be moved by the Front Bench. Towards 11.00 Bonar Law came in and infused rather more point into the gathering. Told us the Front Bench had not yet decided which to make their official amendment. . . . Thought the F.E. meeting very fatuous and ineffective. However, I am now on an advisory committee to discuss TR policy with the TR members in the House.

18 February 1909: Meeting of women. Told them of the desirability, from the public point of view, of imposing the responsibility of voting on them.

L.S.A. to Sir Arthur Steel-Maitland, 5 March 1909

You may have heard of the Trade Union Tariff Reform League, a body of trade unionists pure and simple, organised originally and still financed by Medhurst, at one time connected with the Tariff Reform League but now entirely separate. It contains quite a number of really capable and intelligent working men, but Medhurst is not inclined to go on finding some £1300 a year which it costs him at present and though he is prepared to continue to subscribe £300 or £400 he very much wants the control of it taken over by others. . . .

I believe that if a small and energetic committee devoted itself to working the thing up as an organisation, and also helping it by insisting on getting some of its men into the House, the thing might at the end of a few years stand entirely on its own feet and compete effectively with the existing Labour party but [it] holds views on a great many subjects, not only fiscal but also Imperial, which are thoroughly distasteful to a great body of working men.

Diary

7 April 1909: Found Jack Hills waiting to discuss the Trade Union Tariff Reform League. We went off and lunched at the Savoy Grill Room where we found Gerard Sellar and made a vain effort to screw some money out of him. Then for a short walk and to a meeting of the TUTR where Hills and I were formally adopted as Joint Treasurers. We opened the banking account with £200, being Medhurst's half-yearly subscription, and the responsibility of finding an income of £2000 a year in the next few months. Rather an undertaking.

29 April 1909: Lunched with Ware for our gathering of the informal committee which has been going on since 1907. Milner, Austen, Bonar Law, Lee, Hills, etc. present. Milner started discussing land tax during lunch over which we all fell into confused controversy.

7 May 1909: Went to Milner's, Steel-Maitland there. Tried to get Mackinder to come too but he was lecturing at the School of Economics. Decided desirable to get the Bureau [an informal bureau of information on Imperial matters] started as soon as possible. As regards the work on Tariff Reform we had hoped to do last summer, we felt that as regards the home part of it it was already being done elsewhere and that the main thing was that we should stick to the Preference side. M. told us in strict confidence that he, Austen Chamberlain, Bonar Law, and Hewins were meeting and thrashing out every single item of a Tariff Reform Budget. He told us they had just been having an hour's discussion on the subject of margarine.

6 June 1909: Looked up Robin [Dawson] at 47 Duke Street with Lord Milner and had a short talk, chiefly on the desirability of relieving South African millionaires of their surplus, during the present boom, for good public objects, Imperial organisation, national defence, etc., etc.

3 July 1909 (Oxford): The *History [of the South African War]*, by the way, came out on Thursday [1st], and so far has had very fair reviews, the *Westminster [Gazette]* alone being violently angry.

4 July 1909: Went down by the 11.15 to Woking to stay at Sutton Place [Lord Northcliffe's house]. Discovered that a large contingent of the Russian Duma was going down too. Enormous crowd at lunch. . . . When the ladies departed [after dinner] Garvin poured forth some most interesting reminiscences of the early months of the fiscal business. On one occasion while trying to rest down at Lulworth, he was suddenly seized with a feeling that Joe was going to resign. He came straight up to town, insisted on seeing Joe next morning, and put the question to him. Joe at first extremely surprised, then acknowledged that it was true, and added that to show that he was not going out in any hostile spirit he was going to leave Austen to become Chancellor of the Exchequer to which Garvin replied: 'I hope to God you won't find that a fetter on your freedom of action.' Joe was dead silent for a full minute afterwards.

Milner to L.S.A., 7 July 1909

The last thing which would occur to me was to think anything you say 'slush'. You are the 'unslushiest' of mankind and that is the very reason why, whether I differ from or agree with you, I always find there is something in your views which appeals to me and which is worth weighing.

F. S. Oliver to L.S.A., 17 September 1909

Our Anglesey visit filled me with horror in anticipation (unlike you I'm not accustomed to staying with Dukes and Marquesses). . . . Both here and at Lovat's dinner Milner took hold of the thing with his claw and his beak and kept us hard to business. . . .

P.S. Do you use scent into [*sic*] your bath? If so is it crystals or powder or liquid that you toss in? At Anglesey's we had all three, and half of us were nearly poisoned by mistaking them for effervescent drinks and liqueurs put out for our matutinal solace.

Diary

5 November 1909 (London, on his return from Canada after breaking his leg): In the afternoon Jameson came in looking better than I have seen him for years, and in very good spirits. Told me that my particular fracture was one common with babies but very unusual with grown-ups. Buckle came in later, also Bell and F. E. Smith. All three of them held the view that it would have been better political business to have let the Budget pass and produce its effects which seems to me absurd.

13 November 1909: Went to lunch with Mr Chamberlain and found him looking a great deal better. His face is a good colour and more filled out. His utterance on the other hand struck me as showing no sign of improvement. . . . I sat on some time talking with J.C. about S. Africa, and more particularly about my idea of breaking up the Colonial Office into an Imperial Office and Colonial Office proper.* J.C. did not think that the Imperial Office would have very much to do, but I urged that the Minister in question could be free to travel in between sessions, and in Parliament would stand as the advocate of the Imperial point of view rather than as the head of the administrative department. Mrs C. made the very sensible suggestion that the office might be combined with that of Lord President of the Council.

*This view was reiterated in 1918 (see p. 223) and eventually implemented by L.S.A. himself in 1925.

Milner to L.S.A., 16 January 1910

It is no use swearing at Dame Fortune, no use either tho' much temptation, to d—n a party management or want of management which wastes our best men on hopeless fights and provides noodles with safe seats.

[In a separate letter of the same date Milner added:] For the moment it is a very hard blow for you – *and me*. . . . There are some half-dozen men I want above all things to be in Parliament and you first of all, and more than any other two.

Diary

8 February 1910: Dined with the Colefaxes. The Lytteltons, F. E. Smith and Goulding there. Also Lady Northcliffe. With one accord they all told me it was desperate folly to go off to South Africa at this critical moment. Afterwards however I went home with F.E. and he agreed . . . I could leave my affairs in his hands, say with Steel-Maitland to help. . . . On one of the days I was in town after the election I saw Northcliffe in bed and he expressed himself extremely anxious to secure me a safe seat and to use all his influence with the leaders of the party on my behalf.

9 March 1910 (South Africa): Went back to Government House where there was a 'moot' or gathering of Kindergarten, etc. Curtis held forth on his Home Rule theory of Imperial Union, all of us, myself in chief, going for him with great vigour. During one of his most eloquent passages the bathroom pipe burst overhead and deluged him.

11 April 1910: After lunch I went to the House of Commons. Just as I got in I saw Mr Thorne* so made him take me into the Lobby where I got hold of Steel-Maitland and talked with him and a number of others about the possibility of getting anything. At 5.00 went up to a sort of committee to hear the report of the working men candidates who had been in Germany. They all said that we Tariff Reformers had never said one half of what we might about the prosperity of Germany, the cheapness of food and clothing, and were in fact almost lyrical in their descriptions of German prosperity. Their experience ought to have a very good effect in making their speeches go down in the country. After the meeting had a short talk with Austen Chamberlain and with Goulding about prospects. A.C. thought there was no chance of getting any of the Birmingham members to retire. Both Lowe and Middlemore† were convinced that they

*His victorious opponent, the Liberal MP for Wolverhampton East.
†Two senior Birmingham Unionist MPs.

were the actual hubs of the Empire and it was quite impossible to hint the possibility of retirement to them. Goulding thought that if A.J.B. went straight to Middlemore and offered him a Privy Councillorship he might possibly stand down.

6 May 1910: The new King, judging by his speeches, does understand Imperial questions.

26 May 1910: Talking of King George, Miss Chamberlain said she was struck by the fact that both her father and Mr Balfour had separately expressed their very high opinion of him. As Balfour only admires intellect and Chamberlain chiefly admires purpose and force of character, she thought it probable that he had a fair share of both these qualities.

30 May 1910: Went off to second tea at Mrs Humphry Ward's where there were about a score of people gathered together to meet the Roosevelts. I found the great [Theodore] Roosevelt somewhat shorter than I expected, even more nubbly but less repellently ugly than in the caricatures. He talked with great 'go' the whole time. . . . When I first came up to him he was telling Ian Hamilton all about the sending of the American fleet to the Pacific. It was at the time when the Japanese had been inclined to be nasty, and he had just got information through the Austrian military attaché in Japan that the Japanese military people were frankly boasting that they could wipe out the American navy and annex the whole Pacific slope. On top of this news came a letter from Ian Hamilton on the subject of the Japanese in general which decided the President to send the fleet round. In doing so he thought there might just possibly be a chance about 1 in 10 of the Japanese declaring war and going for him, but if so he thought it just as well that it should come then as later. However, as soon as the fleet got through Magellan Straits in fine shape and showed itself thoroughly well handled, the Japanese tone turned completely and by the time it got to Japan it had a reception that even Australia could not equal. 'The ant-like unanimity of these people is something wonderful,' said Mr Roosevelt.

7 June 1910: To a gathering of the Imperial 'moot' at Kerr's office. Oliver in the chair, and present Malcolm, Brand and Lord Robert Cecil. Resolved that the magazine* should consist of a general survey of the quarter by the editor, followed by surveys written in each part of the Empire by responsible people, and that there might also be articles on

---

*This became the *Round Table*, now the quarterly of Commonwealth affairs, launched in the summer of 1910.

general subjects, but any likely to be controversial should be clearly indicated. The following sub-committee decided on to study –

Financial relations between England and Ireland: nucleus Hichens and Craik.

General congestion of work in Cabinet and Parliament: nucleus Bob Cecil, Dougie Malcolm and Steel-Maitland.

Next Imperial Conference: myself, Oliver, Steel-Maitland.

Imperial Defence: Lovat and myself. General idea that these sub-committees should take outside experts into their confidence as far as their particular work was concerned, but not disclose the fact of its dependence on a central body.

8 June 1910: Breakfast with Lovat and Kerr to discuss the defence sub-committee. Decided to consult informally Kitchener, Esher, Henry Wilson, Repington, some of the officers of the Imperial Defence Committee, etc. Went on to 17 Belgrave Square to see Kitchener whom I had not seen since I saw him off at Pretoria Station just after the peace. Thought he looked younger and thinner. Began by raising very indignantly the subject of a *Times* leader which I had not yet read, which while praising him in general terms scouted the idea of his going to India. Any chances he had of going to India, he said, were dished by this, and he was very curious to know how the article was inspired. I told him it was probably written on quite general grounds or else because *The Times* had already been informed of someone else's appointment. . . . I steered him off the Indian grievance on to Imperial Defence and told him that Lovat and I wanted to consult him more especially with a view to the next Conference. Very interested to find that K. had come on his own to the conclusion that no forward step can be taken on Imperial Defence worth speaking of till there is some form of Imperial representation. His own solution was typically crude, viz. asking the High Commissioners to sit in the House of Lords, and I pointed out to him the difficulties in the way. Generally speaking he was very pessimistic and said that nothing would cure us till we got a beating. Thought the existing state of the War Office and the Army here as bad as it could be, but also said he was by no means sure that he favoured Roberts' scheme. A real Imperial General Staff outside the War Office and attached to the Defence Committee he agreed would be a good thing, but then he said that the Defence Committee had been a fraud from the first, a mere instrument for registering the Prime Minister's view. I tried hard to impress on him the desirability of his not being committed to any particular post for a year or two when there might be an opportunity for his taking part in a really big scheme of organisation. But that wasn't at all to his mind. He wants something definite and if he cannot get it talks about going abroad and doing something else, presumably finance. His general view was well summed up when he said 'After all I have done for England all these years, I don't see why they should not do something for me', meaning India.

Further sub-committee of the 'moot'. Milner, Oliver, Malcolm, Kerr and myself. Practically a repetition to Milner of our conclusions of the previous day. Oliver in great glee. His 'Pacificus' letters suggesting a convention behind closed doors actually led to a definite result. After several hours spent in conjecturing who 'Pacificus' might be and rather concluding that he was Esher, the Cabinet on Tuesday decided to accept the notion, which Buckle heard of forthwith and communicated to Oliver. In view of suggestions from the Government side that the scope of the discussion should be defined beforehand, Oliver wrote another short letter insisting that the deliberations should be secret between principal only and as few of them as possible, and above all that they should be free. Result great triumph for Oliver; also for Garvin who in a general way has been pegging away at compromise in the *Observer*.

After the Anglo–French *entente* in 1904, in 1906 the new Liberal Foreign Secretary, Sir Edward Grey, had, with the knowledge of his senior colleagues, authorised naval and military discussions with the French with a view to joint operations in the event of an attack by Germany. These went on up to 1914.

Diary

10 July 1910: Went across to the Staff College and there spent most of the morning in keen discussion over a map of the Belgian and French frontier. Wilson told some extraordinarily good stories about General Foch, the head of the French Military College, the best being a description of his interview with Haldane. Haldane asked him what he thought of our troops, and, after being fairly complimentary on their quality, he said, 'But you have not got enough, *monsieur le ministre*'. Haldane replied to this, '*Ah, mais nous avons des réserves dans la Méditerranée, dans l'Afrique, et dans les Indes.*' The little Frenchman thereupon slowly counted on his fingers '*Dans la Méditerranée, au Cap, dans les Indes*' and then shaking his fingers in Haldane's face, '*Tra, la, la, la.*' Haldane, not disconcerted by this, said, '*Nous avons aussi les territorials*'. . . . The Frenchman just screwed up his face and wagged his head up and down.

John Simon to Hamar Greenwood, 10 October 1910

[The letter, now in the Amery papers, reminded Greenwood that he was to speak at two major Liberal pre-general election meetings for Simon in Leyton and Walthamstow, and hoped this would not be disturbed by Amery's engagement to Greenwood's sister.] Amery is my *fidus achates* and he will want to see you today. Can you do that either before or after our show? Don't desert me – though I know of nothing in the world of friendship more entirely satisfactory than the great news he told me last night. Miss Greenwood will not mind my saying that no one ever deserved warmer congratulations than she.

Milner to Miss Greenwood, on her engagement to L.S.A., 27 October 1910

Leo is one of the people in the world that I must value and am most attached to. We have been and are *very close allies* in our public work and aims, differing rarely even in opinion and never in the spirit in which we approach public questions. Beyond that I have a very genuine affection and admiration for him as a man – for his strength, his simplicity, his kindliness, his utter lack of vanity or pettiness. . . . This is between ourselves. I don't want even Leo to see this letter which is written from the bottom of my heart.

F. S. Oliver to L.S.A., 8 November 1910

The other thing my informant* gave me is that Lloyd George's present intention is to follow up the Colonial Conference by visiting Canada and earning there – as he can easily do with his oratorical gifts – a great personal popularity. Of course this probably will mean the conversion of Lloyd George to Protection, but that is another matter. It has always been common talk that he is shaping his career upon Mr Chamberlain's so that a development on Imperial lines is now about due. [c.f. p. 343.]

Milner to L.S.A., 20 November 1910

I thought 'if I ask Balfour to do *a particular thing* and he tries it and fails he is absolved'. I want him to feel that it is 'up to him' to get you in *somehow, anyhow,* and that he is not absolved *until he gets you in* [to Parliament].

J. Chamberlain to L.S.A., 12 December 1910

I have received your letter and I am sorry but not surprised that you were defeated at Bow and Bromley [in the general election of December 1910]. Do not contest another seat where there is really no chance. I do not know who sent you to Bow and Bromley but all your friends would be certain that you could not succeed.

*Unnamed, but 'one who has the very best sources of information and whom I can trust'.

L.S.A. to Bonar Law, 16 December 1910

My only conclusion from the elections so far is that we must at all costs, and whatever the row and friction, reconstruct the whole party organisation. It is that, and nothing else, I am convinced, which has prevented our sweeping the country this time, and will prevent our ever winning or ever holding our own if by any fluke we do get in on the demerits of our opponents.

Let me point out that first of all while our opponents [the Liberals] have an effective central organisation we really have three – the Central Conservative Office, the National Union, and the Liberal Unionist Council. The division between Conservatives and Liberal Unionists is nowadays pure fiction. . . . If it is too much of a business to bring about an absolute amalgamation and abolish both the names 'Conservative' and 'Liberal Unionist' for Unionist, I would at least suggest a rearrangement of seats by which Scotland, the Midlands and possibly London were given over to the present Liberal Unionist organisers, and all the rest of the country to the Conservative Central Office.

Much more serious, however, than that anachronism is the utter badness of the Conservative Central Office. If that were really efficient, I believe the other organisations would soon come into line. The key of the position is Acland Hood, and till he is poisoned or pensioned we shall not get a step forward. At present there are I believe combined in him three different functions which no one man, however able, could fulfil effectively, and none of which he is capable of fulfilling at all. These are –

(a) the Chief Whip of the Party in the House of Commons;
(b) the chief organiser of the party in the country, responsible for the campaign as a whole, for the selection of candidates, and for the general efficiency of all the local organisations;
(c) the man who collects an adequate party war chest.

As to (c) it seems to me quite absurd that our Party with the enormous reserve of wealth behind it should actually have less money for its election campaign than our opponents. As far as I can make out no attempt is really made to get at the people who have money. I have been told that the whole of Cadogan Square does not subscribe more than £5 a year to the Unionist Party. . . .

Now as to (b). As far as I can make out the whole thing is completely out of hand. The local organisations pay no attention whatever to the central office, and the central office has no control over them. Nothing has become clearer to me in my own inquiries after a constituency than the fact that the central office have practically no influence with the local committees. It has never really attempted in the past to see that places get the best and most suitable candidates to help struggling constituencies, or in fact in any way to further the cause, and the consequence is that if nowadays it occasionally offers suggestions nobody pays any attention to it. It doesn't apparently try to discover what the organisation is in the constituencies or to make any effort to see that it is improved. Each constituency is consequently a little autonomous oligarchy of half a dozen men, very often of only two men, the chairman and the agent. Of these the agent has to live, and the chairman and other members of the Committee have a natural reluctance to embark on a campaign of collecting subscriptions. Consequently the one thing they bother about is a candidate who will pay for the whole of the organisation, and if they can get that they have no use for the Central Office or for anything else. If candidates and rich people in general paid to the Central Office and that Office contributed towards the local organisation in proportion to their needs and to the sums they can raise locally, the Office would be in a much stronger position both to insist on efficiency and to have its advice followed in the selection of candidates.

Again, the whole housing arrangements of the Central Conservative Office make any real efficiency and decency impossible. Fifteen or twenty men at a time, candidates, deputations wishing to interview candidates, newspaper men wishing to interview Percival Hughes, etc., etc. are shoved into a little coal hole which is also a main thoroughfare for clerks, and kept waiting by the hour. The officials themselves are packed into little dens with no room to spread their papers, with the incessant noise of half a dozen telephones, and with clerks running in and out all the time. All this, though trivial in itself, seriously impairs efficiency. The whole thing wants clearing out and putting into a decent building, well lit, and reasonably spacious, and candidates, deputations, Members of Parliament, and others should have at least two or three tolerable waiting rooms not inferior to those of the ordinary dentist.

There are lots of other minor points about the organisation, but it is no use discussing these now. The real thing to do is to get hold of someone who will lick this thing into shape, sack superfluous people, knock heads together and make the machine run. Now I have a strong notion that your friend Max Aitken* might profitably be turned on to that work. He is full of ambition. But at the same time I doubt if as an ordinary member his ambition will ever succeed in carrying him very far. I cannot conceive his attaining a Cabinet rank for instance. On the other hand he has from all I hear got really remarkable organising power, and if he took to that side of the work and really threw himself into it he would very soon enjoy an actual power and position greater than that of most

---

*Later Lord Beaverbrook, and at that time MP for Ashton-under-Lyme.

Cabinet Ministers. There ought to be no difficulty in getting him on to some of these advisory committees on the National Union to begin with, and then as soon as we are ready for a complete revolution and for the firing out of Acland Hood (which must not be delayed too many weeks) it might be possible to put him in as chief organiser, nominally subject perhaps to a new Chief Party Whip but practically with a free hand to run things.

If you think there is anything in the idea, I hope you will encourage Aitken in that direction and do what you can to prepare the path for slipping him into the organising machinery.

4

To the Brink
1911–14

After the election Amery was faced with a libel action by one ex-Sergeant Major Edmondson, who had denounced Amery during the January 1910 election for a 'damnable libel' of the British Army and quoted certain sentences from *The Times History* out of context. In order to repudiate him as dramatically as seemed to be required, Amery declared at one of his meetings that his accuser had been sent home in disgrace from South Africa for running from a certain battle. Edmondson brought a libel action. The case, as Amery realised, could have been fatal to his political career if it had gone against him. As it was, it brought him into contact with two important men: Tim Healy, Edmondson's counsel and an Irish Nationalist MP who was to become the first Governor General of the Irish Free State, and F. E. Smith once again, who was his own counsel.

There followed speedy developments in the search for a seat. No sooner had Amery been adopted for Bedford than a vacancy occurred in South Birmingham, and with the support of the Chamberlainite chiefs, he was swiftly adopted. The seat, being what would now be known as a 'safe' Conservative seat, was not contested, which was most fortunate as there was no general election until 1918, when the sitting Liberal MP for Bedford, Kellaway, received a 'coupon' as a supporter of Lloyd George.

One of Amery's earliest speeches was on a subject which official and 'polite' circles preferred to ignore (see the diary entry for 17 July 1911). It was provoked by his witnessing the ravages of syphilis among the natives of Uganda, and the immediate occasion of his speech was Lloyd George's announcement that part of his insurance fund was to be devoted to research into and treatment of tuberculosis. Having approached in vain several medical MPs asking them to urge the same course for venereal disease, Amery himself made the necessary speech. Although little was done immediately a Royal Commission was appointed two years later and progress in this neglected field was encouraged by the requirements of war.

More immediate was the fight against the Government's Parliament Bill to deprive the Lords of their veto. On 15 May 1911 the Commons gave a third reading to the Parliament Bill. The Lords gave it a second reading and made wrecking amendments, and on 20 July these returned to the Commons, providing for a referendum on any Bills passed under the new system which affected the existence of the monarchy, or the Protestant succession, or established a national Parliament or council or any of the Three Kingdoms, or which raised any other issue of great gravity.

On the same day Asquith revealed to Balfour that the King had agreed to a creation of peers if this were necessary to overrule the Lords. Balfour, Lansdowne and other chief Unionists decided that they had to climb down, but the following day ex-Lord Chancellor Halsbury denounced surrender, and was supported by various Unionists. Amery's diary at this time shows him taking part in numerous meetings of the 'die-hard' group. On 10 August the Lords debated the issue again and after much heat, marked by Curzon's desertion of the die-hard cause, the Lords voted to accept the Government's ultimatum, with 111 Unionist peers voting against but 30 voting for.

A direct result of this split was the downfall of Balfour. 'Balfour must go' had long been a watchword in those parts of the Party where devotion to tariff reform coincided with die-hard support for the Lords, and various pressures caused his resignation in November, and the 'emergence' of Andrew Bonar Law as his successor in preference to either Austen Chamberlain or Walter Long. (There is, unfortunately, no Amery diary for this period.)

Diary

22 January 1911: Read [H. G. Wells's *The New*] *Machiavelli*. In it he gives a bitingly faithful picture of the Sidney Webbs, their ways, their little dinners, not a single trait left out. Also a description, not quite so literally close, but still very recognisable, of the Coefficients' discussions in which I rather fancied I saw myself as the groundwork of Mr Crupp. The rest of the story deals with his own love affair with Reeve's daughter. Altogether one of the nakedest books ever written but very remarkable.

25 January 1911: Opening of the Edmondson case. Tim Healy led off for the plaintiff, this being his first appearance in the English Courts. Paid me a pleasant little tribute.

26 January 1911: Edmondson in the witness box all day. F.E. cut him to pieces pretty unmercifully.

31 January 1911: F.E. continued his speech, and the second part was even better than the first. Altogether a most masterly presentment of the case. Our witnesses then followed – Lord Roberts, who refused to answer most of the questions on the ground that they were against the public interest; Sergt. Morley, whose story was very clear and emphatic and whom Healy was quite unable to shake on any point.

2 February 1911: F.E. decided to leave out several witnesses, partly because we have got enough evidence and partly because he thought one or two of them had been got at by the other side. . . . Healy had half an hour before the adjournment and devoted it to generalities, at the end of which the judge drily asked whether Mr Healy proposed to deal with the facts next day.

3 February 1911: The judge summed up undoubtedly very strongly in my favour, though naturally worded with great care. The jury retired at 5 minutes to four and reappeared after 5.0 to say they were in difficulties and wanted tea. . . . At half past six they emerged to say that they were disagreed, one or possibly two having apparently held out against the rest who looked very flushed and angry. The judge then took them carefully through the main points for about 10 minutes or so. . . . This was enough for the dissident or dissidents who fell into line, and the German foreman then announced that the jury found the defendant not guilty. It was a great relief, as any other verdict, though not making much difference from the financial point of view would have been very inconvenient politically.

L.S.A. *to Mrs Amery, 27 February 1911*

Bedford may adopt me as candidate. It is a practical certainty – a very bad Unionist candidate was only beaten by 19 and has now been got rid of. It is small, easily worked, and only just over an hour from London.

L.S.A. *to Mrs Amery, 5 March 1911*

I liked the agent at Bedford. I thought his organisation was good, I liked the Executive Committee, so I consented to become their candidate.

Diary

4 April 1911: When I got home I found a communication from the Secretary of the Athenaeum to the effect that I had been elected a member for distinguished eminence under Rule II, proposed by Lord Roberts. A very pleasant piece of news.

18 April 1911: Heard in the morning that Lord Carlisle* had died suddenly and that there was a vacancy in South Birmingham. Communicated with Jenkins to find out whether they were considering me. Also with Mr Chamberlain, and proceeded to await events.

Milner to L.S.A., 18 April 1911

I have been writing letters about you all the evening and am pulling all the wires I can think of.

L.S.A. to Mrs Amery, 21 April 1911

Vince met me at the station to tell me that all rivals had been eliminated and that my name (with one or two others just for appearance's sake) would be up before the full committee at 6.30 and that they would want to meet me at 7 p.m. to tell me their decision personally. . . . I made a few remarks expressing the pride I felt at the idea of representing Birmingham and being a fellow member with Joe, and as I really was moved . . . I gather I owe it nearly all to Neville Chamberlain who saw and persuaded a number of people. . . .

The next year or two, as long as we are in opposition, will be a great chance, and I must make use of it. I have got a great deal more reputation than I really deserve for knowledge and I shall have to work hard to sit up late, and get up early and keep in training to justify it. . . . I do so hope there won't be an election: I want to be in the House at once, and to learn it all, and possibly to speak before the summer is out. . . . It is an immense advantage having the absolute conviction of being in the right and fighting for great ends, and, for one so good natured and easy going as myself, it is good, too, to feel real indignation against one's adversaries as I do. Anyhow, one big stage in my life, that of preparation, is over, and the new stage of full action begins. What I shall achieve in it I cannot tell. I know I have great weaknesses, but also great strength, and if I really grow in inner and outer stature during the next five years, and if fortune is not unkind, I may really play my part in getting big things done.

---

*His heir, Lord Morpeth, was Unionist MP for South Birmingham, and on succeeding to his father's peerage would be forced to resign his Commons seat.

Diary

3 May 1911: Formally returned in the absence of any competition as Member for South Birmingham.

17 May 1911: Down to the House distinctly inclined to speak.* Sat for a considerable time while Pretyman and others were speaking and House rapidly emptying. Got up with great hesitation in face of an almost empty House and with a strong desire to get it over. Spoke for about 35 minutes and House filled up rapidly and gave me a good hearing. Not a very great effort but quite favourably received and kindly commented on in the papers. Lloyd George who had heard the last two or three sentences delivered himself at Simon's instigation of some very laudatory remarks.

9 July 1911: Fetched by motor from Sutton Court for lunch and found there the usual gathering – Austen Chamberlains, Olivers, Garvins, Cole-faxes, etc. Went with Garvin on the river after lunch. He told me that the King had agreed as far back as last November to give Asquith the peers he asked for, and that consequently there was no question of an election. He told me his information was of the best, and I rather conjectured that his informant may have been Lloyd George. All the same I am not sure that from what I have heard elsewhere the King does consider himself so absolutely bound, and in any case the Government may possibly prefer an election to the business of making the peers.

17 July 1911: Made a short speech urging on the Chancellor the consideration of the national treatment of syphilis. Spoke with considerable hesitation and awkwardness in view of the difficulty of the subject, but the House was very sympathetic and several members came up to me afterwards and congratulated me on having raised so difficult a topic. Lloyd George went out almost as soon as I began, but McKenna replied sympathetically.

Dined at the Allens. F.E. was there and I had a good talk with him on the situation. I gathered that Selborne, Austen, Carson, Wyndham and himself were about the only real stalwarts for holding out.

20 July 1911: To dinner with Lady Dawkins. Only people there – Lord Milner and Steel-Maitland. Steel-Maitland unsound on the resistance question, chiefly because he thinks that the Liberals by making the new peers will pocket an enormous campaign fund which will last for years

*This was the day after Lloyd George's Budget speech. L.S.A. spoke on the inadequacy of British spending on both social welfare and defence.

and years; very strong in fact that it was relative poverty of the Unionist Party that was responsible for much of the so-called bad organisation. Maxse came and picked me up and we went down to the House and had some talk with such members as we could catch to try and encourage them. Found all the Whips, Balcarres, Bridgeman, Monsell quite sound.

21 July 1911: Lunched at the Bath Club with Lady Betty Balfour, Lady Selborne, Lady Constance Lytton, Miss Balfour and Miss Christabel Pankhurst, together with several other men, to be encouraged or exhorted on the subject of the suffrage. Sat next to Miss Pankhurst and found her most amusing and clever. We fenced a great deal, but I did not commit myself to any undertaking on the various things she wanted me to do for her.

23 July 1911: Went to call on Mr Chamberlain and found him looking well, and very strong on the necessity of the peers forcing the issue. I had about ¾ hour's talk with him, and he wound up by saying 'Beat them'.

24 July 1911: Spent most of the morning and part of the afternoon in concocting reply to long letter of Curzon's in *The Times* advocating surrender. Went down to the House to hear Asquith open on consideration of the Lords amendments [he was proposing that they should be rejected]. House very crowded and tempers strong. From the first it was clear that a score or so of Unionists (instigated I believe originally by Hugh Cecil and Carson) were determined not to hear Asquith and the rest joined in spontaneously with a good will. Balfour did not look altogether happy, but the Whips were quite pleased and made no attempt to interfere. Some of the interruptions were unseemly and undignified but the general effect was good. Asquith had come down like Brennus to throw his sword into the scale and deliver himself of a pompous triumphant oration to the cheers of his supporters; instead of that he could do nothing but interject occasional sentences, turning round from time to time to Churchill and other supporters to ask if it was any use going on. The demonstration was undoubtedly meant quite as much to keep Balfour up to the mark as to defy Asquith, and to some extent did so. At any rate Balfour's speech, which the Liberals and Irish, with admirable discipline and self restraint, listened to quietly, contained no hint of surrender. [The next day, Balfour and Lansdowne issued letters counselling surrender.]

25 July 1911: To a meeting in one of the committee rooms originally called together by Cripps, Anson and others to deplore yesterday's outrageous proceedings. It was very soon discovered that the majority of those present by no means shared the views of the conveners of the meeting, and it was found impossible to pass any resolution on the subject or on a subsequent point which was raised by Sir George Younger that we should ask for a party meeting. There was a general consensus on the subject of loyalty to Mr Balfour much resembling the warm loyalty to King George shown by the American rebels both before and after the actual outbreak of the revolution.

29 July 1911: Got to the meeting* soon after 11.00. Found there Lord Halsbury, Salisbury, Selborne, Lovat, Willoughby de Broke, F. E. Smith and Wyndham.

8 August 1911: Debate on Lords' amendments opened by Hugh Cecil who produced an undoubted impression on the House, followed by a good incisive speech from Carson and a very fine debating effort from Bonar Law. All of them struck the note of meeting revolution by force in the last resort, and it was interesting to watch the faces of Ministers on the Front Bench, especially of men like Lloyd George and Simon, as they gradually began to realise that they really have committed themselves to a revolution. Churchill in his reply to Hugh Cecil and Carson showed the real revolutionary demagogue more than once, especially in his reference to the 70,000 dock strikers. He also announced the Government's intention to insist on the rejection of all the important amendments but a very trifling amendment.

9 August 1911: Dinner to Hayes Fisher. Sat next to Hamar [Greenwood] and bet him a grey top hat a year for life that the No Surrenders would win. [Later L.S.A. note: 'I fear I only paid once!']

10 August 1911: Listened to the finish of the Lords debate. A few dull speeches and then as a wind up, after the Chancellor rose to move the Question, a somewhat pompous oration from Curzon, followed by another short vigorous appeal from Halsbury. We thought the debate was over, but Rosebery got up and made a last effort in favour of surrender. He sat down and Selborne leapt to the table and in a short speech of amazing eloquence denounced Rosebery and asked the House not to perish in the dark by its own hand, but to die in the light at the hands of its enemies. It was the last speech made under the old order and a fine one. Then came the division. For a few breathless minutes we were all huddled together in the Lobby. The first we heard was that 111 peers had gone into the No-Surrender lobby and we thought ourselves safe, but a minute or two later

*Of the 'committee of stalwarts' on the Lords issue. This was a die-hard 'ginger-group' organised by Lord Willoughby de Broke on 13-15 July.

came the news that the Government had won. First report by 11, after-wards corrected to 17. Apparently over 30 peers, not counting a dozen bishops, had voted with the Government for the destruction of the consti-tution. Went home very angry.

17 August 1911: Dined with Lord Milner alone at the New University Club and had a long talk about future policy for the Party. He insisted that the only thing was that a small group of younger and independent men should get together, agree on a common policy and advocate it in the House and outside without bothering one way or another about Balfour and the authorities. It was no good trying to turn Balfour out; the only thing was to let events take their course and to go ahead with our own policy. As to that policy he was strongly for dropping heredity out altogether and going for an elected upper chamber, proportional represen-tation, ten or twelve years' tenure and rotation, so as to avoid any coinci-dence with general elections, possibly also an age limit of 30 or 40 for the electors, also a certain amount of referendum. As regards Home Rule, he was at first a little inclined to consider Home Rule All Round for the four nations. I think I convinced him that the only possible Home Rule was one which made Ulster separate from the rest of Ireland and that the right basis therefore was a system of provincial devolution giving say something like 15 provinces in all. On Tariff Reform he seemed a little inclined to consider the possibility of dropping the food taxes if the Canadian elections went wrong, to which I demurred strongly. He agreed entirely as to the desirability of treating Tariff Reform and Preference not as separate subjects but as entering into every subject discussed.

L.S.A. to Mrs Amery, 19 October 1911

This morning Mrs C[hamberlain] and I had breakfast alone and we sat on and talked and she told me lots and lots about Mr C., both about the troubles with A.J.B. and also about the fearful time when he first broke down and she deliberately minimised things for fear of any collapse of the movement. She is really a very splendid woman.

The last two and a half years of peace were dominated by the drift to civil war over the future constitutional status of Ireland. Amery's visit to Ireland in January 1912 clearly showed him that the Protestants, especially those in Ulster, meant to resist their incorporation in a state ruled by devolved power from Dublin. He published a series of seventeen articles in the *Morning Post* explaining his views and these were reproduced as a booklet entitled *The Case Against Home Rule*. As he wrote later, summing up one of these articles, 'The real issue was whether a purely artificial and temporary Parliamentary coalition was justified in disrupting the United Kingdom' (*My Political Life*, I, p. 399). Although he was throughout concerned with the need to preserve the Union the issue inevitably centred on the reactions of the people of Ulster.

Asquith introduced the Home Rule Bill on 11 April 1912. Two days before in Belfast, Bonar Law, Carson (the Ulster Unionists' leader) and some seventy MPs had reviewed 100,000 Irish Unionists who marched past in military formation – a process of preparation which had started the previous September when Carson announced that the Ulster Unionist Council intended to set up a Provisional Government to take charge of the Province the moment the Home Rule Bill was passed. Then in September 1912 came the signing of a Solemn Covenant by half a million men and women pledging themselves to 'use all means which may be found necessary to defeat the present conspiracy to set up a Home Rule Parliament in Ireland' and, if such a Parliament was set up, 'to refuse to recognise its authority'.

The new leader, Bonar Law, was a 'hawk' on opposing Home Rule but was less vigorous on tariff reform. Years later, Amery wrote of him that 'when it came to a crisis in the Party over its main constructive policy, he lacked nerve', and he quoted Joseph Chamberlain's words at the time of Law's taking up the leadership – 'he is no Tariff Reformer' – meaning that Law saw the subject in terms of trade figures and not as an Imperial policy of expansion of which trade was merely the economic factor (*My Political Life*, I, p. 387).

Early in December 1912 there were signs of 'wobbling' on the subject of Imperial preference – which inevitably would involve some duties on food imports – on the part of Unionist MPs for Lancashire (where free trade dominated all three Parties). On 14 December Amery, with two tariff reform MPs, George Lloyd and Rupert Gwynne, pressed Law on the subject, but he dismissed as 'ridiculous' the idea that 'there could be any change of policy'. Two days later Law made a speech in Ashton-under-Lyme (the seat of Max Aitken, later Lord Beaverbrook, who was also a strong tariff reformer) in which he limited the scope of all proposed taxation on food imports and said that these duties would be proposed only if the Dominions insisted. This led to a general stampede in the Party and the Unionist press against the full Chamberlain policy. Amery's diary entries describe in detail the developments leading to the acceptance by most of the Party – excluding Amery and his closest allies – of a memorial to Law, who was thinking of resigning, urging him not to do so but suggesting the postponement of any food duties required to make preference effective until after a second election.

Diary

4 January 1912 (Belfast): Lunched out at Craigavon with the whole of the future provisional government of Ulster, including Carson. Talked with Carson, and he told me that the suggestion I had sent him in a letter in September, namely that the Ulster people should as far as possible keep within the letter of the law, and adopting the provisions of the Home Rule Bill simply exercise them in their own way to the exclusion of the Dublin authorities, had commended itself to the Council to whom he had forwarded my letter. He let me see their draft scheme for the organisation and administration of Ulster which seemed to me thoughtfully and practically worked out.

L.S.A. to Mrs Amery, from Dublin, 5 January 1912

Into [Omagh] poured some 20,000 Ulstermen and to the sound of innumerable drums and pipes and trumpets and bagpipes processed past Carson who stood up in an open carriage and acknowledged their cheers with a genial mephistophelian smile. They are a solid determined looking lot these Ulstermen – no more Irish than they are Chinese and with not much more use for 'Papishes' than they have for 'Chinks' or niggers.

Diary

25 January 1912: I think I convinced Lord Milner that there could be no question, for many years, of any form of Home Rule All Round which included Ulster in the Irish unit.

26 January 1912: Went to hear Bonar Law at the Albert Hall. A very useful fighting speech. Some of the earlier criticism a little thin and the whole in a tone and language very different from the elegant philosophy of A.J.B., but clear, incisive and quite definite in its leadership. The audience very greatly pleased.

31 January 1912 (Birmingham): Had an interview at the Midland Hotel with Lady Willoughby de Broke and a suffrage deputation. I told them that in view of the seriousness of the political situation I could not pledge myself to anything and that my vote would be entirely governed by the general interests of the party.

17 February 1912: Went to gathering of Trade Union and Tariff Reform Association to discuss attitude at the approaching conference for the creation of the new Labour Party – Unionist Labour Party was finally selected as the name.

14 March 1912: Arrival of my son [John Amery] who came about 8.30 p.m. – a long and anxious day.

26 March 1912: Dined with the Irish Proportionalists downstairs. Gathered that Redmond's line is that he will accept proportional representation if Ulster asks for it; somewhat like Brer Fox offering to consider any suggestions from Brer Rabbit as to sauce.

28 March 1912: Turned up for the last hour or so of the 2nd Reading of the Suffrage Bill. House in a rollicking mood, and the narrow defeat of the Bill was welcomed with wild cheers. I was sorry that our people had not insured its getting a second reading for the Government would have been put in a very difficult position to find the time, and their own feelings among themselves were very bitter about it. Personally, I voted [for the Bill] because I thought it deserved discussion, though I don't think I could have supported it for the third reading.

11 April 1912: Asquith introduced the Home Rule Bill in a speech which seemed to me to lack any real conviction or keenness. The Bill on pure Gladstonian lines but with the most hopelessly entangled finance. At the opening of the proceedings I introduced my Scotland and Ireland Firearms Bill, a harmless measure for the proving of gun barrels, but the House generally scented some deeper meaning and cheered loudly when I introduced it.

26 June 1912: Dinner with Mark Sykes and Grigg. A very cheerful gathering. Mark Sykes's imitations of French with a Turkish accent quite inimitable; likewise his stories of the monk who rode from Jerusalem to Egypt with a camel, a horse, a mule and a donkey, riding them alternately in order to make quite sure that at least part of the way he was doing it exactly the same as the Holy Family.

15 July 1912: Tea with Locker Lampson on the Terrace to discuss educating Unionist working men on the Insurance Bill with a view to their becoming trade union secretaries.

1 August 1912: Chiefly occupied with the Imperial Fund and with the initiation, together with Worthington Evans, of a small committee under one Will Edwards of the Central Office to consider the question of what steps might be taken to organise the working men in the trade unions. The committee started considering the possibility of forming a separate political trades union, but afterwards abandoned that in favour of special labour organisation under the Central Office.

L.S.A. to Mrs Amery, from Hatfield House, Herts, 1 October 1912

It's nearly 12.30 and we have been at it ever since dinner, discussing constitutions for the House of Lords – we, that is Selborne, Austen, Wyndham, Halsbury, Northumberland, Mackinder, Willoughby de Broke, Hugh Cecil, Salisbury, Winterton, Hope, Ormsby Gore and Sposo.* Tomorrow we meet at 10.30 when we discuss the powers of the House. The real bust will come tomorrow afternoon or evening between those who wish to patch up the existing House and those who are prepared to go for a brand new elected House and let the Peers get elected if they can. Austen, Wyndham, Mackinder, Willoughby de Broke, myself, and, I rather think, Selborne are the latter persuasion, but Halsbury and Northumberland won't have this at any price.

Diary

21 October 1912: Dined with Abe Bailey. Slipped away early from his dinner to go to the House. When I came back about 11.30 I found Bailey very distressed because Churchill had asked whether I had left the dinner table in order not to have to meet him.

During the winter of 1912–13 Amery also served on a parliamentary Joint Select Committee which had been set up in October 1912 to inquire into the rumours of ministerial speculation in the shares of the Marconi company. The party political strife over the inquiry bears witness to the bitterness of those years. A contract with the Marconi company for providing a chain of wireless stations linking the various parts of the Empire had been signed on 18 July 1912. Lloyd George himself, the Master of Elibank (the Liberal Chief Whip) and the Attorney General, Sir Rufus Isaacs, had earlier bought shares in the American Marconi company from Isaac's brother Harry, who in turn had bought the shares from another brother, Godfrey Isaacs, managing director of the British and the American Marconi companies. It was alleged that these shares had been bought at below the market price and that the Ministers had committed an impropriety by accepting through an intermediary a financial favour from a

*L.S.A.'s name for himself when writing to his wife.

Government contractor. Furthermore, the contract was still under discussion, and the favour consisted of shares which were bound to appreciate as a result of the success of the British parent company in securing such an important contract.

Amery's diary gives a somewhat sparse account of the Select Committee's proceedings in late March and he does not describe the Commons debate which opened on 18 June and discussed the thoroughly unsatisfactory report by the Liberal majority. He did, however, help to draft the report of the Unionist minority, which was much more critical of the Ministers' impropriety.

During the last six months of 1913, a period for which there is no diary, Amery travelled with the first delegation from the United Kingdom branch of the Empire Parliamentary Association to South Africa, Australia and New Zealand.

Diary

27 October 1912: First meeting of the Marconi Committee, [examination] of Sir Alexander King, Chief Secretary of the Post Office. A shifty looking fellow and pretty unscrupulous in his statements.

24 November 1912: After tea Mrs Astor insisted on having a parliament to discuss the question of the poor in the country. [The speaker's] main theme was the necessity of giving a really decent plot of land, say an acre, with every cottage. A very interesting discussion followed. At the end of it all, when it was time for dinner, Mrs Astor, with a wave of the hand, said, 'Now let us put on our expensive dresses and forget about the poor.'

8 December 1912: Talked with John Buchan who told me that he had been informed on good authority that Lloyd George had speculated in St Katherine's Dock shares at the time of the Port of London Bill.

17 December 1912: Read with bewilderment and even consternation Bonar Law's Ashton speech. Some of it quite fine but there were two passages in it which seemed absolutely inexplicable, one transferring the whole onus of the food taxes on to the Dominions after a conference, the other indicating that nothing was to be done for agriculture and that the only articles of food to be taxed at all . . . would be wheat, meat and possibly dairy produce. The effect was one of hesitation coupled with an ignorance of the real problem, which was bad enough in its effect upon those of us who knew what he wanted, and apparently precipitated the stampede on the part of the weaker brethren. *The Times* of course came out at once with a strong condemnation from the *Round Table* point of view (written by [Edward] Grigg) of the passage dealing with the conference, and the *Daily Mail* followed suit. All through the Christmas holidays the stampede seems to have continued in the columns of the papers and at country houses.

L.S.A. to Austen Chamberlain, 27 December 1912

I wish I knew what to make of the Ashton speech. So far from clearing the air it seems only to have made confusion worse and everyone is appending a different meaning to it. . . . We must make it clear that preference as such, upon whatever duties we impose in our local interests, is an integral part of our policy in any case. . . .

The second outstanding thing is that the speech, unless re-explained very carefully, would seem to preclude all protection of any sort to British agriculture. It seems to me essential to make clear that 'food' in the Ashton speech only referred to bread and meat in the ordinary sense of the food of the masses and that we are not precluded from protective as well as preferential duties on barley and oats, fruit, hops, poultry and I should like to add, dairy products. This is all the more vital in view of the Irish situation. If Home Rule is to be killed for good and all by the defeat of this Bill it must be by a really rapid economic development in Ireland following our return to power.

Diary

31 December 1912: Saw Austen who was very concerned and said it was the most serious stampede there has ever been on the question. So many people had been at Bonar Law that B.L. was beginning to doubt the possibility of carrying on. He urged me to speak to B.L., Balcarres and others. His views confirmed by Astor who seemed to be trying to get together the stalwarts. Talked to Baird and Stanley in the office and found them quite on the scuttle. No hope of carrying Lancashire or winning seats in Scotland, only chance lay in persuading B.L. to adopt the *Daily Telegraph* or Second election policy.

1 January 1913: Long talk with Balcarres who assured me 90 per cent of the party were on the scuttle and that they could not be stopped. Very sympathetic, and rather impressed by my arguments, but doubtful of possibility of rallying them. Talked to a great many others, the general tendency being to assume that the Lancashire members made it impossible to carry the whole policy. Went for a short walk with F.E. who admitted that the whole policy might quite well have been carried if the rot had not been precipitated by the Ashton speech, but considered that some jettison was now inevitable. Later on Rupert Gwynne, one of the few really staunch ones, and I had a talk with B.L. He seemed very nervous and hesitating; declared it was quite out of the question for him to change his policy, but feared that he could not hold the party for long. Even if he had a party meeting and enthused them, which he thought he could, they would be all over the place later, and it was useless leading an army that thought itself beaten. I scented change in the air and asked him if he could assure me there would be no change for three months, an assurance he readily gave. Gwynne said frankly that if there was to be change and wobbling we might just as well have kept Balfour who could do that sort of thing better, and I also expressed the conviction to B.L. that he had better resign than yield to pressure.

2 and 3 January 1913: Papers indulging in great campaign against each other, Garvin belabouring 'Uncle Five Heads' [i.e. Northcliffe] in *P[all] M[all] G[azette]* and taking daily tea with Lady Northcliffe afterwards! *Times* declares only 17 stalwarts [on food duties] left. *Daily Graphic* gives names of 16 'food taxers'!

4 January 1913: Down to Wittersham and thought out in train my ideas of a possible compromise that might work, viz. the exemption of wheat and meat from our general tariff subject to a subsequent referendum if the House so resolved, leaving it free to members to pledge or not pledge themselves to a referendum.

5 January 1913: Wrote out my compromise scheme in a letter to Austen – the scheme itself workable, but doubtful as to whether it really would be any use now.

L.S.A. to Borden, 6 January 1913

You will no doubt have heard with some surprise . . . the news of the extraordinary Christmas panic in the Unionist party over preference on foodstuffs. There are several causes, some general and some purely accidental and local. . . . There has always been a large element in the party of members who, while in a general way in favour of the whole policy of Imperial Preference, have through laziness or timidity never had the courage to argue the case properly to their constituents, and with whom the disinclination to do so has increased rather than diminished. . . . There is the particular fact that in Lancashire, where the element of real 'free-fooders' has always been strong, Balfour's referendum policy for the 1910

THE LEO AMERY DIARIES

election seems to have been regarded as still standing, with the consequences that Lord Lansdowne's Albert Hall speech,* followed by the
comparative failure of a personally highly undesirable candidate at Bolton
a few days after, created a temporary panic. This was precipitated into a
general stampede by a certain note of hesitancy and change about Bonar
Law's Ashton speech. I don't believe that that speech was really meant to
indicate any deflection in policy. Nor do I believe that Bonar Law had
the slightest intention, in his reference to an Imperial conference, to
suggest throwing the onus of the new policy upon the Dominions. But
the awkward phraseology, coming at such a moment, added to the general
insecurity. . . . At this moment the facts . . . are roughly as follows:

A small section of the party, possibly 20 or 30 members, including
most of the Lancashire members, are really determined to get rid of the
preference as far as foodstuffs are concerned, at any rate for the next
election, and will probably in any case pledge themselves individually
against it. The great middle body, perplexed, puzzled, and frightened, are
for the moment inclined to call for compromise mainly in the direction of
suggesting that the issue at the next election should only include preference on such duties as we shall be imposing anyhow for local purposes,
excluding however all food duties and possibly some form of preference
on investments or some bounty on shipping, leaving the carrying out of
the whole Imperial trade policy to a second election. Finally, there are
some 40 or 50 who are absolutely convinced that quite apart from Imperial
considerations it would be the height of folly, in view of a coming election,
to change our front and practically to recant from the line we have taken
up for all these years. Austen Chamberlain is the natural spokesman of
this group. . . .

Now as to Bonar Law. Though very deeply impressed by the seriousness of the stampede and the attitude of the Lancashire members, I have
the best reasons for believing that he means to stand firm and may refuse
to carry on the leadership if the great majority of the party will not come
into line. We shall therefore see in the next month whether his attitude
will bring them back, always excepting possibly some of the Lancashire
and Yorkshire members, or whether a permanence of the present attitude
may in two or three months' time compel him to resign or to acquiesce in
a change in the party policy, still remaining nominally leader but with
grave loss of reputation.

*The speech to the Unionist Party Conference in November which L.S.A. regarded as
supplying a 'steadying note' (*My Political Life*, I, p. 474).

Diary

6 January 1913: Dinner of stalwarts at Constitutional Club given by Page Croft: some 28–30 present, of whom 5 privately told Bonar Law that it was really no use. Ronald McNeill led off the speaking, beginning strongly but ending feebly. Wyndham rather good, vowing that he would never accept office in a Government which did not give a preference on wheat. One or two others, and then I gave them five minutes' straight talk . . . insisting that it was our character and not our policy that had hitherto been our obstacle with the electorate. I think I made a considerable impression, at any rate for the moment, and Goulding and Hewins followed up effectively in the same vein. Later on Worthington Evans urged blind following of Bonar Law whatever he did.

7 January 1913: Lunch with Rupert Gwynne. Page Croft and Ridley there: general agreement that B.L. meant to give way. . . . At the House rumours of B.L.'s threatened resignation freely current. . . .

[In the evening] was asked by Hewins, Croft and Goulding to help them consider a memorial drawn up by Carson to induce B.L. not to resign as he had definitely declared he would do. I read the thing, a long winded screed treating Preference as a very subordinate issue and directly suggesting its postponement. I urged that we could not possibly agree to such a thing. But the others all vowed it would be discourteous to Carson not to consider it carefully and see if it could be amended. Presently Carson and F.E. joined us and the thing was turned into a sort of drafting committee, I standing on one side and telling them that while it might be worthwhile including reference to Preference for the benefit of the scuttlers who did sign, we ought to have no truck with it. However, I could see that Croft and the others were more and more succumbing to the idea that all would be well if the principle of Preference were reasserted sufficiently vigorously in words, regardless of the real meaning and effect of the document. They were also influenced by what F.E. told them about Austen, to the effect that he would not dissuade any of his friends from signing it.

L.S.A. to Borden, 10 January 1913

Bonar Law told his colleagues on Tuesday he could not go on and must resign, as he was not prepared to change his policy. With no other possible leader in prospect – Austen Chamberlain after all being very much stronger on the question of preference than Bonar Law himself – a tremendous effort was made to induce him to stay on at all costs, and a memorial was drawn up, with a view to its being signed by the whole party, asking him to reconsider his decision, affirming the adherence of the signatories to the whole policy of preference but suggesting its postponement as regards foodstuffs till after a second election. This has been signed by practically the whole party (though I could not bring myself to do it) and on these terms Bonar Law is retaining the leadership.

Diary

15 January 1913: Third reading of H[ome] R[ule] Bill opened by Balfour. . . . The only thing I regret is that not a soul throughout these debates ever says anything to suggest that he feels that the United Kingdom really is a nation and that Irish nationalism in any shape or form means the end of United Kingdom nationalism. If only a single name could have been invented for the United Kingdom in 1800 and the Vice-Royalty abolished I don't believe Home Rule would ever have been considered.

17 January 1913: Lunched with Lady Vera Herbert to meet the Albanian delegates.* They were fearfully delighted to meet someone who really knew a little about their country, its language, and history, and before I quite knew where I was I found myself let in for the task of taking a small deputation to Grey to put the Albanian case.

25 January 1913: Dined at Austen Chamberlain's to discuss the Tariff Reform situation on the basis of Bonar Law's Edinburgh speech. The speech itself was rather what I expected. It reaffirmed preference more or less on the Ashton [speech] lines but ruling out all foodstuffs for the present. . . . All the loopholes in fact opened the wrong way, which to my mind clearly showed no really strong constructive mind or intense desire to carry the whole policy through. Fabian Ware told me at dinner some days after that when Bonar Law was first appointed Joe had said 'He is not a Tariff Reformer', and there is a real element of truth in that. To come back to the dinner, we were there the remnant of the Die-Hards, Selborne, Wyndham, George Lloyd, Hewins, Ridley and myself. There was no end of confused discussion, Hewins exceedingly optimistic and to my mind rather muddled. Wyndham very strong on the necessity of really enunciating our cardinal principles, but as usual, marring the effectiveness of his argument by his frequent reference to his own speeches. Selborne clear

*What is now Albania had been evacuated by the Turks after their defeat by the Serbs and Greeks in the First Balkan War of 1912. A conference in London had met in December 1912 to decide on the borders and the status of the area which became Albania. See the diary entries for 28 January and 31 March 1913. Cf. Julian Amery's liaison with the Albanian Resistance in 1944, described in his *Son of the Eagle*.

on the main point that what has to be avoided at all costs is finding the party muddled when we return with a number of men who will not vote for an agricultural tariff or for preference on any pretext. Decided that really the great thing was to go ahead with the T[ariff] R[eform] L[eague] but yet keep touch with the party.

28 January 1913: Took in an Albanian deputation to interview Grey on the subject of Albania. . . . My main point was the mischief that would result of incorporating large blocks of purely Albanian territory such as Prizrend, Jakova, Ipek and Scutari town in alien states. I quite agreed that wherever the population was mixed the allies [i.e. Greece, Serbia and Montenegro, who all had claims] should have the benefit of the doubt!

22 February 1913 (Rome): After dinner we had some amusing talk with a wonderful old sea captain called Briscoe. . . . Once in '82 he asked Mr G[ladstone] whether Randolph Churchill would ever lead the Conservatives. The old man waved his arm and with fierce emphasis exclaimed, 'God forbid that a great English party should ever be led by a Churchill, one whose family has never had a shred of moral principle', etc. or words to that effect, and then proceeded, 'But there is a young man whom the House of Commons has not yet appreciated who for all his lackadaisical academic manner has got ability and principles who might yet lead the Conservative Party, I mean Mr Arthur Balfour.'

12 March 1913: Having drawn 19th in the Ballot I put in a Proportional Representation Bill, though with little hope of its getting discussed.

25 March 1913: Rufus Isaacs before the [Marconi] Committee. His main statement did not add very much to the Matin case except the fact that he got the shares through his brother Harry. He was rather too voluble and elaborate for a good witness and too inclined subsequently both with [Lord Robert] Cecil and myself to come out with prepared outbursts of indignation.

27 March 1913: 3rd day of Rufus [Isaacs]. In the afternoon it was my turn for examining him which I did at some length and with considerable difficulty. Cross examination is an art that requires practice and in that respect he has all the advantage over me. However, I pressed him as closely as I could.

28 March 1913: Finished my questions to Rufus. Listened to greater part of Lloyd George's statement describing himself as a poor man, etc. It really requires an Aristophanes to do justice to these situations.

31 March 1913: I saw the Albanian delegates at the House and promised to stir up Grey again about their southern boundary which according to them the French were anxious to see drawn as far north as the north end of Corfu.

1 May 1913: Marconi. Chesterton being unable to turn up and witnesses on the corruption question being pretty well exhausted we separated after a short discussion. On a motion of Cecil's that members of the Committee should go into the box to declare their disinterestedness, this met with a wall of blank refusal on the Liberal side, and the extent of agitation showed by [Handel] Booth [Liberal MP and member of the Marconi Committee] indicated to me pretty plainly that he had been in the business.

2 May 1913: Lunched with Joynson-Hicks and Du Cros to discuss the formation of a committee to worry Seely on the air question.

25 June 1913: Lunched with Joseph Chamberlain. He summed up his views as to the attitude of the Unionist Party over Marconi in the phrase 'too bloody polite'.

L.S.A. to Sir Henry Wilson, from Australia, 14 October 1913

Have the General Staff at home yet started a special section for studying the influence of aviation on the whole of our tactics and organisation? . . . I know you have always been sympathetic to my rather revolutionary ideas, so I will throw a few more at your head.

Quite apart from aviation, I should say that the modern rifle had called for new developments in tactics. . . . It necessitates greater extension of front and greater individual dispersion. It enormously enhances the importance of individual efficiency and self reliance and of mobility. . . . It increases the importance of mounted troops, cyclists, motor cyclists, etc., though (in both our opinions I believe) it reduces the opportunities for cavalry shock tactics to a point at which it is not really worth training men for it and diverting their minds from modern cavalry ideas. Lastly, I am inclined to think that it reduces the value of artillery for field purposes, partly because it is slow and needs so much transport behind it, partly because the dispersion of the firing line on both sides gives it so much fewer definite targets. . . .

Now add to these inherent, but not yet fully grasped, factors of the situation, aviation as it is and as it is sure to become in the next few years. Except in rare cases, where one army has an overwhelming superiority in aircraft, both armies will be frequently flown over. . . . All solid compact bodies of troops, whether battalions or batteries on the march, or cavalry divisions waiting behind the traditional 'fold in the ground' for the great opportunity, will be given away at once. . . . The existing importance of dispersion is consequently greatly enhanced. So is that of mobility, for you will in future often want to change your dispositions entirely between the time you are spotted by an enemy's aeroplane and the counter-moves taken by the enemy's general on receipt of an aero-wireless. . . .

Now it seems to me, that you can only successfully meet the needs created by aerial scouting by calling the same mobile medium into play. In other words I believe aircraft for reconnaissance have got to be followed up by aircraft for the conveyance of troops. Already today Grahame White totes round 7 or 8 passengers at a time on his 'aerobus' at Hendon. What is to prevent our organising military aerobuses which will carry a similar number of men to an important position? A hundred such aerobuses could dump the best part of a battalion of infantry down at a point 30 miles away within the hour, come back and dump down another battalion within two hours, and another every subsequent two hours. . . . Of course it will cost money. But I believe that once you begin turning out aircraft wholesale, like Waterbury watches, the price will come down with a run, and I believe the aerobuses I am thinking of could be turned out for £200 a piece, i.e. at less cost per man than mounting them on horseback and providing horse transport. . . .

Just fancy the play even a few hundred men suitably dumped down on the flank of an advancing German column could make with the strategical *Aufmarsch* of the army! Think of the trouble they could cause to station and bridge guards, and of the effect upon an enemy's advance of the need of strengthening all these and of guarding in force the flanks of his whole supply column, and then feeding these flankguards. Have you also considered the possible effect of a few aeroplanes, boldly and recklessly handled, in throwing massed cavalry into confusion?

The first seven months of 1914 were dominated by the deteriorating situation in Ulster, but unfortunately only January is effectively covered in the diary. In September 1913 Ulster had announced the constitution of a Provisional Government, and by the end of the year the Ulster Volunteers totalled nearly 100,000, only partially armed but regularly organised. The Unionist leaders in England tended to concentrate on the need to exclude Ulster, but Amery preferred to stress the central issue of the Union: to drop or suspend the Home Rule Bill and try to work out a genuine federal constitution for the United Kingdom. The only Unionist leader who kept that issue in the foreground, however, was Austen Chamberlain (see Amery's letter to Neville Chamberlain, 25 July 1914).

On 10 January 1914 Amery suggested to Lord Milner that what was required was a British Covenant, on the lines of the Ulster Covenant, which would provide an organisation to paralyse anything the Government did aimed at coercing Ulster. The diary and correspondence for mid-January describe the steps to be taken and the limits to which Amery and even more senior Unionists were prepared to go. Here the diary is interrupted, but Amery recounts in *My Political Life* (I, p. 441) how he visited Ulster then and in May to co-ordinate plans with the Ulster leaders, and how Milner assisted in recruiting significant names for their manifesto published on 3 March. Their Covenant included the threat that they would take or support 'any action that may be effective to prevent it [i.e. the Home Rule Bill] being put into operation. . . .'

But while this was being done, the chances of the Government using the Army to coerce Ulster were being frustrated by Sir Henry Wilson and Brigadier-General Hubert Gough in the Curragh Mutiny and connected developments in late March, when officers in Ulster indicated their preference to resign their commissions rather than to be used to coerce Ulster. As they clearly had the support of their men, the Government had to give way and claim that the whole affair was an 'honest misunderstanding' and there never had been any intention of using the forces in Ulster. We find traces in Amery's letters to his wife of his vigorous activity in the House of Commons during April in debates and question sessions on this débâcle.

At the end of May, Asquith introduced the third reading of the Home Rule Bill and at length admitted that there would be an Amending Bill to supersede the 'suggestion stage' provided for the House of Lords by the Parliament Act. This would embody his own compromise proposals made on 9 March 1914 as a basis for further discussion. These 'derisory and unworkable' proposals, as Amery later called them (*My Political Life*, I, p. 457), involved a scheme for a referendum by counties and county boroughs in Ulster providing for provisional exclusion from a Dublin-ruled Ireland for six years to be followed by automatic *inclusion*, unless Parliament decided otherwise. The proposals were introduced into the House of Lords on 23 June 1914. But after a second reading on 6 July they were converted by the Lords into a measure to exclude the whole of Ulster. In a last attempt to break the deadlock, the King summoned a conference of all the Party leaders – the Buckingham Palace Conference – which met from 21–24 July and failed to find a solution.

With the Commons debate on, and inevitable rejection of, the Lord's Amending Bill imminent, on 26 July a yacht steered by Mrs Erskine Childers landed rifles and ammunition at Howth on the north side of Dublin under the protection of a body of Irish National Volunteers who then clashed with troops with losses in dead and wounded. As Amery later wrote (*My Political Life*, I, p. 458), the emergence of the INV, who by then numbered 100,000, killed the Home Rule Bill so far as this made any pretence of retaining any United Kingdom control over any Dublin Government. 'Their avowed object was to get rid of all restrictions upon full independence.'

The whole issue was about to be defused. On 28 June Archduke Franz Ferdinand had been murdered in Sarajevo and with the despatch of the Austro-Hungarian ultimatum to Serbia on 23 July, the European powers began their drift to war. On 30 July Bonar Law agreed with Asquith on a postponement of the Amending Bill.

Diary

5 January 1914: Lunched with Henry Wilson at White's. He was very pessimistic about the whole political situation and above all anxious that the army should not be drawn in. At the same time he was convinced that nothing would induce Asquith to listen to reason except a big stick. His view was that years of too good living, bridge, etc. had made him quite incapable of any real decision, at any rate that was the impression that he received at the Defence Committee, and therefore he was certain that he would drift where Redmond and his party pushed him till the crisis came. We discussed the possibility of the Territorials doing something that would make the Government realise the situation, e.g. transferring themselves bodily to a Union Defence Force. Lord Roberts, he told me, was tremendously keen and prepared to go to any length if the situation demanded it.

12 January 1914: Came up to town and attended meeting of Willoughby de Broke's Committee* to discuss what measures of organisation might be taken in this country if the Government refused all compromise. Lord Milner explained his views to them, including the possibility of himself and others coming on to the League† to transform it into a body to organise the signing of a declaration. The idea of utilising a public declaration in order to emphasise matters and provide a list of those who really take things seriously had been suggested to me by Lord Milner in a long letter a day or two before and he took it up keenly. On to the dentist's whom I found also a member of Willoughby de Broke's League thirsting to go and fight in Ulster!

13 January 1914: Went to the Ulster League's office and discussed things further with their committee who approved of the new draft declaration.

*See diary entry for 29 July 1911.
†The League for the Defence of Ulster and the Union which had enrolled some 10,000 members to go over to Ulster if necessary.

We then went on to see Bonar Law at 2.30 and Willoughby [de Broke] laid the situation before him. Bonar Law had already been primed by Milner and was quite sympathetic. He put it to us that if the names of the Committee who were prepared to organise this thing were good enough to ensure certain success he would back it with the general support of the Party, though the actual organisation would be separate.

14 January 1914: On the train [to Birmingham] I showed the declaration to Neville Chamberlain who seemed entirely to agree. After the meeting I put the declaration business before Austen, Neville and Lord Dartmouth. Lord D. was willing to support, but Neville meanwhile, Austen agreeing, took the line that the declaration was too vague and that they did not like binding themselves to a form of words which might contemplate subsequent support of extra-constitutional action. I had some correspondence with both of them afterwards but they maintained their view, and their objection, as well as that of Robert Cecil, clearly indicated that one could not have got a unanimous party meeting to start off the signature of the declaration to give the meeting its blessing.

15 January 1914: Saw Lord Milner at 10.00 . . . and put some of the difficulties before him. He left me a free hand to discuss the matter [i.e. the 'Covenant'] with Lord Roberts and certain other people.

L.S.A. to Neville Chamberlain, 16 January 1914

You will have seen in the morning's paper that Bonar Law has not only repeated* for himself and his colleagues a definite pledge to use any means which may seem effective to prevent the coercion of Ulster, indicating that those means will 'involve something more than making speeches', but has definitely declared that that pledge rests on the party as a whole. Now it is quite true that the party as a whole has endorsed it in the sense in which things are endorsed at public meetings and in the sense that there has been no criticism. But it should infinitely strengthen the position of the leaders and make the situation clear if that pledge were really firmly and seriously endorsed by a large body of people. It is only if the Government realise in time that we are really serious that there is any chance of civil war in Ireland being averted, and if it once starts in Ireland I feel certain that it will spread over here. It was from this point of view that the idea of getting a declaration generally signed first commended itself to

---

*This was presumably the 'Bristol Speech' (see diary entry for 17 January 1914). At Cardiff on the 15th Bonar Law announced that negotiations for a compromise with the Government were ended.

a few of us after we had exhausted all the alternatives that occurred.

Again, if it were not inadvisable and unseemly, it would really be impossible at this moment to lay down an exact programme of the measure you are going to take. So much depends upon what the state of public feeling will be and on the actual course of events. That is just the criticism I would make against the existing effort of Willoughby de Broke and Co. to organise a certain number of men with rifles to fight in Ulster. What is demanded is too specific. If there is to be fighting on such a scale it may not be in Ulster, nor does it follow that there is to be fighting at all, at any rate of a kind in which rifles are wanted. It still seems to me that the only possible course is to find out how many people there are in the country who share the same view as the leaders of the party do, viz. that they are determined at all hazards to prevent the coercion of Ulster under the Parliament Act. The exact way in which effect will be given to that pledge depends on the course of events, on the plans which commend themselves to the leaders, and on the capacity of individuals. But you can have no beginning of organisation until you know at any rate the total of men who really mean business, and when you have that you can begin to classify them and consider your plans as the situation moves.

I know it is undesirable to do things prematurely, but, looking at the time table, there does not seem really to be very much time to lose if we are not to be too late to avert an outbreak in Ulster.

Diary

17 January 1914: Weekend with Lord Roberts. Unfolded Lord Milner's views to Bobs who was of course thoroughly in sympathy. He is in a great state about the effect of the whole thing on the Army and is prepared to do almost anything. The only thing really is to prevent him from using his great name except in the most effective fashion. I spent a good part of Sunday drawing up a memorandum for him starting off with the closing sentences of Bonar Law's Bristol speech which were really a veiled invitation to the Party to take up the sort of scheme we were at.

L.S.A. to Mrs Amery, 21 April 1914

I don't think the dear Radicals [i.e. Liberals] love me very much. This afternoon when I got up to ask a supplementary of old Squiff [Asquith] the mere sight of me caused a roar of execration to rise from the Radical and Nationalist benches, which of course our people answered by giving me a good cheer. [*22 April 1914*] I was rebuked today in the House for telling Asquith he had lied.

99

L.S.A. to Mrs Amery, 29 April 1914

I've come home thoroughly vexed and dissatisfied with the turn of things. Our party are such 'mugs' – it is the only word to describe them. Just because Churchill at the end of most offensive speech threw out a few sentences of soft sawder about federation meaning nothing and not committing himself, still less Asquith, to anything – all our Front Bench allow the whole sting to be taken out of their speeches and gush in response and allow Asquith to ride off triumphant at the end of a speech which was most monstrous evasion of the issue.

L.S.A. to Austen Chamberlain, 4 May 1914

What I feel we must aim at is to press home the fact that if there is to be a compromise on some form of federalism or devolution it cannot be by tinkering with this Bill without regard to United Kingdom conditions, but it does involve a start *de novo*. Meanwhile I don't believe that the Government is in a position to concede even the exclusion of Ulster, i.e. the 6 counties, so I doubt really if anything arises except the one question when we can get them [the Government] out. And this can now only arise at the point when they have to make the attempt to coerce Ulster. I don't believe they can do it and if so will have to confess it to their own people. That will be their deathblow. I cannot help thinking that if last week we had boldly justified the gun-running and dared the Government to punish anybody, we should have had them out there and then.

L.S.A. to Carson, 22 June 1914

I have been thinking about the possibilities of an ultimatum when the Amending Bill breaks down, and certain general conclusions have suggested themselves to me. The principal one is that the ultimatum period should be a reasonably long one. In an ordinary international dispute, by the time it has come to the ultimatum stage it is usual to give only 24 or 48 hours' notice. If in this case you gave notice as short as that it might be impossible for the Government to do anything but meet the challenge by instant military measures, and it would have its majority and a good section of public opinion behind it. If, on the other hand, you gave them ten days or a fortnight in which to make up their minds, there will be reasonable time for them to collapse under pressure from the more timid elements in their party, while influence could be brought to bear on the King.

My suggestion therefore would be a reasoned statement of the whole Ulster case, coupled with a definite request for information within fourteen days as to whether the Government intend to consult the people before presenting the Bill to the King or not, and announcing the intention of Ulster, in the event of an unfavourable answer, to take over the administration of the province, and to insist on all persons acting under the instructions of the provisional government. Any movement of troops into Ulster during the period of waiting would of course have to be treated as a hostile act. All this may now of course become necessary, though it is conceivable that the mere failure of the Amending Bill may in itself bring about the Government's collapse.

L.S.A. to Neville Chamberlain, 25 July 1914

It seems to me that we have a splendid opportunity now* for clearing ourselves completely from the entanglement of this Ulster exclusion idea. We only drifted into it really, if we are to be honest with ourselves because Ulster was the easiest thing to talk about when public opinion was apathetic, and because on the face of it it seemed a moderate and reasonable attitude. That it could have led to peace was to me almost inconceivable from the first. But if it had nothing could have been more unsatisfactory from the national point of view and more disastrous from the Party point of view than such an agreement. From all I was able to gather from the tone of people in the Lobby and from the many letters I get, even the acceptance by the Government of the 'clean cut' for the whole province of Ulster would have led to a tremendous explosion of indignation from our Party against our leaders for bringing us into a position where we should virtually, if not theoretically, have accepted Home Rule for the rest of Ireland. I have never seen such a scene of anger in our Lobby as there was when the Conference was first announced, and it was only when assurances spread round that there was no likelihood of anything coming of it that feeling was in the least mollified.

As it is we are now in a splendid position to say that for the sake of peace we have explored a certain path to the utmost and found it led nowhere, and that we are now back on the broad ground of the maintenance of the Union and of the right of the nation to decide.

*Just after the failure of the Buckingham Palace Conference.

5

The War: Defeat
1914–16

Although there had been periodic bouts of 'war fever' before July 1914, the First World War in many respects took Britain by surprise. Amery's papers for July 1914 show clearly that MPs were then absorbed in the Irish crisis.

The assassination of the Archduke at Sarajevo gave Germany and Austria-Hungary (the 'Central Powers') their chance. They felt they should strike while Germany possessed a temporary advantage over France in numbers of reservists and while Britain was paralysed by the Irish crisis and in any event very largely unprepared to make a major military effort. Lord Roberts' campaign for National Service had been disregarded by the Government and not endorsed by the leaders of the Opposition. Similarly, Grey's colleagues – the majority of whom were appalled by the revelation – had not been told until 1912 of the arrangements made should France be attacked. Even when they were revealed the details were not given. Yet Amery had often discussed them with Lord Roberts and Henry Wilson, then Director of Military Operations (*My Political Life* Hutchinson, 1953, vol. II, p. 13). This refusal to reveal openly the nature of Britain's obligations and preparations, Amery believed, led Germany not only to prepare for war, but to insist on attacking France through neutral Belgium as laid down in the Schlieffen Plan.

After a month of alternate bargaining and blustering, Austria-Hungary declared war on Serbia on 28 July. Amery's diary takes up the story on 31 July by which time Germany had declared war on Russia. It describes how he was instrumental in assembling the Conservative leaders scattered about the Home Counties that Bank Holiday weekend, and getting them to assure the Government of full Conservative agreement in supporting France and Russia. It was clear that he was in close touch throughout these days with various French diplomats who kept him informed of the international situation, and with Henry Wilson, from whom he learned much of British moves in military preparations.

Diary

31 July 1914: Down to the House, everything very uncertain. The Government's intentions still quite unknown and Asquith's statement at the end mentioning Germany's declaration of the state of war and deferring all further announcement till Monday did not look well.

Some time after dinner George Lloyd rang me up to say that he felt that something more definite was required in the way of a statement by our Government as to where they stood. He came round for a talk and we both agreed strongly that it was essential that our leaders should voice even more definitely than they had done their readiness to support the Government in doing its duty by France. He had already written a letter to Austen and I wrote another, as well as one to Lord Milner. Subsequently I rang up Henry Wilson and heard from him that the Government was absolutely rotten and in favour of betrayal all along the line. I got on the telephone to [H.A.] Gwynne to urge him to write as strongly as he could, while Lloyd went off to see Robin [Dawson] and also if possible to get hold of Charlie Beresford.

1 August 1914 (Bank Holiday Saturday): No news in the morning except that Wilson confirmed that things were worse then ever, that no soldiers had been taken into consultation by the Government at all, that the Committee of Imperial Defence had never been summoned, and that the Cabinet which was sitting that morning was as wrong as could be. After 1.00 Lloyd rang me up to come round at once to lunch. He confirmed all that Wilson said. He had been round both Benckendorff and to Cambon* where he saw both Cambon himself and Charles Roux.† The French regarded themselves as completely betrayed and were in an awful state of mind. They delayed their mobilization at our instance and Cambon said quite straight to Lloyd that if we stood out and the French won they would gladly do everything to crush us afterwards, whereas if they lost we should naturally follow suit. He added that it would be worse for us even than Napoleon was. Leo Maxse and [Eustace] Percy both turned up during the course of lunch, severally confirming the bad state of affairs.

All the Unionist leaders had departed out of town and we decided that the only thing to do was for us to go out and fetch them. Lloyd had already managed to get hold of Balfour in the morning and induce him

---

*The Russian and French Ambassadors respectively. Cambon wrote of the British position: 'There isn't a scrap of paper. But there is something more. Every act of yours over the last few years gave us the assurance of your support . . . *est-ceque l'Angleterre comprend ce que c'est que le honneur'* (*My Political Life*, II, p. 16).

†The First Secretary at the French Embassy.

to stop in town at any rate till the evening instead of going to Hatfield. Apparently all the Unionist leaders had been given to understand that everything was perfectly all right and Balfour was flabbergasted at the news Lloyd gave him. I accordingly wired to Austen who was down at Westgate on Sea that I was coming down at once as grave developments had arisen, and also to Lord Milner [at] Sturry suggesting that he should come over to Westgate and be prepared to come back to town. After first ringing up Garvin and telling him to write all he could in the *Observer* to stiffen things, I caught the 3.20 at Victoria due to arrive at Westgate at 4.50, with the idea of bringing Austen back by the 5.50. As was only to be expected from the South-Eastern Railway, the engine duly proceeded to break down this side of Rochester, and eventually reached Westgate about 7.30. . . . Austen, whom I found at dinner, fully realised the necessity of coming back at once and seeing what the Unionist leaders could do in town next day. From Lord Milner no message, and I assumed he may after all not have been at Sturry. [Later L.S.A. holograph note: 'He was in London all day.'] We got back to Charing Cross about 1.15 [in the morning] and Lloyd met us and went with us to Egerton Place [Austen Chamberlain's house] to report his part of the day's work. He had gone down to Wargrave with Beresford, and he found Bonar Law at tennis, F.E. and Carson having gone up the river. Bonar too, like another Drake, insisted on finishing his set before discussing the matter. When he heard the situation he thought it would be well to come up to town next morning, but Lloyd very firmly took him in hand and made him come up at once. Carson and F.E. did not come up. Meanwhile Lansdowne had apparently come up from Bowood. Anyhow a council of war was held at Lansdowne House at a late hour in the night – Bonar Law, Lansdowne, Devonshire, Edmund Talbot and Henry Wilson. Balfour had gone off to Hatfield with a promise to return in the morning. According to Lloyd, they all agreed in a general sort of way that something should be done and that things were not satisfactory, but none of them showed the slightest conception of the fact that war was on or that it signified anything.

We both urged on Austen the absolute necessity of the Unionist leaders really taking some action to make their position clear to the Government. Apparently – and this was one of the things that Lloyd heard from Cambon, while Maxse had got it from someone in touch with the Foreign Office – the Government had been busy asserting that they were hampered by the knowledge that the Opposition were against them and opposed to intervention in the war, and it was essential to put an end to any excuse the Government might have had in that direction from the rather vague assurances of mere support which they had so far had. As a matter of fact, except Hugh Cecil, and in a milder degree Robert Cecil, there was no section in the Unionist party in favour of neutrality, though of course the Jewish influence generally, in so far as it affected the *Daily Telegraph* and some other circles in the party, looked with great aversion on the idea of war. Austen promised to get them all together the very first thing and we left him soon after 2.00.

2 August 1914: Went round to breakfast with Wilson and found things still very bad. Absolutely nothing being done at the War Office. Lloyd came round and presently Maxse, and we went round to the French Embassy where we saw Charles Roux who told us that Luxemburg had been entered and the treaty of [18]67 violated, that the Germans had declared war against Russia in spite of the fact that Austria and Russia were actually getting into direct discussion on the basis of a settlement of the Servian question; that Sir Edward Goschen had asked at Berlin for a guarantee of Belgian neutrality and had been met by von Jagow* with a direct negative. He had already rung up Tyrrell to ask if Cambon could see Grey, to which Grey had at first replied suggesting 2.30, but Cambon rejoined that that was too late and that he must see him at once. This he had done but with no satisfactory result. The only thing he was prepared to say was that we should probably not allow the German fleet to operate with offensive intent against the French Channel coast,† apparently by inference leaving it free to them to sail to the Mediterranean and stop French troops coming across from Algiers.

We went back to Lloyd's house in Wilton Crescent and a few minutes later Austen turned up and told us that he had gone to breakfast with Lansdowne and then to Bonar Law's where eventually he had drafted a letter assuring the Government of the complete support of the Unionist leaders in fulfilling their obligations of honour and their maintenance of the safety of the United Kingdom. This was signed by Lansdowne and Bonar Law and sent down to Asquith at the Cabinet meeting. It was pretty obvious that Austen had taken the situation in hand. I had already talked with Bonar Law over the telephone from Wilson's house to tell him about Luxemburg, and his only line had been to say that he did not know what the Unionist leaders could do and that any attempt to bring too much pressure on the Government would rally the coalition in opposition to the war.

Lloyd and I agreed that we had done all we could do in getting the Unionist leaders to town and bringing them to the scratch of doing something. So I spent an afternoon sitting about feeling pretty miserable and

*Goschen was British Ambassador in Berlin: von Jagow was German Secretary for Foreign Affairs.

†As a result of the British arrangement with the French their fleet had been concentrated in the Mediterranean.

taking occasional short walks. The first brighter news was when Mrs Wilson rang through to say that Henry Wilson had been allowed to hold back some 60 or 70 railway trains intended for the transport of the Territorials (for holiday camps) and keep them available for mobilisation.

After dinner I went round again to Wilson's, meeting Lloyd there and heard further on the military situation that he (Wilson) had been able to get the various detached camps of regulars and training corps allowed to come back to their peace centres, an essential preparatory to mobilisation. The Cabinet had sat again in the afternoon, and Grey had seen Cambon after 4.00, apparently telling him that we should not let the German fleet pass the Straits of Dover. Lloyd's news too was not reassuring.

I left Lloyd at 4 Carlton Gardens and went on to the *Times* office. Owing to Bank Holiday the paper was already going to press, and Robin could not see me for a few minutes, but I saw Freeman who told me that as a matter of fact things had taken a much more favourable tone between 5.00 and 6.30, that the rotten element in the Cabinet had been largely talked round. I went on to the *Daily Express* and saw Blumenfeld and then Gwynne at the *Morning Post*, both of whom confirmed the better turn of affairs and from whom I learnt that Grey was seeing Cambon again at 10.30. I went back to see Robin who told me that he had seen both Grey and Churchill after 6.30 and they assured him that things were going right. I went on to Egerton Place and gathered from Austen that the discussions between the Unionist leaders and the Government were continuing, that Churchill had been to see Balfour and that things were decidedly better.

3 August 1914 (Bank Holiday Monday): Round to Wilson's after breakfast. Heard that Germany had presented an ultimatum to Belgium with regard to the passage of troops through Belgian territory; that Cambon was very much happier with the statement that Grey was going to make in the afternoon; in fact we were really beginning to get round the corner. . . .

Down to the House to listen to Grey's statement. As an effort at persuading his own party to move along, it was very adroit. As a statement of British policy on the eve of a great war, it seemed to me narrow and uninspiring. . . .* He was received by his own party very much better than apparently the Government expected. . . .

Ramsay MacDonald expressed somewhat clumsily his disapproval of the whole business, and then a string of the radical crank section aired their protests against our interfering with Germany's 'right' to march through Belgium.

*Later L.S.A. note: 'I found it so long and dull that I more than once fell asleep.' Legend has since made it one of the great speeches of all time.

4 August 1914: Round to Wilson's immediately after breakfast. Heard the bad news that Haldane was reinstalled in the War Office and the Government determined at all hazards not to send the Expeditionary Force. Wilson particularly worried because unless the mobilization order sent out that afternoon added the words 'and embark'* to mobilise the moving of the Territorials to their various stations would delay the mobilisation of the Regulars by something like four days. It was anyhow too late in all probability to get our forces to the points on the Belgian frontier which had been arranged in the joint plan of campaign but every hour gained was important. I suggested that we had better get up another 'pogrom'† and mobilization of the Unionist leaders, so Lovat went off to Bonar Law, while Wilson and I went to Milner and explained the situation to him. Wilson went on the War Office while I rang up Austen and as soon as Milner had explained the situation to him they both went on to Lansdowne leaving word for Bonar and Lovat to follow. I heard subsequently from Austen that their representations greatly influenced Lansdowne, and Austen also went to see Balfour who at his suggestion wrote a strong letter to Haldane. I don't know what representations were made by the Unionist leaders to the Government besides this, but I believe that by the afternoon the idea of keeping Haldane in the War Office was abandoned.

Down to the House after lunch to hear Asquith announce the violation of Belgian neutrality and our ultimatum to Germany. [Later] Lovat came into the Lobby and told me he had seen Cambon who very strenuously denied the rumour which was being busily put round in Government circles that the French did not require the Expeditionary Force. On the contrary Cambon said it represented something like 33% of their actual fighting strength in the field where the armies would meet. Everything had been arranged for it and to do without it would upset their mobilisation and be an immense handicap. There was also the other false rumour vigorously spread, that Kitchener was absolutely opposed to sending the Expeditionary Force. Lovat urged me to do all I could not only with our own people but with all reasonable Radicals [i.e. Liberals] to make them realise the urgency of the situation and the need for conducting war with both hands once we were in it. Meanwhile Lord Milner came along into the Lobby too, and as Lovat mentioned that he was going to

*There were two mobilisation orders: 'mobilisation and embarkment' which would give priority to the six regular divisions to go to France; or 'mobilisation' which would give the Territorials precedence in order to man the coastal defences.

†Henry Wilson's word for a private discussion or 'plot'. Perhaps derived from the 'plot' of the Asquith Government to coerce Ulster into a Home Rule Ireland, frustrated by the Curragh Mutiny, described by Lord Eustace Percy in an article entitled 'The Pogrom Plot' in *National Review*, LXIII. In the previous decade attacks on Jews in Russia had caused the word to be extensively used in this, its more usual, meaning.

see Kitchener, I urged Lord Milner to go too, which, after some protes-
tation, he agreed to do. I stirred up several Liberals and then went down
to the *Times* office and did the same by Robinson. Then back to Duke
Street where Lord Milner told me that Kitchener had stoutly denied his
ever having expressed an opinion at all on the matter and that he could
not express one unless he had all the military material before him. He was
very annoyed with the Government who had hauled him back just as he
was embarking on his steamer the day before and since then left him
entirely alone though he had just received a note from Asquith hoping
he would postpone his departure in view of the situation.* Milner and
Lovat urged him not to allow his time and the public time to be wasted
like that but to go at once to Asquith and ask leave to return to Egypt
immediately unless the Government had some other work for him to
do here, and they prevailed upon him to leap into a taxi straight away
and go.

Soon after dinner walked . . . to Draycott Place where I spent the rest
of the evening with the Wilsons, cheered first of all by a message from
Maxse that Haldane was definitely going, followed presently by Maxse
himself in a very exuberant state. Later on we received a message from
the Foreign Office that Germany had declared war on us. This was
apparently the message; the actual declaration came *from us* after the
unsatisfactory reply from the Germans.

Poor Henry Wilson, though outwardly cheerful and lively, is evidently
tired and must be very mortified that he has not been made Chief of the
Staff to French which he was practically promised, but only Assistant Chief
of the Staff. A. J. Murray, who is to go as Chief, said to him 'You will
have to do the work while I keep the little man [L.S.A. holograph note:
'i.e. Sir John French'] from making a fool of himself' or words to that
effect! We also heard from Maxse that Cambon had definitely pressed that
afternoon for a declaration from the Government whether the Expeditionary Force was going over or not, to which they gave the answer that
was naturally to be expected from such people, viz. that they could not
say but would let him know tomorrow. I rang up both Austen and Lord
Milner to see if the Unionist leaders could put any further pressure on
the Government next morning to put Kitchener in Haldane's place and
get the sending of the Expeditionary Force agreed to. Austen replied a
little stuffily. He thinks I am asking too much of the Unionist leaders
and fears that if they press the Government too hard the latter may get
irritated. We separated feeling that anyhow whatever the hesitation and
cowardice had been and however serious the delays we were now in it
and that events would force the Government's hands to do its duty.

*Kitchener was not appointed Secretary of State for War in place of Haldane until 6 August.

5 August 1914: It was this afternoon that Hamar [Greenwood] told me that a majority of Cabinet had only agreed to war on condition that no Expeditionary Force was sent abroad. It was on this day, too, that the question of Expeditionary Force was discussed pro and con and that K[itchener] came down on the four division compromise which upset all the mobilization and transportation schedules.*

From 5 August, the day after Britain entered the war, until the opening of 1917 Amery kept no diary. He was, in fact, constantly on the move, first within Britain and later in France and Belgium and in 1915 and 1916 in the Balkans. The main sources for this period are his regular letters to Mrs Amery, but certain letters to him which describe the war situation or illustrate the personalities with whom he was in close contact have been included.

In the first weeks of the war Amery was involved in aiding recruitment efforts in Birmingham. A letter (4 September) from Hamar Greenwood to his sister Mrs Amery describes how Amery persuaded Kitchener to invent a scheme designed to avoid congestion of recruits. However, Kitchener gained time in which to change his mind and chaos resulted. Later in September Kitchener discarded Amery. The latter thought (*My Political Life*, II, p. 32) this a result of pressure from Asquith who had discovered his role and resented both his earlier criticisms of the Government and his close co-operation with Henry Wilson, especially over the Curragh Mutiny. Amery then crossed to Belgium. The letters to Mrs Amery do not refer to his interrogation of German prisoners on 19 October which revealed the existence of three completely new German divisions raised after the outbreak of war and ready to fall on Ypres. Thanks to Amery's warning, Rawlinson, commanding the Fourth Corps, was able to withdraw his troops from the trap.

Milner to L.S.A., 4 August 1914

[There is] one thing I regret with so splendid a case against the appointment of Haldane on other grounds. Why bring it up against him, as *The Times* does, that he has sympathies with Germany? So I hope have many of us, certainly I, and I fancy you on general grounds and under normal conditions. If it is necessary for good and effective patriotism to hate the nation to which your country happens to be opposed, I am afraid I don't possess that virtue.

---

*L.S.A. suggested in *My Political Life* (II, p. 24) that the absence of two divisions from the Expeditionary Force might have been a decisive factor in the battles up to the Aisne in September.

Amery recorded (*My Political Life*, II, p. 22) that he and his friends did not feel that Haldane as Secretary of State for War – as he had been from 1905 to 1912 – would 'appeal to the country or provide the sheer driving force required'. In the event, Haldane remained Lord Chancellor until 1915, when the first coalition was formed.

Hamar Greenwood to Mrs Amery, from the War Office, 4 September 1914

[Leo] saw K[itchener] of K[hartoum] and suggested the only possible way of dealing with recruits now pouring into depots, camps, etc. and overflowing into yards and fields. K. of K. was reluctant to accept this, the only possible scheme, but Amery told him he must, and he has.

I write this down now, so as in years to come, the facts will be known as they are. . . . All the soldiers here are afraid to argue with K. of K. who is not mentally a giant, but he listens to Leo and agrees – though reluctantly – with him.

L.S.A. to Mrs Amery

17 October 1914: I have had to read a great many prisoners' letters lately in case they should contain something of military value, including so many from mothers and wives and sweethearts, letters full of love and affection and trust in providence. They are at bottom a very affectionate and simple people, the Germans – the common folk I mean.

20 October 1914 (Ypres): I was over at General Headquarters the day before yesterday and had tea with French who was very friendly. He recalled a great debate we once had on cavalry tactics in which I argued for the rifle against lance and sword, and said that he was now inclined to think I had the best of the arguments.

28 October 1914: These new German recruits seem to fight splendidly for all their want of training, and there are such lots of them. The poor peasants I am sorriest for. The Germans shoot them freely on almost any pretext: if our fire is at all accurate, it must be spies, so shot they are without more ado. The French, too, don't bother much about evidence, and we, though we don't shoot in the same way, are forced to clear them out and arrest them if they come near their houses.

15 November 1914: We heard late last night that Lord Roberts had died. No one could have wished him a more fitting end. Life for him was full of interest and vigour to the very end. I doubt if he ever enjoyed two days more than he did the last two before the sudden end. Meeting the

Indians was a special delight to him and he insisted on stopping his car and talking to every turbaned soldier he met, and visited them in their hospitals. . . . The last thing Lord Roberts did was to insist on walking up a hill here where he could get a good view of the fighting, and it was doing this that caused him to catch the cold which proved fatal.

After Ypres, both sides entrenched in France and there remained dead-locked until the spring of 1918. While most of the British generals believed that the only way to relieve the pressure, first on the Russians in the winter and spring of 1914–15 and later on Serbia in autumn 1915, was to attack in France (a costly and unproductive exercise), Amery and a few others (for example Lloyd George and General Galliéni in France) preferred to strike the enemy on his 'underbelly'. Amery drew up for General Rawlinson a plan of action to reinforce the Serbs and advance into the plain of Hungary. This was not adopted, but it led General Callwell, the Director of Intelligence, to ask Amery to compose a military handbook on Serbia and a phrase-book for the assistance of the British division which with a French division was to be sent through Salonika into Serbia. When all this was complete Amery learned that the divisions were to go to the Dardanelles.

Asquith had expressed his disapproval of Amery's presence on Rawlinson's staff and Amery therefore sought to go to the Dardanelles. Asquith also heard of his attempts to be appointed to the staff of General Ian Hamilton. An old friend of Amery's, Hamilton was to command at the Dardanelles, but this move, too, was blocked. Amery applied to Balfour for help. 'It was conceded that I might be allowed to serve my country in any capacity in which my special experience might be of use, so long as it was not on the personal staff of a senior commander' (My Political Life, II, p. 49).

At length, in the spring of 1915, he was despatched to the Balkans on a special mission to study road, rail and river communications and also to act as liaison officer between the British military attachés in the Balkan capitals. The letters to Mrs Amery tell of his travels. Early in 1915 the Allies had all to play for in the Balkans, as it was just possible that Greece, Bulgaria and Rumania, despite their own rivalries, might be brought into the war alongside Serbia and Montenegro against the common enemies Turkey and Austria-Hungary. The British Foreign Office embarked upon what Amery regarded as a foolish attempt to bribe Bulgaria by offering her Serbian and Greek territory – to the great anger of those two countries. Amery preferred that Britain should strive to bring Greece into the war by offering her the assistance of British forces and territory at the expense of Turkey. This, he believed, would encourage Rumania, which had territorial claims on Austria-Hungary, to come in, and with these two involved, Bulgaria might not be able to avoid the temptation of pickings from Turkish Thrace.

Amery's interest in Greece was stimulated by his renewal of an old acquaintance with Venizelos, whom he first met in Crete in 1896. Venizelos supported the Allies whom he believed would win, and hoped that Greece might obtain Asia Minor. King Constantine however, feared that Bulgaria would seize Salonika if Greece became involved in the Dardanelles, and his Queen was the Kaiser's sister. While the British did nothing to influence the outcome favourably, the French arguably made matters worse by intriguing with Venizelos and against the King.

In a key letter to Churchill on the Dardanelles situation sent in July 1915, Amery suggested the landing of a mobile force on the shore of Asiatic Turkey to turn the position on Gallipoli and cut the communications between Constantinople and the rest of Asiatic Turkey. This plan was later put forward by the French, but was ignored amid the growing opposition to 'sideshows' and the growing threat to Serbia.

L.S.A. to Mrs Amery, from the Grand Hotel, Belgrade, 5 April 1915

The train instead of reaching here at 7 next morning didn't do so till 5.30 in the evening, during which time I sustained life on sugared almonds and the conversation of some friendly Serbian officers. Eventually the train reached Topchidere a small station in a park about three miles out of Belgrade – it can't come further as the line then goes down to the river front where the train would be shelled, and anyhow the station is wrecked. As for the general situation imagine Chelsea and Battersea at war with the Chelsea bridge blown up, and a mutual understanding between both sides not to shell into the town opposite, so that unless you go down to the actual river bank where the Austrian sentries can see you and pot at you, you are perfectly safe and go about life and business as usual.

L.S.A. to Mrs Amery, from the Athenee Palace Hotel, Bucharest, 17 April 1915

Here I am, suddenly transported from the primitive squalor and simplicity of Nish to the splendours of a highly modern cosmopolitan hotel in this gay city. I have just been for a walk, or jostle, through the main street. Bond Street at its fullest is quiet and empty compared with the animated crowd of highly dressed and highly painted ladies, gorgeously uniformed officers and *flaneurs* of all kinds which fills the pavements while endless victorias stream past driven by coachmen in long dark green or dark blue velvet gowns reaching to the ankle and tied by a sash round the waist. And I felt quite homesick for Nish and its mud and discomfort and ever present fear of typhus and the faces of people who know how to fight and to suffer. These Rumanians of the capital look soft and sensual, mostly concerned with having a good time in the most elementary carnal sense of the term. We want to get them in with us, of course; but I don't feel sure of their army as I would of Serbs or Bulgars.

L.S.A. to Milner, 27 April 1915, from off Lemnos

Here we have got to see the thing through at almost all hazards and I don't believe we shall get it done unless we have a far larger force on the spot. . . .

There is a sort of notion about that we can get somebody else, Greeks, Bulgarians, Rumanians, to provide it for us if we can discover terms which will suit them. There are no such terms unless they are accompanied by a display of force on our side, which will convince them that our offer can be made good. . . .

Take first of all the case of Greece, the neutral which is more friendly than any other and to whom Germany can offer nothing.

So certain in fact are the Greeks that Bulgaria means mischief afterwards that they are all for forcing Bulgaria to declare herself now. There are strong strategical reasons in favour of this. By far the best line of advance for an Anglo-Greek force attacking the Turks is from Kavalla and Dedeagatch across Bulgarian territory. If Bulgaria were directly asked by us to give passage through her territory she could either say 'yes' and be practically committed to our side, or 'no', and we should then smash her before going on to the next business. I suggested to a young Greek officer that British rectitude would hardly approve of such a sincere testimonial of our admiration of the German treatment of Belgium. He thought this a rather pedantic attitude but suggested as an alternative to quiet our moral scruples that he could easily himself in a fortnight get up a good *casus belli* on the frontier – atrocities and all included. . . .

If we send out six more divisions at once we shall probably add the whole Greek Army of 250,000 or so to our side, but risk drawing Bulgaria in against us. Rumania might go for Bulgaria in that case and we shall still be to the good but by a small margin, on paper, and of course no one can be certain what the military effect of Bulgaria going wrong might be. On the other hand if we send out not six but twelve divisions, then not only Greece, but Bulgaria as well will probably join us, or at least give very tangible pledges for her benevolent neutrality, and Rumania will be free and willing at once to launch her whole army into Transylvania.

Rumania is chiefly concerned with two things; firstly, she doesn't want to be a mere left wing of the Russian Army, secondly she doesn't want to exhaust the limited staying capacity (in ammunition especially) of her little army before the war is over and then to have no say in the terms of peace. She wants to march alongside with the Italians or ourselves and to start marching not earlier than two or three months before the final collapse of the enemy. . . .

If there is any advantage at all in sending men here instead of to Flanders it is because we hope, firstly to bring in others with us, and secondly to fight on less congested and less fortified ground. The present force under Ian Hamilton is not going to draw in others and is not likely to do more than achieve – if it does achieve – the storming of a few miles of rocky peninsula far more congested and fortified than even Neuve Chapelle or La Bassée.

I don't see how it can do more. It won't accomplish the Dardanelles business under 30,000 casualties and the expenditure of all its ammunition. The balance won't be in much of a position to tackle Constantinople. As for the advance up the Danube or the Salonika railway and thence to Budapest – they will obviously be out of the question.

The whole of this business out here will have been a gigantic mistake unless it is done properly. What I mean by properly is (1) send another 6 divisions to help Hamilton and bring in the Greeks in the Turkish campaign. (2) Send six more divisions up the Salonika Railway to occupy the Banat and encourage both Serbs and Rumanians to advance at once on Budapest.

L.S.A. to Mrs Amery, on train to Sofia, 2 May 1915

The Serbs are very agitated at the rumours that Italy wants to grab most of Dalmatia.* As the population is Serb and as Serbia badly needs a coast line all my sympathy is with them and against the Italians. Besides the Italians are foolish to try and secure now territory they will always be turned out of later by people who can fight better than themselves.

L.S.A. to Mrs Amery, 3 May 1915

They told me at Tsanbrod on the frontier that the quarantine† was now so strict that they wouldn't even let us enter the refreshment room at Sofia station and that I had better buy provisions for the next 24 hours.

While the first six months of war had brought one and a half million recruits, the disorganisation of services meant that hundreds of thousands could not obtain any real training for want of equipment and weapons. During 1915 the wastage at the Dardanelles and on the Western Front

*Italy declared war on the Central Powers on 24 May 1915.
†On account of the Serbian typhus epidemic.

made it necessary to obtain more men. Wilson's letters to Amery in late 1915 (for example, those of 19 August, 17 September and 18 December 1915) show the complaints being made against Kitchener, who had been deprived of able personnel as half the General Staff and other able officers had gone to France.

The wastage at the Front in early 1915 brought about the 'reconstruction' of Asquith's Liberal Government – an attempt to strengthen it by incorporating the Unionist leaders. One beneficial result was that Lloyd George became Minister of Munitions, and made good certain deficiencies, but there was no general British strategy relating to all theatres of the war to give a thought as to priority. Otherwise the coalition did little good. As Amery wrote in his memoirs: 'The Unionist leaders joined it because it seemed the right thing to do. They made no stipulations as to the policy to be pursued . . . worse still, they abdicated for themselves and very largely for their followers the essential function of active and authoritative criticism' (*My Political Life*, II, p. 66).

During 1915, Amery became involved in the issue of conscription which was to continue into 1916, pressing the case for it through speeches in the Commons and articles that summer. On his return from the Dardanelles he was given a post in the Balkan section of the War Office as cover for this activity, and there he discovered just how bad the situation was. He prepared a series of memoranda for members of the Cabinet Committee under Curzon who were looking into the question. On 28 September Asquith urged the House to abstain from discussing the subject until the Government was able to announce a considered policy. Amery referred to the actual situation in the Balkans, where Bulgaria, with German aid, was preparing to attack Serbia: 'Are we to ask Hindenburg to "wait and see" till we have decided?' On 21 October the Government asked Lord Derby, who had just become Director of Recruiting, to make one last attempt to secure enough volunteers so that if he failed, everyone would recognise that compulsion was inevitable. He did fail, and by the end of 1915 the Cabinet had accepted the principle of compulsion. Only Sir John Simon resigned.

L.S.A. to Mrs Amery, from Kraguyevatz, 26 May 1915

I wrote a long letter to Lord Milner from Nish yesterday and asked Tallboy to send you a copy. . . . There are things in it which I would write otherwise to no one but him – perhaps Kipling or Jameson. Men like Bonar and even Austen would be puzzled and slightly shocked.

L.S.A. to Milner, from Nish, 26 May 1915

Here the news is that Italy has joined the Allies and that a coalition

Government is being formed in England. No details have reached here yet except that Squiff and Grey and presumably Kitchener will stay and that sundry Unionist and Labour leaders are to come in. . . . They have not, I suppose asked you and if so, that is just as well. The real crisis when you'll be wanted has to come yet. . . .

It may come through military failure. I am not at all certain that Italy's coming in even if followed by Rumania, Greece and Bulgaria is going to be an easy or speedy victory. Against the extra numbers provided by the Italians we have got to set the possible effects of intense German indignation at Italian treachery. We are only just beginning to reach the period of the war where the moral factor is going to tell and when personal generalship may do wonders. And so far it seems to me that the growth in moral strength is all on the German side – even Austria is beginning to share it. Serbia and to some extent France have gained too. But there is nothing in Russia or with us parallel to the moral exaltation of Germany at this moment. What Revolutionary France did a hundred years ago, Germany may do again; there is nothing inherently impossible in the German armies being in Paris, Milan and Warsaw by the end of the year. And I am not sure it wouldn't be the best thing for us. We want to have our backs to the wall and have such thwacks as will make us see the world clearly as it is and give us a new will and purpose for action. . . .

But even if we do have this easy victory then all the more need for a crisis and complete change of government. While our military task is rightly to crush Germany, our political writers of all shades are forgetting our political object is the defence and welfare of the British Empire. All this harping on Prussian militarism as something that must be rooted out, as in itself criminal and opposed to the interests of an imaginary virtuous and pacific entity called Europe, in which we are included, is wholly mischievous. It all tends to drag us into a false Little England position. We are not a part of Europe, even if the most important unit of the British community lies off the European coast. This war against a German domination in Europe was only necessary because we had failed to make ourselves sufficiently strong and united as an Empire to be able to afford to disregard the European balance. When it comes to the terms of peace and after, we have got to get back to a British point of view. . . . We shall have to fight the people who will be prepared to sell every Imperial gain the war may have brought us in order to secure what they think the proper frontier of certain foreign nations in Europe and who, after the peace, will be hypnotised for years by the emotions and the claptrap of the war.*

*Cf. L.S.A. to Lord Robert Cecil, 23 December 1916 (see pp. 133–4).

L.S.A. to Mrs Amery, from Nish, 1 June 1915

I wonder whom they'll make Under Secretary for War – if indeed Asquith will ever allow Jacky Tennant to be displaced. I imagine I could, if need be, work very well with Lloyd George! But it wouldn't be the same as working under a man like Lord M.

I've just had a wire from Callwell to say that he has seen Lord M. and that there is no reason for my coming home. He doesn't want me to go to the Dardanelles where there are enough special service officers already but does want me to go to Sofia to study the Bulgarian situation. So I'm off to Sofia tomorrow and will I suppose continue perambulating the Balkans for some time longer.

L.S.A. to Mrs Amery, from the British Legation, Sofia, 5 June 1915

As far as I can see the Powers have been singularly maladroit in their diplomacy. They have frightened and annoyed Serbia by telling her she must give up Macedonia in order to secure the valuable co-operation of the Bulgarians, without first making sure whether even that bribe would tempt Bulgaria to come in. As a matter of fact it won't and the only use Bulgaria is going to make of it is to get some concessions from the Turks through the good offices of her dear friend Germany. . . .

The list of the new Government i.e. as far as Cabinet Ministers is concerned, not as regards under-secs. has reached us here . . . What surprises me most is Churchill's staying on in an inferior position with no work to do, and everyone presumably saying he is remaining for the sake of the salary.* I should have thought he would have gone straight to the front somewhere and come back for a fresh start six months later.

L.S.A. to Mrs Amery, from Bucharest, 7 June 1915

Our diplomacy has, for the present, failed here also, and Rumania which when I left three weeks ago was on the verge of coming in has now quite cooled off. . . .

I read John Buchan's articles in *The Times* and thought them excellent. He is a born journalist in the very best sense of the word – he can sense a situation quickly and can with the minimum of effort make a vivid story of it. And I'm not a journalist, though I suppose I have nominally been one for many years. I can write well in my own fashion, but it's

---

*Churchill had been demoted from the Admiralty and made Chancellor of the Duchy of Lancaster which, as Lloyd George wrote, was 'a post generally reserved for beginners in the Cabinet or for distinguished politicians who had reached the first stages of unmistakable decrepitude' (Lloyd George, *War Memoirs*, I, p. 139).

always with an effort, and with an object. I took to it because it was the easiest way open to me to try to get things done, and if I can get anything done without writing the instinct for it isn't there. If John had seen all I've seen of this war he'd have made three most readable books of it.

L.S.A. to Mrs Amery, from Athens, 18 June 1915

I have acted on your suggestion and written a little note to Lloyd George expressing my admiration of his speech as Munitions Minister. I hesitated a little because I don't want any of them to think that I am making up to them with an eye to an odd plum from the coalition cake later on. But I know they have a sort of notion that I am a rather truculent, rancorous person, and I don't want that to get stereotyped in their minds. . . .

I'm quite prepared to back up Lloyd George to any extent now if he does the right thing and to forget Marconi and other causes of offence. The speech I admit was good and had something of the ring of action in it. But we still want the real word of command. If only Lord M. had a little touch of the demagogue or the actor what a stir he could make at once.

Milner to L.S.A., 23 June 1915

I at once took the most energetic steps I thought appropriate to see that you were not overlooked owing to your absence, but I very soon found that the class of considerations, which were weighing in my mind with regard to the formation of the Ministry, were not at all the same as those filling the minds of either party to the coalition. . . . It is essentially a Government of the United Mandarins. I mention, as a mere illustration of this and not the least from any feeling of personal annoyance, because I was in fact very glad of it, that from the first to last no man on either side approached me with reference to the matter at all. . . .

I may say that Austen Chamberlain subsequently told me that he had made very strong efforts to get me as a colleague, even offering to take an Under-Secretaryship himself, if I had a seat in the Cabinet. He told me also that he found, to his surprise, that I was the one man to whom the Liberals most objected. My answer to him was, that *I* was not at all surprised, and that I regarded it as a compliment. . . .

When all is said and done, there is no doubt that the new Government is a great improvement on the old one. But it is an improvement in points of administrative detail. I cannot see, as yet, much change in spirit. . . . The right men have got into the right places, for McKenna, who is no good for anything else on earth, really has financial ability, and Lloyd George, who is the antithesis of a financier, has driving power and enthusiasm.

L.S.A. to Mrs Amery, from the Hôtel d'Angleterre, Athens, 23 June 1915

Today has been baking hot. I went out . . . in the evening by myself round the slope of the Acropolis, and up to the Pnyx, where the great orators of Athens addressed the crowds. The evening light was wonderful, golden on the marble of the Parthenon and purple and pink on the slopes of Hymettus. I stood on the platform where Pericles and Demosthenes stood, and came down the steps wondering what Demosthenes must have felt after all his vain pleas to the Athenians to arm against the coming danger. All this place is holy ground to those of us who have been brought up in the classics, holier even than Rome – I felt transported with deep ecstasy and reverent joy, immortal in the sense of union with the past. Even an immense happening like this war seemed to sink back into its perspective along with the Persian war, far greater in all it meant for mankind, or the long destructive war between Athens and Sparta which is so much more like it, and all the wars and changes of Empires in between. Even Rheims Cathedral and Ypres Hall seem natural and commonplace mischances beside the shattered pillars of the Parthenon. . . .

I am sorry the old faith of Greece and Rome was allowed to die out utterly. I could go to a service in the Parthenon or the Temple of Jupiter or the Capitol so much more naturally and easily than to church, just as I feel that this place gives me a thrill and speaks to my heart as Jerusalem never could. Happily here, unlike Rome, the churches do not obtrude their presence with a counter claim to attention. You will shake your pious little head over my Paganism, but there it is. . . . But my heart is with the Gods of Greece, and Pallas Athene is so much more real to me than Mary of Nazareth. It may only be because the ancient faiths are now beyond criticism: no one even asked me to believe them as literally true; I am not sure whether the Greeks themselves even took them too literally. It may be, too, that they are in themselves less dogmatic and less directly challenging to the reason. That the Goddess of Wisdom sprang fully armed from the head of Father Zeus or that the Goddess Aphrodite rose in all her beauty from the foam of the sea is a statement that no one wants to deny, and it made no difference to their worship if it was believed or not. But to state that God was incarnated in a child born to the wife of a Jewish carpenter in the reign of Tiberius, and to make your whole religion turn on that, is too definite to be treated as merely a way of illustrating spiritual truths – it directly challenges you to believe it as a historical fact or to be only a fraudulent member of the Church.

By the end of August 1915 the Allied failure in the Gallipoli peninsula and Russian defeats in Poland were driving Bulgaria towards the Central

Powers. Only powerful Allied reinforcements and a serious diplomatic effort could encourage Greece, and possibly Rumania, to dissuade Bulgaria from entering the war. A month earlier Amery had urged this and suggested the immediate evacuation of the Dardanelles and an offensive in Asiatic Turkey. On 28 September Sir Edward Grey warned Bulgaria not to enter the war and promised Serbia all support. Bulgaria attacked Serbia on 11 October. The Anglo-French commanders had now decided on an offensive by the British Expeditionary Force at Loos and by the French in Champagne. By mid-October these had failed dismally and the Serbs had been routed.

Carson resigned on the issue of failure to support Serbia, but even then a swift decision could have saved more of the Serb forces in their retreat on Salonika. The decision to evacuate the Dardanelles was not taken until 22 November and it took place, without loss, on 18 December. Simultaneously a start was made to build up a force at Salonika, which, after two and a half years of inactivity was to have a decisive effect in the autumn of 1918.

Extract from a memo by L.S.A. on the Dardanelles position
[Written in Athens in early July 1915, and sent to Churchill on the 13th of that month, with the note: 'I have come to very definite conclusions and I feel bound to state them.']

To put the matter baldly: the forces at Sir Ian Hamilton's disposal, even after the arrival of the new divisions, are quite inadequate to deal with the Dardanelles problem, let alone the subsequent problem of Constantinople. . . . The worst possible method of undertaking the task [of defeating the Turkish Army] is to continue attacking the Turks on a narrow front in a series of strongly entrenched positions where all their peculiar military virtues have the fullest opportunity for display and where they can lose nothing by the weakness of their staff work and their transport. . . . The next way to solve the problem is [to create] a mobile field force and compel the enemy to fight on ground of our own choosing by striking at some vital spot in his territory.

For this purpose it is essential to despatch at least another six divisions of infantry and two or three mounted divisions. Adding two or three divisions of the force now at the Dardanelles, whose task would then be reduced to a purely defensive one, we should get a field force capable of dealing with any force the Turks are likely to be free to bring against it.

The new field force must be despatched at once. . . . Once the rough weather begins with the September equinox we must be prepared for the contingency of the forces on the peninsula being cut off from all supplies or reinforcements for days and possibly weeks, together. . . .

There are two main theatres in which a British Field Force could operate against the Turks: in European Turkey, or in Asia Minor. A landing between Enos and the head of the Gulf of Saros offers, at first sight, the easiest way of turning the Gallipoli position and the shortest road to Constantinople. But there are considerable practical difficulties. The existing [Allied] naval bases at Mudros, Imbros and Tenedos can barely cope with their present work. It is very doubtful if they could deal with the landing and subsequent support of a large additional force on the European coast. . . . The main Turkish forces are close at hand to organise their resistance and would have no difficulty in maintaining supplies and reinforcements from the railway behind their positions.

Another more general objection to the European line of advance . . . is that it does not necessarily solve the problem. The retention of Thrace is not essential to the Turks either for holding the Straits or for the defence of Constantinople. As long as they can hold the lines of Chatalja and Bulair as in 1912-1913 . . . their defence is still unbroken.

On the other hand the occupation of the Asiatic shore of the Straits would speedily make the position of the Turkish forces on the Peninsula impossible and so effectively open the Straits. And a further advance, whether by land or sea, which severed the connection between Constantinople and Asia Minor would paralyse the whole Turkish defence and compel unconditional surrender.

Operations on the Asiatic side would have the further advantage that the Turkish troops would have to be hurried over from Europe and marched long distances over bad roads, i.e. we should meet them under the conditions least favourable to their organisation and most favourable to us, especially if our force is well supplied with mounted troops. Last, but not least, providing Greece is with us, we should be able to make use of Mytilene, which is admirably suited to serve as a base both because of its excellent and secure harbours, and because of its position which is equally convenient for landing on any point of the Asiatic coast. . . .

The plan of campaign suggested is that the British Field Force based on Mytilene, should land at such point or points as may be selected between Besika Bay and the head of the Gulf of Adramyti, and advance with its left in touch with the sea and the mounted troops well out on its right, and clear the whole Asiatic shore of the Straits. . . . Meanwhile the Greek Army of which some 150,000 at least should be available, should seize Smyrna – working from Mytilene and Khios as bases – and then advance along the line of the narrow gauge railways by Soma towards Panderma. Local insurgents could be armed in large numbers in the district between Smyrna and Andremyti [sic] and would help to keep contact between the two forces.

After the clearing up of the Straits the next step would be the cutting of the communication between Constantinople and Asia Minor. The British Force might be re-embarked and landed between Scutari and Ismid or it might march through Brusa upon the Anatolian railway between Ismid and Eskishehr [sic], the Greeks at the same time pushing up to Afium Karahissar.

Such a plan of campaign would naturally be acceptable to the Greeks who would be making good the territory they hoped to retain after the war, and would enjoy the assistance of a mainly friendly population. It would at the same time leave the Thracian area of operations clear for the Bulgarians, at whatever stage they decide to come in, and thus avoid the friction which would be inevitable if Greeks and Bulgarians were operating in the same area.

Extract from a memo by L.S.A., dated July 1915, on the Near Eastern situation
[This was probably written in Athens, which Amery left to return to London in mid-July.]

To help Serbia effectively it is essential to get Greece in on our side at once. It is only the fear of Germany that is responsible for her present attitude. The obvious answer is to meet that fear by effective help, by substantial territorial rewards, and, if necessary, by fear of the conse-quences of our displeasure. The 150,000 men originally stipulated by Greece should be sent to Salonika at once, and the Dardanelles evacuated to enable this to be done. Greece should receive the Dodecanese, South Albania and Cyprus with immediate occupation, and the promise of fur-ther expansion, after the war, in Asia Minor and possibly also at the expense of Bulgaria. Lastly as a positive threat we can use blockade and the refusal to recognise Greeks rights in Salonika on the ground that they have been forfeited by failure to observe the conditions of the Treaty of Bucharest....*

The real function of the Allied Force in Macedonia should be that of Wellington's Army in the Peninsula, to create a constant drain on the enemy's resources, and only to attempt the advance on Bel-grade when the enemy's resistance has begun to crumble everywhere else. . . .

It would, however, probably be as well if our Mesopotamian force could anticipate the Germans in occupying Baghdad and establishing contact with the Russians left in Armenia, but in any case we and Russia between us should effectively occupy Persia and prevent it drifting to

*The Treaty which brought to an end the Second Balkan War in 1913.

anarchy and becoming a highway for German adventurers and arms to the North West Frontier. Additional reinforcements for Mesopotamia and Persia might be drawn from Australasia as well as from this country and should consist largely of mounted troops.

L.S.A. to Mrs Amery, from London, 21 July 1915

Tea and a real heart to heart talk with Carson whom I found resting in bed, having been rather seedy. He is very depressed about the hopelessness of the present system of governing by 22 gabblers round a table with an old procrastinator in the chair.

F. S. Oliver to L.S.A., 23 July 1915

I agree that Squiff and Squiffery (Simon, Birrell and *hoc genus omnium*) must go. 'Liberalism' in the worst sense of that vile word – which they most worthily represent – is dead, *dead, dead*. It is a dead foetus in the womb of Government, and more dangerous being dead and putrescent than it would be were it still alive.

Nor can we wait philosophically, as you suggest, for three months. Squiff was due to be extruded and buried under quick lime (along with all his horrid rout) by 1st August. What prevents it? I will explain.

I am, as you know, a man of moderate counsels. I am repelled by all extreme courses. Therefore I venture to urge upon you the need for the interment and physical dissolution of Northcliffe. He it was, who by attacking K[itchener] like a cad, rallied the country around that oblique-eyed hero, and made impossible that reform and reconstitution of the War Office which was vital, and which I believe K. himself was willing to assent to. . . .

Therefore as a man of moderate counsels I say to you – take unto yourself (O D'Artagnan!) three other wild cozels, to wit Porthos (who men nowadays call Ronald McNeill), Aramis (who masquerades under the sobriquet of Johnnie Baird) and Athos (who it is customary to refer to at dinner tables as Edward Wood). Beyond them you will need a swift and large motorcar, a box about 7 ft long and 3 ft square, a carpenter with some screws, three bottles of Perrier and an opener and a cold ham. You will then captivate both Squiff and Northcliffe, and float them off into a minefield in the estuary of the Weser.

L.S.A. to Mrs Amery, from London 11 August 1915

Jos. Wedgwood came to dinner instead of tea. He reports Churchill as being much in the dumps and engaged in painting pictures to while away his spare hours!

L.S.A. to Mrs Amery, from London, 13 August 1915

I hear the Cabinet had a real debate on N[ational] S[ervice] two days ago – finally Asquith pointed out that it was already late for lunch and so the subject was adjourned.

Sir Henry Wilson to L.S.A., from GHQ in France, 19 August 1915

I heard last night that K[itchener] was really deciding at last to fall over on the compulsion side and was having a paper drafted in that sense. The remainder of the miserable pack of Hesitations and Hiccoughs, the Squiffs and the McKennas, and Lulus and Runcimans will trim quick enough.

If K. wants a disaster he has only got to remain on the Gallipoli till the winds begin and he will get his heart's desire! I propose we shall come away altogether at the same time that the next big attack is made on this front. Nobody will notice or care a d——. You remember the quack dentist who used to pull out teeth when the patient was sitting on a platform on the village green. He had an immense drum and the man behind the patient hit the drum with incredible violence as the quack pulled out the tooth. The patient felt nothing!

Sir Henry Wilson to L.S.A., 17 September 1915

What is going to be the result of these debates? Will 'wait and see' win, or can that part of the Cabinet that is in earnest and is honest force that d—— old Squiff into action? . . .

Wait and see, wait and see. And K. seems to have joined that crowd. Poor England.

L.S.A. to Mrs Amery, from London

27 September 1915: I took Harold [L.S.A.'s brother] to his rays: he looks pretty bad but is feeling much better. A large piece of bone came away in his mouth yesterday and that has greatly relieved him. Muriel Wilson says he was really very bad last week – I never realised it and feel rather ashamed I made so little effort to see him.

28 September 1915: Today old Squiff, by way of putting off any decision for weeks longer, earnestly implored the House in answer to a question of Guest's, not to discuss National Service. We refused to be taken in.

30 September 1915: I had a talk with Carson this morning and he tells me that they are nowhere near a decision on anything. The prospects of further success on the Western Front are dubious, in spite of very heavy losses, and Bulgaria looks worse again – though Callwell tells me she doesn't mean to go to war, but only to squeeze Rumania to let through munitions for the Turks. Leaving Carson in Downing Street I ran into Lloyd George who shook me warmly by the hand, wished to tell me that he thought my memorandum on N[ational] S[ervice] a very able and helpful document, and then bustled on to the Cabinet.

Sir Henry Wilson to L.S.A., from GHQ, 9 October 1915

Our attacks, Champagne and Artois, have failed, and I fear will fail to break the line – chiefly from lack of men and therefore from lack of a big enough front (by the way, I define breaking the line as allowing of Cavalry to pour through), and so we are all very disappointed. . . . On the other hand I am not dissatisfied, because we rattled the Bosh, and in short, in my opinion we have given the final push which makes certain that Brother Bosh is forced to begin crossing the great dividing line between offence and defence. This passage will take months because the Bosh army is a superb machine and the Bosh a glorious fighter, but he has started to cross and once over he is done.

L.S.A. to Mrs Amery, 13 October 1915

K. has come down definitely for National Service and I hear several Ministers may resign any minute. There is an awful row in the Cabinet as to whether Serbia is to be deserted or not and Carson has refused to take any part in their deliberations for two days past – I saw him tonight just after the Zeps had passed.

Sir Henry Wilson to L.S.A., 22 October 1915

What a pie we are in. Oh, if someone would *kill* Squiff.

Christabel Pankhurst to L.S.A., 27 October 1915

I am glad to know that you feel so strongly about Serbia. Sir Edward Grey's crime against Serbia has put the Empire in danger and has stained our national honour with a stain that cannot be wiped out. . . .

The Coalition Government has turned out to be a sad snare, has it not? The same people have continued to hold the real power and criticism has been gagged. Also the development of a party to cope with the situation to arise after the war has been to a large extent checked.

L.S.A. to Mrs Amery, 10 November 1915

After dinner (tonight) Ronald McNeill and I went and had a talk with Carson. He told us that Bonar was very unhappy about the hopeless drifting of the Cabinet and had all but resigned two days ago, only they kept him on to wait K.'s 'report'. While we were talking Bonar rang up to say that the new War Council has been fixed and he is not on it – only Asquith, Balfour, K. (or his successor), Lansdowne and McKenna. A nasty slap in the face for poor Bonar; but the worst of it is he can't resign now because it will be attributed to pique on his part for being left out. So he must defer it a bit, and share the odium of the smash that may come before his chance of jumping ashore comes again. The Serbian tragedy is drawing to a close very fast – may God forgive us.

Wilson to L.S.A., 18 December 1915

I saw Milner yesterday, the outlook is certainly not bright, and the darkest point is the difficulty of getting rid of Squiff. And yet it must be done if we are to win the war. We can't win if we have to carry him.

Squiff – Grey – K. Even the Bosh could not carry that load.

1916 marked for Amery a relative lull before the enormously hectic but satisfying work of 1917–18 on the War Cabinet and Inter-Allied staffs. He was away from the Western Front, dominated by the battles of Verdun and the Somme. For the latter half of the year he was in Salonika, at that time the quietest of the 'sideshows.' The timing of his return to England, together with his adventures en route, caused him to miss the dramatic fall of Asquith in December 1916, and as a result no comment appears in his papers.

The conscription issue which had developed apace in 1915 drew to its climax. In January a Military Service Bill was introduced to enforce compulsion on unmarried men of military age, but by the time it had come into force at the end of March it was clearly inadequate. After an attempt to introduce a further unsatisfactory measure Asquith himself introduced a Bill in early May which became law by the end of the month.

During these months several condemnations of Asquith's way of managing affairs are recorded, and increased attention given to alternatives. Amery later wrote that he regarded the three men best equipped to lead the nation as Lloyd George, Carson and Milner, although he realised the inadequacies of the last in running what was, despite wartime restrictions, still a parliamentary democracy requiring suitable theatrical and political abilities. His main achievement in early 1916 was to bring the three together in a dining group which first met in Amery's home in Lord North Street, a few hundred yards from Parliament and Whitehall. Apart from these three, Geoffrey Dawson, Waldorf Astor, the proprietor of the *Observer*, F. S. Oliver, Henry Wilson, Philip Kerr and Dr Jameson, the Prime Minister of Cape Colony, attended dinners. In his memoirs (*My Political Life*, II, p. 82) Amery pleads agnosticism as to how far these meetings contributed to the fall of the Asquith Government, but Milner and Carson both received major roles in the new Lloyd George Government. Amery, however, was to be once again disappointed of office.

Milner to L.S.A., 9 January 1916

I never succeeded in getting hold of Carson last week. He's a queer fish. We are the best of friends when we meet, but he's always engaged, when I ask to see him, and never makes any counter proposals, which is disconcerting. Just Irish casualness, I expect. . . .

About our scheme for regular meetings, it either means a great deal or is not worth doing. I could no doubt start it, I could not, nor do I think we two together could carry the whole thing on our leaders, unless the others were equally keen. So far I am not quite sure about anyone except yourself, though Robinson [i.e. Dawson] is certainly in favour of it and would I think stick to anything he took up. But he of course has his hands very full with a most important job of his own, . . . he could not spare any time for the hundred and one jobs which are sure to arise out of your consultations if they materialise.

The whole thing does therefore hang very much on the unknown quantity, Carson. I have a great belief in him, but I feel that, as far as he is concerned, the thing will only be a success if he goes into it *con amore* and not if he just lets himself be persuaded to take it up in a half-hearted fashion to please us.

My own attitude to the thing is therefore rather an undecided one. I am prepared to go into it wholeheartedly, as I did with the 'Covenant' Movement,* and, once in, I am prepared to make any sacrifice of time and energy necessary to make it a success. But I want to see the *possibility* of success before starting. . . . Really important things are the Commons, the Press and, if Victor Fisher turns up trumps, the new Labour Party.

*Over Northern Ireland before the war, see p. 96.

L.S.A. to Mrs Amery

7 March 1916: Then to H. of C. heard A.J.B. deliver a dreary rambling disquisition without life or purpose, followed by Winston very much alive full of purpose and self-assertion. Culminating in his dramatic demand for Fisher's recall.

21 March 1916: Robertson sent for me this morning – I thought it was to tell me I was to stop speaking in the H. of C. or else leave his department. On the contrary it was to open his soul to me about the gravity of the present situation and the complete refusal of Squiff (as he too calls him) to face it. He is clearly anxious that we should do all we can to force the Government to act. I am very glad at last to have got in touch with him and I am now trying to fix up an evening for him to meet Lord Milner alone.

Down to H. of C. at 4 to a meeting of the Unionist War Committee – a very large gathering, all in an awful stew at the idea of passing a resolution about universal compulsory service but [*sic*: lest?] it should in any way make things awkward for Bonar Law! We formally voted a mild resolution that a deputation should see him and express our views.

22 March 1916: The deputation to Bonar from the Unionist War Committee met with an evasive and non-committal answer, and now we have to wait for another meeting next Tuesday when I hope Carson will be there.

25 April 1916: First day of secret session over. Asquith what might have been expected, no real grip or life in it. Carson very good. Our Committee is not proceeding with its motion, but we did binge up Carson to move a resolution of dissatisfaction with the delays of the Government. I am afraid Carson is no real leader, good though he is as a speaker. Altogether I feel rather depressed about things tonight. How can we beat Germany with our Asquiths and Bonars and Walter Longs?

27 April 1916: A great day. After all the gloom and sense of failure of the last few days today was sheer satisfaction and largely unrelieved comedy. Long came in and introduced a most absurd ramshackle bill composed of a string of clauses each one of which was the acceptance of something we had pressed for in the discussion of the Military Service Act. Then Carson got up and in twenty minutes polished off the absurdity and unfairness of these detailed measures without general compulsion. . . . And then Stephen Walsh, a jolly sound patriotic little Labour man, whom

I had seen being converted by Carson's speech as it went along, jumped up and gave a most rousing speech condemning it all as foolery. The Bill was dead straight away and not a soul got up except to condemn it. Asquith was hurriedly recalled and put up both hands in surrender, and said the Bill would be dropped.

24 May 1916 (Hotel Ritz, Paris): I had a very interesting talk with Clemenceau this morning. The only thing I was sorry about was that he insisted on starting in English and keeping to it all the time – quite well, of course, probably better than my French, but not the same thing as the flow of thought in his own tongue. He is all against diversions of strength to side-shows such as Salonika – in this almost alone among Frenchmen – reasonably confident about things, but all the same anxious as to what the attitude of France might be if we gain no successes this summer and have to face another winter.

[Esher] was very interesting and rather discouraging. He believes the Caillaux and peace crowds are quietly strengthening their positions, and that the danger of France losing heart about the war and being ready to snatch at any tolerable sort of peace may be great in the autumn. Meanwhile he is convinced the French will have their way about Salonika.

Amery was at this time on his way to take up a post attached to General Milne's staff in the British section of the Salonika Army. This, under the command of the French General Sarrail (the French, for reasons of internal Greek politics, were the prime movers in the despatch of forces to Salonika), consisted of a nucleus of British and French troops from the Dardanelles reinforced by Serbs, Italians and Albanians. For much of the years these Allied forces were side by side with a royalist Greek garrison, while a political feud raged between Venizelos, who wanted Greece to enter the war, and King Constantine who, with his General Staff, preferred neutrality. Amery describes (see diary entry for 2 September) the Venizelist 'revolt' contrived by the French in Salonika. This rising was, however, accompanied by a more spontaneous one in Crete and led to the reinforcement of the Allies at Salonika by freshly recruited Venizelist forces.

L.S.A. to Mrs Amery

4 June 1916 (Athens): Col. Fairholme . . . tells me that my appointment came as a complete surprise to Milne, with whom he was at the time, who had not asked for an extra staff officer and was rather annoyed to have one thrust upon him without any consultation by the W.O. That would confirm the notion that my coming out was due to political intervention.

9 June 1916 (HQ Salonika): Lord K.'s death* creates a temporary problem as to who is to be successor. But I am not sure it doesn't also mean a death blow to the Asquith Government which largely rested (as far as the opinion of the masses was concerned) upon K.'s reputation. If I am right the crisis will come before the autumn, possibly as early as next month, and I may then feel compelled to ask leave to go home and 'attend to my parliamentary duties'.

2 September 1916 (HQ Salonika): Such a busy and rather amusing week. We have had the excitement of the Bulgar advance followed by the counter excitement of Rumania's entry† and initial successes and the screaming farce of the great Salonika revolution. The solemn uprising of outraged Macedonia (arranged by Gen. Sarrail) started the other day with 2 officers and a flag and all the gendarmes and a few scallywags with rifles going and cheering French HQs and processing the streets among mildly interested crowds. That night they attacked the Royalist troops in their barracks and a few shots were fired at 4.30 a.m. (when I slept the sleep of the just) and three or four were killed, and at daybreak French guns and troops arrived on the scene and Sarrail (who had arranged it all) came down and said he really couldn't have this sort of thing going on, and so the Royalists surrendered to him and were interned, but have since been spoken to and coaxed and have nearly all joined the noble Macedonia Army and Provisional Government. What Tino [King Constantine] will do about it all no one knows. But the revolutionaries have already rechristened the Boulevard Constantine the Boulevard de la Revolution and I doubt if they will be content unless he abdicates. Very comic, but also tragic for Greece and even for stupid well-meaning pig-headed Tino – and we might have had him and the whole Greek Army with us so easily, instead of the mere fragment of it we shall have now.

5 December 1916 (Hospital ship Bien Hoa): We left Salonika on Saturday the 2nd on the good ship *Caledonia*, . . . Yesterday afternoon we were somewhere about the middle of the Mediterranean when – *wump*, a most almighty bang which seemed to hit the ship, just where I was, woke me up with a start. I started inflating my Gieve, put the brandy flask in the pocket, seized my little despatch case and ran out to the foot of the

---

*Kitchener had been drowned when HMS *Hampshire*, taking him to Russia, was torpedoed four days earlier.

†Rumania declared war on the Central Powers on 6 August, following Russian successes in S.E. Poland, but was quickly overwhelmed by a pincer attack from Hungary and Bulgaria.

companion, where a certain amount of water was streaming about, and people running up rapidly to the boat deck. I gave a moment's pang of indecision to a pair of eyeglasses, safety razor and British Warm I might have taken but forgot in my haste, but everyone seemed in such a hurry I decided it was hardly worth returning. As it was I had to jump 6 or 8 feet down to the nearest boat where I found General Ravenshaw and about 20 half naked stokers. In less than 10 minutes the whole of the crew and passengers, 216 or so, were off in ten boats and well clear of the ship which was slowly settling. We watched her for nearly half an hour, at the end of which she slowly turned round in a circle, like a wounded creature turning on itself. Then suddenly the stern broke right off with a rending tearing sound, and the bow rose up in the air, 200 ft perhaps, like a great tower, and then with a roar of snapping masts, and engines shifting about inside, and immense jets of water and air spurting geysers round her, she slid vertically down into the abyss, leaving a couple of detached boats and a few bits of wreckage bobbing up and down on the waves. The boats then drew together and the Captain shouted to us to head south, to get into the probable track of steamers. The General got in a very nervous fussy state, and wanted to stop their hoisting sail, and then asked to be taken into the Captain's boat, which after some shouting came along side and took him off. I preferred to stay where I was. How lucky my decision was you'll hear in a minute. Just after this someone sighted a steamer coming up behind us, but a minute later we realised it was not a friendly steamer, but that infernal submarine in pursuit, looking enormous out of the water, with two guns on deck, and signalling to us to stop. The submarine searched one boat first, then called for the Captain's boat and hauled out the Captain, General Ravenshaw and his ADC, Captain Vickermann, had a casual glance at us 30 yards range or more, and decided that we were nothing but unkempt firemen, looked at one or two more and then told us to go off, adding that there was a ship in the offing. Sure enough, there was 10 miles away. It was just getting dark and she showed up brightly lit with green lights – a hospital ship by all that was lucky! Any other ship would probably have been sunk by the submarine if she had stopped to pick us up. Eventually we fetched up and were handed in by cheery French sailors, and overwhelmed with kindly hospitality.

6 December 1916: What is rather annoying about losing a week or more is that apparently there must be some crisis on at home. We got a very garbled wireless on the *Caledonia* from which it was only possible to make out that Lloyd George had resigned or had offered his resignation, but no indication as to the cause of it.

12 December 1916 (SS Ivernia*)*: We have had the names of the new Cabinet. It's all good – though W. Long is a bit weak for the Colonies. We have had nothing as to under secretaries. If I were under Derby it would be a big thing. But I fear the candidates are many and for all my friends may urge as to my capacity for the work, Bonar and others will say I am not popular in the House.

Austen Chamberlain to Mrs Amery, 9 December 1916

Bonar Law has not consulted me about any appointments.

I did, however, take occasion to speak to him about an Under Secretary in the recent Government. From what he told me I gather that Lloyd George having been obliged (through failure of Liberal co-operation) to give all the more important posts to Unionists was in urgent need of minor posts for Liberals, there was little or no prospect of Unionist Under Secretaries receiving promotion or of any vacancies occurring.

I am afraid that I should only be deceiving you if I held out any hope that in these circumstances your husband is likely to be offered office. But be that as it may, Bonar Law is not seeking my advice and has not sought it at all in recent times.

Amery's papers contain a fascinating exchange between himself and Lord Robert Cecil, who later devoted most of his energies to advancing the cause of the League of Nations. For the first time in the papers this exchange refers to the vexed issue of 'war aims' on which Amery was to do much work in 1917 and 1918 (see letter to W. M. Hughes, 12 October 1917). The rather imperialistic territorial 'aims' set out here – most of which were successfully obtained at the Peace Conference in 1919 – were extremely important. If Germany had retained footholds in Africa up until 1939, campaigns of annexation on the same scale as those which took place in 1914–16 would have been required in that war. Furthermore, if Britain had not held Palestine, Transjordan and, in effect, Iraq in 1941, she would not have been able to mop up the Vichy French in Syria and pro-Axis elements in Iran, while keeping Turkey neutral, when Germany was sweeping over the Balkans, Russia and North Africa.

The exchange further suggests the two types of mind at work in British politics and even inside the Conservative Party: Cecil, moralistic, internationalist, and significantly, perhaps, a free trader; Amery, concerned merely with British political, military, material and territorial power, a tariff reformer.

C. P. Scott* casts further light on the issues underlying this exchange

*T. Wilson (ed.), *The Political Diaries of C. P. Scott* (Collins, 1970), p. 305.

of letters. L. T. Hobhouse, a Liberal MP, learned from a confidential source 'last year' that Amery and 'the little group acting with him' had put before the Cabinet a proposal that 'we should not concern ourselves in the European settlement – that Europe should be left to stew in its own juice – and that we should ride off with the German colonies and Mesopotamia'. These suggestions 'had been rejected as they deserved'.

L.S.A. to Lord Robert Cecil, 23 December 1916

Listening, as a humble secretary, to discussions of statesmen this morning one or two points occurred to me with regard to the desirability of formulating our terms not only about Belgian restoration, and Polish and Serbian national union, but about Turkey and the German Colonies. A statement of the Allies' need to keep the German Colonies and partition Turkey, which means we shall keep South-West Africa, East Africa and Mesopotamia with overlordship over Arabia and Southern Persia, will appeal (a) as you observe to the humanitarians in the USA and at home (this applies to giving back niggers to German rule as well as Armenians to Turkish rule), but also (b) to the interest and imagination of the Dominions. The elimination of Germany from the African, Indian Ocean and the Pacific Zones, and the creation of a belt of continuous British and British-held territory from Cape Town to Rangoon, encircling the Indian Ocean, will appeal enormously to Colonial and very largely to English imagination, and stimulate their keenest efforts.

On the other hand 'guarantees', 'reparation', etc. are very hard to define, and in practice impossible to secure. The best guarantees for the future will be the increased manpower and economic resources of the Allies and Germany's deprivation of opportunities for recovering quickly from the strain of the war.

Now consider the effect on Germany. The German people and soldiers are essentially, whatever their publicists and professors may be, a home-loving people, who believe they are fighting a defensive war for the existence of Germany. If they gather that they are being asked to continue the war because the German Government won't let us keep East Africa and Mesopotamia, they will be inclined to say, as Bismarck did, it isn't worth the bones of a Prussian Grenadier. On the other hand any demand for guarantees can always be represented by the German Government as a demand for the destruction and enslavement of Germany, and will stimulate their utmost efforts. . . .

Guarantees for German good behaviour, leagues of peace, disarmament, etc. are all fudge. The demand for them arises largely from the habit, dear to the Squiff and indeed to the Radical mind generally, of treating this great tragic cataclysm with all it means for the saving or losing of our own souls as a nation and empire, and all the opportunities it may afford of increased greatness and security, as a scuffle amongst schoolboys where the master wants to find out 'who began it' in order to punish him and keep him in for the next three half holidays, till he learns to be a fit associate for young gentlemen!

Lord Robert Cecil to L.S.A., on receiving the above letter

Many thanks. But I am afraid I disagree with almost every word of it. It seems to me pure Germanism.

6

The War: Deadlock
1917

Amery arrived home from his adventures on 19 December just after Lloyd George had become Prime Minister. He did not start the diary for 1917 until 22 January, but the events of the weeks prior to this are covered in a summary written up in the diary for Boxing Day 1918, which reflects on his role in helping to construct the administrative organisation which brought victory (see diary entry for 26 December 1918, p. 137).

Amery was particularly pleased to find that a small War Cabinet of five members had been set up (it first met on 9 December 1916). The five were Lloyd George himself, Curzon, Milner, Bonar Law and Arthur Henderson; the last two were the Conservative and Labour Party leaders. Carson joined in July 1917. In the Boxing Day 1918 entry Amery describes how he discovered that the Dominions were to be invited to send representatives (in most cases, their Prime Ministers) to an Imperial Conference such as had taken place earlier, in 1907 and 1911. Amery describes his part in ensuring that the Dominion representatives were invited to take part in the deliberations of the War Cabinet. Protests from the Colonial Office were met by an arrangement in which the Imperial Conference was to sit on alternate days to the Imperial War Cabinet. The former was to discuss inter-Imperial relations generally as was customary, and the latter to concentrate on the conduct of the war and peace objectives. Much of the first half of 1917 was taken up with preparing for this gathering, the more significant because it recognised that much of the effort being put into the war by the British Empire came from outside the United Kingdom.

Amery's own role during the first half of 1917 had been arranged by Lord Milner: he was to be a political secretary to the War Cabinet, at the disposal of its members and free to submit ideas on all subjects. For administrative purposes he was attached as assistant secretary to Sir Maurice Hankey, who had been secretary to the Committee of Imperial Defence and who now became secretary to the War Cabinet. Amery's duties involved the taking of notes at meetings (it normally met daily) and drawing up minutes. With Mark Sykes, he also provided a weekly summary of the world situation. As Amery says in his memoirs, his position was 'delightfully vague'. The War Office eventually decided that he was Personal Assistant Military Secretary to the Secretary of State for War – who was Lord Derby in 1917 and Lord Milner for most of 1918. (Amery described the War Cabinet system to W. M. Hughes, in a letter dated 8 January 1917).

Because the diary does not start until 22 January Amery has no record of a conversation which Hankey records:

10 January 1917: Walter Long the Colonial Secretary lunched with me. He was full of complaints of Amery, who, he said, was quite untrustworthy and ought not to be present at meetings, particularly owing to his intimate association with *The Times*. . . . In the afternoon I saw Amery, who asked to have two Assistants to *him* appointed. When I asked what he wanted them to do he said that he himself proposed to keep up a regular correspondence with the Dominion Prime Ministers and that he proposed that one of these fellows, namely Howard d'Egville, the Secretary of the Dominion's Inter-parliamentary Association, should send variants of his letters to various parliamentary 'bottle-washers' in the Dominions. This fairly took my breath away, but I reserved judgment.

12 January 1917: Saw Amery first thing and told him I could not possibly have his scheme of a subterranean line of communication with the Dominions . . . and he frankly admitted that his ultimate idea was to displace the Colonial Office, and substitute my office as the means of communication between the Dominions and the Prime Minister. I don't mind his principle so much, though I doubt its desirability, but anyhow I won't have his methods and told him so flat. He is a scheming little devil and his connection with *The Times* would make it possible for him to oust me, so the position is delicate.*

It is only fair to add that Hankey seems soon to have changed his impression of Amery.

Internationally, 1917 was marked by the two Russian Revolutions in March and November, and the entry of the USA into the war in April. The course of the military operations in 1917 – even more than the events of 1915 and 1916 – justified Amery's views on the folly of concentration on the Western Front as opposed to the East. Hindenburg's memoirs bear out the shock to German morale of the capture of Baghdad on 11 March 1917. But by then the Russian forces in Persia and Armenia were in retreat, and the Turks were able to detach troops to hold up General Maude's further advance on Mosul. Similarly in Palestine: the General Staff would not permit an extensive advance despite the fact that British forces in Egypt greatly outnumbered the Turks.

There is relatively little in the Amery papers on the dismal progress of

*S. W. Roskill, *Hankey, Man of Secrets* (Collins, 1970 and 1972), I.

the war in the West: the unsensational British attack at Arras in April, followed by General Nivelle's disastrous failure on the Aisne which led to mutinies in the French Army and to the spending of time, lives and munitions on Passchendaele, the terrible 'battle in the mud'. This, and the failure to exploit the breakthrough by the 'tanks' at Cambrai in November along with the Italian catastrophe at Caporetto in late October, led to the establishment of the Supreme War Council at Versailles and the growing pressures on both Haig and Robertson, the British Commander-in-Chief and Chief of General Staff respectively. Amery fully records these developments later in the year.

Diary

26 December 1918: I am afraid I didn't keep any diary for the first month after my return from Salonika at the end of 1916, but my recollection of [the] particular Imperial Cabinet idea is fairly definite. I arrived home, or rather after wandering about in a taxi discovered that we were living in Curzon Street, about half-past two, had a little lunch with B. and then went down to the House of Commons where I found L.G. making his first speech expounding the nature and policy of the new Government. I came in just as he was explaining what the new War Cabinet was, i.e. practically the scheme which Mark Sykes and I had advocated in the teeth of Asquith's contemptuous objections at the beginning of the year. He then went on a little later to say that he was proposing to ask the Dominions to an Imperial Conference. It at once occurred to me that the real thing was to invite them to come as members of the new inner Cabinet, and as soon as he had finished speaking I went out and wrote a line to Lord M. urging this. As a matter of fact I saw him later that evening before the letter reached him and suggested it again verbally. He tumbled to the idea at once and next day or the day after suggested it at the meeting of the War Cabinet, having previously written to Curzon and one or two others to back him up. It was my first day as Secretary and I was sent out with him, Walter Long, Austen, and I think someone else, who were to be a small Sub-Committee to draft a telegram of invitation to the Dominions. I drew up a draft which they accepted.

That afternoon, or possibly the next day, I discovered that Fiddes had modified the telegram in such a way as to make attendance at the Imperial Cabinet a quite subsidiary matter to the Conference which he proposed also to hold, and which as far as the War Cabinet decision that morning went was to have dropped out altogether. I went round and saw Fiddes and Long about it, both of whom were extremely cross at being found out and have never forgiven me since for it, and also at once saw Lord M. who weighed in with the PM and we got the thing rectified at the Cabinet the next day or the day after. Anyhow, though the Colonial Office got its way to the extent that the Conference was to be allowed to take place at the same time as the War Cabinet, it was made clear that the latter was the essential feature of the invitation and of the visit. Subsequently I drew up all the Agenda and also introduced the differentiation between Imperial Cabinet and British War Cabinet. So I think I had some little finger in that particular pie both as regards its original conception and as regards the decision as to the subjects which should be covered by it. I think most of them hadn't realised that the essential thing was to get them to discuss foreign policy and peace terms, and it was only by various memoranda as well as by drafting a scheme of Agenda and worrying Curzon and others individually that I succeeded in getting the sort of Agenda I wanted.

L.S.A. to W. M. Hughes, Prime Minister of Australia, 8 January 1917

I have been attached to the War Cabinet as a member of this new Secretariat which has been developed out of the old Committee of Imperial Defence. The work is of the greatest interest as it not only keeps me in close touch with Milner and other members of the Government, but also because I have to attend a very large part of the actual Meetings of the Cabinet. We have, in fact, swept away altogether the old system which you saw working at the very height of its inefficiency when you were over here, of twenty-three gentlemen assembling without any purpose and without any idea of what they were going to talk about, and eventually dispersing for lunch without any idea of what they had really discussed or decided, and certainly without any recollections on either point three months later. Under the new system the Cabinet has definite agenda; there are no speeches but only short, business-like discussions between the four or five Cabinet Ministers and the Departmental Ministers or professional experts brought in for the discussion; full Minutes are taken, more particularly of the actual decisions arrived at; these are circulated the same day, and unless they are corrected by one of the Cabinet Ministers concerned, the Secretariat assumes that the decisions hold good and makes it its business to see that the Departments are informed of the decisions and carry them out.

The output of energy on the part of the new Cabinet is amazing. It held twenty-three Cabinet Meetings – not counting a series of prolonged Conferences with French Ministers – in the twenty-three days between its taking office and the end of the year. What is more, at each Meeting some, and not infrequently quite a large number of decisions were arrived at.

Lloyd George is of course wonderfully quick and active, and his eloquence and imaginative gifts will appeal to our Allies. But it is invaluable having Milner, with his steadiness and strength of mind alongside of him....

As regards the invitation to the [Empire Prime Ministers'] Conference, the main idea which decided the Cabinet to make it a Meeting of the War Cabinet and not of the Conference in the ordinary sense, was to lay emphasis on the full equality of status between the Dominion Prime Ministers and the Ministers here, and the right of the Dominion Ministers to have the fullest say, and to have it in good time, on the question of the terms of Peace we can possibly accept when the time arrives....

What is really happening at this moment is that the Imperial Government is being carried on by a small Committee of Public Safety, which, though it has not been called into being by a vote either of the Electorate or the House of Commons, does command general confidence; and that Committee of Public Safety will be temporarily enlarged to include men to represent the public confidence of the rest of the Empire. Later on we shall no doubt have to have a formal Imperial Conference to consider how some form of Imperial Government, better than the existing one, can come into being. Meanwhile, the urgent thing is to get the half dozen or so strongest men in the Empire together to make sure, first, of winning the war, and then of not allowing that victory to be thrown away in the Peace negotiations.

I do not suppose that the *post bellum* questions of Inter-Imperial Preference, etc. will arise in the Cabinet discussions on its own merits. But obviously the Germans will try to make it a condition of Peace that the Paris Resolutions* should be upset and that no system of Preference in Tariffs or in shipping arrangements to the detriment of Germany should exist either between the Allies or between the different parts of the British Empire. The question of what line we mean to take on that issue during Peace negotiations is obviously an important one for the War Cabinet to discuss.

Diary

22 January 1917: Dined with Carson in the evening, our usual Monday gathering, only Lord Milner being absent. After the others went I stayed some time with Carson, talking about the submarine matter and also about transferring transport to the Director of Shipping, on which he was quite open minded, though doubtful of Maclay's capacities; as well as about Ireland – with regard to which I expounded my views on allowing the Irish to find a constitution for themselves, but he would not get [*sic*: go?]

*These were designed to erect tariff barriers round the Allies and their colonies.

139

further than that it was impossible for them ever to arrive at an agreement on anything.

L.S.A. to Milner, 26 January 1917

As regards John Buchan, the propaganda question came up before the Cabinet a couple of days ago, and I found Lloyd George inclined to think that Buchan was too purely a literary man, and had been told to get the help of a Manchester Professor called Ramsay Muir but happily Curzon suggested that I should be asked my opinion of J.B., whereupon I delivered an eloquent oration which Lloyd George told me afterwards had impressed him considerably. I think, however, he feels that he ought to look at this other man first, as he is under some sort of promise to Henderson to do so.

In January 1917 Hankey asked Amery to act for him as secretary of the Inter-Departmental Committee set up by the Asquith Government to study the question of the territorial changes outside Europe which Britain should either aim at obtaining in the terms of peace or might secure by exchange with her Allies. As Amery wrote (*My Political Life*, II, p. 102):

The secretary of such a committee, if he has any skill at drafting and is supported by the chairman, can usually get what he wants or most of it, for the single reason that no-one is prepared to take the trouble to recast the document from beginning to end. . . . My main argument was the need for eliminating the German colonial empire, both because of the actual dangers it had created for us in the war and because its return would always renew the temptation to Germany to enlarge it at our expense. My draft also urged the special importance of securing continuity of territory or of control both in East Africa and between Egypt and India. All this was adopted with little alteration.

But Amery was unable to persuade the Committee of the desirability of having a chain of aerodromes under British control in East Africa and the Middle East. References in the diary to this work are frequent during 1917 (see letter to W. M. Hughes, 12 October 1917, for a statement of Amery's views).

Diary

1 February 1917:   Attended Cabinet in connection with Japanese request for assurances about Shantung and Pacific islands north of the Equator. Drafted outlines of Territorial Changes report on German African Colonies. Very glad to see in the morning that Walter Long had declared publicly that we did not mean to give them back.

3 February 1917: Temperley came in with a suggestion that we should have a small historical staff to look into the past history of some of the debatable questions, more particularly in the Balkans and Poland, which will come up at the Peace Conference. This entirely fitted in with schemes I had been revolving for the last day or two for a co-ordination committee to consider peace questions in all their aspects, including what to do about our Allies' debts to us, etc. I put up to Hankey the suggestion that, while using the Royal Geographical as much as possible, I should also get under way a small staff, statistical, historical, etc. here. He entirely agreed.

6 February 1917: After lunch had a word with Brancker, who entirely agreed with my view as regards the future importance, both civil and military, of securing continuous British territory whenever we can for air traffic purposes.

7 February 1917: Went with Mallet and Tyrrell to the War Office to see whether we could coax General Macdonogh into acceptance of the draft report [on territorial changes]. Found him very difficult to deal with. The difficulty is that he in particular and Maurice to a lesser degree are entirely occupied with high policy, more particularly with the idea of leaving Germany strong after the war (a matter which I think she is looking after sufficiently well herself), and will make no real attempt to deal with the question of the African Colonies as such.

8 February 1917: Had some talk with [Philip] Kerr about the arrange-ments for Conference and the getting [*sic*] necessary Memoranda. Went again with him in the afternoon to see Hankey, who had as a matter of fact anticipated us on almost every point. We got a clear understanding as to the division between the work at the War Cabinet and at the Colonial Office Conference, and he, Hankey, had in fact got Walter Long's entire consent to leave the War Cabinet business alone. The want of clearness in public speeches as to the distinction between the two things is causing endless confusion in South Africa and everywhere else – Botha furious because the Constitution [i.e. of the Empire, federation, etc.] is going to be discussed, as he thinks, at the War Cabinet, Sir J. Ward disappointed that it is not going to be discussed, as he thinks, at all.* Neither Bonar Law nor Curzon were in the least clear on this point in the House on the pre-ceding evening, in spite of all the elaborate notes I had made for Curzon on the matter.

Went with Mallet and Tyrrell to confer with Macdonogh and Maurice. At the end of a long discussion I thought we had really got Maurice to

---

*See the diary entry for 14 March 1917.

swallow the thing, subject to a new paragraph pointing out that there might be over-riding considerations arising from European or other conditions.

9 February 1917: T[erritorial] C[hanges] Committee assembled at 11 and we spent the morning struggling through the report. A more hopeless body for the purpose it would be impossible to devise: most of these old departmental gollywogs were only concerned that some other Department should not score off them, e.g. Islington's one fear was that if we put the case for keeping East Africa too strongly, the Government might eventually wish to keep East Africa rather than something which interested India. The only exception was Macdonogh who, refusing to take any interest in minor military details or to furnish any strategical suggestions, confined himself to the broad political case of defending Germany's claim to have Colonies and objecting to any argument adduced in favour of our keeping them. The one thing they were all unanimous on was in greeting with shrieks of laughter and voting the immediate suppression of the paragraph which suggested that continuity of territory would be important in view of the future developments of aviation. It ought to be really possible under the Defence of the Realm Act to have the Departments overhauled and a certain number of the fossils buried there and then. Anyhow, it seems to me quite essential to get together a small effective Committee under Lord Milner to go into things seriously. These sort of people might be called up as witnesses, but ought never to be members of a serious consultative body. The upshot of the Committee's discussions was that the general arguments should be left out and the report to some extent re-cast. The next thing will no doubt be that the General Staff will produce a minority report in which all the general arguments will be trotted out in favour of the Germans.

10 February 1917: John Buchan's appointment as Head of the Propaganda Department at last decided on, thanks I think in no small measure to my efforts with L.G. last week.* He ought really to be operated on for appendicitis, and if Lloyd George had only told him at the start that he would take a month making up his mind, John might have had the operation and been fit to return to work by now.

Lloyd George had decided to establish a Ministry of National Service to ensure the proper use of manpower, and appointed Neville Chamberlain straight from being Lord Mayor of Birmingham to head it as Director-General. The appointment was a notorious failure and poisoned relations

*Buchan became Director of Propaganda in Allied, enemy and neutral countries. See *John Buchan; A Biography*, by Janet Adam Smith (Hart-Davis 1965), pp. 200 et. seq.

between Lloyd George (who had dismissed Chamberlain as 'that pinhead' on account of the shape of his forehead) and Chamberlain. One aspect was the failure of Sir Edward Hiley, the Town Clerk of Birmingham, as chief executive. Chamberlain resigned in August.

Diary

14 February 1917: After lunch Macleod came in and told me that Neville Chamberlain's Department was bidding fair to wreck the whole Government by its want of grip of the situation, and strongly urged that Hiley, who may be an excellent Town Clerk but is not, he thinks, an organiser of labour, should be superseded.

15 February 1917: Went to second half of the Cabinet Meeting for discussion on Imperial Conference, or rather for the arrangements for the Cabinet Meetings. Hankey's programme was in the main approved of, though they kicked a good deal at first at the idea of spending several days on bringing the Dominion people up to date with the general situation. However, I think we shall get our way, at any rate to the extent of a couple of days' preliminary exposition and discussion. . . .

The conclusions of Lord Balfour of Burleigh's Sub-Committee [favouring] Imperial Preference are really a great triumph, and that cause is now fairly won.

20 February 1917: Read, of the Colonial Office, wanted to re-cast the paragraph [in the Territorial Changes Report] about the advantages of securing the German Colonies lest it should be thought that we might actually be guilty of desiring territory for the sake of the profit we might draw from it! The amended aviation paragraph, in spite of Brancker's memorandum, was ignominiously turned down, both the soldiers [presumably Macdonogh and Maurice] voting for its omission. The Board of Trade had sent in a memorandum on the economic policy it wished to pursue, which seemed to me a deliberate attempt to go behind the resolutions of the Balfour Committee in favour of Imperial Preference.

26 February 1917: Dinner at Carson's, present Oliver, Robin, Waldorf and Jellicoe. Carson and Jellicoe did most of the talking.

I argued somewhat vehemently against Jellicoe's last memorandum saying that we would have to cut down one of our overseas expeditions. My point was that we could think of such things when we had saved one million tons on compressed forage, or five million tons by getting rid of all the cavalry and horse transport in France.

Amery's main preoccupation in the early months of 1917 was with the arrangements for the Imperial War Cabinet: he was Hankey's chief assistant in the Joint Secretariat created with the help of the private secretaries brought by the Dominion Prime Minister. The meetings eventually included more than the Prime Ministers. They needed, for reasons of internal New Zealand politics, to include in all meetings Massey's coalition partner, Sir Joseph Ward. In addition, it was necessary to include Borden's three Canadian colleagues, and Austen Chamberlain's three Indian 'assessors', the Maharajah of Bikaner, Sir S. P. Sinha, and Sir James Meston. This destroyed much of the intended intimacy of the meetings (*My Political Life*, II, p. 106).

The Imperial War Cabinet met formally for the first time on 20 March. (Australia was not represented at this stage as Hughes was in the middle of a political crisis.) It held 14 meetings between 20 March and 2 May 1917. As Amery later wrote (*My Political Life*, II, p. 107), 'it deserved the title of Cabinet as fully as any Cabinet that I have ever attended. It was bound together by a common sense of responsibility for a common cause, even if it was not, in the narrower sense, collectively responsible to a single Parliament.' As Lloyd George told the House of Commons on 17 May, the experiment had been so useful as to merit becoming a regular constitutional procedure. As a result, the Imperial War Cabinet met again in June and July 1918.

Diary

2 March 1917: Went to the Cabinet, Borden, Perley, Massey, Ward, Morris all present. A.J.B. opened up with a [peace] proposal from the Pope which L.G., instead of turning down at once, skilfully utilised to give Jellicoe and Carson a chance of stating the seriousness of the submarine campaign from their point of view. Result, a spirited discussion of great interest to the visitors, and the Pope's suggestion was only turned down after everybody had fully realised the difficulties of the situation and after a special Committee had been appointed to investigate the whole shipping problem on the assumption of the war continuing to the end of 1918. . . . The whole thing was excellent because, although quite formal, the visitors could feel that they were up against reality from the start and not invited merely to be talked at.

6 March 1917: As a result of an urgent appeal from Violet Markham to come over and discuss the parlous state of the National Service Department I went over and had a talk with her and Mrs Tennant. . . . I spoke about it to Hankey, who promised to put it to Lloyd George. I also sent in a memo to Lord Milner, who rather feels, however, that he has too much hay on his fork to try and tackle National Service as well.

10 March 1917: Came up early from Birmingham. Meditated sundry schemes of possible Irish government in the train, more particularly taken with the idea of utilising the principle of separate religious electorates as in Bohemia and India, e.g. one might have two equal houses of parliament, Protestant and Catholic, and the supreme executive entrusted to two consuls, or one might have separate Nationalist and Ulster Governments but with a common Second Chamber consisting in equal number of Protestants and Catholics elected by religious electorates.

12 March 1917: Dinner at Oliver's – Robin, Waldorf and Lord Milner. Lord M. very much perturbed by the appalling congestion of War Cabinet business and the difficulty of getting L.G. to face any question of organisation.*

14 March 1917: Dined with Lord Milner at Brooke's – present Smuts, Ward, Massey, Hythe, Hankey and Kerr. Great fun to see Lord M. and Smuts hobnobbing like the best of old friends. After dinner we drew chairs in a circle in the smoking-room and opened up the Imperial Constitutional problem generally. Massey was all for tackling the Constitution and convinced that New Zealand would be bitterly disappointed if some progress were not made. Smuts very cautious. Switched subject off on the possibility of keeping touch after the present Cabinet meetings, but here too Smuts was very shy and ingeniously argued that this would spoil the perfect simplicity of the small Cabinet of 5. I did *advocatus diaboli* all through, urging difficulties and not rushing in with solutions. No progress, but quite good ventilation of ideas.

15 March 1917: Had Agenda [for Imperial War Cabinet] ready for Lord Milner just before meeting of the Sub-Committee on the subject, he being so rushed, however, that we had no chance of discussing them properly. Sub-Committee consequently rather a failure. Curzon fell foul of the proposed Agenda at the outset, not quite understanding them, and was very tedious and pragmatical. Lord M. had been all in favour of restricting the Cabinet to the smallest possible number, whereas Balfour and Walter Long wanted them all to come, and there was some misunderstanding on

*Cf. Hankey, who writes (diary, 18 March, quoted by S. W. Roskill, *Hankey, Man of Secrets* (2 vols, Collins, 1970 and 1972), I, pp. 310–11) 'far worse than it ever was under the so-called "wait and see" Government'. The War Cabinet did not discuss their Agenda paper and Lloyd George would not initial the conclusions so that they became effective.

that, all of the others coming it over Lord M. by saying that the Agenda had been made while he was absent, which as a matter of fact existed only in their imaginations. Also Curzon more or less assumed that he and not Lord M. was in the Chair. Finally he undertook to draft a new and better Agenda. Lord M. and I went off rather depressed.

17 March 1917: Went at 11 to the Privy Council Office for the Sub-Committee and found Curzon had prepared an elaborate new Agenda, repeating in all essential respects the Agenda which he had so vigorously pooh-poohed on Thursday . . . all agreed at the end that it was a very fine document.

20 March 1917: Opening meeting of the Imperial War Cabinet. After short discussion on the question of sending a telegram to Hughes, the Prime Minister led off with a long statement to the aims and objects of the War, mostly rather tosh. There was much too much of the League of Nations and general platform bunkum about the democratisation of Europe, and only a very short and by no means satisfactory reference to the Colonial question. However, they seemed fairly pleased and the others made short statements to follow. Of these the ablest was Smuts's, who pinned things down to the necessity of really considering our future strategy.

22 March 1917: Imperial War Cabinet all morning. A.J.B. gave a typical Balfourian exposition of foreign policy, delightfully interesting and suggestive, but not coherent or leading to any definite conclusions. It was taken from the usual half-dozen notes on the back of an envelope, and naturally he left out a great many subjects – the whole Balkan and Turkish question was passed by practically untouched; there was no reference to Bulgaria, and no discussion of the effect of the Russians getting Constantinople. Austen helped a bit in this quarter by drawing attention to the great importance of German ambitions in the Near East. There was no suggestion from beginning to end, except in Austen's remarks, that British interests in particular were concerned or that we had to face a definite end to the War. The whole thing was delightfully vague, but the audience were all greatly interested and realised something of the complexity of international affairs.

23 March 1917: Further discussion at the Imperial War Conference [L.S.A. holograph note: 'Cabinet']. Smuts launched out in a long dissertation which was a curious blend of the influence upon him of Massingham & Co. on the one side in favour of moderate terms of peace, and Milner and myself on the other in favour of defining the relative priority of our aims. The Massingham element rather spoilt the discussion for practical purposes, because most of the discussion was devoted to that, L.G. more particularly handling it with great tact and skill. But the practical and urgent question of settling the relative importance of our objects got rather side-tracked, Balfour most characteristically deprecating strongly any attempt to define our objects beforehand as unscientific. In the end the recommendation that peace terms should be considered by a Committee fell through. L.G. put it forward without attempting to argue on its behalf; Milner said nothing, and in fact nobody really went into the question. Meanwhile the Imperial War Cabinet decided that in the event of not being able to achieve the results desired in 1917, the Empire should make every preparation for continuing the War in 1918.

27 March 1917: Imperial War Cabinet in morning. Sir Joseph Ward and Smuts again raised the question of the relative importance of peace terms. This time Smuts was very effective, everybody agreeing with him, even A.J.B. going so far as to say that the essential thing was the security of the British Empire and not Central European philanthropy. Curzon came forward with a definite suggestion that a Committee should be appointed to go into peace terms, but L.G. for some reason or other was rather negative, and the matter was left unsettled. Meanwhile, the necessity for having Committees was rubbed in during the next hour by a thoroughly rambling, inconclusive discussion of problems arising out of shipping.

2 April 1917: Dined at Astor's. Present, Carson, Sir William Robertson, [F.S.] Oliver and Robin [Dawson]. Old Wullie [Robertson] very genial and very funny on the subject of Lord Curzon, whose pompous orations are evidently much too much for him. He feels very strongly the absence of anything approaching a plan on the part of the Foreign Office, as he puts it very justly they seem to live from telegram to telegram.

12 April 1917: Imperial War Cabinet. As far as I can remember, a rather fluffy discussion. The Prime Minister reported a conversation he had had with Ribot [then French Prime Minister], who is absolutely set on a policy of renewed interference in Greece and the breaking of all our pledges to the Greek [Royalist] Government in order to pacify the French Chamber when it meets on 24 May. Apparently he thinks that King Constantine's head on a charger might keep his Government in some weeks longer. Personally I wonder if it will survive till then. L.G. seemed to have been captured by the idea of doing something, though the Cabinet generally didn't like the way in which Sarrail was obviously delaying his offensive in order to use his troops in Thessaly instead for the occupation of Larissa. . . .

At last, after many postponements, L.G. was induced to divide the Imperial War Cabinet into two Sub-Committees for the purpose of considering peace terms – one under Curzon, with myself as Secretary, to consider territorial terms, the other under Milner to consider non-territorial terms. My Easter work [6–9 April] fortunately came in very handy, and Lord M. at once sent on my memorandum to Curzon and told me to send another copy direct to Smuts.

After I had done the Cabinet Minute, I wrote a hurried memorandum summing up the whole history of the Greek business since the beginning of 1915.

At the Rome Conference in early January 1917 the Allies decided to order the Greek Government to withdraw all its forces from the Peloponnese and they complied.* On 23 April in Paris Lloyd George, who generally sympathised with the pro-Ally Venizelist Liberals, laid the foundations of an agreement that if the British acquiesced in a forward policy by the French in Greece under General Sarrail they would agree to the British force at Salonika being reduced. Meanwhile the French had squared the Italians, who agreed at St Jean de Maurienne in Savoy on 19 April not to oppose French manoeuvres in Greece provided the French supported Italian claims to an area in S.W. Turkey. At a further conference at Paris on 4 May, Britain was permitted to withdraw part of her force at Salonika and Lord Robert Cecil and Hankey put forward an ingenious plan by which the Thessaly harvest should be bought by the Allies, who would then be able to occupy Thessaly to prevent its illicit removal (see Roskill, p. 386). While the British Cabinet wished the French to go no further, the latter bombarded and occupied Athens, and deposed King Constantine in early June, whereupon Greece, under Venizelos, entered the war on the Allied side.

Diary

13 April 1917: Imperial War Cabinet in afternoon. Opened on the Greek subject and Maurice, on behalf of the War Office, weighed in with an absolutely uncompromising document against the French intrigue. The Admiralty document was equally strong and the Foreign Office one fairly so. L.G. tried to put in something to the effect that the unconstitutional system at Athens could not be allowed to go on and that an Election ought to be held. To this Bob replied by drawing attention to my memorandum. L.G. said, 'Oh, Amery is a noted anti-Venizelist.' 'No,' said

*The position in Greece earlier in the war and Amery's perception of it have been described on pp. 112 and 129.

Bob, 'these are facts referred to by Captain Amery and not his opinions' and then read them a passage saying that the Allies had refused the holding of an Election last autumn because they knew it would have gone in favour of the King. L.G. collapsed completely and the Cabinet decided to send strong telegrams to say that they were against interfering in Greece and in favour of Sarrail's getting [*sic*] ahead with his operations against the enemy.

14 April 1917: Went to see Lord Curzon about the arrangements for the Sub-Committee. Found him still in bed and in pain. He was very much taken with my memorandum* which is useful (said no-one but myself could possibly have written it).

Smuts asked me to come round in the afternoon and I spent over $2\frac{1}{2}$ hours with him. . . . He has got a very good grip of things and evidently feels that if only he had some decisive say in things here he could make a great difference to the course of the war. It is quite clear that he would stay if a definite job were given him, but the difficulty is that he could hardly be made an extra member of the War Cabinet without offending the other Dominions; he could hardly be their collective representative; and as one of the ordinary representatives to stay and keep contact, he might hardly have enough scope.

17 April 1917: First meeting of Curzon's Sub-Committee. Got through Mallet's First Report and definitely decided that neither South West Africa or East Africa could possibly be given back to the Germans. Progress a little slow owing to Massey's volubility.

18 April 1917: [Curzon's Sub-Committee] We got through West Africa and Somaliland.

19 April 1917: Met Parkin on my way to the office, who told me he was likely to go shortly to the United States. Urged on him the necessity of explaining our acquisitions in Africa, Mesopotamia, etc. as part of a Monroe doctrine for the southern half of the Empire.

Lunched at the Carlton. In the afternoon we got through quite a lot of work at Curzon's Committee, more particularly polishing off the Near East.

---

*This memorandum, on what territorial settlement should be sought, was circulated to the War Cabinet and the Dominion prime ministers and is summarised in *My Political Life*, II, pp. 104–5. Amery's priorities were: first, the acquisition of all German possessions in the Indian Ocean and the Pacific and the detaching of Syria, Palestine and Mesopotamia from Turkish rule; second, the liberation of Belgium and the return of Alsace-Lorraine to France; third, a stabilisation of Central and Eastern Europe. With regard to this third point, Amery was prepared to leave Czechs, Poles, Rumanians and even 'Yugoslavs' in the Austro-German orbit as the price of a compromise peace. He later wondered whether such a solution might not have contributed more to the peace of Central Europe over the following twenty-five years.

20 April 1917: Spent 1½ hours in the evening with Curzon over the minutes of the previous meetings. He was in a fearful state to begin with because he didn't figure sufficiently in the proceedings. He asked if I had a personal down on him and only very partially mollified by my assuring him that he had been fulfilling the proper function of a chairman by eliciting the views of others and summing them up in the conclusions which I had put down as conclusions of the Committee. He has a very comic side of him. . . . We then discussed things in general, he being very anxious to ascertain my views as to the efficiency of the Admiralty, and as to whether Smuts could not be kept as a sort of representative in the War Cabinet of the Dominions.* I told him that he might be put in the War Cabinet on personal grounds, but that the Dominions would never collectively accept anyone from any one particular Dominion as representing them. The whole idea in fact of their being classed in one lump and contrasted with the United Kingdom is entirely different to their conception of the Empire.

21 April 1917: Talk with Smuts on the Salonika and Palestine situation, our general line being that if the French insisted on a free hand in Greece, we had better withdraw some of our divisions from Salonika and see if we could use them more effectively, viz. in Palestine.

23 April 1917: Attended War Cabinet for L.G.'s report on Paris Conference.† Apparently the Italians are now more or less satisfied as to the area in Asia Minor they are going to get and are clamouring for fat compensation elsewhere if they don't get it, and will have to be told that any question of compensation will depend entirely upon the effort that they put in. Greece is apparently to be left to the tender mercies of the French, who are now doing the wolf and lamb business with a vengeance. . . .

Meeting of Curzon's Sub-Committee after lunch, at which we polished off Constantinople, the Balkans and Europe generally, Curzon, after a few general remarks, reading out the sentences of my draft conclusions. A few odds and ends, such as Greenland, the Azores and Alaska were also dealt with.

*On 24 April Hankey asked Smuts on behalf of the War Cabinet to give his views on the strategic situation – the first time the War Cabinet had straightforwardly asked for Smuts's guidance (Roskill, *Hankey*, I, p. 379).

†A conference planned for 4 May, attended by Lloyd George, Haig and Robertson. Its main purpose was to discuss Allied strategy in the light of the failure of General Nivelle's offensive on the Aisne a few days earlier. An earlier conference in Rome on 5–7 January 1917 had discussed Italian assistance for the French schemes in Greece.

24 April 1917: Imperial War Cabinet. Full dress discussion on Imperial Preference, most diverting for me to listen to though I should have liked to have my say. Massey stated the case rather long-windedly and evidently gets on the nerves of some of our people. Borden made the amazing statement that Canada had no interest in preference apart from preference on food and suggested that her main interest was in improved transportation. L.G., while also running transportation here with vigour, frankly declared that the war had revealed fundamental facts which it was necessary to recognise, and entirely accepted a summary of the case laid down by Milner to the effect that preference on customs duty was certainly included within his purview wherever customs duties either existed or were imposed in future. All he stipulated was that, when the Resolution was published, it should be made clear that we were not actually committed to taxes on food. The actual wording of the Resolution was however left to be drafted by a small Committee.

26 April 1917: Went to see Curzon before the Imperial War Cabinet about my draft resolution and found that he didn't like my arrangements but wanted [to alter] the sequence in a fashion which seemed to me much less logical and to give a less clear lead on policy to the Foreign Office. As I put in some queries he got quite hot on the matter and suggested that if I didn't want to do his Report he would sit down and try and do it himself. However, this was pure bluff as he could not possibly have found the time.

Went down to the Imperial War Cabinet, where we considered the amended Resolution on preference. This was in a single vague but comprehensive sentence advocating a system by which each part of the Empire should give more favourable consideration to the rest of the Empire. Smuts at once raised the hare that this was so indefinite that it might mean a great deal more than was intended and that he had no mandate to agree to the imposition of any general system upon the Empire. He preferred something stating definitely that each part of the Empire should have whatever tariff it liked, but should give preference upon that tariff. L.G. also liked the idea, and although those who had been on the drafting committee said that Henderson had rejected a Resolution drawn up on those lines Kerr was deputed to go and draft something again pending Henderson's reaching the I W C later on. In intervals between taking notes I also drafted a version which I sent down to Kerr and which he somewhat improved. When they came back to the subject the Cabinet all agreed upon my draft, and it would have been rather a satisfaction after all these years to have drafted the words of the Resolution which finally settled the whole business. However, Henderson, who seemed to think that something had been altered in his absence, dug his toes in and said that he must record his dissent from any Resolution which by implication suggested the possibility of customs duties being imposed in this country. It is the typical contrast between the woolly British mind, which was frightened of particular words but didn't mind giving away the whole case in general language, and the Roman-Dutch lawyer [i.e. Smuts] anxious for precision. However Smuts gave way, being helped in so doing by a suggestion of Bob Cecil's that the word 'principle' should be substituted for the word 'system'. Thus ended the 12 years' fight on Imperial Preference.

The middle of the meeting was occupied in discussing the Report of Lord Milner's Committee, more particularly on the subject of the League of Nations and the limitation of armaments, on which L.G. has every sort of visionary and unpractical view – the last remnants of his earlier political creed.

27 April 1917: Milner ... showed me a letter from Austen [Chamberlain] in which it appeared that Borden had expounded both to him and Walter Long the idea that the [Imperial] contact should be maintained by having an Imperial War Cabinet annually pending the post-war reconstruction. As this commends itself to the Colonial Office there is no doubt that it will go through, and I dare say we may still devise a means of keeping effective contact in the interval.

30 April 1917: Went to our usual Monday night dinner at Waldorf's. Borden had got Admiral Sims, of the American Navy, and Lloyd George; also Philip Kerr, Milner, Carson, Oliver and Robin present. Everybody in very good form, and L.G. related with great gusto the story of the lunatic who made Beaverbrook say the Lord's Prayer for hours on end, 'more fervently, Beaverbrook!' Oliver capped this with the story of the man who called at the Treasury with a visiting card with nothing on it but 'GOD' and explained that he had come down in such a hurry that he had forgotten his cheque-book. After dinner I moved round next to L.G. and had some talk with him on the military situation and on Greece. I am sure he doesn't quite like Curzon's Report and it will be very necessary to get him to understand the Dominion point of view about keeping the German colonies.

1 May 1917: Imperial War Cabinet in afternoon. There was a good deal of further talk on the subject of the League of Peace and disarmament. L.G., whose opinions are still very primitive, thought that the difficulties in the way of disarmament might be got over by an agreement in favour of a general militia system in place of professional standing armies. When, however, Bob Cecil at my instigation suggested that this argument might also be directed against the British Navy, he waved it aside airily by saying that it took at least 3 years to train a sailor properly! The *pièce de resistance*, however, was Curzon's Report. I had warned Curzon that he was to expect difficulties from Lloyd George, and suggested to him the sort of line he might open on. This he did quite adroitly, and evidently to some extent spiked the PM's guns. The latter however laid considerable stress on the difficulty that would arise if our Allies had to fail in all their claims [in Europe and Asia Minor] while we got all we wanted in the Colonies. Borden and Bob Cecil also rather endorsed this view. Nobody really tried to draw a sufficient distinction between the nature and character of an annexation in Europe and the transfer of Colonial possessions. Eventually the Report was accepted subject to a certain amount of qualifying rigmarole. . . . [Then] Henderson declared that he would not consent in any case to any conclusion which contemplated the desirability of any annexations if they could be secured. When pressed as to whether he really wished to give back Mesopotamia to the Turk or African natives to German rule, he got very red and almost tearful and said that he could not express his own views, but as representative of the Party which had sent him to the Cabinet he was bound to vote against any annexation of territory.

L.G. duly dismissed this as absurd, but then proceeded to trot out a general flapdoodle resolution designed for publication as to the object of the Empire, in which *inter alia*, the Imperial War Cabinet was committed to endorsing Asquith's previous speeches, [President] Wilson's address to the Senate and, last but not least, the Allied terms as communicated to Wilson in the winter – a document from the enemy point of view far more annexationist and unacceptable than the whole of the objects of the Curzon Report. Happily, however, Bob Cecil and others protested against the inclusion of the references to previous statements, and the resolution was left entirely harmless, except in so far as it put the security and integrity of the British Empire in second place, after such generalities as the re-establishment of public right in Europe and the liberation of oppressed nationalities in the Turkish Empire.

2 May 1917: Last meeting of the Imperial War Cabinet. The Prime Minister set forth a proposal for annual Imperial Cabinets more or less on the lines of the wording I had drawn up and it was received very heartily by Borden (the real author of the idea) and by the others. Smuts however discreetly tempering his acceptance by the word 'tentative'. Lord Milner suggested later in the discussion that the annual meeting should also, as at present, be accompanied by a Conference. This was generally agreed to, but a further suggestion of his, really borrowed from Borden, that the Conference should now be enlarged by admitting representatives of Oppositions, was criticised pretty vigorously as a too revolutionary departure both by Long and Curzon.

After that we discussed Greece. Bob [Cecil] . . . concluding that we should balance our withdrawal from Salonika by handing over a unified political control to the French, but under a definite stipulation that they would pursue a moderate policy. L.G. followed this up by an eloquent exposition of the case against King Constantine as held by the French. I am afraid he is a thorough demagogue, and if he has a good case for the platform for something which suits him politically the actual facts and actual justice don't matter much to him. Lord Milner, while agreeing that the policy proposed by Bob was the only practical one if we wished to avoid a split with France, felt bound to lay before the Dominion representatives something of the other side of the story. I wished I could have had 10 minutes to give them the actual facts. I can't help feeling, awful as friction with the French would be at this moment, that letting things go on is going to land us into worse troubles. I dread the possibility of the Germans coming down in force once the French are thoroughly entangled in Greece and sweeping the whole of Sarrail's army into Salonika.

To bed well content with my handiwork with the I W C. I had suggested the idea to Lord M. the day I landed and heard L.G. refer to a Conference,* drafted the original invitation, worked up all the Agenda, suggested topics as it went along, supplied the arguments and conclusions of Curzon's Committee, drafted all the minutes – the only thing that was not mine is the annual renewal as I had been more intent on securing continuous contact by subordinate Ministers.

L.S.A. to Milner, 3 May 1917

You have always been interested in the question of the proper name for the British Empire. I see a phrase of Borden's, which was taken up very warmly by Massey at the Conference, is that of 'United Nations'. I am not sure that when an act of definite political reconstruction takes place it wouldn't much facilitate it by giving the formal and official title to the result of 'United Nations of the British Commonwealth' or 'of the British Empire' as the case might be.

Diary

8 May 1917: I fixed up with Hankey that Ministers here should continue to have access to the information in the office, and to receive the Eastern and Western Reports. I also fixed up that he should see Long about sending out regularly the more important documents to the members of the

*Cf. diary entry for 26 December 1918 on p. 137.

Imperial War Cabinet overseas. The great thing is to keep alive the idea of the Imperial Cabinet as a permanently existing institution and not as a thing which lapses and is called into being again at intervals.

10 May 1917: Down to the Secret Session, where Churchill opened up with a very adroit but rather unsound speech, mainly in the direction of passive defence on the Western Front till America can come in. Lloyd George met his points very ably and went on to a very optimistic account of the food situation, wholly ignoring the really essential things, namely the effect of the submarine upon supplies to our Allies and upon our strategic freedom of action.* Churchill had suggested modifying our proclaimed policy and L.G., in replying to this, to my great surprise came out flatfooted and most emphatic against giving back the German Colonies or letting Turkey have Palestine or Mesopotamia. Evidently the arguments used at the Imperial War Cabinet have sunk into his mind and came to the top spontaneously in this impromptu reply.

12 May 1917: [Conference at Foreign Office to discuss the probable effects of Russia's secession, on the basis of notes by L.S.A. Present; Curzon, Hardinge, Robert Cecil, Hankey, L.S.A.] We all agreed on the basis which was also the basis for my notes, that there was now no motive for any of the Central Powers to try and make a separate peace, and that the question of Palestine† was for many reasons connected therewith of increasing importance. I undertook after lunch to draw up a report for Curzon. I did so, incorporating as much as I could of the morning's discussion, as well as of my notes, which had meanwhile been typed out. When Hankey and I went over to see Curzon about it at 7.30 he objected that I put in rather too much of my notes and not enough of the morning's report, and insisted on re-writing it himself.

13 May 1917: Went to the office, where they were busy typing out Curzon's document, which came to the same thing as my own but was considerably more long-winded. . . .
[War Cabinet on Curzon's report on the consequences of the Russian position:] L.G. instead of discussing the report, launched a fantastic notion of his own that it might be possible to get Austria to go out of the war altogether by making her make a separate peace with Italy, so that we

*After long opposition by Jellicoe, the convoy system was tested with the sailing from Gibraltar of an experimental convoy on 10 May. It arrived safely at Plymouth on 20 May. Convoys were thereupon introduced on all the main shipping routes and shipping losses fell steeply from the disastrous level of April.

†According to Sir Keith Hancock, *Smuts*, I, *The Sanguine Years, 1870–1919* (Cambridge University Press, 1962), pp. 433–5, Lloyd George was pressing Smuts in early May to take command of the Army in Palestine. Smuts refused as he claimed that the War Office was treating Palestine as a sideshow and starving it of forces.

should be relieved of an enemy and a rather tiresome Ally at the same time.* After the discussion had proceeded a little while Bonar, whether out of consideration for the P M's feelings or mere silliness, suggested that the Secretaries had better leave (Hankey had already left, having just had a tooth out and feeling bad). It was really rather absurd in one sense, as after all, apart from the fact that I know the situation better than any of them, I shall certainly be put on whatever Committee eventually works the thing out in detail.

The Irish question, which had threatened to plunge Britain into Civil War in 1914, had temporarily shown signs of improving during the earlier part of the war as North and South rallied to aid the war effort. But the Easter Rising of 1916 and the bitterness left after the trials and executions which ensued had exacerbated the situation. Amery believed that partition was no real solution and the only way to approach the problem was to start with a fresh constitutional convention, and he urged this in memoranda and talks with Lloyd George, Carson, Long, Smuts, Milner and F. S. Oliver. Lloyd George thereupon put the idea of a national convention to the Irish leaders, Redmond and Carson respectively, on 16 May, which they both accepted. The convention met at the end of July but the atmosphere was sufficiently bitter to encourage the extremists, especially on the Sinn Fein side, and the Convention failed after sitting for eight months. This led to new pressures in 1918 for conscription to be imposed on Ireland without any concession of Home Rule.

Diary

19 May 1917: Caught L.G. for a few minutes on the Irish question. He assured me he entirely agreed with my memorandum as to leaving the matter one for the Irish to do themselves. His great suggestion is that Smuts should act as Chairman [presumably of L.S.A.'s proposed convention]. This idea is certainly rather tempting; as an old fighter against England he ought to appeal to Sinn Fein, as a nationalist to the Nationalists, while the Ulstermen should approve of a kinsman of King William of immortal memory and, if they knew it, a naturally strong Unionist on the constitutional issue. I put it to L.G. that that would upset Palestine, but he seemed to think six weeks could settle the Irish Convention and that Smuts could go on to Palestine afterwards. He certainly is an optimist.

22 May 1917: Cabinet in the morning. Discussion on Salonika, the Cabinet beginning to wake up to and feel rather unhappy about the con-

*This culminated in the Smuts mission of January 1918 (see p. 196).

sequences of the recent agreement with France. . . . The question of letting Hughes have the Imperial War Cabinet papers also came forward; Long, having promised to back Hankey, rather ran away from it, and L.G. took a rather silly line about the danger of the documents becoming public by capture on the way. Eventually decided to ask Hughes whether he is coming over soon and if so whether he would like the papers kept for his arrival.

At the House part of the afternoon and talked with various people about the Irish position. Swift MacNeill talked to me about the days of the Curragh crisis, and I showed him my speech urging a Convention as solution of the Irish problem, which I made in the middle of those excitements. He was greatly delighted with it. Had a talk with Murray Macdonald as to the composition of the Convention. He and Hills and some Nationalists had worked out a body of about 60. The Cabinet, I gather, spent about two hours discussing the composition of the Convention in detail.

23 May 1917: Walter Long asked me to come round and tell him all about the previous evening's Cabinet meeting. He urged me, as having influence with L.G., to suggest to the latter to leave Convention making alone and to entrust the selection to the Chairman together with the Irish leaders. This of course fitted in entirely with the views I had already been pressing upon L.G. . . . [Long] said that hardly less important than having the right Chairman was getting the right Secretary, and did me the compliment of suggesting that I was the person best qualified. I told him that there was nothing I should enjoy so much, but that my previous record would probably give the ordinary Nationalists fits, though there might be a few of them who knew the essential moderation of my character! I suggested Brand instead, and he was inclined to agree.

L.S.A. to Milner, 24 May 1917 [*See note on p. 167*]

The more I have seen of the work of the War Cabinet the more convinced I am that while it had done good in getting some sort of general co-ordination of policy, it is quite incapable of dealing consistently and in any detail with the problem of strategy. The most vital questions get pushed aside for weeks by Ireland, drink, the Jockey Club, an Anglo-French excitement, or whatever the cause might be. When they do come up, the First Sea Lord or the CIGS produces some categorical statement which nobody on the Cabinet has had any opportunity of really examining. Neither Jellicoe nor Robertson are really strategists in the highest sense of the word, i.e. capable of seeing the remoter political and military bearings of any particular policy, and I always half suspect them of playing into each other's hands for the policy which seems most convenient to both of them. . . .

The only remedy for this state of things it seems to me, is a small Committee which would meet continuously, say three times a week, and which would include the First Sea Lord, Chief of the Staff and yourself, and Smuts while he is over here. Nominally, perhaps, it might be necessary to include Lloyd George at the start, and then get so busy with detail that he would drop off. The essential thing is that on such a Sub-Committee you and Smuts between you could really effectively cross-examine the experts, get at the documents on which they base their statements, and what is more get them to prepare documents in accordance with questions drawn up by yourself (my own experience of the War Office is that there is always a tendency to send down for information to the branches with a pretty definite hint of the sort of answer that would be welcome).

I don't see anything resembling a plan of any sort on our part. And you may be sure of it that the Germans, in view of the possibility of Russia's revival later in the year, have been working for weeks if not months on some scheme, the fruits of which we shall see in Italy, Greece or Rumania before the summer is out.

L.S.A. to Mrs Amery, 24 May 1917

[At dinner was] told a story new to me of the polite Japanese attaché who apologised to Lord Hardinge for 'cockroaching upon your valuable time'. Lord H. very politely explained that the word was 'encroaching'. 'Ah yes, but I thought you only used that when talking to ladies!'

Diary

29 May 1917: Had a talk later in the afternoon with Smuts about Palestine. He had had assurances of support both from the PM and Robertson which seemed really satisfactory, and he was evidently prepared to decide in favour of going. I strongly backed him up, urging that it was the one place where a strategical success of any importance could still be achieved and that though here as everywhere it was a matter of chance there were many favourable possibilities, e.g. an easy settlement of the Greek crisis or the revival of Russia. The Greek question was finally settled that morning in the Conference entirely in the French sense, except in so far as the occupation of Thessaly was to be the first step and troops were only to be sent to the Isthmus of Corinth in an emergency.

31 May 1917: Lane came round in the morning and showed me a letter from Smuts to the Prime Minister definitely declining the Palestine command. Apparently, after the very encouraging promises given a day or two earlier, Robertson at the last moment told Smuts he could not really hold out any hope of his getting substantial reinforcements – in fact changed his tone about the prospects of the expedition completely. Whether this was due to Knox's latest telegrams about the state of the Russian Army or to Robertson's fears about Salonika complications I don't know. Smuts seems also to have had similar advice from Lord Milner, to whom he had gone as his best friend and counsellor. I told Lane that I thought L.G. would not let the matter rest there and that I hoped Smuts would stay for at any rate a few weeks to get something in the nature of a small strategical committee started. [Later holograph note by L.S.A.: 'It may really have been Botha's telegram "don't go: you and I know that you are no general", or words to that effect.']

4 June 1917: Having thought over my idea for a small Policy or War-plans Committee I came to the conclusion that it would be more acceptable to L.G. if Lord Milner were not on it. That might at once make him think it was an attempt to oust him from the supreme direction of policy. I walked down to College Street and had a talk with Lord M. who quite agreed, and we arranged that, in view of the urgency of the matter in so far as it affected Smuts, whichever of us first had the opportunity should tackle the P M. . . .

Weekly dinner at Oliver's: present, L.G., Milner, Carson, Robin, Astor and Philip [Kerr]. The P M was in great form, chaffing Robin about the service he had rendered him in despatching Northcliffe to America, etc. The conversation turned early upon Smuts and the absolute necessity of finding some form of occupation which would keep him here. After some hesitation I rushed in and expounded my plan. L.G. seemed interested; but I was not quite sure whether he fully seized it or liked it, so I followed it up in the morning on paper.

L.S.A. to Lloyd George, 5 June 1917

Are any plans being worked out now to consider how either a favourable outcome of the next month's happenings in Greece is to be further exploited or an unfavourable outcome dealt with before it leads to a real disaster? The answer is no: there is neither an organ for doing it, nor men of the right type of mind at work on these problems.

Now Smuts is one of the rare men who have got precisely the type of mind required, namely that which can simultaneously keep the military and political bearings of a question in view the whole time. Further he has got the personal qualification of being on very good terms with both

Robertson and Jellicoe, who are naturally likely to be the chief obstacles to anything in the nature of a real, as distinct from a departmental, plan. The question is in what way you can most effectively harness him to the job.

What you want, in fact, is a sort of Chief of Staff to yourself. But the line of least resistance to take would be to appoint him vice-chairman, under yourself, of a small Committee which might include the First Sea Lord, Chief of Staff, and Foreign Secretary, or their representatives, but should be as small as possible, all other experts being called up as witnesses when required. The specific object of the Committee might first of all be to consider the future development of the Balkan situation and of the Palestine campaign. Later on it could go into the question of where best to use the Americans, and eventually, when its footing was secure, it might even discuss the sacred Western Front. The Committee need not have other members of the War Cabinet on it besides yourself, but would report progress to the Cabinet at frequent intervals.

Diary

6 June 1917: Admiral Troubridge came and lunched at the House of Commons and drew a very gloomy picture of the Serbian attitude. His solution is to get rid of Sarrail and have a real military campaign with Smuts in command. The outcry against Sarrail is so strong from every quarter that I heard later in the afternoon that L.G. has sent over an urgent message to Ribot urging him to get rid of him. Troubridge confirmed the view I have always held that a frightful amount of shipping is wasted in connection with Salonika, more particularly with hospital ships. . . .

Dined with Smuts in his rooms at the Savoy, Lord Milner, Ivor Philipps, Lionel Philips, Bob Brand and Lane present. It had originally been intended as a little farewell dinner when Smuts was meditating going off this Saturday, but L.G. has now insisted on his staying. . . .

We discussed peace terms and the future of the Empire, Smuts insisting that it was not safe to let the future control of the Empire depend upon the working-class electorate of this Kingdom, but that there must be some common government. Taking this in conjunction with his various previous declarations against Federalism, it suggested to me that he is thinking of something in the nature of a supra-national government, generally supported by the governments beneath it but not directly based on any democratic representation. Possibly he may be right. I am not sure that his views have not been influenced a good deal by Naumann whose book we discussed in the course of the evening, Smuts suggesting that

Philip Kerr and myself ought to combine as the visionary idealist and the practical thinker to produce a similar book for the British Empire. As we broke up it was very nice to see Smuts taking Lord M.'s arm and walking along with him, with the sort of affectionate deference that one would pay to a favourite uncle. Oom Alfred!

7 June 1917: Went off to see Smuts before he went down to spend the night with L.G., and discussed with him both Salonika and my particular scheme for utilising his services as a sort of Chief of Staff for war policy. He agreed entirely with my views on this, and said that he had been struck by the fact that we really had no policy at all and that the whole War Cabinet proceedings were most [*sic*] amateurish kind.

8 June 1917: Heard that all has been fixed up about Smuts, who is to attend the War Cabinet while over here and to be Vice-Chairman, under L.G., of a Committee on War Policy. The only difference between my scheme and this is that Milner and Curzon are also to be there as makeweights to enable S. to hold his own against Robertson and Jellicoe. Hankey is to be the Secretary and tells me he will use Swinton as assistant secretary, but get me in as much as possible. My own idea is to get M. to make me his 'alternate'.

18 June 1917: Dined at Carson's: Milner, Oliver, Waldorf and Robin present. We talked a good deal about the defects of our present organisation and how desirable it would be if only Lloyd George would devote himself for a bit to stirring up Parliament and the country, both of which need it badly, and leave the War Cabinet and War Policy Committee to get on with the work. According to Lord Milner, the warm weather has made L.G. as mad as a March hare latterly; he simply bubbles over with every sort of wild notion, which makes any consecutive work on the Policy Committee impossible. They had one day when he was away and Curzon took the chair, and they really got through a lot of business.

22 June 1917: Dined at the Holborn Restaurant with a mixed gathering of Unionists and patriotic Labour men presided over by Victor Fisher and Steel-Maitland.* This was the outcome of a number of preliminary informal talks between Fisher and Seddon on the one side and Hope and Worthington Evans on the other. After dinner we discussed at length the

*This casts a light on the process by which the National Democratic Party developed out of the British Workers' League as a working-class group supporting the war and financed by Conservatives and Lloyd George Liberals. Ten of its candidates were returned as M Ps supporting the Lloyd George coalition in the 1918 general election, including two who defeated Henderson and Ramsay Macdonald. (See p. 162 in connection with Amery's support for proportional representation.)

question of safeguarding essential industries by State control and touched on the question of division of surplus profits between employer, workman and State.

3 July 1917: Did a paper for the War Policy Committee on the Balkan situation opposing any minor offensive as calculated only to lock up our troops and urging the creation of a united command for the whole of the Eastern Mediterranean so as to make possible the use of our inner line position as between Salonika and Palestine.

Amery later wrote: 'So far as I can remember I only spoke once [in the House] during the whole of 1917, and that was in support of the recommendation of the Speaker's Conference on Electoral Reform in favour of proportional representation in the larger boroughs' (*My Political Life*, II, p. 112). Amery's motive, as he explained in his memoirs, was not to give the voter an abstract right to vote for a candidate who precisely represented his particular views, nor to give minority parties a right, as such, to be represented in Parliament. He wished to give voters a wider choice between candidates and wings of the same Party. No doubt one motive was to assist vigorous Conservative tariff reform candidates against some of the less effective Conservative candidates which successive leaderships had found it convenient to promote. But his stated motive (*My Political Life*, II, p. 112) was to assist the small group of Labour and Trade Unionist people who were anxious to create 'an essentially national and patriotic Labour Party'.

Diary

4 July 1917: Down to House for PR debate. Called [to speak] soon after Austen [Chamberlain], who made a most impassioned speech denouncing the proposals. . . . I replied in a considerably milder key, at first dealing with his particular arguments and then taking the general line that democracy will be on its trial after the war and can only survive and avert revolution if it brings its methods up to date. All the younger Unionists of the Sykes, Billy Gore and Wolmer persuasion were with me. . . . In the end we were beaten by 201 to 169. [*See also p. 180.*]

5 July 1917: Attended a Committee convened by Duncannon, Spender Clay, Guinness and others, the former [i.e. Duncannon] no doubt directly inspired by Henry Wilson* who put forward the thesis that we ought to

*Wilson, whom L.S.A. otherwise greatly admired, was however, a fervent 'Westerner', cf. letters Wilson–L.S.A. in 1915.

make peace with Turkey in order to get more troops to the Western Front to beat the Boche. Mark [Sykes] criticised their argument from the detailed Turkish point of view with regard to Armenia, Mesopotamia and so on. I went for them hammer and tongs.

L.S.A. to Milner and Smuts, 9 July 1917

I cannot help suspecting that the real crux of the air situation* is the refusal to treat the air seriously as a separate department of warfare which, for the purposes of offensive and defensive strategy, requires its own separate Air Staff and Air Force, over and above the General Staffs of Armies at home or in the field or of the Naval detachments at Dunkirk, etc. Let the Army abroad and the Navy have their necessary proportion of air-men for their tactical and air reconnaissance purposes, but reserve air fighting on a large scale, whether offensive or defensive, to an Air General Staff. This Staff could then decide for itself where and how it could most effectively combat German air raids. . . . At present all the aeroplanes kept in this country are practically tied down to passive defence. . . .

Also, as I think I said to you the other day, the inevitable tendency of the Army authorities is to look upon aeroplanes as a military adjunct to be distributed to the various military forces in proportion to their importance, much as artillery is distributed. An independent Air General Staff studying the problem from its own point of view might very well come to the conclusion that in a particular area, say for instance Palestine, a powerful air concentration might make the enemy's position wholly impossible.

Diary

10 July 1917: Wrote a memorandum on the possibility of Austria making a separate peace, treating this as very improbable.

13 July 1917: Went down to Woldingham with Lord Milner after being delayed while he had a flying interview with L.G., who told him he was reconstructing the Government by bringing Carson into the [War] Cabinet and putting Geddes in his place, Montagu to the India Office, Addison to Reconstruction, and Churchill to Munitions. The merit of this will be getting Carson in the Cabinet and eventually, we hope, leader in the House in place of Bonar, who is a very serious source of weakness.

---

*This may have been stimulated by L.S.A.'s witnessing a German air raid two days previously – 'a very impressive sight'.

14 July 1917: Cabinet from 12.30 to 2.30, most of it on Ireland, about which the reports are very discouraging. The alternative throughout is that of upsetting the hopes of the Convention by being firm now, or letting things drift to a state where a Convention or any other settlement except shooting will be impossible. On Mesopotamia there was a general agreement that if Hardinge resigned and the War Office dealt with the officers implicated, the House would be glad to hear nothing more of Tribunals or Inquiries. On this point Balfour absolutely dug his toes in, and threatening resignation, refused to allow Lloyd George to see Hardinge himself and finally postponed any decision over the weekend.

15 July 1917: Wrote a letter to the PM on the question of Hardinge, pointing out that what the country was after was not a scapegoat but the putting an end to the system under which a failure in one sphere is promptly promoted to prepare for worse failure in another sphere, adding pretty plainly that I didn't consider either Hardinge or A.J.B. would be a loss if they left the FO.

18 July 1917: Listened to the tail end of the debate on Dillon's motion for the adjournment regretting the Government's decision to retain Hardinge. I abstained from voting myself and so did a great many others. Balfour's speech was coldly received. The retention of Hardinge and the bringing of Churchill and Montagu into the Government have shaken its prestige and reputation seriously.

28–29 July 1917: Heard that Henderson had run amok on the subject of the Stockholm Conference.*

30 July 1917: Monday dinner at Oliver's: present, the PM, Milner, Carson, Waldorf, Robin and myself. Very lively discussion. L.G. very depressed about Russia and convinced that there is no more to be hoped from her. I saw in the papers next morning that he had made a speech in the afternoon that Russia would soon be stronger than ever! He asked us round the table in turn what we should each do if we were Dictator, and I started off with my unified command in the Near East, which started a

*This had been initiated by the invitation of Russian socialists to socialists in other countries, including Germany and her allies, to meet together and press for peace. Arthur Henderson, the leader of the pro-war section of the Labour Party, who had just returned from Russia, and Ramsay Macdonald, who was anti-war, went to Paris to discuss the Russian invitation. A special Labour Party Conference voted on 10 August 1917 in favour of representation at Stockholm. At this Henderson not only argued in favour of sending delegates but refrained from reading out – as Lloyd George had asked – a message from the Kerensky Government, which had taken power after the fall of the Czar and which was being assailed by Lenin and the Bolsheviks for continuing the war, dissociating itself from the Conference. Henderson had to resign from the War Cabinet.

long discussion. L.G. is all for concentrating on Turkey but feels that he can't get the CIGS to see eye to eye with him sufficiently. The real thing is that, in spite of his flair about military things and his feeling that the War Office is all wrong, he doesn't really know enough to go nap on his own judgment and issue orders accordingly and then impose them on the Allies. I strongly urged Wilson, or Smuts with Wilson as Chief of Staff, for my proposed command. The PM was also back on his notion of a separate peace with Austria, which he said he knew was possible and I insisted that I knew that it wasn't.

1 August 1917: Debate on Duncannon's Motion for the Adjournment. D. put his case tolerably well, and then Henderson followed and laboriously and confusedly tried to justify himself to a House which listened in unconvinced silence. . . . Mark [Sykes] drew from the Prime Minister a definite statement that the Government would not let any member go to Stockholm and would not let its own peace terms be influenced by anything that happened there.

4 August 1917: Took part in a long discussion with Lord Milner and Smuts, firstly about the recruiting and manpower situation, and secondly about strategy. On the first we came to the conclusion that recruiting ought naturally to go to National Service, and that the department would have to be reconstructed and put under somebody who would carry more weight with Lloyd George than Chamberlain. Milner suggested Carson, but both Smuts and I urged that he ought really to take it himself. We left it on the basis that he should see the PM about the whole matter of principle first. As to strategy, we discussed several plans, the main point being that in any case we ought to do something as a proper counter to Falkenhayn's advance against Baghdad.

7 August 1917: Cabinet. On the subject of Sarrail L.G. is obviously unwilling to tackle the French and rather inclined to take Sarrail's part. Smuts raised the question of securing a British commander, but L.G. paid no attention. The real trouble with him is that when he doesn't want to think out a question he won't listen, but floats off on to something else, so that his colleagues can do nothing with him unless they are prepared to come in a body and put him with his back to a wall and give him an ultimatum.

10 August 1917: Heard later in the afternoon that the Labour Conference, by a four to one vote, had committed themselves to the Stockholm absurdity. A hurried Cabinet meeting followed, at which I am told a good deal of strong language was used.

11 August 1917: Lunched at the Athenaeum and motored down to Woldingham with Lord M., who told me the full story of the Henderson incident. L.G. had been furious on Friday afternoon [10 August] when he heard of the trick Henderson had played him, and had come down to the Cabinet with an extremely trenchant but not too grammatical letter dismissing H. from the Cabinet. Whilst some of the periods in this letter were being rounded by Curzon in another room and some of the most violent passages softened down, and while M. Nabokoff was being asked whether he would object to any reference to his letter being quoted, Henderson smelling danger had weighed in with his own resignation, so that the letter of dismissal as edited had to be further modified into a letter of acceptance.

With the Western Front deadlocked, Amery's attention again turned East, this time to Palestine.

L.S.A. to Smuts, 18 August 1917

The Turkish campaign this autumn is going to be a really serious thing and they may make an attack on us in Palestine the preliminary to a Mesopotamia campaign. If so, then surely we shall have an immense opportunity for countering them. In Palestine we ought to plan, now we have the Arabs with us, a mobile desert column which will move up the east side of the Jordan to the Hauran and make complete havoc of their communications and sources of supply. Better still, if we had the troops or shipping available, would be Ayas Bay or the Dardanelles. . . . If we haven't the transport to send large forces of infantry and artillery, why not at any rate send all the aeroplanes we can spare. In a very few weeks now we ought to know whether there is any real chance of our getting to Ostend. If not, wouldn't it be sound business to cut down our air force there to whatever is necessary for ordinary quiet operations, and send the whole balance to Palestine, bringing them back if need be next spring?

At a conference at Criccieth, Lloyd George's residence in North Wales, on 17–18 September with Milner and Hankey present, it was agreed that Turkey should be the first priority, but there was no discussion of the need to remove Robertson before this could be done (Roskill, *Hankey*, I, p. 436). However, at a conference at Boulogne on 25 September the French made it clear that they were not keen to send an expedition to Alexandretta (now Iskenderun).

Diary

20 August 1917: Dined at Waldorf's: present, Robin, Oliver and Lord M. We discussed various things, including John Buchan's difficulties. He can never get access to Lloyd George, who on the other hand continually sees that ruffian Donald of the *Chronicle*.* He has no sufficient power to deal with questions like censorship, and the question is whether he should resign or confine himself strictly to foreign propaganda.

Germany had been able to impose on her Allies a degree of strategic unity by her ability to assist all of them with her own troops, usually making her own terms for the use of those troops. The Allies were disadvantaged in a number of ways. Britain, France and Italy were separated by enemy territory from Russia and Rumania. France and Italy saw almost all their forces committed to the defence of their own territory, and were thus in no position to exert influence over what Britain did with her own forces. In addition, although conferences occasionally took place between the Western Allied Governments to decide strategy, these were disadvantaged by the instability of these Governments, especially of the French. Yet France benefited from certain inconsistencies: a Frenchman, General Sarrail, commanded the Army at Salonika because, although this Army depended on British supplies and shipping, the British General Staff had no interest in the expedition.

Amery had circulated in January 1917 a memorandum suggesting that Britain should take direct command of all overseas expeditions. She could then 'ration' the French with whatever British troops were considered necessary to meet what the British saw as Allied offensive or defensive requirements in France. What was needed for this to succeed, however, was agreement between the British Cabinet and the British Service chiefs on what their strategy should be. Amery hoped that his continued pressure for such agreement had at last succeeded when on 8 June the Cabinet War Policy Committee was set up, under Lloyd George's chairmanship, consisting of Milner, Curzon, Bonar Law and Smuts and the two Chiefs of Staff. This Committee was not able, however, to prevent the launching of the disastrous Flanders offensive in mid-July, which at an appalling cost in casualties absorbed so much of British resources until the end of October.

*Robert Donald was editor of the *Daily Chronicle*, a Liberal newspaper. A 'propaganda committee' had been appointed to 'control' Buchan (the word is that of C. P. Scott, the editor of the *Manchester Guardian*, diary 21 June 1917, in Wilson, *C. P. Scott*, p. 293). The committee consisted of Northcliffe (or Beaverbrook while Northcliffe was in America), Lord Burnham, managing proprietor of the *Daily Telegraph*, Donald and Scott himself.

Lloyd George therefore did not reconvene the Committee, and came to rely more and more on advice from General Sir Henry Wilson. Wilson had returned to England in July 1917 from the post of chief liaison officer to the French. He now held the post of commander of the Eastern military district, but this did not fully occupy his time, and in the following weeks he evolved a plan to secure strategic and political unity of action between the Allies and to provide Lloyd George with authoritative military advice which would make him more independent of Robertson, the CIGS. Wilson proposed an Inter-Allied Supreme War Council which would meet once a month, and would be assisted by a joint strategic staff drawn from all the Allies in the West (Russia was torn by revolution and about to withdraw from the War). This plan was put to Lloyd George at the end of August, and discussed more fully with Milner and Amery at Woldingham (see diary entry for 24 August).

The first official mention of these proposals by Lloyd George came on 14 October at Chequers (Roskill, *Hankey*, I, p. 443) and he suggested that the Inter-Allied War Council and permanent general staff should be set up in Paris. Hankey was 'horrified' at the thought of what this would mean for relations with Haig and Robertson. However, Churchill was complaining at the misuse of munitions (for example, tanks at the Battle of Cambrai) and Wilson sent in a memorandum which developed his views (see diary entry for 20 October).

The Italian collapse after the Battle of Caporetto on 23 and 24 October clinched the argument and on 2 November the War Cabinet approved both Wilson's proposals and his appointment as British representative on the advisory general staff. The Allies as a whole agreed to the scheme at their conference at Rapallo on 7 November.

Diary

24 August 1917: Motored down with Lord M. and Henry Wilson and went for a walk along the edge of the Downs near Tatsfield. Had a long talk after dinner . . . I discovered that there was a new suggestion afloat, which he [Wilson] had put to Lloyd George. This is that the Italians, French and ourselves should form a small committee consisting of the three Prime Ministers or leading politicians and three soldiers under the Chief of Staff, to arrive at a command plan for the whole Front and more particularly for the use of our troops in the winter months when nothing can be done either on the French or Italian Fronts. L.G.'s idea for the politicians is Milner, Sonnino and Painlevé. Henry [Wilson] would naturally be our soldier.

29 August 1917: Saw Lord M. for a moment, just back from Haywards Heath where he had had a most difficult evening keeping the peace between L.G., who is crazy to send the whole Army off to Italy, and Robertson.

30 August 1917: Dined with Worthy [Sir L. Worthington-Evans] to meet Keynes from the Treasury to discuss the question of Empire currency. We sat there till 12, but didn't really get on very much. Keynes is very clever, and when dealing with details I often found myself out of my depth, but his whole mind is based on the crudest doctrinaire free trade foundation and I doubt that much good can be done with him.

Turkey's entry into the war had excited the hopes of the leaders of the Zionist movement. Amery recognised that the liberation of Palestine could only be achieved by British troops and the British people were second only to the Americans in their understanding of Jewish national aspirations. In the Asquith Coalition Cabinet of 1915 Herbert Samuel had been the Zionists' main protagonist, and while Lloyd George and Balfour were very much in favour Asquith was unconvinced. In 1906 Balfour had met Chaim Weizmann in Manchester and in 1916 they met again and had talked late into the night about the Zionist dream. Now Balfour was Foreign Secretary in the Lloyd George Cabinet. Other new factors were Milner and Smuts – both wholehearted sympathisers – and Mark Sykes, who handled the negotiations which led up to the Balfour Declaration. Amery himself (*My Political Life*, II, p. 115) confessed to a gradualism of approach. He wished to ensure the lasting separation of Palestine from the Turkish dominions by the establishment of a pro-British group there and this was enhanced by his doubts as to the permanence of our position in Egypt. Later he developed an enthusiasm for the regeneration of the whole Middle East through Jewish energy: 'Most of us younger men who shared this hope were, like Mark Sykes, pro-Arab as well as pro-Zionist, and saw no essential incompatibility between the two ideals.'

By mid-July 1917 Balfour was able to let the Zionists know that he was prepared to agree to the designation of Palestine as 'the national home of the Jewish people', but objections came from some of the leading British Jews, notably Edwin Montagu, by now Secretary of State for India, who feared that such a move might jeopardise the status of the Jewish community in England (see Amery's letter to Carson dated 4 September, and diary entry for 18 September). This caused the decision to be delayed through August and September. Shortly before the vital Cabinet meeting in early October Milner showed Amery various unsatisfactory drafts which had been suggested. Amery was asked to draft a declaration that would satisfy both Jewish and pro-Arab objections to the Zionists and he substantially produced the agreed text which referred to 'a National Home' and emphasised that Jews did not, as such, necessarily belong only to Palestine (*My Political Life*, II, p. 117). Amery does not describe the drafting of the declaration in his diary, except in a manuscript footnote to the entry for 31 October, on which day the Cabinet agreed to issue the declaration.*

L.S.A. to Carson, 4 September 1917

Apart from those Jews who have become citizens of this or any other country in the fullest sense, there is also a large body, more particularly of the Jews in Poland and Russia or those who have recently come from there, who are still in a very real sense a separate nation, not likely to be absorbed without endless friction and suffering and many other unsatisfactory results, into the nations among which they live, or to which they may emigrate.

The great majority of these do genuinely desire a 'National Home', and that desire is shared even by a great number of those, who though they have long since ceased to be Jews in the national sense and have become Englishmen or Americans or Frenchmen, still feel a great deal of sympathy with the conditions of their co-religionists elsewhere.

I do not think, myself, that the position of the English Jew would be prejudiced by Zionism – on the contrary, once there is a national home for the Jewish persecuted majority, the English Jews will no longer have anything to trouble about. On the other hand an Anti-Semitism which is based, partly on the fear of being swamped by hordes of undesirable aliens from Russia, etc., and partly by an instinctive suspicion against a community which has so many international ramifications, will be much diminished when the hordes in question have got another outlet, and when the motive for internationalism among the Jews is diminished.

The other point, and the one which is most important to my mind, is that the Jews alone can build up a strong civilisation in Palestine which could help that country to hold its own against German–Turkish oppression; and by enlisting their interest on our side in this country, we will gain a very great deal. It would be a fatal thing if, after the War, the

*An article in *The Times* on 2 November 1977 by S. J. Goldsmith describes a conversation with Amery 'shortly before his death', in which Amery claimed, somewhat graphically, to have written the Balfour Declaration in the War Cabinet Offices on *31 October* while the members of the War Cabinet were eagerly awaiting this final form of words. This was challenged by further correspondents who referred to the dates given in Amery's memoirs. A more restrained account of this drafting appears in the memoirs (*My Political Life*, II, p. 116) but clearly refers to a date 'when the matter was to come up for definite decision *early in October*'. Amery added in these memoirs: 'I was not present at the Cabinet on 31st October when it was finally decided to *give publicity* to the declaration, as this was really Mark [Sykes']'s subject' (editor's italics throughout).

interest of the Jews throughout the world were enlisted on the side of the Germans, and they looked to Berlin as their spiritual home.

The Under Secretaryship of State for the Colonies had fallen vacant. Milner had urged Lloyd George to appoint Amery but Walter Long, the Secretary of State, had secured the post for W. A. S. Hewins, former director of the LSE, and a noted tariff reformer. Amery was not dismayed: it would have 'consigned me to a departmental backwater' at such a time.

Milner to L.S.A., 5 September 1917

[The] C[olonial] O[ffice] business has gone wrong.

Carson wrote to Long. The latter replied civilly enough about you, but saying he had already put forward another candidate, whom he pressed strongly. This turned out to be Hewins. I don't think there was any collusion, as Bonar Law showed me Long's letter, which evidently was a spontaneous one and which urged Hewins with 'horse foot and artillery'.

I doubt whether under these circumstances I could have carried my recommendation anyway, but I felt, even if I could, it would be a dubious service to you to ram you into a post against both B.L. and your immediate chief. So I contented myself with a very strongly worded reiteration of my view that you were the best man for the post, and that, while not prepared to fight *à l'outrance*, I regarded the result as very disappointing on personal and public grounds.

Diary

10 September 1917: Met Kipling as I went into the Athenaeum for lunch and we had a good talk. His view is that the British people profoundly distrust the present Government, mainly because of Marconi, and assured me that a man in the train had told him the other day that the only reason why Churchill had been brought back was that he knew too much about that business and so was able to blackmail the Prime Minister. The best story he told me was about his village grocer who, when he heard of Kitchener's death, remarked: 'There! I always said that Haldane would do him down in the end.'

18 September 1917: In the afternoon Weizmann came to see me in great distress about the fact that the British declaration in favour of Zionism had got submitted to President Wilson and hung up by him. However, Sykes was going to take him to see A.J.B. next day and he [Weizmann] was going to cable freely to his confederates in America. He was very interesting in his scorn for Montagu and all that class of 'tame Jew' who doesn't want to be bothered with Zionism or national aspirations, and only regards the nuisance it may be to himself.

25 September 1917: Dined with Smuts. . . . A good talk with Smuts, in the first instance about his memorandum in which he renews my plea for a small War Plans Committee [i.e. the War Policy Committee], which got corrupted by L.G. He told me all the members of the War Cabinet were in favour of the proposal, which is that one member of the War Cabinet should, in consultation with the representatives of the Army, Navy and Air Board, work out combined plans. But he feared that nothing would induce L.G. to get out of his head that he was a strategist and competent to arrive at strategical decisions by mere talk.

L.S.A. to Mrs Amery, 25 September 1917

I invited myself to dine with Smuts. He told me it was perfectly insane putting Hewins at the CO at a time when it was vital to have men who really understand the Imperial problem and could think Imperially, and said he was going to talk seriously to L.G. and Bonar Law about them not having made proper use of me. He is much impressed by the want of clear thinking in all the odd lots of old politicians who run the Empire's affairs; especially worried about Balfour and the lack of any intelligible purpose in our foreign policy. He would put Curzon at the FO in spite of his defects, because he can administer, knows the Empire, and knows what he wants. L.G. he says is just like Botha, or Kruger, or any old Boer; he can only think while he is talking, and is incapable of the clear sustained thought which alone can see daylight through a complicated and big situation. This is all the more fatal because he fancies himself as a strategist. Lord M. he puts in a different class to the rest as a trained thinker, administrator and man with a big intellectual background.

[Later] I'm afraid Carson has come back from the Front full of the grievances of GHQ against L.G. – I must talk to him, for though L.G. has been very tiresome he is really right in substance. The trouble is our so-called experts aren't really experts for a big war of this sort. I know my judgment on the strategy of this war is better than Robertson's and that I am really more of an expert on it than he, because the war involves a lot of politics, history, economics etc. that have not come within his province.

Diary

9 October 1917: Attended the War Cabinet for the discussion on 'Economic Offensive' precipitated by a recent paper of Carson's. A Committee was appointed consisting of Carson, Barnes, Long, [Robert] Cecil, Stanley and Baldwin, with myself as Secretary. This may prove rather a heavy job and interfere with my 'Prevention of War' memorandum. But it is probably worth doing from the point of view of getting a comprehensive grasp of peace terms and also of seeing to it that the Imperial Preference situation is not damaged in the process of making agreements with our Allies or bargaining of [*sic*: over?] economic concessions of territory with the Germans.

10 October 1917: Lunched with Austen. Discussed . . . the dolefulness of Bonar Law, which latter Austen says is largely due to his sister who is always telling him things are going wrong or that he is losing position, etc. A. also spoke very frankly of his dislike for the Beaverbrook entourage. He said what I always felt, that unless you can be with him [i.e. Bonar Law] the whole time pumping blood into him and keeping him going, he was always relapsing and becoming estranged [*sic*].

The following letter to the Prime Minister of Australia reflects Amery's views over desirable territorial changes.

L.S.A. to W. M. Hughes, 12 October 1917

The great danger to my mind is that the Foreign Office and the public of this country should take too European a point of view about peace terms, instead of looking at them from the perspective of an Empire which is distributed all over the world, and is mainly interested in the maintenance of its sea power and of the safe inter-communication and capacity of mutual support between its different elements. From this latter point of view I feel that the really important thing is to eliminate German ambitions, German submarine bases, or German organised Turkish armies, from the whole area which lies round the Indian Ocean.

If the whole of the great semi-circle which runs from Cape Town to Cairo, thence through Palestine, Mesopotamia and Persia to India and so through Singapore to Australia and New Zealand, is either under British control or in the hands of small neutral Powers like Portugal and Holland who cannot menace our security then all the parts of the British Empire which lie on that semi-circle will be in a position to render each other mutual support. They will have the Indian Ocean free for their shipping; as aviation develops they will have a continuous chain of aerodromes, etc.; and to a very large extent it will be possible to secure railway communication as well. The more they can thus effectively support each other, the less the need for any one population to devote an excessive portion of its revenues or of its manpower to defence, and the more each can devote itself to development – the Dominions to making good their free systems of government by securing abundant population, India to attaining a free system of government by gradual internal development. What we want, in fact, is a British Monroe doctrine which should keep that portion of the world free from future interference of ambitious powers, as the American Monroe doctrine promoted the pacific, or at any rate undisturbed development of Central and South America.

Compared with achieving this end, and it involves the retention at any rate of German East Africa, Palestine and Mesopotamia, the precise settlement of Central Europe is a matter of lesser importance. And in any case I have a strong feeling that, whereas what we embody in the British Imperial system will remain permanent, any artificial arrangement set up in Central Europe, even if it satisfies the claims of nationalities with which we sympathise, may break down in the future under the stress of economic forces, i.e. we can never be absolutely certain that any German barriers we may set up in the shape of a Greater Serbia or Greater Rumania may not, when the immediate bitterness of the war is forgotten, cease to be barriers and become affiliated to the German system. . . .

From the point of view of the future peace of the world, too, I feel that the more that this war gets rid of scattered and interlocked interests and aspirations, and substitutes compact and connected groups of territory with the shortest possible frontiers and the fewest possible outstanding problems, the better. As long as Germany retains a substantial portion of her Colonies she will always feel that her possessions exist by our sufferance, and will be tempted to begin again the struggle for the challenging of our Naval position. Therefore, if she has to have a certain area of tropical or sub-tropical territory to supplement her industries, I would sooner let her have it in Asia Minor, which she can reach by railway.

Diary

15 October 1917: Lunched at the Carlton with Johnny Baird who told me that the War Office is trying in every possible way to obstruct the creation of a new Air Service and that as part of this scheme Brancker, who knows all about the War Office work, is being sent out to Egypt and Salmon, who knows all about the air work in Egypt, is being brought to sit on the Army Council. It is typical of War Office ways that, having originally objected to Brancker's being on the Army Council owing to his lack of seniority, they now appoint someone three years his junior. Smuts apparently seems to have shown no fight in the matter. I told Johnny that he ought to try and see Lloyd George personally and stiffen him. He himself talked of retiring and slipping away to Egypt, but I told him that if he retired he was bound to make a statement in the House to make it quite clear why he had done so. The alternative was to stay on quietly, swallow the rebuff and go on working away. I afterwards saw Lord M. and told him that if Robertson was really unreasonable over this, and at any rate L.G. was bound to have a row with him in the end, he had much better have a row over a question with regard to which he would have the House of Commons with him than over issues of strategy. I saw afterwards that the Cabinet in the morning had come to some sort of rather half-hearted decision on the Air business in the nature of an Air Policy Committee with Smuts, Geddes, Derby and Cowdray.

L.S.A. to Smuts, 15 October 1917

It would be good business to have some investigation made into the actual cost in manpower and effort of each kind of military operation and also of each fighting front. . . . When we talk of the success achieved by our operations on the Western Front we generally compare our battle casualties with the German, and are satisfied if the balance sheet shows in our favour. But what we ought also to compare is the volume of material expended and of effort involved. I heard Churchill say the other day that in the last week of his Ypres operations Haig had thrown 85,000 tons of shell at the enemy. Translate that 85,000 tons, the guns required to throw them, the extra railways and roads required to bring them up, the personnel of the depots in France, the ships required to carry them and the actual workers to make the shells, into so many manpower hours or years additional to the casualties, and measure the corresponding effort on the German side, and that would give us a much fairer estimate as to whether we were really in these operations wearing down the Germans as much as we are wearing down ourselves. On the other hand we might take a campaign like Salonika or Egypt where the consumption of munitions is small but the sea carriage is a very large item, and balance it against the long distance railway carriage on the enemy side. My impression is that if you took such a balance, Maude's recent success at Ramadieh* might come out as a much more lucrative undertaking than the recent fighting in France [i.e. Flanders].

L.S.A. to Smuts, 16 October 1917

Have you ever thought whether Falkenhayn's great and much advertised expedition against Baghdad may not really be meant for Caucasia and North-Western Persia? The whole of this region from a little distance west of Teheran up to Baku is peopled by some five million of Turkish

*Town on the Euphrates, eighty miles west of Baghdad, captured by Maude on 28 September.

race, while west of Tiflis the Georgians are kept politically together with them by a common hatred of the Armenians. To overrun this region would from a Turkish nationalist point of view be far more effective than recovering Baghdad, and might even lead up to a still further linking up with their Turkish kinsmen on the other shore of the Caspian Sea. We have no evidence that the troops which pass through Aleppo to Nisibin do in fact go further towards Baghdad. The Turks have recently completed a branch railway up to Mardin, and it is at any rate conceivable that the demonstration towards Baghdad might cover a very strong Turkish reinforcement from Mardin to Bitlis, while other troops might be sent from Mosul by the Rowandus Pass into Persia. It is quite true that operations in this mountain country would be very difficult in winter, but that applies equally to the Russians, and Falkenhayn will remember Grand Duke Nicholas's successful winter thrust at Erzerum.

Diary

19 October 1917: Henry Wilson [and others] to dinner. I sketched to them the outline of the variegated course of the war to be expected during the next five years, ending with the final arrival of the German advance guard at Vladivostock and the British capture of Zandvoorde.*

20 October 1917: Lunched at White's with Henry Wilson who showed me his memorandum on the military situation, culminating in the necessity for a real inter-Allied organisation to formulate a common policy. His idea of that is that it should consist first of the Prime Ministers *ex officio*, secondly of some big statesman, e.g. Lord M[ilner] on our side, and thirdly of a soldier. As regards actual policy, he carefully refrained in the memorandum from directly criticising the 'Western' policy or suggesting alternatives, but confined himself to insisting that a number of separate military policies cannot be as effective as a common policy, and that it is no use talking about the decisive attack at the decisive point at the decisive moment if the decisive moment hasn't yet arrived. My only comment on the scheme would be that, to make it work, you ought still as far as possible to leave each power in effective control of a particular area, and therefore that we [i.e. the British] ought to take over the direct command of everything east of Brindisi, and on the other hand frankly put Haig [i.e. in France] under the French supreme command, a thing which would wear a very different aspect now that the policy of that supreme command was in its turn subject to an inter-Allied supreme

*A village six miles from Ypres.

council in which we had a voice, and probably a decisive voice. H.W. was quite prepared to agree. He laid great credit to himself for the unprovocative character of the document, and told me that [Sir John] French on the other hand had weighed in with a memorandum criticising the whole of Haig's operations and bringing out that the ratio of losses in this year's operations had been much heavier than the last.

31 October 1917: After lunch Weizmann and Aronson came in, the Cabinet having at last agreed to issue the declaration on Zionism, and fell on my neck with gratitude for my efforts on their behalf. [L.S.A. holograph note: 'I had drafted the finally agreed text about 6 October for a Cabinet at Milner's request.'] It certainly is pleasant to see the joy of a real enthusiast when, after many years, he gets a step forward. Aronson is a real Palestinian, having lived there since childhood and been a farmer and cultivator. If all the Jews in their own country turn out as sturdy, frank-looking fellows as he, Zionism will certainly be justified.

4 November 1917: Went across to see Derby* to thank him for putting me on his Personal Staff and told him that I hope he will really treat it as such. He then launched out in a rather agitated fashion about the hostility of the Government to the General Staff. I pointed out that there was no such hostility and that there had been no interference, though undoubtedly L.G. had frequently nagged and worried Wullie [Robertson], while Wullie on his side had been suspicious and mulish. I urged that some form of common strategy between the Allies was essential, and that when it came to negotiating there could be no question as to Wilson's superiority to Robertson, while on the other hand Robertson was no doubt just as good a man when it came to really looking after the details of the organisation of the campaign. He quite agreed and readily admitted that Henry was in no sense an intriguer and that, on the contrary, Haig had been greatly impressed by his loyal co-operation when he was with Nivelle. D. then switched off to the danger of moving too many troops away from the Western Front, suggesting that the Germans might break through to Calais. I pointed out that if with 180 strong divisions to 150 weak and an immensely superior supply of munitions, we had failed to do more than slightly dint the German line, we could afford to take away at least 30 divisions from the Western Front even if the Germans brought 30 more, thus more or less reversing the present positions. He would have none of this, protesting that our troops were not all of the first quality, etc., etc. It is very curious how our determined Westerners try at one and the same moment to argue that we are so much better than the Germans that even

*Derby had been upset over the Wilson plan and had threatened to resign.

with a slight superiority in divisions we can break through, and on the other hand that they are so superior to us that they will break through if even half a dozen divisions are taken away.

5 November 1917: Dined at Carson's: present Lord M., Oliver, Robin and Waldorf. Walked back with Lord M. to the end of Victoria Street, and put to him the conclusion which had been shaping in my mind after reading a memorandum on the shipping situation in the afternoon, namely that given existing methods of warfare on our side we could not possibly hope to achieve any decisive success in 1918, and that given the shipping prospects as they stood at present we could not last beyond 1918. *Ergo*, we must find new methods which can prove more successful in some, if not in all the areas of war, and which if possible shall be less expensive in tonnage. This comes back to my idea of a warfare carried on mainly by aeroplane, and at any rate for the next few months mainly in the Eastern theatre, except in so far as we tried to rally the Italian situation by existing methods. Before that, over the dinner table, I had urged that instead of fiddling about sending a few divisions at a time to stem the Italian débâcle, we should send Haig himself with a dozen divisions or more to create a real impression that we were behind Italy.

8 November 1917: Dined at St Stephen's Club with about 40 of the younger and keener Unionists on whom it was proposed to try the effect of the new programme of the British Workers' League. . . . The idea was taken up with extreme enthusiasm by everybody . . . I made a few remarks, mainly to the effect that the conflict of the future was between those who had the national and patriotic and those who had the international point of view, and that I was prepared to endorse and back any programme that was patriotic, even if I disagreed with its details, providing it secured adhesion of the working classes to the national and Imperial idea. The whole meeting was a remarkable success. . . . They were all keen, however, that the Unionist Party should not simply adopt and patronise the BWL scheme which would be bad for them as well as for us, but should come out with a programme of its own not incompatible with the other. Personally, after all the years I spent at the up-hill task of creating a Unionist Labour Party with such defective instruments as Alderman N——, etc., it was a great satisfaction to see the thing bearing fruit at last.

The entries of the next three weeks cover the problems resulting from the assignment of Amery to liaise between the War Cabinet Secretariat and the new inter-Allied Supreme War Council, and the teething troubles of the latter. It had been proposed by Lloyd George in a provocative speech at Paris on 12 November when he deplored the futile offensives on the

Western Front while Serbia, Rumania, Russia and Italy were being over-run or defeated. On 17 November Amery received a message from Wilson, then on the Italian front, to come over with General Sackville-West to meet him in Paris in order to make initial arrangements. The diary re-counts both the situation in Paris, where Clemenceau had taken over on 14 November after the fall of the Painlevé government and was beginning a purge of the old regime of officials, and, on the British side, how Lord Derby, the Secretary of State for War and a close ally of Haig and Robert-son, was making difficulties for those who were to act on the SWC's Secretariat as part of the Generals' policy of ostracising that organisation. Hankey's diary for 27 November records a report from Colonel Edward Spears that Clemenceau was trying to wreck the scheme as Foch had been at work on him (just as, Hankey thought, Robertson in Italy had been at work on Foch). Clemenceau had suggested that the chiefs of the various general staffs should be the SWC's advisers, rather than the 'permanent military representatives'. The reason for establishing these latter posts had been to bypass Robertson. On 28 November Wilson and Lloyd George saw Clemenceau, and the outcome of their discussion was satisfactory with regard to the SWC, except that Clemenceau made clear that Foch could not be the French permanent representative.

Diary

12 November 1917: Attended the Cabinet, the general feeling a good deal that L.G. had carried them further than they were quite willing to go. Derby and the CIGS both in rather a touchy and contentious state of mind. On the subject of Palestine Wullie [Robertson, the CIGS] showed complete absence of any ideas as to what ought to be done next and seemed to be genuinely afraid lest Allenby should really push on rapidly and eventually ask for reinforcements. It is quite hopeless to expect to win a war in that attitude of mind.

Looking back over the best part of a year at the Cabinet, I cannot re-collect Robertson on a single occasion indicating what he thought the enemy was really likely to do or what we might do ourselves, beyond expressing the general hope that we were going to obtain our objectives in the West.

13 November 1917: Hankey told me that he and Henry thought that I should either be a liaison between the War Cabinet and the Council, whether staying mainly in Paris or mainly here to be considered later, or else to be the head of the Secretariat over there. Hankey rather leant to the latter. My own feeling, which I put to Lord M., was that that would tie me down too much and be too purely a routine and bureaucratic a job, though undoubtedly it would be immensely interesting and give one great opportunities.

L.S.A. to Geoffrey Dawson, 17 November 1917

I hope you may manage to put in a word on behalf of proportional representation in the next few days. The question comes up again on the Report Stage early next week and there is every hope of a decidedly better vote, and perhaps even of a reversal of the decision on the last occasion.

The thing would have been passed easily but for the way in which certain of the Party organisers have got hold of Unionist Members, more particularly the London ones, and suggested to them the possibility of their losing some seats in the near future. What they will not understand is that the only chance in a future somewhat ahead both for the Unionist Party, and for the Patriotic Labour Party, lies in P[roportional] R[represen-tation] which at any rate will help to defeat the power of mere caucus organisation which will be here, as in Australia, dominated by the extreme wing of the Labour Party.

Diary

19 November 1917 (Paris): Went to the Ritz, where Henry [Wilson] and Duncannon arrived about an hour later. Presently, after a general talk, I sallied forth to find out what was happening as regard the Supreme War Council and to arrange for an interview for Henry with Clemenceau. The first person we saw, General Mordacq, Clemenceau's new *Chef de Cabinet*, knew nothing whatever about the Supreme Council, or whether M. Clemenceau had any ideas on the subject, or whether General Foch was on it, or where it would sit. They advised us to see General de l'Allemand at the General Staff. On the way we called on a Captain Bontal, Foch's ADC, who knew even less, but strongly was of the opinion that nothing would induce Foch to agree to having the Council at Versailles and upset his domestic *ménage* in Paris. However, he had no idea who was going to be Chief of the General Staff or when Foch would return. General de l'Allemand knew less than the others, but said that the one person who could tell us all about it was General Mordacq's *sous-Chef* Colonel Herscher, and said that it was probably owing to the rush of new work that General Mordacq was possibly not aware of the existence of his second-in-com-mand. . . .

I gathered afterwards that Henry had found Clemenceau had hardly given a thought to the Supreme Council, and, as far as he had, didn't think it much use. Henry convinced him in a few minutes that it was of use and as far as one could possibly go at present in the direction of unity of control, and also that it must be at Versailles. C. had then called in Herscher and ordered him to make arrangements. This was a great initial victory.

22 November 1917 (London): Saw Henry [Wilson] and he told me that he had a talk with Derby the previous evening, who refused to let him have any of the officers he wanted for his staff, and more particularly Duncannon because he was a member of the National Party! Then saw Carson, who expressed to me his anxiety both about the Economic Offensive Committee if I went away, suggesting however that Fred Oliver might take my place, and more particularly urging me not to forget my own personal position in this matter. He thought I had better think over carefully the conditions of any appointment there I should accept, and get a definite stipulation on the subject before going. Drove down together to the office, and subsequently I attended most of the morning's Cabinet. In the afternoon I saw Lord M. about my own position and put to him that in addition to the necessary military rank I ought to have a definite undertaking from L.G. that he would really regard me as his representative when he [Lord Milner] was not there and use me as his channel of communication and not short circuit. I also put to him what I thought he might say as regards my future claim to take Cabinet office if a proper opportunity arose without having gone through the intermediate stage of an Under Secretaryship. He seemed to think it might be difficult to pin L.G. to anything and was generally rather anxious about the advisability of my entering on the thing at all, feeling also some of the same anxiety about it myself.

23 November 1917: Saw Lord M. on my way to the office and suggested that as regards myself it was not necessary to get L.G. to give any promise if he would only definitely inform Clemenceau, House [President Wilson's special envoy in Europe] and Sonnino next week that he did in fact regard me as his representative and that they could speak to me freely about anything about which they would speak to him.

Went with Storr and Duncannon to the War Office. Met Henry there, who told me that Derby has now given way about all the staff except Duncannon, adding that Bonar Law shared his view. This seems to me quite monstrous.

24 November 1917: A busy day tidying up all sorts of odds and ends. Hankey after the morning meeting of the War Policy Committee tackled Derby about my GSOI and being made Lt Col. in France, L.G. being too lazy to speak to D. himself. Poor D. determined to thwart the Supreme

War Council in every way, distraught by poor Neil Primrose's death, and not too well anyway, absolutely refused to do anything. This is only on a par with his behaviour over H.W.'s being made General, and over Duncannon, whom he wants to compel to wear civilian clothes in France.

27 November 1917: Caught the 8.25 at Charing Cross and joined the Noah's Ark collection for Paris. There were 109 on the train: L.G. Lord M. and A.J.B.; Reading, Northcliffe, Geddes, Maclay; Wullie [Robertson] and Macdonogh and H.W. with Sykes (whom I had keenly pressed on him in Paris); Admiral Sims and half the US Navy; half the Jap Army and diplomatic service; Venizelos & Co.; not to mention Storr and a score of clerks, etc. for Versailles. I travelled down with Sykes and we had a good talk.

28 November 1917 (Versailles):   Round to Clemenceau to tell him that if he didn't mean business about the Supreme Council and only treated it as a personal arrangement between him, L.G., and Painlevé he, L.G., would go back to London that night, whereupon Clemenceau climbed down and vowed he was keen on the thing. L.G. produced a document about the state of affairs in Turkey which he thought showed we ought to push hard there militarily as well as politically. I had brought in my memo as to information required and L.G. suggested it should be cast into resolutions for Saturday's meeting of the SWC. Lord M. urged he should begin this by a meeting of the PMs only or rather himself, Clemenceau, Sonnino and House, where naturally all would talk English and after that convoke the crowd, which is to include not only the Military Representatives, but CIGS, A.J.B., myself, etc.

After he left I had a talk with Lord M. about Turkey; deprecating the idea of doing too much by opening negotiations, but urging the need of political action in another sense, by working up an anti-German propaganda in the country – L.G. talked before in his naïve way about the desirability of assassinating Enver! While redrafting the memo into resolutions in H.W.'s room we began discussing the whole situation and decided that the whole thing would be frozen out unless Lord M. stayed and so forced Clemenceau to deal with him. So I drafted additional resolutions urging that the normal meetings should be monthly, but that there should be meetings in between which, in so far as PMs couldn't attend, would be attended by second members.

After dinner H.W. and I went in to Lord M. and tackled him very straitly on this question, pointing out that if he stayed and got Clemenceau to deal with him then the whole thing would crystallise round them and Sonnino would have to come, followed later by House or some other American, whereas if Clemenceau relapsed into dealing with the British

Government via Foch and CIGS or via Bertie [British Ambassador in Paris] and A.J.B. the whole thing would be left in the air. . . . Lord M. accepted our contentions, and H.W. and I are to go into Paris early in the morning to catch Hankey and Foch and see how we can get things started off on right lines.

29 November 1917 (Paris): To Hankey's rooms where I found H.W. and between us we again recast our resolutions in a somewhat ampler form as L.G. wanted more detail. In this form we then took it over to L.G. who thought it would just meet the case. L.G. went off to the Quai d'Orsay and presently Lord M. came into the Crillon after a talk with Clemenceau. Afterwards M. told me that Clemenceau had expressed himself rather sceptically about the Council, but had said he would do his best to make it work, as L.G. was keen on it, and thought it might do some good. He then added that he had decided to appoint as French Military Representative General Weygand whom Foch thought highly of; Lord M. of course did not know that W. is merely Foch's personal staff officer, and that intentionally or not, this is reducing the Council to a farce. H.W. was much concerned with this when he learned it.

30 November 1917: Went in after breakfast to Paris with Lord M. and H.W. Had a few minutes with L.G. who took a much more optimistic view of the Weygand appointment, said we couldn't interfere with their choice and that it might work out all right. Afterwards Henry saw both Clemenceau and Foch and was persuaded that it would work somehow, largely by Henry coming into Paris to see Foch.

1 December 1917: The first Versailles meeting of the Supreme War Council opened at 10.30 by Clemenceau and three other first representatives, L.G., Orlando and House having a confab in Clemenceau's room upstairs. They then all gathered together in the Conference Chamber. British in a great majority, eight officers (including Hankey and Spiers, Wullie and Macdonogh, besides H.W., S[ackville]-W[est], Storr and myself). Spiers sat on Clemenceau's left and did the interpreting, very well, but much better from English into French than *vice versa*, showing that he really thinks better in French. Clemenceau's allocution was then read out, and he explained that it had been concocted between him and L.G. – as a matter of fact L.G. concocted and Clemenceau added a bit. Then came the resolutions about information drafted by Hankey and myself, passed without a waste of breath. Then Italy and railway transport, on which L.G. suggested getting Geddes to do a report on the whole transport situation by land and sea as well as the immediate local railway situation as regards Italy and Salonika. Then Balkans, for which Venizelos was brought in, and by voluble earnestness talked down every one else and brought home his point of view to the gathering. What he did not tell them of course was the internal state of Greece and the very doubtful value of the 9 or 12 divisions he is ready to mobilise if they can be fed. But no doubt Royalism in Greece has been strengthened by the Allies' failure to relieve her since V. came back, and L.G. did well to make a handsome apology to V. on behalf of the Allies. When V. left the room most of the people stood up.

Altogether we raced through a vast amount of business in very good style. Clemenceau is an excellent chairman and finished each subject promptly and so on to the next. L.G. was the most effective talker, and his effectiveness was doubled by having Hankey at his side ready to draft a resolution at five seconds' notice while also taking notes of the whole discussion. As Wullie was there Foch was telephoned for and arrived half way through. H.W. discovered by the way that the best room at the French end of the passage was reserved for Foch! So much for Weygand's independence as French Adviser! After the meeting poor little Weygand, a little man with the dependent smart air of one who is always in attendance, came up to Storr and myself very anxious to know what we were at, and rather overwhelmed when we announced that we meant to circulate a *procès verbal*, etc. that same afternoon. Storr and I spent the afternoon at the office dictating *procès verbal*, etc.

L.S.A. to Mark Sykes, 3 December 1917

I am sure the whole of Transcaucasia offers a most promising field for real propaganda, i.e. not only words and pamphlets, but political organisation. It is a very sound thing to organise and arm the Armenians, but to guard their rear I think we ought to be busy with the Georgians as well, and even do what we can to keep the Tartars quiet and convince them that an independent Transcaucasia is better than the Pan-Turk scheme.

Milner is keen on all this as I discovered from a talk I had with him the other night on the Turkish question.

Diary [mostly Paris and Versailles]

3 December 1917: In the evening Lord M. and H.W. went to dine with Poincaré. They found Foch and Weygand there who tried to bluff: F[och] saying they were dealing with the whole problem in Paris, for which he got a sharp answer from Henry that things were not going to be done with that way; W[eygand] having the cheek to say that he couldn't come down to a Conference of the Advisers here tomorrow because he hadn't a car.

H.W., letting him down rather lightly, said one of our cars would be at the door of 4B half an hour before the meeting to fetch him. Lord M. also seems to have talked severely to Foch and Weygand. Duncannon who dined with Esher hears that Cadorna is furious about the impertinence of the French in the matter of Weygand; so we can reckon on his help in dressing W. down and letting him learn his place. I shouldn't wonder, if Henry plays his cards properly, that before a month is out Foch will be compelled to take Weygand's place himself. Anyhow the next few weeks promise to be full of interest. All depends on L.G. and Lord M. backing the thing whole-heartedly and consistently.

6 December 1917: After dinner we had a good talk as to what Lord M. should push for when back in London, the first and most urgent thing being quick information. A War Cabinet decision on Monday about countermanding the 5th and 6th Divisions for Italy only reached here in the shape of a War Office telegram today [Thursday]! Nor have we had a single FO telegram since we left London.

Foch came over in the afternoon for a talk with H.W. and Lord M. which was all to the good. He told H.W. that Pétain reports that we are in no condition to take over any more line, our divisions are simply used up, and we shall have to look to ourselves if the Germans attack. What a result for the fruitless efforts of 1917! H.W. says the one thing is to settle down to peace and quiet for the next few weeks or months, or as long as the Boche let us, in order to get our men rested – no raids or shelling or other provocation. Foch also definitely asked us to convert our divisions into 9 battalions if we are short of men, and not keep them at 13 and cut down the number of divisions as Haig talks of doing. H.W. and Sackville-West and Sykes, who have gone closely into it, are all of the same opinion, and the case seems to me unanswerable. But for some reason Haig, backed by Wully, wants to do the other thing. This, like the question of the extension of the line, ought really to be settled here [i.e. at Versailles] as it affects convenience of co-operation, train movements, substitution of English for French divisions in Italy, etc., etc.

7 December 1917: H.W. very angry firstly about a foolish letter of Derby's refusing him his staff (on false information that the French staff consists of two officers only – there were fourteen to sixteen there today) and insisting that Duncannon should wear civilian clothes and secondly about a woolly effusion of Maurice's which Robertson has sent along as his 'plan' or appreciation, a vague document without a fact or a single positive suggestion except that he ought to have all the men that can be found and then may possibly have a plan in the spring, and that troops shall be recalled from Mesopotamia and Palestine. The real truth is that we ought to have somebody with a better head as CIGS and we may have to be quick to avert disaster. I had a good talk with Lord M. before he left and urged him to tackle Derby and the WO generally firmly this next week when they are really so rattled that they don't know what to do. Lord M. left tonight.

8 December 1917: Drafted some notes for a paper on the Salonika front. Attended Conference of Military Representatives in the afternoon and intervened occasionally more particularly on the question of a separate Air Service and air strategy. Proceedings were very confused and inconsecutive owing largely to the difficulty of language. The only remedy is to have everything cut and dried beforehand, memos to read out, full explanations of what everything means, etc., etc., and nothing left to improvisation that can possibly be prepared beforehand.

L.S.A. to Smuts, 10 December 1917

I don't believe he [Allenby] requires extra troops from Europe. . . . After all judging from the figures provided us here by the War Office we are in enormous superiority over the Turks in the whole of that theatre of war, and our superiority ought to increase as we advance by the fact that we shall be joined by Druses and other local populations, while Turkish troops belonging to these regions will tend to disperse.

What is important is that he should have aeroplanes, any railway outfit that can be spared, and that the Admiralty should be making arrangement to enable Haifa Bay to be netted, and opened up as a Supplementary Base for his Force. Another most valuable means of helping this Campaign would be by systematic and properly organised air attack against the three points at which the Turkish Line of Communication is most liable to damage, viz: (a) Bridge over the Maritza which can be reached from Imbros or Samothrace; (b) The Railway Stations and dumps at Constantinople and Haidar Pasha; (c) The railway near Alexandretta. The bombing of Constantinople would of course have a very valuable moral effect. . . . The Naval people have no conception of air strategy, and simply use their machines for isolated and unco-ordinated raids and scouting here and there.

It seems to me so clear that we shall have to be on the defensive along the whole Western and Salonika Fronts for the next 6 or 8 months or more that it is vital that we should retain the initiative and gain successes somewhere. The only field in which we can do that is Turkey, and there I confess I cannot see anything to stop us this side of Aleppo. Of course the Germans may send troops down there. If so it is so much pressure taken off the Western Front and incidentally involves for the Germans a very heavy effort in the matter of transport, etc. It seems to me much better policy to force that effort upon them than to bring our troops back from the East in order that they should fight the Germans on the front where the latter can concentrate most easily.

I don't see, if the last War Office statements are correct, and our force in Mesopotamia three times the strength of the Turks, and the Turkish force in Armenia likewise sorely dwindled away, why we should not push on, as Allenby advances, either up the Euphrates so as eventually to get in touch by flying Arab columns, or even by armoured cars (which as you know were used to great effect in the Egyptian Western Desert) via Tadmor, or also northwards up to Mosul. A move in the latter direction would require the co-operation of the Armenians. The War Cabinet has, I gather, already in general terms agreed to find money for the mainten- ance of the Armenian and Georgian National movement in Transcaucasia; the thing now is to translate that general concurrence into a concrete policy. I believe, in the present state of Russia, you could buy up not only rifles and rifle ammunition but machine guns and even batteries, for the merest trifle.

Diary

13 December 1917 (Paris and Versailles):   Dined with Fabian Ware at the Meurice and heard a lot about the isolation, ignorance and trade unionism of GHQ and the efficiency of Plumer's Army.

Back to hear that H.W. had had an interview with Clemenceau who had that morning seen Pétain and promised him that he should have at least 200,000 men from the interior to dig trenches, and that he would compel us to extend [the line] to Berry au Bac or resign. All this with much abuse of D. Haig and of our attitude generally. H.W. chaffed him for his tigerishness and persuaded him to put the whole question up to Versailles instead of sending L.G. the ultimatum he intended. On this H.W. thought I had better go home and put the whole story to L.G. and get him to play up.

15 December 1917 (London):   Saw Lord M. and then caught L.G. . . . . He made me repeat my story to the [Manpower] Committee and then said, 'Very well, if the French send their case to Versailles so must we', and ordered Maurice to wire to Robertson, then at GHQ to concoct the British case together with Haig.

16 December 1917:   Lunched with L.G., Smuts and C. P. Scott also there. L.G. very outspoken in his denunciation of the stupidity and obstinacy of Haig and Wully. I don't think however he wants to get rid of either, but to buttress up the one with a new staff and to let the other carry on the routine, with H.W. giving the general policy from Versailles. Smuts was very non-committal, and I suspect him of being a good deal in Wullie's pocket. L.G. full of gratitude to Scott because *The Guardian* had not joined the Cocoa and Old Port cabal against him.* To tea with the Carsons. . . . Carson is a strong Westerner and under the spell of the *ipsi dixi* of GHQ.†

23 December 1917:   Into Paris to dine at the Crillon with H.W., M[ilner], Bob [Lord Robert Cecil], Clerk and Duncannon. . . . The war is going East with a vengeance and we shall find ourselves fighting for the rest of it to decide where the Anglo-German boundary shall run across Asia. The French, as usual, have pushed into the first place and are going to run Rumania, Ukraine and the Poles. But their show may collapse and will anyhow never be under permanent French control, while we poor meek British will probably find our non-aggressive little Empire at the end of the war including Turkestan, Persia and the Caucasus!

L.S.A. to Mrs Amery, 24 December 1917

I hear that M. Jules Cambon who was offered a high post abroad by Clemenceau has declined on the ground that his *maîtresse* has just lost her husband and he feels it would be wrong of him not to stay to console her. Isn't it touching and truly French. As old Clemenceau said 'one of the worst troubles in life is losing the husband of your mistress'. It introduces an element of responsibility and bother into a relationship which otherwise is purely amorous and sentimental, and mixing up things which your Frenchman would sooner keep apart. A Frenchman cherishes his wife, is glad with her over their children, mourns with her if she loses an aunt, shares good and evil financial fortune with her. But with his mistress, that's another story: she ought to have a husband with reasonable means to keep her free from all anxiety, and able to devote all her talents and charms to the serious business of being a gifted man's Aspasia or Egeria without distracting him with mundane cares.

Diary

31 December 1917:   At midnight we all drank punch and the Americans led off with songs. Eventually we got away and . . . drove out through the

---

*Presumably the hostility, for differing reasons, to Lloyd George's conduct of the war, of the Asquithian Liberal Quaker Cadbury–Rowntree group and die-hard Tories.

†Carson resigned on 21 January 1918.

snow to Versailles. So ended a year of great events. Not too successful
for the Allies as a whole, but one in which England has come increasingly
to the front as the centre and mainspring of the Alliance. The Imperial
question, in spite of the very successful establishment of the Imperial
Cabinet, has not moved as it might, and in the military sphere we are only
now beginning with fearful searchings of heart to extricate ourselves from
the Western obsession, and beginning to operate in those regions where
we can achieve results, and results which matter to us. The Russian
collapse has indeed forced that on us. The real struggle during the year
will be to extricate ourselves from all the rot talked about our war aims,
in which not only our Socialists and pacifists but even L.G., Bob Cecil and
our diplomats and soldiers are entangled, in order to find our own safety
and for a peace which will really solve questions instead of trying to restore
a false balance. . . .

My first and most useful piece of work, both in the idea and in the
execution, was the Imperial War Cabinet. Next perhaps all the work on
Peace terms which gradually drove into their heads the importance of
East Africa, Palestine and Mesopotamia and the Imperial outlook generally. With Zionism I helped too but there Mark Sykes was the mainspring
of action. The Irish Convention was my other child, whether destined to
live has got to be seen. . . . The idea of unity of Allied control and a better
strategy I've worked at all the year, and I think I can claim part credit, at
any rate, both for the Palestine advance and for the establishment of the
Supreme War Council. . . .

Last, but not least, I have learnt a lot – I suppose, indeed that I've spent
three hours learning and absorbing for every hour that I've been trying
to put out anything or get anything done. Books I have read very few;
the only one I can think of at the moment which really mattered, and that
mainly because I had thought so far in the same direction myself, is
Naumann [*Mitteleuropa*, see p. 160]. At home much happiness.

7

The War: Victory
1918

It is fortunate that Amery's diary gives a much fuller account of the war in this, its final year. The diary and correspondence for both 1917 and 1918 are important contemporary sources for the criticisms and manoeuvrings of those politicians and soldiers who were opposed to the expenditure of lives and resources on the Western Front. The military issue was entwined with a political issue, as the critics tended to be the victors of the political coup of December 1916 – Lloyd George, Milner and Wilson – while those vanquished then – Asquith and most of his Liberal Cabinet colleagues – were tempted to come to the aid of the soldiers most under attack, Haig, Robertson and Maurice.

The close of 1917 had seen the setting up of the Supreme War Council as a means of outmanoeuvring Haig and Robertson so far as the Western Front was concerned. The opening weeks of 1918 saw the controversy over the 'Western' and the 'Eastern' strategies escalate. Although the 'Easterners'' opportunity did not come to fruition until the autumn, this delay occurred as a result of actual developments in the war rather than their being defeated in council. In fact, by the end of April, Robertson and his ally Derby, the Secretary of State for War, had been displaced by Wilson and Milner respectively, and a final attempt by Asquith to exploit an indiscretion by Maurice and regain power had been decisively defeated.

Before these various intrigues are examined, reference should be made to the fact that, in recent years, the Haig–Robertson 'Westerner' school has received powerful support from the pen of John Terraine.* His emphasis lies on the immense success of the Allied armies in 1918, but he defends the whole notion of concentrating on France and implies that little else could have been done; he does not attempt a detailed critique of the Eastern campaigns. His argument (*Haig*, p. 136) that the Central

*John Terraine, *Douglas Haig: The Educated Soldier* (Hutchinson, 1963); *The Western Front* (Hutchinson, 1964); *The Road to Passchendaele* (Leo Cooper, 1977); and, in particular, *To Win a War* (Sidgwick and Jackson, 1978).

Powers enjoyed interior lines of communication which would have enabled them to repulse Allied offensives against Bulgaria and Turkey is examined, in effect, in Amery's letter to Smuts of 15 October 1917 and somewhat refuted by Mr Terraine's own recent admission (*To Win a War*, p. 32) that by 1917 the strain on the German railway system 'had become too great'. In his unpublished draft for Volume IV of *My Political Life*, on which he was working when he died, Amery noted how the railway system of Central Europe, while well designed to transport eastwards or westwards, was inadequately equipped for transport towards the Balkans and the Levant.

Those critical of the conduct of the war by the Allies on the Western Front might also cite in support a number of points admitted or omitted by Mr Terraine. The French army was not able to make a full contribution to the victories of 1918 because its finest troops had been 'squandered in 1915 and 1916' (*Western Front*, p. 172). The relative successes of the Ancre (early 1917) and Messines Ridge and those parts of Ypres III which were not drowned in mud (autumn 1917), in terms of ground gained and prisoners taken, compared to the bloodbaths of 1915 and 1916, were simply a tribute to improved tactics, the availability of more trained soldiers and better artillery preparation. Such victories hardly compare with those won by the Germans and their allies elsewhere. Ypres III, for example, may have greatly worn down the German army, but such tactics of attrition demanded that the British Army (in particular, the Third and Fifth Armies which were to bear the brunt of the German attack of March 1918) should lose 'a large proportion of their best soldiers whose places had been filled, if filled at all, by raw drafts and transfers'.* Just as the Western offensives of 1915 had not helped the Russian forces in Poland or the Serbs, nor those of 1916 the Rumanians, neither did the extravagances of late 1917 save either the Russians or the Italians from disaster. Each of these German successes helped to take the pressure off Austria-Hungary at a crucial moment: as one perceptive historian has recognised, Caporetto ensured that 'the prospects for luring or forcing Austria-Hungary out of the war had disappeared. . . . The five English divisions dispatched . . . to Italy's aid finally forced . . . Haig to cease offensive operations in Flanders. The dismay . . . provided a suitable atmosphere for Lloyd George to launch . . . the Allied Supreme War Council.'†

While 1918 proved that relative successes were possible in the West,

---

*British Official History of the War, France and Belgium: 1918, The German March Offensive, (ed. Edmonds and others, HMSO, p. 254. See Corelli Barnett, *The Sword Bearers* (Penguin, 1966) pp. 325–6 for reference to rising figures for drunkenness, psychological disorders and desertion in 1917 and 1918, 'all illustrat[ing] increasingly shaky nerves in the British Army'.

†Paul Guinn, *British Strategy and Politics* (Oxford University Press, 1965).

fortunately for the Allies, the onus of proof did not initially rest with them. Mr Terraine condemns Lloyd George for 'starving' Haig of troops, and cheerfully argues that the Army's demand for 615,000 men – which was not met – was 'too few' considering that 'British casualties in 1917 had approached 900,000' (*To Win a War*, p. 48). He does not, however, draw attention to the fact that if the military Moloch had been supplied with a sufficient array of victims, Haig would most certainly have attacked in Flanders. Haig told Repington, to promote a press campaign to force the Government to provide the desired men, that 'the continuation of the Flanders offensive is the best way he knows of attracting and using up the Boches, [but] he cannot go on with it if he is not adequately supplied with drafts'.* Professor Liddell Hart would reply to this: 'we should not forget that the Government had the heavy responsibility of being the trustee for the lives of the nation' and that the 'real ground of criticism was that the Government was not strong enough to change or check the military command which it did not trust'. Hart blamed the public, 'for they had already shown themselves too easily swayed by clamour against politicians'.†

The War Cabinet had earlier received vigorous military advice. Lord French, former Commander-in-Chief in France, wrote a twenty-six-page report in October 1917 of which twenty were an attack on his successor, Haig, who 'had lost over a million men to no particular purpose' (Guinn, *British Strategy*, p. 261). Both he and Wilson, in their separate papers, 'condemned the continuance of the Flanders offensive next year, which is the course that Robertson and Haig recommend'.‡

In less than three months in the spring of 1918 (late March to June) the Germans made gains in territory, prisoners and war material in France compared to which the Allied efforts of 1915–17 paled into insignificance. Weight and concentration of artillery was certainly a prime factor, but of equal importance was the German revolution in tactics (Barnett, *The Sword Bearers*, pp. 320–1). While shortage of Allied reserves was also a factor (caused as much by wastage of manpower in 1917 as by British Government policy), Barnett argues that in terms of odds and of density of troops within the actual defence system, the British in March 1918 were better placed than the Germans in July 1917 (at Ypres) who had succeeded in blunting the first British assault (*The Sword Bearers*, p. 327).

Barnett criticises the failure of the British forces to fortify the attacked

*Quoted by Guinn, *British Strategy*, p. 280. See also Barnett, *The Sword Bearers*, p. 313 and p. 325: 'the extreme lateness of Haig's acceptance of the fact that 1918 might open in a major German offensive, not a continuation of Passchendaele'.

†Liddell Hart, *History of the First World War* (Cassell, 1970), p. 470.

‡Lord Hankey, *The Supreme Command, 1914–18*, (2 vols, Allen and Unwin, 1961) II, pp. 712–16.

sector effectively, and their failure to imbibe the spirit, as well as the letter, of captured German fortification manuals. The failure to fortify arose from Haig's 'persistence in the face of news from Russia in thinking more of his own offensives [i.e. in Flanders] than of a German one, bigger than them all, in 1918' (*The Sword Bearers*, pp. 328–9). Amery's diary for 29 and 30 January 1918 refers to the results of a war game played by the Versailles staff, which were reported to Lloyd George and Haig. In his memoirs, Amery records how Brigadier Sir Hereward Wake suggested that the Germans would be most likely to launch their attack on the British front just north of its juncture with the French, and would then seek to thrust the two armies apart, forcing the British back on their embarkation ports and the French on their capital (*My Political Life*, II, p. 139). This was precisely the point at which the attack came in March, and where it found the British relatively unprepared.

While the German successes on the Amiens–St Quentin front (March), the Lys (April) and the Aisne (May) all owed much to superior numbers, firepower and tactics, each success can also be attributed to particular Allied weaknesses displayed at the precise place and time of attack. In these areas, once a line of reserves had been established, and elsewhere (for example, on the Arras and Reims fronts), where the Allies were better prepared, the Germans encountered the same disappointments as had the Allies in previous years. The military historians are agreed on the more general reasons for German failure: the steady arrival of the Americans, the German lack of sufficient cavalry, motor transport and tanks, the excellent work of the Allied air forces, the lack of discipline in the advancing German forces (in which Bolshevik deserters from Russia were already at work), especially as they came upon abundant supplies of food, drink and other necessities, and the onset of the world influenza epidemic, which hit both the physically weakened German forces and civilians as early as June.

Amery was probably right to suggest (in a later footnote to the diary of 21 March 1918) that the Germans would have been wiser to have stood on the defensive in France while their forces' morale there would have been boosted by the troops from Russia being used to overwhelm Italy and then perhaps to 'mop up' the Salonika force and Greece. They would thus have protected the 'soft underbelly' and secured valuable food resources in addition to those in Russia. Even subsequently, there would be no pressing case for an offensive in France, where the Americans would be making their presence felt. The Germans and their allies could drive across Transcaucasia for the Baku oil wells and then across Persia on to India. It would be the old nightmare of British strategists throughout the nineteenth century which was to appear again in 1941–2. In 1918, however, there would have been no Red Army, no Stalingrad.

Once the Germans had, with immense losses, failed in their Western Front offensives and then been thrust back at Amiens in August, the collapse of their morale, followed by that of their effective resistance, was inevitable. This collapse was not so rapid or so clearly apparent that the Allies were able to predict an end to the war that year. What brought peace was the giving way of the 'soft underbelly'. Although it was the Allied successes on the Salonika front (bringing their forces on to the Danube) and on the Venetian plain which caused the collapse of Austria-Hungary and thus, inevitably, of Germany, Amery had always pressed for an offensive in Palestine. For three reasons he may have been right. First, such an attack was the most likely to succeed, in view of Allied military superiority, Turko-German supply difficulties and the already proven difficulty of making advances at Salonika or in Italy. There was no question of unconditional surrender in this war, no question of invading the Anatolian plateau. The loss of Mesopotamia, Syria and Palestine would have convinced Turkey of the disastrous consequences of the German alliance, even if her surviving armed forces had remained intact and loyal, which is doubtful.

Second, it would have been a uniquely British success in an area where Britain had substantial territorial ambitions. If the war continued beyond 1918 and a compromise peace became necessary, Amery had been persuaded since at least 1916 (see p. 133) that while Germany would be obliged to evacuate Belgium and France in any event, only actual possession at the peace would suffice to bring the Middle East into the British orbit.* Third, it is clear from the Amery papers and from other sources that the Allies greatly feared that the Germans would emulate the 'Grand Design' attributed to them in John Buchan's *Greenmantle*, sweep over Western Asia and arouse the Muslim millions of Persia and India. In late 1917 the Indian Army had established a post at Meshed and another party under General Dunsterville ('Dunsterforce') was preparing to move into the Caucasus to organise resistance against the Turks. After the Treaty of Brest-Litovsk in early 1918 fears of the Germans exploiting the surrendered resources and manpower of Western Russia grew. Milner referred to the need for 'Allied military intervention' in Russia to stop 'Germany, like a *boa constrictor*, gradually swallowing Russia' (Guinn, *British Strategy*, p. 308). These fears were not groundless as, during the spring of 1918, the Turks occupied Batum and Tabriz and the Germans seized Sevastopol. In August, British forces landed at Vladivostok (to reinforce Japanese and American forces which were already there, at Archangel and, more significantly, at Baku), and command of the Caspian Sea was secured.

*This advice was set out extensively in letters to Sir Henry Wilson as late as 1 August 1918 and to Smuts on 16 August (see pp. 230–2, 233–4).

These considerations were reflected when, at the start of 1918, Amery drafted the Allied plan of campaign for the year, which became known as Joint Note 12. It opted for the defensive on the French and Italian fronts until the expected German attack had spent itself and continued: 'To allow the year to pass without an attempt to secure a decision in any theatre of war . . . would . . . be a grave error in strategy apart from the moral effect such a policy might produce upon the Allied nations.' Amery emphasised the weakness and dispersal of the Turkish forces, and urged 'a decisive offensive against Turkey with a view to the annihilation of the Turkish Armies and the collapse of Turkish resistance'. The diary recounts its passage through the Supreme War Council at the end of January.

Even before this, the War Cabinet had deputed General Smuts to proceed to Egypt to consult with the chief British commanders in the area. Amery accompanied him and while momentous developments were taking place in London, they recommended that two divisions were to be transferred to Egypt from Mesopotamia, where the British were to adopt a defensive role, and that the Indian cavalry division was to come from France; this was generally accepted by the War Cabinet. Allenby had already begun what was intended to be a slow advance with the capture of Jericho on 21 February.

Robertson, the CIGS, had vigorously opposed Note 12, and was also opposed to Wilson's Note 14, which urged as 'imperative' the formation of a General Reserve for the whole of the Allied forces in France and Italy. Robertson's original role, as Chief of Staff, was to control this reserve with his French and Italian equivalents. On 2 February the Supreme War Council decided that this clearly unworkable process for a sudden emergency should be replaced by giving effective control to General Foch. Lloyd George instructed Hankey not to circulate the *procès verbal* of this discussion as he did not wish the Cabinet to see Robertson's outburst (Roskill, *Hankey*, I, p. 492). In fact, even these arrangements for the General Reserve were doomed to failure. While Pétain made some pretence at complying with Foch's request to assign fifteen divisions to it, Haig, asked to furnish nine, made no reply until 2 March when he flatly refused. It led, however, to a dangerous political crisis. It appears that Clemenceau had invited Colonel Repington, now the military correspondent of the ultra-Tory *Morning Post*, to Paris, and after the Supreme Council session had given him detailed information and a request to 'stop the sideshows'. On 11 February, Repington published the crucial details of the Council's decisions: the plan to 'knock out' Turkey, the refusal to provide reinforcements for the Western Front, the creation of a reserve under a 'committee of military busy-bodies' were all summarised. Repington concluded that 'Mr Lloyd George has clearly and finally proved his incapacity to govern England in a great war' and the *Post*'s leader made the remarkable suggestion – given its political hue – that it was Asquith's 'clear duty . . . to probe this matter'. However, Asquith held back and Lloyd George survived the debates of 12 and 19 February. The latter took place the day after Robertson had accepted his removal as CIGS and taken on the Eastern Command.* The subsequent moves of personnel took more time, and it was not until 19 April that Robertson's ally, Lord Derby, was moved from the War Office and succeeded by Milner. The military results of these moves were by now superfluous, as the Allies were fighting for survival in France and the Turkish offensive had been cancelled. It represents, however, the triumph of Lloyd George and his allies over the generals.

Diary [Paris]

1 January 1918: Wrote criticism of Wully's (really Maurice's) hopelessly timid and destructive paper about Palestine and sent it to L.G. and Milner.

In early January, Count Czernin, the Austro-Hungarian Foreign Minister, sent Count Mensdorff to Switzerland to meet General Smuts, who had been sent out on behalf of the British Government. They were to discuss the possibilities of a separate peace with Austria, but this series of talks did not provide any concrete result.

Diary

2 January 1918: Henry Wilson back in evening bringing not too good an account of Lloyd George who he thought was rather on the peace tack, or at any rate completely perplexed for want of military guidance he could trust, and absorbed in preparing an answer to Czernin's last speech. He is evidently hankering after getting Henry back to London as CIGS which he mustn't be allowed to do as this would upset the whole Versailles tree before it has fairly taken root.

4 January 1918: Leo Maxse sailed in, saying as he took off his hat that Lloyd George was a traitor and went on to explain that he had sent Smuts to Switzerland to negotiate a secret arrangement with Austria or

---

*Guinn, *British Strategy*, pp. 292–6, draws on the Repington diary and other sources for this narrative.

at least information as to Austrian views, against Clemenceau and Sonnino's wishes, that he was all out for peace, etc. At lunch he was in great form, L.G. was described as the 'Kerensky of the West', as for Bonar 'there isn't any such person it's only a camouflage'. As neither Henry or I had been told anything of the Smuts trip, we were anxious.

Amery was briefly involved in the controversy over the number of troops which Britain had in France early in 1918, before the German offensive. This arose as a result of his reporting to Lloyd George from Versailles in December 1917 on the question of the British Army taking over more of the line in France from the French. In January 1918, Lloyd George asked him to 'straighten out' the figures. Yet Hankey's diary for 9 January, reporting a War Cabinet discussion on manpower statistics, alleged: 'I found to my disgust that Amery, who is over from Versailles, where he had seen an advance copy of my manpower report, had been butting in and upsetting or trying to upset the figures given by the Adjutant-General [Macready] and interviewing all sorts of people without my authority' (Roskill, *Hankey*, I, pp. 479–80; see diary entry for 10 January). Amery in fact had to straighten out the conflict in the various figures produced by Haig, the War Office and the Ministry of National Service. The variation was largely due to the fact that Haig's figures were based on infantry strengths and ignored the increase in the machine-gun battalions, artillery batteries and transport. One point which Amery emphasised to Lloyd George was the need for *more* machine-guns and gunners.

Diary

4 January 1918: H.'s anxiety was much increased by a letter from Macready saying that even on the 9 battalion [i.e. per division] basis the army in France would shrink to 44 divisions in the spring and to 30 by the end of the year. By the evening the anxiety had grown to such a point that he decided that I had better go over and find out what the real situation was. [To London on the 5th.]

6 January 1918: An hour with Macready who rubbed into me the imminent disastrous state of the army unless a real big step were taken to find men. He assured me Smuts's trip had done no harm and had clearly elicited that Austria while absolutely against a separate peace, was all for working with us at the peace conference and after and that Mensdorff [Austro-Hungarian Ambassador in London, 1904–14], was much reassured by what Smuts told him of our policy. As to the next Supreme

War Council meeting he said L.G. was in a most tiresome frame of mind and quarrelling hard with Clemenceau, who was the first Frenchman he couldn't twist round his finger.

7 January 1918: Attended War Cabinet over SWC. It was decided to go to Versailles this time but not for another ten days or so till the Versailles report on Western Front, Turkish situation and general future had been received and digested. Haig gave his account of the Western front prospects, didn't believe in serious continuous offensive, but only in a few bangs to produce moral effect. He wanted all the men he could get and wouldn't dream of giving up his precious cavalry and produced some lamentably weak arguments to bolster up his case.

8 January 1918: Lunched at Carlton with Macready, General Hutchinson, Col. Lord Carrick, and Col. West, from 3.30 to 5 going through [the Army Council's reply to the Manpower Report]. I cross-examined them a good deal and discovered a serious flaw in one of the figures supplied to Hankey on which the great discrepancy between English and French casualty estimates was based.

9 January 1918: Saw L.G. for a minute before the Cabinet at which the whole question was to be discussed. As the Army Council papers had only just been circulated he refused to discuss it but said that Smuts, Geddes, Hankey and myself had better go into the figures with the War Office. We three, after a little more desultory Cabinet, remained behind and discussed the figures. L.G. very impatient with the soldiers, whose figures he swore were always cooked, incomprehensible and wrong.

Saw Smuts and went with him properly primed to a 4 o'clock meeting with Geddes and staff at Hankey's room. After a few words, Smuts suggested that I and Geddes' staff had better draw up some real actuarially sound tables. I went off with Lloyd-Graeme and one Frazier an actuary and we discussed a series of tables (an expansion of the one I had got Carrick to work out) for F. to work with his staff.

10 January 1918: Down to National Service Department and went over the tables which Frazier and Co. had been sitting up all night preparing. Talk with Lord M. Our Committee met in the afternoon and it was decided that the tables should be sent to L.G. and WO and that there need not be a conference with the WO representatives unless they disputed N[ational] [Service] D[epartment] figures. Had a talk with Hankey about the Turkish campaign in the course of which he revived my old idea of making Smuts commander-in-chief in that part of the world – this time not only for co-ordination but to get things done in spite of Robert-son and Co.'s obstructiveness. We both waxed keen on it and resolved to try L.G. with it on the first opportunity. He asked me to stay and help finish the manpower business. He told me he had felt rather hurt that I had sailed into the matter with L.G. without consulting him: I confess I had never thought, when L.G. sent me to see Macready, that I was trespassing on Hankey's ground. But it was nice of H. to tell me frankly and not to sulk in silence.

12 January 1918: Down to Walton by car from 10 Downing Street. Met L.G. at the Golf Club where we lunched and had a great talk over lunch and afterwards up to his house. On the figures my chief effort was to prevent his being too optimistic: he cannot get out of his head that Haig and Co. are almost indifferent to casualties and are really clamouring about the danger of the situation in order to have men enough to try another bloody attack as soon as the Germans show signs of not attacking them-selves. I talked to him a lot about all I had heard from the machine-gunners, and pointed out that it was one of the explanations of the low French casualty rate. He readily took to my suggestion that the question of saving manpower and casualties by extended use of machine-guns should be referred to Versailles. The Palestine suggestion he fairly jumped at and asked me to go and see Smuts about it at once – I made it clear that Smuts should go as the War Cabinet and not merely as a C.-in-C. under the War Office. I put it to him very plainly that there was no hope of a success in Turkey unless he did that, or else sacked Robertson and Maurice, and that it might not be easy to find successors who would really be good. On the soldiers he fairly let himself go: he told me that in his opinion the two men who had done most to lose us the war were Asquith and Robertson: that R. hadn't the faintest grasp of the very meaning of the word strategy, that he hadn't the slightest confidence in his judgment and that R. now realised this. He is apparently thinking of possibly getting Harrington – as I elicited by praising H. and Mitchell – into his place and admits now that H.W. should stay at Versailles. He told me Maurice ventilated to him the other day the idea of a generalissimo of the reserves in France, viz. Joffre with Robertson as his Chief of Staff – an absurd scheme, but showing that R. realises that his occupation at the WO is largely gone. I think, however, that L.G. himself was rather tempted by this and some similar ideas from what Lord M. had told me on Thursday [10 January].

Altogether L.G. and I found ourselves in very hearty agreement over a very wide field, and when I departed he expressed his delight at having had an exchange of ideas with someone 'who talked sense'! Even about the Western front figures I can't help feeling that he is substantially right – at any rate by keeping them short of men we may get machine-guns, the abolition of cavalry – (on this I pitched into him again) and other essential reforms, and still have Ireland and the men over 41 as a reserve to make good victory.

14 January 1918: Attended a short War Cabinet, at the end of which L.G. asked me to stay with Smuts and Hankey to discuss the Eastern scheme. He was very anxious that the Versailles report should give a favourable handle to the new proposal and I suggested that he should send Smuts over in person with me to talk it over with H.W. and enlist him for it. So it was agreed that we should both go the first thing in the morning. Attended a further meeting of the Smuts Geddes Committee in the afternoon to consider the WO rejoinder to the tables which was right on a small point, but made a curious error in its main contention which was that the NS people had deducted 33% instead of 25% for the reduction from 12 to 9 battalions. . . . To Carson's for the Monday dinner, where there were Philip [Kerr], Astor, Fred Oliver, Robin [Dawson] and L.G. full of talk. We had great discussions about Pitt and Chatham, about Joe for whom L.G. confessed having always had a great admiration much more than for Mr Gladstone, about Unionist leaders. . . . He talked about future co-operation between himself and the Unionists and said that since his last war aims speech, he could count on about 100 Liberals to follow him.

16 January 1918: H.W., Smuts and I had a long talk, H.W. putting all the objections from the military technical point of view, as well as the objection that S[muts] in Cairo would be out of touch and less well informed than in London. I vigorously combated the latter objection, being convinced that anything lost in that respect was more than compensated by personal touch and by the power of action, as against the endless intermittent discussions of the War Cabinet, with no actual steps ever taken. The former had more substance and Smuts was induced to accept this in so far at least as they involved his being made an actual Military C.-in-C. and so, nominally, at any rate, under the War Office. . . . A talk with Storr and Smuts brought back the fact that the task suggested for S[muts] was the very one Asquith and L.G. had planned for K[itchener] when they were trying to get him out of the way in October 1915. If only he had accepted he might be alive now and the most famous general in the war, for whatever his failings he knew his East and could have driven a campaign in that region. . . . In the car on Tuesday S[muts] suggested that I ought to come out with him in some capacity – chief liaison or sub-chief of staff for the political and general aspect of things. I didn't reject the idea but pointed out that it was difficult as I was now doing work both for H.W. and for Lord M. which was important for the success of the Versailles scheme and for which they relied on me and mightn't easily replace me. He quite agreed but said it was simply a question of where I could do the most important work and suggested that in civil life hereafter it might always be an interesting reminiscence to have been a brigadier general and to have helped conduct a victorious campaign!

21 January 1918 (Versailles): The great report [on strategy for 1918] up before the Military Representatives. Fortunately Henry was in the chair and also Weygand was very anxious to please and conciliate as he had been rather aggressive the time before and had been mistaken. (This was the question of the command of the Reserve). Henry gave them plenty of time taking it paragraph by paragraph, and I quickly drafted new words to meet such few objections as were raised. When it came near one paragraph where we expected difficulty, Weygand's chair slid back and he vanished under the table, which helped to cheer up everyone and get things through all the quicker. In an hour the whole thing was through.

23 January 1918 (London): While we were there [L.S.A. and Sackville-West with Milner] L.G. rang up to see M. so we took him round in the car that had met us at Victoria. When I got home Davies telephoned to say that the PM would like me to bring round the Appendices dealing with Palestine, etc. I ran round and drove off with L.G. to Victoria where he was meeting Orlando, thence back to 10 Downing Street, and on to Reading's where he was dining, talking hard all the while. He is very cross with Northcliffe for making it impossible to sack Robertson or Derby for some time to come.*

24 January 1918: Breakfasted alone with L.G. and had a good talk. He is much perplexed over manpower as Macdonogh has suddenly revised his figures of Boche combatants increasing them by over 500,000 in last October and 600,000–700,000 at present. This altogether upsets L.G.'s basis on which his plans are built. . . . On the general question I insisted that the key to the whole situation was the incompetence of the S[ecretary] of S[tate, i.e. Derby] and that he ought to put in Lord M. He said he couldn't spare him from the War Cabinet, as he was the only person he could turn to for advice. Bonar was a quaking reed, Carson had courage but not always judgment, and he was gone now, M. alone had both wisdom and intrepidity. I said all he would have to do was to drop all

*Northcliffe's offence is explained in an entry for 22 January: 'news of a violent attack on Wullie in the *Daily Mail*'.

other committees and become chairman of the Army Council, still remaining in the War Cabinet. I think the idea impressed itself upon him.

I went on to see Lord M. and spring the bomb of my project on him. At first he groaned, then he saw there was something in it, but we adjourned the subject for lunch. At lunch I went into it thoroughly and convinced him that the S. of S. was the key of the position and that he could do it best and could keep WO and Versailles in their proper relation. But he was rather oppressed by the thought of the work it might mean. . . . Went down to H[ouse] of C[ommons] to a Unionist War Aims Committee out of curiosity. Wasted 1½ hours listening to the most awful footle about the danger of W. Churchill getting into the War Cabinet, and the wickedness of criticising Haig and Robertson.

28 January 1918: Smuts rang up while I was still in my bath asking me to come round and see him. He sent his car about ten and when I got there he showed me a War Cabinet resolution he had drafted giving him powers to deal direct on behalf of the War Cabinet with Allenby, Egyptian Government, etc. while on a tour of inspection there and said I was to come with him to Charing X in quite good time [i.e. for Versailles]. The inevitable circus: the whole Italian party with Orlando. . . . Lovely sunny crossing, destroyers and airships circling all round all the time. Had some talk with the PM over tea and reached Paris about 8. Much pow-wow in the evening.

29 January 1918 (Versailles): H.W. had Wake and Studd up to lecture the PM on the W. Front attack. He followed with keen interest and was evidently rather perturbed by seriousness of the possibilities. . . . Went for a walk in the Park with Lord M., PM and Hankey and Lloyd, and saw to it that the PM had a good talk with Lloyd. When I caught them up later they had left Arabia and had got on to home politics and L.G. was explaining that with the sort of leadership we had, he could have kept us Unionists out for 20 years. Mark Sykes came to dinner and the PM insisted on his drawing illustrations to my theme of what Bonar would look like addressing the H. of C. with 3 bottles of port inside him, or Asquith doing the same after drinking a glass of Bonar's ginger ale by mistake. PM much dismayed by Lawrence, Haig's new C. of Staff, whose obvious intellectual inferiority struck him at once. D. H[aig] seems also to have said some very stupid things at the confab, such as that he could hold his line unaided against anything the Germans could do, that the French were no use and that he wasn't going to divert troops to help them.

30 January 1918 (Versailles): D. Haig and Staff came in to hear a new edition of the Wake and Studd lecture. D.H. showed little interest, twiddled his moustache impatiently and read a paper which he had prepared for the afternoon. Lawrence was just puzzled. I grew hot several times as Studd pointedly explained the precautions which he would take, but Haig never even realised that he was being taught his business as C-in-C.

At 3 p.m. the Meeting of the SWC began. No sort of precaution was taken as to who was to come in so D.H. flocked in with Lawrence, and Davidson and Spiers and Maurice and the CIGS while the French had Pétain as well as Foch, and the Americans their whole staff. L.G. got through a 'second reading' of Note 12 on the 1918 campaign quickly and then came a discussion in which Haig and Pétain launched a pre-arranged onslaught of pessimism with the object partly of forcing the Americans to allow their units to be incorporated in our armies (Pershing had agreed to that as regards 90,000 men that morning) partly to explain that there was no reserve to come under a general control, partly also to put a stop on Palestine. The Italians looked horrified, the Americans didn't at all like their army described as quite useless by itself and only fit for amalga- mation. The PM resolved to break up the meeting and said it was no use going on until they had the facts and asked for an adjournment till the general staffs had produced figures of allied and enemy strength and reserves. The Meeting broke up in confusion and dismay.

My conclusion was that tomorrow the PMs must reassert themselves and keep out all these unauthorized soldiers and only let D.H. or Pétain in when called for. I pressed this on Lord M., Hankey and H.W. who all agreed and they have now since dinner rubbed it in hard on L.G. I think they have also had a heart to heart talk (i.e. PM, Lord M. and H.W.) on what to do about Wully, D.H. and the whole show. We certainly can't win the war with that crowd. Lord M. must go to the War Office. There he can keep Wully in order, and if he won't obey, sack him in a few weeks time. As for D.H. he might stay if fitted out with a new Chief of Staff.

31 January 1918 (Versailles): The Meeting began at 3.00. The M[ilitary] R[epresentative]s, CIGS, and C-in-C's were let in and all the rest of us turned out. They sat with a ten minute break for tea till nearly 7.00. Foch made an immense statement to prove we weren't doing enough. L.G. replied very effectively. Clemenceau denounced the Eastern plan [i.e. the Palestine operation] and was again replied to by L.G., also by the Italians. Bliss [of the US Army] spoke very sensibly about his own force and rather exploded the exaggerated depreciation of it which Haig and Pétain had indulged in. L.G. sat heavily on Haig. All this from Lord M. and H.W. afterwards. After dinner long confab between Lord M., L.G. and H.W. as to how to tackle the situation tomorrow and defeat the Haig–Wullie– Foch–Pétain–Clemenceau combination which at first sight looks pretty formidable.

1 February 1918: Not very happy about the prospect of the Council
agreeing to differ over Palestine, feeling sure that this will be exploited
to the full by Wullie [Robertson], Repington and Co. and make it almost
impossible for L.G. to carry out his policy or to make the necessary
changes at the War Office. Urged both on Hankey, H.W. and Lord M.
the necessity of finding some formula of agreement among the Ministers
upon which they could accept Note 12. Tried to catch L.G. but failed
till just as he was going to Clemenceau's room for the private ministerial
discussion. He grasped the point at once, asked me to draft something
and raced off. I scribbled out the first best formula that came into my head,
ran after him and sent it into the room. Five minutes later Lord M. stuck
his head out, waving the sheet in his hand and said 'they've all accepted
it' and I took it off to be typed. At the full meeting afterwards Robertson
got up and made a protest, but was just waved aside by L.G. and so Note
12 was carried, and one stage of my work completed. The next stage will
begin with my trip with Smuts. . . . In the afternoon there was a terrific
battle over the control of the General Reserve. The Chiefs of Staff and
C-in-Cs made a combined offensive to control the whole thing among
themselves as a board – an unworkable suggestion from the physical
point of view alone. The Italians counter-attacked heavily on behalf of
Versailles [i.e. the staff there] and suggested Versailles in consultation
with the Chiefs of Staff. L.G.'s motion was four extra generals affiliated
to Versailles! . . . [At dinner] L.G. had a great confab with Briand . . . on
Clemenceau's draft for a declaration on war aims to be published by the
Supreme War Council tomorrow. I am not sure that this is playing the
game at all and fear trouble if it gets out. We should not like Clemenceau
to come to a Council in England and show L.G.'s confidential drafts to
Squiff [Asquith] and Henderson. But L.G. is beyond all rules of propriety.
Driving up from the morning meeting L.G. told me Robertson's protests
had 'put the lid on' as far as he was concerned. He is determined to get
rid of him and has said as much to H.W. He was much pleased by my
intervention and said I deserved a statue as the saver of Note 12.

2 February 1918 (Versailles): Council sat in the morning and adopted
a scheme for the reserve which Hankey, I think, had devised on lines laid
down by Lord M. There is to be an Executive Committee consisting of
the M[ilitary] R[epresentative]s but with Weygand replaced by Foch,
who is to be Chairman. That is as near a generalissimo as we can possibly
get. As this has knocked out Wullie's scheme for getting himself made a
kind of joint generalissimo with Foch and practically replaces him by
H.W. for the whole front from Nieuport to Sievres, his poor nose must
be very much out of joint. However, he will probably make a stiff fight
of it when he gets home.

L.S.A. to Mrs Amery, 3 February 1918

The great meeting finished yesterday afternoon with a complete victory for Versailles all along the line, and the defeat of Wully and all his schemes. But the fight isn't over. Repington has been over and no doubt, duly inspired, will launch a furious attack on the whole affair in a few days. L.G.'s only chance is to get in first by putting Lord M. into the WO and letting him put the place in order, bringing Wully and Co. into line or sacking them as he may think best.

Diary

3 February 1918: Went for a walk with Lord M. and put the same idea to him. He is beginning, somewhat regretfully, to regard his becoming S. of S. for War as inevitable. He knows he would do it better than anyone, but he also knows that he is the only 'synoptic' person in the Cabinet and is afraid of losing his grip of questions at large.

11 February 1918: [L.S.A. and Smuts arrived in Egypt for their tour of inspection.] Met at Cairo station by all sorts of generals and ADCs, one of them young Ulick Alexander, one of the trio of young Guards adjutants who had come to me by night during the Ulster Crisis for advice as to leaving the service and bolting across to Belfast.

15 February 1918: Off early with Allenby, Bols, Smuts and Taylor (an Australian ADC) to Jerusalem up the vale of Ajalon, a regular defile among precipitous limestone hills, our cars threading their way through endless processions of camels. It was easy to grasp why so few conquerors ever got to Jerusalem, and what a considerable feat it was for our troops to take it even against a relatively weak Turkish resistance. At Jerusalem itself we looked just inside the Jaffa gate for a moment and then outside round by the Damascus gate to the Mt. of Olives to the splendid German sanatorium which now serves the 20th Corps as Headquarters, with its chapel depicting Wilhelm and Augusta [the Kaiser and Kaiserin] on the ceiling among the other divine personages.

16 February 1918: Spent most of the day drafting the strategical and railway sections for Smuts's report, the former very skilfully worded so as to help put ideas into Allenby's head when he reads it. There is no doubt Allenby has got the confidence of his men quite wonderfully, and showed real courage more than once during the recent operations in refusing appeals for help by hard pressed units and pushing ahead. But it has made all the difference having Smuts talking to him and giving him confidence and some constructive strategic ideas, and though there is no reason now for S. remaining out here as co-ordinator-in-chief, it will be a good thing if he can come out every two or three months to find out what help he wants and to give him a new moral and intellectual impulse.

18 February 1918: Reached Luxor which I had left so hurriedly just ten years before on the news of Mother's death. We were met there by Lady Allenby, very charming though saddened by the loss of her only son. Crossed the Nile by launch and then on ponies and in sand carts . . . to the Tombs of the Kings, Dehr el Bahri and Queen Hatasu's memorial shrine, and Medinet Habu. . . . Some of the paintings and reliefs in the tombs were very fine, especially in that of Seti I. . . . This Egyptian Art with its deep thought and symbolism has real attraction in spite of its curious stiff conventions. The annunciation of Hatasu's divine birth – an idea repeated even more fully in the temple at Luxor – shows clearly where the Christian idea of the Annunciation, the divine parentage of Christ and much else in Christianity come from, as indeed much of Judaism before that.

19 February 1918 (Luxor, Upper Egypt): In the morning to Karnak. . . . After lunch . . . the Luxor temple. The impression of what it all must have been like once, the miles of temples and rows of sphinxes, the gay processions up and down the river, the sacred functions, was tremendous. Not a bad check to too short a perspective in dealing with the outcome of this war.

21 February 1918 (Cairo): A chance in the morning of a good talk with Clayton whose views coincide entirely with those that I have already put into Smuts's report. The two important points are not to make too much of a splash locally with Zionism until the Arabs have got a slice of cake themselves, i.e. Damascus, and to get the French to come out clearly with the declaration disavowing any ideas of Colonial annexation and emphasising their adherence to the idea of Arab autonomy – all this without prejudice to their retaining control of one or two ports of entry like Alexandretta or Beirut, corresponding to our gates of entry at Basra and Haifa. I asked Clayton whether the Arabs felt any objection about our position at Basra, and he assured me that they quite accepted that and never thought of questioning it. There is of course no doubt that the whole Arab situation would be much simpler if we hadn't got the French to take into account. The Arabs trust us and dislike the French, and none the less since Picot's carelessness in leaving about his papers in Beirut has caused a lot of them to be hanged by the Turks. . . .

[Symes had told L.S.A. in the morning] the need in Egypt is for a few British officials, but as good as possible and capable not only of treating the natives fairly, but entering sympathetically and intelligently into the views of the educated class. I am afraid our public school system, which discourages general intellectual curiosity and makes everyone flock together for certain stock games and amusements, undoubtedly acts as a great barrier between us and the educated class in a country like Egypt, and gives the native no encouragement to learn English or become anglicised. In spite of the fact that France has been disinterested in Egypt for 14 years, and we have been there for nearly 40, it is French not English that is still steadily spreading. . . .

Back to the hotel and found a Reuter to say that Robertson had resigned and H.W. was CIGS in his stead. This is a great and welcome change, but I don't quite see how Versailles is to work, unless H.W. combines both functions.

4 March 1918 (London): Lunch with Hankey at the Carlton Grill Room and had a good talk about Palestine and things in general. He told me that he had been urging L.G. to put Lord M. at the War Office with myself as right-hand man, Lord Derby going to Paris. As regards the FO H.'s suggestion was that Bonar should take it, being replaced at the Treasury by Austen. I prefer Lord M.'s idea that the PM should temporarily take over the office himself, my own candidate for the subsequent succession being either Lord M. himself or else Herbert Fisher. The idea of Lord M. going there had been strongly urged on me by Smuts one day on the journey, on the ground not only of his general capacity and power of decision, but as being the only man who really grasped the point of view of the outer Empire.

Dined at Carson's, the others present being Lord Milner, Austen, Oliver, Robin, Waldorf and Philip. Austen full of the infamy of L.G. in appointing these Press magnates to ministerial offices and confident that if he and Carson liked to combine in a resolution on the subject, the Government would collapse; but Lord M. told him that he was barking up the wrong tree and that what was wanted was the amending of the ways of Government, which Philip expanded by pointing out that as long as L.G. had no properly organised backing in the House or the country as against Asquith and Henderson, or against the War Office Press Bureau, he was naturally tempted to create a Press following of his own. I told Austen it was useless trying to separate real power from official responsibility, and that the putting of great newspaper proprietors into a Government was no more heinous an offence than putting in great landed proprietors for the sake of their local influence. The real question was whether the individuals in question were fit for the work given them. . . . [Austen] is full of beans over [a] recent successful speech, but I am afraid exhibited all his worst defects, namely his incapacity to realise that we are no longer in the parliamentary world of the '8os, and his lack of proportion in dealing with anything that savours of breach of good form, personal loyalty, or political etiquette. He is too genteel. F. S. O[liver] said afterwards that he must have included someone at Madame Tussaud's among his maternal ancestors.

5 March 1918: Down to the House of Commons and heard L.G. defend himself before the Unionist War Committee against the charge of having been guilty of bringing newspaper men into his Government. His speech was a masterpiece of adroitness: nothing could equal the neatness with which he suggested that Beaverbrook had been selected for Director of Propaganda because he was an unscrupulous ruffian, or that Northcliffe would be ideal for sowing, in enemy countries, distrust of the Government and lack of confidence in the General Staff. Of course he blew away the whole ponderous attack.

10 March 1918 (Paris): I went back and read some of the minutes of the meeting of the Executive Board [the Executive War Board at Versailles] and it was evident from them and from what I was told generally that Foch had been much too sweeping and domineering, and that Rawly [i.e. Rawlinson] hadn't been able to stand up to him at all. On the other hand I gather that Rawly was simply out to please D. H[aig] and that Clemenceau himself was not really backing Foch but inclined to agree with Pétain, who wished to drop the general reserve.

13 March 1918: [Talk with Hankey during the Channel crossing from Paris accompanying Clemenceau and the French Military Chiefs to London.] Impressed on him the impossibility of letting a Commander-in-Chief directly flout the authority of the Government. The same as my theme to Lord M., and H.W. in a talk we had later. I suggested a formula for at any rate nominally asserting the authority of the Council, while giving every consideration to D. H[aig]'s present position. H.W. was rather in favour of definitely admitting that the E[xecutive] W[ar] B[oard] was hung up for a the time being. I urged that if hung up now, it was obviously hung up for the whole summer and autumn and might just as well not be constituted this year. I also insisted that the circumstances would be known and exploited at once by Repington and Co. We agreed in the end that only L.G. by the exercise of his personal authority could set the thing straight, and Lord M. said he would write a letter that night to L.G. who was seeing D.H. in the morning.

14 March 1918 (London): Meetings of the Supreme War Council, and I hung about in case I was wanted, but wasn't called in. The general conclusion rather lame, the existing divisions on the Italian Front being treated as the Reserve, which is to grow slowly as the American divisions roll up. Foch clearly annoyed, but was sat on by Clemenceau.

These deliberations about the organisation of the reserves were interrupted by the great German offensive of 21 March, which as Hereward Wake and his staff had predicted fell precisely on the extreme right of the British line. Pétain, commanding the French forces, convinced that the real attack was going to be in Champagne, kept his reserves back in the Vosges, and reinforcements ordered to the area of the breakthrough were slow in arriving. Amery's diary entries for the remaining days of March form a dramatic account of the course of the battle, so far as news was reaching headquarters. He reached Versailles from London on the evening of the 23rd and early the following morning he told Milner that it was essential he came over. This led to Milner and Clemenceau agreeing in principle to the idea of a single command in the West under Foch – a remarkable decision as the War Cabinet had repeatedly rejected the idea. Lloyd George had disclaimed it in Parliament, and Clemenceau and Foch were at the time open enemies. While Lloyd George in his *War Memoirs* (p. 1731) claimed that he had 'authorised Milner to do what he could to restore the broken Versailles front [i.e. with regard to reserves, etc.] by conferring upon Foch the necessary authority to organise a reserve and to control its disposition', Amery, judging from what Milner said as he left Clemenceau (see Amery's note to his diary entry for 25 March), doubted whether Lloyd George had gone so far as to suggest a unified control of the front. This decision was confirmed at a conference at Doullens the next day, where Haig agreed. The tardy but inevitable movement of reserves to the Amiens front enabled the German advance to be halted east of that city.

One incidental result of Doullens was that Rawlinson, who had succeeded Wilson at Versailles, should resume command of the Fourth Army, while Sackville-West took his place at Versailles. With Wilson as CIGS, Foch as Supreme Commander, and Robertson removed, the British section of the Versailles staff lost much of its earlier independent initiative and Amery's own function as liaison with the War Cabinet lost importance.

Diary

21 March 1918: Attended a meeting of the War Cabinet where the CIGS gave us his news of the German attack on a 50 mile front. I don't yet feel convinced that this is the real thing and more than a gigantic raid to be followed by similar attacks on the French before Italy and Salonika are seriousl yattacked.* An interminable discussion on Japanese intervention in Siberia followed. The Cabinet are still clearly divided into anti-Bolshevists, whose propagandists are Milner and Bob [Cecil], and pro-Bolshevists led by L.G. and Bonar.

23 March 1918: News from the West Front very bad and worse as day went on. Vth Army evidently collapsed, a true punishment for the crime of keeping on Gough in command. . . . L.G.'s only chance is to take drastic steps as regards Labour and Conscription in Ireland, to reorganise his Government, and not to lose his head and sacrifice Palestine or the East – though things may be bad enough to involve bringing back men from Allenby. . . . If he hesitates or bungles he will be out and we shall have Squiff and Wullie back. . . . Boche this morning began shelling Paris at 75 miles range – shades of Jules Verne!

24 March 1918 (Versailles): Duncannon rang up to say Lord M. was thinking of coming over and if so would an officer who knew the way go to meet him. Later Lord M. rang up himself and asked what I thought: I said he should come and get in touch with Clemenceau. He agreed. . . . [Later L.S.A. note: 'I remember that I was very definite and Lord M. rather doubtful.']

25 March 1918: Motored in [to Paris] after breakfast with Lord M. who was to see Clemenceau whom he found in great form, calm, determined and with a clear notion of what he would do.† He would have made a great soldier. Someone on his staff, however, is a bad Berthier to his Napoleon, for a conference which he and M. and all the generals were to attend in the afternoon was so arranged over the telephone that Haig, Wilson and Weygand met at Abbeville and the others [i.e. Milner, President Poincaré, Clemenceau, Pétain and Foch] went to Compiègne. And this on the most critical day of the whole war. . . .

During dinner H.W. turned up with the Lord [Duncannon] and presently Lord M. Each had been separately discussing the question of who was to control the reserve situation, i.e. do that for which the Executive Board was set up two months ago. Henry's suggestion, which Haig

---

*L.S.A. later noted: 'Throughout the previous three months I gave the Germans credit for more sense than risking all on a W. Front offensive. The W. Front has proved their undoing as it had ours for three years.' Cf. letter dated 1 August 1918.

†L.S.A. footnote: 'It was at this talk that Lord M. offered to agree to the single command if Clemenceau would accept Foch, asking me afterwards, "I hope I was right – you and Henry always tell me Foch is the best man." '

apparently agrees to, is that Clemenceau should have the actual decision, with Foch as his technical adviser – a good idea which I trust will be given effect to at the meeting at Doullens tomorrow morning. H.W. afterwards went in to see Foch who objects to being only technical adviser and wants to be co-ordinator, Clemenceau only deciding what ground should be held or given up, and in any case wants the position definitely endorsed by Lord M. for England tomorrow. Evening news rather better: IIIrd Army holding its own; Vth Army, behind the Somme, not being attacked (Pétain, who is very severe on Gough, describes it as non-existent), French heavily attacked at Noyon but doing well. Germans still have some 30 untouched divisions in hand, and if they can bring them up quick enough it may go ill with Amiens, or even worse befall. But as long as we hold a line somewhere his victories won't save him if he can't get food enough from the Ukraine to see him through till the harvest.

26 March 1918: Lord M. and H.W. started off at 8 for Doullens Conference. I urged both of them to arrange that Plumer should be given Vth Army to reorganise and Rawly [Rawlinson] & Co. go back to their old IVth Army. Agreed that H.W. and Lord M. should both go back home and see to keeping L.G. straight through the measures required in this crisis. The day's news better on the whole, at any rate on the British front, but French hard pressed. . . . The Germans are clearly trying to break through S. of Amiens and force us up N. towards Abbeville. If they succeed it's all up with the French situation and we shall have to see how we can let them and the Italians out and carry on without them. But I don't think they can do it. The elastic resistance of the modern line is tremendous as long as any fight is kept up and there are any reserve divisions to put in.

27 March 1918 (Versailles): News on the whole better; most of our front holding. . . . [The French] divisions are coming up fast and the enemy are not likely to get Amiens from the S.E. Last news in the evening that our line had been attacked with great violence all the way from S. of the Somme to Arras without giving way anywhere. Two or three days more and we shall be out of the woods. M[ilitary] R[epresentatives] had a conference with Pershing and got him to be reasonable about Americans sending all their infantry and m[achine] g[uns] first. Heard about 6 p.m. that Gough had at last been unstuck and that Rawly [Rawlinson] was to go and take over the Vth Army.

Despite the news from France the Irish question could not be avoided in 1918; both because the convention under Sir Horace Plunkett set up in 1917 reported on 13 April, and because of the drastic need for more soldiers. On 9 April Lloyd George introduced a new Military Service Bill which was rushed through in ten days. This provided for a drastic mobilisation of available manpower, and raised the upper age limit from forty-two to fifty. At the same time, the War Cabinet decided to attempt to extend conscription to Ireland. This pill was to be softened by the promise of the early introduction of a Home Rule Bill. In the debate on conscription on 12 April, Amery, who had returned from France, pressed the Government to bring in that Bill as soon as possible (but see diary entry for 7 April).

However, the report of the convention provided no basis for an agreed Bill. The Ulster Unionists and the Irish Nationalists both issued dissenting reports, but the nature of the debate convinced Amery that a true federal system, as part of one for the whole United Kingdom, might be acceptable.

Working closely with Lord Selborne, F. S. Oliver and both Unionists and Liberals, Amery bombarded Lloyd George and other members of the Government with letters and memoranda and drafted the heads of a National Government (Ireland) Bill to serve as the first of a series of parallel Bills to be applied to all parts of the United Kingdom.

The resistance in Ireland to conscription led Lloyd George to postpone this plan and it was finally abandoned in October, when it was no longer required. Similarly, there was no federal Bill.

Diary

28 March 1918 (Paris): The long drought broke later in the day and we had a heavy rain which may impede the German transport. Afternoon news from the French much better. They have counter-attacked all along between Montdidier and Noyon and gained some ground. . . . To Ritz to meet Winston [Churchill, then Minister of Munitions] and gave him L.G.'s message which I had got over the telephone to stick to Paris and not go directing strategy at French GHQ. We had a good talk while he wallowed in a hot bath and then went to bed. He had found our GHQ very worried about Montdidier and the French, and down in the mouth generally – also evidently without information of what the French were doing. His own preoccupation was whether the French were only counter-attacking piecemeal or were getting everything together for a real big stroke. He reports well of the War Cabinet, though they are still very worried about Ireland, mainly because L.G. doubts if Irish conscripts will fight. Bonar too was facing the storm all right, though, as W. C[hurchill] said, he is a vessel with very low freeboard and the deep waters roll over his soul very easily.

31 March 1918 (Versailles and Paris): Motored up to Paris to see Churchill. Having first suggested myself to join him on a trip he was doing round the front I afterwards thought I wouldn't, as these stray tourists are not popular with staffs in a crisis. I found Bendor shared that view very strongly and was going to ask me not to come. He said Churchill couldn't realise that he wasn't popular on these occasions, just because people received him reasonably politely. We lunched at the Ritz and I talked over Irish conscription with Churchill who is sound on it – complained that if only my party had not insisted on hounding him out of the front rank he might have saved the country from so many disastrous hesitations. He showed me a very good wire from L.G. to [President] Wilson asking for 120,000 American infantry a month. He is full of admiration for old Clemenceau with whom he spent 15 hours in the car yesterday going right up to the fire zone and walking about.

L.S.A. to Mrs Amery, 31 March 1918

I sent you a very measly little scribble from the Embassy today, after a fat lunch with Winston and Bendor – a dozen huge blue Marennes oysters, a fried sole, roast chicken, Barsac, and all round hundreds of people eating the same and more. They say many people have left Paris but the Boulevards and Parks looked full enough of Easter Sunday crowds. The shelling has been going on steadily and shells fell yesterday in the Place Vendôme and the Rue de Rivoli. . . . From what I see in the papers I believe the Yanks are just waking up to the fact that there is a war on, and that they may miss the last call for the dining car.

Diary

3 April 1918: Hereward Wake and Ollivant both come back from the battle. O. puts the collapse of the Vth Army down to undue extension and bad placing of reserves, as also does Hereward. Both agree that there is no one at GHQ who has any brains or approves of brains in any one else. Hereward in a moment of bitterness summed it up by asking what was to be expected with a fool like Haig and a liar like Pétain, or as Sackville-West put it 'if Haig and Pétain had only spent half the energy they spent in defeating Versailles [over the reserve] in preparing against the Boche the line would never have been broken'. Hereward is convinced the Boche means to attack next with 40 divisions north of Arras.

4 April 1918: The Boche after all seems to be continuing his attack between Montdidier and Amiens. Nothing could be better. By the time he has taken a few more villages he will be stone cold and in no very good position to face Foch's counter-attack. What he has achieved so far, besides his actual captures, is to aggravate the coal crisis enormously as the French coal supply is the wrong side of Amiens.

5 April 1918 (Paris): Feeling very uncertain about the Government's line over Ireland, I decided I had better get back.

6 April 1918: Wrote short note on a possible policy in Russia, i.e. that we should offer to recognise the Bolshevists at the end of a definite period of weeks or months if meanwhile they accepted Japanese help, allowed us to get through to Trans-Caucasia, and showed signs of really creating a proper army.

7 April 1918: Crossed over by morning boat. Beautiful passage. Had most interesting accounts of the retreat of the Fifth Army from one Mackenzie, General Staff Officer 1 of the 29th Division. The picture he gave of the Fifth Army, enormously strung out and no reserves posted behind at all, was a most damning indictment of Gough and Haig. As to the troops, he was more convinced than ever from what he had seen of the importance of discipline, the units with weak discipline going to pieces badly. . . .

Had a short talk with Carson, from whom I learned that the Government's idea was to hang up the application of conscription to Ireland while they introduced a Home Rule Bill, a most fatuous proceeding calculated both to wreck Home Rule, by treating it once more as a means and not as a question to be dealt with on its merits, and to prevent the men being got.

8 April 1918: Went round after breakfast to see Lord M., whom I found looking very cheery in spite of a hard week. He was not at all satisfied with the way the Government was handling the Irish question, but as he had managed by exercising all the pressure he knew to get a definite pledge from the PM that Conscription and Home Rule were not inter-dependent and that he would go on with Conscription whatever happened to the other, he felt he could hardly make it a case for going out. The real question was whether the PM really was going to stick to what he said. . . .

Had a talk at the War Office with Derby, whom I tried to get out of the delusion that Haig has an unanswerable case against the Government. Our discussion was cut short by the arrival of Gough in order to get his final *congé*. I had never seen him before, but a look at his face was enough to show that he was not a man who could command an Army however good he might be with a smaller unit. Had some talk with H.W. in the passage. He was very pleased with my memorandum on the future of Versailles and had acted upon it in the way of sending or rather getting L.G. to send messages to Clemenceau both about keeping Versailles going and about limiting Foch's activities to the French theatre.

On 9 April, in their second great attack, the Germans broke through the British front between Armentières and La Bassée. Over the next two weeks, the British were driven back but held on to Ypres. On 13 April Haig issued his famous 'backs to the wall' appeal.

Diary

10 April 1918: Geddes in rising to wind up was barracked for nearly ten minutes by shouts for Duke. This demand was started by that horrible pair [of Liberal MPs], Pringle and Hogge, who had been keeping up a running fire of interruption throughout the debate and are out for mischief. The only way to deal with them would be for a dozen stalwart members to give them a good man-handling in the Lobby. All this time bits of news came dribbling in about the loss of Messines, and the contrast between the thought of the men dying in the mud out there and the obscene leers and jests of Pringle and Co. made the House seem a pretty intolerable place.

13 April 1918: Tried to catch L.G. just after the Cabinet, and as it was already late for lunch he took me upstairs. The party consisted of Megan and three other girls of her age. . . . Presently H.W. also joined us. The question of the constitution of the Government was raised by his [L.G.'s] asking me if I thought he should add Austen [Chamberlain] to the War Cabinet. I said certainly, but it was even more important to get rid of the present weak members of his administration; that unless he sacked them promptly, the public would insist on getting rid of him. H.W. then raised the question of an urgent message from Clemenceau asking the PM to come over and a telephone message from Capel saying that Clemenceau had been fussing round in the zone of the British Armies and was dissatisfied about things. L.G. decided that he could not leave but that it would probably be better for Milner to do so. So I went round afterwards to tell Lord M. that he was expected to go that evening. I offered to go with him, but he wanted me to stay behind to look after both the Irish situation and Sykes. He was afraid that while he was away things would relapse all over the place and no decisions be taken. I urged him to go and see L.G. before going and insist on getting a definite declaration from him about the War Office, Foreign Office and Irish Secretaryship. He quite agreed; so he went round to Downing Street. . . .

[Amery saw him later.] The interview had been only partially conclusive. L.G. could not make up his mind about the Foreign Office, but he definitely promised to settle the War Office in the next few days. As regards this, he was however not quite certain whether he should send Lord M. or, by way of a really bold experiment, try Hankey.*

14 April 1918: [Talk with Henry Wilson.] We discussed the possibility of Hankey [for War Office] but came to the conclusion firstly that Hankey was indispensable where he is, secondly that he wouldn't carry the necessary authority with the public and the Army, more particularly if it was a question of shifting Haig and making other drastic reforms, and thirdly that if L.G. was going outside the ranks of men of authority and trying experiments, I should be better for the post myself. So H.W. agreed that if L.G. asked him, he would press in the strongest possible manner for Lord M.

19 April 1918: With regard to Robertson, he [Henry Wilson] told me that he had offered him first to Foch as British member of his Staff and been refused, and secondly to Haig who declined flatly to give him an Army, which he said he was entirely unfit to command, or to make him his Chief of Staff or Quarter-Master General, as he thought his present men better. The only thing Haig thought he could do with Robertson possibly might be to put him in charge of Inundations! It is really a pity one can't publish this side by side with the Press clamour for Robertson's return. . . .

I put to [Lloyd George] very strongly the federal case both on its merits and on his being able to find in it the makings of a genuine new party. He was very much taken with this idea, as well as the notion of giving Ireland the land. I tackled him about getting rid of Duke and he told me the difficulty was that no one was prepared to take on the job, which had been offered in succession to Cave, Walter Long, Austen, Avon Clyde, Hewart and I think one or two others. He asked me if I could think of anyone. The only name I could suggest at all was that of Worthington-Evans, which seems also to have occurred to L.G. We also discussed A. J. B[alfour], Haig and other matters, L.G. rather taking the line that it was very difficult to get rid of people when things went wrong. *A propos* of Lord M.'s leaving the War Cabinet, L.G. insisted that it had to be done nominally to prevent a row from Geddes and Walter Long, and he assured me that I underrated the strength that old political associations still had, or the political weight of a man like Long. He admitted

*c.f. Roskill, I. pp. 525–6.

they did not count for 23 hours out of the 24 just now, but there was always an hour where they might count, in which case the Government might go out. I thought this rather feeble.

21 April 1918: Wrote some letters to Selborne, Austen, etc. on Home Rule question. . . . To the office, where I drafted a long screed to Lord Curzon and then had a talk with Lord M. He liked my draft outline very much and is keen that I should give as much time as possible to Ireland at present, for the rest of my time helping in any way I usefully might. We fixed up that I should provisionally occupy the room next to his, but I think I will also continue to keep a *pied-à-terre* in the War Cabinet office.

22 April 1918: Monday dinner at the Athenaeum: L.G., Carson, Lord M., H.W., Oliver, Kerr, Astor, Brand and myself, and Robin as host. A good deal of sparring between L.G. and Carson, L.G. very strong on the question that if the Nationalists decide directly to raise the issue of the right of the United Kingdom to levy men in Ireland, and practically to claim the right of secession, this would have to be suppressed unrelentingly. The only question was whether the Government ought to interfere with any seditious doings and risk precipitating a conflict before it could produce its Home Rule Bill. On this I rather agreed with him. We afterwards walked back together to 10 Downing Street, and he urged that it would be better to have any sort of Bill and get it quickly than delay any longer by drafting a new Bill, and told me that Austen was rather tiresome on this question. I quite agreed with the need for urgency, but told him that it would not do to produce a Bill which would cause Ulster to go off at half-cock. He agreed.

L.S.A. to Curzon, 22 April 1918

A Bill which definitely and avowedly contemplates federal reconstruction of the British Isles is easier, even for the Nationalists, than one which gives Ireland alone self-government in leading strings, and what applies to them in this respect applies equally to the Dominions and America. The kind of government to be set up is one perfectly familiar to them, and they would regard it as monstrous if Ireland rejected the measure which was to be applied equally to England and Scotland.

As regards the future of the United Kingdom, there can be no doubt as to which is the better solution. A dual system, as Norway and Sweden, and Austria and Hungary, have shown, always tends towards increasing separatism. But for the strength of the outside pressure in the shape of Serb and Rumanian ambitions, and the fear and hatred of Russia, Hungary would have broken off from Austria long ago. Federal arrangements on the other hand, tend to be stable or even centripetal. There are few occasions where one unit wants increased powers which all the others want simultaneously, many occasions on which some new circumstance arises which leads to a general acquiescence in the tightening up of the federal control. American, Australian and even Germany's experience all goes the same way. Home Rule for Ireland alone means incessant unrest ending eventually in complete separation or forcible reannexation. Home Rule all round leaves the United Kingdom a reality for all questions that matter most. It is even a positive advantage, for it relieves the Central Parliament of a congestion which, especially in the period of reconstruction, is likely to be well nigh intolerable and may wreck Parliamentary institutions altogether. To some extent too, the setting up of new local legislatures may prove both an outlet for social agitation and a barrier against Bolshevism.

Diary

24 April 1918: Attended a large meeting of Unionist Members, convened by myself and others, to hear Selborne discuss the federal issue. . . . One or two persons got up approving, and then Hugh Cecil went for the proposal root and branch in his plausible and perverse fashion. I got up next and answered his arguments, and then proceeded to rub in the fact that the federal line is the only one on which we can redeem the spirit of our pledges to Ulster and make the present Bill tolerable. Ronald McNeill rejoined on the lines that nothing but a literal fulfilment and the exclusion of Ulster redeemed the pledges, and that the only thing the Unionists could do, if they were not prepared to prevent the Bill being passed, was to keep their 'hands clean'. After the meeting we constituted a small private committee. . . . Wood and I issued a circular to all the Unionists asking them to reply whether they preferred a purely Irish or a federal measure because the real thing that is now going to count is the amount of support we get.*

What Amery in his memoirs called the Robertson–Maurice–Repington combination had not accepted their defeat as the Supreme War Council over the plan for 1918, nor Wilson's appointment as CIGS. They saw their opportunity in the German successes of March and April and blamed these reverses on Haig's having been deliberately starved of reinforcements by Lloyd George, and forced by the Supreme War Council to take up a longer line than could be defended. On 7 May, Major-General Sir Frederick Maurice, who until shortly before had been the

*By 29 April they had obtained support for a federal scheme from sixty-three MPs, with ten against and three 'doubtful'.

Director of Military Operations, published in most of the main newspapers a letter charging Lloyd George and Bonar Law with having deliberately misled Parliament about the strength of the British Army in France, the strength in the Middle East, and the extension of the line in France.

Asquith saw his opportunity in promoting the fall of the Government, decided to reject the Government's proposals for a judicial inquiry and pressed for a Select Committee into Maurice's allegations. He hoped for Unionist support. The vital debate took place on 9 May, and Asquith was beaten by 293 to 106, a vote which both confirmed the split in the Liberal Party and provided evidence for the issue of 'coupons' to Unionist and Liberal candidates opposing 'Asquithian' Liberals in the election later in the year.

Amery was not involved in the process of helping Lloyd George disprove Maurice's figures. As always with statistics, these could be made to mean different things, and both Hankey (Roskill, *Hankey*, I, p. 545) and Amery (*My Political Life*, II, p. 155, footnote) admit that Maurice's claims were not without substance. But the political issue was the essential factor.

Diary

7 May 1918: When I got to the War Office I found it all buzzing over Maurice's foolish letter. . . . There is no doubt that Maurice has been got hold of by Repington and that the whole thing is a plant aimed at creating a Parliamentary situation in which Asquith, by the help of the disgruntled Unionists, may climb back to power. To the House, where we heard Bonar heckled by Asquith and finally promise to give a day (9th May) for discussion. Carson having interrupted Bonar with questions that showed evident animus against the Government, I wrote him a very strong letter urging him not to destroy his influence as leader of Ulster by taking part in any general wrecking tactics.

8 May 1918: To the Unionist War Committee, a very large gathering, which was discussing today's (the 9th) Vote in the House. Salisbury opened, very hostile to the Government, and then Carson suggested that the Unionist War Committee should as a body take an independent attitude by moving the previous question, thus neither endorsing Asquith nor approving of L.G. The palaver went on for about an hour, the meeting being very much all over the place as to what it should do, when I got up and tried to bring them back very firmly to the principal point, that this was a manoeuvre to get in Asquith and that we should only weaken the

Government at this moment in Asquith's interest. Our immediate task therefore was to reject the Asquith motion by as large a majority as we could. Rather to my surprise I found I had got practically the whole meeting with me, and almost every speaker that followed took my line. Carson's suggestion consequently dropped, and the meeting adjourned about 7 without any resolution but with a general sense that, whatever happened, we were not prepared to let Asquith come back.

9 May 1918: Asquith opened very hesitatingly and made the poorest speech I have ever heard from him, his only chance at all being given him by an indiscreet interruption from Bonar. L.G. followed in great debating form and, thanks to an admirable case worked up by Hankey, was able completely to pulverize the attack. Carson subsequently urged Asquith to withdraw, but apparently Gulland [the Liberal Whip] and Co. would not agree to this and he was compelled to go to a division and roundly beaten. I am more than half inclined to think that this finishes Asquith as a possible alternative Prime Minister. People won't follow a man who has shown to such a degree both bad judgment and lack of courage.

16 May 1918: Saw Curzon about preparing agenda for the Imperial War Cabinet. He was very anxious that the question of Indian Home Rule – 'Montagu's silly notions about Home Rule' [Curzon's words] – should not be discussed in front of the ignorant backwoodsmen from the Dominions! We also talked about Ireland where he seems to think that neither Home Rule or conscription can possibly be applied. He really is pretty hopeless. Had tea with Hankey to discuss the same subject. He told me that he was getting overworked by having to take the minutes for the new little meetings between the PM, Lord M. and H.W. which now take place every morning before the War Cabinet. I suggested that I might help out with that, an idea he jumped at.

With Milner's appointment, Amery's duties as assistant secretary to the Secretary of State for War, hitherto merely nominal, became his chief task. But he continued in his role as assistant to Hankey, secretary of the Imperial War Cabinet. This led to helping Hankey act as Secretary to the triumvirate of Lloyd George, Milner and Henry Wilson, known as the 'X Committee'. It usually met at 11 a.m. before the War Cabinet at noon, thus almost once a day and sometimes twice a day during the later spring and summer of 1918. The first meeting was on 15 May. On 17 May, Amery was responsible for taking the minutes and seeing that the conclusions were implemented.

Diary

17 May 1918: Attended the little 11 o'clock conference at the WO to take notes and produce the minutes. A very interesting and free and easy gathering, which may very possibly develop into the real War Cabinet. Anyhow, I live in hopes that it may. [Later L.S.A. added: 'But it didn't'.] However, it is not all-powerful yet, for though at the little meeting they were all agreed to try and stop Lindley going to Russia because he stood for a policy of mere inaction, the FO carried the day in favour of Lindley at the War Cabinet meeting immediately afterwards.

Amery crossed the Channel on 25 May reaching GHQ that evening, and going on to Versailles on 26 May.

Diary

27 May 1918 (Paris): Heard the first news of the German offensive on the Aisne, though I already conjectured it taking place from the fact that the shelling of Paris had begun again. I gathered from Lord M. on the way back to Versailles that Clemenceau had not been in any way upset but rather relieved that the Germans had begun.

5 June 1918: Two X meetings, one in the morning and one after lunch, arising out of Foch's request for three of our divisions to go behind the Somme and the American divisions to be transferred south. This raised questions of such magnitude that L.G. insisted that Lord M. and Henry had better go over at once and hold a council of war with Foch, Clemenceau and Haig. . . .

Long talk with Lord M., who was rather despondent about the whole position, more particularly L.G.'s unwillingness to face the necessity of getting rid of A.J.B.

7 June 1918: Long talk with Bob Cecil who wants to resign because of his dissatisfaction with the feeble handling of the Russian intervention question, culminating in the lamentable performance at Versailles. His view was that he was doing no good and that if he resigned it would be much easier for L.G. afterwards to appoint someone else in Balfour's place, as he felt sure that L.G. was only keeping on Balfour because he couldn't make up his mind to give it to him [i.e. Cecil]. I tried to dissuade him, but saw the force of this particular argument.

L.S.A. to Lloyd George, 8 June 1918

It is not our military situation that alarms me. Nor have I a shadow of doubt, in my judgment or my conscience, as to what the main lines of our policy should be. What terrifies me are the instruments to which these great tasks are entrusted. With Milner and Wilson the purely military side will be all right, though they have come to the business desperately late in the day. But Balfour and Hardinge! . . . To let them stay and paralyse our policy during the war and finally to throw away in the peace negotiations everything we have gained by all our sacrifices is really intolerable. And you are responsible. It is no use blaming Haig for hanging onto Gough in spite of the useless slaughter of Passchendaele . . . if you really do the same thing in your own command. You must make a change. If you won't have Cecil, who in spite of certain defects, is the ablest and strongest, have Austen who is competent, steady and has a good grip of essentials. Or else take the office yourself, in order to control the general policy, leaving the details of current work to your understudy. But do it now.

The Imperial War Cabinet and War Conference (see p. 135) met again in June 1918, with Amery as Hankey's chief assistant. The Conference did some useful work, for example on the Imperial control of raw materials, and concluded at the end of July. The Imperial War Cabinet sat intermittently for the rest of the year until it transferred, under the title of British Empire Delegation, to Paris.

One thing which emerged in their deliberations was the criticism by Borden, Prime Minister of Canada, of the incompetence of Army headquarters. They also discussed constitutional relations between the various parts of the Empire and Allied war aims. The conclusions on the former issue were confined to securing the continuity of the War Cabinet by providing for attendance by Ministers other than the Prime Ministers in the intervals between the annual meetings, and for direct communications between Prime Ministers on Imperial War Cabinet business.

In several letters to the various Prime Ministers Amery set out his ideas for a post-war settlement. These, with his belief in the development of the Empire and Commonwealth and the grouping of nations with common political and economic interests, were directed against President Wilson's 'facile slogan of self determination . . . [and] the specious sham of a world authority' (*My Political Life*, II, p. 163; see pp. 160–5 for a development of these views).

Diary

11 June 1918: First meeting of the Second Session of the Imperial War Cabinet, or rather Fifteenth Meeting of the Imperial War Cabinet as I have since persuaded Hankey to number it, treating it as a perpetual body in continuous session. The PM made a long statement setting out the situation very frankly. To us who were used to all the matter it conveyed, it seemed rather a dull performance; the Overseas members were, however, deeply impressed as well as depressed by it.

12 June 1918: Usual X meeting. H.W. still strongly of opinion that the next German attack is going to be against us. Had a talk with Long of *The Times* about getting Dominion affairs out of the Colonial Office, which Hughes is apparently going to push hard when he comes. Put to him the arguments in favour of having a separate Dominion Minister instead of leaving it all to the PM's staff.

13 June 1918: X meeting at 11, followed by Imperial Cabinet, at which Borden came out with a very strong indictment of our whole Higher Command based on information given him by General Currie, a statement put with such obvious sincerity and desire to help that no one could have taken offence at it, and, as a matter of fact, it will prove most helpful both to Lord M. and the PM.

14 June 1918: An X meeting in the garden. I am afraid these meetings would be more helpful if L.G. were less discursive and if they were reduced to two or three a week. Then came Imperial War Cabinet at which Smuts delivered a very interesting discourse,* the gist of which was that all our troubles had been due to Jellicoe and Robertson and might have been avoided if only the Prime Minister's advice had been followed.

17 June 1918: Attended a further X meeting in the afternoon, this time on the question of the control of forces in the Middle East. Montagu, who has evidently been suffering under the cumbrousness of Curzon and his Eastern Committee, urged either that the whole business should be put under one member of the Cabinet (he mentioned Curzon because to have mentioned anyone else would have been offensive, though I am by no means convinced that he meant Curzon). His other alternative was a Commander-in-Chief in the East. Balfour of course pointed out in his

---

*According to Hankey, he was justifying the Government's doubts over Haig's launching the Passchendaele offensive in 1917 (Roskill, *Hankey*, I, p. 565).

best manner that he really couldn't expect anything else but a muddle in view of the weakness of our military position, and that the defects in our machinery didn't really matter. It is rather interesting finding them coming back to the need to put the matter under a single command, or to my other suggestion of substituting Smuts alone for the whole Eastern Committee.

18 June 1918: A short X meeting, rather desultory talk in Lord M.'s room, followed by Henry's lecture to the Imperial Cabinet in his room. The lecture was admirably clear and impressive, the gist of it being that while the Germans, after failing to obtain a decision against Paris or the Channel Ports in 1914, left the West alone for three years while getting together strength by disposing of their enemies on the East, we had gone on hammering away on the Western Front without ever really considering whether we were in a position to obtain a really decisive result.

20 June 1918: Short X meeting degenerating more than ever into casual conversation. . . . Imperial Cabinet at which Balfour gave a most illumi- nating address on the whole state of foreign policy. When it was all over, Hughes piped in and asked what exactly it was that Balfour was proposing to do, almost like the little boy who said, 'Why, the King has no clothes on!' Much discussion on Japanese intervention [in Siberia], in the course of which Hughes brought out what Balfour had never heard of, that [President] Wilson's Committee on Foreign Relations was quite in favour of intervention. It was decided, i.e. by Hankey and myself, that the Imperial War Cabinet had instructed A.J.B. to send a further direct message to Wilson urging intervention. At the end of the meeting, Hughes followed up Borden [on 13 June] by talking of the need for overhauling our army organisation generally, whereupon L.G. suggested a small committee consisting of the Prime Ministers, Lord M., and if necessary H.W. to go into the whole matter. This was generally accepted, and a new stage in Imperial Organisation has I fancy begun.

26 June 1918: Lunched at the House and had some talk with Mark Sykes, very agitated about the idea of 54th Division being brought away from Palestine [and taken to Italy]. Had some talk with Hankey and Smuts on the matter later. The question was reopened at Committee A in the afternoon and the moving of the Division postponed. [September comment: 'Mark did good work over that'.]

28 June 1918: Imperial War Cabinet in the afternoon; statements on the Air situation by Sykes and Weir. . . . Hughes took the matter up with his usual love of coming to a direct point in an aggressive fashion by suggesting that we had better concentrate on something like the air instead of squandering all our manpower in a fashion which would leave us ruined however victorious.

1 July 1918: [Crossed Channel for Supreme War Council meeting.] The luggage with all the British Government's state secrets never turned up at all till next morning, having been all night in the charge of a couple of French soldiers.

3 July 1918: [At Supreme War Council in Versailles]. Our whole feeling has been that the French are going much too far in the direction of trying to run the war as if it were their concern, and L.G., who had been very cross over several things, more particularly with H.W. for not having come back from Italy to see him before the Council, let loose all his temper by a real vigorous attack on the French, both for having made plans for bringing over American divisions next year without any consultation with us who provide the shipping, and also over Salonika where they sanctioned an offensive directly contrary to the views expressed by the Supreme War Council and without consulting anybody. The general effect of this onslaught was very good, and the French were much chastened on the following day.

4 July 1918 (Versailles): The Dominion [Prime] Ministers attended the afternoon sitting of the Council, and I have heard since from Capel that Clemenceau was much impressed both by Hughes and Borden and that the French generally for the first time realised that there is such a thing as the British Empire. Hughes, who is always quick in his judgment, thought very meanly indeed of Pershing and not very much of Foch; Clemenceau he thinks must be partly a Mongol or Tartar.

[L.S.A. took Hughes, the Australian Prime Minister, to meet Millet and Simon, two French officials, to talk about the future of the various Pacific territories.] Hughes made it quite clear (1) that we would keep the German colonies, (2) that Australia didn't wish to see the French flag disappear from the Pacific, and (3) that the condominion in the New Hebrides ought to come to an end and the islands be taken over by one power or the other. Hughes also adumbrated a rather loosely thought-out scheme for a federation of the various Pacific islands under authorities with headquarters at Sydney, and suggested that the French might come into that federation. The main point, namely that the French Colonies ought to co-operate with ourselves in this region, was easily seized on by Millet, who is sound; the federal part of it, however, obviously rather frightened Simon. As a matter of fact, when Simon asked if America was to come into the federation on behalf of Samoa, Hughes at once shied off; he evidently has no idea that anybody but Australia should play the leading part in the proposed scheme.

Lord M. and I dined quietly with Millet at the Inter-Allied Club. When we came back we found that Clemenceau and Foch had been up to the Villa in a great state of mind. They had originally passed the propositions with regard to the Military Representatives after [L.S.A. holograph query: 'without?'] much discussion. Subsequently they thought that they had discovered that these propositions diminished Foch's powers, and Foch came up threatening immediate resignation. However, the art of the draughtsman sufficed eventually to satisfy all their objections with a few alterations which did not materially alter the sense, and Hankey was sent down to get Orlando to accept them likewise. I have heard since that further trouble has arisen because the French version differs rather widely from the English.

11 July 1918: Imperial War Cabinet put off for a further discussion of the aliens question. I have never known a single parliamentary crisis in which the War Cabinet have been able to make up its mind what to do till absolutely the last minute. There is always an agitated War Cabinet on the question within about three hours of the speech which the PM is to deliver. . . . Missed Cave's speech on the aliens question, the most successful part of which was his announcing that enemy banks would be closed and that enemy aliens should not be allowed to start banking businesses for five years after the war. This is the real key to the whole question. If the Government only had a firm general policy towards German trade they wouldn't have so much fuss about this aliens business. . . . Back to hear L.G. make a very typical little speech in which he placated the House by promising ruthless measures.

12 July 1918: Imperial War Cabinet. Churchill expounded his work and views on Munitions with usual ability and picturesqueness of language, winding up with a strong appeal that more manpower should not be diverted from munitions, but that we should concentrate on the scientific and technical side of warfare.

14 July 1918: [Sir Edward] Grigg came to breakfast and we had a great talk about the situation at the front. He is convinced that Haig and all the Army Commanders ought to be cleared out immediately. They are all tired, have lost all control, and, as I have often said to Lord Milner myself, the British Army is in a more or less feudal condition, each of the great barons being a law unto himself and only carrying out GHQ commands as far as it seems to him desirable.

15 July 1918: Got to the War Office to hear the [German] offensive had started on a 35 mile front from Château Thierry almost to the Argonne. If this is the real thing,* which is not clear yet, I shall have come out as a true prophet, as I have been asserting for the last six weeks or more that the attack would come on this line and have as its object Rheims, Châlons, and Revigny and eventually the cutting off of Verdun.

16 July 1918: X Meeting; L.G. having just seen a letter from some Canadian engineer to Borden condemning the High Command, and being generally in a state of nervous agitation over the offensive, was clamorous to have everything changed at once and urged that the matter should be brought up that same evening before the Dominion Prime Ministers. Lord M. with his experience of L.G.'s methods and not quite convinced himself of what changes to make, rather dug his toes in, whereupon L.G. became most petulant and really rather offensive, and launched out into a harangue in which a good deal of sound argument was mixed up with the wildest and most inaccurate of statements, taking the line as if Lord M. was an obstructionist and never wanted to do anything. Hankey and I both much distressed by L.G.'s tiresome behaviour, and I tried in the afternoon to get Lord M. to have a private talk with L.G. before the meeting to straighten matters out, but he was for leaving him alone in his present mood and straightening it out later, saying that they would have plenty to talk about at the Dominion Ministers' Committee that afternoon without getting on to this topic. And so apparently it turned out, for he told me at dinner that although L.G. had been very wild on all sorts of subjects, this particular trouble hadn't arisen.

Amery later wrote the footnote: 'It was on this day, I think, I was told to make plans for carrying on the war if France and Italy were out.' In liaison with the Admiralty and War Office, Amery concluded (in a memorandum that was left unfinished) that if Britain were forced to evacuate by the Channel ports, it could only hope to get away its men and field artillery; if by the western ports of France the British could take out some heavier material, but their vast depots of munitions and stores would have to be abandoned. Britain would lose all Europe except perhaps Greece to Germany, but would have been able, if the right decisions were taken, to spare resources for the war in the East and for shipbuilding and munitions – what Amery describes as 'the 1940–43 situation' (*My Political Life*, II, p. 158).

---

*L.S.A. footnote: 'It was, but it failed at the outset as [General] Gouraud heard of it and plastered them at zero.'

THE LEO AMERY DIARIES

Diary

18 July 1918: X Meeting at which we discussed the offensive, L.G. strongly holding the whole thing to be mere bluff, Milner still inclining to think that it was seriously intended but that having failed at the outset, the Germans had given up the idea of throwing any serious weight into it. Cheering news of the French counter-attack beginning.* Imperial War Cabinet.... There was a long discussion about the desirability of publishing our casualties in America in order to enable them to realise the extent of our sacrifices.

23 July 1918: Imperial War Cabinet this morning tackled the thorny question of Channels of Communication. The ball was opened by Hughes rather lamely and apologetically. Borden strengthened the case and others supported, Smuts, however, in a rather slim speech urging that the whole matter should be shelved till after the war. Generally speaking the discussion was pretty muddled, no clear distinction being made between the minor question of direct communication and the major one of re-organisation generally. When it broke up I found Winston bubbling over with excitement and frantically keen that something should be done. He tackled Lloyd George who had appeared to be rather indifferent during the meeting but who assured us with a twinkle that he was all with us. I gave Winston my paper on the Future of the Imperial Cabinet as his ideas were very much on my lines....

From 3.30 to after 5 I attended a Conference on Serbian Supplies.... The whole British plan had been to secure direct supply to the Serbian Army through the proposed Joint Commission in order to eliminate French peculation of our stuff. However, we put up no sort of show against the French, who brushed all the charges aside indignantly and stood quite firmly on their right to distribute all supplies and the impossibility of creating a Serbian supply service. I am afraid that as long as the French know better what they want, think quicker and talk louder, we stand very little chance against them at this sort of gathering, more particularly as our people will be foolish enough to talk French themselves.

25 July 1918: Imperial War Cabinet [on inter-Imperial communications]. Walter Long palavered at length trying somehow or other to get things delayed by reference to the Governors General. A.J.B. brushed the Governors General position aside with a sweep as belonging to a past

*This was Mangin's attack on the west side of the German salient on the Marne, starting the process by which the Germans were pushed back.

epoch. Ward made a very sensible little speech insisting on permanent ministerial representation and drawing attention to the financial problems of reconstruction. Rowell also put his points well. Presently L.G. weighed in with an admirable statement in which he accepted completely both direct communication between Prime Ministers and permanent ministerial representation, and went on to urge the appointment of a Committee to study the whole problem of the future organisation of the Empire. This last suggestion elicited most violent expostulation from Hughes who said it would wreck the Empire altogether as far as Australia was concerned. There was the merest span there between those who wished to stay in the Empire and those who wanted to break it up. As for the soldiers in France, 75 per cent of them were against having anything further to do with the Empire in future. He also argued pretty confusedly that participation in Councils only involved more entanglement. On this he was well pulled up by Borden who said that that had been Laurier's views. But as far as he was concerned he would rather be out of the Empire altogether than in it and not have a voice in its decisions. Hughes agreed, and really, as I gathered from a note he sent me afterwards, he had spoken crossly and without much consideration on the spur of the moment. But there is no doubt that he has been much disgruntled latterly by the difficulties of his position in Australia, and by the conviction into which he has worked himself that all his political opponents must be enemies of the Empire. When he had finished, Smuts very adroitly turned the tables on him and smoothed matters down by suggesting that what the PM [Lloyd George] had proposed was really only what was implied in Hughes' own resolution at the Conference, which he himself had been rather inclined to shelve. . . .

To Brooks's where Lord M. had a dinner. . . . Cook stayed on for nearly an hour with Lord M. and myself making a lot of fuss about the Japanese having the islands north of the Equator [including the Carolinas and Marianas, which were then German]. The Australian attitude is not only for a White Australia, but that because they can't develop Northern Australia nobody else should be allowed to come within 2000 miles of it. We have to run some risks.

30 July 1918: Imperial War Cabinet met again to consider the question of channels of communication on which L.G. had put up three resolutions, the first dealing with direct communications, the second with the appointment of permanent Ministers by the Dominions to secure the continuity of the Imperial War Cabinet, and the third suggesting a Committee for studying the Imperial constitutional problem. At the opening of the proceedings Borden announced that he and his Dominion colleagues had met the day before and had agreed in favour of both (1) and (2) but against (3), even in the informal shape suggested. Walter Long made a last plaintive kick on behalf of his Department expressing regret that the matter had been so rushed, but subsided quickly feeling that nobody was paying any attention to his protest. And so a great step onward has been brought about without effort almost, and certainly without the public being aware of it. . . .

We [Lord Milner and L.S.A.] were to start [for a walk on the downs near Woldingham] at half past six, but the King kept Lord M. talking so long that we only got a very short walk. The poor King is very annoyed and indignant over the alien hunt; the latest proposals if applied all round would presumably involve his submitting himself to Justice Bankes's Committee to justify his functioning as king, and would certainly involve his having to drop the name of Windsor again for the original German name, whatever it is. Poor Mountbatten* would also have to lose not only his name but his seat on the Privy Council.

1 August 1918: Wrote a long letter to Henry [Wilson] criticising his paper on British Policy as regards his conclusion in favour of bringing affairs on the Western Front to a climax next July [1919] and his under-valuation of the Palestine–Mesopotamia area both as a field for active strategy in the war and from the point of view of our post-war security. . . . I had a longish talk with him about it late in the afternoon. He didn't really disagree with my conclusions in themselves, but said that Foch would never stand the postponement of the attempt to reach a decision in France, nor would he agree to a diversion of any part of our divisions, more particularly if they were going to drop as seriously as looked likely.

L.S.A. to Sir Henry Wilson, 1 August 1918

Can we do enough to interfere with the German consolidation in the East if all our effort in manpower, shipping and munitions is concentrated on trying to force a climax on the West in 1919? Isn't President Wilson discouraging real serious Japanese action in Russia just because he thinks he can't find munitions for that as well as for the Western Front? Isn't the real danger precisely what it was in 1915–16–17 that the Boche will consolidate in the East, where we leave him alone, while we gain a few villages in France or Flanders? . . . As for the morale condition behind the lines, is there any comparison? The one thing that might carry enemy morale through another year is the successful defence on the West coupled with a few more cheap victories in the East and the actual

---

*Admiral Prince Louis of Battenberg, created Marquess of Milford Haven in 1917.

harvesting of the economic results of previous successes in that region. The worst thing for them would be to have the flimsy structure of their Eastern conquests seriously shaken, while the menace of defeat on the West grew steadily more certain.

Isn't the real danger still impatience? We have fallen into it all the time, from Loos to Passchendaele? The Boche fell into it at Verdun; showed great patience for two years, largely because he couldn't help himself, and then fell into it again this March. Wouldn't he have been much wiser to have concentrated on Italy and Salonika? ... You treat Palestine as an area where the enemy's communications are better than ours and will be increasingly so as we advance. But doesn't that leave out of account our command of the sea, and the possibilities of the coast ports as well as the possibilities of local supply? You rather dismiss an advance to the line Haifa–Tiberias as a mere addition of 60 miles to our communications and an extra strain on our rolling stock. I would, on the contrary, regard it as a shortcoming of our communications and a relief to our rolling stock (or alternatively an increase of the force we can supply) by the 2000 tons a day landing capacity that Haifa can be developed into yielding. ...

Again you treat the Turk as an elusive jelly-fish opponent. But has that been our experience in the past? Whenever anyone has struck quickly at the Turk, whether at Kirk Kilisse, or Erzerum, or Ramadie* he has not eluded the blow but just taken it between the eyes and tumbled down. There is no purely strategical reason why this should be impossible in Palestine. ... And there are the very strongest political reasons why he should stand up and take the knock even if as a matter of pure strategy retreat were advisable and possible. Syria and the Arab world – Damascus, Aleppo, Mosul – are after all a very big part of the Ottoman Empire, as important to the Turks as India is to us. ... And if these blows succeed, and succeed largely because the Germans are busy in Russia and the Caucasus, the endurance of the Turks may reach its breaking point and a separate peace be in sight, with all its immense consequences in opening up the Black Sea, and so cutting the German communications with the Caucasus, the subsequent detachment of Bulgaria, etc. Turkey is the keystone of the German arch in the East. The whole fabric of German control over the Balkans, Ukraine and Caucasus, the hope of getting to Turkestan and Persia and threatening India, the hope of securing in these regions at least a minimum of semi-tropical raw materials so as not to be utterly dependent economically on our mercy – all this goes if Turkey goes.

But even if the Turk is somehow kept under German control it seems to me immensely important from the point of view of our future security to drive him a great deal further back than he is at present. ... You lay

*In the Balkan wars (1912), Armenia (1915) and Mesopotamia (1917) respectively.

great stress on the 'physical gap' element in our future defence. But doesn't it take two to acquiesce in a physical gap? The Boche will soon see to it, if he retains control [of the Syrian area] that his side of the gap is well covered with strategic railways, and that the population and resources on his side of the frontier are organised and developed to take part in the offensive. . . . I would go for the shortest possible frontier against the Boche, the largest number of railways behind that frontier, and the largest resources to develop locally for the defence of that frontier. From that point of view the shortest frontier is the Alexandretta–Caspian frontier. It is one which lends itself to the construction of a much better system of railways. . . . If we conduct [its] development on sound lines from the political as well as the economic point of view it ought in a developed Arab nationality to furnish a real live buffer against German ambitions. If we leave the Arab world halved between us and the enemy at the end of the war we shall have continual intriguing and a new war sooner or later. . . .

An argument I have overlooked with regard to Mesopotamia is the all-important question of the control of oil. The greatest oil-field in the world extends all the way up to and beyond Mosul, and even if it didn't we ought as a matter of safety to control sufficient ground in front of our vital oil-fields to avoid the risk of having them rushed at the outset of the war.

Diary

2 August 1918: [Talk with Lord Milner about Lloyd George's attitude to the question of conscription in Ireland. Milner thought that] it might be possible to bully him [Lloyd George] into tabling an Order-in-Council but not into carrying out the policy effectively. He admitted, however, that if L.G. would only tackle it he could have no better election cry, and at this moment his mind is mainly full of election. Lord M., while agreeing to a large extent with my letter to Henry, is also inclined to believe in the possibility of the war coming to an end this year. The Germans are in bad straits and may offer as good a peace as, given the chances and uncertainties of the war, we might get later on. I don't agree.

7 August 1918: Lunched at the Carlton and had some talk afterwards with James Craig about the possibility of an election and the line the Government should take. He is all for the Government declaring itself on the war issue only and getting a House of more or less the same complexion back. He is all against a declaration on Preference, however broadly worded. I had a talk with Guest in the House after dinner on the same subject and his view was more or less the same, thought 'no peace with the Hohenzollern' the best cry.

8 August 1918: Lunched at Jules's with the Stokeses [later Sir Wilfred Stokes, inventor of the Stokes trench mortar]. He told me that Winston had insisted that he should be allowed to have some say in developments and alterations to his gun, but that people lower down take care that he is really kept well on one side. He suggests that our whole system for dealing with new ideas was entirely wrong. At present they are passed round to everyone concerned for comment, and there is always someone who finds an objection. His idea is a central committee to consider these things and decide on its own responsibility which of them the Army should be equipped with, leaving to the troops themselves to do the best with what they get.

13 August 1918: Imperial War Cabinet, or rather War Cabinet plus Dominion Prime Ministers, in the morning to discuss war aims. Balfour gave them an amiable and mildly interesting survey of the whole field without any perspective as to the relative importance of the objects aimed at or their bearing on what was attainable or not. Borden followed up by saying that Canada was against extensions of territory and that he was all in favour of persuading the United States to take over any German colony or territory we could give her. Reading thought the Americans would quite take to the idea of replacing us as trustees in control of Palestine. L.G. was rather taken by this notion not from any altruism but quite evidently because he thinks that if the Americans take a good deal they won't make a fuss about our keeping what we really need. Lunched afterwards with L.G., Hankey and Philip Kerr being present, and discussed the same subjects, as well as the General Election. With regard to the latter I urged L.G. not to defer it beyond the beginning of November in view both of the growing Henderson organisation [the Labour Party] and the effect of the shortage of coal later on in the winter.

L.S.A. to Smuts, 16 August 1918

I don't believe America will be at all pleased to be asked to take up either East Africa or Palestine, and I am sure that the result will only be friction. To dump the Americans with their vigorous but crude ways into the middle of a problem like that of Palestine so closely connected with adjoining territories will be bound to lead to friction. . . . The great thing to aim at is a compact, continuous, easily defended and easily developed British Empire with the fewest friction surfaces with other Powers. If I had to give up territories it would not be Palestine or German East Africa but things like British Guiana, British Honduras, the Gambia, the Gold Coast, or even Gibraltar. . . .

I frankly do realise the possibility of incomplete victory, and I am not prepared to see the British Empire exhaust itself utterly to secure complete victory, providing only it can make sure of reasonable security. But . . . I would fight on to 1920 for the essentials to security; . . . In the West I believe it is enough to assure military superiority without actually carrying out to its conclusions the physical expulsion of the Germans from France and Belgium. In the [Middle] East I think you have actually got to occupy the territory you mean to keep before you can negotiate. As far as I am concerned I would therefore be ready to negotiate as soon as we have definitely secured a line of defence from the Mediterranean to the Caspian, including Aleppo and Mosul or at least Damascus and Mosul.

Diary

19 August 1918: Our Monday dinner reduced itself again to Robin and Waldorf, to whom, together with Billy Gore, I gave dinner at the Senior. . . . [Gore's] conviction is that Allenby and Bols are really all for pushing on [in Palestine] but still afraid that they are not really wanted to do so by the War Office and may have their troops taken away from them at any moment.

20 August 1918: Attended an Imperial War Cabinet with Bonar in the chair. They discussed minor matters, and Bonar showed himself more than usually terrified about any sort of decision.

Amery, Lord Milner and Hankey travelled to Shrewsbury by train on 22 August. On arrival they met Sir Bertrand Dawson, the King's doctor, with a car, and drove into the Welsh mountains. At Lloyd George's country residence at Criccieth, where they were to have a session on peace terms, they found Dr Addison, Philip Kerr and various friends of Megan Lloyd George. Hankey wrote to Lady Hankey (25 August 1918, see Roskill, *Hankey*, I, p. 593) that Amery had 'invited himself, yet settled down as though he were an invited guest'. Roskill commented: 'Hankey evidently sensed that Amery was hoping to be included in a new government.'

Diary

22 August 1918: In the evening Dawson expounded to us very interestingly his conception for the organisation of Health Centres in each town, at which the doctors, while retaining their private practice and personal interest in their patients, also give a portion of their time to State service and have all the machinery and equipment of a hospital at their disposal.

23 August 1918 (Criccieth): Henry Norman and Dudley Ward [Liberal MPs] arrived and had a long conference with Addison as to the Lloyd Georgite election programme, for which I gather Norman is to act as propagandist-in-chief as he did for the 1909–10 Budget campaign.

24 August 1918 (Criccieth): L.G. in great form after dinner, indeed during the whole of my time there – full of humorous chaff about his own past and about his present colleagues. He was specially delighted with my story of the earnest young radical watching the election results in Trafalgar Square in 1910 who, after a spell of three or four Unionist successes, could not refrain from saying 'damn!', and was reproved by his neighbour, a non-conformist minister, with the words 'Leave language like that to men of the stamp of Lord Milner'. It was interesting to see how greatly L.G. has always admired both Joe and Dizzy and how little use he had for Gladstone. His evolution, like Joe's, is really a very natural one.

Amery's secretary was away from 28 August to 22 September, so the diary was largely incomplete, consisting of occasional rough recollections. The Allied counter-offensive against the Germans had already begun in France, with the successful British attack at Amiens commencing on 8 August and being followed by Anglo-French thrusts along the whole of the Western Front. Amery later recorded, however, that even in mid-September both Foch and Henry Wilson were making their plans on the assumption that the war would continue into 1919 (*My Political Life*, II, p. 168). On 15 September the Allied Army at Salonika attacked the Bulgarians who collapsed in rout after a few days. On 27 September Bulgaria sued for an armistice, and by the end of October the Allies were invading Austria-Hungary along the Danube. Allenby's offensive had been planned for April 1918, but had been postponed owing to the situation in France when one division was brought back to France from Palestine. Amery was able to persuade Wilson to bring back no more full formations and Allenby rebuilt and retrained his army. On 21 September, the long-awaited offensive began with the battle of Megiddo. Feinting on his right

Allenby broke through on his left on the coastal plain and with the aid of cavalry and aircraft routed the Turkish Army. On 1 October, the Arabs under Emir Feisal and T. E. Lawrence entered Damascus and Allenby's forces pressed on to Aleppo and Alexandretta. On 21 October, Turkey asked for an armistice. Meanwhile, Prince Max of Baden became German chancellor and put forward peace feelers. The Italian attack at Vittorio Veneto routed the Austrians who similarly sued for an armistice on 28 October.

Diary

26 September 1918: I never thought the Germans would allow us to bring about so complete a collapse of the Bulgars as we have done. It looks as if the Westernism which we suffered from so badly during '15, '16 and '17 has this year proved the final undoing of the Germans. His only chance to my mind now is to get back to the Meuse, or even the old German frontier, as quickly as possible, try and reconquer the Balkans and save what can be of the Turkish Caucasian and Russian position. But happily we have got him so tied round the neck in the West at this moment that he can't do any rearranging for some weeks to come, during which great things may happen.

27 September 1918: The first news that greeted me at the War Office was that General Toderoff [the Bulgarian commander] had asked for an armistice.

28 September 1918: Had a long chat with Lord M. at his house after lunch, chiefly about Bulgaria and the Eastern situation....
    Down to Birchington by the 5 o'clock train and spent most of the journey reading over the last six months of my diary, beginning with the March crisis. I noticed that for some days after the big offensive opened I couldn't persuade myself that the Germans were seriously going to stake their whole fortunes on a Western offensive, and thought that it was only a big demonstration, which had succeeded beyond their expectations but which was still only meant as a prelude to tidying up first the Salonika and then the Italian situation. The six months have shown how wrong I was in my estimate of the German Higher Command's grip of the realities of the situation. They believed that just a little extra advantage in tactical efficiency could break down the Western front, just as we believed year after year that something extra in the way of numbers or artillery would have the same effect. Happily we had boundless resources which even the Westerners could not wholly dissipate. The question still

is whether we have learnt and know how to exploit our successes properly in all theatres or whether we shall go on indefinitely spending ourselves and pushing the Germans back to the Rhine. Of course if the Germans are wise they will lose no time in getting back to the Meuse or even to their old frontiers, and clear out of France and Belgium. . . . Grant told me at the War Office that Foch considered that they ought to have done that before now and that their present position was exclusively due to the failure of the German High Command.

30 September 1918: Arrived at the Office to find that Bulgaria had accepted the French terms unconditionally, and that her railways and everything else will be at our disposal. General Berthelot is to be sent through to Rumania at once to raise the Allied standard again. Turkey will probably collapse within the next week or so.

2 October 1918: Heard in the morning that we had occupied Damascus; another dream come true. . . .

H.W. went off to France to discuss the Balkan situation with Foch and Clemenceau. My own belief is that we can't really prevent the Germans retaining control of the Danube. We may be able to secure before the winter the frontier of the Balkans from the Shipka westwards to Pirot and across the Vranya to Kachanik. Or possibly we may only be able to hold the line of the Rhodope, i.e. substantially the old pre-1914 Turkish frontier. From this point of view it is obviously more urgent to make sure of getting Turkey out than of pushing prematurely to the Danube.

5 October 1918: Talk with Sykes about what to do with the Sykes–Picot Agreement. He has evolved a new and most ingenious scheme by which the French are to clear out of the whole Arab region except the Lebanon and in return take over the protectorate of the whole Kurdo-Armenian region from Adana to Persia and the Caucasus.

6 October 1918: Max of Baden has celebrated his entry into office by immediate action. The object of the offer presumably is to make it easier for the German Army to fall back to a new line and for the German people to hold out through the winter, and at the same time to affect our pacifists.

7 October 1918: Lord M. interesting in his appreciations of the different generals, French and British, he had come across. Talking about Foch, he said he didn't feel any tremendous personality, either intellectual or otherwise, about him, but thought that possibly at his age and with his experience of men, that was hardly to be expected. But he did think him good, and had of course backed him throughout both with Clemenceau and with L.G. About Henry [Wilson] he thought that his ability and power of clear and convincing exposition was wonderful, and that he had been invaluable through all this crisis. His judgment, however, was not infallible and he hadn't always the courage to see things through where it meant unpleasantness to old fellow officers – plenty of courage otherwise. On the whole he thought that Henry was at his best as a Chief of Staff rather than as Commander-in-Chief. He would be admirable with a man of the type of Plumer. He might have added that he was really at his best with someone like himself to steady him.

L.S.A. to Lord Robert Cecil, 7 October 1918

We should take on the fostering and developing of Zionism and of the Arab state, while France looks after Eastern Christianity. [Sykes]'s idea of the French zone would be firstly an autonomous lesser Armenia including Adana, Alexandretta, Zeitun, Marash, etc. and behind it a great region occupied by Armenians and Kurds, with smaller elements of Turks and Nestorians, which the French would run more directly. Our boundary with the French would then run, apart from the Lebanon, from south of Alexandretta, north of Aleppo, Urfah, Mardin, Mosul. . . . The Turk, on the other hand, would be cut back to the limits of the country which is really properly Turkish. The only person who doesn't come into anything in this scheme is the Italian, and I don't know what is to be done with him.

Diary

20 October 1918: Inspired by Professor [President] Wilson's pontifical reply to Austria to write a short memo on the Austrian situation to the effect that we must eventually take a constructive line about Middle Europe and not merely an anti-German one, which would make a second Balkans of that region. If the Germans and Magyars have any kick still left in them I can think of nothing more calculated to rally them to a last effort than Wilson's reply which leaves the fate of the German Bohemians and Northern Hungary to the Czechoslovak Committee.

Amidst all the expectations of a collapse of the Central Powers came the preparation for the election.

Diary

22 October 1918: Went to a meeting at 12 Downing Street with Sanders, Freddy Guest and [Henry] Norman to meet Mr Higham. He is apparently a professional advertiser, and expounded his advertisement scheme with great enthusiasm and vigour. I was quite at one with him in the idea that advertising in the Press on modern lines is much better political propaganda than the old business of leaflets and posters. The only question between us was whether these articles should be amiable generalisations issued as by a group of citizens, or should directly and frankly appear over the name of the Coalition Publicity Committee and so be able gradually to take on a more definitely political character. We finally decided on the latter alternative.

29 October 1918 (Versailles): Spent most of the morning at Villa Romaine, but put in a short walk in the woods with Lord M., Hankey and Bowly. Suggested to Hankey that as nobody seemed to have thought out armistice terms for Austria I might try my hand at them. . . .

Dined at the Villa, L.G., Lord M., Hankey and I at a table. L.G. was very amusing on the way in which he and Clemenceau had pushed poor [Colonel] House about over Wilson's 14 points. He, L.G., had made it quite clear that we would sooner carry on the war single-handed than agree to the 'freedom of the seas'. He horrified us, however, by telling us that he had offered East Africa to Colonel House; and this because he is now convinced that the Americans would be a nuisance in Palestine and upset all our Moslems. After dinner I had a great go at him over E. Africa and Lord M. and Hankey backed me up. . . . Finished my Austrian terms.

30 October 1918 (Versailles): After lunch Lord M. and I motored out to the edge of the Forêt de Marly and had a very good walk back. He is rather tired of working in harness with so erratic a creature as L.G., and rather doubtful if he can carry on with him after the war is over, much though he likes him personally. I urged him to take on the Dominions work and the Imperial Cabinet which L.G. would not interfere with much once he had begun to be intent on domestic reconstruction. . . .

L.G. [to tea] who was full of a real set to he has been having with Clemenceau over Admiral Calthorpe's [commanding in the Mediterranean] signing the armistice conditions with Turkey alone without the French Admiral. He seems to have been brutally firm and said that all the help the French had ever given towards the conquest of Turkey was a few niggers to prevent our stealing the Holy Sepulchre. He then suddenly thought that I had better rush in at once to the Quai d'Orsay with the revised Austrian terms as the military were just settling them. I drove in and found that they had practically settled them (a combination of a draft of Franchet d'Esperey's with mine, but much inferior and with an awful reference to the Pact of London* which might imply their retiring out of Dalmatia) though they still put in one or two small points. . . . *A propos* of L.G.'s interest in the new map on the wall, Sackville-West says L.G. was much interested in discovering New Zealand lay eastwards of Australia, he had always thought it was the other side!

L.S.A. to Mrs Amery, from Versailles, 31 October 1918

Lord M. tells me that he had had a talk with Bonar about the necessity of fixing me up in the next shuffling of offices, and he was, I gather, quite friendly and promised to settle nothing with L.G. without consulting Lord M. first.

Diary

31 October 1918 (Versailles): Prepared with Sackville-West certain amendments to the armistice note, including substituting the actual line in Tirol and Istria for the reference to the Pact of London. The only copy of the Pact in the office was a hopelessly incorrect translation of the Russian version published by the Bolsheviks. This I amended as well as I could by guessing, and this came very near to being the text adopted and settling the future frontiers of Italy. This is how high diplomatic settlements are made and why treaties are often so puzzling to the geographer. While we were making our amendments Geddes and others met somewhere else and made another lot of amendments and apparently agreed in so many words to the very thing we were anxious to avoid, viz. Italian occupation of Dalmatia and the islands in accordance with the Pact of London, and it was in this form that the text was settled in the afternoon. So the seeds of future trouble were duly planted and Yugoslavia probably definitely committed to the German side in future – unless Italy joins that side first. I shouldn't wonder if these armistice terms don't mean German Austria going straight off and joining Germany at once with such soldiers as can get away and preparing to defend all they can of the Tirol in the spirit of Andreas Hofer. . . . Henry has heard Northcliffe has come over with the deliberate intention of hounding Lord M. out. If L.G. has any decent feelings, he will speak up and say what he owes to Lord M. But elections are near and L.G. is L.G.

*Secret agreement of 28 April 1915 between Britain, France, Russia and Italy providing for the latter to enter the war on the Allied side and to receive territorial considerations in the Alps, Adriatic and elsewhere in the Mediterranean.

Amery also referred to the vain attempts to displace the French from Syria and abrogate the Sykes–Picot agreement of 1915. While the War Cabinet's Eastern Committee were moving along these lines, Balfour and Robert Cecil reconfirmed the agreement by allowing the French to administer Syria 'temporarily'. Even with the collapse of Austria–Hungary, the British staff was still assuming that Germany would continue to resist into 1919. But the plight of the starving German civilian population, communicating itself by letters to the constantly retreating German Army in the west and thus back to the High Command, was decisive. Ludendorff, who in September has scorned the idea of peace negotiations while still fighting, now insisted on an immediate armistice and Germany accepted President Wilson's famous Fourteen Points. On 4 November the harsh armistice terms for Germany were settled between the Allies, and Amery's concerns over the following days were for Lord Milner, who was being attacked by the Northcliffe press as 'pro-German' on account of his having deprecated 'gratifying our feelings of anger or indignation against Germany, however justified'. Thus Milner became one of the first victims of the 'squeeze Germany till the pips squeak' mood to which Lloyd George pandered during the election campaign.

Diary

2 November 1918: Found all the British section at Château Wake [i.e. the quarters of Sir Hereward Wake] at midnight working out schemes for invading Bavaria from Italy.

3 November 1918: The news of Austria's acceptance of the armistice came in the afternoon. L.G. was very cheery at dinner and we drank to the success of the policy of knocking out the 'props' which he always advocated against Wully.

4 November 1918: An informal meeting of the 'hush frocks'* took place at Colonel House's dwelling in the morning at which they finally settled the armistice terms for Germany subject only to their formal ratification by the [Supreme War Council] in the afternoon.

6 November 1918: Northcliffe had a further most offensive attack on Lord M. in the *Daily Mail* this morning.... Had a talk with Robin to see if anything could be done in the matter, but it was clear that the only people whose intervention would be of use were L.G. or Carson. Carson

*Otherwise 'frocks': Henry Wilson's term for the top politicians.

did in fact follow up the next night with a most courageous defence of Lord M. and indictment of Northcliffe's methods.

8 November 1918: Lunched with Guest to meet some leading newspaper proprietors in connection with an idea of his for a committee of Unionist and Liberal proprietors to try and strike the same note during the election. No Unionist proprietor was there, Peter Sanders being the only Unionist beside myself, but three Liberals, Rothermere, Dalziel, and Sir George Riddell. I felt I was in a real den of thieves when they once started talking and realised more than ever that the political strength of the Liberal Party has lain not in its principles but in the thorough-going unscrupu-lousness of its wire-pullers. Rothermere I had never met or even seen at close quarters before; a more perfect specimen of the plutocrat cad it would be hard to imagine. At one moment Guest inadvertently said something about consulting editors. 'Editors', replied Rothermere, 'I have six editors and if any one of them dared to say something I dis-approved of I should have him on the pavement in half-an-hour. My brother [Northcliffe] would do the same to any of his editors.' Henry Norman, the other person present, suggested that one of these days the public would hang the big newspaper proprietors, and I added that at any rate the private ownership of newspapers might have to be effectively limited. Rothermere did not understand the point at all; his only retort was 'Who makes the success of the newspaper? Some of my best papers have been ones of which I have changed the editor half a dozen times.' This kind of creature is one of the biggest dangers we have got to fight in future....

Just before lunch I had been called in to the War Cabinet and asked by L.G. to draft some sort of communiqué in answer to Hughes's attack on the Government for not having taken the Dominions into consulta-tion when they settled the peace terms at Versailles. I drew up one draft which neither the PM nor A.J.B. liked very much, I think because it entered too directly into the issues. A second, which went round the point rather more, was approved of and went into the papers. There are the makings here of a first-class row. Hughes is technically in the right, that is to say if the Allied reply to Wilson really constitutes the definite settle-ment of the peace terms. He has also some grievance because they didn't take him much into consultation during the last week or two before they went over, mainly because he is so irritating to most of them personally both on account of his deafness and aggressive manners. His explosion may possibly do good if things haven't gone too far, by forcing the Government to face the issue of really making Dominion representation adequate.

11 November 1918: Came up in the morning on the 24 Bus and was presently passed by a lorry full of shouting soldiers saying it was finished. When we got near Downing Street I saw a crowd running across, so I got off and was in time to see L.G. at his doorstep telling them (being then about five minutes to eleven) that the war was over at eleven o'clock and that they could cheer with a good will. They did so and also started singing 'God Save the King', a performance politically though not musically quite satisfactory.

8
Colonies and Navy
1919–21

The end of war brought for Amery an immediate return to politics. He had been drawn into the preparation of Unionist election material as early as the beginning of October 1918, and he was insistent that the Unionists should 'stand as the party of Imperial and national reconstruction', even to the point of welcoming a degree of Government intervention and expenditure. Lloyd George was determined to maintain his ascendancy, and early in November he and Bonar Law agreed on a joint programme. While fairly Liberal in character, it envisaged also Imperial preference, anti-dumping legislation and protection for key industries. Home Rule was to be given to Ireland in a form which would leave Ulster free to govern herself. The election, however, turned less on these issues than on the question of making Germany pay for the war, and Amery, in receipt of the Coalition's endorsement (the so-called 'coupon'), found himself swept home for Sparkbrook by a majority of 12,211 votes. It was his first successful electoral contest, since in 1911 he had been unopposed. In the Government reconstruction which followed Milner went to the Colonial Office and insisted that Amery should join him there.

From December 1918 to the end of October 1919 Amery's diary provides a fairly full record of his own activities. Inevitably it contains little of the national picture. His own concerns were largely peripheral to the industrial militancy which seemed to the Cabinet to threaten revolution, and his role at the Peace Conference, which dominated the first half of 1919, was marginal. In the summer he was out of Britain studying the problems of Malta, and in the autumn the diary peters out, perhaps because of the pressure of work. With Milner's departure for Egypt in December at the head of a special mission to review the Government of Egypt, Amery found himself acting as Secretary of State, a position which held good until Milner's return in April 1920. In August Amery wrote a brief account of his stewardship, which was subsequently bound in with his diary. No diary entries survive, perhaps none were written, for the remainder of his term at the Colonial Office. Milner, despite an evident wish to resign, remained in office until February 1921.

Amery may have been disappointed not to succeed him or at least to achieve ministerial rank – in his memoirs he notes that the press canvassed him as a possible successor – but he was not left more than a few weeks as junior to Churchill, who succeeded Milner. Lloyd George offered him the post of Parliamentary and Financial Secretary to the Admiralty, and on 2 April 1921 Amery took his seat at the Board of Admiralty.

Despite his obvious concern with the work of the office, it is perhaps a little surprising to find how little impact the domestic scene has on this volume of his diary. The mutinous outbreaks of January 1919, the earliest of which concerned Amery as a junior Minister at the War Office, were followed by serious disorders in industrial centres, particularly Glasgow, and by a threatened coal strike. Lloyd George bought time with an abortive National Industrial Conference, and a largely abortive Royal Commission on the coal industry. A police strike in August and a rail strike in September were potent reminders that it was time and not industrial peace that had been bought, and the Government created an emergency organisation to maintain essential transport and supplies. Amery was designated Regional Commissioner for the North Midlands, but it finds no place in his diary.

Nor does Ireland rate more than an occasional mention, although Sinn Fein followed a unilateral declaration of independence in January 1919 with a terrorist campaign. An even more serious civil war in which Britain was involved, that between the Bolsheviks and the White Russians, escapes mention altogether, although the Cabinet were locked in argument about the right policy to follow. The Peace Conference figures rather more. At the beginning of February Amery was in Paris to discuss the issue of mandates with the Dominion Prime Ministers, but beyond fixing up the cession of Ruanda to the Belgians in July and writing into the Tanganyika mandate an explicit proviso that there might be closer union between it and the neighbouring British East African territories, Amery played little part in the negotiations which led to the Treaty of Versailles. It was a treaty which he defended against critics like Keynes, and he thought the real mistake of the settlement was Britain's subsequent withdrawal from her guarantee to France.

Perhaps his dominant interest, and one which remained his responsibility even after his departure from the Colonial Office, was the question of overseas settlement – the promotion, by various means, of the settlement of Britons in the 'old' Commonwealth Dominions. He was to be largely responsible for placing the Empire Settlement Act of 1922 on the statute book. Professor Drummond has traced the wartime discussions on the subject,* and has shown how they centred on the pre-war surplus of women and varying estimates of the likely post-war demand for labour. There was little concern for the market impact of Empire settlement which became Amery's major theme.

But for the activities of Sir Rider Haggard and the Royal Colonial Institute, the Government might not have developed a policy at all. That which was put to the Commons envisaged a central migration authority, seemingly designed to discourage emigration, but to ensure also that where it was permitted, the place of settlement would be within the Empire. The Bill had a difficult passage through the Commons and the dissolution put an end to its progress. In place of the central migration authority, the Colonial Secretary therefore established a non-statutory committee, whose vice-chairman and administrative officer, T. C. Macnaghten, had worked for six years on the question in the Colonial Office. In January 1919 Amery became chairman of this body, whose meetings must often have resembled a dialogue between himself and Macnaghten. From his diary it is easy to discern how it became his major concern.

L.S.A. to Mrs Amery, from Birmingham, 23 November 1918

I was just wondering whether you could have rung up Ld Milner and found out if there was any chance of my succeeding Bob Cecil. It would be just the right place for me!†

L.S.A. to Mrs Amery, from Birmingham, 26 November 1918

The great British people are not in the least interested in Social Reform or Reconstruction, but only in making the Germans pay for the war and punishing the Kaiser. . . . I have gradually cut down my social reform programme to a few generalities, plus a little about dumping and British industries and tell them about the Peace Conference and what it means to this country, and go wholeheartedly for a strong policy including the Kaiser punishing as well. . . . I am getting my power of platform oratory again, and I hear my speeches are making a very good impression. They all say now we are quite safe, but we are still woefully short of workers, and practically no canvass has been done yet. . . . I must say Lloyd George is a great help from the electioneering point of view. His speeches and manifestos are good reading and full of zeal – and there is no one who

*Ian M. Drummond, *Imperial Economic Policy 1917–1939* (Unwin University Books, 1974), ch. 2.

†Lord Robert Cecil, Under Secretary of State for Foreign Affairs, had resigned rather than take any share of the responsibility for dis-establishing the Welsh Church.

really holds a candle to him in that line. It now remains to be seen how much of it all we make good.

Diary

18 December 1918: I had a long talk in the evening with Lord M. with whom I had only had brief talks before, about his own position. He is not at all anxious to stay on to do hack work. The only posts he might be willing to occupy were Foreign Secretary and Head of the Dominions Department. I strongly urged him to take the offensive at once on the question and let L.G. know his views instead of waiting. It is of course absurd that he should not be at the Peace Conference. His greatest strength lies in his knowledge and grasp of big principles which makes him a diplomat. As he said, the really serious feature about the situation is that L.G. hardly seems to realise the difference between having him and some-one like Bonar Law or Balfour.

L.S.A. to Lloyd George, 27 December 1918

The task of reconstruction (including demobilisation) is going to be so tremendous and require such constant settlement of interdepartmental issues and questions of general policy, that I am convinced it cannot be carried out by a large Cabinet on the old lines. You will want a 'Recon-struction Cabinet' on the lines of the present War Cabinet consisting of not more than half a dozen Ministers, all, or most of them, without depart-mental duties.

On the other hand Imperial Affairs will no longer want the same day to day attention and can be left to an Imperial Cabinet comprising the holders of the Imperial Offices of State and the Dominion representatives. The Imperial Offices for this purpose would naturally be the President of the Council (under which I suggest Dominion Affairs might now be placed), Foreign Office, Colonial Office, India Office, and possibly the First Lord and the Secretaries of State for War and the Air. You would be head of both Cabinets, and members of the Reconstruction Cabinet could attend the Imperial Cabinet and vice versa, as required. But the two bodies should be quite distinct.

Now as to personnel. Your Reconstruction Cabinet will naturally include the leaders of both Houses: Bonar Law in the Commons, and Curzon (unless you replace him by a younger and more progressive peer) in the Lords. In either case it would be better if these leaders held no other offices, and Bonar Law handed over the Chancellorship to the ablest financier available, while Curzon resigned the Presidency to whoever is to be Dominions Minister in the Imperial Cabinet. Then you must have in it a good Liberal. Fisher is probably your best man for the job, and, if so, it would be worth while to keep him for that rather than let him go to Foreign Affairs or to any other departmental task. You will also need the best Labour man you can get. Lastly you might add one man of general capacity, ideas and drive, e.g. Auckland Geddes.

As regards the Imperial Cabinet Milner is clearly much the best man for President of the Council and Minister for the Dominions. He understands their problems and point of view so much better than anyone else, and the position is one where he could do a great deal to help on the growth of Imperial Unity without having to deal with heavy routine work. The only alternative post for him would be the Foreign Office. I will only venture on two other suggestions in connexion with the Imperial Cabinet. One is that you make use of Carson again – he would make the next best Dominions Minister to Milner, though he knows much less about the subject. The other is that you don't put Churchill in the War Office. I hear from all sorts of quarters that the Army are terrified of the idea. What he needs is a field of adventure and advertisement, and the field that would give him most scope in both directions is the Air Ministry with its interesting potentialities both commercial and strategical, or, failing that, the Colonial Office, minus the Dominions, where there is a great field for a constructive administrative and economic policy.

Diary

29 December 1918: Spent the morning reading the amazing news of the complete disappearance of the Old Gang. I have always said that Liberalism has been internally dead for the last 20 years or more and would have gone the way of continental Liberalism ages ago but for the cohesive force of the two-party system. The break-up of that system by the war destroyed all *raison d'être* for our Liberal politicians; even apart from the failings of Asquith's war leadership. And so the great Liberal party has vanished, and, as far as I can see, for good. All the Coalition Liberals are in by virtue of Unionist votes, and though they may lose their seats to Labour they can only hold them by continuing their alliance with the Unionists. On the other hand the Unionists know equally well that unless this Government goes in for a really bold and constructive policy of social reform, there will be a Labour landslide in the next few years and I don't think we need reckon on too much stickiness from our older Tories

30 December 1918: Imperial War Cabinet in the afternoon to hear L.G.'s report of President Wilson who on the whole seems to have been not quite so tiresome as was anticipated, except perhaps on the question of Indemnity. The feature of the afternoon was a slashing speech by Hughes pointing out that America had made no money sacrifices at all, having not yet spent anything like the profits she had accumulated in the first part of the war, that she had lost fewer men than Australia, that Wilson didn't represent even half of America, and that therefore L.G. should go ahead and look after British interests firmly without bothering too much about the President.

1 January 1919: Had a talk with Carson about things generally and more particularly about the position as between Lord M. and L.G. [relations between the two men were at a low ebb]* and Lord M.'s going to the Peace Conference. Carson felt he could not approach L.G. on the matter himself but would certainly do all he could if L.G. asked for his opinion. His own inclination was to stay outside the Government and contribute friendly criticism. He told me that the Ulster elections had been run with very little reference to Home Rule and on the main general issues, as in England, and with a special demand to share to the full with England in the benefits of reconstruction more particularly in respect of Education. ... General Clayton came round afterwards and we had a long talk about Palestine and Syria and about the situation in Egypt which is evidently drifting into a bad mess from the sheer absence of a really big man at the Egyptian end and anybody capable of giving any decision at this end. I asked Clayton whether making Allenby High Commissioner wouldn't improve matters and his answer was that the whole trouble would shut up like a book. I put these points briefly to Lord M. afterwards.

2 January 1919: Lunched at the Carlton and had some talk with Bob Cecil, who tells me that he is doing what he can to get Allenby made High Commissioner as soon as possible, his only difficulty being to know what to do with Wingate as he doesn't want to treat him in the unceremonious fashion in which they treated MacMahon.† I gathered from him that the chaos in the Foreign Office is now indescribable. ...‡

3 January 1919: Short talk with Lord M. He explained his position to me in almost identical terms I had used in writing to Hankey two days before.

---

*See W. S. Churchill, *The World Crisis* (6 vols, Thornton Butterworth, 1929), *The Aftermath*, pp. 53–4, and A. M. Gollin, *Proconsul in Politics* (Anthony Blond, 1964), pp. 578–80.

†Sir Henry MacMahon (1862–1949) had been High Commissioner in Egypt from 1914 to 1916 and had been replaced by Sir Reginald Wingate.

‡Cecil was acting as Foreign Secretary in Balfour's absence.

The move must come from Lloyd George and L.G. must clearly show that he wants him and is prepared to treat him seriously as a partner.

4 January 1919: [On 3 January 12,000 soldiers in rest camps at Folkestone and Dover refused to embark for France and demanded an extension of their leave]. Lord M. had hoped to get down to Sturry in the morning but was kept by this very unfortunate outbreak at Folkestone. The whole trouble, as far as I can make out, is due to this stupid contract system by means of which men on leave can secure immediate demobilisation. This was forced upon the War Office by the War Cabinet in the middle of the Election as an Election move and was one of the chief reasons of Lord M.'s annoyance with L.G., quite justifiable as the event has shown.

6 January 1919: Had a longish talk with Lord M. who told me he had been seeing Bonar who, as one might almost have expected, had never even thought of the question of dividing the Imperial from the Home Cabinet. He also suggested to Lord M. that he should go to the Colonial Office. I hurriedly dictated a short memo on my ideas on the relation of the Reconstruction to the Imperial Cabinet for Lord M. and then went on to the first revival of our Monday dinners.

7 January 1919: Had a short talk with Hankey who tells me that he had three or four goes at L.G. on the subject of introducing a definite division between the Imperial and Home Cabinets and making the latter a small Reconstruction Cabinet on War Cabinet lines. L.G. listened but on none of the occasions committed himself at all. Subsequently Hankey had suggested to L.G. that if he wasn't prepared to go as far as that, he should have a Cabinet of 22 or so and at their first meeting inform them that he didn't intend them to meet as a whole body but would formally divide them into Imperial and Domestic Cabinets. He also told me that L.G. was meditating asking Lord M. to go to the Colonial Office. I saw Lord M. later in the morning and he told me that after reading my memorandum he had written to Bonar suggesting an arrangement very much on the lines of Hankey's alternative proposal, i.e. a large Cabinet to be divided up formally into two panels, Imperial and Home, plus certain Ministers of Cabinet rank outside the Cabinet but reckoning as full members of either Cabinet if they were called in. With regard to the Colonial Office he told me he disliked the idea of holding an ordinary office, but was I think impressed by my argument that he might be able to do what nobody else would, set on foot the division between Dominions and Crown Colony work and prepare the way for the transfer of the former to a separate Department as soon as possible. . . . . If he did go there he said he would insist on having me with him.

8 January 1919: Had a further talk with Lord M. who told me that he had definitely been offered the Colonial Office and that they were making a great fuss about inducing him to stay in the Government. He said they still seemed to be entirely vague as to what kind or shape of Government they were going to have, though it looked as if they were coming nearer to the idea of a small inner Reconstruction Cabinet for Home Affairs. He disliked the idea of going on as he felt he never knew where he was with L.G. and the rest of them. I urged very strongly that the whole future of Imperial development would depend on the next two or three years and that there was no one except himself who could be trusted not to handle the thing wrongly. There was the Conference which was to discuss the future Constitution, etc., of the Empire and there was also an immense work to do in the development of the Crown Colonies. In all this he would be very little interfered with by L.G., who would be mainly full of domestic and demobilisation affairs, and would not share the general odium into which the Government might very soon fall. In any case he would have behind him a Parliament thoroughly in sympathy with the ideas of Imperial Unity and development. He agreed, but thought the Treasury might prove very sticky when it came to raising loans for the Crown Colonies, especially if Austen went there. I asked if he could make any stipulations. He didn't think any worth making were likely to be kept except about having me with him. . . . All the papers are announcing positively that Winston is going to the War Office, and WO and Army are not at all pleased at the prospect. Dined at a Masonic Dinner . . . General Currie there and made quite a nice little speech, incidentally describing how he saw a Canadian soldier drilling a small squadron of Boches to the swing of 'Rule Britannia', and when they had accomplished this more or less to his satisfaction he said 'And now you may sing the 'ymn of 'ate'.

9 January 1919: Looked in at Great College Street [Lord Milner's house] on my way up to the office to suggest to Lord M. that he should stipulate to have the title of Secretary of State for the Colonies changed to Secretary of State for Imperial Affairs. Found him in a mood between great anger and irresistible laughter. Apparently he had gone round to see Bonar and asked if everything was all right and Bonar had said yes. Lord M. asked, 'I mean all right about Amery?' to which Bonar replied, 'Oh, yes, we can't fit him in just at present but there is sure to be an opening for him shortly', or words to that effect. Thereupon Lord M. went round to L.G. and said, 'This won't do.' L.G. launched forth in high praise of myself, said that the more he had seen of me the more he appreciated and liked me, etc., but made it clear that I was the sort of person who would be friendly and helpful in any case, whereas there were several people who

THE LEO AMERY DIARIES

had got to be fitted into office anyhow who might be nasty if their claims were not satisfied. Lord M. rejoined that he didn't propose to argue the case on its merits but that if I wasn't Under Secretary he wasn't going to be Secretary and that was the end of it, and departed. He assumed that they would give way but hadn't heard and hadn't, as a matter of fact, heard even this morning (10th). He said the only reason why he was taking the Office at all was to get me started in a position by the time he left public life to be able to carry on his ideas on Imperial matters.

10 January 1919: Down to the War Office and saw Thornton who told me the Chief had got his own formal letter of invitation but no information as regards myself and had gone round to see Bonar about me before accepting. . . .

Went across to the War Cabinet Office to do letters and found my letter from the PM inviting me to become Under Secretary for the Colonies. In the dignified days of old these documents were, I believe, lengthy personal letters. In my case it was a short formal typewritten letter asking for a prompt reply as the PM was going to France. I replied in an equally brief formal typewritten note, which I suppose would have horrified a Prime Minister of 20 years ago but will certainly not horrify J. T. Davies or Sutherland [the Prime Minister's private secretaries] who are the only persons likely to read it. So starts a new chapter. I don't suppose I shall be nearly as much in the swim of general policy as I have been for the last two years, but I shall have a real piece of work of my own to do instead of merely hanging round trying to be useful where I could and often feeling that I was only fussing. Above all, it will be work I care most about and under the one chief I wish to serve under. . . . Heard that B. was clamouring for me on the telephone. I rang up and she told me that she had just had a message of enquiry from Lord M. to know whether I had actually received my letter of invitation from the Prime Minister as he was determined not to sign his own answer to the PM till he was absolutely sure. As he said, he was 'not prepared to take any verbal assurance from these rogues'.

11 January 1919: Saw my name duly in the papers. Most of them fell very foul of the Government as a whole, but, except the *Daily News*, they were almost unanimous in approving the CO appointments. Lord M. very much amused at the thought that he should be the one popular person in the Government. He had a good talk with Fiddes in the morning and I gather made it clear that my position in the Office, especially with himself in the House of Lords, would have to be very different from that occupied by Steel-Maitland or Hewins [Amery's predecessors in the post of Under Secretary of State].

12 January 1919: Had tea with Hewins and had a good talk with him, more particularly about Emigration and Raw Materials. He seems to have been completely surprised to find himself not wanted by the constituency on the very eve of the election. I have no doubt they treated him rather unfairly. But he is not naturally a good candidate, he turned R C recently, and he probably had a pretty bad agent too, or he would have heard of these things before.

27 January 1919: Had a talk with Sir Joseph Cook. . . . He suggested that it might help the Commonwealth and State Governments a great deal to get to terms on emigration if the Imperial Government invited them to a Conference here. He also told me that things were going pretty happily over in Paris. This was very different from the information which I had heard from Astor and Beale, as well as that which Lord M. had got through from [Lionel] Curtis. In fact my own endeavours for some days have been to stir up things in order that Lord M. should go over himself.

30 January 1919: In view of the obvious troubles over in Paris about the Pacific Islands I went in to suggest to Lord M. that he should go over to Paris and straighten the thing out. He knows he ought to be there but doesn't feel inclined to go over at this stage or to push himself in at all without being really asked for his help. But he thought it would be a very good thing if I ran over, so I have been busy making arrangements accordingly. We agreed that everything really turned on what was meant by the word mandatory occupation, as after all it may comprise anything between an intolerable condominium and the ordinary British system of colonial administration. I have a sneaking feeling myself that it really makes no difference as long as we actually get our flag up and our administration in as the mandate of a League of Nations which isn't going to exist and won't affect anybody. . . .

Emigration Committee at 3 to consider the Draft Report and we steered it through practically unchanged in an hour and a half, subject only to a caveat by the Ministry of Labour that there might be a shortage of labour in the near future and that they were not disposed to encourage anyone leaving the country.

1 February 1919 (Paris): Read through the Reports of the Conference and discovered that the mandatory question had been settled by a fairly satisfactory compromise agreed upon at a meeting of the British Delegation and accepted even by Hughes. Heard afterwards that both Botha's and Massey's speeches accepting it made a great impression. My impression as to [President] Wilson, confirmed from what I heard from others, was that he is less intractable and unreasonable, but even stupider, than

I had imagined. . . . Went for a walk with Wiseman and heard all about the American point of view. I gather Wilson is hankering after a mandate somewhere, preferably Armenia, but daren't commit himself until he goes back and sees his own people. I urged Wiseman to suggest to him that he ought at least to commit himself as to the particular region where he might accept a mandate, so that the rest of the Allies could leave that in blank and proceed to allotting the rest among themselves. Came back and had some talk . . . with [T.E.] Lawrence who was in attendance on Feisal. Had some talks with Hughes and Ward and I don't know who else. All the world that I had ever known was popping in and out of the big lounge of the Majestic like figures in a cinema show. . . . Smuts wrote to say would I dine with him. After dinner Smuts took me away to discuss ways and means of getting hold of Portuguese East Africa for the Union. I promised to think the matter over further, but meanwhile urged him that the Union should not try and get more than Lourenço Marques and Beira but rather extend on the high veldt to include N.W. Rhodesia. He agreed.

2 *February 1919:* Lunched with Hughes and Mrs Hughes and most of the Australian outfit. Hughes put before me the whole of his case over the *Daily Mail* article which has caused so serious difficulty between him and L.G. Undoubtedly Hughes has been tiresome and behaved rather badly, though not quite so badly as L.G. and most of the big delegates seem to think. I promised to do what I could to set things straight.

Further talk with Smuts, to whom I expounded the various devices for dealing with the Portuguese, including a mandate for reorganising the administration and a scheme for local self-government with permission to the new colony to affiliate itself closely with the Union on a basis of mutual citizenship. . . .

Went over to L.G.'s flat, and as I came in heard weird doleful sounds and found L.G. in the drawing-room singing a Welsh hymn to Miss Stevenson's accompaniment. There was nobody serious at dinner, only J.T. [Davies], Megan, Gwilym and two friends of Megan's, and L.G. was in very high spirits. After dinner we had a quarter of an hour's talk, in the course of which we dealt with the whole question of mandates in the Near East and he incidentally suggested that Egypt, Palestine and Meso-potamia should come under the Colonial Office and that the Dominions should be taken out of it and put under the Prime Minister and Under Secretary or under a special Dominions Minister. I urged the latter as there would be too much work, and he agreed. He asked how Lord M. was and hearing that he was better said, 'We must have him here at once. I can't find out what the French are thinking about the Near East and I must have him to get at Clemenceau. He must come over on Tuesday.' As he went off to join the ladies I stopped him to get a last decision as to whether there was to be preference on sugar. He agreed at once and said that he meant to fulfil his pledges to the Unionist party in this respect in the letter and the spirit. He only hoped we should fulfil our pledges to him as well in respect of social reforms. For the next hour or so he insisted on cavorting round to the gramophone or the pianola, sometimes both playing the same tune in different times, being taught various kinds of dances by Megan's young friends. Soon after 10 they and Megan disappeared, M. ostensibly to bed, though I met her again at the Majestic an hour or two later where she had been dancing. I stopped to urge again that he should make it up somehow with Hughes and send for him. However he would have none of it and worked himself into quite a fine temper over the whole business, striding about and saying that Hughes was quite impossible and that he couldn't play fair with anyone, was a regular little cad, etc. I didn't venture to suggest that one of the difficulties in the case was a certain similarity in temperament between both little Welshmen.

6 February 1919: Went with Macnaghten to see Horne to get him to waive the provisional veto by the Ministry of Labour on our Emigration Report. Had a considerable argument with Sir Stephenson Kent, who is the source of the mischief and is violently opposed to 'exporting our best men', etc. On the whole I think I carried Horne with me, especially in dealing with Kent's economic fallacy that shorter hours in this country are going to mean more employment all round. Anyhow the veto was withdrawn, subject to Horne's raising it in the Cabinet again.

[In the evening] walked homewards with F.E. and looked into F.E.'s house for the best part of an hour's talk. He is very anxious to make his name as a great Chancellor and thinks if he is given four years he can do three things: (1) unify the Supreme Court of Appeal, (2) incorporate the Inns of Court in a great Law University, (3) I have forgotten. His plan for dealing with the difficulty of admitting women to the legal profession is to create a separate Hostel for them which will gradually grow up into a fair sized Inn of Court of its own.

7 February 1919: Saw Bonar Law for a few minutes and ascertained from him that Emigration is to be in the King's Speech unless L.G. knocks it out at the last moment.

8 February 1919: Meditated over the problem of what to do with East Africa, coming on the whole to the conclusion that we ought to take settlement in hand seriously, not only for the white but also for the natives themselves and the Indians.

10 February 1919: Dined at Carson's; Waldorf, Robin and Oliver present. Carson very keen on co-operating with Lloyd George, but independently, and down on the element in the Unionist War Committee which can't get over old hostilities and suspicions.

11 February 1919: . . . down to the House to hear the King's Speech. Disappointed to find the reference to Emigration cut out and also to hear that no decision had been come to about my giving notice of the Emigration Bill.

12 February 1919: Lunched at the Athenaeum with Wimperis who told me about the very important progress the Americans had made in the development of a flying bomb maintained at a constant elevation. Azimuth gyros capable of effectively hitting a target like a town at a hundred mile range and possibly in the future at a five hundred mile range. I told him that the idea had been in the rough in my mind some years ago as I dare say in the minds of lots of people. However our main talk was about his very fruitful idea of using the Crown Agents for creating a real General Staff for Crown Colony development.

Down to the House for a while and spoke to Bonar about the Emigration Bill. He asked me to submit the Bill to the Cabinet.

20 February 1919: To Auckland Geddes's Committee on Unemployment. I never heard anything more rambling and devoid of any notion of a policy than the contributions of Addison and the various Ministers who spoke. However Geddes said something about emigration and I stayed to the end and had a real talk with him. He is not only for emigration, but thinks that unless we can hive off something like five million people as quickly as possible we shall have absolute chaos in this country.

24 February 1919: Went to the Cabinet to raise the question of my Emigration Bill. A general confused scuffle was going on between Ministers, all of them wanting their own particular subjects discussed before L.G. went away. At last Bonar or somebody managed to say that the item Emigration on the Agenda ought to be discussed, whereupon L.G. put his hand through his hair in a bewildered way and remarked that Emigration was an unpopular subject and that he hadn't time to deal with it. So saying he escaped and the Cabinet broke up in confusion.

25 February 1919: Went to a special meeting of the Cabinet at which Geddes was to expound his conclusions. I am afraid he hasn't the art of making himself very clear and his presentment of the case for emigration wasn't at all convincingly put up. A long wrangle followed about whether there was enough capital in the country and about the prospects of employment generally. I got in eventually, urging the case for dealing with emigration as forcibly as I could but I fear without making very much impression, at any rate for the moment. Any impression I may have made was probably dissipated by the solid business men, Weir, Illingworth and Stanley,* who all said they believed we were in for a period shortly of extreme prosperity and of a great shortage of labour, provided a few tiresome restrictions such as the Excess Profits Tax could be got rid of. Eric Geddes alone was prepared to say that there might be a period of unemployment and that it might be necessary to take measures to deal with emigration. . . . Had a long talk with Botha, with whom I got on excellently. He professes to be only too keen to get out a good class of settler and make the country hum, as long as it isn't too publicly advertised. . . . I took Auckland Geddes to dine in the House, and presently L.G. came down and sat opposite to us, very pleased with himself and full of chaff. So I got a chance of arguing the Emigration case again. What sticks with him is the word 'Emigration' and he finally said that if I could completely change the name of the Bill he would sanction my going on with it.

26 February 1919: Talk with Sinha about the possibility of finding suitable land for Indian ex-service settlers in East Africa. . . . Sinha pressed me strongly on the question of absolute equal rights everywhere, but I made it sufficiently clear that the German East African highlands adjoining those of British East Africa, as well as those of German Nyasaland, would probably be reserved as white areas. It was finally left that they should communicate informally with the Government of India and suggest to the latter to have one or two officers in readiness to send over to East Africa to look at the country if things developed somewhat further.

28 February 1919: Lady Londonderry told me that she had Welldon [Headmaster of Harrow School] to dinner the other night. F.E. was there and said to him: 'I have been waiting for 33 years to meet you, Dean, and tell you how little I think of the Harrow scholarship entrance examination, at which they turned down both Amery and myself on the first day.' Welldon ought to have replied that he was glad that we had both improved since then, but apparently he was not quick enough. Sat up and recast the Emigration Bill into an Overseas Settlement Bill.

---

*Perhaps dictated from memory since Weir had in fact left the Government already. Stanley was at the Board of Trade and Illingworth was Postmaster General, but since the latter was not in the Cabinet, Amery's secretary may well have made a slip and the reference may be to Inverforth, the shipping magnate.

8 March 1919: Lunched at the Carlton and had a talk afterwards with Kipling who is full of the notion that this war, like the Crusades of old, might lead to a revival of a real heraldry.

10 March 1919: Attended a meeting of the Home Affairs Committee of the Cabinet where in spite of a certain amount of confused murmuring Fisher and I carried through our proposals for inter-Imperial education and also got the general principles of the thing sanctioned for the offices and works training of the Ministry of Labour. This is a real success. . . . Saw Lord M. for a few minutes and heard that L.G. was still very sticky about the Overseas Settlement business.

24 March 1919: Dined at the Astors'. . . . We discussed the plight of Europe, Lord M. very pessimistic and inclined to agree with my conclusion that if we wished to avoid general Bolshevism coming to the Rhine we had better go to the Germans at once with simple straightforward terms involving no humiliating loss of territory, a reasonable indemnity, and no disarmament but on the contrary a request to the Germans to co-operate with us in defending the line of the Eastern Polish frontier, and take the whole of our Armies from the Rhine across to the other side of the Vistula. His reason for coming back was that he had refused to act as Chairman of the Mandatory Commission on the German Colonies as Wilson wanted the Commission to do nothing more than discuss the character of the mandates and have no say as to who was to be the Mandatory Power. So that is hung up, as well as the mandate question in the Near East, which is going to a roving Commission. That is probably all in our interest, as for all we know France may be bolshevised, or at any rate in terror of her life from Bolshevism, long before the Commission reports, and prepared to give us anything we want in the East.

26 March 1919: Had some talk with Lord M. about getting Austen to face the financial points arising out of the Report of the Overseas Settlement Committee.

27 March 1919: Bryddie's much feared day of trial; a bad business while it lasted. She was very brave . . . and after all the agony all went very normally. The boy,* a fine sturdy little rascal, weighing 8lb 2oz was born after 5.00. It was all a great relief after our long anxiety.

2 April 1919: I had some talk later with Furse about the hopeless inadequacy of our salaries and rubbed into Lord M. the need for taking

---

*L.S.A.'s second son, Julian. This entry is in holograph.

some steps immediately before all the good men are scattered. [L.S.A. holograph note: 'I do this about twice a week!']

Dined at the Democratic Supper Club, to which Whitley expounded the spirit of the so-called Whitley Councils in a speech full of real human feeling and sound thought which impressed them all very much. I didn't know Whitley had so much in him. . . . I spoke for a few minutes, pointing out that industry had been becoming more and more immoral and in-human before the end of the war and that his Councils pointed the way to something that made for industry based in justice and also humanly interesting to those concerned. I also hinted at a council of all the Whitley Councils being the true Second Chamber of the future and the way of meeting the element of real need which underlies Bolshevism.

3 April 1919: Dined at the House with Carson, much pleased with himself over a speech he had just been making on Ireland, in which he had ignored the Home Rule question and devoted himself mainly to education, etc. Had some talk with Geddes afterwards and suggested that the present licence system for imports should be converted by easy stages into one of 'licence fees' charged *ad valorem* so that we should get a tariff that way without ever raising it on the Budget. He was much taken with the idea, and as he is now running the Board of Trade for Stanley, who is ill, he may be able to do something in that direction. It has just been announced that he has accepted the Presidency of McGill [University, Canada] and is going there this autumn. . . . I am not sure my own ambition would not be to return from whatever political *fastigium* [pinnacle] I reach on to the Mastership of Balliol.

10 April 1919: Attended a Treasury conference from ten to nearly twelve on the question of Preference in the forthcoming Budget. Austen, Baldwin and Bradbury were there, Guillemard, Gallagher and Reade for the Inland Revenue and Chapman and Ashley for the Board of Trade; I had to represent the Chief [Milner] who is in Manchester. Thanks to his previous intervention with Guillemard, the original recommendations of the Committee which had played about with the question, hearing all the foolish fears of merchants etc., were disregarded and a general flat rate of $16\frac{2}{3}$ per cent accepted. For the kind of duties in question this is not bad, and I afterwards successfully persuaded Austen to make the duty $33\frac{1}{3}$ per cent as regards motor cars, matches, etc. – in fact I flatter myself that I secured the general adoption of the principle of $33\frac{1}{3}$ per cent on ordinary duties and half that for duties where there is a corresponding excise. The only point on which I was not satisfied was wine and brandy, and Austen won't have a brandy preference for fear of annoying the French, and $16\frac{2}{3}$ is too little on wine to amount to any real help. . . . My hope is that Lord M.

may still do something over the matter in Cabinet but I mustn't complain for Austen was really very reasonable and broadminded over the whole business.

8 May 1919: Received a native deputation who appealed to the Imperial Government to amend the Act of Union [of South Africa]. The spokesman gave a full and not unfair recital of all the grievances suffered by the natives under the Union and went so far as to suggest that these things would strain their loyalty to breaking point. He kept on insisting that the ordinary native understood nothing about ministerial arrangements or grants of self-government. All he knew was that he had been justly treated in the reign of a Queen Victoria and that now he had no access to the King and that unjust laws were passed over his head in the King's name. I replied sympathetically . . . but it was very clear to me that trouble is coming in this way, possibly very much sooner than we have generally thought, and that the only hope of any constitutional development on this question lies in the increase of the British element of the population in the next few years. The Dutch left to themselves will certainly head straight towards general native rebellion, and only a British majority would tolerate anything like the constitutional evolution of native rights.

9 May 1919: Went over to the Cabinet for Lord M. and by using his authority, and with the warm support of Austen, knocked on the head a scheme for including Belgium in the Imperial preferential scheme. The proposal had been put up by Steel-Maitland and Curzon, but we successfully convinced Bonar and Co. that whatever concessions we might make to Belgium it would not do to let her in to the preferential scheme itself.

There appears to be little of interest in the diary for the following two months, with no particular comment on the signing of the Peace of Versailles on 28 June except a reference to the jubilation in the West End. The period has obviously been written up from Amery's pocket book of engagements and contains remarks such as 'Attended Cabinet – I forget what about' (24 June). Extracts from letters to his wife have been used where these are more revealing.

Diary

15 May 1919: Received a deputation of Gibraltar native workmen . . . and was very much impressed by the need for trying to bring the place up to date in respect of social legislation, education, etc. if we can't do anything for them constitutionally. Personally I should like to bring these little places like Gibraltar and Malta directly into the United Kingdom.

L.S.A. to Mrs Amery

27 June 1919 (morning): Dined with Mrs Elinor Glyn (the girls and Rhys Williams made up the party) at the Berkeley. She is over to present the girls at Court today, and then hurries back to be present at the signing of the peace to which she is to be officially admitted as reporter – by what devious devices she wangled this out of L.G. I didn't ask, but according to her story L.G. gave a whole evening to her recently talking about her book.

27 June 1919 (evening): By the way I gathered at dinner last night that it was Lord M.'s enthusiastic praise that created Eleanor [*sic*] Glyn's new-found interest in me. She asked for a frank opinion on her book and I told her that it lacked structure.

28 June 1919: Lord M. comes back tomorrow by special train. I know he hates travelling with the PM and a big circus, and the idea of a cheering noisy welcome at Folkestone also repels him. I rather share his feelings, but it is a real weakness to him politically.

Diary

4 July 1919: Went to L.G.'s great Ministerial dinner. . . . L.G. looked radiantly happy, not proud or self-conscious but just like a child who was thoroughly enjoying himself.

L.S.A. to Mrs Amery

5 July 1919: The PM's dinner was a great function, some 70 of us sat down and there were quite a lot of members of HM Government whom I didn't know by sight! . . . After dinner L.G. made a nice little speech of thanks to his colleagues to thank them for their loyal help, etc. and specially coupled it with Bonar who rose amid great cheers and made a typically Bonarish little speech. . . . F.E. rose in response to many calls but was rather dull and tried to improve the occasion by a homily on the need for House of Lords reform.

6 July 1919: The Service this morning was very impressive though I was sorry they didn't have 'Oh God our help' or Arkwright's 'Oh Valiant Hearts', and did have 'Now thank we all our God' which is German both in tune and words and therefore not appropriate to my mind on such an occasion fine though it is.

10 July 1919: Hamar [Greenwood] has succeeded Steel-Maitland: everybody agrees he has done very well at the H[ome] O[ffice]* and I daresay he will do well in the Overseas Trade job, though in some ways it is not quite so much his *métier.* Johnny Baird goes off to HO, not really a good appointment because in the HO you must have nerve and decision in rows and Johnny gets too anxious and alarmed. I'm going in for gaiety tonight. Mrs Glyn is taking Lord M., Rhys Williams and myself to the play and I've asked them all to dine here first. The Glyn family seems to have taken to me greatly. . . . I'm not quite sure yet how much I like Mrs G. – I think she is really a very good sort when you get over or through the wicked looking surface.

Diary

17 July 1919: Down to the conference at 10.30 at the Colonial Ministry, Simon in the chair, Marconi and someone else for Italy, Beer and another for America, a Jap, and Baron something or other, and Count de Grunne for the Belgians. The Belgians stated their case and withdrew, and Beer then put up the arguments against Belgium having any part of East Africa. I expressed my agreement with them but said we were not anxious to press our claims against a small nation beyond what was essential from the point of view of the development of the communications and of the country. I must confess the Chief has been extraordinarily generous to the Belgians and I daresay it is really wise, though I expect we shall get pretty heavily attacked in Parliament. After the conference broke up I spent some time justifying to Beer our giving preference to mandated territories and then had some further talk with the Belgians, who were waiting outside, largely on the alternative scheme of getting the Portuguese out of North-Western Angola.

For nearly twenty years the so-called Mad Mullah had been in revolt in British Somaliland, now the northern part of Somalia. Despite heavy expenditure, he had resisted all attempts to suppress the revolt and Britain's wartime preoccupations had enabled him to occupy and fortify much of

*Where he had been Under Secretary.

the country. While the War Office took the view that success would entail the deployment of two or three divisions and the building of a railway, Amery urged that aeroplanes would be most effective in open country with no cover. Churchill, who was Secretary for Air as well as War, agreed and a dozen planes from Cairo dispersed the Mullah's forces in three weeks in January–February 1920 at a total cost, according to Amery (*My Political Life*, II, p. 202) of £77,000 (the year of the campaign was erroneously stated in the memoirs as 1921).

Diary

23 July 1919: Conference about the proposed Somaliland raid. The War Office and Air Ministry both urged that they could not do anything at present in view of shipping difficulties, Allenby's commitments, possible trouble in India, etc. Even a pure aviation scheme seemed ruled out. I suggested that the whole thing might be done by an airship cruising across from Cairo and the idea rather smiled on them, as also on Seely to whom I put it afterwards. Meanwhile the Air Ministry promised to draw up a scheme and if it comes to the worst we may accept Brancker's offer to organise it for us on a commercial business.

9 August 1919: Lunched with Lord M. and we decided that I *had* better go to Malta more particularly in view of Plumer's latest messages about the financial tangle the Island has got into.

13 August 1919: Longish conference with Lord M., Seely, Trenchard, and WO representative . . . to discuss an air expedition against the Mullah. Settled the matter in principle and the experiment may possibly be of immense value from the whole point of view of keeping order in the Empire at a reasonable cost. The air expedition in this case is likely to cost less than £60,000, whereas the War Office would prefer us to have a proper expedition next year at the cost of about £2,000,000 which I wager would end in achieving nothing. [L.S.A. holograph note, added 11 October 1919: 'L.G. agreed to this a few days ago.']

On 22 August Amery and his wife left for Malta on the SS *Lancashire*, which was carrying reinforcements to Palestine.

Diary

30 August 1919: We reached Malta in the early morning of the 30th, our ship stopping for just half an hour or so about a mile out while a launch came and took us off. On the launch were Robertson, the Lieut.-Governor, and Colonel Mercer, Plumer's ADC . . . Robertson seems to have had quite a shock at his first sight of us, having been prepared for something elderly like the Hewinses. He jumped at the opposite conclusion when he saw B. and myself in summer clothes and thought we had come out to Malta for our honeymoon. He expressed the appropriate incredulity at dinner that night when she told him of the two sons she had already got. The next fortnight was spent in going down to Valletta after breakfast every morning, where I had an office in the Palace and interviewed deputations, officials, elected members, chambers of commerce, etc., etc., all the morning and sometimes a good part of the afternoon. More usually we got back to lunch at Verdala [Plumer's house in the country] and spent the afternoon seeing some sight or object of interest.

Amery concluded at the end of his visit to Malta that the Imperial Government was to blame for Malta's financial situation. In his report he urged a substantial refund to the island from the Treasury, pending a settlement of financial relations, an immediate pay increase for the scandalously underpaid dockyard workers, and the encouragement of emigration. But the financial and economic situation, in his view, could not be dealt with unless there was a fresh start politically, and he urged that internal self-government should be conceded to the Maltese over a period of two to three years. Plumer endorsed this view.

Diary

22 September 1919: Dined with Lord Milner and had a good talk with him both about Malta and things in general. He agreed entirely with my main conclusions and is prepared to back them with the Cabinet before he goes. [Milner secured an immediate payment of £250,000 to Malta, but it took two years for the new constitution to be formally inaugurated, despite Milner's decision to do it in a single step.]

14 October 1919: I went and lunched at the Crown Agents' Office, a building in every way superior to the Colonial Office, as indeed most of the arrangements of the Office seemed to be. I am not sure that the real solution of the problem of organising the Colonial Office doesn't lie in transferring it to the Crown Agents.

15 October 1919: Told Lord M. how, like Christopher Columbus, I had discovered a new world in the Crown Agents' Office 200 yards from this doorstep. He was delighted with my discoveries but suggested we should say nothing about them till we could really make effective use of them.

23 October 1919: Dined at St Stephen's Club with Walter Faber, who is having a series of dinners for the discussion of the Home Rule problem organised for him by Hannon. Plunkett was there as the chief guest, also Hubert Gough and Colonel John Ward, just back from Siberia, next to whom I sat. It was rather interesting that Gough, Ward and I should all sit together when I look back on the great debate on the Curragh affair at which Ward and I went for each other over Gough. More interesting still was it to find Gough coming out in a speech in favour of Home Rule because the Irish were the worst soldiers in the field, which he attributed to want of national pride, while John Ward came out with a statement that he had been prepared to suppress Ulster before the war but wasn't prepared to do so today.

30 October 1919: Went to a further dinner of Faber's and spoke again, outlining a scheme for a single upper house and separate lower houses for Ireland, the powers to be those of a federal union in the United Kingdom but with the right for the whole of Ireland to have Dominion status when and if Ulster agrees. Plunkett got up afterwards and talked the most appalling nonsense. His idea is that the Irish Convention was on the eve of settling everything and would have produced a unanimous report (excepting for the misguided Ulstermen and Sinn Feiners – big exceptions) if F.E. hadn't made some remarks in America which annoyed most of the Nationalist members.

With the departure of his secretary for South Africa and the rush of work while Milner was absent on his mission to Egypt, Amery ceased to keep a diary. On 24 August 1920, however, he set down the following account of his period as acting Secretary of State.

Notes, 24 August 1920

I took over from Lord Milner about 20th November as far as my work was concerned, not actually occupying his room till he left, i.e. about 27th November. My position was regulated in accordance with the precedent set by Mr Chamberlain in the case of Lord Onslow; i.e. I acted for the Secretary of State in all matters, including submissions to HM, except those that required the final signature of a Secretary of State. I was summoned by the Cabinet to represent the Office whenever specifically Colonial Office questions arose, and somewhat intermittently also for general questions of foreign policy, e.g. Turkey, when I spoke strongly

THE LEO AMERY DIARIES

against the eviction of the Sultan from Constantinople, and such occasions as King's Speeches, etc. In the Cabinet summons, and elsewhere, I was usually described as Acting Secretary of State, but as a matter of fact, nothing definite was ever settled as to my exact description.

I found the sense of having a completely free hand very exhilarating – not that Lord Milner had imposed many restrictions on my discretion before, or had even questioned my decisions on the large number of matters I used to settle without reference to him – and the work not very much harder than being Under Secretary. I discussed all matters of any consequence personally with Fiddes, with whom I usually had half an hour every morning – I did not attempt to carry out my idea of having a sort of Colonial Office Council and settling most questions verbally with the heads of Departments at regular meetings, because I felt Lord Milner might not keep it going and it was anyhow my business to carry on for a few months and not to try and reorganise the office. I got on excellently with Fiddes – his shrewd, incisive judgment was a great help, especially if one did not feel obliged to agree, and he always fell in with my views if I differed and worked them out most loyally. Almost the first thing I did which raised me greatly in his opinion as a champion of the Colonial Office against any other was when I managed by seeing Henry Wilson to secure a reversal of the War Office decision to send us General Ironside as Inspector General of W[est] A[frica] F.F. and give us Lt. Col. Haywood instead, a less distinguished and much junior officer but one who knew West Africa well and whom the Office wanted. Lord Milner had abandoned the fight with the War Office and his last Minute was one acquiescing in Ironside, so that my taking it up again and winning greatly pleased old Fiddes.

Thornton was a great standby, especially in all matters where the Court had to be dealt with. He always took great pains to see that HM was properly informed and so, in spite of his rather brusque manner, he was a great favourite with Stamfordham and all the Royal entourage.

I had no little work with the Royal family, as it happened, during the next three months fixing up the arrangements for the Prince of Wales' tour to Australia and New Zealand. After a really great effort and repeated telegrams I induced Hughes to let the visit to New Zealand come first, as any other itinerary would have involved the Prince's visiting New Zealand in the middle of their winter. But this meant getting to New Zealand as early as possible, anyhow not later than the middle of April, and I thought both the Prince of Wales and Halsey understood this quite clearly and were ready to start in good time, i.e. by the beginning of March. Grigg certainly did and also made it clear at a lunch they both had with Lloyd George. However, later on the Prince felt he didn't want to go so early, in fact, wished to put off going till about 21st March, and put up

Halsey to argue both that this date was the one agreed on, and that the *Renown* couldn't be ready earlier. The latter business I cleared up quickly enough with Walter Long. The general question involved a whole series of long talks with the Prince whom I pressed very hard, both on this and on the question of Grigg's position versus Halsey – it being essential that Grigg should have complete control of all arrangements.

Quite apart from the narrative printed above, Amery's letters to his wife provide some substitute for the diary which does not begin again until March 1922.

L.S.A. to Mrs Amery

28 December 1919: ... read Ludendorff* for an hour or so: what stands out is that the Germans were beaten not because Foch was a better soldier than Ludendorff but because Lloyd George and Clemenceau were so infinitely bigger and more daemonic than anything the Germans had behind their front.

2 May 1920, (All Souls College, Oxford): [T.E.] Lawrence was in the smoking room too last night and very entertaining in his quiet shy way. He gets called at 11 a.m., never breakfasts or lunches and very rarely appears at dinner – a quaint elusive creature altogether.

7 June 1920: I had a good talk with Sir R[obert] Borden yesterday afternoon and dined and had a long and most intimate talk with Rowell, the leading Liberal member of the Cabinet who is keenly interested in Imperial constitutional problems. It is this getting into real personal touch with people here that makes so much difference, and would be worth the trip over quite apart from the West India Conference which is going well and will do good.

15 June 1920: There is a real hitch in the Conference, and the members of the Canadian Cabinet have suddenly got frightened of the whole thing for fear of its lending a handle to their political opponents who want a 50% preference with England. I am seeing Sir R[obert] Borden after dinner and will do what I can with him, but I confess I am anxious that the whole thing may have a lame conclusion. . . . My West Indian colleagues had arranged a little dinner to express their appreciation of my efforts for them, and now I fear it may be rather a piano little affair.

*Erich Ludendorff, *My War Memoirs* (1919), English edition published by Hutchinson.

9 August 1920: Just been sitting with House and W[orthington] Evans and Pollock and Craig all discussing Mrs Asquith's 'revelations'* and unanimous – disapproval of her vulgarity and snobbery. The Polish situation is the chief topic of course: House of Commons unanimously against any active intervention and I don't think L.G.'s statement tomorrow will go against that feeling.

Throughout 1920 the idea of the Empire Settlement Bill had remained alive. Early in June Milner asked the Cabinet to agree to its early introduction and he renewed his request in July. The Cabinet agreed that it should be introduced 'forthwith' – once the parliamentary recess was over and the Treasury and Colonial Office had settled 'certain points of detail'. Late in November the two departments were still at work on the Financial Resolution and White Paper, but on 6 December Amery wrote that there was 'no chance of Bill being introduced this session'. The previous month, however, the Cabinet had agreed to extend the free passage scheme for ex-servicemen for a year, and on the same day as Amery's note the Cabinet agreed to negotiations with the Dominions to 'formulate a scheme for assisted emigration on a large scale, for submission to the Cabinet'. Austen Chamberlain was later to protest that in the specific proposals cabled to the Dominions late in December Milner and Amery had exceeded Cabinet authority, but he had agreed to spend £2 million a year, and Amery was quick to translate this into £1 million for passage assistance and another for advances to settlers. Amery's settlement conference met from 20 January to 4 February 1921, and he took the initiative on land settlement schemes. His officials were already negotiating one such scheme with Western Australia, and the Treasury was far from happy with the result. Winston Churchill, Milner's successor as Colonial Secretary, encouraged the Dominions therefore to bring forward schemes to the Imperial Conference scheduled for the summer of 1921 and on 6 May, with Churchill's full backing, Amery urged the Cabinet to endorse the recommendations of his Conference as the basis for the Conference discussion. Policy he wrote, should aim at the redistribution of the Empire's population so as 'best . . . to promote development, stability and defence', and he urged the importance of British aid to land settlement lest the Dominions 'reach the limit of their powers to absorb our unemployed or other classes'. The treasury for its part insisted that nothing should be done until the Conference had met.

By then, with Milner's decision to leave the Colonial Office and his replacement by Churchill, Amery had been appointed Parliamentary and Financial Secretary to the Admiralty, a job which once again made him

*In *The Autobiography of Margot Asquith* (1920).

principal Commons spokesman for his department since the First Lord, Lord Lee of Fareham, was a peer.

Milner to L.S.A., 26 February 1921

The interruption . . . this morning prevented me from giving you a piece of news about myself, which I should not like you and Florence to learn from the newspapers. It is that I am not going abroad alone but with Lady Edward Cecil, to whom I shall be married tomorrow morning.

I hope you managed to see Bonar today and had a satisfactory interview. I fear that I may have given you a wrong impression about him. He is not unfriendly to you, but he is a queer fishlike sort of creature and does not seem to take a warm personal interest in anybody. My only regret in leaving office is, that I feel I am leaving you rather alone, among people who have very little real sympathy with the things which we both most care about. I have not the least doubt that you will ultimately get your proper recognition, but I should certainly have been much happier if you had come to your own at this stage. As things are, I incline to think that it would be best for you to take the Admiralty, though it will be a great loss to the CO.

At the Admiralty Amery was almost at once involved in the 'searching examination of current expenditure' demanded by the Chancellor of the Exchequer on 9 May.* He had not had a great deal of time to learn 'the financial business of a vast and complicated industrial, transport and personnel organisation' (*My Political Life*, II, p. 215). By a minute scrutiny the Sketch Estimates for 1922–3 were brought down from £88 million to £82 million and a further million of savings had been found by the time the estimates were put to the Geddes Committee in August.

Just before Amery joined the Admiralty, however, an inquiry by the Committee of Imperial Defence into the future of the capital ship had concluded in effect that there was no adequate evidence that it was obsolete. The sub-committee had been evenly divided: Bonar Law, Horne and Geddes admitting that they could reach no conclusion on the evidence before them while Churchill, Long and Beatty insisted that to maintain equality with any other naval power four new capital ships should be laid down without delay. The issue of the four 'Super-*Hoods*' went therefore to the Cabinet, and a compromise was reached. In addition to estimates totalling just under £80 million, £2½ million was approved for the replacement of obsolete ships, but no details of the ships to be built were to be announced until the Standing Defence Committee of the CID had con-

*Adm. 167/64; CP 2919.

cluded its review of the RAF's role in Imperial defence. It reported finally on 26 July, but a decision on the four battleships still hung fire. In part no doubt this was because the United States had on 8 July invited the powers to a disarmament conference at Washington.

Lee had put the case for four battle cruisers and for four battleships to follow to the Conference early in July, and there was a powerful argument, voiced by Churchill among others, to approve their construction to improve Britain's bargaining position at the conference table. That argument eventually prevailed and the go-ahead was finally given in October. Serious doubts about the step had been voiced, however, in the Commons at the beginning of August when Amery had the unenviable task of introducing a supplementary estimate for nearly £12 million – and that despite the peremptory instruction given to his predecessor on 16 March that there were to be no supplementary estimates. With powerful help from Churchill, Amery secured his vote, but Churchill's argument implied that the battle cruisers were to be a bargaining counter, and that proved to be the case. In November work on the 'Super-*Hoods*' was suspended and in February the orders placed for them were cancelled.

The Washington Conference replaced the Anglo-Japanese alliance with a tripartite agreement between Britain, the United States and Japan while the naval treaties agreed there limited the total tonnage of battleships and aircraft carriers permitted to each nation, regulated the size of battleships and established a ratio of 5:5:3 between the three powers. There was to be a ten-year building holiday so far as capital ships were concerned, but Britain was specifically permitted to complete two new 35,000-ton battleships, the *Nelson* and *Rodney*. It fell to Amery to introduce the much reduced estimates for 1922–3 on 16 March, totalling just under £65 million, and to boast of the lead given to the world by the Washington Conference. Later in the year, during June and July, Amery piloted the Naval Treaties Bill through the House of Commons.

In speaking of the Washington Conference Amery had claimed that it gave 'increasing proof of the capacity of the British Empire under its new organisation, to unite in, and give effect to a single Imperial policy'.* In one respect, however, 1921 and its Imperial Conference had been disappointing. Amery and Smuts had corresponded about the need to turn it into a constitutional conference, and Smuts had produced a detailed memorandum about the Commonwealth concept on which he asked Amery to comment (see letter, 20 June 1921). But when it came to the Conference, Hughes, the Australian Prime Minister, was able to prevent it from being discussed. Nevertheless Amery's letter of 20 June shows how far embarked already he was on the road which led to the Balfour Declar-

Hansard (16 March 1922), vol. 151, cols. 2409–2528.

ation in 1926. Both the memorandum and letter subsequently passed into the hands of Hertzog and led directly to the Amery–Hertzog correspondence, which began in 1924 and continued until the eve of the 1926 Imperial Conference. Amery's views were his own – they had been embodied earlier in memoranda prepared for the 1921 Conference – and differed from those of Smuts in the stress laid on the unifying role of the Crown in the Commonwealth. Nor did Amery share the South African's desire to try to compress the Commonwealth idea into a single formula. Amery aimed rather to emphasise the autonomy and equality of the Dominions by removing all constitutional anomalies and that seems to be why he spoke of 'certain general declaration of constitutional rights' rather than 'the general declaration of constitutional right', which was in fact the suggestion from Duncan Hall, endorsed by Smuts in 1921.

The major event of the year politically was the signing of the Irish Treaty in December 1921, by which Ireland (Ulster remaining free to stand outside) was conceded independence, but as a Dominion within the Commonwealth. There was to be an oath of allegiance, Canadian in form and practice, and a boundary commission should Ulster stand out. Safeguards important to the Admiralty were included: in time of war Britain might reoccupy key ports, and Ireland would at most share in her coastal defence. 'Granted from strength after the definite suppression of armed resistance,' Amery thought 'there might have been much to be said for such a solution' (*My Political Life*, II, p. 230). He had watched with resentment the opening of negotiations just when the efforts of his brother-in-law, Hamar Greenwood, to suppress the rebellion seemed on the point of success, and in after years he remembered 'the sense of shame and indignation with which I walked out of the House after the announcement' (*My Political Life*, II, p. 231). There is no record of his reaction in the letters to his wife, although his concern can be gauged from the reference to the Annual Conference of the Conservative Party at Liverpool. This had been crucial for the Coalition Government since the die-hard element in the Conservative Party intended to challenge the Government's Irish policy and had been encouraged by the knowledge that Austen Chamberlain's predecessor as leader of the Conservative Party, Bonar Law, had just attacked any attempt to coerce Ulster into accepting unity with the rest of Ireland. In the event the pressures for Party unity prevailed. The most hostile motions were withdrawn, and a critical resolution successfully amended, but the overwhelming vote for continuing the negotiations concealed a deep undercurrent of feeling against the Coalition and a determination to defend Ulster.* When the Irish Treaty resulted in civil war and not a settlement, the Conservative Party nursed

*Cf. Salisbury to Law, 18 November 1921, printed in Lord Beaverbrook, *The Decline and Fall of Lloyd George* (Collins, 1963), pp. 119–20.

a corrosive bitterness against the Coalition which proved a major factor in its downfall.

There is no evidence that Amery considered resignation. Bonar Law's endorsement of the treaty (and Ulster's exclusion from it) appeared to exclude the possibility of effective revolt, and he had the Empire Settlement Bill to get through. But his discussion with Birkenhead on 8 January does not suggest that he was contemplating a break. Lloyd George was contemplating an immediate election, and the press was full of inspired rumours to that effect. In the end the project was nipped in the bud by the hostility of the Conservative Party Organisation and its chairman, Sir George Younger.

In his memoirs Amery noted another possible reason for remaining in office, the necessity of dealing with the Geddes Report on National Expenditure, which proposed substantial cuts in naval expenditure of £21 million. In the absence of Lord Lee, who was still at the Washington Conference, Amery and Beatty, the First Sea Lord, had to deal with the proposition. The account in Amery's memoirs is for once not quite accurate. The Cabinet appointed Churchill to chair a Cabinet committee to go into the proposals; this met for the first time on 9 January and reported on 4 February. The Board of Admiralty forwarded as a result of their deliberations on 10 January a full statement of the reductions they regarded as acceptable and there followed detailed discussions which led eventually to a reduction of the naval estimates from £81 million to £62 million. Churchill paid tribute to the Admiralty for their efforts, and although he singled out Beatty, it is only fair to add that as Parliamentary and Financial Secretary Amery must have been responsible for much of the work done on the case Beatty presented so effectively.

The Geddes Report was to be published on 10 February with a rider that the Government was not bound by its recommendations. Contrary to the statement in his memoirs, Amery was not present at the Cabinet which decided on publication. This met on 6 February (not 10 February, as Amery suggests). However, it seems probable that Amery was the first to see the possibilities inherent in the rider to the decision that 'Ministers should be free to take such steps as they might deem advisable to rebut any reflections made on their Departments by the Report',* since Beatty clearly thought that no reply to Geddes was going to be published.† The rejoinder was drafted by Amery and Sir Oswyn Murray and issued on the same day as the report. Amery escaped with a private rebuke from a shocked Austen Chamberlain, who had publicly to defend the publication as being in accord with Government policy.

*Cab. 23/29, p. 101.

†Letter to his wife, 7 February 1922, printed in W. S. Chalmers, *Life and Letters of David Beatty* (Hodder and Stoughton, 1952), p. 371.

The Cabinet discussed the report on 15 and 17 February. Amery was present with Lee at both meetings, the first of which was very acrimonious, not least because of the publication of the Admiralty rejoinder. Amery told the Cabinet that the true savings suggested by Geddes had amounted to £7 million only, but that Geddes's arithmetic would have been accepted as correct had no rejoinder been issued. A letter of 18 February describes the second and more amicable meeting, as a result of which a further paper was put in to the Cabinet making it clear that few extra economies could be found.* On 24 February the Cabinet met and finally ratified the Naval estimates. Amery presented them to the House on 16 March 1922.†

L.S.A. to Mrs Amery, 1 April 1921

I came in from a lovely spring walk round the fields this morning . . . found the PM's letter which I enclose and I leave the CO with rather a sinking heart at the thought of what may become of so many of my pet schemes, but on the whole satisfied that I am doing right and that a big new chapter of work to learn and do is opening. The CO chapter must have its continuation later on, meanwhile I must try and draw up a list of some of the things that most want doing for Winston in the hope that he may prove a useful executor. And anyhow, if I haven't achieved a quarter of all I wanted at the CO I expect, looking back, that there has been quite a useful total of really new things done, as well as all the usual things kept going in a keen and sympathetic spirit. . . .

I am glad [Sir Herbert Richmond] is here and we have already had a great talk (without sitting up till morning hours) on naval problems. My feeling is that I am more made for First Lord than for Financial Secretary but as the H. of C. representative I think I am sure to have some say in strategy, training and high policy generally.

L.S.A. to Smuts, 20 June 1921

I have read your draft Memorandum with the greatest interest and with complete agreement on the main points. Working separately it seems that we have both arrived at more or less identical conclusions, not only on questions of principle but also of actual machinery, and that is at any rate not unhopeful as to the feasibility of what we advocate.

I entirely agree with you that it is desirable not only to secure at the forthcoming Constitutional Conference certain general declarations of

*CP 3765 (22 February), Adm. 116/1776.

†*Hansard*, vol. 151, cols. 2409-2528.

constitutional right, as Duncan Hall suggests, but also to frame the draft of those declarations now at the present Prime Ministers' Conference and have it in circulation during the next 12 months, in order to focus public opinion in the Empire. While we do not want anything in the nature of a fixed or written constitution for the British Commonwealth, we do want a general agreement and public understanding on fundamentals, and not always to be questioning these afresh or pulling our institutions up by the roots. The suggested declarations would have that desired effect and the process of constitutional evolution would then go on both as between the different parts of the Empire, and in each part of the Empire severally, without further questioning of the underlying fabric.

These declarations would, of course, include an affirmation not only of the complete independence and equality of the several partners but also of the indissoluble unity of all of them under King and Crown. That is the issue which you have recently fought so successfully in South Africa. But in your anxiety to lay stress on the other aspect – the one which requires action and a measure of re-organisation – you have omitted to mention it in the draft Memorandum. I think it would make it rather more complete in itself, and more acceptable to the Members of the Conference, if you put in a few sentences making that clear.

The peculiar characteristic, it seems to me, of the British Empire is the combination of the complete independence of its parts (at any rate of the self-governing parts) as political entities and the underlying unity based on the fact that these independent political units are composed equally of British subjects and have thus a common and interchangeable citizenship, and that the same Crown is an integral part in the constitutional frame-work of each. The unity created by the Crown is an inherent constitutional unity and not a mere accidental and personal connection. The relation is quite different to that between say England and Hanover a century ago, or even Austria and Hungary up to the other day. In those cases the Crowns are separate even though they happen to be worn by the same Monarch, and the identity of the Monarch did not make a Hanoverian a British subject or a Hungarian an Austrian subject. With us not only the King but the Crown and the status of British subject are one. That status may be limited from the point of view of citizenship in various parts of the Empire by restrictions as to franchise, immigration, etc., etc., but fundamentally it remains one everywhere, and this is of course one of the greatest assets of belonging to the British Commonwealth. It means that each member of it can aspire to not only the ordinary rights of citizenship in other parts of the Empire but to its very highest posts. Nothing could be more typical of this community of citizenship than the fact that you, while a South African Minister, were actually for a time also a member of the British War Cabinet or the converse fact, that you picked a member of the British House of Commons as one of South Africa's representatives at the Assembly of the League of Nations. . . .

As regards the machinery for co-operation my conclusions are the same as yours. We require an enlarged Imperial Conference which ought to be a Conference of Parliamentary delegations and no longer a Conference of Governments only, to discuss with the fullest publicity broad fundamental matters of common interest, not only questions of constitutional right but of defence, trade, shipping, etc. in so far as they can be discussed in the general aspects and embodied in broad resolutions. Under present conditions of communications, I do not think you can summon this body conveniently more than once in 4 years. In the interval you would carry on firstly with the Prime Ministers' Conference or Imperial Cabinet, meeting not less often than once in two years, and the Imperial Committee or Commission sitting more or less continuously, though with no doubt a frequently changing personnel.

L.S.A. to Mrs Amery

13 July 1921: This morning I carried my Overseas Settlement business a stage further at a Committee presided over by Winston. Lunched at a gathering of Unionist Members at House, a series of lunches to enable backbench Members to meet Ministers in general and Austen [Chamberlain].

19 July 1921: We haven't got a Cabinet decision for our 4 Capital Ships and if we don't get it there will be no end of a row – if so you must be there to hear as I shall have to be a central figure. However the odds are we shall get our way.

1 August 1921: I feel fearfully lazy and not in the least in the mood for a speech on Naval Estimates or anything else, but perhaps I may wake up by Wednesday.

17 August 1921: Have just got through my reply on the Naval Officers' Marriage Allowance (11 p.m.), my last bit of parliamentary work for the session. I thought I was rather halting and not as clear as I wished to be but [H.A.L.] Fisher seems to have told Austen that it was excellent and Austen beamed and expressed approval when he came in. So I think he will now consider that I am reasonably capable of answering in debate as well as of making a set statement.

19 August 1921: Talk with Arthur Lee [then First Lord of the Admiralty]. He has strained himself badly, hernia, caused by tennis he thinks and has got to go into a home on Tuesday, for an operation which will keep him laid up till the beginning of October. He had an operation for stone in lieu of his holiday last summer and now this – it really is too bad luck. . . . Anyhow that puts an end to the *Enchantress* [the Admiralty yacht] part of my summer holiday.

16 November 1921: Lunched with Neville and Annie [Chamberlain] and had a long talk with Neville over Ireland and persuaded him to modify a resolution he is bringing before the B[irmingham] Unionist Management Committee this evening. Liverpool [where the Conservative Annual Conference was to meet] will be interesting. I am very anxious to judge the *real* feeling of the Party, not the mere voting – but I have no doubt the Government can satisfactorily deal with the dissidents.

8 January 1922 (Buffet, Gare du Nord, Paris): I didn't join F.E. and Co. till after Chur – we dined together and talked till about midnight or later: politics, classical quotations, college reminiscences. His classical memory is wonderfully good – quite as good as mine in Latin, though not in Greek. He never goes to bed till after 2 or sleeps more than 5 hours and that gives him a lot of time for reading and work which my sleepier nature doesn't! He is immensely pleased with his recent achievements especially with a judgment on 'Contributory Negligence' which Finlay pronounced a permanent contribution to jurisprudence. But he won't connect these triumphs with his year of sobriety and is, I fear, drinking much more than is good for him – and I noticed a shade of anxiety in Lady F.E.'s reference to the subject. He is rather in favour of a general election soon, but not dogmatically or violently. His trouble with Hamar [Greenwood] was simply that Hamar against his express advice and entreaties, and after promising not to do anything without consulting him, sacked Campbell the Lord Chancellor of Ireland in order to put in Ross, an inferior man. He is very bitter against Simon, as always, and was very anxious to know if Simon had said anything to me about him. Happily I could truthfully reply in the negative as far as I myself was concerned. He told me he had recently said to Austen that I ought to be in the Cabinet, and that A. had heartily concurred. He also added that it was absurd that Horne was where he was when I was a better man in every respect. His explanation of Horne is that L.G. does not like to put strong and possibly difficult men in the posts of real power and looked on Horne as tame and useful. For a while L.G. consulted no one but Horne, Balfour and Austen, whereupon F.E., Winston and Curzon put their heads together and blocked everything in the Cabinet for three weeks till L.G. climbed down and changed his advisers!

10 January 1922 (London): I got back only just in time for the new Winston Committee to go into the Geddes Report, as it affects the fighting depts., started on the Admiralty yesterday – Winston is understanding and not unsympathetic and we shall come out not too badly. There is a growing volume of feeling against the election idea and I hope we may defeat it.

17 February 1922: We had a long Irish day in the House – the whole position is very unsatisfactory but we are all, I fear, committed to this crazy treaty.

18 February 1922: I went with Lee to the Cabinet yesterday to have a first class tussle with Horne over our figures. But L.G. cunningly stopped the discussion at the outset and said we should never convince each other, and appealed to the Admiralty to see if they could possibly do any more. So we have a few days in which to think over it and see if we can scrape a bit more here and there. I don't believe we can.

9

The Fall of the Coalition
1922

Amery's diary entries begin again in March 1922. He gives no indication of why he should have resumed his earlier practice, nor is there any mention in the entry for 12 March that he has done so. There may well have been earlier entries therefore that had disappeared by the time he came to bind the diaries in volume form.

From the entries which follow one can trace the corrosive effect of the continued violence in Ireland on the fortunes of the Coalition. Amery had acquiesced reluctantly to the Treaty which conferred Dominion status on Southern Ireland, but, in common with the Conservative die-hards, he watched with dismay the events which followed.

The Irish Dáil did not approve the Treaty until 8 January 1922 and then by the narrow margin of sixty-four votes to fifty-seven. De Valera at once resigned as President of the Dáil and was not re-elected. Michael Collins took over as the head of a Provisional Government pledged to carry out the terms of the Treaty. The evacuation of British troops began at once and there even seemed some hope of an agreement between the Irish Free State and Ulster. This foundered on the question of modifications to the border and there was renewed tension, which shortly gave place to a terrorist campaign against Ulster, waged by the IRA. Churchill protested privately to Collins and Arthur Griffith about the course of events and late in March invited Craig and Collins to London to meet under his auspices; the meeting took place on 29 and 30 March and reached full agreement. Lord Hugh Cecil denounced the agreement as a 'statue of snow' and it is evident that Amery shared his scepticism.

The Irish Free State Bill became law on 31 March, but at once rebellion threatened in Ireland. De Valera denounced the legality of both the Provisional and Northern Governments. The British Government agreed that they 'could not allow the Republican flag to fly in Ireland' and that if Collins could not restore order, they must do so. On 12 April Churchill made a personal appeal to Collins, which embodied this warning. Next day, Rory O'Connor and a large force of armed Republicans seized the

Four Courts – the Law Courts of Dublin – and held them against the Provisional forces. In England the violence and the continued murders of Loyalists aroused considerable anger which was accentuated when Collins and De Valera negotiated in May for 'an agreed election'. In Ulster Sir James Craig announced that whatever the Boundary Commission established by the Irish Treaty should decide, there would be no change in the border.

Further talks which Churchill had with Collins late in May led to a Cabinet decision to accept the result of the Irish election. On 31 May Churchill appealed to the House of Commons to show patience towards the efforts of the Provisional Government, but he repeated also the Government's hostility to any form of Republic in the South, and in answer to Henry Wilson made clear that in such an event the British would hold Dublin as a preliminary to military operations. 'The House was decidedly sceptical', Henry Wilson noted in his diary, and the Republican seizure of Pettigo and Belleek across the border together with the early drafts of the Free State constitution – described by Lloyd George as 'purely republican in character' – seemed to give them cause.

Early in June British troops recaptured Pettigo and Belleek, but this did not hold up the negotiations on the draft constitution. Agreement was reached and the revised draft published on 16 June; that same day the Irish election resulted in a victory for Collins and the Treaty. There followed a struggle between the Free State and Republican forces. The patience of the Conservative backbenchers, already strained, came near breaking point on 22 June when Henry Wilson was shot dead on the steps of his house by two Irishmen after returning from unveiling the War Memorial at Liverpool Street Station. Meeting that day, Lloyd George, Austen Chamberlain, Churchill and Shortt concluded that they must force Collins to destroy the power of the Republicans and in particular to recapture the Four Courts. Churchill made public the substance of the warning, which in private they had already given to Collins on 26 June, the day of Henry Wilson's funeral. Bonar Law endorsed the warning but there was a clear threat in his speech, lent emphasis by his words to Churchill that evening: 'You have disarmed us today. If you act up to your words, well and good, but if not . . .'*

On 28 June the attack on the Four Courts began and two days later O'Connor surrendered and was shot. The fighting in Dublin continued until 5 July, but it was evident that the Provisional Government were determined to vindicate their authority. By the middle of August they had largely done so. The struggle, however, lasted into the winter, well

*W. S. Churchill, *The Aftermath*.

beyond the fall of Lloyd George's Government, but on 6 December the Free State came into existence.

In September Amery's concern with Ireland fades under the impact of a fresh crisis, this time fatal for the Coalition. Lloyd George had backed Greek aspirations in the Near East. The peace treaty with Turkey concluded at Sèvres in 1920 had handed to the Greeks Smyrna and its hinterland, East and West Thrace, Gallipoli and most of the Aegean islands. The Dardanelles, Bosphorus and the Sea of Marmora had been declared an international waterway. Kemal Ataturk and the Turkish nationalists had never accepted the Treaty and established a Government at Ankara. January 1921 had seen the Greek advance into Anatolia checked, but an attempt to revise the Treaty of Sèvres by agreement broke down in the face of Kemalist demands that they should control Smyrna, the Straits and Constantinople. Without telling Curzon, Lloyd George encouraged the Greeks to launch a fresh offensive, which came within an ace of taking Ankara. Defeated there in August 1921, the Greeks retreated and stood on the defensive. In August 1922 Kemal in his turn launched an offensive and tumbled the Greeks into the sea. The holocaust at Smyrna on 13 September marked the end of Greek hopes of empire and all that stood between the victorious Turk and control of the Straits were twelve battalions of troops under the command of Sir Charles Harington, stationed in the neutral zone securing freedom of passage through the Straits.

The Cabinet on 15 September decided that the neutral zone should be defended by force, and asked by telegram for support and reinforcement from the Dominions. They decided also that the public must be told and on 16 September Churchill and Lloyd George drafted a communiqué for the press embodying the substance of their decisions. In Canada, Australia and New Zealand the communiqué was published before the telegraphed appeal to them had been decoded, and this caused a great deal of resentment. In the end only New Zealand and Newfoundland responded favourably to the Government's appeal. In England the *Daily Mail* headline STOP THIS NEW WAR in all probability encapsulated public feeling, and the Conservative Party, by tradition pro-Turk, found the idea of unilateral involvement in a war against them intolerable. On 18 September the French and Italian Governments withdrew their contingents from the defence of the neutral zone and all Curzon's diplomatic skill was needed to persuade them into a joint proposal for an international conference at which, it was made clear, Constantinople and East Thrace would be conceded to the Turks. This invitation was despatched on the 23rd, but as the days passed without a reply tension mounted. On 29 September the Government decided upon an ultimatum to Kemal, which Harington, confident that there could be successful negotiations, refused to deliver.

The Cabinet, although angry, acquiesced finally in his decision on 1 October and the danger of war receded. It took ten days to arrange the Mudania Convention which allowed the Turks possession of Eastern Thrace after a brief delay while the Allies retained Constantinople and the neutral zone, pending a formal peace treaty.

At the height of the crisis, on 17 September, the leading members of the Government (meeting at Chequers) had decided on an early election, to the evident dismay of the Conservative Chief Whip, Sir Leslie Wilson, and Sir George Younger, the Chairman of the Party Organisation. Further discussion of the question was deferred during the crisis, but there seems to have been some Conservative suspicion that a fresh 'khaki' election was intended. On 10 October the Conservative members of the Cabinet agreed to an early dissolution, Baldwin and the Chief Whip alone dissenting. At a further meeting on the 12th Boscawen joined them, and on the same day Austen Chamberlain wrote to Birkenhead that they might have to take the matter to a Party meeting.

Historians, perhaps prompted a little too much by Beaverbrook, have seen in a letter Bonar Law wrote to *The Times* on 7 October a declaration against the Government. It finds no mention in Amery's diary and was construed by Austen Chamberlain as support for the Government. But whatever the letter's intent, it provoked appeals to Bonar Law to return to the leadership and led him to consider his position. The negotiations which followed need not be detailed here.*

While the major interest of Amery's diary in these months is the light it throws on the break-up of the Coalition, it documents also his own involvement departmentally in the aftermath to the Geddes Axe, princi- pally in settling the terms of compensation for the officers and men who were compulsorily retired from the Services. He was concerned also with instituting airship development. There are references also to the consequences of the Washington Naval Treaty, which led to the scrapping of twelve capital ships and twenty-seven submarines, a reduction in the Atlantic Fleet's destroyer flotillas, the abolition of two home commands, and a major reduction in both Naval and dockyard personnel. The four battle cruisers approved in 1921 were abandoned and two 35,000-ton battleships, the *Nelson* and *Rodney*, substituted although they were not to be laid down until 1922, and then only after a constant battle against 'economists' elsewhere in the Government.

Finally Amery's work for Empire settlement reached its culmination. Perhaps prompted by Amery the Australian Prime Minister had in November 1921 asked Britain to pay half the interest on a £50 million

*For further details see Robert Blake, *The Unknown Prime Minister* (Eyre and Spottiswoode, 1955), and Keith Middlemas and John Barnes, *Baldwin. A Biography* (Weidenfeld and Nicolson, 1969).

development loan. The Overseas Settlement Committee backed the request on 30 November, recommending a short Bill which would allocate £4 to £5 million a year to overseas settlement including this proposal. Amery told Churchill that the idea meant large, quick outlays which would have an immediate impact on unemployment. Churchill was already well disposed to the scheme, and so too were the Board of Trade and Sir Alfred Mond, chairman of the Cabinet Unemployment Committee. On 8 December Mond suggested that Amery should raise the question of overseas settlement at his Committee and Amery did so. Although the Treasury were hostile, the Chancellor, Sir Robert Horne, was not and after a conference with Amery, he put the subject on the Cabinet agenda. Late in December 1921 the Overseas Settlement Committee put its case for the draft Bill which Amery had already begun to prepare. This endorsed Hughes' proposal as well as migration assistance. 'On 16 February, the Cabinet', as Professor Drummond notes, 'was still waiting to hear from the Geddes Committee' on whom, no doubt, the Treasury were pinning a great deal of hope. But Geddes failed them. He gave Empire settlement qualified approval, and on 24 February the Cabinet, deciding only that £5 million was too much, referred the matter to a committee. With Amery and Horne in agreement on principle, the detail could be compromised: £1½ million in the first year and £3 million a year for the next fourteen, while the principle of interest sharing, despite Horne's departmental opposition, was included in the Bill. The Home Affairs Committee agreed to the immediate introduction of the Bill on 4 April, and it passed through the House of Commons almost without debate.

Amery proceeded at once to cable Hughes and to write to Mackenzie King, seeking to generate projects, but the only immediate interest was from Western Australia and Victoria. Financing agreements for their land settlement schemes were, as Amery's diary indicates, settled without undue delay and the UK and Commonwealth Government agreed an assisted passage scheme. Canada, despite Amery's efforts, was less than helpful, but the British Government, faced with heavy unemployment, would not be checked. It set up a committee on trade policy in July, but Amery warned them that until the current negotiations were complete, further initiatives by the British Government would be superfluous. Instead he urged aid to Imperial shipping and transport. But with the collapse of the Lloyd George Government the trade policy committee lapsed, and the ground seemed clear for the more ambitious schemes of Empire development which Amery had in the middle of 1922 urged on his masters in the Cabinet.

Diary

12 March 1922: Lunched with Grigg at Vincent Square. His view is that the PM ought to resign and he has apparently been telling him so hard. He thinks the old politics largely dead and the public much more influenced by personalities. Once L.G. dropped current work and came before the country he would carry all the fluctuating mass of people with him. I would have agreed if L.G. at this moment had got anything in the nature of a policy or even a definite cry. . . . The Creedys . . . came to dinner . . . apparently the WO were rather buzzing with the notion that Worthy [Worthington Evans] might go to the India Office and I take his place. Sundry papers had been running that or pushing me for the India Office myself, but I felt certain it would go to Peel if Derby and Devonshire refused.

13 March 1922: Meeting of Baldwin's Committee on Terms of Compensation for Officers and men turned out of the Services. I am glad to say he is thoroughly sympathetic and I trust that we shall get reasonable terms. I am specially anxious that the terms for the men should not be, in principle, worse than those for officers.

17 March 1922: First result of the new reduced programme is that the whole of the Industrial North came up in a deputation to the PM which Lee received.

21 March 1922: Lunched at the Hotel Cecil with Sir J. Connolly and a large crowd to meet Sir James Mitchell, the Premier of Western Australia. I sat next to Mitchell who was almost speechless with a bad cold. The gist of his conversation was that if only we could take the lead and tell Western Australia what to do and how to do it, they would do their best to play up but that it was really a little absurd that we should take the line that because 300,000 people had been given self-government in an area of a million square miles we should disinterest ourselves in the possibilities of development of that area. He appears to have come over here mainly to see me but the trouble is that while all these people think that I am in a position to do great things for them, I cannot get a move on when the Cabinet or rather Horne, whom the Cabinet appointed Chairman of a Sub-Committee to look into my Bill, simply won't convene the Sub-Committee. I tried to tackle him yesterday but he only gets cross and almost tearful when anything involving expenditure is mentioned.

27 March 1922: A long discussion at the W. Australia Offices with Sir

J. Connolly, Mitchell, Stevensons and others on the W. Australian scheme. Mitchell is incredibly inarticulate and incoherent in exposition but I believe the scheme is really a sound one and I should think he had a good business head in action. We lunched there and continued the discussion until nearly 3. After questions I had a short conference with Baldwin and [G.F.] Stanley on our Naval compensation terms and at the time secured complete acquiescence from Stanley as to the reasonableness of our terms as compared with the Army terms in spite of the fact that they are higher. But I had misgivings about him knowing the family instability and was not surprised when he came out two days later with an Army protest against our terms.

30 March 1922: Conference at the Treasury of Horne's Cabinet Committee on the Empire Settlement Bill. Both Winston and Worthy [Worthington Evans] were kept away by the Irish Peace negotiations and I had only Mond to back me which he did rather less effectively than I had hoped. The Treasury began with a very negative attitude treating the two millions previously promised as a maximum and suggested that practically nothing should be spent this coming year. I fought stoutly for my proposed 5 millions maximum and eventually came down to 4, but when Mond concurred with Horne in thinking three sufficient, I was beaten and accepted the inevitable. However, if it is much less than I hoped, it is as much as I expected and I think I can make a fair beginning with it. The Treasury also wanted to put in a time limit of 5 years. I insisted that 15 years was the least period that would fulfil the Conference demands for a permanent scheme and carried my point. . . . At dinner Gwynne urged me to come out of the Coalition and lead the true Conservatives. His thesis is that every Unionist who remains in contact with L.G. is ruined sooner or later. The Die-hards according to him are quite willing to take us all back save only F.E., whom they cannot forgive.

31 March 1922: The newspapers full of the new Irish Settlement which as far as I can see contains only one element of certainty, viz. that the British taxpayer should contribute £500,000 to relief in Belfast. As a typical contrast to all this optimism I found on arrival at the office a telegram describing how a ship load of munitions being transferred from Haulbow line to Devonport was captured by IRA raiders on the high seas, taken to Ballycottin Bay and 80 tons [L.S.A. holograph note: 'Proved to be much less.'] of munitions taken out of her and conveyed away by lorry before destroyers arrived on the scene. This is quite enough to weigh down the scales against Collins and his shadow government. So far nobody seems to have lifted up their voice at this office as to who should be punished for sending the ship load out unprotected.

5 April 1922:   Had quite an interesting talk with [H.A.L.] Fisher about our colleagues in the Government. He puts the PM, Winston and F.E. in a class by themselves, and is inclined to put F.E.'s abilities highest of the three for sheer brain power. Austen he considers good second class, a highly finished parliamentarian. Milner he was inclined to put into the same class on the ground that he could never command public enthusiasm. I demurred pointing out the wonderful enthusiasm he excited in S. Africa but admitted that he could never win his way to the top though if by chance put there he might have held the country and enthused it. Fisher said that what had impressed him most since he had been in the Cabinet was the importance of physique. He doubted if anyone, except by a fluke, could get to the top without tremendous physical strength and staying power. He felt himself that he was physically below par to be a real match for the work or to be able to enforce his views.

11 April 1922:   Long meeting of Baldwin's Committee, ministers only, in his room at end of which he appealed to me whether I could make at any rate some further concessions, but if they did not satisfy the Treasury, might at any rate enable him strongly to support us before the Cabinet. I went back and discussed this with the Second Sea Lord and suggested a slight further reduction of the Lieutenants and a partial revision of the scale for ratings by which one way or another some £200,000 could be saved. [L.S.A. holograph note: 'This was eventually accepted and the Navy owe me some gratitude for having secured such fair terms at so difficult a time. Baldwin a great help.']

27 April 1922:   Press generally backed me very well over the Bill and I hope they won't turn round later.

3 May 1922:   Went to the War Office to see a cinema film of the destruction of old battleships by bombs from the air; interesting but did not prove more than that ships could be sunk if the aeroplanes bombed long enough and flew low enough. It proved nothing as to the value of air bombing under war conditions.

10 May 1922:   To the Cabinet which accepted the Compensation scheme without alteration. . . . Dined at home but went back to the House afterwards for the finish of a discussion on the kidnapping of [three British] officers in Ireland. A good many outside professed Die-hards voted against the Government this time and they will be joined by many more if this sort of thing continues indefinitely.

25 May 1922:   Received a letter from the PM telling me that HM had been pleased to make me a P[rivy] C[ouncillor]. Austen had mentioned to me some weeks ago that he was putting my name forward though he was not quite certain as to whether it would be accepted and Leslie [Wilson, the Conservative Chief Whip] had also told me that he had declined to have his own name put forward unless mine was in the list too. [L.S.A. holograph note: 'I hear Austen was really rather sticky and wooden about it, and that George Younger insisted that it was long over-due.']

31 May 1922: Heard Winston make his interim statement on the Irish situation, an admirably well arranged and well balanced performance, very moderate in its wording, so much so that the House as a whole rather missed underlying seriousness and threat of action. Collins, Griffith and Co. were up in the Gallery. The interesting feature of the debate was the intervention of Fitzroy, Lane Fox and the other moderate Unionists to tell the Government that things had really gone far enough and that it must put its foot down. The Irish situation has now reached the critical point and I fancy we are within a few days of a complete break-down of the famous Treaty. Whether the tactical advantages of having made the Treaty will ever compensate for the far worse mess which we shall have to face now, remains to be seen. I only hope that my original prophecy on the day on which the Treaty was signed, namely that it would lead to war with the United States, will not be fulfilled.

1 June 1922: Irish situation I hear increasingly critical. The constitution handed in by them quite unacceptable and in spite of vague expressions of desire to fulfil the Treaty no real evidence of either the will or capacity to do so. Collins going back to Ireland when he will no doubt fall under the De Valera influence and atmosphere, Griffith almost alone in realising the seriousness of the whole position.

3 June 1922: [L.S.A. holograph]: My name in Birthday Honours – but alongside of J. B. Robinson and some other shockers.*

17 June 1922: Admiralty Board to consider the site of the future Naval War Memorial. The Committee recommended the Temple Arch on the Embankment and I have no doubt that short of taking over the whole of Trafalgar Square that will be the best. Beatty however is keen on a Britannia or other symbolic object to be stuck on the top of the Admiralty

---

*Written presumably on 11 August. Robinson was a South African financier of dubious reputation, and his honour was one of those questioned in the controversy of 17 July 1922 about the sale of honours.

Arch. [L.S.A. holograph note: 'A subsequent effort by Beatty to get HM to give up York column and put Britannia in the Duke's place was coldly received!']

20 June 1922: Duly kissed his Majesty's hand and a little red Testament and became a member of the Privy Council, . . . Arthur Balfour and Munro were there, the former in his delightful vagueness quite surprised to find that I was being sworn in and that I was not already a member of the Council.

22 June 1922: Down to the House hearing just before the end of questions of Henry Wilson's assassination. The whole House very much upset and adjourned at once. I have lost one of my best friends and his death raises in my mind again all the doubts I have felt about the whole hateful Irish business. I cannot help feeling that it is to these very men we have handed over Ireland.

23 June 1922: Down to the House at Question Time and found Members in a very angry mood with the Government and in particular Shortt [then Home Secretary]. There is no doubt that Henry's murder has given a definite impetus to the growing dissatisfaction of the moderate Unionist with the whole of the scuttle policy. For the first time there is a general feeling even among those who have supported the Treaty that we should have insisted on maintaining order till the Treaty was confirmed by the passing of a proper constitution. After lunch Gwynne of the *Morning Post* tackled me and appealed to me very strongly to break with the Government and lead the Die-hards and asked me whether I did not ask myself every morning when I was shaving what business I had to stay on. I could have replied that is precisely the question I have been asking myself most mornings since last December, but I thought it wiser to say nothing.

26 June 1922: [Wilson's funeral.] The crowds were wonderful both in numbers and demeanour and the service deeply moving, the Last Post more particularly. . . . A very crowded and tense House assembled for the Irish discussion and I have no doubt that but for Churchill's very definite concluding threat that no more nonsense is to be allowed in the shape of IRA at the Four Courts, etc., the Government would have been very roughly handled, if not turned out. Later on Baird and I had a talk with Stanley Baldwin, all of us having felt very much the same for some time past and decided we were bound to give the Government another two or three weeks' trial. After Churchill's speech the position from our point of view was still more cleared up by a speech from Bonar thoroughly facing both ways in manner but in substance very definite and practically telling the Government that this was their last chance.

27 June 1922: Going up to the House I met L.G. in the lobby going to hear Balfour in the House of Lords and he offered to take me round for the first time to the steps of the Throne as a PC. We stood together sometimes listening to Balfour and Grey, and *à propos* of my telling him a story of the dinner where five of us independently put to him, Milner, Henry and Hankey in the same order as the men most responsible for winning the war, he showed me a letter from Henry to himself in 1919 in terms of the greatest affection saying that he had been more responsible for winning the war than anyone else. He also told me that he had a very friendly letter from Henry quite recently. He evidently feels very keenly the sort of attack made on him by the *Morning Post.*

7 July 1922: Introduced the [Washington] Naval Treaties Bill in a short matter-of-fact speech for which Asquith applauded me but Elliott and certain others complained. They had evidently hoped for a good deal of general 'flapdoodle' by Cabinet Ministers and protested that the matter was not being treated seriously. In reply I said that action is the best test of seriousness and that a live shell from a gun of minor calibre was worth much more than many salvoes of blank ammunition from all the big guns of the Cabinet. Much laughter from Lloyd George who had happened to come in just before this and sat behind me. [L.S.A. holograph note: 'L.G. retorted *sotto voce* – so he told me later – you look more like a trench mortar!']

20 July 1922: Conference between Austen and the Junior Unionist Ministers who spoke their minds to him very freely about L.G. and the Party position generally. I re-asserted my policy and insisted that that policy had to be economic and Imperial. I cannot say that I met with much support on the particular question of economic policy: they are all so frightened of reviving Tariff Reform lest it should upset some of the Lancashire members. It looks to me as if we should have to get on to definite party lines first before we can get a less wobbly attitude.

21 July 1922: Lee told me afterwards that the PM and Horne really mean to have a serious go at getting rid of the two capital ships and that he means to make it quite clear that the Board will stand no nonsense but will go out in a body rather than submit to that.

23 July 1922: Devonshire House at Roehampton for lunch and tennis.

. . . There was no one at lunch besides Lee, Lady Lee being seedy, who afterwards showed me the memoranda we are sending in on the Naval control of our air service, and a very stiff letter he has sent to the PM to make it quite clear that we mean to stick to the capital ships. There is some sort of intrigue between him [Lloyd George] and Horne at this moment to drop the ships and pocket most of the money appeasing the country with a few more aeroplanes but it won't come to anything. [L.S.A. holograph note: 'The latest development of the attack on the ships is a scheme by Winston to have one built at Devonport which would involve 18 months' delay. I think we shall defeat that also.']

24 July 1922: The PM told me in the Division Lobby that he wanted me to take only a short holiday and take Winston's place on a committee over which the whole problem of trade and employment, my part being to explore all the possibilities from the point of view of both Empire trade and settlement.

26 July 1922: First meeting of Airships Committee. . . . Locker-Lampson brought down Burney to my room and I told him the main points on which we should wish to have evidence from him and put him off from submitting a paper containing very much exaggerated claims for the airship as a fighting weapon. . . . Talk with George Younger about the meeting of Unionist Cabinet Members to whom Austen had related the proceedings of his conference with the Junior Ministers. Apparently it is all very inconclusive. [L.S.A. holograph note: 'Chief decision not to decide anything before October.']

31 July 1922: Airship Committee from 10–12 to consider my draft report. It was evident that the Air Ministry people disagree with my general conclusion and were likely to be supported by the War Office. However, I got them to put off discussing the conclusion while we worried through the report paragraph by paragraph and by dint of a few small concessions I got them up to the edge of the final conclusion before we separated. . . . At 6 the Airship Committee reassembled in my room at the House and by dint of qualifying sentences here and there and obstinately sticking to my main points an exhausted committee finally accepted the conclusions in their original form, which was on the whole preferable, that the Admiralty should consider whether it could find enough out of its estimates in order to make a commercial scheme possible, and that failing that the Admiralty and Air Ministry should both contribute something to research on service lines and that at any rate the existing air stations should be kept.

1 August 1922: Went to the first meeting of L.G.'s Trade Committee at 10 Downing Street and found to my surprise that everybody had been supposed to prepare memoranda saying what great things they could do and that there was only a skimpy little memoranda from the CO about which L.G. was very contemptuous and I gather quite cross with me for not having something more ambitious. A lot of inconclusive discussion with no attempt to get near the real question of principle which is whether we should continue the policy of deflation and economies or go in for a policy of development and employment regardless of the Budget.

2 August 1922: Meeting of Junior Ministers to discuss who should be their spokesman and what lines should [be] taken at the meeting with the Unionist Cabinet Ministers next day. I again expressed my view that the issue was really one of policy and that unless the Prime Minister were really personally anxious to resign it would have to be on policy if at all that any cleavage could take place. However, I agreed that it would do no harm their putting the case for the difficulties of the position in the constituencies if no decisions were taken before October.

3 August 1922: From 6 till nearly 8 we were at a meeting of Unionist Ministers. The case was introduced quite temperately and fairly by Sanders, Pike Pease, Gilmour and Pollock and then Austen asked F.E. to reply. F.E. began by rating them for their impertinence in having asked for a meeting at all when they had already been informed of the Cabinet Member's [*sic*] views, and went on in the most astonishingly arrogant and offensive manner to lecture them for their silliness and want of loyalty. I could see them all bristling more and more with every sentence. . . . Whatever chances F.E. may have had of the Unionist leadership of the future are not likely to have survived this unfortunate performance. A.J.B. tried to make amends by a conciliatory speech pointing out that only difference of policy could justify any action and that no shade of such a difference existed. I held my peace not wishing at that particular moment to emphasise my own conviction that the difference of policy does exist both retrospectively on Ireland and prospectively on the fiscal question. Austen wound up with a few rather pontifical sentences and we dispersed, most of the Juniors spluttering in indignation.

24 August 1922: [On holiday in Switzerland] Walked with [H.A.L.] Fisher and discussed the state of the Government, etc. He feels he could serve under Balfour much more easily than under Bonar or Austen if L.G. went, which he has more than once urged him to do. He thinks Co Libs may return 50 strong, I said they might be [L.S.A. wrote '20 or 30 strong' presumably meaning to write 'stronger' and deleted it subsequently writing in the margin 'much stronger'] if L.G. were not PM for Unionists will vote for them as supporters of a Unionist PM who would not under present conditions.

12 September 1922: Back to the office. . . . Had some talk with Lee who has been pretty seedy during his holiday. He is full of his impressions of the Turkish situation. The Greek collapse has now put an end to Lloyd George's disastrous Near Eastern policy – perhaps it is not fair to blame it on Lloyd George alone as Balfour and Curzon – not to speak of smaller men like Philip Kerr and Mark Sykes – were equally crazy. If only Milner could have pressed more vigorously for the saner views on which we were agreed in 1919.

13 September 1922: Conference with the First Lord to discuss line to be taken with Churchill's Economy Committee. A message reached me from L.G. through Grigg that he thinks I ought to concentrate on the Imperial side of the T[rade] P[olicy] Committee rather than go to Canada. He does not realise of course that there is practically nothing on the TP Committee that is not covered by the proposed alteration of the Trade Facilities Act, or realise in the least the importance of the work I could do in Canada.

14 September 1922: At 3.30 attended the Churchill Committee. Churchill very hectoring about his proposal to postpone one of the battleships. I left soon after 4 to catch the Birmingham train, thinking that part of the discussion was over. I heard afterwards that he kept going at it the whole time and had been very rude and overbearing to the Controller [Third Sea Lord, responsible for all Naval construction] till the latter finally shut him up. If I had known I should have stayed to keep him in order.

18 September 1922: Came up and read with stupefaction and no little annoyance the latest *pronunciamento* about the Turkish crisis, with its challenging tone, and its very dubious appeal to the Dominions. I have heard since that the document was mostly Winston's, as perhaps I ought to have guessed, and as far as I can make out the appeal to the Dominions has been reasonably well received and may not have done much harm. But the whole thing is unfortunate as we are bound to climb down and hand over Constantinople and Eastern Thrace to the Kemalists, just saving our faces as best we can over the Straits. The final collapse of L.G.'s Near Eastern policy will I think weaken him greatly and may strengthen the movement for independence in the Unionist Party. . . . After hanging about all day I at last saw L.G. just before dinner. He was very friendly and did not object to my going to Canada on principle but insisted that it was necessary first of all to work out a great scheme for Empire Development. He talked about a 100 million loan, said he was discussing it with Milner, etc. I mildly tried to suggest that such a loan could only be profitably spent over a considerable period of years and that surveys, etc. would be required before new railways could be constructed, but he waved all this on one side. I daresay I may be able to work out something with Stevenson of the CO as well as with the Indian Railways. But these sudden bold head-line plans are really very trying.

19 September 1922: Talk . . . with Worthy [Worthington Evans] who had not much to suggest as he is too full up with the Eastern situation. He is advising strongly that we should clear out of Constantinople and confine ourselves to Chanak and Gallipoli, holding these points till Kemal makes a satisfactory arrangement about the Straits. He is also prepared to let the Turks have Eastern Thrace. This is perhaps the most sensible way out but Heaven knows what may happen in Constantinople and it is certainly very hard on the Greeks if we abandon Constantinople to Kemalists when we would not have allowed them [the Greeks] to enter.

20 September 1922: Walked home in the evening with Edward Wood and discussed affairs generally. He is now definitely of the opinion that the Government had much better break up and thinks that the breakdown of L.G.'s Eastern Policy will hasten the process.

27 September 1922: Dined at the Conservative [Club?] with George Younger and Willie Bridgeman and heard from the former all about the schemes which have been on foot for an election before the National Union Conference, and the queering of the pitch by the Turkish crisis. He has urged Austen if they do have an early election to call a special conference of the same composition as the National Union to avoid the charge of having tricked the latter. Meanwhile he has got Austen's assurance that he will call the Junior Ministers as well as the Seniors into council on the whole question in the next week or so. Afterwards Worthy joined us and when the other two departed I had some talk with him alone. The Eastern situation is still very critical and even if we do mobilise the two divisions, which is all we can produce, can barely hold Chanak, and do nothing else. I said if it was war we should obviously co-operate with the Greeks in Western Thrace and that it by no means followed from their recent skedaddle that the Greeks would not fight well in Europe on a narrow front and with even the slightest British stiffening. He also mentioned the danger of the French handing over to the Turks all the dumps of rifles, etc. in Allied charge in Constantinople if we evacuate.

I told him that it was quite essential that Harrington [*sic*, i.e. Sir Charles Harington] should in that case replace the French guard by British even if it had to be done forcibly in order to destroy the arms. I gather from him that if the Turkish question really settles down in a few days that the possibility of an election may still crop up. Anyhow it will be decided one way or another before the 13th for which date I am still holding my booking for Canada.

2 October 1922: Peel told me that things had been desperately anxious on Saturday and Sunday and very near war. The danger in this sort of situation is Winston who is always perfectly intoxicated at the thought of war and was visibly disappointed when the more pacific telegrams came in. F.E. seems to be in the same lot and Scatters [i.e. Wilson] told me that he had freely expressed himself at a dinner table as to the desirability of war. They are really a dangerous couple and all the more so because of Winston's influence over L.G.

3 October 1922: Peel still very anxious at the attitude of Winston, F.E., and other colleagues who he fears mean to make trouble over the Greek evacuation of Thrace. Happily Venizelos seems to acquiesce in the idea himself so I do not think that any of our fire-eaters will want to go beyond him.

10 October 1922: Spent three quarters of an hour hanging about 10 Downing Street to see if the PM would give me an answer about my going to Canada or not and finally got a message to say that I had better wait till the Near Eastern situation cleared up as it might in a day or two. Went on from there to Austen. He strongly urged me not to go but proceeded to develop his general thesis which is that in order to defeat Labour it is necessary to have a Coalition, that the only possible Coalition is the existing one and that neither he nor any of his colleagues are prepared to suggest to the PM that he should go, or that the Coalition should be modified to make room for a Unionist Prime Minister. He thought that the only thing was for all Unionists in a responsible position to stand together and urge this upon the Party in the hope that they would at any rate in the great majority of cases fall into line. If his advice were not accepted he would not continue to lead. His view is to have the election as quickly as possible. I might add that this was after a meeting of the Cabinet in the afternoon at which he expressed the same views and seems to have been more or less supported by most of them. The only one who took a definite line against him being Baldwin. I do not think Austen yet realises the position in the Party or the fact that in the present temper of the country the half is a great deal more than the whole, i.e.

that the Unionist Party is likely to get more seats standing on its own than the whole Coalition are likely to get standing together.

12 October 1922: Lunched at the Carlton and had a good talk with Baldwin who told me all about the Unionist Cabinet Ministers' meeting on Tuesday. He even talked about resigning at once but I told him that he ought not to do anything before the General Meeting of Ministers next Monday. . . . Short talk with Lord Milner about the crisis. He is quite resolved not to join a new Government himself though he is quite prepared to support it from without.

13 October 1922: I went round after breakfast to have a talk with Bonar. I found him very pessimistic about the Party, convinced that nothing would avert a break up and fearing a long exclusion from office, something like the fate of the Party after the break between Peel and Disraeli. He favoured my compromise of election as two Parties leaving the question of Coalition and of its terms open until after the election. He did not think that the Unionist malcontents would accept it. I said that on the contrary I thought that the Party as a whole would readily accept it but that Austen and his colleagues would regard it as simply another way of giving L.G. notice to quit. He urged us not to be precipitate about resignations even if Austen proves very intractable on Monday, but to hang on for a bit trusting to the chapter of accidents. He thought that L.G., if he resigned now, would be in a position of equal power within 12 months, whether he chose to throw in his lot with the Unionists or to unite the Liberals under his leadership, but he feared that his pugnacity would lead him to ignore the fact that there is at this moment a real tide running which no leader could stem and which it would be useless for Austen to try and stem. He is evidently very anxious not to be thought to try and queer Austen's pitch, but he will obviously take the leadership if he is asked. . . . Lunched at the Carlton with Lloyd Greame, Pike Pease, Leslie and King. All of them in very intractable mood, more particularly Philip [Lloyd Greame]. I suggested that we Juniors ought to meet on Monday before and possibly after the Party Meeting and it was arranged that I should summon them all to lunch at the Metropole. . . . The evening papers presently showed that Austen is sticking to his guns and making a big bogey of the Labour peril. I do not think the speech will cut much ice. What is true – as B. keeps on urging – is that a great many people abroad and in the Dominions, and not a few at home, will be puzzled as to why the crisis should have arisen just at the moment when the Government has on the whole covered itself with credit by its handling of the Eastern situation.

14 October 1922: Lunched at the Carlton and had further talk with Lloyd Greame and others; all agreed regarding Chamberlain's speech unfortunate both in substance and in detail, e.g. the reference to Labour as the common foe. *Telegraphed asking all my Junior colleagues to lunch on Monday (Or did I do so on the 13th?)** Lloyd Greame and I had tea with Baldwin and heard such further news as he had to tell us. There was some sign of weakening on Austen's part with regard to consulting the Party and he seems to have written a letter to F.E. to that effect. Baldwin also told us that not only Boscawen and Peel but Curzon would go if it were decided to have an immediate election without consultation. . . . Had a Turkish bath and read L.G.'s speech while cooling. My first impression was that the tone of the references both to our Allies and to the Turks make it quite impossible to secure reasonable settlement of the Eastern situation while he remains PM, and that is my own opinion though so far apparently the papers have not made much of it. I imagine that there will be a real flare up in the French press during the next few days. As for the rest, the speech was perplexing and might have meant anything, retirement, service under Balfour, or a straight fight for the Premiership. On the whole I concluded it meant the latter. Dined at home and worked out figures for a memorandum on foreign trade for the TP Committee in which I restated the case for protection in a more controversial manner and from the point of view of the changed situation.

15 October 1922: Walked round to Hamar [Greenwood]'s and had a long talk with him. . . . He had seen L.G. in the morning and is convinced that he regards the whole thing as a personal intrigue against him and is determined to fight for all he is worth. Hamar much depressed by the whole business, cannot see any difference in principle between the two wings and much regrets that a more determined effort was not made to form a central party earlier, but does not think that L.G. can go back to the Wee Frees.† He thinks that the Wee Frees will disappear and individually creep back into L.G.'s Party, if he remains separate.

16 October 1922: Together 17 of us assembled at the lunch at the Metropole [London] which I had convened, and after lunch we got to business. Leslie Wilson first summed up the course of events in the last month beginning with the mid-September decision at Chequers to rush an election, and anticipate the National Union, down to the dinner at Churchill's house on the night of the 15th since which has come the further decision to hold a meeting of the Unionist Members of the House

---

*Italicised passages added much later, that in parentheses in the early 1950s, and the other probably post-war.

†i.e. the Independent Liberals, led by Asquith.

of Commons. After that I circulated a sort of questionnaire that I had prepared to see if we could agree upon some sort of compromise on the lines of the two Parties going to election separately, leaving the terms of Coalition to be settled by the results of the election. Most of them present thought this too vague and finally we all agreed unanimously upon the following formula to be recommended to our Seniors that evening and to represent what we should recommend to the Party Meeting on Thursday: 'That the Unionist Party, while welcoming the co-operation, during and after the forthcoming General Election, of any party with which it may be in substantial agreement, shall go to the country as an independent party, and that the leader of the Unionist Party shall be prepared to accept the responsibility of forming a Government if the Unionist Party after the election should be the largest party in the House of Commons.' I confess, knowing the point of view of Ernest Pollock and one or two others I was surprised that they were so unanimous on a stronger form of wording than I had contemplated, and was not altogether unprepared for defections. This happened quickly enough when we came to the main meeting at 5. Austen led off with a general appeal for unity and then propounded his formula which was that we should go to the country as a Coalition Government, Members individually however going as Conservatives or Liberals without a Coalition label, and leaving the question of the reconstruction of the Government quite vague. I followed, and as briefly as I could, stated the conclusions we had come to, explaining that for the sake of being clear as to what our views really were, we had tried to lay them down in definite language. Austen was indignant and wanted to know if this was an ultimatum which we had decided upon before even hearing what he had to recommend. Of course I disclaimed this but before I could even say three words Pollock chipped in to explain that not only was that not meant but that he unreservedly accepted Austen's solution and he was subsequently more or less backed by Leslie Scott and Gibbs, while the rest of us tried by question and answer to find out what Austen's formula meant. We pressed him repeatedly to tell us whether as ministers we should be free to say that we wanted a Unionist Prime Minister, or even as Mike [Mitchell-] Thompson put it, hoped for a Unionist Prime Minister. Austen's main plea was that it was essential to keep the situation open, and F.E. chimed in to say that it was more probable that the Prime Minister after the election would not be L.G., whereas we took up the line that by saying nothing ministers would be more committed than ever to the Prime Minister and indeed that there was no argument against displacing him today which would not be infinitely stronger after the election. (More than one of us has since been told from the inner circle that the idea is for L.G. to assert his position by winning his victory and then resigning in favour of Austen.) I intervened pretty frequently and I am afraid Austen, who always takes things personally, was hurt that I should have taken a lead in the matter at all. We separated about 7 and we Juniors agreed to meet again next morning. I went home with Edward Wood and Baldwin, the latter told me that everything depended upon whether Bonar's doctor would agree that he was well enough to undertake the strain of leadership if he was called on. I hear he examined him once yesterday and said he would have another examination today. I rang up Boscawen late at Baldwin's suggestion to ask him to come to the Junior Ministers' meeting to-morrow and he asked me to come round after dinner. So I went and had a talk with him, his views coinciding very much with Baldwin's. He also told me that Curzon is very much inclined to the same conclusion, especially after L.G.'s outburst at Manchester [see entry for 14 October]. My mind during the course of the evening turned round the possibility of accepting Austen's formula as one which private Members could interpret as they liked, and becoming a private Member before the election. The difficulty of this is that if all of us should agree to do this together Austen's resignation would still follow and a break would not be avoided.

17 October 1922: All of us Juniors together with Baldwin and Boscawen and George Younger met at Leslie Wilson's room at the Treasury at 11.30 and had a long discussion as to our personal positions, whether we should resign or what we should do. Baldwin spoke briefly but with very great feeling to the effect that he himself could never serve under L.G. again; Boscawen was pretty much to the same effect and during the meeting went out to see Curzon, who I gather shared his views, but was not certain whether he would give voice to them. Gilmour pressed very emphatically and earnestly the point that it was no use going out into the wilderness unless there was someone prepared to lead us and wanted to know when we could hear definitely about Bonar. Pollock pleaded earnestly for peace, suggesting as a way out that we might make another appeal to Austen to hold an emergency meeting of the National Unionist Association as well as the meeting of the House of Commons Members and he, Gilmour and Edward Wood went down in the evening as a deputation on that subject. I gather that the main theme of the deputation did not come to anything but that they really spent their time discussing what a minister could say at the next election about L.G. without being bound first of all to resign. Before the meeting Locker-Lampson had come to see me to say that Austen was very much hurt by my uncompromising attitude the day before and I asked him to let me see Austen later in the day which indeed I wanted to do in any case. He, Oliver, told me he was sure the great majority of the Party would be swung by the appeal of Austen and F.E. and Balfour: I do not think he realises at all how intense the feeling against F.E. is. He also spoke much about the difficulties in Birmingham. . . . I went in to see Austen about 5.45 for a few minutes. He was as usual altogether on the question of personal obligation and loyalty. I told him that the line I had taken on Monday was not due to any desire to present him with an ultimatum. On the contrary I thought it was a compromise and a way out, but that I had not seen in his proposal anything that will be accepted by the Party as really leaving the position open in fact and would not mean the continuance of the present regime. I also briefly discussed with him the real differences of principle, Near East, appeal to the Dominions, and above all preference and protection, which affected me. The last he seemed to think an almost absurd scruple and I think he has really dismissed his father's policy from his mind entirely. His last appeal to me was to try and see if I could not meet in some way in finding a solution, he having done all the advance so far. This morning (18th) B. showed me a letter from him in which he expresses the same sort of view and I took occasion to write back and once more make it clear that I was trying to secure unity under his leadership, but that the solution must be a real one. Dined with Larkin, the Canadian High Commissioner . . . I sat next to Beaverbrook and had at intervals some quiet talk about the whole position. He felt that the first thing that ought to be aimed at was to keep the Party together and thought that possibly the difficulty might be met by having a Party meeting immediately after the Election. I at once jumped at the idea which seemed to me to solve everything at any rate in the sense of keeping the Party together and avoiding Austen's resignation if he were prepared to accept it as he ought to be if he really meant what he said about keeping the position open. It would at any rate be in a position acceptable to all the rank and file if not to Ministers. Whether Ministers could exercise the freedom of the rank and file and say that they would hold out for a Unionist Prime Minister after the election without resigning is another matter. However, that is a minor point and even if it might be more agreeable for some of us to resign definitely before the election it might be fairer to Austen in order to avoid the embarrassment of a number of us doing so at once, to stay on against a reasonable freedom.

18 October 1922: Meeting of our lot at 10 o'clock. I took up my plan at once (though I gather that the idea had also occurred to George Younger), and urged it very strongly upon them and after half an hour's discussion we were unanimous about it. I also raised the further point whether we could as Ministers stay on if we made it clear that we only did so to avoid embarrassing the Government and to show our readiness to accept responsibility for the past provided that we could speak with reasonable freedom about the future. We were not perhaps altogether agreed on this and left it for further discussion in the evening. Meanwhile I urged that whatever we did we should all do the same. . . . Leslie went off to see Austen about it and I dashed back to the office to dictate my form of words for Baldwin who was lunching with Bonar and wanted to discuss it with him. While I was actually dictating Leslie rang up to say that Austen had accepted it. This was indeed good news and may mean that we shall get through tomorrow with a united Party. . . .

Lunched at the Carlton which is now like a beehive in swarming time and talked with a great many people. My advice to all was to concentrate on the proposed solution and keep the Party united. . . . Oliver Locker-Lampson came up [to the office] and I gathered from him that Austen was meeting F.E. and other colleagues and reading between the lines of what he said concluded that F.E. would not agree to the proposal for consultation after the election. Presently Edward Wood picked me up and we walked as far as Victoria discussing our position and both concluded that if the compromise were accepted we were still personally bound to resign. Dinner at home. . . . Philip [Lloyd Greame] and I deserted the party early to go to a further crisis meeting in Stanley Baldwin's room where we first heard a report from Sam Hoare as to an interview he had had with Austen as a deputation from Pretyman and others who had been meeting in the afternoon. From what he said of Austen's temper and the absence of any reference to the possibility of a meeting after the election I concluded my suspicions were probably well founded and that Austen had been made to go back on the idea. We also heard about Bonar that he had been in such a state of perturbation about the whole business that though his Doctor had pronounced him fit for at least two years' hard work, he had actually drafted a letter to his local chairman announcing that he was going out of politics altogether. It was only with the greatest difficulty that he was persuaded to tear up the letter and go to the meeting. We had a great deal of desultory talk but in view of the complete uncertainty of what Austen would say or what was likely to happen, we all decided to hold our hands but meet immediately after the main discussion.

19 October 1922: The meeting opened at 11 and the much greater volume of cheering for Bonar than for Austen was an indication which way the wind was blowing. Austen opened with a very set speech on the Birmingham lines and it was very soon evident that he had gone back on the proposed compromise [L.S.A. holograph note: 'F.E. and, I believe, Balfour talked him out of it.'] – the idea underlying his remarks being apparently that it was not for Unionists alone to decide the question of Prime Ministership after an election in which they had enjoyed Liberal support. The speech received rather a cold welcome, and Baldwin who followed with a short speech to the effect that he did not want the

PM's dynamic force to break up the Unionist Party as it had broken up the Liberal, got a much greater reception. Pretyman then introduced his resolution in favour of the independence of the Party in a reasonable speech, followed by quite a good one from Lane Fox, Mildmay and Craik whom nobody wanted to hear. There were continuous shouts for Bonar and he pulled himself up and after one of his characteristic soliloquizing speeches made it quite clear that the Party ought to come out of the Coalition and go to the election with a mind to winning on its own. This evoked tremendous enthusiasm and settled the business, the meeting listening with patience but without conviction to a philosophic analysis by Balfour. I rather wanted to answer Balfour's statement that no difference of principle divided us but Austen said he wanted to close proceedings though subsequently let Leslie get up just to put, rather like Baldwin, the views of some of us. [L.S.A. holograph note: 'Leslie really jumped up without asking Austen and A. was very angry about it.']

There was some suggestion about adjournment but the sense of the meeting was for an immediate vote and it was put not on any resolution of Austen's but on Pretyman's resolution. A good many abstained who did not exactly like the wording, while others voted against it from their dislike of a vote of want of confidence in the leader, but it was carried by 186 to 87. Austen briefly thanked them all for their support and friendship and a painful morning came to an end. As a matter of fact the actual result from the point of view of Party unity is much better than would have happened if we had agreed upon the suggested compromise. Presumably Lloyd George will now resign and Bonar form the Unionist Government to which the whole Party will rally. I do not see why he should even have a General Election, which after all was only to have been rushed in order to dodge the National Union. However we shall see.

[Later] went to a [Admiralty] Board Meeting at which Lee made a very nice little farewell speech except for one remark in which he spoke of those who had 'engineered' the business. The PM has resigned and gone to the Palace and I suppose Bonar will be sent for tonight or tomorrow morning. . . . We went round to the Athenaeum [after dinner] to have a talk with Lord Milner who is very pleased at the turn things have taken and thinks it a unique chance for the country to have something of leadership from younger men; his one anxiety was that the old crowd in the Party should preclude themselves from being invited to join at once (this morning's manifesto has secured that!). On my way home I looked in for a few minutes on Stanley Baldwin, very happy over the result. I suggested to him that it would be in every way a good move and heal present battling if Bonar could invite Neville Chamberlain to be Minister of Health or Labour for both of which posts he is eminently fitted. I also suggested to him Mackinder as Minister of Education or

Board of Trade. He also discussed briefly the pros and cons of a General Election at once while the country is clamouring for alternative Government or waiting to meet the National Union, deal with the Turkish affair, etc. So ends a varied chapter, the last year of it increasingly unsatisfactory from my point of view and evidently so from that of the Party, and I think the elections will show, the country.

IO

Bonar Law and Baldwin
1922–3

The break-up of the Coalition resulted in both a new Government and a general election. There was no certainty that Bonar Law's Government would win, much less that it would have an overall majority, and there was a good deal of co-operation with the Coalition Liberals. Only 144 of these came into the field, and only 24 of them intervened where there had not been a non-Conservative Coalition candidate in 1918. Kinnear* asserts that the Conservatives and Lloyd George Liberals conflicted in 55 seats and co-operated in 160. More striking still was the benevolence shown by the Chairman of the Conservative Party Organisation to the Asquithean Liberals. Bonar Law himself took good care to leave every option open for an anti-socialist arrangement after the election. Amery had wanted the Colonial Office, but it was offered first to a former Speaker, Ullswater, whose prestige, it was hoped, would ease the Irish Treaty legislation through in December. Baldwin too was second choice for the Exchequer, the post being offered first to the Liberal McKenna. Another Liberal, Lord Novar, found a place in the Cabinet. Linking together die-hards, free traders, protectionists and those supporters of Austen Chamberlain who would serve, the new Government could not afford to raise divisive issues like the tariff, and indeed concentrated on creating an atmosphere of 'honesty, simplicity and balance'.† There was in all Parties a remarkable disposition to avoid issues, and a celebrated *Punch* cartoon pictured the Party leaders with variants of the same slogan, peace and retrenchment, or, as Bonar Law put it, 'tranquillity'.

At the last moment Amery was transferred from the Colonial Office to the Admiralty – it was felt wrong to leave both the major Service departments in the hands of peers – but this did not prevent him from advocating the calling of an early Imperial Economic Conference, and, together with the Duke of Devonshire and Lloyd Greame, he amended the draft agenda prepared by an interdepartmental committee, and had the

*M. Kinnear, *The Fall of Lloyd George: The Political Crisis of 1922* (Macmillan, 1973).

†R. R. James, *Memoirs of a Conservative* (Weidenfeld and Nicolson, 1969), p. 154.

satisfaction of seeing this amended draft go through the Cabinet without change. It was at his insistence that overseas settlement was added to external commercial relations and co-operation in the development of the Empire's resources as the principal subjects for discussion. The proposed agenda was forwarded to the Dominions on 29 November.

By then the election had been fought and won. It was at Amery's suggestion that the tariff issue was played down, rather more perhaps than Bonar Law at first wanted,* but Amery's drafting of the relevant passage in the manifesto was intended to leave the Government a free hand. However it was Bonar Law who on 7 November pledged the Government to no fundamental change in fiscal policy in the new Parliament, a pledge which led directly to the disastrous election of December 1923. Amery kept no diary during the campaign, perhaps because of the very active part he played in it, and the two-page summary he wrote after the end of the campaign throws no light on Law's decision. Nor did he at once resume his diary once the campaign was over. From 18 November to 8 December the entries are rarely more than terse summaries made after the event on the basis of a pocket diary in which it seems evident he had recorded little more than his daily engagements.

The new Government faced a number of problems. Indeed Amery had not been able to attend his own election count because the Cabinet had been summoned to discuss the Eastern question, an issue which had rumbled on throughout the campaign, and which, early in November, had seemed momentarily on the point of erupting into war. As First Lord Amery had a double involvement. There was a powerful naval presence at Constantinople under the command of Sir O. de B. Brock, while the presence of oil in Iraq gave the whole question of Britain's continued mandate for that country considerable importance in the Admiralty's eyes.

The Beaverbrook press were urging the Government to evacuate Mesopotamia and Palestine 'bag and baggage *and at once*',† and Bonar Law was sympathetic to the demand if unsure about its practicability. The decision was deferred, and a Cabinet Committee set up in December, with Devonshire in the chair, to consider the question. In the meantime the RAF and the Army agreed on a forward strategy, and towards the end of January the RAF commander in Iraq, Sir John Salmond, moved his forces up to Mosul. The Turks did not react.

---

*Derby's diary for 20 October records that Bonar Law 'gave it to be understood his views on Tariff Reform were unchanged and of course if he is going to bring that up he is going to split the Party again at the beginning. However Amery smoothed matters down by saying he only meant Trade within the Empire and a tariff if necessary for the purposes of revenue', quoted in R. S. Churchill, *Lord Derby* (Heinemann, 1959), p. 455.

†*Sunday Express*, 5 November 1922.

In part no doubt this was due to Curzon's masterly handling of them at the peace conference in Lausanne which opened on 20 November. Effectively he isolated the Turks from the Bolsheviks, securing from them the freedom of the Straits and agreement to join the League of Nations. The question of the correct frontier line between Turkey and Iraq was more troublesome, and not least because Bonar Law was unwilling to go to war for the *vilayet* of Mosul.

Curzon kept his nerve, and on 23 January, after exposing the weakness of the Turkish case, offered to submit the whole dispute to arbitration by the League. The Turks compromised on a period of direct negotiation, with ultimate reference to the League should there be no agreement. The Treaty presented to the Turks at the end of January was virtually accepted intact although it was July before it was finally signed. The negotiations on Mosul followed almost a year later in May 1924 but no agreement could be reached. The matter stood referred to the League for arbitration and it chanced that when Amery became Colonial Secretary in the autumn of 1924 it was he who had to deal with the closing stages of the dispute.

In the spring of 1923 he was concerned only to put an end to the policy of 'scuttle' and in March 1923, after nine meetings, the Cabinet Committee on Iraq confirmed the policy that had been determined by Churchill at the Cairo Conference in March 1921.

Part of Curzon's difficulties in dealing with Ismet at Lausanne had been the direct result of the growing rupture with the French over the handling of the reparations issue. These payments, intended to be Germany's contribution to the cost of the war it had provoked had been scaled down technically to 132 milliard gold marks and effectively 50 milliard* in 1921, but had still proved an almost impossible burden. The necessity to procure the foreign exchange with which to make payment had combined with bad management of the economy to bring about a major devaluation of the mark,† and it seemed evident to the British Government that the first essential in this situation was to stabilise the German economy. The French regarded the total collapse of the mark almost as a deliberate act and would make no concessions to the Germans. Instead Poincaré proposed to seize Germany's industrial assets in order to exact direct payment. That the proceeds might be in paper marks incapable of translation into any worthwhile currency did not seem to worry him. Indeed there must be more than a suspicion that his actions were designed to weaken the German Government and fragment Germany rather than to exact reparations.

*About £6600 million and £2500 million at the official rate, May 1921.

†In May 1921 the mark stood at 62.3 to the US dollar, by September 104.9 and by November below 260; from 317 in June 1922 it fell to over 1000 in August and over 7000 in November. By the end of 1922 the rate was 7589 marks to the dollar.

The details of the British plan offered in January did not concern Amery. It was clearly unacceptable to her Allies and on 11 January the French and Belgians occupied the Ruhr. The Germans resorted to passive resistance and, later, sabotage. French proceeds from an increasingly coercive occupation were minimal, but the effect on the German economy and currency was catastrophic. In the latter half of April in response to Labour pressure for a statement of British policy, Curzon called upon Germany to make a firm offer and made it clear that German capacity to pay should be determined by an international commission. The Germans on 2 May offered a lump sum payment and failing that an international commission. The French and Belgians rejected the move out of hand, but on 13 May the British reply begged them instead to reconsider and expand their proposals. The German Note of 7 June was more conciliatory in tone, accepting unequivocally the idea of an impartial tribunal to determine German capacity to pay and setting out ways of guaranteeing payment. The Allied powers were sounded but the French and Belgians suggested only a joint demand on the cessation of passive resistance. To Curzon it was clear that this would mean not only continued occupation of the Ruhr, but active co-operation by the Germans in transferring both certain revenues and industrial enterprises. The Cabinet backed him in seeking clarification of what cessation meant and of what was intended to happen to the occupation. By the beginning of July, with the mark falling irretrievably and the Belgians restive, the Cabinet was ready to take a definite line. The French remained obdurate. Amery's diary records their and his own part prefacing it in the entries for 4, 7 and 9 July. He also throws considerable light on the final drafting of the statement which Baldwin made to the Commons on 12 July. This was to be followed by a draft of a joint reply to Germany which Curzon would circulate to the Allies. Effectively this envisaged three stages: the cessation of passive resistance; an impartial committee to settle Germany's capacity to pay, the means of payment and the guarantees; and the evacuation of the Ruhr as soon as the plan was in operation. There were to be also inter-Allied discussions leading to a general financial settlement.

The French and Belgian replies to this proposal were courteous but unyielding. The Ruhr would be released only when Germany paid. One group, including Amery, Derby, Joynson Hicks and Salisbury, now proposed to let events take their course, but the majority, spurred on by Curzon, resolved on a further Note, designed to enlist the support of world opinion. Amery summarised his own approach in a letter for Baldwin, and both he and Derby expected to be consulted in the text of the Note which was put before the Cabinet on 9 August. Amery's doubts, as he notes, concerned the threat of unilateral action embodied in the Note, since no thought had been given to what this meant. In the event to his own and Derby's anger the Note was despatched before their comments reached London.

Germany was heartened and Poincaré stung to an equally brilliant piece of dialectic in reply. Baldwin's private secretary at the Treasury acidly recorded in his memoirs that when 'this exchange of compliments was over the mark was at thirty millions'. In the Ruhr there was a general disposition to end passive resistance and in the rest of Germany widespread labour unrest and Communist-instigated riots. In the middle of August Cuno's Government fell, and Stresemann, who replaced him as Chancellor, declared that Germany would 'abandon passive resistance when the conditions of the treaty had been restored'.

In Poincaré's reply there had been one encouraging phrase, that France had 'neither political views nor any idea of annexation' with regard to the Ruhr, and when the new German Government announced plans to reconstruct Germany's finances even at the cost of aid to the Ruhr, Baldwin decided to take the invitation and see Poincaré. His chief aim was to restore French confidence in London and if that could be achieved, to point out how French conduct was alienating British opinion and risking the *entente*. He was working for a prompt settlement in which Britain and France would work closely, and he secured this much from Poincaré that he was 'quite prepared to allow a certain latitude subject to conditions, in order to allow Germany to stabilise her position' and that he was entirely prepared to work with Britain in a practical solution once passive resistance ceased. Davidson summed up their agreement for Lord Stamfordham: 'The French Government and the British have arrived at complete agreement on principle, namely that reparations are what is wanted, and any question of annexation or the breaking up of Germany is far from the intention of the French Government.'

But the announcement that Britain and France were agreed, in a communiqué designed to conceal the fact that no immediate progress towards a settlement had been made, was enough to precipitate the abandonment of passive resistance and the opening of local negotiations on a resumption of work. The next stage was an attempt to draw in the United States by canvassing the possibility of an American representative joining the Reparations Commission. Curzon was far from optimistic, but when on 11 October President Coolidge revived the suggestion of a committee of experts to investigate Germany's financial position, both Prime Minister and Secretary were agreed that they should ask in the name of the British Empire how far the United States was prepared to go. (They failed to consult the Dominions first, however, which led to a minor storm when the Dominions were told what they had done.) The German reply made it clear that Germany would take part in an economic conference only in an advisory capacity, or unofficially in an inquiry under the auspices of the Reparations Commission. Baldwin and his colleagues endorsed the first proposal, expecting Poincaré to go for the second and reckoning that even this would be a great advance. Baldwin had begun to be suspicious of Poincaré's honesty and, with serious disorder in Germany, felt it necessary publicly to say on 25 October that his Government would not countenance the disruption of the German state.

Reluctantly on 28 October Poincaré agreed on an inquiry under the auspices of the Reparations Commission. The occupation of the Ruhr would continue and certain other conditions were set which Baldwin feared might destroy the plan. However, on 30 October the United States was informed of Allied agreement to an expert inquiry and was asked to nominate a representative. Poincaré tried to hedge his acceptance further and the Americans drew back. At the very moment of apparent failure, the Reparations Commission saved the day, setting up on 30 November two expert inquiries, and the American General Dawes was chosen to chair the first and most important which led directly to the Dawes Plan and the settlement for a lengthy period of the reparations problem.

Amery's diary, however, contains little or nothing on the last stages of this long drawn-out episode once the Imperial Conference had broken up and Britain had plunged into an election. It was to be a Labour Government under MacDonald which reaped the credit.

Diary

20 October 1922: At 5 o'clock we held a meeting of Party leaders including Curzon, Derby, Salisbury, Gretton and even Esmond Harmsworth, so that all wings were represented, to arrange about the Party meeting on Monday and to ask Bonar to allow himself to be nominated as Leader. Curzon conveyed to us that Bonar was anxious to have our views on two subjects, Ireland and fiscal policy. Salisbury and one or two others expressed their views on Ireland and then I spoke up as the leading Tariff Reformer and said though more convinced than ever of the urgency of our policy, I felt that this next election would be run really on one issue, a change of Government, and that it was not desirable to confuse it by putting Tariff Reform as such in the forefront. I thought it was essential that Bonar should keep the door open for himself but thought it would be enough if he dwelt on what preference had achieved, on the need for Empire development generally, and suggested an early meeting of an Empire Economic Conference. On the home side of the situation

I thought it would be enough if he laid stress on the need for fresh sources of revenue and relegated the matter to the consideration of the Chancellor of the Exchequer. As they all rather expected that I wanted to raise the Tariff flag aggressively at once they were some of them, e.g. Derby, very much relieved, unanimously approved of my line and asked me to go to explain this to Bonar as one of the deputation which had asked him to be nominated. Accordingly Salisbury, Derby and I drove round. . . . On the way Derby asked me what we were to do with Mesopotamia and I said that we could not scuttle but might, if we were making peace with the Turks, simplify the whole situation as bringing in the Turk as co-guarantor of our treaty with Feisul [sic]. This was a brain wave of mine early in the afternoon when I had been discussing the matter with Lloyd Greame. We had a friendly little half hour with Bonar and he entirely concurred in my exposition of the situation as regards Tariff Reform. [L.S.A. later noted in pencil: 'i.e. promised that he would keep a free hand for himself. This he didn't do being talked over, I believe, by Derby.'] I think I have succeeded in allaying the fears of those who thought I might damage the situation by my strong views, but I only hope that Bonar won't use this in a way that will shut any doors for the future.

21 October 1922: To see Bonar. I had some little talk with him about preference and also put to him very strongly my personal ambition to be at the CO, but asked him not to say anything in reply. He was very nice and said that of course he would give me a good place and that I was the best fitted person for the CO, except possibly for one point which was the need of having someone of greater acquired status for the immediate urgent business of settling Irish Constitution with the Irish, and he told me that in that connexion he had thought of Milner if he could possibly be induced to serve, and Ullswater whose authority as Speaker would count for a great deal. So I fear that unless Ullswater refuses I shall have to go somewhere else.

23 October 1922: Meeting of the Party at the Hotel Cecil in the afternoon to elect Bonar as leader. Both Curzon and he made very suitable speeches striking just the right note for the great mass of people who want quiet sober Government. Bonar's reception was very good, and there must have been a great many who voted with Austen the other day. After the meeting he asked me to come with a few others to his house at 7 to discuss some points of policy. We assembled there, what I imagine to be the nucleus of the future Government, and one of the chief points discussed was the Tariff question on which with one accord they all wanted to say nothing whatever. I expressed myself strongly on the need for keeping the door absolutely open to enable us to take at any rate a certain amount of action in varying duties and extending preference and Bonar, to my great satisfaction, entirely took my point of view and commissioned me to see if I could draft something sufficiently vague to secure what we wanted without raising the immediate Tariff controversy. He asked me to wait after the meeting and then told me to try my hand at drafting not only the paragraph in question but his election address generally.

24 October 1922: Worked on [Bonar's election] address most of the day. . . . [L.S.A. marginal note: 'I wrote all the Party Election Addresses of 1922, 1923, 1924, but only one or two passages of 1929.'] Down to Bonar at 7 to discuss it. He had read it and rather agreed with both my own view and Curzon's that it a little lacked precision though it struck the right note of 'safety first'. He told me that it was definitely settled that I was to be First Lord. He had actually put me at the Colonial Office at the semi-final stage of the picture puzzle, with Devonshire at the Admiralty and had then decided that he could not have both the fighting services in the Lords.* He felt anyhow that this was the best initial arrangement if he might move me to the CO later. I did not expostulate; after all the PM's difficulties are great and we have got to get through the election somehow. I shall no doubt continue to carry on Empire Settlement and very probably to speak in the Commons for CO on some bigger issues.

25 October 1922: My first pre-occupation in the morning was to try and find a frock coat. Kingsley Wood could not be discovered on the telephone anywhere – it was he from whom I borrowed one to enter the Privy Council – so I was finally reduced to an expedition to Moss Bros. . . . Was duly sworn in and kissed the King's hand. . . . Had a talk with Masterton-Smith about Empire Settlement, which I fear very much I shall have to give up. Down at 7 to Bonar's where with Curzon, Derby and Carr, we finally revised and settled Bonar's election address, which still retains most of my original framework and a good deal of the original language. . . . [In March 1930 L.S.A. added a note that he had some days before wirelessed Neville Chamberlain not to commit himself and had met him on his return from Canada.] He [Neville Chamberlain] went straight down to Birmingham but I spent some of the evening with Annie [Chamberlain] and travelled down with her [on 26th]. . . . Neville had an awful breakfast with Austen who said he would never speak to him again if Neville took office under Bonar. He then came to see me and I had to work very hard to get him not to acquiesce in [Austen's] ultimatum, but I sent him off in the end fortified and at a further talk with A. in the afternoon he told him he had decided and rang me up to let me know.

*In two marginal notes L.S.A. records that he could only have done this just before he went in since as he came up he heard someone on the telephone in the hall transferring the two names.

There are no diary entries from 26 October to 17 November but Amery
set down a two-page summary of his part in the election campaign. The
result at Sparkbrook was: Amery 13,326; Duggan (Lib) 7283; Hampton
(Soc) 6310. Amery missed the count because he had to be at a Cabinet
on the Eastern position. The entries from 18 November to 8 December
are jottings based on his pocket diary, which clearly recorded little more
than his engagements.

Diary

21 November 1922: Had some talk with Bonar about the Navy. His
whole inclination is to underrate the importance of the Navy and to doubt
the use of capital ships, but I realised that he felt that whatever his personal leanings might be, the case was too strong for him and would weigh
too strong with other Members of the Cabinet. So I made no great effort
to argue with him or to fuss him about the ships [the post-Washington
Treaty battleships, *Nelson* and *Rodney*], more particularly as the tenders
were not yet in and nothing would be lost by the decision being delayed
for a short time. My attitude was justified by events and incidentally also
by the decision of the Law Officers who rule that the true interpretation
of the Washington Treaty was that if we did not lay down the two ships
before the end of the year, we could not lay them down for 9 years to
come. This seems to be nonsense but as it helped I did not mind. Anyhow
we got the ships eventually without trouble. On the other hand Bonar
is very frightened about the Air and afraid of what may happen in case
of trouble with France.

27 November 1922: Meeting of the CO in the afternoon to discuss the
telegram to be sent to the Dominions about the proposed Economic
Conference. My own inclination was to press for an ordinary Imperial
Conference when main business should be to discuss economic questions
alongside of the Imperial Cabinet discussing high policy, i.e. to reproduce
the conditions of 1917–18. Bonar, however, was very keen to have a
special conference and have it before the main conference.

9 December 1922: Dinner at Downing Street to the foreign Prime
Ministers.* Just before dinner Bridgeman, whose French is indifferent
and Italian non-existent, asked me to swop with him and sit next to
Mussolini. I jumped at the suggestion, and had a most interesting evening.
He unfolded to me his whole simple scheme of Government. Except for

*In London for a conference about reparations from Germany.

the monarchy and the existence of Parliament he can do anything he likes by decree. In a decree of two lines he has just abolished all forms of unemployment relief and subsidy and people have to either starve or work. He also raised with me the question of big battleships versus small and submarines, etc. I did my best, but to discuss such points as depth charges, hydrophones, [anti-torpedo] *bulges*, etc. went considerably beyond my rusty Italian. He told me he was anxious to ratify the Washington Treaty. We made good friends over the Macugnaga.

10 December 1922: Millet came to lunch and told me all about the [Ruhr] position from the French point of view. He wanted me very much to sound Bonar whether we would accept a small French detachment at Essen if the French on their side agreed to the whole German indemnity being cut down to about 50 milliards [thousand million marks] (from 132) and France receiving about 30 of them. I dropped Millet at the Ritz and walked across to Downing Street, and as Bonar was still in conference left the substance of Millet's suggestion with Davidson [Bonar Law's Parliamentary Private Secretary].

11 December 1922: Saw Bonar a minute or two before the Cabinet. He told me Millet's suggestion was not worth exploring so long as Poincaré kept on insisting that he must occupy the Ruhr and also have the whole fancy figure for reparations only minus whatever we let off the French. He told the Cabinet that he had managed to solve the deadlock by getting Poincaré to agree to an adjournment till 4th January. Saw Millet in the afternoon and pressed on him very strongly the danger of Poincaré making a forward move before January. He thinks Poincaré will fall very soon.

12 December 1922: Long meeting of the Iraq Committee on the subject of whether we are or are not in honour bound to stay in Iraq and ratify the Treaty with Feisul [*sic*]. Eventually Derby took the view that we were and this enabled us to get a satisfactory majority over Novar, Lloyd Greame and McNeill. McNeill's attitude must be rather embarrassing for his Chief, Curzon, who takes precisely the opposite view.*

13 December 1922: Dined at the Hyde Park Hotel with Beaverbrook who had gathered together a large party to do honour to Tim Healy. I sat between Beaverbrook and Joynson Hicks. Had some good talk with Beaverbrook who spoke in warm praise of my part in the recent crisis, also about Mesopotamia on which I tried to convince him [Beaverbrook

*McNeill was representing Curzon in the latter's absence negotiating with the Turks at Lausanne.

was in favour of complete British withdrawal] that while I agreed to the general desirability of limiting our commitments, I was convinced that the right order of procedure was to get out of Constantinople first and make a real peace with the Turk. Presently Beaverbrook got up and after some general remarks asked Birkenhead to propose Healy's health. This F.E. did in a very long and most egotistical speech all about his own share in bringing about the Irish settlement. Everybody was frankly and visibly bored. Healy redeemed the situation by a delightful speech paying a generous tribute to all that he owed to England and Englishmen and pledging himself to do what lay in him to interpret the spirit of England to Ireland.

14 December 1922: Long meeting of the C[ommittee] of I[mperial] D[efence] mainly on Singapore. We settled the location of the base and after much discussion agreed on our part to a postponement till 1937 of the completion of the home reserve of oil fuel providing we were allowed to complete the Singapore reserve by 1931. We also made it clear that this meant completing reserves on the way to Singapore so as to enable the fleet to get there somehow by 1935.

18 December 1922: Long Iraq Committee in the afternoon. The strength of the case is gradually proving too much for the scuttlers. In any case we suspended the meeting of the committee in view of our unanimous agreement that whatever policy was decided upon it would depend upon the kind of peace we made with the Turks at Lausanne and how it could be carried out.

19 December 1922: Cabinet on various questions, Agricultural Rates, Criminal Law Procedure in India, approval of Curzon's handling of things at Lausanne, etc. Bonar firmly discourages full dress debates and as regards the Indian question would not have it discussed at all but promptly remitted it to a small committee.

20 December 1922: Had a talk with Bonar. . . . He would not listen at all to my suggestion that Barlow [Sir A. Montagu-Barlow, Minister of Labour, facing figures of over a million unemployed] might go to Canada to press Overseas Settlement, a thing Barlow is very keen about. He was very persistent in pressing me to produce estimates on the 58 millions basis pressed for by Baldwin [then Chancellor of the Exchequer]. We also discussed at some length the question of the Air Committee which he now thinks he cannot find the time to take himself. I strongly urged him to get the matter settled quickly. I thought he was looking tired and he had got a bad cold.

27 December 1922: Just before going off I saw a very agitated telegram from Curzon who had apparently first seen in the papers news of certain moves of ships back from the Eastern Mediterranean to Malta including Brock's own return to Malta for a fortnight, which I had sanctioned on the 17th in consultation with Beatty but which somehow was never communicated to the FO in the ordinary course, as I had assumed it would be. An unfortunate incident I am afraid, and one causing considerable annoyance to Curzon and also to Bonar, from whom I found on my return a very stiff letter asking for an explanation.

15 January 1923: Murray reported very satisfactorily as to the progress with regard to the Estimates and perhaps we may get through after all without too serious a crisis. Cabinet in the afternoon on American Debt. Baldwin* and his colleagues had wired unanimously urging us to accept the last American proposal of 3% for 10 years, then 3½%, plus half per cent Sinking Fund on top. This Bonar insisted that we should refuse and had a draft telegram in reply prepared for the meeting. There were not very many there and though some of us had misgivings we let Bonar have his way, my own feeling being that Americans will probably advance a point further when we certainly ought to close with them, but I should be very much distressed if the thing breaks down over our obstinacy. In any case the actual nominal sum of our payment seems to me to matter far less than how that payment is affected by subsequent money policy and fiscal policy. What we do with gold affects the real amount of our debt far more than the number of dollars at which the payment is fixed. Indeed I am not sure that I should not like to see the payment definitely fixed as early as possible in order to make us face both the gold† and the fiscal questions. The difference in the Bonar and L.G. Cabinet is very marked. There is very little talk and things are largely cut and dried. In fact with all his mildness of demeanour Bonar is really much more of an autocrat than L.G.‡

26 January 1923: Cabinet in the afternoon. Saw [Sir Ernest] Swinton who told me that he was trying to put together the ground work of facts for L.G. to write his war recollections as L.G. has kept no diary and

---

*Baldwin was in the United States with Montagu Norman, Governor of the Bank of England, attempting to negotiate a funding operation for the war debt which British owed to the United States, and which was repayable on demand.

†The reference here is to the question of returning to the Gold Standard about which L.S.A. was doubtful. It was thought it would necessitate deflationary policies and to some extent interfere with his own preferred fiscal policy of a tariff.

‡In a pencilled note, added probably when he was preparing his 'Notes for Volume II' of his autobiography, L.S.A. wrote: 'B.L.'s manner was very diffident. I once at a Cabinet counted how many times he began by saying "I am afraid" and got to nine running!'

practically no papers and consequently remembers hardly anything.*
I promised to help him having no objection to L.G. getting the credit he
deserves for his part in the war.

From late in January 1923 a new theme enters the diary, the Admiralty's
battle to control its own air service, which Amery recalled as his most
difficult task as First Lord. The White Paper of December 1919, which
was the 'charter for the permanent organisation of the RAF',† had provided for the probability that the Naval co-operation wing would revert to
the control of the Navy. In September 1921 the Admiralty had raised the
issue of Naval control, but had made the tactical error of supporting a
War Office demand that the Geddes Committee should investigate the
extravagance of maintaining a separate air force. Far from thinking this
to be the case, the Geddes Committee argued against the creation of
separate Naval and Army air arms. The Admiralty were not convinced.
The Cabinet referred the issue of naval and air co-operation to a CID
inquiry, and asked Churchill, as a preliminary step, to bring Beatty and
Trenchard together for informal talks. Beatty accepted the compromise
reached and made it quite clear that he had no desire to break up the RAF.
Trenchard was much less acquiescent, and the argument dragged on into
the summer of 1922 to become eventually the business of the incoming
Conservative Government.

Bonar Law seems to have been persuaded by his son-in-law, the former
Chief of Air Staff Sir Frederick Sykes, that there was everything to be
said in peace-time for reverting to Naval and Army control of the air arm,
and this was made clear to the incoming Secretary of State for Air, Sir
Samuel Hoare, although Law seems also to have indicated that there
would be an inquiry into the whole question by the Cabinet and the CID.
Presumably because the Weir Committee, which examined and rejected
the possibility of amalgamating the common services of the Navy, Army
and RAF, did not report until January 1923, the inquiry did not go ahead
immediately.

Amery raised the question of the Naval air wing on 27 January, and
just over a fortnight later, on 12 February, he endeavoured to persuade
Hoare of the merits of the case. The latter feared that any concession
would spell the end of an independent Air Force, the case for which he
and Trenchard had just set out again in ambitious terms. On 17 February
Amery sent Law his views. Next day the Prime Minister talked to Hoare.

---

*L.S.A. later noted (probably in June 1923): 'Extraordinary contrast between L.G. who
lived for the moment and remembers nothing and Winston who wrote every office minute
with an eye to history and had them all typed out in a volume for the whole time he was at
the Admiralty.'

†Cmd. 467; see S. W. Roskill, *Naval Policy Between the Wars* (Collins, 1968), I, p. 256.

Seriously alarmed by this conversation, Hoare wrote to Bonar Law, sending a copy of his letter to Weir, begging him to intervene with Law. He contended that 'only by a centralised force can we undertake the strategic operation that is likely to be the crisis in a continental war'. To separate the Naval air arm would be to remove one of the principal foundations of this force, and he begged for delay therefore, concluding that the only real solution, a Ministry of National Defence, might in the interval become a practicable proposition politically.

Hoare tells us* that Beatty insisted on forcing the issue in an interview with the Prime Minister on the 20th, and that Law requested Hoare to see Beatty himself. In fact Amery came to see Hoare that evening. 'After pressing the naval case as strongly as he could, he made a proposal, as a compromise, that in order to retain the outward integrity of the air force the naval units – manned by naval personnel and a certain sprinkling of air force officers – should be shown on both the Admiralty and air force lists and that the Admiralty should make a grant-in-aid for the naval personnel.' Amery's diary, written no doubt after the event, has no record of this conversation, which Hoare undertook to put to Trenchard. The Chief of Air Staff subsequently told Hoare there was nothing to discuss. Both Beatty and Amery saw Hoare on the 22nd. The former, having agreed to postponement in 1919, refused to contemplate a further postponement, and the two Ministers agreed to demand the appointment of 'a small outside committee to whose names we would also agree'. When they saw Bonar Law he would agree to it only as part of an inquiry into national defence as a whole.

Boyle's biography of Trenchard describes a further confrontation between Amery and Beatty on the one hand and Hoare and Trenchard on the other on 23 February, but since Amery was in Cambridge that day, this cannot be so. Nor does Amery's diary record any such confrontation between Beatty and Trenchard. The conference described by Trenchard to Sir Philip Game on 12 March took place on the 2nd and must have been lent piquancy by the fact that Amery was supported not by Beatty but by Keyes, who was Trenchard's brother-in-law.

The Cabinet on 9 March approved the setting up of a sub-committee of the CID under the chairmanship of Lord Salisbury whose terms of reference were to examine 'the co-operation and co-ordination between the Navy, Army and Air Force generally, including the question of establishing some co-ordinating authority, whether by a Ministry of Defence or otherwise'. It was Amery's own idea, accepted by Hankey, that the relations between the Navy and Air Force should be left to a

---

*His account may be found in *Empire of the Air* (Collins, 1957), supplemented and corrected by J. A. Cross, *Sir Samuel Hoare* (Jonathan Cape, 1977).

special sub-committee with Balfour in the chair, and that was agreed when the Salisbury Committee met for the first time on 15 March.

The sub-committee met twelve times and considered nineteen memoranda. Its parent body met nineteen times and considered no less than sixty-seven memoranda. Amery played an active part in their deliberations. He was well aware of the potentialities of the air weapon, and he clearly favoured the recommendation, approved by the Cabinet on 20 June, that to cope with the potential threat from France, Britain's metropolitan Air Force should be built up to 52 squadrons. (He would have carried out the expansion on a volunteer reserve basis, however.) Nor did he countenance an attempt by the War Office to call into question the existence of an independent Air Force. The Cabinet confirmed the Salisbury Committee's conclusion that there should be a separate Air Department on 9 July. The Army's campaign against the Air Ministry may, however, have prejudiced the Navy's efforts to establish control of their own arm, since Hoare was quick to polarise debate between the concept of a separate air arm or one under the control of the two older Services. Amery's own proposal, although more limited than that of the War Office, was held to weaken the newly born Air Force too much to be contemplated, at least at this date. Balfour's sub-committee made some minor concessions to the Navy, most notably that the number of Naval officers seconded to the Naval air wing should be increased to 30 per cent of its total strength, but on the central issue recommended that administrative (as opposed to operational) control of the wing should remain with the RAF. Despite Amery's efforts, the Salisbury Committee endorsed this conclusion, and, after a long debate, the Cabinet by a majority agreed to do so also. The Sea Lords were bitterly angry and it was only with the utmost difficulty that Amery dissuaded them from resigning.

Amery's account of his dispute has been called in question by Trenchard's biographer, but the diary entries printed here justify it in every particular, and in their turn dispose of the allegation that what really caused Beatty to hold his hand was a threat from the Prime Minister to investigate leakages in the press of the Admiralty's case against the Air Ministry. Not only was the investigation carried to a successful conclusion (which is rare) but it played no part in the Board's decision to stay. Amery had secured two small but vital concessions from Baldwin. In his statement to the House the Prime Minister made it clear that 'absolute control afloat' was secured to the Admiralty, and in deference to Amery's representation, he stated that it was 'impossible without experience to pronounce a final judgment on these arrangements'. Fourteen years later Baldwin's third administration finally pronounced against them and in favour of Amery's arguments, but by then it was too late to secure the kind of Fleet Air Arm to wage war for which Amery and Beatty had been fighting. Both the Japanese and the American naval air arms had far outstripped the British.

Amery's far-sightedness may be seen also in his observations on the key recommendation made by Salibury's Committee, that there should be a Chiefs of Staff sub-committee to integrate defence planning. Amery did not believe that this could be done from the top down, and the history of strategic planning by the Service departments, at least until the creation of joint planning machinery in 1936, wholly justified his view.

If the issue of the Naval air arm dominates the diary in the summer of 1923, Amery was by no means obsessed by it. As First Lord he was concerned also with the development of Singapore as a Naval base, with planning the strategic redistribution of the fleet and the development of a cruiser building programme (with an eye to a possible war with Japan), and (looking towards the Imperial Conference) with the establishment of a possible basis for Imperial co-operation in the Naval sphere. A good deal of his time was also absorbed by the controversial question of the publication of an official Admiralty Narrative of the Battle of Jutland, since Jellicoe objected very strongly to the account drawn up by the brothers Captain A. C. and Commander K. G. B. Dewar, even after it had been corrected and heavily expurgated.

It should not be imagined that Amery was engrossed solely in his work at the Admiralty. He played a full part in Cabinet debates on unemployment, arguing that protective tariffs would not only create employment in the industries protected but would create additional demand through the wages paid to those freshly employed. He continued to be concerned with the issue of European economic reconstruction, which was bedevilled by the problem of reparations. He also watched with a sceptical eye Lord Robert Cecil's efforts to buy French acquiescence to British policy towards Germany by the draft treaty of mutual guarantee. This was designed to remove French fears about her long-term military security by buttressing the Covenant of the League of Nations. Both the draft treaty and the Geneva Protocol, which was its lineal descendant, were unacceptable to Britain, but they led directly to the Locarno Agreements of 1925.

Amery may well have hoped that his influence on the Government would grow with the succession of his close friend, Stanley Baldwin, to the premiership in May. Indeed it has been alleged that he took part in a 'Baldwinite conspiracy' to prevent Curzon's succession. The principal instrument of the conspirators is supposed to have been a memorandum canvassing Baldwin's superior claims to the job, which was falsely represented to the King's private secretary by Bonar Law's principal private secretary, Sir Ronald Waterhouse, as being a clear reflection of Bonar Law's views. If the King's account of his actions given to Derby on 29 May is taken at face value, he had already made up his mind on Sunday 20 May that Baldwin should be Prime Minister, and the memorandum with any accompanying remarks made by Waterhouse was significant.

The matter needs little discussion here since it is extremely improbable that Amery played the part claimed for him. The only evidence is an assertion, at best at third hand, in Tom Jones's diary. Amery was never reluctant to claim that he influenced the eventual choice of Baldwin, yet neither in the diary nor in the subsequent accounts he wrote for Geoffrey Dawson (1928) and Mrs Dugdale (1935) does he mention the memorandum, much less claim a share in it. Indeed he always believed that the interview he and Bridgeman had with Lord Stamfordham had an important and possibly decisive bearing on the eventual outcome. In fact, the earliest mention of the memorandum, which antedates Lord Blake's discovery of it in the Royal Archives, specifically attributes it to Davidson.* The author of the attribution, A. J. Sylvester, was at the time serving in the Prime Minister's private office, and was Jones's informant. It seems likely therefore that Jones misunderstood Sylvester and conflated two separate pieces of information, that Davidson was the author and that he had met with Amery the previous night.

A close reading of Derby's diary also would suggest that he ran together the events of Whit Sunday and Whit Monday, and that the King did not make up his mind until the Monday evening, which squares with the information passed to Geoffrey Dawson, the editor of *The Times*. If this is correct the memorandum takes on less significance and Stamfordham's interviews on Whit Monday rather more. It may be worth noting in passing, however, that Amery is one of five witnesses, four of them direct, who claim that Law's personal preference was for Baldwin, and it is difficult in the face of their testimony to suggest that the memorandum, even if wrongly taken to be Law's view, did in fact misrepresent it.

Amery's diary account of the interview he and Bridgeman had with Stamfordham differs from that in his memoirs, in that the latter reverses the order of the talks with Stamfordham and Salisbury, and asserts that Bridgeman had come to see him after seeing Salisbury and learning from him that he had treated Curzon's succession to Law as settled. The reason is to be found in Amery's annotation of the phrase 'We found Stamfordham' which reads 'Or did we see Salisbury 1st? I am sure we did' on which he further commented that the entry was no doubt dictated some days later. Internal evidence, however, would suggest that the entry was dictated while the outcome was still in doubt and that it is therefore to be preferred to the account in the memoirs. In fact the intervention was

*A. J. Sylvester, *The Real Lloyd George* (Cassell, 1947), p. 103.

not as crucial as Amery came subsequently to believe, since Stamfordham had earlier refused to see both Bridgeman and Amery as he felt sure they would be in favour of Baldwin and that therefore their advice would not be helpful. He recommended Curzon to the King only to find that the King had made up his own mind in favour of Baldwin.

Diary

27 January 1923: Saw the PM about the Naval Air Wing and thought I had really made some progress with him, though I am not sure that he has not relapsed. Also raised the question of broadening the Revenue on which I found him very terrified of raising anything remotely connected with the Tariff. . . . I dined alone with the Sam Hoares and found there Jack Hills and [T.E.] Lawrence, who after having spent 6 months as a Private in the Air Force in the name of Ross, had been discovered by the papers and discharged by the Air Force owing to the awkwardness of the situation *vis à vis* other ranks and junior officers. After dinner we had a tremendous talk about Mesopotamia trying to get Hills out of the purely 'scuttle' frame of mind. Lawrence insisted that there was no difficulty once we had peace with the Turks in withdrawing all the troops and keeping only such Air Force as was required for Imperial purposes. Gave Lawrence a lift home and told him that if he still wished to go into hiding we might possibly take him into the Naval Air Wing. I said this in jest but he came a few days afterwards to see me and asked if he could get some work under the Admiralty. He wants to be quite clear of the Middle Eastern business for the present, more particularly when his book appears, as he hates the idea of having to discuss things with everybody, being invited out to dinner, etc. What he would like to do is to look after the Naval Stores at Bermuda or something harmless of that sort for a few years. A very strange creature. [L.S.A. added on 22 June: 'Eventually he got fixed up as a private in Tank corps which he hates'; and when writing his memoirs, 'He told me he was some very exalted person's natural son.']

29, 30, 31 January 1923: On Tuesday I was at lunch at Admiral Nicholson's on the *Courageous*, and got through on the telephone to Stanley Baldwin about the Cabinet on the American Debt. In view of what he told me I decided to go up by the 2 o'clock train. . . . At the very outset Bonar said in his firm and gentle way that whatever we thought, he was determined not to agree to the American proposal and would resign rather than do so. This somewhat damped discussion, but I ventured to put, as well as I could, the arguments for accepting the proposal and except for Novar, it was evident that practically all the Cabinet agreed, Derby and Cave being particularly strong. [L.S.A. later added: 'The division in the Cabinet was on racial lines, the 2 Scots being the only ones against paying!'] I had to hurry back to Portsmouth where I was going to be late for dinner anyway, but Cave knew my views and had summoned a meeting of all the Cabinet except Bonar to discuss things next morning. I got through my inspection next morning . . . and left by the 2 o'clock train. . . . Rushed off to the Cabinet to find that it had only sat 5 minutes and that Bonar had given way after receiving a deputation from the other members just before. Had a short talk with Baldwin who is overjoyed at the termination of this sudden very awkward crisis. Bonar is certainly apt to be rather autocratic in his methods but realises that he could hardly force the whole Cabinet to do what they felt to be a great mistake simply to comply with his wishes.

9 February 1923: Cabinet, brief and unexciting as usual. Iraq Committee to cross-examine Cox who made a very bad witness. On the other hand Curzon was in his best and most impressive form and is certainly quite clear in his determination not to sanction a scuttle.

12 February 1923: In the afternoon I had an hour with Hoare trying to convince him about the Naval Air Wing, but we did not argue on the same plane. The case is all our way on merits, but he and Trenchard are so desperately afraid that this means the beginning of the end of the Air Force, and both vow they will resign if we get our way. As I am sure Bonar is not prepared to push things to an extreme, I got hold of [Admiral] Fuller afterwards and asked him to see if he could not work out some scheme by which we could save their face, i.e. by filling the whole Wing with Naval personnel theoretically seconded to the Air Force. Dined at 10 Downing Street and sat between Baldwin and Wood. The King's Speech was like Bonar's customary ginger ale, rather dry and uninspiring but will serve its purpose.

14 February 1923: Went to a Cabinet where we dealt mainly with unemployment. I raised my voice at the end in order to get it on the Cabinet Minutes that the various unemployment schemes were only makeshifts and that our main policy is Empire Development and Empire Settlement.

17 February 1923: Sent Bonar a tremendous screed on the Naval Air question. . . . Back to the office to discuss with Murray how to meet Baldwin's last demand for another £325,000 reducing our Estimates to 58 million.

21 February 1923: Meeting of the Cabinet at which I got formal approval of the Estimates which we have somehow squeezed down to the 58 million demanded by Baldwin; also after some discussion approval for going ahead with Singapore.

22 February 1923: 1½ hours or more of talking in a circle at the Iraq Committee. I spoke a good deal, but the floor was mainly held by Curzon, very eloquent and somewhat contemptuous about anyone who bothered about mere base millions.

In the end we decided that we could not decide anything until we knew whether we were at peace or at war with Turkey. Sam Hoare and I then went in to tell Bonar that the Air Ministry could not accept the compromise I had put forward and that we must have a definite decision on the points at issue between us. Bonar would have nothing to do with a decision on this one point except as part of a general wider inquiry into the correlation of the three Services as part of the whole problem of Imperial Defence. In the course of the discussion I asked whether it might not be possible, pending the decision, to have our men trained by the Air Force so that neither party should lose time whatever the decision was. We all thought that this was a *modus vivendi*. Unfortunately I assented rather unthinkingly to a demand of Hoare's that our men should undertake the training on a definite understanding that if the decision goes against us, they should transfer to the Air Force. I did this overlooking the fact that the men whom we would axe and those whom we would wish to see trained for air work would not be the same. However, I hope that we may still be able to straighten out this point and get the two Services to agree. But even a *modus vivendi* is full of difficulties. Dinner . . . the Baldwins, Stanhopes, Mrs W. W. Fisher and Admiral Boyle. . . . All went well except when at one moment after dinner Stanley and Stanhope began speaking abusively about men who use scent – Boyle turned very pink.

23 February 1923: . . . back in time for the Speaker's Dinner to the Cabinet and Reception afterwards. Sat between Bonar and Edward Wood. Bonar amiable but not very active. His general attitude towards most things is negative and I have been taking in Cabinet to counting how often he begins a sentence with 'I am afraid' or 'I fear'.

24 February 1923: Long and rambling Cabinet on the subject of the answer to be given by Bonar with regard to the decontrol of middle-class houses – Boscawen in his anxiety having largely given the case away in the end we settled on the usual unsatisfactory compromise the main object of which was to reconcile Boscawen's latest promise with Bonar's last answer in the House – a clear cut decision either way would have been much better. I tried at the end to raise the question of Lloyd Greame's and Devonshire's Empire development proposals (a much reduced version of the scheme I drew up for Lloyd George before the crisis) but could not make much impression . . . longish talk with Beatty who convinced me that on our agreement in the PM's room, I had gone too far in accepting the idea of a definite pledge to transfer beforehand. I subsequently wrote a long letter to S. Hoare pointing this out.

28 February 1923: Cabinet at which with Neville's help and a very neat and concise summary from Curzon, I carried my conclusions about Empire Wireless. I also raised no little controversy by protesting strongly against Lloyd Greame's idea of announcing that we did not mean to apply the Safeguarding of Industries Act to French lace.* My protest, with which I think Bonar sympathises a little, was at any rate successful in diverting a decision and having the matter referred to a committee. . . . Had some talk with Hankey to try and fix up the proper sort of committee to enquire into the Air business. He rather likes my own idea of a committee of the CID Ministers plus certain distinguished outsiders, the specific Navy Air Personnel Question being left to a sub-committee from which the Service Ministers should be excluded. Meanwhile the Sea Lords had been getting into a fearful state of mind over the *modus vivendi* and especially agitated as the Prime Minister was to answer the question today. So we had an emergency Board which sat for over an hour. I think I was able, at the end, to reassure them as to the position and as to the real advantages to us to get some of our people trained pending a decision. However I am still very much inclined to think that the *modus vivendi* will break down. . . . Got back [after dinner] in time for the division and fixed up with Sam Hoare and Neville the answers the PM is to give on the Navy Air question and on wireless. I have since heard that Sam Hoare demurs to the form we agreed upon – no doubt under Trenchard's influence.

1 March 1923: Long sitting of sub-committee on the Safeguarding of Industries as a result of which I at any rate gained this much ground, that Lloyd Greame has abandoned the idea of generally announcing that we did not mean to apply the Act to France, Belgium or Italy. Salisbury thinks he can devise some formula on which we can agree. I doubt this and think the only way out is to add lace, and probably silk, also to the McKenna duties.† This would of course be far better from every point of view and Baldwin, whom I saw later in the evening, seemed not indisposed to agree.

*The Safeguarding of Industries Act (passed in 1921) allowed protective duties to be applied to industries which were either important strategically or suffered from dumping.

†Protective duties imposed by the Liberal Chancellor McKenna in the 1916 Budget.

2 March 1923: Conference in my room with Sam Hoare, Trenchard and Keyes, Davidson attending in order to convey the results to the Prime Minister. The immediate purpose of the conference was to settle the answer the PM was to give about the proposed inquiry but it emerged very soon that the Air Force would have no answer and no *modus vivendi* which did not definitely pledge anyone who trained with them to join the Air Force if a decision were given that way. That knocked the whole *modus vivendi* on the head and we decided to leave it out. The Sea Lords are very pleased but I cannot help thinking it might have saved a little time. . . . Saw Hoare again about fixing up the terms of reference for the committee which I had agreed with him and Hankey should consist of the CID Ministers, plus 3 out of the following distinguished outsiders: Balfour, Weir, Esher, Milner, Chancellor.

3 March 1923: Salisbury rang up during lunch to say that Lloyd Greame would not agree to report so carefully framed between us. Went out early to be in good time to meet the King whom I had to sit next to [at the Navy and Army Rugby match]. He had a good deal to say about airships which he has a prejudice against, as indeed against all modern weapons, submarines, aeroplanes, poison gas and all the rest of it.

7 March 1923: Cabinet at which I defended the case for giving modern artillery to the Indian native states with much earnestness but without succeeding in carrying anybody with me, except Derby.

14 March 1923: Came up in time for a Cabinet. We got through the Agenda in 25 minutes and then did a little talking at large on the Eastern situation, and the Ruhr.

15 March 1923: First meeting of the new Defence Committee, i.e. the Ministers on the CID plus Balfour and Weir – the latter not yet arrived. Salisbury handled the business well and before Sam Hoare knew what he was about it was arranged that a special sub-committee consisting of Balfour, Weir and Peel should inquire into the Navy Air work question at once, concurrently with a larger inquiry with regard to which a general programme of investigation was agreed to, divided, at my suggestion, into three main heads, viz. (a) War with the Western European powers affecting narrow seas and home defence, (b) Japan, (c) War with Russia and possible Allies affecting the Middle East.

19 March 1923: Iraq Committee in the afternoon at which we passed an admirably lucid report written by Curzon.

20 March 1923: Lloyd Greame and myself with the Duke of Devonshire tackled Stanley Baldwin about the Empire Development Bill (a very much reduced version of the scheme I prepared before the last government went out) and succeeded in getting his general agreement, in view of the fact that very little money will be wanted in the first year.

10 April 1923: Cabinet on agricultural conditions at which they decided to do precious little in the way of an announcement for next day and to refer most things to a special Committee.

11 April 1923: Spent the morning at meeting of CID giving instructions to the staff representatives who are going to Geneva to discuss some futile scheme of Robert Cecil's for universal disarmament.

12 April 1923: Cabinet at 11.30 to discuss Budget which, I think, will be fairly popular. My own part in the discussion was mainly confined to expostulating against the omission to make any little advance in preference, more particularly on dried fruits as an earnest of our goodwill. All the rest took the view that we should keep that in hand for bargaining when the Conference comes off.

17 April 1923: Meeting of the General Committee on the Services at which Beatty gave his evidence in chief. I re-examined him more particularly to bring out, from the parallel of the Falkland Battles, what an enormous number of aeroplanes would be required to carry enough bombs to sink one battleship. After the Committee Weir and Sam Hoare came into lunch and we had some further talk. I think Weir is coming pretty rapidly to my conclusion which is that the air is not for a long time going to affect the problem of naval warfare nearly so seriously as that of land warfare, and that it is the Army rather than the Navy which will be displaced by air developments. . . . Heard from Davidson the story of the very active intrigues of the last week or so due to the crazy notion of F.E. and others that the Government was just falling and that a Carlton Club meeting might be called to displace them. Somehow or other, however, they seemed to have upset Rothermere who has suddenly gone against them and has led off by praising the Budget for all he is worth.

18 April 1923: Cabinet at which we discussed the report of the Agricultural Sub-Committee. The proposal to tax imported malting barley was accepted. I pressed very strongly that the half million or so of revenue from this should be definitely earmarked for helping agriculture, and at any rate got so far by my insistence that Sanders was authorised to say that it would help in covering the many other schemes we had in view.

23 April 1923: I had a quiet talk with Neville [Chamberlain, then Minister of Health] after dinner as to the need for looking ahead and having some policy on Social Reform. We also agreed that, in order to break the new habit of treating the Cabinet like a business committee and hurrying through a few items on the agenda, and then separating, that we should take the opportunity to ask occasional questions of the state of foreign and other general matters in order to start discussion.

26 April 1923: At six o'clock there was an emergency Cabinet which first of all settled, without further discussion, to accept the Report of the Iraq Committee. . . . After that Bonar told us that he had seen his doctor about his throat who told him that he was doing neither one thing or the other at this moment, neither resting his throat nor doing any good in the House and that he had consequently decided to go away for a complete rest until after Whitsuntide. If that did no good he said he would seriously have to think of resigning. We naturally declined to let him discuss that contingency but agreed that he was right in going away at once. After the Cabinet Willie Bridgeman spoke to me about the desirability, if Baldwin is to lead during Bonar's absence, of the work of speaking for the Government on important debates being divided up. I agreed and said there were certainly some subjects like Iraq that I would willingly take up.

27 April 1923: I had some talk over dinner with Derby about the more immediate future, i.e. as to what will happen if Bonar cannot carry on. He is willing to serve under Baldwin but vows that nothing will induce him to stand the autocratic rule of Curzon. However, we shall see when the time comes. 'Nothing will induce me' from Derby is never a final pronouncement.

1 May 1923: Walked up to the Carlton with Edward Wood and we dined together. He feels, as I do, that while it may be possible to take back Austen and most of the others when opportunity offers, that F.E. has made himself impossible.

2 May 1923: Cabinet – Curzon presiding. Derby told me afterwards that Bonar had told him that he had arranged for Cave to preside so presumably Curzon may have weighed in with his claims in the interval. He was most conciliatory, however, and gave us plenty of rope.

5 May 1923: Had a long talk with Beatty about the Imperial Conference and was delighted to find that his views entirely coincided with mine, i.e. that we should wholeheartedly accept the principle of Dominion

Navies; in fact he was not even startled by my proposal that we should directly subsidise them, and will I think come into line with it. He also entirely shares my view that we must present them with a definite concrete programme of the Empire's needs over a period of years and ask them to put up their share of it.

7 May 1923: Cabinet in the morning to discuss the proposed reply to the German offer [a conciliatory move in the Ruhr dispute] which we went through with a rather fine tooth comb, a thing poor Curzon had never seen done to an FO despatch before. Curzon was very down on the Belgians for having backed us at first and then having turned down our policy.

16 May 1923: Special Defence Committee at which we considered a draft interim report. Both Derby and I went for it as too panicky and asking too much in the way of theoretical equality with the maximum French Air Force, and Peel backed us up. In the end we did not arrive at sufficient agreement to send in the report at once though we shall no doubt agree on something a little toned down after Whitsun.

18 May 1923: Caught the 12 o'clock train for Grindlewald. . . . I reached Paris shortly before 7 and drove round to the Embassy to see Phipps and make sure that the Greeks were not getting out of hand. He told me that Bonar was staying at the Crillon and Davidson at the Vouillemont, just round the corner. So I went round thinking to dine with Davidson and hear the latest about Bonar's health before catching the night train to Basle. I found Davidson in the hotel lounge just as I came in, and he took me upstairs where he and Mrs Davidson (in her dressing gown) told me that Bonar's voice was worse, that his throat gave him pain, and that he had entirely lost heart and wanted to resign at once. Could I help their efforts to try and persuade him to go away for a cure and keep things going until August? Davidson went over to see Bonar, who asked me to dinner. So I decided to put off my journey for that night anyway. I found him looking very seedy and miserable, but he cheered up a little during and after dinner on hearing the latest Cabinet gossip and in fact I finally persuaded him that if the specialist he was going to see in London could assure him that his voice would be right in about a month he would hang on. A good part of our talk was occupied with discussion of a successor, Bonar's view on the whole leaning towards Baldwin, but inclined to doubt the possibility of displacing Curzon against his will. About 10 o'clock we sent Bonar to bed and the rest of us, viz. the Davidson's, Young Bonar [Richard Law, later Lord Coleraine] and myself went on to hear the last part of the *Valkyrie* at the Opera.

19 May 1923: By this time I had decided that the Alps were off and so I caught the 8.40 train back to London. Bonar and Davidson were in the same train but we were not actually together except on the steamer. . . . Got home about 5. Went for a walk and dined at the Carlton. Presently Davidson rang me up as promised and told me the doctors had not given a definite period for Bonar's recovery though they had not found anything malignant, and that he was determined to resign at once sending Sykes down with his letter the next day. Meanwhile Baldwin got up to Town about 10 o'clock and I went round at 11 and had a good talk with him and Davidson. He is of course quite willing to serve under Curzon, though I think equally willing, if necessary, to become Prime Minister himself. He is rather hankering after getting back Horne and encouraged my going down to Rupert Gwynne's, where Horne was staying the week-end, in order to judge of his attitude.

20 May 1923: Caught the 9.30 to Polegate. . . . After lunch we motored over to see Douglas Hogg, who was very alarmed and perturbed at the news I brought him. . . . After dinner Rupert and I had a go at Horne who clearly had not realised the strength of the feeling of the Party against F.E. and to some extent against Austen. He is still entirely of the view that they all, including even Winston, should be brought back as quickly as possible. For himself, he professed not to want to come back again and I rather fear if he were brought back he would spend all the time trying to urge the re-admission of the others. He would not face the fact that the fiscal issue has got to come uppermost again and that, in such a case, people like Winston would be a handicap. Afterwards we joined the ladies and he bubbled over with his usual endless flow of stories.

21 May 1923: Came up by an early train. . . . Willie Bridgeman came round to talk about things, being himself strongly inclined towards Baldwin. I suggested we should both go and see Stamfordham in order to let the King know the views of the rank and file of the Cabinet. We found Stamfordham at the doorway of his house and walked about St James's Park with him putting to him all the pros and cons, while I took advantage of the occasion to give him a summary of Bonar Law's own views as given to me on Friday night. We both made it clear that there should be no question of F.E. returning. We then went on and had a talk with Salisbury who on the whole is rather inclined to the Curzon solution. We gave our reasons for the other but made it clear that we were equally prepared to serve under Curzon. Derby of course has announced to everyone that nothing will induce him to serve under Curzon, but I daresay a little straight talking from his colleagues and if necessary the

King, will make him behave. The real trouble with Derby is that he thinks he might be Prime Minister himself and bring in the Coalitionists again. In fact he had already gone so far as to offer Horne the War Office if he had to leave it for more exalted work. Salisbury came on and lunched with me and we further discussed the crisis and also our defence problems. Presently B. came back and we went and looked round the Academy before tea. We dined with Neville and Annie who had come up to Town to be in touch with things. [L.S.A. later holograph note: 'Neville told me he did not think Austen should come back just yet.']

22 May 1923: Office most of the morning, but went down to 10 Downing Street about one and had a talk with Baldwin, who had by then already received an intimation that he would be called for and that the King would do what he could to reconcile Curzon to his disappointment. I told him of the general impression which my talk with Horne had given me of his attitude. Baldwin said this was very different from the impression Jackson had conveyed to him – I fancy that Jackson must have sounded him already on Saturday, if not before and that to him Horne had expressed himself willing to come into the Government, and had not laid stress on his eagerness to bring back the others. [L.S.A. holograph note: 'I told Baldwin, when he said he couldn't think of a Chancellor, that I should like to do it and believed I could inaugurate the new imperial and fiscal policy better than anyone else.'] After that I had a talk with Davidson who thinks that Baldwin will be bound to make a considerable re-arrangement of the Government after the session, possibly immediately afterwards, in order to come within the 9 months rule. He dwelt particularly on the general collapse of the Colonial Office with regard to which I pressed my own point of view that it ought to be divided, and that even if it were carried on temporarily by one man it should be as two offices with two permanent and two political under secretaries. Robin came into lunch and expressed doubts about the desirability of bringing back Horne to the Exchequer, suggesting that I was the best man for that. . . . Willie Bridgeman came to dinner and we had a good talk afterwards. He told me what I had not gathered from Baldwin's conversation that he was thinking of inviting Austen to become Privy Seal, not so much with any idea that Austen would accept but as a demonstration of goodwill and to put an end to any idea that we were waging a vendetta. I am not sure that the gesture would not be premature, though there is something to be said for it.

24 May 1923: Meeting of the Ministers not formally constituted as the new Cabinet. Curzon opened the proceedings by a felicitous little speech congratulating Baldwin and assuring him of our united support.* We then went on to the Russian position and decided that the Soviet answer was still a bluff and that they would give way if we pressed them for the recall (but not the dismissal) of their representation at Teheran and Kabul. Oswyn Murray into lunch and shortly afterwards Hamar [Greenwood] came in full of excitement over the fact that a number of papers had put me down as Chancellor of the Exchequer. I had not seen these and in view of what I had said to Baldwin before, I thought it better to go round and make clear to him I had not been talking about the matter and certainly have had no hand in starting the report.

25 May 1923: . . . came up [from Bury Green] for dinner. Heard that Horne had definitely refused [the Exchequer] and assumed that Baldwin would carry on himself until the end of the session.

26 May 1923: Saw in the papers that Baldwin has asked McKenna to come in as Chancellor which he is to do at the end of the session. This coupled with Robert Cecil coming in as Privy Seal seriously perturbs me as they both so far have been Free Traders and on the whole little Englanders. If the balance of the Cabinet is to be seriously shifted in the wrong direction it will have lost its usefulness so far as I am concerned.

28 May 1923: The big Party Meeting to install Baldwin as our new leader was a great success. . . . I gathered from Lloyd Greame that McKenna has very much changed his old doctrinaire attitude about Free Trade and that he may be helpful to us in getting round the corner easily. Had a subsequent talk with Davidson who is likely to act to some extent in a political general staff capacity, indicates to me that Baldwin also is contemplating a gradual progress on the subject which interests me most. This greatly relieves the anxiety which I confess had worried me considerably over Saturday and Sunday.

31 May 1923: Privy Council at 10.30, after which the King kept me back and with much vehemence and at considerable length expressed to me his fears that the Services generally, and more particularly the Army were being cut down too much. Derby has evidently been working on his feelings, more particularly *à propos* of a Treasury reply to one of Derby's latest papers on the size of the regular Army. I agreed with him wholeheartedly on the main issue, though when he began to suggest that capital ships were a waste of money that could be spent on cavalry or aeroplanes I found myself contradicting him very firmly.

*L.S.A. added in the early 1950s: 'C. always behaved as a great gentleman over his disappointment, especially to me whom he always regarded, rightly, as responsible for Baldwin being chosen.'

I spoke to Baldwin afterwards about this and he assured me that he was going to let Derby make an announcement that there would be no further reduction in personnel.

5 June 1923: Walter Faber's Derby Dinner. . . . The American Military Attaché made quite a clever speech, the best thing in it being a summary of the Irish situation, viz. that Ireland never forgot, England never remembered and America never knew.

9 June 1923 (Oxford): Went round to Magdalen [College] after breakfast and had some talk with Baldwin and Hogarth about Lawrence, who is now a private in the Tanks, and not particularly happy there. I am afraid he is too mad for it to be possible to help him in any official way. I also walked round Magdalen Park for a few minutes with Baldwin afterwards and told him that I hoped he would let me take part in the Economic Conference.

11 June 1923: Longish Cabinet on reparations, the only practical conclusion of which was to ask the French to clear up further what they meant by the cessation of passive resistance, etc. I urged that the direct line of procedure was to go direct at the French on the economic issue and get them to reduce their unreasonably high expectations.

12 June 1923: Special Defence Committee all the morning mostly on the general staff paper saying that the Air Ministry should be abolished altogether, a point of view to which I did not agree and to which I mean to send a rejoinder.

13 June 1923: Cabinet, largely on the difficult question of compensation to Irish Loyalists. I wonder when, if ever, we shall get clear of that tangle? . . . Dined at home and back to the House where I finished a memorandum in answer to the General Staff advocating that there should be a separate Air Ministry.

19 June 1923: National Defence Inquiry and definitely decided that there should be a separate Air Force, the only one voting for its inclusion in the Army being Derby. . . . Before dinner I asked Baldwin what I should say about Austen in proposing his health at the Canadian Club on the 21st. He said that the only true thing I could say was that he was the stupidest fellow he knew. All the same he thought for old times' sake he ought to be brought back and he would try and persuade Salisbury to acquiesce. If so he would bring him in just before the House rises.

20 June 1923: Cabinet in the morning at which the interim report recommending an Air Force adequate to defend this country and provisionally fixing the figure at 600 machines was approved of. . . . Much talk [at lunch] largely about Lloyd George's services in the war and after. Lord M. compared him to a racer who was very good while on an actual straight course, viz. the war, but who became quite unmanageable when he got out on to the open heath, peace. . . . Drafted a short memo on co-ordination of the Services, my specific proposals being to add to the CID a joint war staff on the lines of the Versailles staff, and making the financial adjustments between the Services go through the CID.

21 June 1923: Canada Club Dinner. . . . I said a few nice thing about Austen at the end and as we drove back to the House for a division, he asked me whether, in view of the way I had spoken about him, it was really a fact that I had been one of the people who had objected to his being re-admitted into the Cabinet. I was able to make him happy over this; apparently he had been told, on what he thought good authority, and was very sore. It may be that Horne conveyed to him a somewhat garbled impression of what I had said at Rupert Gwynne's, namely that there was a strong feeling still in the Party against his re-admission.

22 June 1923: National Defence Committee from 3-5 on the question of co-ordination. I think my idea of joint financial bargaining with the Treasury through the CID will be adopted. But I find it very difficult to get them to understand the differences between separate strategic policies co-ordinated by the chiefs of staff and a common strategic policy worked out from the beginning from a single point of view.

25 June 1923: Had some talk with Beatty both about the joint staff question and about Jutland. He told me that two days after Jutland Jellicoe broke down in his cabin regarding himself as a man who had wrecked his career and the chances of victory and that it was only gradually that he had come to think of himself as having done the best possible. B. undoubtedly feels – and I daresay it has vexed him ever since – that the whole German Navy might have been sunk and that there would be no criticism of the value of the navy such as there is to-day. On the staff side, I think I got him to see my point as to the desirability of joint plans being built up from the very bottom and not merely combined at the top.

27 June 1923: Cabinet, largely on the troubles of the Irish Loyalists for whom, I am afraid, there is really rather a lack of sympathy. The report of the Pre-War Pensions Increase Committee came up and I took the opportunity of expressing my dissent from the very limited recommendations made by them. A breeze between Peel and Curzon who is inclined to consider himself a super Secretary of State for India and objects to anything affecting India being raised without full previous consultation with himself.

29 June 1923: Interesting morning at the CID discussing Bob Cecil's scheme for the reduction of armaments with corresponding guarantees, and made myself the protagonist of the opposition to his scheme or any scheme based on the 'Holy Alliance' of guarantee and the status quo.*

3 July 1923: Last morning of listening to evidence on the Navy Air question. Trenchard very impassioned. I am afraid we are not likely to get a unanimous conclusion from the sub-committee as Weir, who I thought was coming round latterly, has I think relapsed.

4 July 1923: Cabinet at which we discussed pretty fully the unsatisfactory position as regards Poincaré and came generally to the conclusion that we must now take a definite line, in the first instance trying to carry the French with us, failing that answer the German Note on our own together with the Italians and Japanese.

5 July 1923: Hankey came to see me with a compromise he had worked out on the Navy Air question which in substance gave us what we wanted subject to having 40% of Air Force men seconded to our Air Wing and to the Air Ministry still doing supply and preliminary training. I told him that I could not commit myself to this and pointed out some difficulties and urged that the only chance of compromise going through would be if the sub-committee themselves decided what was a reasonable compromise and forced it upon us.

6 July 1923: National Defence Committee at which we finally passed the report on co-operation between the Services. This does not go quite as far as I might have gone but undoubtedly leaves the field open for further development in detail.

7 July 1923: Down to Birmingham. . . . I had to say a few sentences about the European depression and in what I thought perfectly vague and colourless sentences indicated that we should have to take a somewhat more definite line to emphasise our own policy with regard to the Ruhr. This and something to the same effect said after me by Neville was taken

---

*Cecil's draft treaty of mutual guarantee was an attempt to make the security provisions of the League of Nations Covenant absolutely watertight. By this means he looked to reassure the French about their long-term position in Europe and promote both disarmament and a French evacuation of the Ruhr.

up by all papers as a great state pronouncement of policy and has filled the press of this country and the continent ever since.

8 July 1923: After breakfast had some talk with Neville and Austen in the library.... [Austen] says that only Birmingham and Neville keep him from criticising the Government more vigorously for their feebleness in dealing with Turkey and with France. On the other hand he says that if we were to take up the Imperial Preference question with vigour that would naturally bring him in support of us and separate him from others with whom he is associated at present. I am afraid I forgot to ask him why he did not come out on the subject actively himself. I think the trouble with him is partly that he is rather stupid and also that he is too much worried about what people think of him. It would be better if he were keen on some definite political object and went ahead with it.

9 July 1923: Cabinet at which we discussed the Ruhr situation first; Curzon though thinking what Neville and I had said [in Birmingham] was quite useful, hoped that in future his colleagues would consult him before making 'pronouncements' on critical issues in foreign affairs. We decided to make a definite statement on July 12th preparatory to a draft reply to the Germans and an accompanying memorandum to the French which we hoped to get off a week or ten days after that. We then discussed Derby's proposal to put the Air Force under the Army again – really rather a perfunctory attempt to justify himself in the eyes of the War Office. He was backed up by Worthy [Worthington Evans] but otherwise the Cabinet were against him and I put in a strong plea for the strategical justification of a separate Air Force.

10 July 1923: The result of the whole budget of critical notes on my part on the Board of Trade proposals for Preference was that I attended the Economic Conference Committee from 4.30 till 7, and I shook them up well. They nearly had a fit at first when I wanted the sugar preference not only fixed for 10 years but doubled, but I believe in the end they were seriously shaken and the Treasury have at any rate got to look into the question of an increase in preference from 1926. Similarly Jix [Joynson-Hicks, Financial Secretary to the Treasury] was rather rattled when I proposed that the £2,000,000 a year for Empire development should be made £10,000,000 though I assured him that like Clive I was astounded at my own moderation. I found Jix very anxious to penalise India by not extending preference to her unless she first gave preference in return, a wholly unsound point of view. It is amazing how few of those who were supposed to be in the Chamberlain movement before the war ever really understood it or if they understood it remember anything of it today.

12 July 1923: Before going to the Cabinet I read Curzon's draft statement on the Ruhr position. It was all right in substance but there was enough in the way of rhetorical questions and sarcasm to bring about an immediate rupture with France. I hurriedly started toning it down and rang up to ask if I could see Baldwin about it and heard to my satisfaction that Baldwin had prepared another draft of his own. When I saw the two at the Cabinet it was obvious that Baldwin's was much better from the point of view of tone though in the latter part he had rather too much compressed and slurred over the conclusions made clear by Curzon. So when the Cabinet at first was rather stampeded in the direction of taking Baldwin's *en bloc* I urged that a combination of the first two thirds of Baldwin's and the last third of Curzon's would make the better paper. This found general agreement and we left the two to fix up among themselves.

17 July 1923: Cabinet Committee on the Strike organisation at which I was able to devolve my Chief Civil Commissionership on Mr Davidson. It is possible that the situation may develop rather more seriously in connexion with the Dockers' Strike as there is barely a week's supply of flour left in the country. Went to Beatty's dinner to the King . . . sat between the King and Madden and found the former in an extremely chatty and cheery mood. He really loves the Navy and is fearfully pleased when he finds himself among old shipmates, more particularly if he finds that many of them who are his juniors have grown a good deal whiter than he has. He was quite interesting on the subject of Northcliffe and Rothermere and told me that he had seen both Northcliffe's letters, the first suggesting that he should be included in the War Cabinet and the second demanding peremptorily that he should be one of the peace delegates. Lloyd George had answered the first civilly by saying the War Cabinet was meant to be a very small body and had not answered the second at all. As for Rothermere he seems to have repeated with Baldwin what he had done with Bonar, asking as the price of his support for a place in the Cabinet for himself and an under-secretaryship for Esmond. Baldwin asked if there was anything else that he wanted so Rothermere added that he would also appreciate a further step up in the Peerage, and then Baldwin replied that there was no question of him getting any of the things he wanted.

19 July 1923: Cabinet in the morning at which we discussed at some length both the draft reply to Germany, which everybody liked and the accompanying Note to the Allies, which we all thought too argumentative and less sympathetic in tone to France. We threw our various suggestions at Curzon['s] and Baldwin's heads and asked them to meet in the afternoon and redraft.

20 July 1923: Cabinet at the House at 12 at which we submitted the revised draft of Curzon's Note to the Allies with [*sic*] still further corrections to Curzon's disgust as he had already had it printed and had hoped to give it to the French Ambassador before 2 o'clock. . . . Salisbury came to see me later to tell me of the compromise arrived at on the Navy and Air question. He seemed to think it was extremely favourable from our point of view but I confess from what I gather from him it will be anything but pleasing to the Navy. However, he was really very vague as to what its details were.

21 July 1923: Soon after lunch I got the report of the Navy and Air Sub-Committee – a thoroughly bad document in itself and one likely to give a fit to the Sea Lords. How Balfour could have come to sign it I cannot understand. All the same I believe it provides sufficient handle for securing a reasonable compromise by getting rid of the absurd 'seconding' scheme and accepting the basis that the Naval Air Wing should be composed of 70% Naval personnel and 30% Air Force.

23 July 1923: . . . had a good talk with Beatty who is naturally very upset and talked freely about a general resignation of the Sea Lords. I think, however, he was somewhat encouraged by my suggestion that we should break the proposal down into a more reasonable compromise and I have since written letters to Balfour and to Peel. To the latter I also talked pretty seriously, to bring that about.

24 July 1923: Saw Salisbury . . . and impressed upon him the necessity of getting rid of this idea of 'seconding' our people to the Air Force while with the Navy. I told him that would wreck any possibility of settlement.

25 July 1923: Very anxious special Board meeting to consider the Report of the Sub-Committee, Fuller, Keyes, and some of them were all for claiming our maximum and nothing else. Beatty I think would be willing to find a compromise.

26 July 1923: Meeting of the National Defence Committee. I had expected that Weir and Peel would begin by expounding their Report, but Salisbury asked me to lead off. I stated as fully as was reasonable under the circumstances the general case put forward by the Navy and pointed out that the Report had implicitly accepted one main contention of the Admiralty, namely that the Fleet Air Arm exists for the purposes of the Navy and not for the purposes of the Air Ministry and was not to be transferred in war without Admiralty consent, and that the rest of their recommendations were largely inconsistent with this. I concluded by saying that while we adhered to the point of view that the Naval Air Wing should be under the Admiralty in all respects, I was prepared personally to urge upon my colleagues that we should give up both supplies and training and be satisfied if 70% of both officers and men were naval and remained under naval authority and organisation and 30% of the Air Force being attached to them. This Weir and the Committee discounted and after a long morning of arguing the Committee adopted the Weir Report, Derby and myself dissenting. . . . Had a full talk with Beatty after lunch and also with Oliver who has come back from Scotland for the crisis and told them what had passed. They both took it very seriously. . . . Back to the House and presently Salisbury came to my room having a great idea that all that was wanted to ease the situation and make it acceptable was to alter the word 'seconded' into 'attached'. We had quite a vehement argument. I am afraid he has also been completely nobbled by Weir or perhaps it would be more correct to say he has worked himself into the determination that the Report shall go through.

27 July 1923: To Harley Street first. Back soon after 10.30 to find that Salisbury was clamouring to see me before the 11 o'clock meeting of the NDC. I walked down with Beatty and put to him that if we have got to accept the Report it would make it easier if the Air Ministry definitely constituted its Fleet Air Arm a separate unit which would then gradually come to identify itself more and more with the Navy. I had a few minutes with Salisbury and Weir before the Meeting in S.'s room and did not find him helpful. He has taken the Air Ministry view entirely. However, I strongly pressed the point as to its making some difference if our attached officers retain naval uniform and if the Fleet Air Arm is in some sense a separate unit. At the meeting of the Committee Salisbury read out their note on the Report which suggested that 'seconded' should read 'attached' and upon this, while dissenting from the general conclusion, I pressed first the point about uniform, which was conceded, and secondly that the Air Force personnel with the Fleet Air Arm should wear a definite distinctive badge if they were not to be treated as a definite unit, which Hoare was not prepared to agree to. . . . Further talk with Beatty, who was in a very considerable state of agitation. In the afternoon attended a Palestine Committee which swallowed a perfectly masterly memorandum drawn up by Curzon, the upshot of which is that we stick to our guns, subject only to the creation of an Arab Agency to balance the Jewish Agency if such an Agency is regarded by the Arabs as a final settlement. Back to the Admiralty and had a long palaver with Beatty and Oliver, impressing upon them the disastrous results of using the threat of resignation, equally disastrous if we failed or succeeded. I made it clear throughout, of course, that there could be no question of their resigning without my doing the same. And, I think, I made them understand something of the attitude of mind of the Cabinet and the public towards an attempt to force their hand.

28 July 1923: Worked in the morning at the memorandum to the Cabinet summing up the situation. Board at 12 where I put the general situation before them pointing out what I would still try and get through the Cabinet but deprecated all talk about anything in the nature of resignation. The Sea Lords had trooped straight into the Board from a prolonged conference in Beatty's room and I gather that that particular danger was ruled out. Unfortunately an awful lot of nonsense got to the papers, some of it through young [Viscount] Curzon who runs in and out of the office far too much. About one o'clock I got an urgent message from Chequers with regard to things in the *Daily Express* and other papers which amounted to practically a verbatim transcript of 20 lines or more of the latest Admiralty memorandum to the Committee. This sort of thing is an infernal nuisance and seriously weakens our case with the Cabinet. I sent for Beatty at once and he made inquiries but could find out nothing and this morning (30th) reports that he is quite sure that no unauthorised copy got out or was shown to anybody. I have also asked young Curzon who swears he has not seen it. Beatty in fact suggests that the leakage was deliberately done by the Air Ministry. Meanwhile my anxiety over this tiresome business has been greatly lightened by the fact that someone in the PM's own office seems to have given away that I asked in the morning whether he could see me and Beatty over the weekend and this has got into the Central News as an attempt to waylay the PM and courteously refused by him.

30 July 1923: Had a talk for nearly an hour with Baldwin on the Navy Air question in the afternoon and found him sympathetic but inclined to think that the compromise of the Balfour Committee could not well be rejected off hand and would have to be given a trial for some time at any rate. I was followed by Beatty who was also with him for nearly an hour and to whom the PM spoke not only about the Navy and Air question but also very seriously about the recent leakage of the preamble of one of our memoranda into the papers. . . . Hannon let slip to me that the leakage into the papers was from a memorandum which Gaunt was carrying around for the purpose of inducing Members to sign a petition or protest against the Admiralty being overruled.

31 July 1923: Saw Beatty about the leakage and told him he was to find out as quickly as possible who had communicated with Gaunt and let me know in the Cabinet. The Cabinet began with a discussion of French and Belgian replies to our Note about the Ruhr – both very unsatisfactory. Neither of them paid the slightest attention to our draft reply and the position clearly is that the French demand the immediate cessation of passive resistance before they even mitigate the severity of their rule in the Ruhr and mean to stay in the Ruhr for the next 50 years. We then came on to the Navy and Air question and I delivered a long and earnest plea for an alternative compromise I put forward which at any rate did not preclude us from utilising our own personnel to handle our own aeroplanes. I laid great stress upon divided and indeed muddled responsibility of the proposed scheme and on the fact that what we were asking was not for a separate Service but simply for the lifting of the veto against our being allowed to use aeroplanes ourselves. After Hoare had replied we adjourned until the evening. Meanwhile during the Cabinet I had had a note from Beatty to tell me that the memorandum that Gaunt had shown about was one prepared by Fuller and was part of the material they had used in compiling the other memorandum. So at 2.45 I took Fuller with me to the Cabinet Office where Bob Cecil, Hogg and Bridgeman were investigating the question and they interrogated both Fuller and Beatty. At 5.30 the Cabinet resumed its discussion. I was well backed by Derby and Neville and also more briefly by Lloyd Greame, Novar and Bridgeman. But the majority could not bring themselves to go against the Balfour Report, especially when they were told that Balfour had written the document himself, and finally Baldwin summed up in the same sense, though making it clear that the question was not finally settled. I replied that though I had grave doubts as to whether the scheme could possibly work, I would loyally do my best to make it succeed though I could not regard it as a final settlement, and then suggested one or two amendments in the covering note by the main Committee. These were accepted.

1 August 1923: The Sea Lords came to me in a deputation, very distressed and restive and through Beatty laid a special stress on the necessity for its being made clear in the Prime Minister's statement that the settlement was only provisional. Cabinet mostly occupied with the Ruhr business. We reached the conclusion that we should publish the papers including a last word to the French, but we reached no conclusion as to what our future policy really is to be. To my mind we must either get our reparations through the French, making them responsible and letting them do with Germany what they like, or we must get our reparations from unoccupied Germany leaving the French to do what they like with the Ruhr and Rhineland but giving them an explicit 'hands off' as regards the rest. I have put this in a letter to Baldwin since. . . . Answered my questions and then back to the Admiralty where I saw Beatty who gave me a couple of sheets with certain points which he insisted ought to come into the Prime Minister's statement, failing which the Sea Lords would resign. I went down to the House to see Baldwin about these points but hearing that I could not get at him and that Salisbury was drafting the statement, went up to see him at the Cabinet Offices. Meanwhile I got a letter from Beatty definitely asking me to tell the PM unless these points were met the Sea Lords would consider that they had lost the confidence of HM Government and would have to make room for others. I pressed Salisbury very strongly on the main point which was to make clear that the settlement was not final. . . . Salisbury did not like the tone of Beatty's letter at all, which was not surprising and when I saw the PM later in the evening I did not actually show it to him, though I read him out the sentence about their feeling that they had lost the confidence of the HMG. Baldwin refused to be seriously perturbed and I did not press matters, rather agreeing with him and also unwilling to make him angry with the Sea Lords. I had by now clearly come to the conclusion myself that unsatisfactory as the compromise was, there was no justification in it for anyone resigning.

2 August 1923: Saw Beatty and had a pretty stiff altercation with him as to the right of the Sea Lords to resign if they did not think the statement sufficiently satisfactory in its tone. Down to the House by 11.30 in time for the statement which I think sufficiently met the point as regards non-finality. It was received without enthusiasm by the House which I think on the whole shares the naval view. . . . Cabinet at 3.30 at which we got through a large number of matters including the proposed arrangements for preference at the Imperial Conference. Lloyd Greame also brought up his suggestion that we should drop the Safeguarding of Industries Act Part 2, and definitely clap McKenna duties on silk, lace, tyres and possibly woollens. Bob Cecil promptly shied at this and Baldwin also suggested that at any rate it would not be settled off hand in a moment. Possibly he may have been thinking of what McKenna might say if he came in and found this already settled – though of course nobody seems to know whether McKenna is coming or if a seat can be found for him anywhere. Saw Beatty at the Admiralty and found him more amenable but still complained very much of the ungraciousness of the statement and of the absence of any assurance that the Board still had the Government's confidence. I subsequently rang up Davidson and got him to draft a suitable letter from the Prime Minister which I read out at the Board next morning.

3 August 1923: Board at 11.30. Made a brief statement on the air question after reading out the PM's letter and there was no dissent from my view that we try and work as well as we can and that the better we

work it the more likely it is to break down in our direction before long. . . .
Afterwards I brought Beatty along to discuss with him one or two points
outstanding on the Battle of Jutland before finally settling the narrative. . . .
He assured me that all Jellicoe's arguments as to his not knowing during
the night which way the German Fleet was going are purely moonshine
and that two days after the battle Jellicoe told him that he knew quite
well and never suggested anything else but that he was not prepared to
run the risks of a night engagement. B.'s whole view in fact is that
Jellicoe from start to finish funked an engagement both in the afternoon
and during the night and that it is owing to him that the German Fleet
was not sunk there and then and the war shortened by a couple of years,
for if we had sunk the fleet we could have pressed our blockade home,
prevented the submarines coming out and induced Germany to throw
up the sponge before the Russian revolution started.

5 August 1923:   Off for the holidays [to Chamonix].

9 August 1923:   . . . wires and telephone messages from Derby at Évian
asking me to come over and discuss the note to France which a King's
Messenger was bringing out to him.

10 August 1923:   We had a short go at the note before lunch and [I]
glanced through it and said at once that I could agree to all of it except
the last sentence which threatened separate action, as I did not believe
that we had any definite separate action in view and were merely bluffing.
Derby said that had been exactly his conclusion, so after lunch I wrote a
fairly full letter to Baldwin on that point in which D. concurred in a
covering note. We also drafted a telegram but eventually decided not to
send it as he said there was a clear understanding that the reply would not
go off till our messenger got back. As a matter of fact they did not wait
and D. was very much upset, but the course of events has since superseded
it all.

There is still a good deal of controversy about the genesis of the tariff
election of December 1923, but it seems clear enough that during his
walks in Aix in the summer recess Baldwin had convinced himself that
protection had to come. There is confusion only because he changed his
mind at least twice about the exact timing of the election, which his decision
to adopt protection rendered almost inevitable. It was not lack of conviction but doubt about the electorate's readiness to accept tariffs which
held him back as it had led Law in 1922 to pledge the Party against
major fiscal change. As late as 25 July Baldwin had referred to Law's
policy in a by-election message; by 10 August he was dwelling on the

need to find a satisfactory solution to the unemployment problem which had begun to concern him greatly. The possibility of using the traditional tariff reform banner to reunite this Party and to detach Joseph Chamberlain's eldest son from Lloyd George was also obvious to him.

The McKenna duties imposed in 1916 and the Safeguarding of Industries Act, which Baldwin had piloted on to the statute book in 1921, provided substantial protection for a number of British industries, notably the nascent motor industry. They could well be extended. Amery had tried to add silk and lace to the McKenna duties in March and had been countered by a threat from Derby and Devonshire to resign. Early in August Lloyd Greame urged the extension of the McKenna duties to silk, lace, tyres and possibly woollens; he also raised the possibility of extending the Safeguarding of Industries Act to protect employment. Baldwin deferred a decision and Amery, while agreeing he was right to do so, wrote nevertheless at some length to urge the case for protective duties.

It is possible that in appointing Neville Chamberlain to the Exchequer, once it was clear that McKenna was not fit enough for the job, Baldwin gave an overt sign of his intention to seek an alternative to the existing policy of trying to settle Europe. Amery's diary makes it clear, however, that as late as 1 October Neville Chamberlain still adhered to Bonar Law's pledge. Indeed at Chequers over the weekend of 5-7 October both he and Baldwin distinguished carefully between the extension of the McKenna duties and 'taxes on bacon, cheese and butter' which they thought would stir 'the fundamental question',* but Baldwin was disposed to go a long way in the direction of new duties with preference designed to help the Dominions and to develop Empire sugar, cotton and tobacco.†

They were, however, conscious of the hampering effect of the Law pledge. From the constituency point of view Amery had no doubt that a definite policy was a necessity and he was both surprised and delighted to learn on 8 October how far Baldwin was prepared to go.

Neville Chamberlain had thought of the new duties as the first shots in an educative campaign leading to an election some eighteen months ahead, but on 10 October he noted that Baldwin thought of an immediate dissolution and that he had asked the Party Chairman two days earlier whether he would be ready for a November election.‡ The pressure from the Australian Prime Minister Bruce for preference therefore fell on ready ears, and over the weekend of 13-14 October Baldwin settled his policy

*Neville Chamberlain's diary, 6 October 1923 (Birmingham University Library).

†Neville Chamberlain to Hilda Chamberlain, 7 October 1923. Baldwin had consulted that veteran tariff reformer Hewins on 4 October (Middlemas and Barnes, *Baldwin*, p. 214).

‡Middlemas and Barnes, *Baldwin*, p. 221.

with Amery, Lloyd Greame and Davidson. The four of them envisaged announcing the McKenna duties immediately, and holding an election in the New Year.

There were already faint ripples of concern about Lloyd George, who was in the United States and who it was thought might come out for preference. Younger spoke of the rumour as early as 8 October, and Davidson learned from Gideon Murray on the 11th not only that Rothermere would support Baldwin on tariffs provided they were not extended to corn or meat, but that he 'did not think that [Rothermere] intended to run Lloyd George'.* In fact it very soon began to look as if that was precisely what Rothermere did intend to do.

Contrary to Amery's impression at the Cabinet on 23 October, Baldwin had done a good deal of consultation beforehand. Almost without exception the advice he received was either against a dissolution or at least for caution† and by 20 October he 'had quite abandoned the idea of an early election . . . no longer thought it practicable to advocate food taxes but had it in mind to say he had concluded that a general tariff was necessary to meet unemployment'.‡ In fact the opposition he met with in the Cabinet on 23 October, and the subsequent letters of protest against early abandonment of the Law pledge which he received from Devonshire, Novar, Bridgeman, Cave and Gretton, compelled him to be vague in his speech to the Conservative Conference at Plymouth, to speak of his personal conviction that a tariff was necessary but commit himself that autumn only to an extension of safeguarding.

The intention was to avoid an election until the New Year and it is quite clear from Amery's description of the initial campaign planning that this remained the case in early November. Amery was himself for waiting and going to the country on the Budget. He wrote to Baldwin on 5 November to confirm that was still his view: 'Every Free Trader would in fact be put on the defensive to explain by what fresh taxes he is to make the Budget square if he foregoes the tariff revenue.'§ The option was a real one. As late as 5 November Baldwin gave his close friend, Edward Wood, no inkling that he would go for an early election even though Wood urged him not to exclude thoughts of one in December.

Twenty-four hours later it was a different story. Amery's diary, tantalisingly, throws no light on the reasons for Baldwin's change of mind and is indeed, from 8 November onwards, the product of recollection, the

*Middlemas and Barnes, *Baldwin*, p. 221.

†Middlemas and Barnes, *Baldwin*, pp. 222–4; M. Cowling, *The Impact of Labour 1920–24* (Cambridge University Press, 1971), pp. 309–10; C. Cook, *The Age of Alignment* (Macmillan, 1975), pp. 114–21.

‡Neville Chamberlain's diary, 26 October 1923. Cowling, *The Impact of Labour*, p. 310.

§Baldwin Papers, F35/60.

entries being dictated on 6 January 1924 on the basis of his pocket book. He himself notes that he could recover the days only 'very sketchily'.- In his memoirs, on the basis of Baldwin's own testimony passed to him by Dr Thomas Jones, he attributed the decision to Baldwin's fear that Lloyd George would return 'from his visit to the United States and Canada full of ideas of a bold Empire policy with Imperial preference well in the forefront' (*My Political Life*, II, p. 280). He claims that in his innocence this did not occur to him at the time nor for a long time afterwards. That must be bad memory. There was suspicion at the time, which Amery shared, and he publicised the suggestion 'that a tariff campaign was to be conducted this winter, whatever the Baldwin Cabinet decided to do or leave undone, and it was to have been conducted by a Liberal leader, who, even before the war, was described by the leading Liberal editor as "Joseph Chamberlain's natural successor" – Mr Lloyd George'.*

Lloyd George had certainly given Beaverbrook cause for hope sufficient to encourage him to a series of hortatory telegrams as Lloyd George returned from New York after 3 November, and his own supporters raced on his arrival in Southampton to secure a 'Free Trade pronouncement . . . for fear Beaverbrook should capture him'.† It may be that Baldwin feared that Lloyd George would outbid him or that he would prevent reunion of the Conservative Party. Certainly he warned the King as early as 6 November that he might seek an early dissolution, and he was not disturbed by the efforts of the Unionist free traders to delay the election. He even drafted an announcement to deliver at a special meeting of the Imperial Conference on 9 November. But the opposition he ran into from the Cabinet that same day, and perhaps concern that the Empire should not be drawn into domestic politics, caused him to hold his hand.‡

There was no real room for hesitation even though Amery urged it still. Liberal reunion might be welcome as putting an end to the chance of Coalition but before it could solidify, the election must be won. The Conservative Chief Whip was in any case not certain of his ability to keep a majority in the House for the autumn session.§ The decision seems to have been taken on the 12th, and that same day, Baldwin told Derby that Birkenhead and Austen Chamberlain were rejoining the Cabinet. Amery's diary confirms that this was discussed by the 'inner circle who settled most of the election business', and tells how it was frustrated. What he does not make clear and almost certainly did not know, was that Baldwin had asked Beaverbrook on 5 November to arrange a meeting

*Quoted in the *Yorkshire Post*, 26 November 1928.

†H. A. L. Fisher's diary, 9 November 1923 (Bodleian Library, Oxford).

‡Middlemas and Barnes, *Baldwin*, pp. 237-8.

§Lord Derby's diary, 12 November 1923, cited by R. S. Churchill, *Lord Derby* (Heinemann, 1959), p. 531.

with Birkenhead and had written to the latter on the 7th. Birkenhead refused Baldwin's invitation to call on the 9th, but after a weekend at Cherkley with Beaverbrook, Lloyd George, Churchill (still a Liberal), and Austen Chamberlain, both he and Austen Chamberlain were ready to rejoin the fold. Baldwin clearly thought that they should become Ministers after a successful election campaign but Austen Chamberlain insisted that he and Birkenhead should join the Cabinet at once as Ministers without Portfolio and that places should be found for one or two others. Effectively the free trade group under Salisbury exercised a veto on Birkenhead, but they were not alone. Curzon, Bridgeman, Sanders, Elliot, Ormsby Gore, and McNeill voiced their opposition, and Davidson reported that Hall and Jackson thought his return would have serious electoral consequences. Baldwin had already warned Birkenhead of the position, and he was determined to retain Salisbury. On the 14th he told Birkenhead that the deal was off. Austen Chamberlain wrote an apparently cordial but hurt letter of complaint. Although both men campaigned on the platform for the Party, reunion seemed to have suffered a distinct setback.

Nor was the election itself a success. Both the *Daily Express* and the Rothermere press moved into opposition to the Government, and the Conservatives lost 108 seats and gained only 20. They faced a new Parliament in a minority of 99.

Diary

30 August 1923: By 6.30 a.m. train to Aix and drove up to the Hotel Albion. . . . We lunched with the Baldwins and afterwards Stanley and I went for a three hours' walk along the hillside talking about people, politics, books and nature as the fancy took us. On the Ruhr question I urged very strongly that Poincaré's last note made it imperative for us to assert publicly and promptly that we did not regard France's debt to us as theoretical, but that we expected it paid, and that any arrangement we had proposed for limiting our net gain over reparations to nil was off if P. stuck to his position. Stanley agreed, but was also very anxious to put it to P. personally and in a friendly way that he really had to choose between breaking the *Entente* and keeping it. We discussed appointments and I suggested Guinness for agriculture vice Sanders, the weakest link in the Cabinet, and A. M. Samuel for Financial Secretary to Neville. I rubbed in a bit of protection *à propos* of Neville's appointment (as Chancellor of the Exchequer) and Stanley is evidently convinced it has got to come and is only seeing how he can get round the corner. He also told me he realised that we have come to the end of the possibilities of economy and declined to discuss the arbitrary figure for the fighting services which he seems to have laid down on Jix's advice.*

31 August 1923: I had another short talk with Stanley before leaving. He is rather concerned about Curzon's health; also about the health of Crowe and the FO senior staff generally whom Curzon overworks most desperately.

Amery joined the Admiralty yacht, *Bryony*, at Marseilles on the 31st, and, by way of Malta and the Gulf of Corinth, she took him to the Dardanelles and Constantinople. He returned to London on 18 September.

Diary

20 September 1923: Neville Chamberlain and Annie dined with us alone and I had a good talk with Neville about many things including the amazing development in the direction of protection which has come about in the last few weeks. It is a great relief to know that he is at the Treasury as he is bound to move in the right directions, though perhaps a little more slowly than I would in his place. Anyhow, between us we ought to get a move on.

22 September 1923: Looked in first at Downing Street to see if there was any chance of seeing Stanley Baldwin, but he was already full of inter-viewers and went off to Chequers in the afternoon. However, I had some talk with Davidson who tells me that Poincaré has waked up to the fact that he is helpless without us and that he does not know what to do with the Ruhr when the Germans cave in, hence the new tone of effusive-ness in the French press.

25 September 1923: Had a short talk with Baldwin and told him I should like to be a member of the Economic Conference both on account of Overseas Settlement and generally. He said he would think about it which presumably meant that he still wanted to make sure that Devonshire and Lloyd Greame had no objections before he said 'Yes'. I also pressed upon him the need of doing something for unemployment by adding the most seriously hampered industries to the McKenna Schedule. I think he is coming round to that view himself but feeling his ground cautiously. . . . Long conference at the CO to discuss Imperial Conference documents on the economic side. I strongly pressed Neville to consider the feasibility

*Joynson Hicks, the Financial Secretary to the Treasury, had just laid down a ceiling on total Service expenditure in letters to the three Service Ministers.

of giving in respect of sugar and other matters a long dated promise, as we are going to do in the case of sugar of a specific preference. Smuts came and dined quietly with B. and myself and we had a good talk in the Library afterwards. He has come evidently prepared to go much further in respect of preference than he has been in the past. His view is that in the general chaos of the world outside the only real stable and feasible factor is the British Empire and it is worth developing for that reason. He talked a good deal about our need for increasing preference in order to transfer our purchases from the American exchange. I told him that the extension of preference should be mutual and that South Africa ought to go beyond her present 3% rebate. He replied that he had come prepared to go up to 33% preference and I urged him seriously to consider the possibility of going as far as 50% and helping to give a lead to everybody.

26 September 1923: Cabinet in the morning. Curzon set forth at great length the story of the Italian–Greek business* and explained how in view of the wording of the declaration by the Italian Ambassador at the Ambassadors' Conference on 13th September, he felt obliged to let Crewe [British Ambassador in Paris, representing Britain at the Conference] assent, owing to the Commission of Inquiry's suggesting that there had been some slight negligence on the part of Greece, to the monstrous imposition of the full penalty of 50 million liras. I pointed out in the discussions afterwards that this was really a bad blow to the League of Nations, which might have survived the reference to the Ambassadors' Conference with credit if the decision had been a just one, but that the present result was bound to shake the faith of all the small powers in the value of the League. I also pointed out the test had shown that the sanctions imposed by the League were quite unworkable. I added that I thought we ought to show our displeasure with Italy by beginning now to press them for our money [i.e. war debt]. We shall not get their gratitude anyway. At the end of the Cabinet Baldwin announced that he was putting me on to the Economic Conference. But I was only to be on the Imperial Conference in so far as defence matters come up for discussion.

29 September 1923: Saw . . . Winston who is now employed [L.S.A. marginal note: 'at a figure of £10,000'] by the Burmah Oil and Shell Co., to try and bring about the amalgamation with the Anglo-Persian which

---

*Mussolini had seized Corfu, ostensibly in order to exact from Greece compensation for the assassination of Italians serving on an international commission defining the boundary between Greece and Albania. Greece had appealed to the League, but Mussolini made it clear that he would accept only the verdict of the Ambassadors' Conference, who had appointed the commission. The British Government reluctantly agreed that the League should refer the matter to them to determine the terms of a settlement.

was rejected last year. He certainly made suggestions which might make the scheme more capable and promised to let me have them as draft heads in a fortnight or so. He sounded me very anxiously about what our intentions were on the tariff issue strongly urging us not to throw away a good position but to continue peacefully in office for the next two or three years. He told me that the Liberals were very anxious to have him back but that he was not having any and was enjoying his present holiday immensely. I have no doubt that he has hesitated as to whether he should wait and rejoin us later or join the Liberals now and the tariff question will no doubt decide him. As I did not want him to decide too soon, I assured him that my lectures,* which had started his alarm, were purely academic and that I could not tell him what line Baldwin would take.

1 October 1923: The main Conference began. . . . Stanley struck a note which pleased them all very much but I was astounded to read in the morning that he had regarded the Italian–Greek business as a great triumph for the League of Nations and his generalities on the Ruhr seem to have dissatisfied most of the Press. I spent the time when he was speaking dictating to him a strong exposition of my own opinion on foreign affairs the gist of which was that the Italian business had bust the League, that we ought to get away from Europe as much as we can and keep France and Italy well behaved and doing what we want by applying a direct financial squeeze. After lunch I had a long talk with Neville, first of all about our conflict with the Treasury over the Clyde tanks and the oil question generally and then about the Economic Conference and how far we could go. I gather that while he thinks it possible to clap on extra McKenna duties in view of the urgent industrial situation and justify them by existing duties and by the Safeguarding of Industries Act he does not think we can go as far as Peto's proposal, . . . viz. take so much off tea and sugar duties and put it on to ham, butter and cheese. He thought that would upset the tranquillity which was the essence of Bonar's pledge. I suggested that Bonar had not foreseen the critical state of unemployment we should have to face this winter and that we should have no tranquillity until that is settled.

2 October 1923: Opening meeting of the Imperial Economic Conference – a large crowd. . . . Philip led off by reading a carefully prepared statement which on the whole struck the right note very well. Of the speeches in reply the best by far were Smuts', who laid stress on the American

*On 26, 27 and 28 September L.S.A. gave three lectures at the Philip Stott College at Ashridge, Hertfordshire, on National and Imperial Economics, aimed at preventing the Party from 'drifting into a mere acceptance of the old *laissez-faire* individualism as an alternative to Socialism' (diary, 22 September).

exchange aspect of things, and Innes for India. Mackenzie King was not bad and certainly, though vague, less negative than I had feared. He is certainly coming on in the Imperial atmosphere.* CID in the afternoon at which the strong line taken by Derby and myself over the need for keeping troops in Egypt not merely on the Canal but within reach of Cairo and Alexandria evidently impressed Curzon and he promised to try and make the best arrangements he could on these lines. . . . At the end I raised the question of the Treaty of Mutual Guarantee which Bob Cecil has apparently agreed to at the Council of the League without any warrant from the Cabinet here, and asked that it should be brought up before the Conference.

8 October 1923: Baldwin asked me to come down and see him at 6 about the economic situation. I went across the [Horse Guards] Parade determined to pitch into him very strongly if he suggested our standing still at the Conference, or wanted me to tone down my speeches in the country. I had even thought, if he really were going to be wholly negative, of asking him to let me go free when the Conference was over and campaign in the country on my own. I do not know why I had this momentary doubt of the way his mind might be working, but it was relieved by his telling me at once that he had come to the conclusion that we must go all out on the Conference, and as regards domestic protection, and that he wanted me to cut my attendance at Birmingham at Neville's Banquet and come down with Philip for the week-end to Chequers to shape our policy. This is the best news I had heard for many years.

9 October 1923: Economic Conference. Bruce opened with a statement which took him nearly one and a half hours to deliver embodying the whole case for thorough-going preference on meat, wheat and all the rest of it, very well done and not aggressive. Then we went back to settlement and I spoke for about half an hour.

10 October 1923: Economic Conference. . . . We purposely adjourned early to enable Philip, Neville, myself and Bruce to have a talk in Neville's study on the whole question of how far we can go at the Conference and also what we are to go to the country upon and when. A most useful talk.

11 October 1923: Dinner at Buckingham Palace. . . . [The King] is very down on both Poincaré and Mussolini and delighted with Smuts' description of the three mad dogs of Europe, de Valera, Poincaré and Mussolini,

---

*That evening at the Colonial Institute Dinner to the Conference Amery found it 'great fun to hear Mackenzie King roll the word "Empire" from his lips every second sentence'.

the first in prison, the second with his teeth in Germany so that he cannot disentangle himself and the third running about biting everybody.

13 October 1923: Bruce came in after breakfast and we had a further good talk of what was possible or not possible as regards preference, his views generally being that we should try and keep the wheat and meat question in suspension or under investigation while we pushed our main campaign in the country. At 11.30 or so I went off with Philip in a car, B. following by train in the afternoon, and got to Chequers somewhat latish for lunch. Philip has been looking into the details of the meat situation and has, *pro tem.* at any rate, convinced himself that it is quite hopeless to give any preference to Australian beef. I have noticed that he is very apt to come to too definite conclusions on departmental evidence. After lunch the three of us [i.e. including Baldwin] had a good long walk, first to get the wonderful view from the top of the hill and then through some of the delightful coombes full of box and other almost sub-tropical vegetation. B. came in time for tea after which we walked about a bit more and talked a lot in Stanley's study. After dinner we sat in the long gallery, a very beautiful room.

14 October 1923: Another very good walk during which for a time we deserted tariffs and policy and talked about religion and other things. Davidson came for lunch, and after lunch the four of us paced the sunk garden till nearly tea time in further conversation. This pretty well exhausted our great political talk which the general conclusion was to announce a whole-hearted policy of protection and preference at Plymouth [where the Conservative Party's Annual Conference was to be held], but to meet the House and impose such McKenna duties as we could in November and give the country a chance of understanding what it is all about by postponing the election until after the middle of January. We discussed wheat and meat and a good deal and I think my earnestness finally persuaded Stanley that whatever we did we could not go to the country and give definite pledges not to do something which we might want to do very much during the next three or four years. On the other hand I was quite willing to let that particular question remain open on the basis that we would inquire into it and would only delay it by some months. I also urged and think succeeded with them both that it would be a worthwhile [L.S.A. emendation to original 'worn'] thing to declare at the end of the Conference that we meant in our own tariffs to embody the principle of the 50% preference but to do no bargaining with the Dominions this time, leaving them to go home and reflect on what we are giving them. I am sure we have got to do the thing on broad and generous lines. There was much talk of the attitude of Rothermere and

Beaverbrook who have now coalesced into a monstrous press syndicate and whom Jackson and Davidson are to meet at a dinner tomorrow night. They are all out to back us providing we do not touch wheat or meat except by subsidy. I daresay we can meet them and get their help but we must not rely on them and I believe we can win without them. The point I insisted on again and again was that once the announcement of policy is made we shall open the flood gates and a great stream will carry everything else away and that we shall have to fight on the main principle and not on the kind of details that appeal to Philip and the Board of Trade.

17 October 1923: Imperial Conference which I opened with a general survey of the naval position which took nearly one and a half hours. . . . Except for a few sentences here and there there was nothing in the speech that could not be published and I was rather anxious that it should be, more particularly in order to let the Dominions know that we definitely favour the policy of Dominion navies. However Smuts and Mackenzie King were not for it and so nothing appeared, except reference to the Empire cruise which they all very cordially welcomed. Mackenzie King followed with a very remarkable disquisition to try and find some sort of excuse for not saying that he was going to do something and we had not really got very far in the discussion by ten minutes to two when we broke up.

19 October 1923: Imperial Conference on defence. . . . At the beginning of the proceedings Curzon made a very lame explanation of why he had telegraphed both the US and to the Allies about American participation [in a conference on reparations] without consulting the [Imperial Conference].* I spoke very strongly to Stanley after the meeting and Salisbury did the same.

20 October 1923: Breakfasted with Derby who is furious with Curzon for not having consulted his colleagues in the British Cabinet. Sam Hoare was also very equally annoyed about that and also about his disregard of the Conference. I told Derby that I was going to write a strong letter to Stanley anyway and he told me he was doing the same. We also discussed the protection campaign. Derby is quite prepared to accept the position. He feels very strongly that we ought to have the support of F.E. as a speaker, and of the Rothermere press. I told him that there could be no question of any bargaining with F.E. as to his position after the

*The telegrams had been sent in the name of the whole British Empire although none of the Dominion Prime Ministers had been consulted. Mackenzie King had made clear throughout the Conference his opposition to any attempt to secure a common foreign policy for the Empire.

election. On the other hand if he really worked all he was worth I knew that the natural instinct of our Party was forgiving. At the Office – wrote a very stiff letter to Stanley about Curzon's performance.

22 October 1923: Stanley asked me to come down and see him. His feeling is that in view of the critical foreign situation he ought to say nothing at Plymouth which would cause things to drift towards the immediate election or lay us open to the charge of levity in the matter. I entirely agreed saying that I still thought we should be forced to have the election at the beginning of the year but that it would be very undesirable to create the election atmosphere immediately. As regards the Curzon business he said he would try and make an explanation at the beginning of the Cabinet, but himself feeling that he was partner in it at any rate to the extent of having over-looked that aspect when Curzon asked him for his concurrence in sending off the telegrams. Cabinet which cleared off several outstanding matters.

23 October 1923: Cabinet at 2.30. This was by far the most interesting Cabinet I have yet attended. Stanley opened in a very serious vein on the subject of unemployment and very soon came to the point and made it clear that he was going out quite definitely in favour of protection at Plymouth and that he could not make himself responsible for any other policy. I thought he had consulted with a good many of his colleagues about it but it was very soon obvious to me that besides Philip, Neville and myself and Derby the thing was a bombshell to most of the others.* Bob Cecil was of course in a state of great excitement, and Curzon was also obviously annoyed at the sudden prospect of so formidable a political issue coming to the front.† However, the discussion happily turned very soon on to the question of procedure and the desirability, in which we all concurred, of the statement being so framed as to avoid our being pushed into a general election this autumn. It was eventually decided that the leading spokesmen of the committee, Bob Cecil and Edward Wood on the one side, myself, Sam Hoare and Neville on the other, should wait after the Cabinet and discuss matters with Stanley. We then went on to foreign affairs, and Curzon once more gave us one of his elaborate recapitulations of the position in the Ruhr and Germany generally without any sort of indication of a policy. He did read out some conclusions of a FO committee which went so far as to suggest that we should definitely announce that as we stood for a unified Germany in order to

*But see Middlemas and Barnes, *Baldwin*, pp. 223-4; and Cowling, *The Impact of Labour*, pp. 308-10.

†Neither had been forewarned, although Salisbury, who had been told, was clearly expected to have sounded his brother. They were the leading free traders in the Cabinet.

get reparations we intended to suppress any Separatist movements in our area by force. After the usual long and earnest appeal by Bob Cecil for what he calls a constructive policy, i.e. some general undertaking to let France off what she owes us in the vain hope that that will alter her general attitude towards Germany, I chipped in and tried to bring the discussion to the realities of the situation, which are that the French and Belgian areas will very soon be part of a Rhineland Republic while in our area, whether we use our troops against the Separatists or merely let the German police prevent the population being coerced, we shall find ourselves a part of the *Reich* and our area possibly even at war with the French area. I urged that there were really only two alternatives, one was to drift into a position of definite antagonism to France by remaining in Cologne. The other, not a very dignified one, was to take the first opportunity of clearing out. My own conclusion was that we had better clear out and concentrate on getting what money we could out of the French. They always gape when I say these things but gradually they are getting more familiar with the idea and presently they will all come to it. After the Cabinet broke up we had tea and a little conversation which worked out in a most friendly fashion. Neville was most firm that the speech must be quite definite in policy while I rather played the part of an intermediary between Bob Cecil and him as to the actual procedure. In the end it was left that Stanley should make clear what his conclusions were and that he was not prepared to deal with the second one* without the necessary powers. That will leave it vague whether he means to have an election before the Budget or upon the Budget. As we broke up I told Bob that I hoped he would not leave us. He said it was very difficult for him as he was not only a Free Trader by conviction but had got a good deal of Liberal support in his constituency by pledging himself to Free Trade at the last election. I am inclined to think that he may find it difficult to continue, but that Salisbury, Edward Wood and Devonshire, as well as Derby [all free traders] will manage all right.

25 October 1923: . . . caught the 2 o'clock to Plymouth travelling down with Baldwin, Neville, Davidson and Lord Churchill. I discussed with Baldwin a bit what he was to say with regard to the cruisers which we were going to accelerate in order to provide employment,† and more generally

---

*Not a 'second election' as L.S.A. queried when writing his memoirs but his second conclusion, that personally he had reached the view that unemployment could only be countered by protection.

†The Naval Staff had been pressing the case for seventeen new light cruisers to counter the Japanese building programme and the proposal had been put to Baldwin as Chancellor of the Exchequer in January 1923 (Adm. 1/8702–151/26). It was now proposed that there should be eight in each of the years 1924, 1925 and 1926 and four a year thereafter until forty-eight had been built.

as to the subject of his speech. . . . Davidson and I had dinner. Then to the Meeting which was very large. Stanley spoke slowly, as was inevitable, and I thought rather stickily. He made no attempt at oratory but the stuff was good and the courage and sincerity obvious. He also succeeded in his main object of launching the protection campaign without doing so in a form which would precipitate an immediate election. The audience rose with great enthusiasm to his definite declaration about protecting the home market though some of the Conference delegates afterwards were a little inclined to shake their heads, more particularly Nancy Astor and Eustace Percy with whom we had some talk before catching the midnight train back.

29 October 1923: Cabinet at 5 at which we discussed the foreign situation at length, while at the end of it we got on to the subject of what we were to say in our speeches, Salisbury telling us that he meant to give a score of different reasons why we should not go to the country for some years. We did our best to dissuade him and I hope with some success.

30 October 1923: Emergency Cabinet at 12 at which we had still further discussion on the foreign situation. Baldwin had overnight come to the conclusion, which Neville and I had strongly pressed the evening before, that we must make it explicit in our telegram to Poincaré, that what we contemplate is an inquiry into Germany's capacity to pay and that it is no use starting an inquiry and then finding it made futile by Poincaré's limitations. We also decided to let Curzon send off a fairly strong telegram on the subject of the Separatists movement. A suggestion raised by Bob Cecil that we really ought to have a small committee to agree as to what our foreign policy is and I am not sure that S.B. will not agree to that presently. The trouble with Curzon is that his policy is purely static and argumentative and does not attempt to deal with the development of live forces.

31 October 1923: Long sitting at 10 Downing Street with Baldwin, Neville, Lloyd Greame and Worthy, to work out our campaign organisation.

1 November 1923: Long conference with Worthington Evans and Hall at the Unionist Central Office about campaign arrangements. We discussed a good deal the formation of an independent 'Home Protection League' but afterwards Hall rang me up and also wrote to Worthy suggesting the time was too short for such a separate organisation and that it had better simply be a committee attached to the Central Office or working with it. . . . We had a Board in the afternoon at which Beatty reopened the whole air question on general principles. We argued the matter at great length, my main point being that we cannot go back directly on a Cabinet decision without giving it a reasonable trial, and that after all either way a period of transition was inevitable. In the end as I was clearly not disposed to even consider the memorandum Beatty suggested that the Sea Lords should think over the matter further and we left it at that.

2 November 1923: Had some talk with Lloyd Greame . . . as to whether we could not hold an election on the Budget itself, i.e. in June or July. This would give us time. We could go to the country on something concrete and there could be no question of pledge giving or breaking. Lastly the public would realise that any concession we had given on tea or income tax would have to be undone if a Government came in that was not prepared to have the revenue from the general tariff.

3 November 1923 (The Naval Review): A gleam of sunlight came out during the run between the lines [of warships] and the sight was really magnificent. I got the three Prime Ministers present, Bruce, Mackenzie King and Massey, to come on to the bridge where I also had to take the salutes. Looking down the long line before we turned I told Mackenzie King that what he saw was the reason that he was Prime Minister of Canada and not at best Senator for Ontario.

4 November 1923: Hankey had given me the evening before the draft resolutions on defence agreed to by Mackenzie King and Smuts and I sent him a letter embodying a few important alterations. The timidity of even speaking about the Empire as a single unit is getting too ridiculous [L.S.A. note in the 1950s: 'M.K. had insisted on altering all references to the Empire to "the several parts of the Empire concerned", and I had to give way on this.']

6 November 1923: In the afternoon Imperial Conference at which we ran through the defence resolutions. The language of these and even the sentiment was very washy in deference to Mackenzie King whom even Smuts laughs at for his timidity, but I did not suggest even the simplest verbal amendment for fear of starting a landslide by a new discussion as Salisbury and Smuts and everybody else had had hours in trying to coax Mackenzie King to accept anything. However the substance of the resolution is useful for it endorses the One-Power Standard, the necessity of Singapore and the importance of control of the Suez canal route. . . . I tried to get Stanley to say definitely whether his pledge [of no food taxes] excluded or included bacon and ham but could not get him to make up his mind.

7 November 1923: Economic Conference. . . . We announced our further offers in the way of preference which were accepted rather ungraciously by Graham and in a better tone by others, though nobody came forward with a definite declaration that they would do something more substantial in consequence. Bruce brought forward two strongly drafted resolutions which we had concocted after lunch the day before. These were thrown out after some heated discussion in the afternoon I am told and another resolution passed re-affirming the resolution of 1917.

8 November 1923: Board at which (I think this was the occasion) I agreed after some discussion to let the Sea Lords put their considered protest against the danger involved in the Balfour Air compromise on paper as a memo to me which I then sent to Baldwin and he circulated to the Cabinet. This solved the very awkward position into which we had got, the Sea Lords resolved on some formal protest, and I taking the view that my protest once made in Cabinet I was bound to try and work what the Cabinet decided.

9 November 1923: Cabinet where we discussed policy. I put in a very strong plea for my favourite plan of going to the country on our Budget and gaining the four or five months interval for education. I found some supporters, but Worthy and the other electioneering experts all ruled it out as unpractical, and I found that the tide especially in Baldwin's own mind was setting towards an early election. Looking back I wonder if I should have made a more determined fight for my own plan; it might have enabled us to pull off the election or at any rate get a better result, and we should have had a 'tariff in being' as a standard afterwards. I fear after I made my appeal that morning I gave it up and when it was merely a question between January or at once I was quite prepared to accept the view that the sooner we went to the country the more we should secure a verdict on the broad issue unconfused by a great deal of detailed argument.

10 November 1923: Dined with the Willie Bridgemans – met there the Archbishop and Mrs Davidson. Mrs D. was very anxious F.E. shouldn't be asked to join the Government – thought this would offend all decent people. Baldwin, Neville, Philip, Worthy and myself – the sort of inner circle who settled most of the election business – had had a talk about this and I had on the whole inclined on the side of those who thought the advantages of having him outweighed the obvious disadvantages. On this S.B. subsequently saw both Austen and F.E. who insisted on being treated as a unit, and claimed that they must come in as Ministers without Portfolio before the election. S.B. seems to have demurred but not very strongly and it looked as if things were likely to be settled on this basis when the almost unanimous expression of the view of MPs' wives and other women workers conveyed to Hall made it clear that the arrangement was impossible. The objections of Billy Gore, Elliot, etc. would I think have been got over. But the women of England want either political or moral respectability (if they can't get both!) and F.E. was too much all round for them.

12 November 1923: I fancy we had several meetings of the inner group of the Cabinet during the day. We certainly had one late at night in a small room at the Constitutional Club where we had all gone to attend an immense party squash. I think it was at this last meeting that the immediate election was finally decided on.

16 November 1923: If I remember rightly this day was mostly spent in writing Baldwin's election address of which the first draft was ready for a 3.30 Cabinet and a further revise discussed in detail with the chief actors plus Bob Cecil as chief critic and Edward Wood later in the evening. In the end the address went through very much as I had drafted it.

20 November to 6 December 1923: The election was much like others except that I did not have to do nearly as much of the Agent's work this time. . . . I also had to give much more time away than ever before. We held two or three meetings a night and at an early stage of proceedings I concentrated on the dear food bogey and dealt with it mainly by pointing out that Free Trade was the chief cause of dearness. Naturally on my own topic I found the election an easy one from the speaking point of view and even more so from that of answering questions.

[L.S.A. spoke at Widnes on the 23rd and had supper with Derby] who was pretty cheerful. His chief anxiety was about F.E. as he felt he couldn't stay on in the Cabinet after accepting F.E.'s help in Lancashire unless he were included. Events have solved that difficulty! From what I have heard since F.E. did not, after his first speech which was good, make very much of an impression anywhere this election.

[He spoke also at Leigh, Warrington, and later at Abergavenny and Newport]. Clarry [candidate at Newport] scraped in so I daresay I really was of use there. On Saturday 1st December I spoke both at Walsall and Wednesbury for Sydney Lewis and H. G. Williams [candidates]. Magnificent meetings and I really did hope that these two first class candidates would be elected. But neither were anywhere near in the end – the last moment dear food lies, etc. having evidently had their deadly effect there as in so many other places.

II

In Opposition
1924

Baldwin's defeat left him contemplating both the resignation of his Government and his own demise as Party leader. Had he followed his own first intention of resigning office immediately, it seems probable that Lord Birkenhead (F.E.) would have engineered a fresh coalition under Derby, Balfour or some other prominent Unionist. It was a project for which he claimed Asquith's support. Amery had other ideas. He had written to Baldwin urging that he 'should go unconcernedly till the House meets in February: give time to Milner's [Tariff] Committee to complete their work; let Neville begin work on his Budget; have a King's Speech framed on the lines of your election programme (as aggressively as you like!) – and then see what they will dare to do'.* In this way Baldwin would retain the strategic initiative and force the Labour and Liberal Parties to combine on a ground not of their choice. On 10 December he travelled to Chequers to add his persuasion to those of Davidson and Bridgeman, and their view prevailed over that of Neville Chamberlain, who would have put Labour into office straight away. Baldwin's decision killed any possibility of a successful intrigue to replace him, but his own reluctance to do a deal with Asquith frustrated any hopes that Buckingham Palace may have had of avoiding a Labour Government.

For a while Amery was hopeful that the Commons might even sustain a minority Conservative Government, 'with Labour support or neutrality, if circumstances should arise which converted the Labour Party themselves to the conviction that protectionist measures were necessary'.† But although certain Labour MPs were ready to flirt with the idea in the event the great majority preferred to remain in the free trade camp.

The remainder of his advice to Baldwin (in the same letter) was shrewd:

The Liberal policy clearly is to push us and Labour out in succession and then come into office with our support, thus gradually building up for themselves

*L.S.A. to Baldwin, 8 December 1923 (Baldwin Papers, 35).
†L.S.A. to Baldwin, 21 December 1923 (*ibid.*).

the position of the real 'moderate constitutional party' and the only 'effective alternative to Labour', reducing us to a rump of 'protectionist extremists'. Our object clearly must be to defeat this policy and do everything in our power to help the natural tendency in the Liberal Party to break up between the section that hankers after Lib–Lab fusion, and the section which will naturally tend to us when it gets over its fear of protection. . . . Our first business will be to make it clear that under no circumstances whatever will we give any support to a Liberal Government. If we should join with Liberals in defeating the Labour Government, it would be either to take office again ourselves . . . or let MacDonald have his dissolution. Till the time is ripe for that we should, I think, make it clear that we are going to turn out the Labour Government but rather concentrate on educating the country in our own policy.

Asquith intended originally to behave in precisely the way Amery had anticipated. Lloyd George demurred, and Asquith allowed himself to be persuaded that it was best to sustain MacDonald in office in order to establish that the Liberal Party was not the party of reaction. He thought he would hold the balance of power and found instead that he was dividing his support. Still more, and to Lloyd George's dismay, there was no sign that the Labour Party was ready for 'the union of all the radical forces for common ends' which his close friend Philip Snowden evidently envisaged.* Instead the Labour Party declared war on the Liberals, and they found themselves ground between upper and nether millstones, the polarisation of the radical forces behind MacDonald and the dismay of those who saw in Asquith's sustaining of a Labour Government the betrayal of all that Liberal individualism stood for.

If Amery's forecast was in that respect triumphantly justified, he was to be bitterly disappointed by the Conservative Party's precipitate retreat from that 'faith and purpose as definite as ardent and true to reality and the instincts of our people'† as the socialism it sought positively to counter. Neville Chamberlain had moved in to take the helm from Baldwin's listless hand, and he felt that 'education must now precede resurrection'‡ so far as the tariff was concerned. To Amery's despair when the Cabinet met early in January the King's Speech was drafted in such a way as 'to leave the impression that we have dropped our policy and have no definite intention of taking it up again in the near future'.§ He begged Baldwin in his own speech to be definite and challenging: 'It is far better for the future both of our Party and of the Country that the Liberals should definitely face their responsibility and put Labour in, or else put us back

*Cowling, *The Impact of Labour*, p. 352.
†L.S.A. to Baldwin, 29 December 1923.
‡Quoted in K. Feiling, *The Life of Neville Chamberlain* (Macmillan, 1946), p. 112.
§L.S.A. to Baldwin, 12 January 1924.

on our terms. Facing that responsibility has already sent Asquith to his sick bed: it will be the death bed of his Party.'

Baldwin had been taught by the electorate to be cautious, and he was not convinced. Instead Amery's diary chronicles the steps by which the Party's policy was adjusted, the commitment to protection becoming instead a policy gradually to extend safeguarding to particular industries following a detailed inquiry into each case. Asquith had in any case already made up his mind to put MacDonald in, and his decision to do so not only rendered the Government's defeat in the censure debate on 21 January inevitable, but paved the way to the reunification of the Conservative Party. 'It would be a curious tit-for-tat if, as a result of S.B.'s uniting the Liberal Party, Squiff were in turn to reunite us!' Neville Chamberlain reflected on 24 January, and he immediately bent all his efforts to that end. In the no-confidence debate Austen Chamberlain had earned Baldwin's plaudits for his slashing attack on the Liberals and on Asquith for putting the socialists into office, and with Baldwin's consent, Neville Chamberlain brought the two together on 5 February. The result was the return of Austen Chamberlain and Birkenhead to the Shadow Cabinet, and it was Austen who took the lead in urging that protection should be put in cold storage for the time being. Apart from Amery and Bridgeman no one said anything against that step and Baldwin to both the parliamentary Party and to the National Union explained that he did not 'feel justified in advising the Party again to submit the proposal of a general tariff to the country, except on the clear evidence that on this matter public opinion is disposed to reconsider its judgement'.

Despite his threat to Baldwin on 28 January that he could not acquiesce in running away from tariffs, Amery contented himself with a public letter of dissent and an attempt to organise a successor to the Tariff Reform League. He was allowed also to establish a Policy Secretariat for the Party, forerunner to the Research Department, although despite his pleas, it was dismantled when the Conservatives returned to office in the autumn. But his influence was significantly diminished and that of his coadjutor, Neville Chamberlain, checked.

One clear aim of the decision to diminish the emphasis on protection in the Conservative programme was to ease the path of Liberals desiring to identify with the Conservative Party. Hamar Greenwood, Amery's brother-in-law, was one, but by far the most distinguished was Winston Churchill. His first effort, fighting the Abbey division of Westminster as an Independent against the official Conservative, Otto Nicholson, was necessarily without Baldwin's approval, although the latter was fully conscious 'of the advantages of getting Winston over'. Churchill asked Baldwin on 7 March not 'to fire upon the reinforcements I am bringing to your aid', and in face of Baldwin's evident hesitation about doing so and the neutrality he imposed on the Shadow Cabinet, Amery decided to force his hand. The letter he published in *The Times* on 15 March did in the end bring Baldwin out in support of the official candidate but it did nothing to prevent a gradual *rapprochement* between Churchill and the Conservative Party. This was to prove a major blow to Amery's hopes of reviving the issue of protection.

The Labour Government moved swiftly to its predestined end. Snowden's Gladstonian finance at the Treasury appalled Amery and did little or nothing to stem rising unemployment. The Liberals predictably had been put on the rack in the House of Commons and were proving unable to hold together as a Party. The Labour Government refused them any influence and were determined to kill them off in the constituencies. Reluctantly Asquith was brought to face the need to bring the Government down, and the issue of the treaties signed with the Soviet Union, agreed finally after left-wing pressure, seemed a suitable one. The Conservatives too were waging an anti-Bolshevik campaign, but the election when it came was precipitated by a more minor issue, the withdrawal of a prosecution for sedition against the editor of the Communist *Workers' Weekly*. It was evident that the matter had been discussed in Cabinet and MacDonald made matters no better by telling an untruth to the Commons and then in part recanting. The Conservatives put down a motion of censure, but, when it became apparent that MacDonald would treat the Liberal motion for a Select Committee as a vote of confidence, switched their vote to support that. Inevitably the Government fell and in the subsequent general election the Conservatives swept back to office, with 413 seats to Labour's 151, and the Liberals were left very weak.

Once again Amery had tried to draft a manifesto which left the incoming Government a free hand over protection but Baldwin in his speeches had committed himself against a general tariff. Even so the creed in which Amery believed and for which he campaigned so strenuously might have borne fruit if Neville Chamberlain had accepted the Exchequer from Baldwin. There could well have been a fruitful partnership between Amery at the Colonial Office, Lloyd Greame at the Board of Trade, and Chamberlain, all of them protectionists at heart. But Neville Chamberlain was as intent on the Ministry of Health as Amery was on the Colonial Office. The result, disastrous to all that Amery had hoped for, was the quite devastating appointment to the Exchequer of Winston Churchill, until recently an advocate of the purest free trade. With that appointment the battle lines were set.

Diary

8 December 1923: Returned to town to face the new situation. A hundred seats lost, no clear majority to anyone. I had wired to Stanley to cheer him up and had to console myself with Kipling's 'If'. Found Willie Bridgeman at his office and heard that Stanley was thinking of resigning both the Premiership and the Leadership of the Party. We agreed that he ought not to do either, least of all the latter. Willie had already written a letter and as the car with the special messenger hadn't gone off I went across to No. 10 and dashed off a strong appeal to Stanley urging him to realise that he stood head and shoulders above any man in the country and that if he now threw up the sponge he would cart all of us who had pinned our faith to him and would smash the Party. I also pressed him to stay on and meet the House so as to state the issue his own way and force the Liberals to face the necessity of supporting Labour which is bound to mean their eventual break-up and disappearance as a Party. My whole object in this and subsequent talks and letters has been to convince him that our main object in the immediate future is the destruction of the Liberal Party and the absorption of as much of the carcass as we can secure – this in opposition to all the born idiots, from Austen and F.E. downwards who are clamouring for us to support an Asquith Government which would mean the final break-up of our Party. One of the three parties has to disappear and the one that is spiritually dead and has been so for thirty years or more is the natural victim. I shall have my job cut out, as the Party are full of funks who naturally do the wrong thing in their terror – as true in politics as in skiing that – and have got to be argued and perhaps frightened out of that. Had a good talk with Neville who generally agreed.

9 December 1923: Motored with B. down to Chequers for lunch and found David [Davidson], the Bridgemans turning up presently, likewise Johnny Baird. We had a great talk and a good walk and all agreed that the Government should stay on and present its own King's Speech with its own policy. Stanley was in very good form and much heartened. Neville and Annie came for tea and we left soon after, feeling we belonged to a true band of friends and that even if we had to go out for some months or years and give up things like the work at the Admiralty which I have grown so fond of, and Admiralty House which will be a sad heartbreak to Brydde, that all will turn out right in the end.

11 December 1923: Cabinet. A brisk and by no means too despondent assembly. We found ourselves all of one mind as to the main immediate issue, viz. to face Parliament at the earliest possible moment and propound our own King's Speech. It was obvious we should differ a good deal on the form of the latter but Stanley wisely insisted on postponing all reference to that. . . . Cabinet met again at 6 to discuss and pass draft of statement.

13 December 1923: Walk after breakfast with Neville from whom I heard a certain amount additional to what I know already about intrigues to get rid of Baldwin and have a mugwump combination under Balfour or any one they might find. Worthy had already come round to me on this tack and I was not surprised to find him in the list. Jix was apparently even worse, having so swollen a head that he thinks his retention of office is the only thing to be aimed at. Derby had (so I heard from Rupert [Gwynne] and Stanley himself) on a word from F.E. run round to offer his services to Balfour who told him he had no idea of coming back and that Stanley was the only possible leader; so Derby at once ran back to Stanley and with charming naïveté told him all. Even Philip seems to have been rather shaky over all this business; he is much too impressionable I fear.

17 December 1923: . . . . goodbye to Massey who is very unhappy over the election result. He, Smuts and Bruce have each made it pretty clear that they will be greatly disappointed if the Economic Conference understandings [on preference] are not kept. . . .

18 December 1923: Cabinet to consider King's Speech. I had prepared a rough draft which served as a basis for discussion and my paragraph reiterating the tariff policy was the main theme. Except Curzon and one or two others who were frankly for dropping it, most of them followed Cave who was for reasserting it but in an 'unprovocative' manner. Willie and Neville the soundest. We left it over till January and I after a further talk with Willie worked out a fuller draft which I sent Stanley and Hankey.

9 January 1924: Cabinet at which we went through the King's Speech and finally left it in the hands of a drafting committee consisting of Curzon and myself to polish up. Board in the afternoon and subsequently went with Tom Jones, Ac[ting] Secretary [to the drafting committee] to the FO. . . . We drafted for a couple of hours, more particularly struggling to cut down the length of the document which had become quite preposterous, but after all our efforts we did not get it down to less than 1500 words. After dinner I tried my hand at a completely new edition cutting out all the reference to detailed bills and not exceeding half the length of the other.

11 January 1924 (but written later, certainly not before 15 January): Further Cabinet at which we considered our joint version and my new version together and eventually by a blend of the two produced a document of tolerable length covering all the items that everybody wanted in. . . . Saw Lord Bearsted who wanted to talk to me about the Anglo-Persian Shell combination, etc., on which I had to tell him that I had definitely decided against the merger (I had in fact just sent into the Cabinet a long memorandum against it prepared for me by Murray [Secretary of the Admiralty]) and also to ask me if I could not possibly get him a GBE or something of the sort for his services to the Admiralty. I inquired from Murray who told me that his services had been fully covered by his Peerage.

13 January 1924: The Davidsons to lunch and I went for a walk with Davidson in the Park afterwards and discussed things generally. There has been an enormous amount of intrigue aimed at displacing S.B. but it is mostly fizzling out in the absence of any inspiring alternative for the Leadership.

14 January 1924: Cabinet in the afternoon. Various odds and ends. I raised the question of the Dye Stuffs Agreement which I had only heard of during the weekend and protested very strongly, Philip [Lloyd Greame, President of the Board of Trade] and myself being quite vehement on the subject. Certainly an agreement by which our Dye Stuffs are tied up over 50 years by the terms and limited to the British islands and a fraction of the Empire market seems to me monstrous.

15 January 1924: Opening of the House. The King's Speech generally well received. Meeting in Stanley's room to discuss procedure more particularly with regard to election of a deputy Speaker and we decided that if this were opposed we should not proceed with an election but let Whitley carry on suspending the sitting whilst he had tea and dinner. . . . The session did not open very well as Stanley's answer to MacDonald was very poor and dispirited. I think he must have been worrying too much about the whole position and both Neville and I have been seriously exercised about his depression and his incapacity to come to any decision about the Party meeting, or other matters. No doubt this is only a passing phase.

17 January 1924: Cabinet. My proposal supported by Neville that we should definitely turn down the Anglo-Persian merger proposal was in view of Philip's protests not agreed to. On the other hand my vehemence on the subject of the Dye Stuffs agreement was successful in persuading the Cabinet to refuse to ratify that and this matter also has consequently been left in suspense for a new Government to deal with. Clynes led off in the afternoon with the 'No Confidence' Amendment and spoke very reasonably more particularly on Preference and Empire Settlement. I had to go out to discuss Estimates and other matters with Beatty and during that time Asquith made what I am told is one of his very best performances in his old easy manner. Jix replied with great vigour and spirit ragging the Liberals for their anti-Socialist election addresses. A good pot and kettle speech which has now confirmed Jix in his belief that he is the real person to lead the Party.

I subsequently fixed up with Neville both the Navy Estimates and the Special Cruiser Programme, the former at £57,250,000 and the latter at an extra estimate of 5 millions, Neville being very unwilling to sanction the Naval Loan as this might give a precedent to the Labour Party for loans for all other sorts of purposes.

21 January 1924: [Simon] was answered by Austen in what was a good debating performance but weak in its exaggeration of the danger of Socialism and its appeal even at the last moment to Asquith to lead a Liberal Conservative Coalition. Stanley made quite a good fighting speech and entirely undid the bad impression his previous speech had made. I think his position is all right now and altogether the Party have gone out feeling as if they had got very much the best of the opening debates.

22 January 1924: Meeting of the Cabinet. A very desultory and chatty character as half the time Hankey was away on the telephone talking to B[uckingham] P[alace]. The original programme was that Stanley should resign in the morning MacDonald being sworn into the [Privy] Council and kissing hands immediately afterwards. Owing to Pringle's performance* that had become impossible for it would have meant our meeting Parliament in the afternoon with MacDonald as PM and all the rest of us except Baldwin still Ministers, and the idea of MacDonald sitting with us on the Treasury Bench and Stanley sitting alone with the Opposition was too incongruous, so it was eventually fixed up that Stanley's resignation and MacDonald's swearing of the Privy Council should take place in the morning and MacDonald's kissing of hands after the House in the afternoon.

23 January 1924: To Buckingham Palace to bid my respects to the King who thanked me very nicely for my services and explained that he would have liked to have a longer talk if the new lot had not been due in a few

---

*He had prevented the adjournment of the House being carried after the Government's defeat on the vote of censure the previous evening.

minutes. The new Cabinet announced. I had already heard in the last day or two that Chelmsford was likely as my successor and was told at the Milners' that he had taken the post on a definite pledge that the Navy would not be cut down and that the Air Force would be brought up to the French level. . . . The House of Commons members of the departed Cabinet met for the last time at 10 Downing Street at 12 and we discussed various matters in view of the session, more particularly a very useful idea which Stanley put forward of creating a 'Shadow Cabinet' Secretariat to match the Cabinet Secretariat. We also discussed who should be invited to the Front Bench and the Shadow Cabinet and as far as we House of Commons members were concerned agreed that we had better invite both Austen and Horne and swallow F.E. As regards the latter there was no immediate question of his taking office but simply of his being treated as an ex-member of the Cabinet. . . . Had a short Board at which we finally settled the last outstanding points of the vexed Jellicoe–Jutland controversy. I then said goodbye in a few sentences, Beatty replying for the Board saying how sorry they were to lose me, etc. I then spent a sad hour taking farewell of senior officials generally. They were all very nice though much the best and most amusing compliment paid me was the remark of old Hodden, the Messenger, to Hodges that evening. Hodges remarked, 'we shall have a new chief tomorrow' to which Hodden replied, 'I daresay he will be all right, Sir; we could not beat this one and we could not have a worse one than Mr Winston Churchill.' . . . So ends my brief span of office as First Lord. The time was too short to effect much but I think we have made a definite move forward in various directions towards making the Navy Imperial. The shift of the main base of our Fleets away from the North Sea is now practically certain and I doubt whether even Singapore can be reversed. The Imperial Conference marked considerable progress even if Canada was thoroughly unsatisfactory, and the Empire Cruise ought to lay useful foundations for the future both in the minds of the Dominions and those of the Navy. I failed to get the Naval Air Wing definitely transferred, but at any rate the compromise which we secured has started a process which is bound to continue and very possibly the whole thing may break down under the new Government.

24 January 1924: The House of Commons members of the ex-Cabinet met in my library and we discussed the forthcoming Party Meeting and wisely decided to have it immediately before the meeting of the N[ational] U[nionist] A[ssociation] on the 12th and to include defeated candidates. We also discussed organisation generally, Jackson [then Chairman of the Party Organisation] insisting strongly on the point which I have long felt keen about that to secure efficiency the Central Office must have a financial hold over the agents directly by some system of either a grant-in-aid towards the cost of the agent or by actually paying the agents and getting their pay, or most of it, back from the local organisations. . . . At tea time Stanley, Sam Hoare and Philip came again to discuss still further the question of [the] Secretariat. We got afterwards on to the question of policy and I found both Sam and Philip thoroughly unsound and unwilling to realise that you can only get efficient organisation if you have got people who are really keen and enthusiastic about a policy. Stanley laid low and said nothing but we had already arranged in the morning that we ought to meet the Thursday before the reassembling of Parliament and that meanwhile Stanley was to send round to us his ideas on the line to be taken at the Party Meeting.

25 January 1924:   Had a long talk with Storr whom we propose to make head of the new Secretariat and discussed the way the thing should be arranged and the assistance he would require.* We shall probably take on Pembroke Wicks, who has long experience of this work and shall want somebody possibly from the Board of Trade on economic questions as well as someone with special acquaintance of Labour problems and probably also a woman with special social experience. I saw Davidson afterwards about one, Granville Ram, who he is keen that we should take on for the Labour side of things and subsequently had a talk with Ram himself who would I think suit very well if we can afford to pay him a salary sufficient to justify his leaving the Ministry of Labour. . . . Had an hour with Chelmsford putting him wise on a number of outstanding points. I was much distressed to hear from him that in the absence of a confirming letter from Neville to my last figure for the Estimates which I had finally agreed with him, viz. £57,250,000 for the main estimates and £5,000,000 for the special programme, the new Chancellor of the Exchequer was treating the whole matter as open and demanding drastic further reductions in the light of Stanley's memorandum to the Cabinet of last spring. This is a great nuisance for my successor and I only wish I had written my own letter in a more definite form or insisted on getting the answer before I went out. I have written to Neville since to ask him to write to Snowden but I fear the mischief is done. I found Chelmsford very much concerned by the cruiser situation and surprised that we had not really faced the building of more cruisers before. He did not seem to think his Government would last long and told me incidentally that Lloyd George, Birkenhead, Beaverbrook and Co. were still intriguing. It looks as if L.G. would try and lead a stampede against the Labour Government in the course of the next two or three months. To tea with Mrs Baldwin with whom I had a long talk on social reform and other questions while waiting

*Storr had been working for J. C. C. Davidson at the Duchy of Lancaster office, but in effect as part of Baldwin's political ménage.

for Stanley to whom I definitely reported the results of my discussion with Storr, etc. and he gave me a free hand to fix the whole matter up with Jackson.

27 January 1924: Wrote a long letter to Stanley at his request suggesting the line he should take on the fiscal question.

28 January 1924: Saw Jackson at the Central Office about engaging rooms and fixing up things for the Secretariat. Found him a little alarmed at being rushed into so large a definite commitment. However, I got him to realise that at any rate the rooms and Storr and Wicks would have to be taken on at once.

4 February 1924: Had a talk with Neville in the afternoon from which I gather that Austen is coming gradually to a much better frame of mind and is convinced that our first duty now is to smash the Liberal Party though still inclined to think that we have got to pledge ourselves for the next election against a general tariff. He also thinks that once we have brought Austen and F.E. in Austen will think that he has discharged his obligations of loyalty to F.E. and that the link which now binds them together will disappear.

5 February 1924: Went round to Hill Street and had a good talk with Stanley who, I think, will be reasonably all right on the fiscal issue; also with Storr who has started work on the new Secretariat.

7 February 1924: Went at 3 o'clock to the Shadow Cabinet at 93 Eaton Square, Austen, F.E., Balfour and Crawford attending. Austen led off by suggesting that Baldwin ought clearly to take the chair himself at the Party Meeting and that this had always been done except when there was no leader and the choice of one remained in doubt. He was obviously right and I am surprised we had not thought of that before. We went on to policy. I had strongly urged Baldwin on Tuesday to begin by giving a definite lead expressing his views pretty fully, and then leaving others to make criticisms or suggestions. I thought he had agreed but to my great disappointment he began by simply asking Austen for his opinion who thereupon propounded the view that we should make it clear that the election having gone against us [we should revert] to the *status quo ante* the Bonar Law position of preference where we happened to have duties and a possible extension of the principle of the Safeguarding of Industries Act. They all tumbled over themselves to emphasize their agreement with this point of view though Neville stood out against Sam Hoare's suggestion that we should make this a decision not only for the immediate present but one to bind ourselves with at the next election. The only person who said anything against the folly of practically dropping our policy and discouraging our workers was Willie Bridgeman. I followed pointing out that the obvious and inevitable result of what was proposed would be to send all our best and keenest working men supporters in disgust into the Labour camp, going further than I had done on previous gatherings. I said that I had no doubt that the really wise course for us would have been to have announced that we should refuse to take office until our policy was accepted, knowing that a Party that had the courage to do that would very soon have the country asking it to take office on its own terms. As that was obviously out of the question I urged that what Baldwin should say was to decline to commit himself as to whether he would go as far or further when another election came but that we did stick to the general principle of protecting our industries against unfair competition and developing the Empire. I spoke possibly for 10 minutes altogether, very earnestly, but I think without any touch of resentment. F.E. followed and after some complimentary remarks as to how deeply he had been moved and how his soul agreed with me, etc., took the line that there were too many great causes beside protection bound up with our Party which would sink with it. This noble way of stating that it was essential for the existence of the country that we should be in office at the earliest possible moment greatly appealed to everyone. However F.E. did some service by producing a wording rather less disastrous than some of the things suggested. Before this Derby had read out a resolution from Lancashire both condemning Baldwin and declaring that protection must be abandoned, and announced that while he proposed to get them to drop the first part he should support the second. Curzon also had made a little speech telling Baldwin that he had been a naughty boy but that he would be forgiven and nothing more said about it if the unpleasant subject were dropped. Balfour urged the maximum of vagueness and in answer to me suggested that if protection and preference were once carried there was nothing left to put up against Socialism. Finally Baldwin summed up by saying, 'I think I see what the general opinion is. I shall have to do some skilful tight-rope walking on Monday for which my figure is not very well suited.' That was all; no indication of his own view and indeed I am beginning to have doubts whether he has a view beyond 'the unity of the Party', as expressed in the consensus of the Shadow Cabinet and other such like people who are in no real touch with the democracy. F.E. said one thing which struck me as very true namely that he had come to the conclusion sorrowfully that the Conservative Party by itself was not an instrument capable of carrying out so difficult a policy. I felt inclined to retort that I agreed but that the incapacity in this respect lay in the handle and not in the sword. In any case the clear conclusion is that one will now have to try and create some outside organisation on non-party lines to get to work with the education of the country. I went on to tea with Neville afterwards and found that he took a much more acquiescent view of the situation than I did. He seems to think that the mere fact that we have not committed ourselves for the next election leaves things open. But of course what will happen is that the whole propaganda machine of the Central Office will now be on other subjects and that the word of command will be to let the unpleasant subject drop altogether. That has somehow or other got to be fought and it seems to me that for the moment, at any rate, there is no one left to fight it but myself which is not a very adequate basis, remembering how even Chamberlain failed with a similar attempt.* On the other hand the case is much stronger and the ground has in an intermittent sort of way been prepared. What is the best step and how I can best dissociate myself from the conclusion arrived at without breaking with my colleagues has got to be thought out in the next few days.

8 February 1924: Lunched at the Marlborough with Hodges [Naval Secretary to L.S.A. as First Lord] from whom I gather that Chelmsford is putting up a good fight against Snowden's Departmental effort to cut down his Estimates. Hodges thought that Chelmsford would probably get his way in the end though the Cruiser Programme might be cut down from 8 to 5, but he was not certain and quite contemplated the possibility of Chelmsford deciding to go out if he failed.

10 February 1924: Went round to Eaton Place [*sic*] and had a talk with Stanley in the morning. We both discussed what he should say and he showed me some notes of Edward Wood's which were rather well put and which he, to some extent, afterwards adopted. I told him that as regards my own position I was bound in some way or other to make it clear that I was going straight ahead and could not agree personally to any limitation on the policy and that I had great doubts whether if our Party were returned on a very restricted policy I could agree to take office. He thought it was best not to worry about the future but I gathered that he had no real objection to my sending him a letter. Presently Neville came in and we discussed things a good deal further including the formation of some sort of outside league, 'Fair Trade Union' or whatever we might call it, of which I should be the active organiser probably but which Neville and other members of the Shadow Cabinet might also join even if in my capacity I might prefer to be outside it.

11 February 1924: Down to the Hotel Cecil after lunch to the Party

*Joseph Chamberlain. The reference is to his departure from the Cabinet in 1903 to lead a movement to educate the country.

Meeting. Baldwin led off obviously rather nervous and tired. He was received with a somewhat half-hearted singing of 'He is a jolly good fellow' before he began but the audience warmed up more as he proceeded and he had, on the whole, a very friendly though not on the whole enthusiastic reception. What he said about the election and fiscal policy was quite well received but it was clear to me from the tone of the meeting at his remarks, and still more at the general shouts of 'No, no', which met a subsequent attempt by Clifton-Brown to ask for a definite abandonment of protection, that the meeting would have welcomed a stronger and more definite line of policy. In fact I felt that carefully stated he could have carried the whole of his policy with just a little vagueness and shading off at the edges. As usual the 'panic-mongers' were wrong again this time and we have submitted to the weakening of our policy and to all the trouble and fuss and disunion which that will cause and done it quite unnecessarily. What he said later about social reform and idealism was very warmly approved, but nobody seems to realise that you cannot do much in the way of social reform unless you put industry and finance on a sound basis, or that there can be much talk about idealism when you run away from your policy whenever it proves a little unpopular. . . .

Walked away from the meeting with Neville who told me he saw no objection to my making my point of view clear in a letter. So after a little further deliberation I sent my letter round to Stanley and to the Press at the same time. The object of the letter was just to make it clear that I stood for the whole policy and that I should not be accused of changing or of disloyalty if presently I began to assert it on the platform. I also wanted it as a signal in order to get into touch with others who shared my view in order to get a move on with a new organisation. Judging from the letters received in the 28 hours since it appeared it has exactly done what was wanted, and has caused no trouble.

12 February 1924: Meeting of the N[ational] U[nionist] A[ssociation] Council to which Baldwin gave more or less a repetition of the previous day's speech but in a much more cheery spirit, in fact made a very good speech of it. There was a strong resolution of Harry Foster's urging education so that at the next election the full policy of tariff preference, etc., could be triumphantly vindicated. I suggested to him that if he altered 'next election' to 'earliest practicable opportunity' he could claim that he was only following up Baldwin's view that more education was required and claim to be fully in line with his policy. Foster adopted my suggestion and saw Baldwin at the end of the morning meeting who expressed his approval of the resolution as amended. I sat through all the morning's proceedings and went back in the afternoon instead of going to the House in order to make sure that the resolution, which was rather low down on the Agenda, would be reached. Happily two other resolutions were dropped out and Foster came on before 4 o'clock. I spoke to the resolution. . . . Clifton-Brown, who, like me, had been waiting for it, got up to oppose urging that this was a violation of the understanding on which the Free Traders had accepted the Baldwin policy but when it came to a vote he only had two supporters out of 150 or 200 which was all that by then was left of the Council. However, the great thing is that the resolution was passed though it was not in the summary in the next day's papers and has not yet apparently been published.

13 February 1924: Lunched with Caillard in his flat in Mount Street to discuss the best means of getting a new fiscal organisation under way.

15 February 1924: B. and I lunched with Lady Hogg, the good Douglas being kept in Court. A large mansion with many treasures and an enormous meal. No wonder Lady Hogg is so ample.

19 February 1924: Lunched at the Athenaeum with John Buchan. . . . A good talk, as always with him. He told me that Ramsay MacDonald was really the son of the former Lord Dalhousie and consequently a relation of the King's by marriage as half uncle of Lady Patricia's. . . .
To the Institute of International Affairs at which Bob Cecil was holding forth on his Treaty of Mutual Assistance. I followed him and went for his Treaty tooth and nail to the considerable consternation of the large and amiable audience who had been sucking in his scheme without realising any of its absurdities.

20 February 1924: Back to the House and spent a most agreeable hour from 11–12 watching the fun between the Labour back benches and their Ministers. Day by day at question time and otherwise the back benches are discovering that their Ministers take, in office, practically the same view of things as the late capitalist Government.

21 February 1924: At the end of Questions Ammon announced in answer to a private notice question that the Government would lay down 5 cruisers and two destroyers, viz. about half of the programme I had announced on 21st January.

23 February 1924: Neville came to tea and we had a long talk in the evening about the future fiscal campaign both agreeing that the great thing was to find a really first rate organiser to run it.

24 February 1924: When I arrived home I found that B. had gone on to the Baldwins' for supper where I joined her. Stanley asked me my view about Winston standing for the Abbey Division and I was very clear as to its being a mistake on our part to encourage it and foolishness on his part to want to do it just yet. I gather Austen (whom Stanley had gone down to see in the country), Jackson and others were quite in favour of it.

26 February 1924: Had a long talk with Bessboro' about the old TRL. He strongly advised that we should have nothing to do with the old organisation which was never really competent.

27 February 1924: Had a long talk with Hamar [Greenwood] who feels that the only thing for a large body of the Liberals on the right is to come over to us at the proper time. He entirely agreed with me that to do this they ought to get together as Liberals first and move in a body and that Winston was making a great mistake from his own point of view and theirs by trying to rush ahead at Westminster. He said he would do his utmost to stop Winston if he could, but I am afraid here again it is a case of true to type and Winston will desert his Liberal colleagues with the same swift decision that led him to climb over the railing at Pretoria and escape without Haldane and Le Mesurier 25 years ago.

4 March 1924: Dined at the House at the Birmingham Dinner where I had some argument with Austen as to the desirability of Winston standing, afterwards walked back with Neville. I found he entirely shared my view and thought that Baldwin ought to have called some of the leaders of the Party together and had it out with them definitely that they must all take the same line and back up the Party's candidate.

5 March 1924: Lunched at the Carlton where everything is buzzing on the subject of Westminster, Jackson very depressed but Neville and I managed I think to put a little more spirit into him. Both at the Club and down in the House afterwards I took the line with everybody that there could be no possible question as to their duty to do everything in their power to return Nicholson and resist Churchill's attempt to force our hand to create disruption in our Party for his own end.

6 March 1924: Informal meeting of ex-Ministers in Stanley's room after Questions. We discussed ordinary business for a while and then got on to the Abbey Division. Austen agreed that under the circumstances Stanley had no choice but to write a letter to Nicholson backing him up. But it is quite clear that he wants Winston to get in at all costs. He got very angry and excited at the idea of Neville and myself going to speak for Nicholson and threatened in that case to speak for Churchill himself. We both made it clear that, unless there was a general formal renewal [of the rule] by which the arrangement that ex-Ministers are not to speak at by-elections, we should speak.

7 March 1924: Speaker's Dinner at which I sat between Hogg and Roundell. Hogg has been told by the Whips not to speak for Nicholson which really seems to me incredible as he is not even an ex-Cabinet Minister. I tried to have a word with Stanley afterwards but found him so miserable about the whole business that it was no good going on talking. He said that if I insisted on speaking in Westminster it would bust up the whole Party.

8 March 1924: Received a letter from Vesey to say as it had been decided that ex-Cabinet Ministers were not to speak during the Abbey election he had cancelled my proposed meetings. I went round after breakfast to see Neville about this and found he had received the same letter. This has apparently been done without any definite arrangement with the other side and Neville like myself feels strongly about it but is at present inclined to submit in order to avoid having any share in creating a breach in the Party though I am afraid the breach is creating itself fast enough. He told me that he had said quite frankly to Baldwin last night that it was all part of a general scheme to oust him from the leadership, and we both agreed that Baldwin's hesitation and uncertainty in dealing with the matter was coming perilously near to committing suicide. His letter to Nicholson giving him the official commendation has now been held up day after day. The last idea is that Jackson is going round to see Winston this morning to ask him if he will withdraw on the understanding that Erskine is to resign in the next few weeks for St George's [the other Westminster seat]. I do not suppose anything will come of it.

13 March 1924: Took the chair at the Imperial Affairs Committee where we dealt first with Egypt then Palestine. . . . We then had some discussion on East Africa on a memorandum on federation put up by Ormsby-Gore. I think we shall get this moving eventually. I shall always regret that Lord Milner did not carry it out when I wanted him to do so in 1919.

14 March 1924: Sent a short letter to Nicholson backing him up. I had postponed doing so day after day hoping Baldwin would send in his first but after worrying B. half a dozen times I gave it up.

19 March 1924: After lunch B. and I drove to the City Hall, Charing Cross Road, and duly voted for Nicholson.

20 March 1924: Lunched with the Cazalets after just hearing that Nicholson had scraped in. B. was very pleased that she had contributed [by canvassing] so substantially to the result. As for myself I hope I did some good by my general attitude and by my letter than I may have done harm by provoking Balfour's letter in favour of Winston.

Apparently Balfour showed that letter to Baldwin on the previous Friday and at his urgent instance decided not to send it. When he saw my letter in the paper next day he sent his on to Baldwin saying that he thought it ought now to appear but still giving Baldwin a chance of suppressing it, meanwhile going off to Cannes himself by the morning train. Baldwin might have suppressed it but while he was still deliberating Austen rang up from Sussex in a great excitement threatening to write a letter himself and was in the end appeased by Stanley's sending on Balfour's letter. I fear I gave poor S.B. a bad time over it all but really the fault was his for not taking a more definite line sooner and again for his slowness in writing a letter to Nicholson.

2 April 1924: Shadow Cabinet at which Curzon pulled to pieces the statement of Unionist Policy created by Sam Hoare, Edward Wood and myself proposing something much more detailed and precise. We therefore saddled him with the job of drafting it. We then discussed our attitude towards the Liberal group who are meditating joining us. Most of us made it clear that we did not think that this group amounted to very much in point of numbers and that only definite evidence of works would justify our making any arrangement with them. So I do not think very much will come of it although it will need further watchfulness to prevent a still further watering down of our policy. After the meeting Edward Wood talked very straight to F.E. about a recent speech of his in which he had talked about the imbecility of our leadership and found him in a very humble frame of mind anxious to be on his very best behaviour.

14 April 1924: Had a talk with Beatty at Mall House about Singapore which he is very anxious for us to keep alive. He takes the view that the Government have only very temporarily suspended the matter [i.e. building the base] pending some [disarmament] negotiations with other countries and that he wants to begin pressing the matter again. Haldane's intervention seems to have settled the interminable air controversy for the time being on lines substantially in favour of the Navy while still saving the Air Ministry's face.

16 April 1924: In the evening George Lloyd came and dined and we had a good talk. He is as keen as ever on protection and preference but still quite uncertain as to what his own line should be. His ultimate ambition is the Indian Vice Royalty, and I suggested to him that his best line thither would be to make himself a position as the leader of the fiscal movement outside of Parliament until we got in, then take his peerage and either join the next Cabinet or go out to India straight away.

29 April 1924: Down to the House early for Snowden's Budget statement which was well delivered, clear and from his point of view boldly conceived, i.e. wherever he had to cut he cut clear; a typical Gladstonian budget in fact and typically Gladstonian too in the crudeness of his Free Trade pedantry, McKenna Duties abolition, Empire Preference cut down in every direction, the whole thing most disastrous. The only hope is that some reasonable measure of indignation will be wakened among our own people, but so far I have not seen much sign of it. The Liberals were of course delighted. . . .

Dined in the House with Samuel Samuel and a large company of financiers, etc. . . . I told Bearsted about my fiscal scheme and he promised financial support. Incidentally he told me that he had already given such support to Austen, Birkenhead and others though when I questioned him more closely I found it was for some schemes to help Liberals to come over. I could not pump him more but I wonder very much what intrigue is on foot.

1 May 1924: To a Leader's Conference where we discussed the various texts of party programme which had been drawn up and decided to leave it to S.B. to produce his own blend either in a letter or in his speeches.

Amery neglected his diary in the months which followed and wrote it up from his engagement book at the end of August.

---

11 May 1924: In the afternoon I went for a walk with Hudson who was most entertaining on the subject of his unsuccessful efforts to get L.G. to disgorge his private Liberal Coalition funds into the common Liberal purse. In his view the only satisfactory solution of the problem of Lib-leadership is for a railway accident to deprive the party of Asquith, Lloyd George and Simon simultaneously and leave them with Donald Mclean whom they all trust and like.

14 May 1924: Leader's Conference – I forget now what we discussed, probably the never ending statement of policy which did eventually appear and gave mild satisfaction all round, though there will be no real fighting spirit, or feeling that we have a live policy, till we really get committed to the fight against Free Trade.

23 May 1924: After dinner F.E. asked me to join him, Austen, Winston, Buckmaster [the former Liberal Lord Chancellor] and the Prince [of Wales] at a little table upstairs to drink wine and talk. F.E. told old stories of our jaunt to Asia Minor while Winston recounted our first meeting in Ducker and the armoured train business; generally my expeditions and physical condition framed the main topic of conversation for a long time!

Later on F.E. made a personal appeal to me to see more of him and work more with him and appealed to Winston if he hadn't always defended me to him as a splendid fellow! Winston drily said 'not so much lately'. I also had a good talk with Winston about conditions which it was necessary for him to face if he came with us. . . . With the Prince I mainly talked climbing, keeping fit, etc. Drove home with Hamar who is, I think, rapidly coming our way.

31 May 1924: Breakfasted with George Lloyd to discuss the fund, his own movements, etc. He was still very undecided; very cross with Austen for showing so little interest in him on his return and on the whole inclined to throw in his lot unreservedly with Baldwin, but asked me if I had any objection to his seeing Beaverbrook, Rothermere, etc. and getting at their views. I said no, let him sound them by all means. I forget whether it was at these conversations, or whether it was from Euan [Wallace], that I heard that Beaverbrook had announced that he meant to 'kill' Baldwin first and me next.

Thence to Bath Club to see Sir J. Power whom Lascelles had suggested as a probable contributor, and worker, for the fiscal movement. I found him shrewd, keen, a self made man very interested in his creation but a good fellow. Lionel Curtis whom I saw at the CO about him said the same and told me the story of how he had worked to get Power the baronetcy promised him for his generous gift to the Institute of Foreign Affairs which L.G.'s herdmen [*sic*] then refused to give unless he added another £30,000 for Party Funds!

6 June 1924: Sitting on the bench next to Austen I asked him what final arrangements had been made about the Preference debate.* Stanley had several times told me I was to speak on this, and I had always assumed I should do the chief speaking with Lloyd Greame as a fellow member of the Conference and also as having organised the whole discussion in the Imperial Committee. Austen told me he had advised Stanley that it would prejudice matters if I spoke more particularly in view of my activities with regard to raising money for protection and preference (he seems to have been unaware up to the last moment that Neville was in it), and that

---

*On the issue of the Government's refusal to implement the 1923 Imperial Conference preference resolutions.

Stanley had acquiesced and put in Tryon as well as himself and Austen. I was really annoyed, not that I often worry about speaking in the House, but because my friends here and still more in the Dominions might not understand my silence. However, Stanley had gone away and I was not prepared to make a fuss about the actual speaking, though determined to clear up the position generally, and after long talks with Neville at Culmhead wrote very strongly both to Stanley and to Austen.

16 June 1924: At the House I had a talk with Stanley who was genuinely sorry for the affair over the Preference debate, but had evidently been talked into it by Austen without realising that I attached any importance to it. At the Imperial Affairs Committee there was no little puzzling and some rather strong protests when it leaked out, at the end, that I wasn't speaking but I glossed it over on the ground that there was quite enough front bench talent.

18 June 1924: Back to the House in time to hear Austen wind up. It was about the best speech I have heard him make, an admirable parliamentary performance. And yet one couldn't help feeling behind it the lack of real will-power; his father's policy has always been to him a hereditary incubus about which he has felt dutifully zealous or dutifully bored, but which has never been to him a great object in itself. The division on the first resolution was very close (6) and but for some stupid backchat by one of our backbenchers the whole Clyde brigade would have voted for us and carried it. L.G. was paired for the resolutions – a miserably weak perform-ance, and the loss of a great opportunity to rehabilitate himself in the eyes of the Empire. Hamar has told me since that when L.G. landed last autumn he, Hamar, went to see him and urged him to back Baldwin. L.G. admitted that Baldwin was right and said 'if it were Austen or Horne or one of the fellows that stood by me I could do it, but I won't help Baldwin who knifed me'. The decision of the House will be disastrous unless it can be reversed within the next year or two.

19 June 1924: Informal Leader's Conference in H. of C. to discuss position of Neville and myself. We both made it clear (a) that the proposed [Tariff] organisation was not to advocate a different policy from that of the Party, but only to propagate principles whose acceptance was equally necessary to the restricted as to a wider policy; (b) that neither he nor I wished to remain on the organisation once it was started. Austen was rather muddled in his criticism of our doings, and the general feeling was that the organisation was in itself desirable but that it was undesirable that Neville and I should be on its formal executive, some expressing the opinion that my own position was rather different in view of my February

THE LEO AMERY DIARIES

letter. Stanley afterwards said he rather doubted its being desirable my being in the leader's official councils if I did take a leading part in the formal organisation, adding that it would of course make no difference to my taking office when we come in again. Neville and I both wished the matter to go further and come before the whole of the Leader's. But Stanley wouldn't have it, and dealt in his own way with Curzon who hearing of what had passed wrote a truly Curzonian letter of protest about the whole business and the ignoring of himself and his House. Neville and I then suggested [on 4 July] that Stanley should write us a letter which we could answer, putting our position in black and white, not for publication, but to show to colleagues. But Stanley evaded this too, and possibly for the best, for it looks as if events would compel us to take a more active fiscal line very soon.

3 August 1924: Off to the Alps in some hopes of getting in a few really good climbs with a guide like Joseph Pollinger – alas, I took no account of the worst summer yet known.

12

Secretary of State
1924-5

By September the Conservative mood was in marked contrast to the shock and demoralisation that had followed their election defeat in December 1923. The Russian treaties agreed to under pressure from the Labour left in August 1924 were to be the subject of parliamentary debate before ratification, and Lloyd George was determined to force an election on the issue. His view reflected that of a majority in the Party, and by September Asquith was moving towards outright opposition. When MacDonald made it clear on 27 September that the treaties would not be amended in any significant way, an election was certain. Labour, however, chose to accept defeat over the Campbell case. The Communist edition of the *Workers' Weekly* had published an article on 25 July which was held to be seditious, and the Attorney General decided that charges were to be pressed. There was anger on the Labour back benches, and the prosecution was abandoned. The Attorney General gave a reasoned explanation to his Conservative and Liberal critics, but MacDonald lied to the House about his own involvement. The Conservatives put down a motion of censure and the Liberals called for a Select Committee of inquiry. MacDonald decided to treat the Liberal amendment as one of censure, and the Conservatives in the course of the debate decided to support the Liberal amendment, which was carried by 364 votes to 199.

Parliament was dissolved on 9 October, and polling day fixed for the 29th. The election campaign began quietly and ended sensationally with the release on 24 October by the Foreign Office of the text of an alleged letter from Zinoviev urging the British Communist Party to campaign for ratification of the Russian treaties as a means to revolutionising the British proletariat, accompanied by a Foreign Office protest. It now seems certain that the letter was forged, and that MacDonald had not authorised publication of the protest. The Labour Party's tactics in handling the issue varied from protests against the forgery to MacDonald's statement that his protest showed the Labour Government as a staunch defender of the

379

country against Bolshevism. The Conservative victory was already inevitable: the extent to which it was further boosted by the Zinoviev letter is uncertain, but the publication probably polarised the electorate and harmed the Liberals.

There was never any doubt that Amery would go to the Colonial Office, and there he remained for five years, engaged on developing the Colonial Empire and strengthening the Office's ability to aid its officials in the field. He has described his achievement in a chapter of *My Political Life* (II, ch. 11) and a fuller account can be found in the White Paper on Progress and Development of the Colonial Empire from November 1924 to November 1928, published in 1929 (Cmd. 3268). Part only of his activities in this connection figures in his diary and that in the form usually of a terse note that he had talked with Clifford, for example, or Guggisberg. Valuable to the scholar, perhaps, when set alongside the official papers and Amery's correspondence, it has not seemed worth selecting *in extenso* in these pages. Sufficient only has been kept to indicate how his days were filled. The more major questions figure where the diary touches on them and suggests the contribution he made to the development of research, to the extension of specialist advisers and services, and to furthering both transport and agriculture. Perhaps the most important innovation in his first year in office was the Empire Marketing Board, product of a deal with Churchill, now Chancellor of the Exchequer in a Conservative Government but still too much of a free trader to contemplate with any equanimity the extension of Imperial preference.* At Lloyd Greame's suggestion £1 million was set aside each year to honour the pledge given to the Dominions at the 1923 Imperial Conference by promoting the marketing of Empire produce in Britain. Amery reluctantly acquiesced, and with the indispensable help of the Board's secretary, Stephen Tallents, devoted the allotted sum not merely to publicity and marketing, but also in very large measure to research (*My Political Life*, II, pp. 348–50). When the Committee of Civil Research was established in 1925 as a civilian counterpart to the Committee of Imperial Defence, Amery also made good use of it to further the research work which the particularist finance of the Colonial Empire was unable to further.

Amery had just under two years in office before the Imperial Conference reassembled, and he used them to lay the basis for the restructuring of the Empire's institutions and constitution which was its principal work in 1926. He had made it a condition for his acceptance of office that he should be allowed to implement the proposal he had made in 1911 for a separate Dominions Office, whose task would be quasi-diplomatic. His correspon-

*Middlemas and Barnes, *Baldwin*, pp. 286–7.

dence with Smuts in 1921 reveals clearly his grasp of the transformation of the Empire into Commonwealth, and while he did not like the term, he was prepared to further the reality. There would need to be a network of High Commissioners to link the Dominions, since the Governor General could no longer represent both the Crown and the British Government. Much has been claimed for Hertzog and for the Irish in the outcome of the Conference, but it is now clear that the changes, far from being forced on a reluctant British Government, had been anticipated in almost two years' patient spadework under Amery's direction.

During 1925 the Conservative Government was engaged on a major effort of appeasement both at home and abroad, and an attempt also, through the return to the Gold Standard, to re-establish international trade and Britain's part in it. Amery was intensely suspicious of the economic thinking behind the move, and would have preferred a policy of tariff reform. He felt that the Treasury was unnecessarily deflating the economy, but he does not seem openly to have opposed the decision to return to gold, which had in effect already been taken by Baldwin, Churchill and Austen Chamberlain well before the Cabinet were told that it would form part of the Budget. He was concerned at the application of the embargo on overseas lending to the Empire, despite its justification in the avoidance of a high bank rate, and his diary records his arguments with Churchill on the subject and of how in the end he succumbed to the arguments of Montagu Norman, the Governor of the Bank of England. He was deeply suspicious of Churchill's Cobdenite economics, and was far from surprised that the Chancellor's brief flirtation with safeguarding at the outset of the year had so little concrete result.

The crunch came over the iron and steel industry's application for a safeguarding inquiry in June. They had a strong case, but a doughty opponent in Churchill, who argued persistently and in the end successfully that to concede the industry protection would be in breach of Baldwin's campaign pledges. Discussion of the case was conducted in the Committee of Civil Research, a parallel body to the Committee of Imperial Defence, proposed by MacDonald to improve the economic foresight of the Government and to improve the co-ordination of its policy. Rescued by Baldwin after the downfall of the Labour Government, this new body was seen as an admirable instrument to tackle the steel inquiry. Amery records a little of its extensive investigation, but it was in the end terminated with the Cabinet's decision in December that, while the case seemed made, to move in this field would precipitate the issue of a general tariff against which the Government was pledged.

This was far from the only issue on which Amery and Churchill were opposed. As befits a former First Lord, he supported Bridgeman in the dispute over the next instalment of the cruiser construction programme which he had himself set in train just before he left the Admiralty in 1924. It was remitted to a Cabinet committee under Birkenhead, which broadly found for the Chancellor. But the Board of Admiralty were determined to fight and, if necessary, to resign. When the Cabinet considered the question in July a majority backed Churchill, but Bridgeman refused to budge and there were rumblings on the back benches. Amery played a full part in the final compromise, that two cruisers should be laid down in October 1925 and two in February 1926, but his diary is silent as to what it was. This is unfortunately a fairly typical problem with his diary for 1925. The record is sufficient to indicate his active concern with these events, but it is never complete, perhaps because Amery was too active and too busy a Minister to achieve complete regularity with his diary. There are few days without a luncheon party at 112 or a luncheon to attend, and a very full tally of speeches, too tedious to report at length, which must have left all too little time for domestic life or autobiographical record.

One minor conflict with the Treasury which figures constantly is the battle waged by Sir Fabian Ware to secure permanent endowment for the Imperial War Graves Commission. The Treasury were reluctant to envisage the graves as a permanent feature, hoping that 'they might ultimately be allowed to disappear'* and they were still more opposed to the creation of a fund in place of an annual vote. But with Amery's support and that of Bruce and Mackenzie King, Ware secured his fund from the Cabinet in March 1925. There was conflict over the size of the capital sum necessary which limited investment of Government securities at the period over which the fund was to be created, but eventually in June 1926 the Bill went through Parliament. The Treasury never hid its dislike of the scheme, and in 1928 unilaterally recommended postponement of its annual contribution. Ware engineered a successful appeal to the Cabinet, but the guerrilla war between the Commission and the Treasury continued into the early 1930s.

If Amery and Churchill were usually to be found on opposing sides, they were at one in their suspicion of Austen Chamberlain's projected pact with France. The context in which he had elaborated this idea was the need to find some alternative form of security for France in place of the Geneva Protocol. This had been elaborated in 1924 to ensure that the procedures under the League Covenant would be automatic and certain. Arbitration in disputes would be automatic and the aggressor against whom sanctions would be enforced would be the power which refused to accept an arbitration on its result. The Service Ministries and the Dominions were bitterly hostile to this proposal and the incoming Conservative Government as a result seemed almost certain to drop it.

*P. Longworth, *The Unending Vigil* (Constable, 1967), p. 138.

Chamberlain, who thought maintenance of the *entente* the cardinal object of British foreign policy, felt that a particular and specific guarantee to France was the only way to relieve French fears for their security and so pave the way for a relaxation of tension in Europe and consequent disarmament.

Amery's diary, written up in March from his pocket book, telescopes a good deal of history into a few brief entries. The CID decided on 4 December 1924 that the Protocol was unacceptable. On the 16th Chamberlain broached the idea of a tripartite pact with France and Belgium. Curzon, presiding over the CID, did not commit himself to this particular proposal, but agreed that there must be an alternative to the Protocol. A sub-committee under Hankey was set up to consider whether the Protocol might be amended or whether an alternative should be elaborated. Not only Amery and Churchill but also Curzon, Balfour, Birkenhead and Hoare seem to have been opposed to Chamberlain on this issue, and Churchill propounded an alternative, a demilitarised zone guaranteed by various signatory powers who would take action against whichever of the two powers, France and Germany, violated this zone. It is just possible that it was the British Ambassador to Germany who put the idea into Churchill's head since on 20 January Germany revived an earlier proposal of its own for a mutual security pact of which the British Ambassador was regarded as part parent. Fearing that the French would never contemplate the inclusion of Germany in a security pact, Chamberlain warned the Germans that discussion on their proposal would have to await a bilateral arrangement between France and Britain, and that remained his aim even after the French Government had expressed its willingness to include Germany in any arrangement.

Hankey's sub-committee, which reported on 23 January, rejected the Protocol in favour of a declaration of mutual guarantee of territory against unprovoked aggression signed by France, Belgium and Britain, which it was felt might serve as a model for other similar declarations elsewhere. A Foreign Office discussion on the 28th did not rule out the eventual inclusion of Germany, but set as preconditions to a new concert of Europe German membership of the League and the quietening of France through Britain's influence as an ally. The evident fear in the Foreign Office was that if Germany were included, France would seek to extend the guarantee to Germany's eastern frontiers also.

Nevertheless the CID on 13 February revived the idea of a four-power pact to include Germany. Chamberlain believed that Herriot in conversation with him had consented to Germany's inclusion, but his real plea was for the pact with France, not least because it would lead to the abandonment of the occupation of the Rhineland by British and French forces. Amery favoured a guarantee only of Belgium and Luxemburg, but in the end the Foreign Office were asked to prepare a draft four-power pact. Amery's diary telescopes this meeting with that on the 19th which finally determined the rejection of the Protocol along lines suggested by Balfour but at the same time turned against the idea of 'little local protocols', which Amery thought had found favour on the 13th. By now Chamberlain had support for his proposed pact with France from Bridgeman and Worthington Evans. Hoare would not risk guaranteeing France, and Churchill, while he had not abandoned his support for a pact including both France and Germany, was all for a three-year delay. Birkenhead and Amery agreed with him, the latter because he wished for a Dominions Conference to discuss the issue. Curzon attacked the whole concept of regional arrangements, and only Balfour reluctantly backed Chamberlain.

The Foreign Office had returned to the idea of a pact with France alone: a powerful memorandum advocating this was circulated on 20 February. The prospect of a four-power pact had not, however, been withdrawn, and, on 2 March, it became the Cabinet's approved alternative to the Protocol when Chamberlain's proposed Anglo-French pact foundered in the face of opposition from Amery, Churchill, Balfour, Birkenhead and Curzon. Apparently only Baldwin's support had enabled the proposal to go through. Curzon and Balfour declared their opposition immediately after the Cabinet to what had been agreed, and in Baldwin's absence on 4 March, the Cabinet came down against any definite commitment even to a four-power pact should it involve a guarantee of frontiers. The door was left open, but only just, and the whole process made subject to consultation with the Dominions, as Amery wished.

The French were dismayed, and it seemed evident that, if Britain wished to secure the evacuation of the Rhineland and the pacification of Europe, she would have to commit herself to the pact. Baldwin called together an informal meeting on 11 March at which Amery was present. There is no record in his diary, unfortunately, but the outcome of an evidently stormy meeting, at which Amery had denounced all specific commitments because the Dominions would never agree to them, seems to have been a decision 'to continue the policy of refusing any pact with France unless a quadrilateral arrangement could also be made to include Germany'.* Amery does not record the final approval of the pact by the Cabinet on 20 March, but Hankey records the reason for his eventual acquiescence: 'Amery accepts it, only because he is certain the French won't take it – a bad

*Bridgeman's Political Notes (unpublished; courtesy of the 2nd Viscount Bridgeman). This is denied explicitly by Sibyl Eyre Crowe in her article 'Sir Eyre Crowe and the Locarno Pact', *English Historical Review*, January 1972, and implicitly by Jon Jacobson, *Locarno Diplomacy: Germany and the West 1925–29* (Princeton University Press, 1972), p. 20, but the evidence of Bridgeman seems to be borne out by Baldwin's letter of 12 March, printed by Middlemas and Barnes, *Baldwin*, pp. 354–5. The letter as Baldwin himself interpreted it makes more sense than in any rival interpretation.

reason.' In the event the French did accept the Locarno Pact, and Amery in retrospect came to find it defensible as an instrument of policy. However, as his diary for 26 May shows, he remained almost as watchful as Hankey about the over-extension of British commitments and the reservation to the Government of the power to determine its own actions.

Appeasement at home and in Europe was accomplished also by the settlement of differences between Northern Ireland and the South over the boundary question.

As a consequence of the decision of Ulster to opt out of the Free State, a Boundary Commission representing the Governments of Northern Ireland, Eire and the United Kingdom automatically came into existence to delineate the boundary 'in accordance with the wishes of the inhabitants, so far as may be compatible with economic and geographic conditions' (Clause 12 of the Irish Treaty). The Northern Ireland Government refused to act under this article of the Treaty, while the Government of the Free State prepared its case and, in July 1923, appointed MacNeill as their Commissioner. The British Government did not act immediately on the request to set the Commission in train, perhaps because of widespread disagreement over the scale on which the Commission could act. Privately the South hoped for transfers substantial enough to force the North into union, but the view of the Northern Ireland Premier, Sir James Craig, was that only limited frontier rectification could be involved. It was not until the Labour Government took office in 1924 that a joint conference was called, although this had been the strategy of Baldwin's Government also. No agreement could be secured, and when Craig refused to appoint the Northern Ireland commissioner, the Labour Government secured from Parliament – the Conservatives reluctantly assenting – power to appoint for them. The Commission was constituted with Feetham as chairman and a staunch associate of Carson and Craig, the journalist and barrister J. R. Fisher, as Ulster's representative. The new boundary was virtually settled by mid-October and agreed early in November, but a premature leak of the findings in the *Morning Post* on 7 November 1925 suggested that they would not be very favourable to the South. In fact this was not accurate. Craig, naturally enough, was now disposed to implement the changes while the South reacted fiercely. They would cede no territory to the North. MacNeill resigned. The Free State leaders came to London to confer on 25 November and eventually the two sides were brought together at Chequers on 29 November. Amery's diary should be compared with that of Tom Jones* to get a full picture of the discussions which led ultimately to an agreement to bury the report, and settle on the existing frontier. Such an agreement could not have been reached without

*Thomas Jones, *Whitehall Diary* (Volume III Ireland 1918–25, Oxford University Press, 1971).

a major concession by Britain, the relief of Eire from its obligation under Article 5 of the Treaty to undertake a share of the National Debt. In its turn the Free State took over responsibility for the compensation due in respect of damage done in Ireland due to the truce as assessed by the Wood Renton Commission and a proportion of the compensation payable for damages done during the Civil War. Northern Ireland gained the powers hitherto reserved under the Treaty for the abortive Council of Ireland. Final agreement was reached on the night of 2–3 December and was speedily made law. The Boundary Commission's report was buried in the obscurity of the Cabinet Office from which it was rescued by scholars forty-four years later.

Diary

19 September 1924: Saw . . . Haden Guest who is evidently rapidly drifting away from the Labour Party and to us. He seems to have assimilated my fiscal writings to some purpose and told me that he was coming out with a series of four articles in *The Times* both advocating protection and preference and severely criticising the policy of the Government. He is by no means sure that the result of it will not compel him to leave his Party and join us and his is [*sic*] that while there are some reactionaries in our Party with whom he will find it very difficult to work he could very happily follow Baldwin and myself and work with younger men of the Eden and Lumley type. On my way to the station in the afternoon I had to see Jackson about a cable from Hamar [Greenwood] who has been invited to stand as a Liberal for Central Cardiff. He informed Jackson that he would only do so if supported or nominated by our Association there. I told Jackson that I had no doubt that Hamar would very much sooner stand on our side than as a Liberal and I hope it may not be too late to get the Cardiff Conservatives not to decide on the candidates before them but wait for Hamar's return. All these things are straws showing that the tide is turning our way. Then I had a short walk with Baldwin who is very anxious if possible to avoid the Lords making Ireland and their own powers the election issue. He seemed well and cheery.

23 September 1924: Went to the Central Office to see Jackson who wanted my advice about Hamar. I agreed with him that it was much better to secure Hamar directly for our Party and get the full advantage of his effectiveness on the platform at our meetings than merely to fix up some local pact . . . and that therefore we should get him to stand on our nomination with

Liberal support if available and not on Liberal nomination. Anyhow Jackson is cabling him not to touch Cardiff.

25 September 1924: Meeting of the Shadow Cabinet on the Irish question. The general conclusion was that we ought not to let the Lords wreck the [Boundary Commission] Bill but confine ourselves to insisting that the supplementing of the Treaty to fulfil the intention of the signatories ought no less to be supplemented in order to fulfil the full intention of Parliament as to the scope of the Boundary Commission. If over-ridden we must warn the Government that we should resist any attempt to enforce against Ulster a decision based on what we regard as a false interpretation of the Treaty. I confined my remarks to observing that the really serious issue we should have to face sooner or later would be the Free State's tearing up the Treaty and that meanwhile the important thing was while avoiding anything that could suggest to Ulster that we were weakening, also avoid saying or doing anything that would be against us when it came to dealing firmly with the South.

27 September 1924 (Birmingham): A long walk with Neville round Harborne and back by the Canal. We amused ourselves among other things by doing a little Cabinet making. Neville's chief anxiety is firstly to get Curzon out of the FO and see Austen there, and secondly to get Jix out of the Ministry of Health where he splurges about without much understanding. Neville is quite disposed to go back there again if Stanley should want to put Horne or anyone else at the Exchequer. [The entry for 27 September is unfinished, and there are no further entries for that month.]

8 October 1924 (written on 7 November): The events of this day put a stop to my diary for a whole month. I can only resume very badly. At question time MacDonald explained to a frigid and astonished House that his previous answer about the Campbell case [see p. 379] was all untrue and due to the 'heat of the moment' and that he had known all about it. The vote of censure was duly moved by Horne. . . . MacDonald was high falutin and unconvincing. Then old Asquith in a most witty mellow bantering speech brought the whole thing down to a low temperature and offered to accept any sort or kind of inquiry, in fact giving the Government a pretty easy let out if they had not had too much to conceal or had not decided to rush an election over this sooner than over the Russian business.* Then followed much discussion behind the scenes. We realised

*The reference is to the Russian treaties. One was a commercial treaty granting most favoured nation rights and diplomatic status for certain members of the Russian trade delegation. The second would have guaranteed a loan to the Soviet Government if a satisfactory

that the Labour people proposed to vote with us . . . in order to defeat the amendment and then vote with the Liberals against our vote of censure. On the other hand we did not wish to make fools of ourselves by dropping our own motion, and indeed voting against it, if the Libs ran away as so often. However, Asquith assured Baldwin that he could rely on all except a dozen or so to vote straight and said that he would resign the leadership if they didn't. This was good enough so B. announced we should withdraw our motion for the Liberal amendment. The Cabinet met after dinner and apparently the Die-hard section prevailed. After Hogg wound up for us in far the best speech of the debate, Thomas replied, much against his own views, in a truculent speech refusing all consideration. We divided and the Government were beaten hopelessly, only a baker's dozen of Libs running out [fourteen Liberals and two Conservatives voted with the Government]. It is interesting to think that if they had accepted any sort of inquiry and gained time, they could have got rid of the Russian Treaty on the plea of the Zinovieff letter and carried on for months longer.

10 October 1924: Meeting at Palace Chambers to discuss Baldwin's Election manifesto. As usual it fell to me to draw it up and I set to work, embodying sundry fids from others about Housing, Agriculture, Education, etc., and had a first draft reading by 5 o'clock.

11 October 1924: Back by the 7.30 which was very late, but had enough time to go over the draft with Stanley and Sam and make a few additions and alterations in time for the Sunday papers. This is the third party manifesto I have now drafted and I think the best one. Contrasting it with our opponents' it struck me as much clearer and more practical, and I think it helped materially in influencing the election from the start.

21 October 1924 (Pembroke): I discovered before the meeting that L.G. had through the *Daily Chronicle* been preparing the ground for me by saying that I was the person who had tried to close Pembroke which he had prevented and was told I might expect a rough time from the hecklers. It was a wonderful big meeting, at least 4000 tightly packed. I began straight away on Pembroke and told them the true story adding that I did so to free the L.G. family from the unfair charge of having misused power for family ends. This went down very well and the whole attitude of the great audience inspired me to make the best election speech I have yet made. Both the Chairman and Price [the candidate] referred to me after-

settlement could be made of British subjects' claims in respect of pre-Revolution Russian Government bonds and of property confiscated by nationalisation. The negotiations had broken down on 5 August, but, after left-wing pressure, the negotiations were resumed and an agreement concluded.

wards as the future Prime Minister, and the cheering at the end, after a dead silent meeting, lasted a long while. L.G. came down for two days to counteract it, attacked me for all he was worth (to which I replied in a letter for last hour publication) but failed to save the seat for Gwilym [Lloyd George]. Here I think I definitely turned the scale.

29 October 1924: We all adjourned to the Queen's for supper and while we were finishing the first results began to come in, one Unionist victory after another. Then to the count, a weary and hateful business. There were many more Potters* than seemed at all pleasant at first, and it was soon clear that the Socialists had gained very heavily at the expense of the Liberals and would have a large total poll. In the end I polled just under 16,000. The Socialist nearly 10,000 and the Liberal 1500. My majority of 5959 was 1600 less than last year's, but my majority over both opponents combined was about 1400 up. My percentage of total votes polled went up to 59% as against 56% last year and 49% in 1922....† After our count was over and other counts turned out all right, we turned our attention to King's Norton where H. Austin was defeated by 133, the reward of slackness, and then to Ladywood. At one stage Neville [Chamberlain] was in by 30. [Oswald] Mosley demanded a recount and Neville was down to 7. Then one of N.'s packets was found to contain only 13 papers and M. was 2 up. Then the 7 were found attached to another bundle and N. was 7 up again but the totals over 30 out. So the Lord Mayor took the whole count over with new tellers and scrutineers and at 4.20 announced the final result N. 77 up. B. and I stayed right through to cheer up Neville and Annie through the ordeal. . . . Mosley behaved very badly, accused everyone of cheating, etc., a hairy heeled fellow.

30 October 1924: Got up late to read the amazing results of the great landslide. I had secretly believed we should get 100 majority, but had no notion of the strength of the swing against Socialism and for a stable Government. It made me wish we had taken a stronger line on fiscal policy for we could easily have afforded to lose 50 seats. I had implored Baldwin when the election began to make no negative commitments, but I fear he has rather narrowed things down.

1–3 November 1924: Went for a good walk with Neville on Monday 3rd and discussed new Cabinet and policy. He was very anxious to go to Ministry of Health rather than Exchequer, his view being that he preferred

*The Labour candidate whom L.S.A. described (on the 16th) as 'a young ex-Captain of Air Force called Potter, a fluent but silly young man'.

†The relatively low swing suggests how well Amery in particular and Birmingham in general polled for the Conservatives in the 'tariff election' of 1923.

to make a big name in the job he knew and cared about rather than a mere average reputation as a Chancellor. He was inclined to think that Baldwin had made it difficult to carry through the [Imperial] Conference [preference] Resolutions [of 1923] involving additional duties (salmon, apples, etc.), thus rather endorsing the view Euan Wallace had taken of Baldwin's speeches. I do trust that may not be the case. It would be a great pity if we started off our preferential policy with practically nothing for Canada and a bar against all future development. I shall have to explore and see whether there are not some raw materials on which we couldn't give preference. Here at any rate we have no pledges and no mass fears to encounter.

5 November 1924:   Met Winston looking very cheerful, and no wonder, getting, as we learnt afterwards, in the shape of a fatted calf what he had failed to get for all his effort while sojourning with his former depraved associates. While there was told Baldwin had fixed me up for the CO 'after a good many vicissitudes' – this I think referred to what I have heard since about both Winston and F.E. being anxious to get the post. His one anxiety about it was that I might be in bad odour as a 'die-hard' among the Irish and he was anxious that I should take an early opportunity of getting to know Cosgrave, etc. He told me he had fixed up Steel-Maitland for Labour – this is what I had suggested to him and I hope it will turn out all right. I did not know then that he had pressed Horne very strongly to take it, and that without even suggesting the Exchequer, whereat I gather Horne is now very annoyed, though I see no reason why he should regard the fluke which made him Chancellor in 1921 as giving him a prescriptive right. Jix came in just after me and emerged in a moment looking fairly cheerful. I heard from him later that it was to be Home Office for him. He may be disappointed at not getting the Exchequer, but he isn't really quite up to it. The other he will do well if only he doesn't fail at a critical moment for cocksureness and lack of tact.

6 November 1924:   Looked in at Chatham House for a talk with Curtis about the Irish situation. He is all for my writing to Healy [Governor General of the Irish Free State] and saying frankly that I wish to know his ministers personally and would be willing to go over and see them.

7 November 1924:   The new Cabinet duly announced in the Press and no little surprise and some annoyance at Winston's preferment. If he means to play the game about Empire development and Preference no one could be better. If he doesn't he may make my position very difficult. . . . Had a very pleasant half hour's talk with Thomas,* who is overflowing

---

*J. H. Thomas had been L.S.A.'s immediate predecessor at the Colonial Office.

with friendliness and assurances of willingness to help and co-operate in every way. I congratulated him on his work at the CO and on the tone of his speeches since the election.

The next set of entries were written up on 5 January 1925, presumably from an engagement book.

Diary

8 November 1924: During the night I felt seedy and apparently started a gastric flu which kept me more or less in bed for four days – my most serious illness since 1907.

12 November 1924: Our first Cabinet. I found myself between Curzon and F.E. nearly opposite Baldwin, a much better position for getting a word in.

13 November 1924: Attended Cabinet Committee to fix up terms of reference and personnel of proposed Royal Commission on Food Prices. We had already on 12th decided to send off a definite telegram to Dominions to set the Imperial Economic Committee going on the limited *ad hoc* reference agreed to by Canada. . . . Trevor Dawson came to see me about oil in Mosul – evidently in connexion with Inverforth's most shady and unpatriotic negotiations with the Turks. I gave him no encouragement. The Beits, Neville Chamberlains and Davidsons to dine, our first dinner at 112 [Eaton Square, London SW1]. The Library makes a really 'homey' place to sit in, and has something of the feel of a library in an old house.

14 November 1924: Saw all the High Commissioners at the rate of half an hour apiece. I had meanwhile arranged with Austen and Stanley that the latter should receive them all at tea one afternoon the next week, and that Austen would informally tell them something about the general foreign situation. They were all greatly pleased about this. After, the High Commissioners saw Blain and Sam Hoare about the Secretariat which Jackson wants to abolish. Blain was all for keeping it and regarded it as most valuable. I produced a strong memo: had it up before the next Cabinet and also with S.B. But he gave no real effective backing and in the end the whole organisation was disbanded; Wicks going to Curzon again – a job he by no means relishes though he says Curzon has much improved – and Storr to the Lord Chancellor as Secretary to deal with ecclesiastical patronage.

18 November 1924: Saw Colebatch, the W. Australian Agent General, who is very anxious that we should fix up the big settlement scheme with the Commonwealth, as all W. Australian activities have been hung up for months waiting for this. . . . High Commissioners' Tea Party at No. 10. Austen gave a short survey of the world situation, laying special stress on Egypt. Both in the matter of wishing to consult the Dominions and in his foresight over the Egyptian situation Austen started off very well. When Stack was murdered a few days later Allenby was already fully primed as to our general purpose if a crisis arose. The High Commissioners were all very pleased and no doubt communicated very fully with their Governments. In this matter we went as far as we could go without forcing the hands of the Dominion Governments by treating the High Commissioners as their diplomatic representatives.

19 November 1924: Cabinet – I think this was before Stack's murder [on 20th] but am not quite sure. Lunched with the Carsons . . . James Craig was there and we had a long and useful talk afterwards. He is convinced that the Free State can't survive, but is bound to break down financially and otherwise in the next three years – a pretty prospect for me!

20 November 1924: Had a talk with S.B. about my idea of dividing up the CO and having two Parliamentary Under Secretaries and two Permanent Under Secretaries possibly also giving myself an extra Patent as S. of S. for Imperial Affairs. He was quite sympathetic but wanted me to discuss it fully with Warren Fisher and Winston.

Cabinet on the Egyptian situation. All of us quite clear that firm action had to be taken, and that we should more particularly use this occasion to clear up things in the Sudan. Our general line was not to ask for anything outside the terms of our declaration of February 1922 but to make that declaration effective.

21 November 1924: Saw Winston for a few minutes. . . . On the question of dividing the office he was not at all sympathetic, taking the view that the CO was lightly worked and that he had never had any difficulty in doing it all. (I couldn't very well reply that except for Ireland and Iraq he had largely neglected the work and that no one had really done it since Milner and I left in 1921, and anyhow I had to rush off to catch a train to Birmingham.)

22 November 1924: My 51st birthday. Saw Mr Casey, Bruce's new liaison officer for Foreign Affairs. Hit upon the happy idea that he should be quartered not at the Foreign Office but with Hankey and this has since been most satisfactorily arranged. I see in this move of Bruce's the germ of a real practical development in inter communication. Meanwhile the crisis of the day showed how difficult it is in practice to consult with the Dominions by cable. We had an emergency Cabinet at 12 to consider the first draft of the ultimatum Allenby was to deliver. In it Austen had eliminated some of Allenby's crudities of language and also the undesirable and invidious demands for a fine and for unlimited irrigation of the Gezirah. It was in every way a good document and was telegraphed off at once. Two minutes before its first sections arrived in Cairo Allenby went off in state, with escort of lancers, etc. to deliver his own ultimatum (already aware from previous cables of our objections to part of it). Such of us as were in London were hastily summoned to a Cabinet at the FO at 6 p.m. – myself from the Turkish bath. Austen had decided to send a very stiff wire to Allenby and compel him to take back the original ultimatum and substitute our text. Baldwin had agreed with this over the telephone from Chequers and so did I. Winston and F.E. very strongly the other way pointing out the humiliation and absurdity of going back on the dramatic action taken and making light of foreign and Dominion objections to the Allenby version. Hogg and Steel-Maitland hesitatingly went with them and between them convinced Austen and (over the phone) S.B. I held out on the ground that our regulations and authority were far more important than Allenby's and that the convenience of giving way and accepting the situation would be outbalanced by the later consequences. In a subsequent note to Austen I compared our acquiescence with Rhodes's after the Raid and contrasted it with Joe's instant disavowal of Jameson. So far, however, it looks as if I overestimated the disadvantages. All went well and though the points we objected to were also objected to abroad, in the Dominions and here the criticism was not serious. Allenby was terribly difficult though those days especially about the sending out of Nevile Henderson, and after showing infinite conciliation and almost humiliation Austen had to accept his resignation to be acted upon later on. . . . As for Dominion consultation, what with Saturday afternoon and the continual changes of the day no wire went off till after our late Cabinet to explain how it came about that they got the press details of the ultimatum actually delivered. In the next few days, however, we kept them well supplied with our views and the stages of development of our policy.

It was not until 25 March 1925 that Amery began to keep a diary again, and his first entries are an attempt to recapture the events from the previous November.

Diary

26 November 1924: [Saw] Hankey about my ideas of reorganising the office. He is inclined to put Sammy Wilson above Chancellor as a P[ermanent] U[nder] S[ecretary] on the ground that Chancellor does not get on with his subordinates.

6 December 1924: George Lloyd to dinner and full of most interesting talk about India and his own hopes. Quite miserable that I should have thought of the possibility of his going to Egypt when it might side track him. Cannot understand how any one could compare Ronaldshay's work with his. B. and I both much taken with his life and keenness and not worried, as I fear some are, by the naïveté of his interest in himself.

8 December 1924: Cabinet Sub Committee on Economic Conference, S.B. in the chair. I found them all against me on the question of the literal fulfilment of the pledges given at the Economic Conference on the ground that S.B.'s election pledges were taken as excluding all new food duties whatsoever. After a long fight I had to give way and content myself with securing the full money equivalent of the bounties which might have been imposed in lieu (this when inquiries showed that bounties were very awkward to administer) to be devoted to the better marketing of Empire foodstuffs. I was anything but happy about this and have the gravest doubts as to the effective spending of the £1,000,000 a year that the Economic Committee are to make recommendations about. The only consolation is that it gives the latter something very definite to set to work on, and may offer a precedent for further development on similar lines.

24–31 December 1924: So ended 1924. Looking back I don't seem to have done very much though busy all the time. Politically it began in disappointment and, for me at any rate, ended in the disappointing feeling that we, with all our great majority, were shackled by the pledges which I had vainly urged S.B. not to give, and not free to do anything really big in the way of grappling with unemployment at home or with the centrifugal forces in the Empire.

Amery returned from holiday on 10 January. His diary until 24 March is written up from his office list of engagements and pocket book and has many omissions.

Diary

15 January 1925: [Saw] McDougall, who has come back again from Australia, about the Preference situation and the Imperial Economic Committee (of which he has since become a member). He is evidently very distressed at our failure to carry through the Preference proposals unaltered and not too sanguine about the million a year idea [for the Empire Marketing Board].

17 January 1925: [MacNaghten] came about the long drawn-out Australia negotiations which I brought to a conclusion in the next few days, by conceding some of Bruce's further requests and rejecting others, as far as we were concerned at this end. He then submitted them to the six States in conference with the result that a far-reaching lot of amendments were telegraphed back at the end of February, of which again I accepted most with one definite proviso, viz. that not less than 50% of the men actually settled on the land should be migrants, doing so on my own responsibility as the Treasury disclaimed any, and telegraphing accordingly.

19 January 1925: [Saw] the PM about things in general, and more particularly about my desire to get a move on over the reorganisation of the office. This led to Fisher's being called in and to the suggestion [of] a small Committee of Scott, Hopkins of the Customs and Hamilton of I[nland] R[evenue] to investigate the whole matter. I accepted this rather too easily and should have stood out for Hankey or Oswyn Murray to be head of it. However, no great harm came from it in the long run, except that they simply reported what Fisher had made it plain to me was his conclusion at the beginning viz. against two Permanent Under Secretaries. Otherwise as I wished.

20 January 1925: Had a long talk with the new Committee, drafted their terms of reference, and gave them my own views as to office organisation. I ought to add that at our talk the day before the principle of creating a new S. of S. for Dominion Affairs was agreed to, and the reference was based on how most efficiently to carry out this principle.

23 January 1925: Long conference in the afternoon with Northumberland, Gretton and others about Irish Loyalist hardships. They were really most reasonable, but it is very difficult to know what to do. One cannot compensate in practice against all the consequences direct and indirect of a successful revolution, as the old American example showed.

25 January 1925: Dined with Sam Hoares to discuss our project of visiting Iraq in order to get the new defence policy put into effect. S.B. had already after the policy had been raised at the Cabinet privately agreed to our going.

28 January 1925: Cabinet at which I think the Iraq reorganisation of defence, etc. was finally approved in principle.

2 February 1925: [Saw] Halsey about the rather unfortunate press statement that the Prince was going over to Ireland for Masonic purposes and made it clear that it would only do if the Masonic business was one incident in a visit for some general object such as the Horse Show. . . . Talk with Hankey about Protocol arrangements arising out of the excellent report of his Committee which, however, was dropped when it came to our discussions in favour of an ingenious, but I always thought, somewhat nebulous argumentative negation by Balfour. . . . Winston and F.E. to dinner and a great evening's talk at the end of which F.E. went away protesting that he had not been allowed to get in more than ten per cent of the talking. We discussed a great many topics, including naval expenditure, and my counter criticism that the only real way of meeting the burden was to increase production by protection and Imperial development. We also had a long discussion of the pros and cons of Birdwood and Jacob for the C.-in-C. India, and on balance decided for Birdwood.

4 February 1925: Long interview with Turkish Petroleum Co. to see if their differences with Iraq Government could be settled, and sent off strong telegram to Dobbs to bring matters to a head.*

5 February 1925: Singapore Sub-Committee of CID at which Winston, instigated I suspect by Leveson, raised anew the whole question of the site for the base and floating dock at Singapore. After several meetings he was successfully overridden and the old Strait settled on as the site for the floating dock. But the rest is still left in suspense and he is being very troublesome about it.

13 February 1925: Meeting of CID, I think on the Protocol, the discussion turning mainly on guarantees to France and on whether the last part of Balfour's memo should be retained. In the end it was rewritten in a form suggesting something more in the nature of joint and mutual pacts, i.e. little local protocols and no defensive pacts against any one, and as

---

*The Iraq Government were seeking a shareholding in the Turkish Petroleum Company as the price for allowing development of their oilfields.

such the whole thing was eventually delivered by Austen as his speech to the League Council.

17 February 1925: CID on Singapore: we definitely recommended to Cabinet that floating dock and ancillary buildings water supply, etc. should go ahead at cost of about £750,000 over three years. Subsequently Winston made a considerable fuss in the Cabinet because he claimed that this excluded the cost of completing the floating dock itself before sending it out. I have forgotten to mention that we had had [11 and 12 February] great Cabinet discussions about the Navy, one at the Cabinet where I went bandaged and spoke with some fervour against Winston and in Willie's defence. [Later L.S.A. holograph note: 'At some stage I told S.B. that if Winston forced Willie's resignation I would resign too.'] In the end the whole construction programme was remitted to a Sub-Committee and Winston was left to settle with Willie and Beatty the rest of the Estimates. At the conference I was told Beatty completely talked round Winston and the figure agreed on was far better than the Admiralty hoped. So while the Press were giving headlines to Winston's victory over the Admiralty, the Sea Lords were quietly chortling over their successful defence.

20 February 1925: Walked to office with Lane, Smuts's old P S, now S. African Exhibition Commissioner. He expressed to me Smuts's anxiety already conveyed by cable for a really first rate man, in sympathy with the white ideal, in Kenya.

21 February 1925: Long talk with Zakiki Bey, the Turkish Minister. Z. has been intriguing for months with Inverforth to get us to surrender Mosul. I. seems to have made, or claimed to have made some progress with MacDonald and tried again not only with S.B. but with almost every member of the Cabinet. I was made to lunch one day with Tommy Platt and met Sir G. Armstrong who was one of the I[nverforth] crowd. Winston and F.E. had both found themselves asked to dinner and then found themselves side by side with Z. They tried via Simon to get me to meet Z. at dinner with Wimborne and I refused. Eventually he asked Austen to see me. I fear he got no change out of me in an hour beyond a parting word of friendly advice that he was merely wasting his time if he thought Lord I. had any influence with the Government or that we would alter our policy in any way.

25 February 1925: Cabinet. It was on this occasion I think that I raised question of a definite ultimatum to Iraq Ministers about the oil concession on which they had now reopened the issue of their right to share participation. The Cabinet evidently thought this too strong a measure and I suggested a Committee under Curzon to go more closely into what we might do. . . . [Talk] with Nichols of Turkish Petroleum to tell him that he must try and find some device by which Iraq could still be given shares without prejudice to the fact that the contract was already as favourable as it could possibly be made.

26 February 1925: Compatriots' Annual Meeting and dinner. G. Lloyd in the chair and we had an excellent address by Gore on E. Africa. I spoke to Lloyd about the possibility of his taking Kenya, but he didn't think he could look at it unless I could federate for him at once – which I really can't – and even then he doubted as it might prejudice his chances of India for good.

27 February 1925: Cabinet. I think this was the Cabinet at which we discussed the Political Levy Bill.* F.E. reported the Cabinet Committee's conclusion in favour of promising an inquiry adding his own personal conviction that we ought to go straight against the Bill. We others all talked round and about it, I rather attracted by Churchill's idea of putting most of the cost of elections on the state, not so much as an alternative to the Levy, but as a direct encouragement to our own working man. In the end S.B. summed up with simple homely eloquence in favour of industrial peace, and what carried no conviction as put by F.E. carried us all away. We went out wondering if S.B. could possibly put it over the House and the Party as he had over us round the table. Meeting of the Iraq Oil Sub Committee at which we worked out the outlines of a plan by which the dividend on Iraq's shares should come out of the 4s royalty. Saw Cranworth and Grogan [white settler leaders] very anxious to persuade me to get G. Lloyd for Kenya and assuring me that Kenya could swallow federation at once if it could get him. The trouble is not only Gore's report and the promises given† but the physical obstacles to any High Commissioner getting round the different colonies till the railways are linked up.

28 February 1925: Conference with Turkish Petroleum Co. at Board of Trade at which we hammered out a workable scheme. After all this was done and the assent of the various groups secured and cables sent out to Dobbs the Iraq Government suddenly agreed on the old terms, two

*A Conservative backbencher, Macquisten, had proposed to reverse the legal position on the political levy paid by trade unions to the Labour Party. This would have made the individual trade unionist contract to pay rather than have to contract out of paying. Since most Conservative backbenchers believed that there was a great deal of intimidation of those trying to contract out, this was a very popular move, but one which would be taken by the Labour movement to be intensely provocative. Baldwin secured its withdrawal by his 'peace in our time' speech on 6 March.
†See pp. 507–8.

ministers apparently resigning. So that is, I hope, happily out of the way. . . . Down to Chequers in time for tea. . . . As S.B. was dining in Oxford with the 'Ad Eundem' I went on with him to dine at All Souls. . . . We had a great talk both going and coming on many topics, among others Australian Governor General, as to which S.B. had no definite views except that he was rather glad that I proposed to include Johnny Baird's name as well as Evelyn Cecil's and Seely's. We also discussed Kenya and G. Lloyd and S.B. told me, to my surprise, that he and Austen had suddenly thought of Ronaldshay as better suited for Egypt than Lloyd, apparently in conjunction with an idea of prolonging Reading and then judging how R. might do for India. R. had apparently been offered Egypt so it was no use saying much though I expressed the view that Lloyd was really the better man. I took S.B. into All Souls where he had never been before for a few minutes before his dinner.

1 March 1925: A quiet Sunday. S.B. and Mrs B. rather piano because of his mother's illness which looked like being the end. He was also meditating his speech for Birmingham and for the Political Levy Bill and asked me to postpone discussion of CO organisation.

2 March 1925: Sir D. Cameron to say goodbye. I broke it to him that I might begin to move federationwards before very long. . . . Cabinet at which, in spite of my pleas of Dominion opposition, Austen talked the Cabinet round to agree to some kind of promise of a pact to be more or less given to Herriot, on the way to Geneva, where A.C. was to bust the Protocol, based on the German proposals but not excluding a preliminary pact to France and Belgium. On this I had managed to draft a telegram to the Dominions making the thing look as plausible and innocuous as possible.

4 March 1925: Cabinet. Since Monday Curzon and others had got together and made it clear to Austen that his ideas of what was to be said to Herriot went too far. My telegram was, to my great relief, scrapped, and to Austen's bitter disappointment the Cabinet (Baldwin away with his mother) definitely told Austen to make it clear to Herriot that there could be no question of an Anglo-Franco-Belgian Pact but that we were prepared to favour a joint pact with Germany, though as Winston insisted even this should not involve more than mutual consultation if one party to the pact showed signs of breaking it. The definite adhesion of Curzon, Winston and F.E. to the anti-pactites of whom Hoare and I had so far been the protagonists has completely defeated the FO scheme (which captured Austen) for rushing the country (forgetting the Empire) into a definite commitment to defend France on the ground that she would never behave rationally till we relieved her fears of what may happen twenty years hence. Austen faithfully carried out the Cabinet's wish and made things quite clear to Herriot with, I have no doubt, good results. Now I come to think of it all this happened at an afternoon Cabinet at the House of Commons the same day. The ordinary Cabinet in the morning dealt with other and less exciting matters I think.

6 March 1925: S.B.'s speech in the House, simple, quiet, reminiscent about his own days as an employer and his old workmen, carried the House away more completely than even the Cabinet. Neville had previously induced the leaders of the movement for forcing the Bill through to accept a most innocuous amendment, and after B.'s speech they all most loyally accepted the situation, the only real malcontent being Horne who was very cross. It was by far the greatest political triumph S.B. has ever had and when he sat down there was a moment's silence and then applause from all sections of the House.

7 March 1925: We dined with the Milners, no other company. He was in good form, but I felt somehow as if he had aged quite appreciably since he went away. His reception by old friends in South Africa seems to have gone very much to his heart.

12 March 1925: Walked to office with Casey who has heard from Bruce that he wanted something more showy than my suggestions for Governor General and mentioned Derby, Salisbury and Cavan as names which Bruce had suggested. I promptly tried S. in person who though very appreciative couldn't do it – I am not sure he wouldn't look at Canada later. Derby I wrote to and as expected got the telegram 'impossible'. Cavan wants to complete his time as CIGS. . . . Took chair at Imperial Affairs Committee addressed by Boyd-Carpenter and the others who have recently visited Iraq and are all strongly for our permanently staying there. The whole atmosphere on this question has changed. Had a talk with George Lloyd about Kenya – deferred day after day – and had to break to him the fact that he might not be going to Egypt after all. He was in a dreadful state and talking of throwing up public life, thinks it all due to personal animosities, etc. Had a dinner in the evening for the High Commissioners, all there except Allen, and to meet them Milner, Hogg, Willie [Bridgeman], Philip, Arthur [Steel-Maitland] and G. Lloyd. After dinner we discussed Dominion representation at length, their main point being that the Dominion Governments would never appoint or designate them or anyone else, but that they would only too gladly accept the situation if we began gradually to take the High Commissioners into our confidence. I doubt it, but I think I shall try. Anyhow they may have written to their PMs and I have also done so since.

17 March 1925: Up with Edward [Wood] in the train. He was very worried about George Lloyd as he had told him with S.B.'s authority that he was going to Egypt and thought George was really in a mood to do almost anything in his despair. . . . Saw Hankey and conspired with him as to how to hang up things at the CID till my return. He is never very happy about things when I'm away, as his views generally coincide with mine. . . . To York House to see the Prince for ten minutes before his departure. He kept me for over three quarters of an hour and impressed me more favourably by good sense and a real interest in things than ever before. He himself raised with me the question of dividing the CO and changing the name and was delighted to hear of what I proposed. He also spoke very nicely about his brothers and is anxious Henry [Duke of Gloucester] should go out and soldier in India. His references to the climate of Buckingham Palace as depressing were rather amusing.

18 March 1925: Cabinet at which my proposals as to CO reorganisation were accepted in principle except as regards Permanent Under Secretary. Even here, however, I think I have got most of what I want. The Committee's suggestion of a deputy to do most of the work on the Colonial side is dropped and there is to be a 'deputy' on the Dominions side as near as possible in pay and status to the PUS. And I shall see to it that the PUS is PUS for Colonies only and the Deputy, deputy for Dominions only. The whole thing is, however, not to come into effect till I have time to put it before the House on my return. Meanwhile I was told informally to consult the Dominions and got leave to do it via the High Commissioners.

Amery's responsibilities as Secretary of State included not only the great Dominions and the colonies of direct rule in all five continents, but also the League of Nations mandates based on the territories administered by Britain as a result of military conquest during the war. Of these, the most troublesome was to be Palestine, where the contradictions involved in the Balfour Declaration regarding a 'Jewish national home' and Arab aspirations were endemic. However, earlier difficulties were encountered in Iraq, where the Turks, reinvigorated by their defeat of the Greeks in 1922, and their expulsion of all Greek settlers in Western Turkey, were claiming Mosul province, in the north of Iraq where oil had been discovered. In 1924 they had attempted a large-scale invasion which had been broken up by the RAF. This issue had been referred to the Council of the League of Nations, which had decided to send out a commission of inquiry early in 1925. Realising the importance of local opinion, Amery decided to inspect the area for himself, and was accompanied by Sir

Samuel Hoare, Secretary of State for Air, as the fledgeling RAF was crucial to the country's defence.

They first visited Amman, arriving on 25 March when they met the Amir Abdullah, who was to be visited by Amery again in the late 1940s before his assassination in 1951. In Iraq, where King Feisal, the devoted friend of T. E. Lawrence and Abdullah's brother, had been driven out of Damascus in 1921 by the French, Hoare and Amery held conferences with Iraq Ministers, visited Mosul and more ancient places, such as Nineveh, Hatra, Arbela, Kirkuk and finally Ur, and assisted in the organisation of the country's defence forces.

On 14 April they flew back to Amman, visiting Jerash, one of the Greek cities of the biblical Decapolis. This encounter encouraged Amery to insist on withholding from Churchill's expenditure cuts a few thousand pounds required to restore many of the columns and arches with their own stonework. They went thence to Jerusalem, where their time was similarly spent in conference on future arrangements for defence and the maintenance of internal order. By comparison with the French, who had 40,000 troops in Syria, Palestine was policed on a shoe-string: the Arab Legion, with a mounted British gendarmerie which Churchill compelled Amery to disband, and a few armoured cars in Transjordan. As Amery records these proved sufficient to preserve internal peace while he was Colonial Secretary, but were unable to cope with the communal rioting that broke out in 1929 over the Jewish use of the Wailing Wall, leading to a situation that gradually deteriorated during the 1930s. His memoirs give a full account of this short but fruitful visit (*My Political Life*, II, pp. 319–24).

The commission of inquiry appointed by the League had ruled that by far the greater part of Mosul should be incorporated in Iraq on condition that Iraq continued under a British mandate for another twenty-five years. Amery secured the Cabinet's agreement to his promises that Britain would renew her treaty with Iraq (thus fulfilling her mandatory obligations) for whatever time might be required to enable Iraq to enter the League as a member. The League Council met on 3 September, and though Austen Chamberlain was there as senior British delegate, the handling of the Mosul question was left largely to Amery. Amery asked also for a further readjustment of the frontier in his opening speech, but there was never any real chance that this would be agreed. Amery was on strong ground tactically since he could and the Turks would not accept the League's ruling. The Council referred the matter to a sub-committee chaired by the Swedish Foreign Minister, Unden, to whom Amery submitted a formal letter on 14 September.

Upon his return to London at the end of September he found the Rothermere–Beaverbrook press ready to attack him. The press lords were still anxious to destroy Baldwin and sought to use the desirability of 'economy' to justify their clamour for a British withdrawal from the Middle East. The Labour and most of the Liberal press joined the campaign with a will. 'For weeks on end Amery the spendthrift, the wrecker, the warmonger, was the theme of leading articles and cartoons' (*My Political Life*, II, p. 328). More serious were the press appeals to the Council of the League not to provoke war with Turkey by adjudicating in Iraq's favour, and the claim that several influential members of the Cabinet were opposed to Amery.

As a result, perhaps, the League's sub-committee was 'very wobbly', Unden in particular being prepared to give the Turks half the disputed province. However, Amery's hand was strengthened by reports from Iraq that the Turks had again crossed the frontier and deported many of the Assyrian Christian villagers there into the interior of Anatolia. As a result of his protests the Council appointed General Laidoner, the Esthonian Commander-in-Chief, to inquire into the facts on the spot. His report, confirming the accounts of Turkish misbehaviour, arrived when the Council was assembling in December, and greatly helped Iraq's case. Meanwhile Amery ensured that Baldwin successfully defended the Government's Iraq policy in his speech at the Conservative Conference on 8 October. During November he beat off criticisms in Cabinet from Churchill and Birkenhead.

Amery and Austen Chamberlain returned to Geneva in December where there was a momentary panic as a result of Baldwin's reply on 9 December to a supplementary question in the Commons, dismissing with a blunt negative the suggestion that Britain was bound to afford her protection to Iraq for twenty-five years. Hastily drafting the answer Baldwin should have given, they telegraphed to him to confirm that this was what he meant, and with his confirmation, were able to restore the situation. The League's verdict was announced in Iraq's favour on 16 December, so far as the existing frontier was concerned, although Amery's desire to let the Assyrian Christians recover the uninhabited mountains that were once their home was disregarded.

This was Amery's only direct experience of the League of Nations and he was not greatly impressed: 'All the Council was asked to do was to confirm an existing territorial situation, justified on every principle for which the League was supposed to stand, against a purely aggressive demand by a power which refused to recognise its authority' (*My Political Life*, II, p. 331). Only with difficulty did it give a positive response. The new Anglo-Iraq Treaty was approved by the Commons on 18 February 1926 and further negotiations with the Turks ended in June 1926 with Turkey receiving a 'sweetener' in the shape of a small royalty (afterwards commuted to £500,000) on such oil as might be found in Mosul province.

Diary

26 March 1925 (Baghdad): The High Commissioner [Sir Henry Dobbs, described by L.S.A. as 'a shrewd and genial Irishman'] told me that the League of Nations Commission had just gone, having drunk him out of ten dozen of champagne but having greatly improved in their point of view as they got in real contact with things and realised the objection of the Kurds and the horror of the Christians at the idea of coming under Turkish rule. Paulis, in fact, the most friendly of them, left me a message to say that they would recommend Iraq should retain the whole Mosul *vilayet* provided always that the mandate were restored, or the Treaty renewed for 20 years, failing which he would recommend that the Mandate should be given to France. I fear myself that he spoke too optimistically and that we may still find a tiresome compromise giving something to the Turks. However, if that is their decision it will help a great deal, not least in enabling me to get Cabinet and Parliamentary sanction to a new treaty giving us a permanent interest in the country and an obligation to defend it against aggression.

27 March 1925: Up the river by launch to Feisul's [*sic*] palace and had a talk with him and his Ministers and then from eleven spent the morning till nearly two o'clock at a full dress Conference each of us with all our staffs, etc. . . . Dobbs had prepared some very helpful critical notes on our proposals, laying stress among other matters on the fact that our scheme, as it stood, proposed that after all the amazing success of air administration hitherto, Iraq was to be left with no air resources at all, and suggesting the creation of a 'mercenary' Air Force, i.e. British officered and manned under the Iraq Government. On this question and also on any question of finally accepting a lower numerical standard than 15,000 ground troops, Sam was very sticky and negative, showing that same rather prim and narrow monopolistic spirit about the Air Force that gave us so much trouble in the Navy–Air negotiations. In the end we broke up very inconclusively for lunch. . . . Reflecting over the morning's discussion I came to the conclusion that the question of a local air force and the increase of the Iraq Army had better both be left in suspense and that Sam and I could quite well agree on a first stage of three years during which the Iraq Army should not be increased but only improved by the attaching of British Officers, leaving things open for a new military agreement and new treaty generally in about two years' time.

28 March 1925: After breakfast Dobbs, Sam and I met for a short preliminary talk before an 11 o'clock general conference. We found we made such useful progress that we decided to have no conference but only to call in Higgins. We agreed on a first stage of three – subsequently reduced to two – years during which we should definitely tell the Iraqi (after letting the pressure come from them) that we would not ask them to increase their army but only to improve it. We arrived at satisfactory conclusions as to the position of the proposed Inspector General, his relations to the present Adviser in the War Ministry, etc., going clause by clause through certain critical notes prepared by Dobbs. We also agreed, Sam at first protesting, that we should not hurl a cut and dried scheme at Ministers' heads, but have a conference with Yasin, Nuri, Sassoon, etc., and let them raise points and feel that they had secured concessions. I also suggested that we might encourage them to form armoured car units, believing that much more use might be made of these. . . . Went early to a reception given by the King where I was introduced to all the notables of Baghdad and afterwards sat for three quarters of an hour or so with the King, Yasin, Dobbs and Sassoon. At first I exchanged amiable conversation in Turkish and then we got on to more serious talk on the general political relations between Iraq and ourselves which I had to do in English, Yasin translating. Feisul [sic] was much impressed and pleased with the line I took especially when I talked of 'mutual confidence and respect', etc.

29 March 1925: Long conference with Ministers, i.e. Yasin, Sassoon, Nuri, on our proposals which they evidently didn't like at all and which I didn't really like, though I put them as persuasively as possible. My feeling was that for a training scheme it was a mistake to put British officers in all the positions of command in all the units and I felt sure that simply to convert the Iraq Army into levies would set all their national feeling, at present so friendly, against us. I confided my views to Dobbs and made it clear to him that his communication embodying our proposal in detail was to be a reconnaissance in force and that I did not want to press things to the utmost.

[On 31 March Amery flew to Mosul.] The most interesting bit was over Samarra, not so much the city itself with its golden dome, as the miles and miles of outlines of ruined cities very visible from the air and the well preserved Ziggurat near by. The air gives one a wonderful idea both of the past of the country and of its possibilities. . . . Tea with Surma Khanum, aunt of the hereditary patriarch and herself hereditary high deaconess of the modern descendants of Asshur Banipal, . . . who was most interesting on the subject of her own people, now reduced to less than 20,000, most of the able bodied males keeping themselves and families going by serving in the Assyrian Levy Regiments. The thing they naturally wish above all is to get the Iraq frontier extended so as to include their old mountain homes, failing that they would settle further back, providing always that Iraq remains under our control; failing that she would like to settle the lot in some British colony or at any rate in a Christian country. I doubted whether any British Dominion would like them as a national community, and was sure Cyprus had no spare land. I think myself they should remain in Iraq. . . . A small dinner at the Lloyds after which I drafted a short speech in reply to the addresses from notables which I was to receive the following night. Lloyd suggested I should address them in Turkish to which I demurred on the ground that this would be a little absurd after we had been so busy assuring the Mosul Boundary Commission that Mosul was all Arab and contained no Turks and few who even spoke it! I said that if he put it into Arabic I could make shift to learn it.

1 April 1925: Found Lloyd had, with the help of the Mutassarif, produced an eloquent oration in the most classical Arabic which we went through together so that I could construe it for myself; and then I read it several times in the Arabic script – the only possible way of grasping Arabic – and then wrote it out in large Roman script and read it over to Lloyd so as to get the emphasis right. . . . To the Town Hall decorated for our benefit and crowded with all the notables of the place. They addressed a series of Arabic speeches to me after which I got up and replied in kind to their great surprise and delight. I found it quite easy to speak with just a glance down at my notes every sentence or so – I certainly read less and spoke more than most of the previous speakers. They were also very pleased with the substance.

[Amery returned to Baghdad on 4 April.]

5 April 1925: Studied the alternative plan of Iraq Army Reform put forward by Joyce and the Iraq Government and decided myself we should adopt it as our basis. We had a long Conference over this at the end of which Higgins suddenly climbed down and said he would accept it if three infantry battalions were made exemplar battalions. I agreed at once and after this the rest of the business was detail as to when the third battalion should be raised, whether the second should depend on the creating of a 7th Iraq battalion, etc. Anyhow, we got complete agreement eventually and the only difficulty left outstanding was the purely personal one of securing Joyce's position. Dined with Gertrude Bell and had a very pleasant evening.

7 April 1925: At four King Feisul came to be instructed in his rights and duties as a constitutional monarch. He and I and Dobbs sat there for $2\frac{1}{2}$ hours discussing this and other matters such as Ibn Saud which interested him perhaps even more. The real difficulty has been to prevent him deliberately inciting his own tribes to raid Ibn Saud's people in order to bring us into a state of war with the latter. He thinks that when I.S. has conquered the Hejaz he is bound to turn against Trans-Jordan or Iraq next. [On 8 April Amery left for Basra and Abadan.]

10 April 1925: To Abadan where we lunched and then spent a couple of hours going over the vast refineries. It is a wonderful big industry to have planted down in the middle of nowhere, and suggests what a big difference the discovery of two or three fields of the Anglo-Persian Oil Company capacity would mean to Iraq. The new field at Khanikin may possibly be as large as this one and if so, it will soon make a big difference. [On 14 April Amery flew to Amman, and from there went to Jerusalem.]

21 April 1925: At 9.30 I had in the joint deputation of the various Arab sections . . . introduced by Musa Kazim Pasha. The main speech by a blind Imam Suleiman Farukh was violent and much of it absurd – peasants building roads under the lash to Jewish colonies, tobacco duties imposed to compel Arabs to sell their lands to the Jews, etc. After another less violent speaker had repeated the old question of our pledges to Hussein I replied making clear that we could not go back on our policy, explaining what it really meant and how it had actually worked out in practice, referring to all that had been done for the Arab population and how, in fact, it had grown faster than the Jews: 80,000 since 1920 as compared with 53,000. Rebutted one or two of the most absurd charges and ended by assuring them of the Government's determination to do all it could for the Arab population and its willingness to proceed on the path of representative institutions if they really wanted them. Then about 11.15 I went off to another room and faced the Va'ad Leumi, Jewish national deputation whose complaint was that we were not letting in enough immigrants, giving all the land to the Arabs, holding up the promised community ordinance, etc. I told them it was more important to build soundly than in a hurry, and that they had got to realise that they must live with the Arabs who would probably always be the majority, and create a common Palestinian patriotism. At 12 I received the Orthodox Patriarch. Having listened for 2½ hours to Arabic and Hebrew I now had to listen to Greek and found I could follow most of his grievances before the interpreter retailed – and sometimes curtailed them. His finances are being closely controlled in order to pay off the vast debts of the patriarchate and enable its income and expenditure to balance. This stops all sorts of petty corruption and extravagance and is keenly resented by the Patriarch and his immediate entourage. . . . At 1 o'clock I received the Mufti with the Mufti of Haifa and one other as representing the Moslem Supreme Council . . .

they went on to the general national tack to which I replied much as to the Arab deputation. . . . Back at 4 to a two hours' conference with Shuck-burgh, Samuel, Davis the Treasurer and Leys of public works. Settled in principle to raise loan including £1,000,000 for Haifa harbour and exten-sion of railway towards Beirut through Jaffa, sanctioned immediately £4000 being spent on Jaffa urgent improvement and one or two similar things, laid down the lines on which Samuel was to submit a new Com-munity Law on general lines so as to cover Moslems, Jews, Patriarchate, etc. . . . In fact we got through the whole of the 13 items on Samuel's list many of which had been waiting for years. Poor old Shuckburgh looked as if the pace at which decisions were given made him quite giddy. . . . I think I did good work in Palestine on the whole. Apart from settling out-standing points I was able to make it clear that there was no general change of policy and yet that I was sympathetic to the Arabs and under-stood their point of view, knew their language, etc. It is a difficult policy to carry out and I only hope old Plumer [who was shortly to replace Samuel as Governor] will manage with Symes'* help to keep an even keel. [Amery flew to Cairo on 22 April, reading the first five books of the *Odyssey* on the flight.]

22 April 1925: I had a good long talk with A[llenby] who is very bitter and unreasonable about Austen and the FO. He can see nothing but the slight to him of their sending out [Neville] Henderson and cannot in the least realise the difficulties he put us in over his ultimatum. I told him that I alone of the Cabinet was for revoking his ultimatum and thus publicly over-riding him. He is also very sore over the discussion in the Press about his successor. I agreed that this was very unfair to him and that the sooner he now resigned the better – and wrote Austen to that effect.

23 April 1925: Allenby then took Sam and myself to visit King Fuad who talked and barked at us for over an hour, some of it very amusing and full of shrewd hits at our methods as well as at those of his own people. He regards Zaghloul as down and out and his chief fear is that the consti-tutional Liberals will combine to make things difficult for him in which case he made it pretty plain he would intrigue them out again. [Amery left next day for Italy.]

27 April 1925: At five we called on Mussolini in a breakfast room in the Palazzo Chigi. He looked dreadfully ill (he has duodenal ulcer so Graham told us, and can only drink milk) and altogether changed from the rather bombastic theatrical person I sat next to at 10 Downing Street two years

*Stuart Symes (later Sir Stuart) was to replace Clayton as Chief Secretary. L.S.A. had been much impressed with his administration in the northern half of Palestine.

ago. He was quiet, humorous, wise and very attractive. We discussed Hindenburg's election which he thought would cause trouble not now but later as it was bound to bring back the Hohenzollerns, the Communist outbreaks in Bulgaria and elsewhere, aviation especially air control of colonies which greatly interested him *à propos* of Cyrenaica.

2 May 1925 (London): Dined at the Academy Dinner sitting almost directly below my portrait [recently painted by Fildes] which is I think quite good. I sat between F.E. and Jix, the former very cross that he is not being pushed for the Oxford Chancellorship. Stanley made an admirable speech and Sam was quite interesting on our tour. I had some talk with Beit who had been down to Sturry to see Lord Milner who is ill with encephalitis lethargica. It is a very anxious business but there are real hopes of improvement and if once he can turn the corner he ought to recover completely. Meanwhile things are grave. I was glad to talk to the Duke of York who kept me for a long time discussing East Africa, etc. and by the time we were done almost everybody had left.

4 May 1925: Down to the House to take questions and was received with a mild cheer on returning from what the ordinary member still seems to regard as a perilous journey. Had a short talk with Stanley about the Governorships and the new Under Secretary. . . . As regards Australia the last suggestions in are for Willingdon and failing him Baird.

5 May 1925: Saw Stamfordham who showed me letters from Cosgrave to Granard and from Granard to himself which made me conclude that it was after all inadvisable for the King to race his yacht at Kingstown. Then up to the King who was in his chattiest form very anxious to know all about the new appointments, Nigeria, Kenya, etc. As regards Australia he thought either Willingdon or Baird would do quite well but did not think Lady Plumer up to it. He also discussed the new division of the CO which he approved of. The subject he was keenest on was to get Thomas to take Devonshire's place temporarily as Chairman of the Executive Council of the [Empire] Exhibition in order not to throw the headship of the thing as regards all public functions upon Stevenson for whom HM has very little use. The idea is good and I told HM I would see what I could do about it. Seeing Stamfordham afterwards I gathered that they had sort of half taken the thing up and then dropped it as not feasible. From there I went on to see Winston who is very full of his Budget. I was glad to learn that he proposes to have a preference on the raw silk duty. Acting on telegrams from Australia and a letter from the South African High Commissioner I urged him to anticipate the date for giving the full preference to Empire dried fruit but his customs people showed me figures which made it clear that there was nothing in it. He was glad to know that his policy in Iraq had been such a success and that I hoped to be able to show him some further economies.

6 May 1925: To Cabinet where I found that I now sit next to Balfour which is pleasant. We dealt with the recommendations of the CID as regards Japan and Singapore which seem to me to be rather havering and a whittling down of our policy. On the assurance that short of the equipping of Singapore for taking a fleet equal to the Japanese the whole question of how far Singapore should be carried was still perfectly open, I waived such objections as I had raised. We had a discussion on the proposed lace duty which Winston tried to get out of on the ground that one of the White Paper conditions* was not literally fulfilled in view of the Safeguarding Committee. However, we all swept that away, Edward Wood being particularly helpful in pointing out that the conditions laid down in the White Paper were not the conditions for the Cabinet to go by as each and all of them necessarily fulfil them but conditions which the Committee had to take into account before it made a recommendation. . . . Saw Thomas at the House and found that he was quite prepared to face any criticism from his own party and would take on the Acting Chairmanship of the [Empire Exhibition] Executive. He was very anxious that the Duke of York should actually be present at the special meeting of the Council convened to propose this. I wrote straight away to Devonshire and to Stevenson whom I am afraid will now have to swallow it.

7 May 1925: Had a talk with Johnny Baird about Australia. I had also seen the PM for a minute in the morning and he felt that we were entitled to press his claims as against Willingdon both on the grounds of greater Parliamentary experience and of belonging to our Party.

8 May 1925: Saw Seely at the office and broke it to him that he might consider himself definitely out of it for Australia. He was very angry and seemed to think I had behaved with personal ill-faith towards him. Evidently all my warnings to him that he was only one of several candidates and that the choice lay mainly at the other end had had no effect upon his conviction that he would naturally be preferred. His indignation will probably be even greater when the name of the successful candidate is published.

10 May 1925: The George Lloyds came to dinner, George in a very

*The White Paper on Safeguarding, published earlier in the year, had laid down procedures which each industry had to go through to obtain protection, the most important of which was to satisfy a committee of inquiry that protection was needed on certain specific grounds.

funny mood treating Egypt as rather a matter of indifference to him now. He told me he was carefully going through all the papers in order to consider whether it would be better to separate the Sudan entirely from Egypt and have a High Commissioner or not, his view being apparently that if he decided to separate it he would also contend the High Commissionership.

13 May 1925: To the Cabinet where we ran through a large number of not very exciting matters. As I came out they gave me a telephone message from Sturry, Lord Milner had died an hour before. One of the greatest and best men there have been and a father to me. I think one of the things that pleased him most at the end was that I was safely in the Colonial Office and likely to have the time to carry out some of the things he most cared about. [L.S.A. holograph note: 'I am glad to think that the very first thing I did when seated in his old chair at the CO was to write to him and thank him for all I owed him.'] Back to B. who was also very unhappy. . . . Saw Stanley about a memorial service in Westminster Abbey. I could have wished that the public had known him enough to make actual burial in the Abbey possible but Stanley. . . . doubted if it could well be done But I must see to it later that we erect some suitable tablet to his memory there. . . . B. had to give up her party that afternoon as she could not face seeing people but we had the Lugards to dine quietly with us and had a long talk with them about my various schemes for Colonial reorganisation. My talk with him, as well as with Davidson at the House immediately afterwards confirmed me in the view that Clifford would not really do as PUS and Davidson strongly confirmed me in favour of [Sammy] Wilson.* . . . I spent two hours or more that afternoon and evening trying to see if I could write anything in the way of an appreciation for Lord Milner but nothing would come.

14 May 1925: Caught a 3 o'clock train for Sturry as I wanted to have the last look at my old chief. Lady Milner was very calm, unemotional and businesslike at first. Afterwards when I had been in to see him and was walking in the garden she came down and after getting rid of her first bitterness against the doctors for mishandling the case let go to her real sorrow. . . . [Reception] at Australia House where I sat for half an hour or so. Cook told me, talking about Milner, that the last time he had seen him he said, 'Amery is well in the saddle now, though it has taken him a long time to get there. I am very proud of him.'

16 May 1925: [L.S.A. attended Milner's funeral, and as a result found himself discussing the appointment of additional Rhodes Trustees with

*Warren Fisher had favoured Clifford (Diary, 11 May).

Violet Milner.] Found she wished to discuss trustees and the possibility of Grigg going to Kenya, etc. For her the one relief of grief seems to be to discuss practical business issues. I think most other women would have stayed down at Sturry and been afraid to face anybody.

19 May 1925: Discussed [with Mackinder] Balfour's new project of setting up a counterpart to the Committee of Imperial Defence in the shape of a committee of Imperial Development and Research. Balfour had already mentioned this to me [this became the Committee for Civil Research].

22 May 1925: Emergency conference with FO, Air Force and Admiralty on Ibn Saud's march on Akaba. I pressed strongly for being quite firm with I.S. in this.

26 May 1925: Meeting of the Overseas Settlement Committee. I shall be very glad indeed when I have my Dominions Under Secretary available for this. Clarendon has now consented and next to Linlithgow I think is quite the best man I could have got. Incidentally he has actually been a settler in Canada himself. . . . The meeting of the committee on the proposed Pact in the PM's room at the House. The French reply is a good deal more reasonable than it might have been but its proposal of compulsory arbitration treaties between all the parties of the Pact raise a difficulty which apparently Austen does not seem clearly to visualise, namely that committing ourselves to guaranteeing the Franco-German frontier and the observance of a treaty of arbitration between those two Powers was one thing and universal compulsory arbitration as between ourselves and France or Germany for all disputes everywhere quite another, and one affecting the whole Empire very immediately. I found the general body of opinion with me in the necessity of making it clear to the French that we were not prepared to go in for the latter. Saw Austen about Ibn Saud's threatened attack on Akaba and got him to agree that if the actual attack did not materialise at once we could give King Hussein three weeks in which to turn out and look for lodgings elsewhere. . . . Saw Robin for a few minutes about Grigg's appointment [as Governor of Kenya] which he thinks a good one. . . . The King is very pleased about Grigg and sent me a special message through Stamfordham.

27 May 1925: Had a talk with Stanley about the necessity for having a definite announcement on Colonial Office organisation about which I had already written him a very strong letter a few days before. I think I got him to understand the difference as between myself and Fisher and to make him realise that Fisher's way of doing the thing would spoil the whole effect on the Dominions.

28 May 1925: Saw Sir C. Greenway and Nicholls about letting the Turkish Petroleum Company start work without waiting for the final settlement of the Mosul frontier. Thought their case perfectly reasonable. Cabinet at which Sam raised the question of my action with Austen in regard to Akaba and the taking over of the Ma'an *vilayet* [in Trans-Jordan]. I thought it was just as well we acted because the Cabinet were rather vague and sticky, Winston, however, backing me up well. We discussed a large number of other matters up till 1.45, Austen being in the chair as Stanley had to be in the House for the absurd Liberal vote of censure on the Speaker for accepting the closure on the Finance Bill. After a short adjournment for lunch we continued the Cabinet which about 3.30 became the Security Committee at which we settled the draft despatch to the French covering our proposed amendments to their reply to Germany, the essential part in them being the point I had laid stress on namely that we could not commit ourselves to universal arbitration with France and Germany, but were prepared to guarantee such a treaty of arbitration as between ourselves at any rate to the extent of defending their common frontier against an aggression.

8 June 1925: Had a talk with Larkin and agreed with him that we should have periodical weekly regular meetings between the High Commissioners and myself at which we could discuss matters of current interest which otherwise get indefinitely postponed. . . .

[Saw] Grigg about the date of his own going out. . . . He is very anxious to have the Native Reserves put separately under himself as High Commissioner and similarly to get control as High Commissioner of Bukoba and the Tanga district.

10 June 1925: Cabinet, mostly minor matters but towards the end we got on to the fringe of serious discussion owing to Philip bringing up before the Cabinet the question whether he should accede to the application of the iron and steel industry for an inquiry under the Safeguarding of Industries Act. Winston very agitated but S.B. clearly of the opinion that we could not refuse an inquiry. The matter was postponed for a week.

16 June 1925: With the help of Billy [Gore] had a long interview with Dr Weizmann. . . . The gist of Weizmann's talk was that we should not begin any restriction on immigration just yet but give him time to study what is happening and produce figures and conclusions for us – also a general appeal for co-operation.

17 June 1925: Cabinet where we discussed a variety of things beginning with unemployment which has gone up by 100,000 in the last fortnight.

Winston was very eloquent on the theme that there was really nothing in this, that it was all due to coal and would be set right by some agreement between the miners and coal-owners and that we should not do anything in a panic, his whole oration being a prelude to what he will no doubt say when the question of safeguarding iron and steel comes up before a special Cabinet next Monday. I did not let myself be drawn into the discussion beyond drawing attention to the contributory factor of the general check in migration.

18 June 1925: To the first meeting of the Committee of Civil Research under Balfour's chairmanship. We first discussed the tsetse fly campaign and appointed a sub-committee to plan out the general outline of the future campaign. . . . We also brought up the Imperial College of Agriculture and Aspinall came and made a clear statement which greatly impressed Lord Balfour who is prepared to be thoroughly helpful. I see my way to getting a great many things I have wanted out of this new Committee and indeed we may get the whole spirit of research animating the public life of the Empire.

22 June 1925: Cabinet where we discussed Afghanistan at great length, the Pact, and eventually began on the safeguarding of industries, Philip having now suggested a wider inquiry into steel and iron than the ordinary Safeguarding Committee. The Cabinet dragged on until 7.30.

24 June 1925: Talk in my room with Gore and Grigg . . . about Grigg's scheme for dividing up Kenya into self-government area and native reserve. I think he began to realise some of the difficulties in a scheme otherwise attractive and sound in principle. . . .

Sat in the House for an hour or so listening to the FO debate. . . . Austen wound up the defence of his Pact fairly effectively, but I am horrified by the way in which he habitually personifies the League of Nations as a concrete entity capable of giving decisions at critical moments.

25 June 1925: Before the dinner I got Baldwin's letter formally sanctioning the appointment of Wilson and Grindle as P[ermanent] U[nder] S[ecretaries] Colonial Office and Davis Dominions.

26 June 1925: Cabinet down at the House. The first item was C[ash] O[n] D[elivery] which at first everyone was against because of the retail traders. However, I made a vigorous appeal and got some backing and the matter was referred to committee. The safeguarding of iron and steel led to a confused discussion, Winston trying desperately to avert the drift towards the only possible conclusion. His suggestion that the application

for a safeguarding committee should be definitely rejected found no
favour. But it was decided to suspend matters pending an investigation by
the Committee of Civil Research which is rapidly becoming the solution
for every difficulty. After that my proposals for the Irish Loyalists got
through without discussion.

28 June 1925: Burney came over in the afternoon with his wife and I had
a little talk with him. He told me that some of the Labour people had
been approaching him with a view to combining on the Imperial and
protectionist policy, Kirkwood in particular had said to him he did not
see what we kept all our cruisers for if we were to allow all this ——
foreign stuff to come in!

30 June 1925: Rhodes Trust meeting to accept Kipling's resignation
based on the fact that he does not like Philip Kerr's smile or the fact that
he did not serve in the war. If we had had any idea that his doubts about
Philip's appointment [as Secretary] went to that length we might possibly
have reconsidered, but he certainly never gave that impression and his
action in resigning is tiresome. Poor old Beit has been very much worried
and distressed about it. I cannot say that it has worried me much because
Kipling has not really contributed anything really material.

8 July 1925: After Questions Young and I had an hour's hammer and
tongs with Winston and his myrmidons, Barstow, Niemeyer, etc. on
Palestine loan, Trans-Jordan estimates, etc. I got my way very satisfactorily over Trans-Jordan estimates and more particularly over the antiquities
vote. I also think I made a real impression on him as to the need for keeping faith with our Civil Servants in Iraq. With regard to the Palestine loan
on the other hand I went a considerable way in meeting him in admitting
that the whole of the million pounds due to the railways would have to be
found and that if any of the payments were put off it would have to be
with interest. [This and subsequent entries were clearly dictated nearly a
fortnight later.]

9 July 1925: To a Privy Council to receive the seals of office as S. of S.
for Dominion Affairs. This was the end of a considerable flurry. Until
almost the last moment the Treasury had declared that legislation was
wanted. Then Liddell on being consulted said that not only was it unnecessary but it would be actually wrong for a S. of S. to be appointed by
any other means than the simple handing of seals. The Treasury also until
the last moment insisted that it made no great difference whether this was
done before the end of the 9 months of dissolution because a by-election

could be avoided by the device of resigning from the CO and then simultaneously receiving two new sets of seals. I mentioned this to Hogg at the Tuesday Cabinet but he was very reluctant to try this latter dodge which was open to question and urged that there should be a Privy Council before the end of the 9 months i.e. before 7 o'clock on Thursday. Stamfordham was very rattled at having to ask the King to hold a Council at such short notice. However, the King was in the most amiable of moods, treated it as a great joke handing me my own seals which I had sent round in the morning and was much amused when I told him that the real responsibility for all the trouble given him was his guest [i.e. in gaol] Horatio Bottomley who had frightened Bonar out of his intention to make ministerial appointments free from by-elections.

10 July 1925: Attended the Civil Research Committee on the iron and steel trade. These discussions are all quite interesting but really futile as long as we are not prepared to face the obvious and simple remedy. . . .

14 July 1925: Conference with Winston, Cave and others in Salisbury's room about the Irish Loyalists, finally agreeing on the terms of the letter to Selborne which seems to have met the case as far as the following day's debate went and now leaves us with the problem of constituting the informal committee and seeing what resolutions they arrive at.*

15 July 1925: Cabinet on the report of the Navy Committee. This report, with F.E. in the chair to back up Winston, almost inevitably took the little Navy point of view. The issue, however, was narrowed down to a minimum programme not two-thirds of the programme to which we had assented two years before, but which the Admiralty now accepted if it was to be begun at once. The Committee supported Winston's view that it should be postponed a year. Willie led off stating his case very well and was followed by Winston who was also effective and made a great appeal to the weaker elements in the Cabinet generally. I rejoined with special stress on the Dominions point of view and the difficulties we should create for Bruce if we now treated the cruiser construction as in no sense urgent. Several others spoke, all very flabby, though Austen suggested that some compromise was desirable.

16 July 1925: Cabinet for further discussion of the Navy business. Balfour led off very well making a special point of the Dominions position. He was well backed by Cave and somewhat unintelligently by Jix.

*L.S.A. had talked with Salisbury on the 7th 'about the letter he proposes to send to Selborne offering an informal committee on the position of the Irish Loyalists' (diary, 7 July). He had earlier agreed (diary, 24 June) that Salisbury 'might invite Lansdowne and a few others to consult with us and see what we are doing'.

Douglas Hogg to my surprise all wrong, Neville for a reasonable compromise and Salisbury inclined that way.*

30 July 1925: Went to an EPA [meeting] to receive on behalf of the Speaker the pictures of Botha and Smuts presented by Colts. Balfour arrived blissfully ignorant of what it was all about and asked me in a whisper what he was to say. I said, say something nice about Botha and he then got up and delivered a most eloquent and moving speech at the end of which he forgot that he was presenting the picture and expressed his satisfaction at receiving it. . . .

Amery attended the Dublin Horse Show on 4 August at the invitation of Tim Healy. Between 31 July and 25 September he kept no diary, but from a pocket engagement book he established a brief record in 1949 or 1950. This account does not deal with the Cabinet on Iraq on 7 August, but he put together some recollections of the League Council meeting at Geneva in September.

Diary

3 September 1925: If I remember rightly I got up at 5.00 in the morning and wrote my statement to the League of Nations Council so that it could be typed out and ready when the Council met. The statement made a very great impression on the Council and I was told afterwards that it was the best and clearest exposition of a case that had ever been before them. Anyhow, by contrast the Turkish case stated by Rushdi Aras [the Turkish Foreign Minister] sounded feeble and obstinate. Rushdi with his receding forehead looked a regular Armenian type of Turk and certainly did not impress me then, though we made quite good friends afterwards when he became Ambassador in London [during the Second World War] and assured me that though he had to put up a fight of sorts both Ataturk and he were never really anxious to get Mosul.

4 September 1925: Further meeting of the Council at which I dealt with Rushdi's statement pretty devastatingly. Apparently the League had never before had really forceful argument used.

25 September 1925: That is all that I can piece together from my little pocket book, but it was all an extremely busy time while at the same time the

---

*Curiously, L.S.A.'s diary contains no further references to the dispute over the naval building programme although he was involved in the discussions which led to the final compromise on 22 July (see Middlemas and Barnes, pp. 338-9).

League of Nations danced as hard as the Congress of Vienna ever did in old days.... I seem to have no sort of record of the big occasion at the meeting of the Assembly at which Austen made the speech, substantially on lines drafted by Balfour, in which we made it clear that we could not accept the Geneva Protocol, but which pointed at the end to a more limited alternative solution, the solution in fact which became Locarno.* Considering how immensely proud Austen was for the rest of his days about Locarno, never able to stop talking about it, it is curious to think that he was really shepherded into it out of an earlier proposal for an alliance with France, by myself and to some extent by Sam Hoare. Whether in retrospect we were right is another matter. It is at least possible that a policy of actual alliance with France would have been better as things turned out. On the other hand I was mainly anxious about the Empire attitude and could never have foreseen the incredible folly of sanctions against Italy. Austen's speech was received very coldly and Paul Boncour who followed swept the Assembly away with him in a speech of great eloquence ending in effect with 'The protocol is dead; long live the protocol'. Smit, the South African High Commissioner, lunched with me afterwards and remarked casually on that theme, 'How differently these dagos think from us.' Considering what an anti-British nationalist he was I thought that a good unconscious tribute. Austen and I worked together very happily throughout the whole time and again when we went to Geneva that December and finally pulled it off.

29 September 1925: Cabinet Sub Committee on Dyes. It is difficult to see how we can release the Dyes Corporation from Government control which is essential to its commercial success, and prevent it entering into combination with the Germans. My own inclination is to let them do it and counter the danger by direct protective measures.

King Feisal with Tahsin his ADC, Gertrude Bell, and Meriel Talbot came to dinner, Feisal looking ever so much better for having his teeth pulled out, and deeply grateful for the help I have been able to give over Mosul. I told him he could go back and give his people good courage. I am sure that whatever does happen it is right that their spirits should be kept up until the end. He was very anxious that Weetman Pearson should be allowed to fix up a loan with King Ali in connexion with the railway and port concession. I doubted if the FO would agree to this and said I would consult with them.

1 October 1925: Saw [F.S.] Jackson who is very anxious that Stanley should make a good straight fighting speech at Brighton. He feels that the

*Here L.S.A.'s memory is at fault, telescoping Chamberlain's speech to the League in March into an account of the Assembly in September.

Party is rather disgruntled and inclined to think that it is not being led definitely enough.

6 October 1925:   Saw Casey for a few minutes but was interrupted to go across to see Stanley about a statement which had appeared in the *Daily Mail* that Birkenhead, who had been absent from the Cabinet of 7 August, disagreed with the Iraq policy. Neville had rung me up about it in a state of great indignation and had already spoken very strongly to Stanley. Stanley told me he was going to see F.E. and insist on an explanation. As regards the general situation his view was that we should not discuss the future policy at the next Cabinet but that I should prepare a full memorandum for fuller discussion after Austen came back.

7 October 1925:   [J. H. Thomas] talked about Mosul where I found he was all over the place, really under the impression that the Commission had declared that Turkey had a rightful claim to the place. I sent him the memorandum prepared for the PM and hope he will make good use of it. . . . [Cabinet.] F.E. opened by a personal explanation that he had neither directly nor indirectly inspired the *Daily Mail* statement and had certainly not been guilty of such disloyalty towards his colleagues and more particularly to an old friend like myself. He was going to write to the Editor in strong terms protesting. I confess I imagined at the time that this meant a disclaimer for publication but looking at the Cabinet minutes afterwards and in view of the fact that nothing has appeared I imagine that it was only a private letter. The Cabinet was supposed to be mainly on the subject of Stanley's forthcoming speech and to convey suggestions to him about it but most of it was taken up with a rambling discussion on measures to be taken in the event of a general strike.* However, towards the end I insisted on saying a few words about Mosul making clear that while future policy will have to be discussed on merits I hoped the Prime Minister would be able to state very definitely that what had been done so far was done with the approval of the Cabinet and as the right thing to do. There was general assent to this and Stanley suggested that Ministers generally should avoid any discussion of future policy. As far as I can make out the members of the Cabinet most likely to be difficult are Philip and F.E. Salisbury congratulated me very warmly on the line I had taken and I think most of the rest approved though a little nervous about what the Press may do.

---

*In the face of industrial trouble over miners' pay, the Government had set up the Samuel Commission in August to go into the problems of the coal industry, and were subsidising the mines while the Commission sat. The possibility of a general strike when the Commission reported and the subsidy was ended was an obvious one.

8 October 1925: [Amery travelled to Brighton to hear Baldwin's speech to the Conservative Conference.] Stanley was very well received and so was his speech right through, though there were few things in it calculated to create any bursts of enthusiasm. I had been a little anxious about what he would say on Mosul and had sent him a sketch of the kind of thing that I should be inclined to say. To my surprise and satisfaction he produced it with hardly a word altered and gave me not only complete endorsement but warm commendation. His action was characteristic both in its loyalty and in his readiness to accept anything drafted for him which I have noticed before e.g. over his election manifesto. All this was very well received by the meeting and has I think had its effect in the country, though some of the stunt press have since tried to explain it away. . . . Back by the 10.45 train sharing a compartment with the Baldwins, very happy over the result of the Conference generally and the success of the speech.

10 October 1925: Went to see the King in the morning and was kept by him for nearly an hour talking about Mosul, Australian State Governorships, the political situation at large, etc. The King was very critical of Stanley for taking so long a holiday abroad and not calling more Cabinets or getting more of our Cabinet Ministers to sprinkle some of their speeches over August and September. It was no good going back to old ways when you had the Labour Party working all the year round without a break, and in any case he thought the Prime Minister had too big a show to go out of the country at all. I did not ask him whether that also applied to other Ministers or it would be a bad thing for my summer and Christmas holidays! He appeared to be thoroughly sound on the Mosul question and to have a very hearty dislike of the official Turk. His conversation with Feisal seems to have been a decided success. Altogether he seemed very well and in great talking form. Had a few words with Stamfordham as I went out and there met George Lloyd anxious to know whether Lord Lloyd would be too cacophonous a title.

12 October 1925: Attended the Civil Research Committee and spent an hour listening to Winston cross-questioning the iron industry representatives and trying to trip them up. At the end I got in one minute of questions, which I think undid his efforts, before flying off to catch my train to Birmingham.

13 October 1925: Cabinet dealing with a number of odds and ends including the fate of Pembroke and Rosyth [dockyards which were to be closed] leading up to a discussion on safeguarding arising from Philip's demand for an inquiry into the woollen and worsted industry. Winston gave his usual dissertation trying to make out that safeguarding was a term of art implying duties applicable only to specific nations and not general duties. I retorted that these hair splittings were hardly suitable for the seriousness of the present crisis. Anyhow the proposal went through, Winston contenting himself by urging that we ought to call a halt presently or else we might be in danger of sliding into a general tariff. At the very end he brought up Iraq, having suddenly developed the view that if the Turk should suddenly make an attack upon Iraq our only policy should be to retire without firing a shot and put in a wail to the League of Nations. I headed this off at the time but I fancy he is going to be troublesome. . . . Agricultural Policy Committee where we spent an hour while Winston criticised Edward's proposals for small holdings and occupying ownership. I fear Winston is a pure Cobdenite in his outlook and his long dissertations make it very difficult to get ahead with the business.

Then to the Civil Research Committee where we finally settled to let go of the British Dyes Corporation concentrating upon our fiscal system to counteract any danger of combination with the Germans and giving part of the proceeds of the sale of the Government shares to research.

Just before dinner I went across and had half an hour with Winston partly on E. African loan on which I was able to make him understand that we were not going to spend the 10 millions all at once and got him I think into a more reasonable frame of mind; partly on Mosul where I found him difficult and really not very clear in his views, his argument being confusion of the strategical point whether in case of war we should do our main fighting in Iraq or elsewhere, and the political point that we should not fight at all but simply retreat and appeal to the League. Apparently his inclination was to fight the Turk elsewhere but not to make use of our forces in Iraq at all.

Then to dinner with Sam Hoare, the party consisting of Philip, Edward [Wood], Sassoon and Lady Maude. Over dinner they all told the most amazing stories about Jix and his aspirations to the Premiership. He recently offered Philip a good place in his government whenever he should form it, and appears at the end of the session when the [coal] subsidy was agreed to have sent round his P[arliamentary] P[rivate] S[ecretary] Erskine to sound the Smoking Room and Lobby to see what support he would get if he made a declaration of independence and a bid for the head. It really is rather pathetic. We discussed various other things including what Edward might say about the Economic Committee and the Publicity Grant, and after Philip had hurried away to catch a train Sam, Edward and I had a good talk on Mosul. Sam is thoroughly sound, his lips drawn very tight at the thought that the 'scuttle school' is being represented by the general staff who are very jealous of the position of

THE LEO AMERY DIARIES

the Air Ministry in Iraq. I might add that when I spoke to Winston about Trenchard's point of view he brushed Trenchard aside as quite contemptible and having no opinion worth anything. This after all he has said about Trenchard in the past was rather comic. Edward also was quite sound though naturally very conscious of the state of public opinion. We agreed that if the Turks did by any chance attack it would not be a case of sending out a large British force to Iraq but at the most of a couple of Indian divisions, more aeroplanes and more white officers for the Iraq army.

15 October 1925: Saw Trenchard for a few minutes before the CID and was glad to know that he had been lunching with Winston and F.E. and had really opened their eyes on the Iraq frontier situation by explaining to them what happened when the Turks made a similar push last year. Baldwin presided himself at the CID which went very satisfactorily. I was able to agree with Winston that I was not in the least anxious for any large infantry forces, let alone large forces from England, fighting the Turks in Iraq and particularly north of Mosul, but that I am quite prepared to deal with the Turks with the Air Force and troops on the spot. I am sure that this is right as a general principle though no doubt we shall want to call upon the very moderate re-inforcements from India that are being warned to be in readiness. Meanwhile Cavan can arrange for the relief of the British Battalion next month to make an overlap during which both Battalions will be in the country. Anyhow the Committee agreed that a Turkish push should be at once hit hard by the Air Force not only in Iraq territory but across the frontier if necessary. If the Cabinet endorse this we are all right. . . . To CID on Pembroke and Singapore. I joined with Balfour and Air people in deprecating the closing down of Pembroke and Rosyth and with Winston and the Air people in postponing heavy gun equipment for Singapore pending further explorations of aerial defence possibilities.

16 October 1925: Dined at the Laverys . . . I sat between Lady Lavery with whom I got on very happily, and Lady Curzon who did not appeal to me very much. There is a beautiful portrait of her in the studio which Lavery originally painted for Grace Curzon, George Nathaniel's wife. She kept on asking the artist to make her as slender and slim as possible and when the picture was finished Curzon rejected it with indignation saying that it gave her none of that 'snowy amplitude which is the greatest beauty of the female form', whereupon they quarrelled and Lavery painted out the head to put in Mary Curzon's. Lady Lavery suggested that the proper motto for the picture was 'Hail Mary full of Grace'. It was quite an entertaining party, rather Irish and Bohemian.

19 October 1925: Had a short talk with S.B., my chief object being to make him understand that we shall get no progress on any Imperial development question unless he can make Winston definitely understand that it is his duty not simply to defend the Treasury point of view in these matters which is congenitally Little England but to override them. I spoke particularly in this connexion about E. African loans and the present embargo.

20 October 1925: Saw the High Commissioners and talked to them about Locarno and other things. . . . Committee of Civil Research where a miserable fellow called Scarf spent an hour or more explaining to Winston's great satisfaction that anything done for iron and steel would destroy the Rerolling Industry. After him one Whitehead came and dismissed Scarf as entirely unrepresentative of anything but the least efficient employers and definitely expressed his belief in the necessity of iron and steel being safeguarded.

To Victoria to meet Austen on his triumphant return from Locarno. All the Cabinet were there and lots of others and he was fairly beaming, but certainly has handled the situation very ably.

21 October 1925: Cabinet at which Austen began by giving a very interesting and humorous account of the Locarno 'Love Feast'. He seems to have been entirely in his element and at the end to have had 'Roses, roses all the way'. I did not wish to insert a note of scepticism, but I asked him afterwards at lunch whether he thought that the French or German Governments were both certain to survive until December when the Treaty is to be finally signed. He thought that even if the Governments were modified the Treaty would survive. After Locarno came a desultory discussion on Iraq. I refused myself to be drawn into the question of general merits as I had no paper ready and also did not wish to circulate one until I could agree it with Austen, but I got the Cabinet to agree to the essential items in the CID recommendations and sent telegrams out to Iraq accordingly. I think this policy of working step by step is probably the best. Five or six of us from the Cabinet including Austen and Winston went on to lunch with Sassoon where Austen expanded still further.

Back to the Agricultural Policy Committee where I championed Edward's policy very vigorously against Winston. After the meeting I tackled Winston, with some misgivings in view of our recent controversy, about East Africa, and found him in a most reasonable mood. We agreed that if a public announcement were made as to the Cabinet sanctioning the principle of the 10 million guarantee, the actual introduction of the Bill could be postponed. He even, with help from Niemeyer against

Barstow, agreed that something should be put in about research. I promised to draft an announcement which he might agree to.

22 October 1925: Conference with Jix and Anderson on the one side and myself, Davis and Whiskard on the other about the Irish Boundary. I convinced Jix against Anderson that we really cannot do the thing without giving Craig proper notice. But he is still very frightened of the idea that we have somehow or other to implement our Treaty obligation.

23 October 1925: To a further Cabinet at which we discussed a variety of things, more particularly the programme of work for the autumn session. Winston with the usual flourish accepted with good grace the necessity for an emergency Finance Bill dealing with safeguarding measures and presently came round to me with my pronouncement as to East African loan modified in a quite acceptable way. I agreed there and then and we ran the thing through the Cabinet without discussion.

28 October 1925: Cabinet on Pembroke and Rosyth where we again postponed a decision in order to try and get a balance between Admiralty saving and the expenditure in other directions, the obvious point which should have been examined years before. From that we went on to what was to be done over the Ulster Boundary determination, a matter on which I had to see the Free State Ministers the following day. The Cabinet was at once plunged into the regular Irish atmosphere, everyone talking excitedly and most of them irrelevantly. Hardly anyone seemed to be prepared to realise that we should have at any rate to try to fulfil our Treaty obligations whatever the verdict was, and Winston even suggesting that it might be better to tell Ireland to go and be a republic than yield certain places. Of course all these excitements are hypothetical and depend upon the possibility of the Commission giving a foolish decision. But such information as percolated through Cave was that the decision would be sensible. In the end I was instructed to confine my discussion with Irish Ministers entirely to the details of the arrangements and not to enter into any far-seaching assurances or considerations of what might have to be done if the decision was one which Ulster refuses to accept, while S.B. was meanwhile to try and get some idea from the Chairman as to the date and character of the determination.

29 October 1925: Conference with Free State Ministers, O'Higgins, O'Byrne and Blythe, Douglas Hogg and Walter Guinness supporting me as well as a large posse of departmental experts of all kinds. We got through the business extraordinarily quickly and smoothly and even on the matter of prisons got them to realise that prisoners in Ulster hands would have to be moved back with the prison authorities subject always to any legal remedy they might have. We successfully avoided being drawn into any serious discussion of what might happen if Ulster refuses to accept the determination of the Commission and in fact avoided hypothetical dangers altogether. The whole thing for which we had left the day free was over by 1.30 to their surprise and ours. . . . Edward Wood is to be made Viceroy – on the whole the best possible appointment. He has good sense, high character, and though slow to move courage in emergency.

30 October 1925: Attended the Civil Research Committee all the morning and at the end had no little sparring with Winston who is determined by hook or crook to prevent a safeguarding inquiry [on iron and steel]. I pointed out that the Committee had been set up to consider alternative remedies and that not one had been suggested but had been dropped as unpractical, and that we were face to face with the alternative of either saying flatly that nothing could be done or else allowing an enquiry under safeguarding. . . .

Went to St James's Palace to see the Prince of Wales. We had an hour and a half's talk both about South Africa . . . and about things here at home. I let myself go to him pretty freely about the necessity for an entirely new economic policy.

3 November 1925: Talk with the PM . . . about his having a talk to the King or Prince of Wales about the latter's specialising in an interest in migration and Imperial trade affairs . . . and the Irish Boundary question. . . .

In the afternoon saw Fox who had tales of the imminent collapse of the *Morning Post* and its being taken over by Beaverbrook. My next caller was Gwynne, not to tell me that the *M.P.* was collapsing, for indeed according to him it was going very strong and had stolen away some of Beaverbrook's best men, but that Beaverbrook was financially in with Inverforth in the latter's shady schemes to get Turkish concessions in return for pressing the Government to abandon Mosul.

17 November 1925: High Commissioners followed by CID mainly on disarmament. Meeting of the Committee of National Expenditure at which Winston opened up his attempt to cut down the million pound grant for Empire development [i.e. the provision for the Empire Marketing Board] to nothing for this coming year and half a million for next year. We had a spirited contest but I refused to budge beyond admitting the possibility that no money might be available this year or indeed the schemes for expenditure quite ready, and it was left for a further meeting between Winston, Philip and myself to go into the matter.

18 November 1925: Then to the Cabinet where after disposing of some anti-strike business we opened up the deferred discussion on Mosul. I took over half an hour with interruptions expanding the general memorandum on the subject which I had just circulated and was followed by Austen, who dealt very fully with the foreign aspects of the question and gave me the most whole-hearted support. I think the strength of the case has commended itself to the Cabinet as a whole and the only difficult point will be the precise statement I may have to make about the nature of the pledge for the future. We finished after 1.30 with Winston to lead the counter attack at the next meeting.

19 November 1925: Committee of Civil Research which is now getting near the summing up stage on the Iron and Steel business. Philip summed up ably and temperately in favour of a safeguarding inquiry; Winston naturally to the effect that the evidence had obviously shown that we could not grant one. I as naturally in the opposite sense comparing all these efforts to wriggle out of the proper and obvious solution of all our difficulties to bluebottles buzzing in a fly trap. . . .

Took the chair for half an hour at the Imperial Affairs Committee where I received quite an ovation on coming into the room – apparently because of Mosul. This is at any rate encouraging. Then to FO for a talk of 1½ hours with Austen and de Jouvenel in the course of which we managed to get de Jouvenel to raise himself all the points we wanted raised. The only awkward thing is that he apparently is convinced that under the Treaty of Angora the French cannot stop Turkish troops from going through over their railway and that therefore if any more are sent he will take action by telling the Turks that this is something affecting the Mosul frontier and the League and that before he allows them to pass he may ask the League to intervene possibly through its representatives on the spot.

21 November 1925: Soon after I got home for lunch I received a telephone message from Whiskard to say that MacNeill, the Irish representative on the Boundary Commission, had resigned and that the Free State Ministers had cried off our meeting for Monday and Tuesday. Just like Ireland. Sent across the papers to Inskip for an opinion, Hogg being out of Town. Inskip took the view which Hogg confirmed later that the resignation of a Commissioner did not affect the existence of the Commission.

22 November 1925: Sam Hoare came in to have a bit of a talk about Canada and Iraq. I encouraged him on the former at any rate to the extent of saying that I thought his name ought to go forward [for the Governor Generalship] though necessarily with one or two others. On the latter he said that he had heard that F.E. meant to make real trouble and might even leave the Government, being desperate for want of means now that journalism is cut off from him.

23 November 1925: Irish Affairs Committee. This meeting was to have been preliminary to a meeting with Irish Ministers in the afternoon but the unfortunate resignation of Dr MacNeill from the Commission had caused Irish Ministers to cry off. It was decided that I should go with Jix to the Boundary Commission the next day in response to their invitation in order to receive a communication from them but not generally to confer about the situation as the Irish could not be present.

24 November 1925: High Commissioners for a short meeting after which I went on to Clement's Inn to meet the Irish Boundary Commission. Feetham told us that everything had been settled by 17th October and that the subsequent delay had only been due to the absence of map preparation, that the 6 inch map would be ready in a few days and that they would be prepared to issue their award by about 3rd December. They considered MacNeill's resignation as invalid and in any case not affecting the situation. They offered to show us the outlined map of the proposed award but I declined suggesting that it would be better to get the Irish to come and see it. Went on to the Irish Affairs Committee which was all over the place and demurred very strongly to my sending anything to Dublin which looked like an invitation to come to see the map on Thursday feeling that this should only come from the Commission and that until we had seen the map we should say nothing.

. . . had a long talk with MacNeill which I hope he conveyed to his Ministers in Dublin pointing out that after all the award gave them a good deal and that it was in their interest, especially if they looked to the future union of Ireland, to get a prompt and peaceful settlement. I spoke to him very earnestly and it may have had some effect. Anyhow they did telegraph over the next day that they wished to come and consult with us before any meeting with the Boundary Commission.

25 November 1925: Cabinet where we had the long threatened onslaught by Winston and F.E. on the whole Iraq policy. Winston began by hand-somely admitting that he was wrong as to our obligation to defend Iraq under the present Treaty, but used that very effectively as an argument to show that any arrangement involved entanglement. F.E. was mild, chiefly raising the Indian objection and when I read out a formula explaining negatively what our pledges at Geneva did not commit us to he thought that that would meet his views. I thereupon suggested to S.B. that we should have a small committee to settle a joint draft for such statement as might have to be made in the House on this question. . . .

Soon after this I got a telegram from Cosgrave offering to come over and arranged with Stanley that he would meet them himself. Unluckily the word 'personal' got so placed in the reply that the Irish took it to refer to his wish to see Cosgrave personally with the consequence that Cosgrave came alone and did not bring his colleagues as he wished.

26 November 1925: Irish Boundary meeting at No. 10. Cosgrave and O'Hegarty on the Irish side, Stanley, Austen, Jix and myself on the British. Cosgrave stated as well as he could the unconvincing case that the proposed Boundary award was another flagrant injustice to Ireland. S.B. made it very clear to him that there was no question of our repeating an injustice done to Ulster when the Commission was appointed without her consent, and that any alteration could only come by agreement with Craig. We then had a short talk among ourselves and at 12.30 got in the remaining members of the Irish Affairs Committee and Craig. The discussion centred mainly on Craig's demand for compensation which was put in a form well calculated to upset Winston. After a long wrangle on this we tried to get things back to the question whether Craig would meet Cosgrave in the afternoon to which he bluntly replied that he would not do so unless he had an hour with Winston first and got that side of things agreed to. Stanley got over this by saying that he would be at the interview himself and would take the responsibility for any concessions that might have to be raised. . . .

Back to the Office and had a longish talk with the Rt Hon. Andrew Jameson, a Free State Senator, who told me something of the difficulties of Cosgrave's position. Later on Cosgrave himself came in for a few minutes, very tired. The conclusion of his long talk with Craig had been that he was in favour of retaining the existing boundary and seeing if he could get any concessions along with it, and he went back to Ireland to recommend this to his colleagues.

27 November 1925: We had a sub-committee on the Iraq statement with Austen in the chair, and agreed upon a formula. We disagreed as to whether we should push a statement on to the House before we left for Geneva or only make it if required. Winston is all for the latter, but then he frankly wants to create an atmosphere at Geneva which would make the League give the Turks so much of Mosul that we should chuck the whole thing.

30 November 1925: Cabinet on the Irish situation to which the PM expounded all that had happened at Chequers at the weekend between himself, Craig and the Irish Ministers. It appeared as if a settlement could be reached on the basis of the status quo, the dropping of the Council of

Ireland [L.S.A. holograph note: a point about which I had been pushing hard] and some concession with regard to Irish [debt] payments under Article 5. It was decided that Winston aided by Birkenhead and Salisbury should do battle with the Irish on the following day on the Article 5 position.

1 December 1925: Winston told us [L.S.A. and S.B.] that the discussions had gone on all day without very much result except that the Irish were now by way of offering twelve million pounds to be paid over a long period of years as the settlement of Article 5.

2-3 December 1925: Irish discussions continued and we discussed situation in Cabinet I think on both days. F.E. and myself pressed hard for dropping Clause 5 (debt payment) while I also strongly urged getting rid of the Council of Ireland clause. Winston disposed to agree. Salisbury and one or two others hostile. By some time later on afternoon of the 3rd Winston had settled and I went up with him, Craig and Cosgrave in a taxi from H. of C. to Treasury. As we got out Craig and Cosgrave both rushed forward to pay the fare. I pulled Winston [back] and told him not to interfere with the first occasion on which the two factions in Ireland had ever joined to offer to pay for England. We went through the draft agreement in which I discovered that the two parties were described as 'High Contracting Parties' which I insisted on changing. When they were finally corrected and retyped we took them down to Stanley's room at H. of C. and there all those who had been concerned in the negotiations were assembled to sign. Salisbury was summoned on the telephone and came not quite realising what it was. When he read the document he passed it on, tossed a slip across to Stanley 'I cannot possibly sign this' made some lame excuse and bolted. The Irish had got to catch the 8.45 from Euston but I gave them a joint dinner with Winston in Room D of which they ate the first course or two and we drank each other's healths. . . . The whole business was an immense relief to me. Winston really did all the work of negotiating the deal which was as well, as I should have been out of place as a representative of the British side, and equally so, when the Irish were there, as their champion. But I think I can credit myself with having during the year before done much to create the atmosphere without which the settlement would never have been possible. As to the ultimate end no-one can say. But if the Free State settlement is to succeed at all, or succeed for a generation, this new agreement has given it its chance. As for Feetham he deserves immense credit, and his reasoned memo afterwards was a most statesmanlike document.

6-16 December 1925: Geneva once more. I have put the main business into a Cabinet paper. Our September tactics worked out admirably. The Hague decision inevitably shepherded Unden into the position where he was finally faced with the alternative of wrecking the whole thing or falling into line, and the truculent stupidity of the Turks helped greatly, as also did the Laidoner reports. For the idea of sending Laidoner great credit is due to Young. Unden came – so we are told – hoping for two things (1) that I should say I would not be bound unless the Turks agreed to be bound also, in which case the League might wipe its hands of the whole affair, (2) that we would never accept definite mandatory terms. I spiked his guns as regards the first at the opening meeting by announcing that anything I had said in September referred to declarations but that after the Hague decision I regarded ourselves as absolutely bound by the Treaty, and as regards the second by letting d'Avenol (who was most helpful throughout) have a document, prepared by Young showing that our existing Treaty covered everything in the Syrian mandate. At the first public meeting Munir Bey [the new Turkish representative] not only rejected the Hague ruling but by a consummate piece of bluff challenged the right of the Council to accept Unden's report recommending the Hague ruling without his concurrence: the Council adjourned for tea and at the end of nearly an hour I heard that they had come to the lamentable conclusion to take note of Munir's objection and leave things undecided! Then they seem to have pulled themselves together and to have decided that Munir must be overruled, but failed completely to agree as to the reasons to be given. In the end Scialoja [presiding over the Council] was authorised to give any reasons he liked! One of the troubles I might add almost to the end of this session was that Scialoja disagreed with some of the reasoning of the Hague ruling and was for ever harping back to his grievance against their want of logic instead of trying to settle the Iraq frontier. After this the next day or day after I appeared before the Sub-Committee to see whether we could find a compromise. I gave them a very full (and I believe effective) statement of the reasons why a compromise couldn't be reached till a basis of principle had been established – this in English and subsequent discussion in French. From then onwards my role – and Austen's – was hanging about while the Council was struggling to make up its mind. Unden produced one draft report in favour of partition. Quinones [Señor Quinones de Leon, Spanish Ambassador in Paris, and member of the Sub-Committee], greatly helped by d'Avenol, produced a much abler and really conclusive report in the opposite sense and got Quaroni [L.S.A. queried 'Guani', the Uruguayan representative, also on the Sub-Committee] with him. The Sub-Committee then ceased and became merged in a series of tea parties of the whole Council, which must have been incredibly funny. At a late stage we learnt that Hayashi was a strong Undenite on grounds of backing a small – possibly old

Asiatic – state. Meanwhile Unden was weakening and things looked well when a very clumsy answer of S.B.'s to a supplementary in the House created a complete panic in the Council and nearly drove poor Austen (whom I have never known so tired out) to despair. A wire from us skilfully worded got the right reply from Stanley and this enabled us to give private assurances after which we were told that Scialoja and Unden would come and receive from us assurances formally signed by us both. There was some muddle as to when this was to happen and we both hung about for two days waiting. In the interval Unden suddenly decided on a new move which was not to ask for assurances but to fix the frontier conditionally upon our making the required treaty with Iraq in a given time. This was improved by Scialoja in such a way as to prevent a subsequent council going into the merits of the case.

16 December 1925: We were promised the League decision by 10.15 so that we could prepare our remarks on it for an early afternoon meeting. All the morning we waited and heard that Scialoja, who had been drafting since the 13th, had started some new hares. Then we waited longer and longer wondering if a decision would ever come, till finally at 11.15 or so the document came round. I prepared a brief reply and agreed it with Austen, as well as the one he was going to make as to future negotiations with Turkey and we went off to the Council at 6.30. Crowded hall and really tense excitement. Turks invited to take their place – no response. Decision read out in French, English omitted as it was circulated. Then I made my statement and made place for Austen who made his. All over. Dined quietly and thankfully at the Hotel and off by the 10.40 train. Looking back I feel certain that it was only tactics and also good pleading that made it possible for such a body as the Council to agree on such a decision – strong though our case was – against its natural tendency to favour the smaller and more troublesome Power and to split the difference. But I tremble to think what the Council would be like if a really difficult, critical and urgent question arose which divided the Great Powers!

20 December 1925 (Chequers): Wet and snowy. Tyrrell came down and we discussed the next day's Iraq debate a bit in the morning and after lunch, and then I sat down and wrote out what I thought Stanley ought to say finishing soon after tea.

21 December 1925: [Iraq Debate.] Our people filled up the benches and S.B. then delivered the speech, with practically no alterations, and had a great success, disposing most effectively of all the charges of breach of faith, etc.

431

27–28 December 1925: So ended 1925. A busy year in which my two main achievements were the dividing up of the office and Iraq. As for the latter all the abuse I got at one stage did me no harm and in the end I was right as to the dogs barking and the caravan passing on. All the same there was more justice in the attack on me as the author of the Mosul policy than they knew. I think my efforts on the original 1917 and 1918 Committees had a good deal to do with our definite decision to take in the whole of Iraq in a British mandate, and at a critical moment I saved Allenby the cadre of his British divisions as well as a brigade. Later, in 1923, I worked very hard against the scuttle policy on the Iraq Committee and helped to stem the tide there. And in 1925 if I hadn't gone out and persuaded Sam to go too he would never have been so loyal a helper and I should never have had the same certainty of touch or convinced the Cabinet that things were going as well as they are. Hardly less important, though not so directly in my sphere, was the work I did earlier in the year on the CID and in the Cabinet in defeating Austen's idea of a pact of Alliance with France and Belgium and shepherding him into the position of accepting the to him at first by no means attractive notion of a scheme which should ally us equally with Germany against France as with France against Germany – a scheme I pushed from the outset as calculated to disentangle us from our European commitments. So I can claim a very real share in the paternity of Locarno.

13

General Strike and Imperial Conference 1926

With the passage of the Iraq Treaty through the Commons on 18 February 1926, Amery could turn his mind to the Imperial Conference, which was to take place in the autumn of 1926. The League Council crisis, which the Cabinet discussed on 3 March, had emphasised both the need for and the difficulties of consultation with the Dominions, and this was Amery's main concern throughout. They had opposed the addition of any permanent Council members other than Germany, but only in March had made it clear that they would object less to additional non-permanent members. The scheme which Chamberlain put to the Cabinet on 15 March nevertheless envisaged adding Spain and Brazil also to the permanent membership. The compromise finally made public at an informal meeting of the Council was to defer for further inquiry the constitution of the Council, and in the meantime to accept the generous gesture of Sweden and Czechoslovakia to resign immediately their non-permanent seats on the Council in favour of Poland and Holland. Spain and Brazil immediately declared the plan unacceptable, the former threatening withdrawal from the League and the latter to veto Germany's seat. The special Assembly was thus rendered abortive and Germany's entry into the League had to be postponed until September. In May, however, a committee met at Geneva and it was decided to extend the membership of the Council, and that three of the nine elective seats should become semi-permanent by a procedural device and should be given to Poland, Spain and Brazil. This compromise plan was accepted at the price only of Brazil's withdrawal from the League.* In September when the election took place Eire tried for a place on the Council in defiance of Dominion opinion, but with the support of South Africa. This confirmed the right of Dominions to stand

*David Carlton has discussed this crisis in 'Great Britain and the League Council Crisis of 1926', *Historical Journal*, 11 (1968), pp. 354–64; cf. also F. P. Walters, *The League of Nations* (Oxford University Press, 1960), ch. 27.

for election, but emphasised once more that the Empire had become a Commonwealth of equals.

The Cabinet's principal concern that spring was the report of the Royal Commission on the Coal Industry (the Samuel Report), published on 11 March. Although appointed as the direct result of a dispute over the proper level of wages in the coal industry, it pointed to no easy solution and indeed advocated both an end to the Government subsidy and an immediate cut in wages. The miners were certain to resist this proposal. On the other hand the owners, who wished to abandon the national wages agreement for separate settlements in each mining district, were bound to dislike the Report's specific endorsement of a national wages board and a minimum percentage base for the wage. They were opposed also even to the relatively mild Government interference proposed to further amalgamation proposals. For its part the Government also found certain parts of the Report unacceptable. In particular, they had both political and financial objections to the proposal that mineral rights should be nationalised and indeed it was difficult to see how it related to the proposed creation by amalgamation of large undertakings to increase productivity and lower costs. These amalgamations were to be the long-term remedy to the problems of the coal industry and the owners' proposal that the length of the working day should be extended to eight hours was rejected on the slightly suspect ground that it would produce unsaleable coal. This was an argument hard to reconcile with the Commission's evident belief that *per capita* productivity achieved through amalgamation would not lead to a severe contraction of the industry.

At the prompting of the Secretary for Mines the Cabinet decided to accept the entire Report, despite financial opposition from Churchill and on grounds of principle from Amery and Salisbury, but to make their acceptance conditional on an unconditional acceptance of the Report as a whole by both miners and mine-owners. Baldwin announced this decision to the leaders of both sides at a meeting on 24 March, together with promises of a tapering subsidy should both sides reach agreement. He promised that the relevant Bills would be ready before 30 April, but the miners insisted on knowing the details, and the owners refused to say anything. They had already displayed their hostility to the Report and their preference for an extension of hours in a memorandum sent to the Government on 17 March.

Predictably therefore the owners and miners reached no agreement when they met face to face, although there seemed some disposition on the part of the former at least to negotiate a national agreement. No terms, however, were put forward, and the miners took their problem to the TUC's special Industrial Committee. They were not ready to back the miners to the hilt when no proper negotiations had taken place and on

8 April they committed themselves to an equitable settlement only and a continuance of negotiations. Despite the advice proffered to the miners' leaders by Pugh and Thomas in particular, the miners' Delegate Conference next day voted for the principle of a national wage agreement, a national minimum, no extension of hours and no cut in wages. When the miners and owners met again on 13 April there were heated exchanges since the owners wished to be rid of the national minimum and were in effect warned that there could be no reductions in pay. They also wished district meetings to take place and this aroused the miners' suspicions. The TUC also were deeply disturbed by the owners' attitude and agreed to see Baldwin.

Baldwin received the Industrial Committee on 14 April and agreed to call the two sides together, but he made it clear also that he was not going to be pressurised into anything that he did not think right, and later that evening warned Thomas of the Pandora's box a general strike would unlock. Next day he saw the miners, making it clear that he understood their fear of district negotiations, and confirming the possibility of a temporary subsidy. The miners for their part made it clear that any district variations must be nationally agreed. The Cabinet discussed the situation on both 14 and 15 April and it was made clear that the owners had accepted the Report, although rather less definitely than the Government. Baldwin's own mind was now running on an extension of hours as a way to avoid the harsh wage cuts which he had been warned the owners had in mind. The owners' first offer was clearly far too low, and on 23 April Baldwin brought the two sides together in further sterile argument. Both dug in their heels.

The details of the talks which followed find no place in Amery's diary. He was not one of the negotiators, and the Cabinet's only discussion in this period, on 28 April, concerned emergency supply and transport arrangements should a strike come. By the end of the month it seemed clear that the miners would not bind themselves to a cut in wages, and that the owners, while now ready to concede a national wage agreement, would do so only on the basis of the 1921 wage tied to an eight-hour day. Baldwin felt bound to put the offer, although it appalled him, and with the miners' inevitable refusal to negotiate upon it the Cabinet declared a state of emergency. They agreed also that Baldwin should bring the TUC directly into the discussions.

Baldwin met with the TUC and the miners knowing that his colleagues would neither extend the Government subsidy to the industry, nor agree to ask the owners to postpone their lock-out unless a settlement seemed a real possibility. The TUC presence at first seemed to offer a real chance of escaping a deadlock, but they could not trust the Government genuinely to reorganise the industry. In the end the negotiations broke down, largely because the Cabinet were not convinced that the miners would in the end concede the necessary reduction of wages, and feared a continuation of negotiations ending in 'a second deadlock which would leave us in a worse position than we are in tonight'.

On the morning of 1 May the Conference of Trade Union Executives voted overwhelmingly for a general strike. The TUC, to whom as a result control of all negotiations was handed, still hoped for a peaceful outcome. So did Baldwin, even though many of his collagues felt that the call for a general strike had transformed the whole nature of the dispute. It was possibly illegal; it was certainly designed to coerce the Government and hence unconstitutional. Indeed a TUC letter offering to take responsibility for the maintenance of food supplies was rejected since it involved the partial takeover of the Government's function. The talks which the TUC offered seemed more acceptable. Baldwin clearly hoped to explore further the possibility of a comprehensive agreement embodying proposals for the long as well as the short term.

At Baldwin's suggestion the actual negotiations which took place on the evening of 1 May were carried on by two small teams, Baldwin, Birkenhead and Steel-Maitland for the Government, and Pugh, Thomas and Swales for the TUC. Citrine and Sir Horace Wilson were present to advise. Since the TUC was obliged to obtain a withdrawal of the lock-out before further negotiations took place, negotiations turned on the conditions under which the Government would renew its subsidy, and the least Ministers required was a clear recognition that the application of the Samuel proposals would entail a cut in wages. Amery reports the formula reached, although he wrongly attributes it to Birkenhead; in fact the author was Wilson. Not only was it vague but it was clearly subject to slight but significant variations of interpretation. The Cabinet, as Hankey reported to the King, thought the formula 'too vague and indefinite, giving no assurance that the proposed negotiations were likely to lead to a successful issue; and that taken in conjunction with the menace of a general strike, it would be regarded by public opinion as a yielding by the Government to threats. It was felt that negotiations involving the payment of a subsidy ought not to be resumed without a definite answer from the miners on their acceptance of the Report of the Royal Commission, which, of course, would commit the miners to make some sacrifice as indicated in that Report. The TUC for their part learned that the miners' executives, unaware that negotiations were continuing, had departed for their areas and would have to be recalled. A. J. Cook gave it as his personal opinion that the formula was unlikely to prove acceptable and that the Miners' Federation had never intended to accept the Report unconditionally. Since he had not been told of the talks, he was deeply suspicious. He need not have worried. After an initial reluctance to endorse the formula until they knew both what the miners meant by 'negotiations on the lines of the Report' and what the Government's reorganisation measures would be, the General Council of the TUC finally accepted the formula in substance later in the afternoon of 2 May, subject to discovering more specifically what were the Government's intentions with regard to its interpretation.

While their deliberations were going on the mood of the Cabinet hardened. The failure of the TUC to appear at 1 p.m. as arranged, the news shortly before 2 p.m. that the miners had vanished into the country, and above all the information from the Postmaster-General that telegrams had gone out calling for a strike from midnight on 3 May contributed to a mood in which 'Ministers more than ever felt that the PM was a helpless innocent moving about amid dangers unrealised. Only yesterday,' Tom Jones recorded, 'the TUC had informed the PM that they had as yet passed no formal resolution in favour of a General Strike.'* Bridgeman for one was 'very uneasy as to the propriety of seeing the TUC again – as it seemed a most humiliating position for a Govt. to be negotiating with a threat of this kind held like a pistol at their head'.† However, while waiting to see the TUC again on the conditions under which negotiations could continue, they drafted an ultimatum requiring unconditional withdrawal of the threat of a general strike before negotiations continued.‡ Baldwin appears to have been given a discretion as to whether to use this or not, and in the event he kept it in his pocket. The discussions, three to a side as on the previous evening, had been friendly but unproductive. Once again they turned on whether the TUC could guarantee some modification in the miners' attitude about wages if further time were given. The only formula acceptable to the TUC was, however, weaker than that agreed the previous evening, and even without the *Daily Mail* incident (see below), it is difficult to believe it would have satisfied the Cabinet. Birkenhead told the TUC's representatives as much.

The arrival of the miners seems to have brought these indeterminate discussions to an end. While the TUC were showing them the previous day's formula and finding the response sticky, the Cabinet began to discuss the propriety of breaking off any further negotiations. According to Bridgeman 'there was strong difference of opinion', but the news of the refusal to print the *Daily Mail* because of its editorial attacking the strikers 'brought the doubtful people right up against the situation that the General Strike had actually begun'.§ There were no dissentients when it was decided to bring the negotiations to an end.

*Whitehall Diary, II, p. 28.
†Bridgeman's Political Notes, II.
‡The text can be found in Jones, Whitehall Diary, II, p. 30.
§Bridgeman's Political Notes, II.

Amery seems to have written up his diary for the period of the actual strike on 13 May, when it was all over. There is no reason, however, to doubt the accuracy of the entries and they provide a valuable account of the decision to introduce a simple three-clause Bill 'declaring' a general strike illegal, immobilising trade union funds, and prohibiting the expulsion of union members refusing to participate, and of the subsequent decision to drop the Bill. In fact on 11 May Lord Chief Justice Astbury in the Chancery Division stated that a general strike was illegal, and that no trade dispute could exist between the TUC on the one hand and the Government on the other. That same evening it became clear that the TUC were anxious to call off the strike, but the evidence seems conclusive that this had nothing to do with the Astbury judgment.

In fact the end of the strike was brought about not by any weakening of the strike itself, but rather because the General Council were sure it would weaken and in all probability also because they feared that frustration would breed violence. Samuel had returned from Italy to mediate, and although he had no authority to do so from the Government, the TUC's negotiating committee may well have refused to accept at face value his clear statement on the point. At all events they were ready to try once more to link a temporary reduction of wages with reorganisation under the aegis of a national wages board. The miners would not do so, and their refusal even to contemplate any movement at all on wages in effect put an end to any identity of purpose on the trade union side. The TUC endorsed the Samuel memorandum, and then surrendered to the Government. They quickly found that Samuel had not been deluding them about his position, but nevertheless felt that if only the entire Labour movement embraced the Samuel proposals, the Government could not refuse them. The miners had already turned down Samuel's proposals, however, and the Government's terms, while broadly similar to those Samuel put forward, retained control of the reorganisation legislation for itself: the wages question would be resolved by compulsory arbitration. Both sides of the coal industry turned down the proposals.

The Government decided to let time bring them to their senses, although ready always to see if private mediators could secure a settlement. On 15 June however the Cabinet decided to suspend the Seven Hours Act on the advice of the Coal Committee: evidently most Ministers shared the view that Amery put to Baldwin on 1 June 'that the men would prefer the 8 hours day to a lower wage'. That had always been Baldwin's view, and so both the suspension and the Mining Industry Act implementing certain reorganisation measures were put on the statute book in July. The coal owners, however, were much less generous in their wage offers than they had indicated they would be, and the Government perhaps began to regret that they had not written some form of national wages board into the Mining Industry Act.

The difficulty was to find a way of enforcing a national agreement on an industry whose owners obstinately refused to make one, and it was on this rock that Churchill's vigorous attempts to browbeat the owners into a settlement failed in September. The Cabinet agreed on 17 September to a wages tribunal with power to revise on appeal settlements agreed at district level on an eight-hour basis. The owners opposed the step and the miners rejected it. When the General Council made a final attempt at a settlement in November the Government revised the proposal and this time had the support of the miners' executive, only to find the miners still ready to vote it down. Instead the strike had to peter out in a series of district settlements and a bitterness that has lasted to the present day.

Diary

18 January 1926: Back to work feeling very Monday morningish and most disinclined to look at papers or face office problems. . . . In the afternoon I saw . . . the PM. Stanley had been a little worried because owing to a misunderstanding of something I had said to him Shuckburgh had not circulated any telegrams in connexion with the getting through of the Iraq Treaty so that it came upon him as a complete surprise. However Wilson had already explained things and all was well. He was looking fit but I warned him not to take on too many speeches and he himself is very anxious not to overload the session's work after Easter in view of possible troubles.

19 January 1926: Cabinet at which we had a little Iraq discussion arising out of the suggestion of the Air Ministry that the overlapping Battalions could now safely be withdrawn. . . . In the afternoon I attended a meeting of the Standing Committee on Expenditure and agreed with Winston as to a very considerable number of economies on Middle Eastern and Colonial Votes, and also very reluctantly accepted a cut in the O[verseas] S[ettlement] Vote which will prevent my extending to Australia and New Zealand the principles of the last passage scheme with Canada.

20 January 1926: Saw Hugo Hirst and Ben Morgan about the EIA. They have had meetings with Frank Hodges and other Labour men who have agreed upon a statement of policy which, with only a word or two altered, is the one we drafted at the meetings at Neville's house 18 months ago.

26 January 1926: Committee of Imperial Defence meeting. On the question of the Iraq Battalion Beatty raised a new hare and generally upset things by suggesting that the Navy could not do anything in the Sea of Marmora unless it had some previous guarantee as to what other Powers were going to do. The whole discussion rather went to pieces and eventually got postponed pending a telegram to Lindsay to find out if the Turks really were doing anything at the Dardanelles. Meanwhile the withdrawal of the Battalions was provisionally sanctioned. Thence to the Australian and New Zealand Luncheon Club to hear the Prince of Wales who had prepared quite a good little speech on migration. I sat next to him and he talked to me a good deal about it and is really genuinely anxious to show his interest in it in every way and later on to go round the Empire and meet the settlers. . . . To the Economic Committee at which Winston and everyone else made a dead set to get the million a year Empire development money postponed. I made it very clear that I could not possibly consent to such a breach of faith or even suggest it to the Dominions or to such a departure from the whole policy which we had put before the country.

1 February 1926: Saw Stanley about the Imperial Conference which he agreed ought to be held this year, and about the Economic Committee and the million a year. I spoke to him very strongly indeed and said that I could not possibly accept the suggestion of a cadging telegram asking the Dominions to let us postpone things. I was prepared on my own to agree to a shadow cut to £750,000 or even £600,000 if the matter was put under an independent Executive like the Forestry Commission, and I made it clear that I thought I ought to be chairman of it. As usual he was receptive but inscrutable. . . . PM's dinner. I sat between Winston and Willie. Winston very cheery and much interested in discussing climbing and the psychology of danger which tempted me to tell him the story of my accident on the Aiguilles Rouges which greatly excited him. He told me in return his emotion during a bad side slip trying to learn to fly. Fear in his view is quite definitely grey in colour. All this occupied us so pleasantly that I abandoned my idea of tackling him on the Empire million. Then to the Londonderry's squash. . . . The new recruit Mond [a former Lloyd George Liberal who had joined the Conservatives] was there with a large carnation looking rather coy like a debutante.

2 February 1926: Opening of Parliament. Found myself the senior Minister next to Stanley, Winston, Austen and Jix being away. . . .
Had a short talk with Sam about Iraq and other matters including his own prospects of being considered for Canada. Dined at home and back to the House to see Stanley about the Empire million which he had been

discussing with Winston before dinner. I found him with a draft telegram to the Dominions suggesting postponement until the Conference which he seemed to think might very well be sent. He added that he asked Austen whether there were any objections to sending a telegram and that Austen had not seen any. I told him I could not possibly agree and went over all the objections from the Dominion point of view as well as from our own to our turning up at a Conference with nothing really taken in hand, but with a sort of Penelope's web of things agreed at the previous Conference modified and then brought up again for new consideration. All other avenues of preference except that of our publicity and research had been blocked (apparently Philip [Cunliffe Lister] in his German treaty has gone and made impossible any form of preference by prohibition and licence, a damned silly thing to do and one calculated to expose us legitimately to the charge of disregard for Empire development by the Labour people). So there really was no alternative to the Economic Committee's proposal and after all to whom else would the Dominion Governments refer such a question than to the Economic Committee. . . . I said that, as much as I hated it, if Winston had his way with the Cabinet I should have to go out. He was, I think, impressed and at any rate agreed to postpone discussion at the Cabinet for another week to see if we could not get to some agreement outside.

3 February 1926: Cabinet where contrary to my expectation we got the question of the Iraq Battalions through without discussion, and also got an agreement on asking for an Imperial Conference this year without controversy after I had stated the case and had been strongly supported by Austen. On the Empire million Stanley announced postponement and added that he had appointed a committee under Austen to go into the question of the right organisation to administer it.

4 February 1926: Had a long talk at the House with Philip about the organisation of the committee which is to carry out the spending of the million and he produced some rather effective arguments against an executive commission which would need statutory powers. He is, however, determined to oppose any suggestion of detailed Treasury control.

9 February 1926: Attended the sub-committee on Empire marketing under Austen's chairmanship. We had first discussed Philip's proposal for a mixed Cabinet committee and then Winston suggested that much the best thing was to entrust the whole responsibility to one Minister, namely myself, and Austen added that the Imperial Economic Committee might be in fact his Advisory Committee. On these lines we very soon came to substantial agreement and I am to see Mackinder to see how far this would meet the wishes of the IEC.

Saw Stanley for a few minutes about the Empire million and he told me that he thought it would be all right when it came up to the Cabinet on Thursday; that he had talked to Austen who now realised that we ought to do something. I could not press him much further than that though I made it clear that by all rights I understood that at least six hundred thousand should be on this year's estimate.

11 February 1926: CID meeting on oil fuel for the Navy which has been still further cut down in the teeth of vehement opposition from Beatty. My feeling is that if they would only make sure of the tanks and the tankers they could probably pick up the oil fairly quickly....

Imperial Affairs Committee at which I explained the general outline of the scheme for spending the 10 million loan, and then hurried down to Cabinet where we considered the proposals of the Economic Committee. I made a hard fight for Plumer not bearing the whole burden of the Jordan Regiment in Trans-Jordan but the Cabinet insisted on my sending him a strong telegram urging that he should do so. On the Imperial Economic Committee Winston opened and was strongly supported by Salisbury and I think had several others with him. I replied and then Stanley summed up in my favour, at any rate as regards some money being down in next year's estimates. Austen followed agreeing but queering the pitch badly by suggesting that he thought £250,000 would be enough. Neville, who had been very helpful with Stanley behind the scenes, chipped in with a sentence to say that that would look miserable and that something more like half a million was required, and Stanley also said that he thought that was about the amount. It was left for me to settle details with Winston. Afterwards Philip expressed his great delight at the result though I felt it would have been better if he had helped more to bring it about. Altogether not far off 40 million has been whittled off the year's estimates and Winston deserves every credit for his effort in the matter.

13 February 1926: Long talk with Mackinder about the Imperial Economic Committee and the new organisation. I was glad to find that the general scheme worked out by Austen's Committee appealed to him. He said they would be very relieved to know that I would be in charge and not Board of Trade which they regarded as a purely British department. We worked out details together with the result that the thing was likely to be very much on the lines of the Overseas Settlement organisation. I found Mackinder unexpectedly strong on the point that any diversion of the money to specific British agricultural campaigning would be keenly resented. I had seen Casey a day or two [ago] and suggested to him that a private telegram from Bruce asking us to include British agricultural produce might be very helpful; in view of what Mackinder says I am not sure that I did wisely.

15 February 1926: Lunched with Lady Dawkins. . . . Younger was there and told some good stories, more particularly the one about Lloyd George's telling Bonar about Northcliffe badgering him to be made a representative of the Peace Conference, at the end of which L.G. had told him to go to Hell and Bonar's sad reply 'but he didn't and came round to the Treasury instead'. . . . Further meeting of the Empire Marketing Committee . . . at which we made considerable progress. Austen and all of us except Winston definitely in favour of the money being non-surrenderable.

17 February 1926: Cabinet at which we discussed enlargement of the Council of the League [to include Poland] and sundry other matters. Austen asked for a special Cabinet Committee to be appointed to discuss the negotiations with Turkey and Winston not being on it we may get through business in reasonable time. After Cabinet helped Austen to draft answers to questions which raised the ticklish point how far we represent the Empire as a whole on the Council or only ourselves to which I think the only real answer is that at present we represent the Empire if and when they want us to do so but not otherwise.

18 February 1926: Motion [in the Iraq Treaty debate] carried by 260 to 116, no Unionist voting wrong. So ends that chapter of the Iraq story.

19 February 1926: Conference with Sam, Trenchard, Dobbs and Middle Eastern crowd from this office, FO, Air Ministry, etc. about what frontier concessions could be made and also on the position of the Turks in the North Eastern wedge and Syria. General conclusion that we could concede very little territory but that we might encourage through railway communication and perhaps even cede to an Anglo Turkish Company the existing railway from Baghdad to Shergat.

20 February 1926: Long talk with Edward Wood about India and some of our joint problems in connexion with it. I urged him to get away if he could from the atmosphere of constitutional grievances and to buck up India and make it feel proud of itself.

24 February 1926: High Commissioners in the morning all of them very down on the enlargement of the League Council. Cabinet at which the Empire Marketing Committee's Report was accepted and largely thanks to Neville's intervention we got our way against Winston as to the money being non-surrenderable. I still am anything but happy at the idea that only £500,000 should be spent the first year but I certainly have fought my best. . . .

Iraq sub-committee in Salisbury's room at the Lords where we made some progress, the main idea being that we should offer Turkey definite security as to the Iraq frontier, a couple of small slices of mountain country and see whether we could strengthen this further with any economic arrangement as to oil (which I doubt) or as to the Baghdad railway.

25 February 1926: CID where we decided to let the exchange battalions leave Iraq, and then had a long talk on the extension of Soviet influence in Asia and how to meet it.

3 March 1926: Cabinet at which we discussed Geneva Council affair at some length. I only intervened to lay stress on the importance of keeping in touch with Dominion opinion and of Austen's not creating a rent between us and the Dominions in his efforts to heal any rent there may be between us and some of the foreign Powers on the Council. S.B. brought up the tiresome question of leakage, the *Daily Express* having embodied a considerable part of Cave's last memorandum on the House of Lords only about a week after their publishing Cunliffe Lister's paper on films. As a matter of fact the very next morning the *Daily Express* came out with yet a third bad leak, the full details of Bruce's telegram about a proposed shipping scheme, and since then S.B. and others of us have been seriously considering what action is possible. Talked to Robin about it at All Souls last night. He insisted that in all recent cases the leakage never occurred during the weeks or even months while the thing was prepared in the departments, but only after it got into Cabinet Ministers' hands.

4 March 1926: For the rest finished dictating letters for the mail. This is the first batch of letters to Governors and Prime Ministers I have done since Christmas – a most distressing reflexion on my original resolution to write to them all at least once a month.

5 March 1926: Lunched at the office and down to the House afterwards to see Stanley about the leakage business which I had discussed to some extent with Austen and Hogg the evening before. He decided that he could not possibly let Hogg take action without a Cabinet and wished me to consult with F.E. and if possible Cave over the weekend.* Saw Winston and arrived at a reasonable *modus vivendi* with him as regards

---

*L.S.A. saw Cave on the 8th and found him 'inclined to favour a vigorous action with regard to the leakages'.

Palestine, namely to accept Plumer's propositions for the present year and to work by stages to the eventual nominal basis that Palestine should pay for its defence and for half the expenditure required from outside for the defence and administration of Trans Jordan. Saw F.E. about the leakage business. At Wednesday Cabinet I had urged that one of our number should go out to Australia with the E[mpire] P[arliamentary] A[ssociation] as I could not go and F.E. is now quite eager to go himself. He would do admirably if only he would be certain to keep sober.

Down to Oxford for the Bursar's dinner. Simon has come back from India very much impressed with the fact that the Oriental is not really adapted to our English scheme of Parliamentary Government. I think he is rapidly becoming a Tory.

10 March 1926: Cabinet at which we ran through a number of minor matters beginning with some Indian questions, after which F.E. went off in order to deal with telegrams arising out of the attitude of the Speaker of the Indian Assembly. At the end of the business I brought up the question of leakage and on Cave's and Hogg's advice it was decided to summon the Editor of the *Daily Express* to give information as to the source of the leakages and if necessary proceed further. . . . Questions and afterwards some animated talk with Winston about Bruce's telegram expostulating with us over our failure to keep our promise with regard to the current year. Winston quite intractable, nothing but nonsense about Bruce cadging, trying to squeeze the last drop of our blood, etc. It really is a disaster that Stanley put him at the Exchequer where he intensifies all the 'little Englandism' of the Treasury.

Compatriots' Dinner at which Dougie Malcolm gave an admirable survey of the history of Chartered Companies in general and Rhodesia in particular. Afterwards Boyle told the story, apparently quite true, of a Frenchman who noticing Dougie at a dinner and his rather distinguished appearance asked his neighbour who he was. The neighbour replied, 'Don't you know, this is Mr Malcolm who runs Rhodesia.' The Frenchman asked eagerly, 'And who is this Rhodesia; is she very beautiful?'

11 March 1926: Saw d'Egville and discouraged any idea of postponing the Australian visit of the EPA. When I mentioned that F.E. was thinking of going he looked very terrified and not at all happy. Apparently he has been hearing a good many stories about him in India.

12 March 1926: Saw the King at 10.30. He was even more talkative and emphatic than usual and it was quite difficult to get in a word edgeways. He was not at all enthusiastic about the Duke of York going to the opening of Canberra. He seemed to think that he could not possibly afford it. I assured him that the House of Commons would make no fuss about the expense of the journey and that Australia would no doubt look after him at the other end. I shall have to send a temporising reply to Bruce and get in touch with the Duke myself before renewing the subject. He was also very contemptuous of Canberra and the idea of a bush capital generally, though in the same breath he was also very critical of the arrangement by which a Governor and Governor General lived in the same capital [the capital was then Melbourne]. We also discussed the question of a Governor for Victoria and Governor General for Canada and the *Daily Express* leakages. He was very down on Beaverbrook and hopes we may set an example this time. As regards Canada he has no use for Mackenzie King and not much more for Meighen. . . . On the subject of the Coal Commission Report he enunciated the startling doctrine that nobody ought to be allowed to make more than 10 per cent in the way of dividends. His idea was entirely based on his own experience as an investor and the suggestion that when new enterprises are being started those who put their money into them require more than the ordinary interest to induce them to face the risk had hardly occurred to him and did not apparently very much impress him. [Amery began reading the Samuel Report on the train to Birkenhead, where he spoke that evening.]

13 March 1926: Came up by the early train and got through the Coal Report before Euston. It is an able document though I cannot see why they should have dragged in the nationalisation of minerals.

15 March 1926: Emergency Cabinet to sanction a request from Austen to be allowed to agree to a last minute scheme which he thought might save the situation at Geneva and which everybody else including the Germans were willing to accept. The scheme involved bringing Spain and Brazil on to the Council [of the League] as permanent members in September or at any rate the Council recommending that solution to the Assembly. We deprecated this if it could be avoided but gave him a free hand assuming that he had the substantial assent of the Dominions' representatives. I pointed out that it would never do for us to put a proposal forward in our position on the Council of the League which was then to be voted against by all the Dominions on the Assembly.

17 March 1926: Cabinet where we had a preliminary discussion on Coal. I rather took the lead in demurring to the idea of nationalising mineral rights and was strongly supported by Salisbury, but not very much otherwise though everybody agreed in principle. I brought up again the question of increasing the Empire Marketing sum to a million for the first year in view of Bruce's telegram but failed to carry support from anyone except Willie Bridgeman, Neville unfortunately being away. . . .

To the India Office where Worthy and I and Ronald McNeill had a conference with F.E. on Aden. Found F.E. much more reasonable and the three of us against Ronald were prepared to agree on the basis of the supreme military and political control being in the hands of the CO, India only retaining the administration of Aden town itself, India paying normally one-third of the expenses or £150,000 but paying £250,000 for three years. Ronald wanted to press the Treasury view that India should take over the whole place and receive a subsidy from us but F.E. insisted that even in that case India would not pay substantially more than she is prepared to pay under the other scheme.

22 March 1926: Cabinet on the Coal question at which I again opened up on the subject of mineral royalties. As the Cabinet Committee had recommended S.B. to take the line the Cabinet were prepared to accept the report as it stood if both sides could come to an agreement on it. In the end I admitted that if it were essential to an agreement I would accept the royalties business but I wanted it made clear in the PM's statement that we did definitely disagree with it but were prepared to accept it if it were an essential part of a settlement. Salisbury was not prepared to go even as far as that and almost hinted that he could not stay on in the Government if that were conceded. It was agreed that the original draft statement should be altered so as to make it clear that we did disagree and that we would only accept it as a condition of settlement. . . .

Had a talk with S.B. from which I gather that Bob Cecil is in a fearful state of mind about Geneva and thinks that the whole matter should be handed over to the Assembly; wants to leave the Government but will no doubt think better of it.

24 March 1926: Cabinet at which we agreed, myself and Salisbury very reluctantly, to the PM's statement to the Coal people in the afternoon which commits us to nationalising the royalties if both parties agree to accept the Report, and I am afraid rather commits us even if they don't. We also polished off the last revised instructions to Lindsay for his negotiations with the Turk. Winston made one quite helpful suggestion and to my great surprise made no sort of difficulty about the main question. He has obviously accepted the position and I do not think will make further difficulty. [On the 25th Amery had a useful talk with Churchill 'whom I think I have now persuaded to stabilise some of the existing preferences'.]

29 March 1926: Then to have a talk with the Duke of York at Curzon House about the proposed visit to Canberra. He is all for going but

447

desperately anxious that the King should not know that he even has heard of the matter but that it should come entirely from the PM and myself pressing the King on public grounds that he must go. He told me very frankly that the King's natural instinct is to say 'No' to everything that is suggested, more particularly about his family and specially if it comes from them! He fully realises the importance of the experience, and the chance of taking it, and is looking forward to the time when somewhat later in life he might perhaps become Governor General in S. Africa or some other Dominion. He inquired whether it might not be possible to have a cruiser rather than to land in full uniform somewhat mixed up with the ordinary passengers on a P. & O. I must try and see if Willie could possibly rise to this. We also discussed the idea of going on to New Zealand and coming back through Canada and I have since urged Stanley to press this upon the King.

31 March 1926: Cabinet. Got approval for Palestine and E. African Loan Guarantee, but my attempt to secure the issue for the Crown Agents against the wholly unreasonable claim of the Treasury that it should be done by the Bank of England (who collar the commission) failed when Winston's dramatic appeal to 'fundamental principle' was pompously upheld by Austen. *En revanche* I defeated Winston over the War Graves Bill and he was forced very reluctantly to give up the parts of it which were not only unnecessary but offensive to Dominion sentiment. . . .

Had a good talk with Winston in the afternoon about rubber on which I expressed my willingness to accept 100 per cent as the maximum percentage of release, and he, on his side, promised to consider further the idea of putting a protective duty on British tyres. He also renewed his promise to be sympathetic about stabilising existing preferences. Imperial Communications Committee.

1 April 1926: To H. of C. where I found Violet Carruthers waiting to tell me something of importance. To my amusement it was a message from Mackenzie King to indicate that if J. Buchan's name was included among the candidates for Governor-General it would be welcome! I gave Violet to understand, as gently as I could, that he really had not quite the experience or qualifications – much as I loved him and Susie – and that these appointments could not be settled by Dominion PMs' picking out their personal friends.*

14 April 1926: Cabinet at which we dealt with the long and most interesting report of Burton Chadwick's Committee on Key Industries which

*Buchan was appointed Governor General in Canada in 1937.

the Cabinet swallowed *en bloc*. The only doubtful point was whether the protection should be renewed for 5 or 10 years. Philip and Winston both said 5 and it looked as if this was going through without discussion when I raised the point that defence after all was a permanent matter and the longer the security given the readier capital would be to come in with development and research. I found one after another backing me and we carried the 10 years by a large majority. We also talked a lot about the coal situation, the suggestion I put forward being that we should make it clear at once what was the maximum sum of money we could provide to ease the bump after 1st May and let the two sides between them agree as to how they could best utilise that sum. I am sure that is the best way of averting a strike. Winston was vehemently of the same view but others were all for some dilatory tactics. Nothing was decided.

15 April 1926: Cabinet at which we discussed certain projects of Winston's with regard to petrol duty as an alternative to higher licences. Next with Mond who is now such an Imperialist and a jingo that I can hardly keep pace with him.

16 April 1926: Had a short talk with Tallents whom I had designated to act as the pivot of my Empire Marketing Board and found that he is . . . completely taken up by the anti-strike work at the Home Office for this month and for longer if the strike continues. . . . Went round to see Jix at his house to find out if he could release Tallents. This he cannot do and I must therefore try and think of some provisional arrangement.

21 April 1926: Cabinet at which we discussed the League of Nations Committee which is to try and arrive at the future composition of the Council, not a very hopeful task.

22 April 1926: Sir Charles Cottier to lunch and had a good talk with him about the EIA and the fiscal future generally. I told him that one of my chief anxieties about the EIA was that I felt it imperative at the next election we should be free from the present restrictions as regards protection and preference, that I hoped that by 1928 the Cabinet would be sufficiently advanced, even with Winston, to be prepared to face the new policy but that if it was not I might be compelled to break off and force the issue single handed. . . . I asked him whether he would be prepared to back [me] up whole-heartedly if I were forced into an independent campaign and he promised to do so.

I stopped for a moment to talk with Blain [Principal Agent, Conservative Central Office] and he told me that he had sent in his resignation some time ago finding it impossible to carry on with Jackson, not because of any personal difference but because of the impossibility of ever getting him to decide anything or stick to a decision when arrived at. Linlithgow seems to have left for the same reason.

26 April 1926: Lunched at the Carlton and then down to Questions after which we had the Budget. Winston dealt with it very skilfully and had the House with him right through though the only cheers he got, and these were remarkably enthusiastic, were whenever he used some protectionist argument.

28 April 1926: Cabinet – not much progress to report on the coal situation though the PM with infinite difficulty had got them as far as being willing to confer under his chairmanship. We discussed the Angora negotiations and decided to press Iraq to stump up a portion of the TPC Oil royalties. It really is very amusing to find the terrible danger of war with Turkey is now reduced to this. Apparently all because the Turks have become alive to the danger from Mussolini.

2 May 1926: Sunday. I had planned to go down to Maidenhead. . . . But before starting I got word that there was to be a Cabinet at 12. We were most of us there I think, the only absentee being Austen who had lumbago down at his cottage, the almost invariable result in the spring time of his trying to do a little gardening. The PM told us of the long conference he had had the night before with representatives of the Trade Union Committee who were trying to get him to continue the subsidy for another fortnight for further negotiations in which case they would call off the General Strike which had been proclaimed on Saturday afternoon but which they assured him had not been definitely and finally ordered. As the outcome of this discussion which had lasted until after one o'clock in the morning and at which F.E. and Arthur had stayed until the end, Willie and Neville having been present at the earlier stages, F.E. had produced a very vague summary of the situation to the effect that the PM was satisfied that the TUC representatives were confident that if the subsidy were continued for a fortnight negotiations might be resumed on the lines of the report. The Cabinet were all very down on this document which they regarded as both meaningless in itself and likely to lead to some very feeble and ineffective negotiations while in practice accepting the general strike as quite a natural thing. We adjourned until the afternoon by which time we hoped to get a reply from the TUC people as to whether they concurred in this colourless version of what had happened.

We met at 5 and walked about in the garden or chatted in the Cabinet room for nearly two hours without anything much happening. The rumours that the TUC people did not think they had the miners' authority to say even that much in the end came somewhere after 7. We had more or less been sitting in Cabinet on what was to be said to the TUC people when they did come and agreed on the combination of certain wording of Bob Cecil's with regard to the mining question and words of Winston's with regard to the general strike, and these were combined by a small sub-committee of us in Winston's room about the time that the TUC people arrived. As far as I can remember nothing special happened on their arrival except that they hoped to get the miners along later in the night and we left about 7.45 on the understanding that some members of the Cabinet were to come back at 9 to meet the TUC with the PM while the rest of us were to go to No. 11 at 9.30 and wait until we were wanted. I took Douglas Hogg back to dinner and at 9.30 we assembled in Winston's room and passed the evening as best we could until about 11. Then Stanley came in very tired and threw himself into an armchair leaving it to F.E. to read out as far as they had got with the discussions. What he read out was dictated to him by Thomas and amounted to this, that if the subsidy was continued for a fortnight and the lockout suspended, the TUC would urge the miners to enter into discussions on the basis of the report, understanding that this might include some reduction of wages.

The Cabinet as a whole who had thought F.E. had gone much too far in the way of compromise did not at all like this. They thought there was no real assurance that it would lead to anything nor did it take any notice of the general strike about which our feelings had stiffened considerably when we discovered during the course of the day from the Post Office that the actual telegrams to the different Unions telling them to cease work had gone out on Saturday evening. F.E. and Stanley were both inclined to go on with negotiations on that basis, that is to say to wait and hear what the miners who had meanwhile arrived, would say to this last formula, but except myself no one else in the Cabinet was prepared to do so. I had taken the line in the morning that the coal issue and the general strike were two very different problems and that even if we came to any sort of agreement at this moment to re-open the coal discussions and continue the subsidy we ought at once to announce legislation which would make a general strike impossible in future. At this stage of the evening I felt great reluctance to break even if the advance made by the TUC was very tentative and even if its acceptance by the miners only meant another fortnight of futile discussion. I said that while my reason inclined me to believe with the majority that we should now send in to them the Cabinet's decision both as to resuming negotiations and as to the removal of the general strike, my instinct was against anything that might look like breaking off negotiations.

While we were discussing the news arrived that the *Daily Mail* had been suppressed altogether by the printers because they did not like its leading article. We had already had information that in the *Sunday Express* and other papers articles had been considerably censored or dropped out. This turned the scale and made it clear that the only issue that really mattered for the Government and with the public now was the issue of the general strike. The Cabinet decision which was adopted in the afternoon was toned up a little further so as to make it quite clear that there could be no discussion until the general strike had been withdrawn and it was then sent in to the TUC and miners who I gather went home shortly afterwards. Whether the miners were or were not prepared to look at Thomas's formula before they got our decision I do not know. Baldwin certainly did not think they would, mild though it was. We dispersed about 12.30. [Amery clearly did not know of the TUC leaders' return to find the Cabinet gone, which fact he noted in his diary when preparing for his memoirs.]

3 May 1926: Saw Campbell Stuart at the House just back from the West Indies and Canada. He tells me that Mackenzie King is determined not to have any of our three candidates and that if he cannot have Buchan he will push for Willingdon. Apparently he got his first information about our three candidates from Beaverbrook which looks as if Sam had unwisely talked to the latter.

Debate on the adjournment on the Strike. Stanley very quiet understating the case throughout but quite firm at the end. His speech made a great impression and was listened to with hardly any interruption. . . . During the evening there were constant conferences in the PM's room, the gist of which was that Ramsay and Thomas tried in vain to find some formula by which the calling off of the General Strike might be made to appear as a bargain in return for the continuation of the subsidy. This Stanley declined to do and at midnight the General Strike started.

4 May 1926: First day of the General Strike. Tremendous congestion of road traffic. . . . To the House where the Labour Party had decided not to debate anything except the General Strike issue and so we got through the whole of some 17 Budget resolutions in a couple of hours' continuous dividing.

Dined at the Japanese Embassy where we met the Danish Minister and Countess whom I took in. The Countess was very strong on the need for firmness. She told me what an admirable time they had had in China when there was a certain amount of brigandage and trouble on the railways when the local Chinese General dealt firmly with the situation and adorned all the trees of the railway stations and elsewhere at intervals on the line with the decapitated heads 'looking like radishes'. I am not sure whether she meant us to be equally drastic with Thomas and his men.

6 May 1926: A short Cabinet to report progress after which the main business of conducting the strike passed on to the Supply and Transport Committee [chaired by Joynson-Hicks, the Home Secretary]. Work at the office very soon began shrinking in dimensions and I found myself able to catch up a certain amount of arrears of papers and, not being upon any of the main organising committees, a little freer generally. With no record of any particular appointments and over a week of varied events already passed I have not much idea of what I did for the rest of the day.

8 May 1926: [Meeting with] the Duke of York's Private Secretary, to talk about arrangements for the Duke's visit to Australia. The King seems to have been completely reconciled to the idea after his talk with the PM. He broached the matter to the Duke of York (who I gather pretended it was all news to him) in the following characteristic manner, 'Now, Bertie, no more babies for a while – you have got to go to Australia.'*

Sadie drove me up to the Bath Club from where I walked to the Athenaeum and met Robin [Dawson] and Cecilia, he having just got back from Florence where he was laid up with fever. He was full of complaints against Winston for having threatened to commandeer *The Times* paper for the benefit of his *Gazette*, and also like myself, very doubtful of the wisdom of preventing the *British Worker* appearing by the device of confiscating its paper. Later on we had a Cabinet at which we decided to bring in legislation declaring the General Strike illegal. Hogg had pressed for this for some days but had only just succeeded in getting the PM to allow it to come before the Cabinet. We were all quite clear on the point.

9 May 1926: Sunday. . . . Walked across to Downing Street in the morning and again in the afternoon to see the PM about the general tangle in propaganda matters and the danger of Winston upsetting the whole Press by his methods in relation to the *British Gazette*, but the first time he was crowded out and in the afternoon he had not come back from his walk.

10 May 1926: Cabinet at which, in view of certain indications that the strike might be petering out as afforded by the railway companies and from other quarters, Stanley urged that we should hold our hands for a few days longer about the Bill and not introduce it until the beginning of the following week, and at any rate not to make up our minds for a day or two. Austen followed Stanley's strong expression of opinion and the

*Princess Elizabeth who became HM Queen in 1952, was born on 21 April 1926. Princess Margaret was not born until 1930.

Cabinet concurred though very reluctantly some of us e.g. Neville, Winston, Cave, Balfour and myself opposing. My own view was that the sooner we got the thing on the basis of legality the better knowing that as long as it was an issue between the Government and the strikers a great section of the public would always treat it as a party battle; the moment it became a matter for the strikers versus the law the position would be quite different. I could not wait until the end of the discussion as I had to go to see the King and report progress to him. This also postponed the discussion on publicity methods which I had asked Stanley to bring up. The King was full of talk, very glad to know that we were postponing legislation for the moment, being very much afraid that it would be regarded rightly or wrongly as an attack on Trade Unionists. We afterwards also talked about Canada and I had to tell him that Mackenzie King was lying low at present, probably rather sick that we had paid no attention to his suggestion about John Buchan, a suggestion which the King treated as frankly ridiculous.

11 May 1926: In the evening we had a Cabinet at which I raised the whole question of publicity suggesting that while the *British Gazette* had been an excellent emergency newspaper we ought to get back to normal newspaper publication as soon as we could. This let loose Winston in a munificent tirade on the wonders achieved, the selfishness of *The Times* in wishing to increase its circulation at expense of others during the crisis, the impossibility of letting go at the moment without unfairness to one or other newspaper and ended with his determination to suppress the *Daily Express*, if, as they intended, they started an evening paper in the next few days.

Against his vigour and enthusiasm nobody except Eustace Percy had the courage to say anything and most of those who for days had been going round and complaining rather left me alone when I belled the cat. However, they did in fact agree and in general terms Winston gave the assurance that he would allow other newspapers to appear as soon as possible. We then had a discussion on whether MacDonald should be allowed to speak on the Broadcasting where I found myself quite alone except for mild support from Salisbury in favour of allowing him to speak if he were duly corrected and certainly if Lloyd George were allowed to speak as I felt that the latter would be far more mischievous. My efforts were successful in getting a decision that no political speeches were to be allowed to be Broadcasted except statements by the Prime Minister himself, and also that this should be done by the Broadcasting Company on their own and that there should be no taking over and running the BBC purely as propaganda which is what Winston and F.E. had been trying to bring about.

At the close of the meeting the Prime Minister received information that the TUC were holding a meeting with the miners and that it was quite possible that we might hear later in the evening that the strike was to be called off. Soon after dinner we were warned that there might be a Cabinet late in the evening and it was not until midnight that the messages calling it off reached us. I understand that the TUC had 4 hours with the miners trying to get them to agree to certain proposals of Samuel's which he made on his own and without any authorisation from the Government. These have since been published and seem to me eminently unsatisfactory and quite unacceptable from our point of view. However they seemed to have sufficed the TUC as a sufficient argument to enable them to get out of the difficult position in which they were placed by [Lord Chief Justice] Astbury's judgment that morning declaring the strike to be illegal and consequently making it impossible to pay out strike pay as well as exposing the leaders generally for action for damages.

12 May 1926: ... found a crowd outside Downing Street and a reporter told us that the Strike was off unconditionally, the TUC leaders having come round to Downing Street to tell the PM. Apparently they did so against the miners and undoubtedly did it unconditionally though with every effort since to try and make out that it was linked up with Samuel's proposals. Since then we have discovered that the actual orders to go back to work were not sent to various Unions and I expect we shall have plenty of trouble still. ... Lunched at the Carlton, and with other members of the Cabinet got a great deal of congratulations on our triumph – a little premature I fancy.

We had a short Cabinet at 2.30 at which Stanley told us what had happened and what he proposed to say in the House. I am afraid what he did say about 'no malice or vindictiveness' was bound to encourage the idea that this strike was to be ended on the 'no victimization' line.

13 May 1926: Cabinet at which I could only attend the first few minutes as I had to go on to the Opening of the West Indian Conference. The strike seems to be continuing in most directions owing to the insistence of the men being taken back in a body with no exclusion of ringleaders or even of those who are in prison for acts of violence. After I left the Cabinet discussed Samuel's proposals which I am glad to say they rejected, and a rather better proposal of their own.

17 May 1926: Cabinet on the question of a cash payment to Turkey to settle the Iraq business. Winston not only prepared to fight to the death against having to find the money himself even as an advance but opposed even to Iraq finding it. Six or even two months ago the Turk was for him a terrible neighbour; now he was contemptuous at the idea of giving anything. I explained that the Crown Agents could finance the money for Iraq directly and the Cabinet generally were only too delighted at the thought that a settlement might be arrived at at an expenditure of not more than half a million. Instructions sent to Lindsay accordingly. The remainder of the Cabinet taken up with the question of disciplinary action by Admiralty and War Office with regard to ringleaders among the established men in the recent trouble.

20 May 1926: First preliminary and informal meeting of the EMB and a great deal of talk on research and other problems. . . . To FO to have a hammer and tongs with Austen in front of Buxton on the subject of the Willingdon mission going to Canton which I vehemently opposed. As no Cabinet could meet for a fortnight I offered to leave the matter to the PM to settle and we went round afterwards. He decided in Austen's favour mainly I think because it was less trouble.

31 May 1926: A 10 o'clock [p.m.] Cabinet on Egypt. The upshot of it all has been excellent; Zaghloul having been full of swollen-headedness climbed down precipitately before George Lloyd even had to pull his revolver (i.e. our ultimatum to say that on no account would we accept him as PM) from his pocket. The whole thing came to a head at the end of that week, I think within 24 hours of the signature of the Angora Treaty, the two between them marking a great enhancement of our prestige in the Middle Eeast.

1 June 1926: Long meeting of the CID to listen to Bob Cecil's summary of what happened at the Disarmament Conference. Balfour finally summed up the whole situation by saying it was all nonsense anyway, and the only instructions he thought we could give Austen were to do as little mischief as possible.

. . . Imperial Conference Documents Committee under Salisbury's chairmanship. From what Winston said on the subject of assistance re Imperial Development loans it is quite clear that he and I will have to have a stand up fight on the matter. At present the Treasury policy inspired by the Bank of England is to discourage all Empire loans. At the Western Australian dinner Glendyne told me that Norman [Governor of the Bank of England] is working for all he is worth in that direction and is responsible for the way in which the financial editors of *The Times*, *Morning Post*, etc. have been crabbing Australian loans. If we are not to have preference or financial development I do not see how I can stay on in the Government at all. At the same time I must either persuade Winston or get Stanley to persuade him or get him made Minister of Defence, or in the last resort go.

7 June 1926: Lunched at the Carlton with Chatfield who was giving a big party of a dozen or more. As I went in I saw Shefki Pasha who congratulated me in a very friendly manner on the final settlement of the Mosul business. The whole thing has been a great success. I never doubted myself that the Turk would be unreasonable. My only fear lay in some of my colleagues and the squealing in the Press. In the end we were helped partly by Mussolini but I think no less by a growing realization at Angora that managing their own Kurds was already just as much as they could do and that they could not now afford to take on any more without the whole thing breaking down.

Talk with Cadman on the results of his visit to Persia and Iraq. He is very satisfied with the developments in the transferred territory and is already talking of a pipe line down to the Mediterranean as well. If oil in the Mosul *vilayet* should be discovered in anything like similar quantities the finances of Iraq will be assured and incidentally the Turk may really get a nice little dividend in 10 years' time.

8 June 1926: The King seems to have taken Cromer's willingness to go very much amiss and to have done everything he could to avert it. It was of course his instance that forced Baldwin to include Willingdon's name in the list and so knocked Cromer out. Lady Cromer was much amused when I told her of the gloomy picture the King had drawn to me of her delicate state of health and how it would never do to let her face the rigours of the Canadian climate. All this in the intervals of Kreisler and Elizabeth Schumann, both perfect.

9 June 1926: Delamere came to the House to put forward his views on East Africa, Gore and Wilson being present. In the main he was rather pushing at an open door, his chief requests being for some announcement that Tanganyika really did remain with us and that the dual system apply here.

11 June 1926: [Saw] Count Coudenhove Kalergi, a young man half Austrian and half Japanese who is the great exponent of the idea, which I have always held, that the League of Nations should be decentralised with the British Empire as one of its constituent unities. He promised to send me his book. . . . Billy Gore having suddenly developed flu I had to go to the E. African dinner at the Savoy to take his place. . . . This gave me an opportunity of stating clearly that Tanganyika is permanently a part of the British Imperial system and explaining what the mandate really means, as well as of stating that we meant the dual policy to apply in Tanganyika as well as in Kenya or Nyasaland. My speech consequently was received with immense approval all round and even Delamere could not find anything in it with which he could differ.

22 June 1926: High Commissioners and then on to a meeting of the Central Unionist Council at the Hotel Cecil where F.E. made a rather indiscreet but very much approved speech indicating action with regard to the Trade Unions.

25 June 1926: Talk with Delamere and made it plain to him that I did not think the time had come or would come for some time, for an unofficial [settler] majority in the Kenya Council.

2 July 1926: Weizmann looking wary and rather piano; put his complaints about inadequate consideration given to the Jews very reasonably. It must be a tremendous responsibility to have to raise half a million and more a year by begging.

Amery was writing up the following entries from his engagement book, at least one month in arrear and sometimes nearer two, which explains the lack of detailed reference to Cabinet or to Parliament.

---

23 July 1926: Saw a very keen young man called R. A. Butler, nephew of Sir Harcourt Butler of Burma, who wishes to go round the Empire before going into politics and gave him such advice as I could.

26 July 1926: After the business the King asked me to stay to discuss the Duke of York's trip. He began by being very emphatic that it would never do to have a man-of-war but I got in some of the arguments in favour edgeways and gradually he came round to the position that it was all right as long as he did not have to make the request himself and that the matter was a decision by the Government. He also talked about Byng* whose conduct he thoroughly approves of and from whom he has had long letters. I gather from what Lady Willingdon told me at

*The Governor General of Canada, Lord Byng, had refused Mackenzie King a dissolution in June and King had resigned. Subsequently Byng conceded a dissolution to the succeeding Conservative administration on the grounds that it had been defeated only after being sustained by the House in three major decisions. King insisted that he should have been restored to office, and that the Conservative Prime Minister Meighen had proffered wrong advice to the Governor General (see E. A. Forsey, *The Royal Power of Dissolution of Parliament in the British Common-Wealth*). In the Canadian general election on 14 September Mackenzie King's Liberals won 116 seats, and with the support of ten Liberal Progressives, twelve Progressives, three Labour and two Independents, had a clear overall majority to form a Government.

dinner that Byng has very much prided himself on sending the very minimum of information to me and writing freely to the King. This is all on the line of the theory of present developments and certainly worked out well as far as Byng's decision not to consult me in the crisis was concerned. But it goes unnecessarily far and I hope Willingdon will continue to keep in reasonable close personal touch with me like Stonehaven and others.

30 July 1926: To Cabinet to hear Lloyd make a very interesting and effective statement on Egypt which we all approved of, and he can go back heartened by our support and know he can see things through.

24 September 1926: Meeting of the Empire Marketing Board all the morning and got through a good deal of business including a very serviceable report drafted by Tallents for the Imperial Conference. Cabinet on the coal situation in the afternoon. Walking down with Neville he told me that the Coal Committee had decided that the only thing we could do was to introduce a bill for compulsory arbitration on district settlements, not waiting for settlements to take place first as in our previous scheme but to introduce the scheme straightaway. I expressed considerable misgivings when we got to the Cabinet. Winston unfolded the scheme at considerable length but it soon became obvious nobody liked it very much. I championed the extreme opposite view that we ought not only not to take up this scheme but announce definitely that we did not mean to intervene in the matter again believing that the more definite our announcement would be the quicker the men will come in. Nobody else was inclined to burn boats to the same extent but one after another they damaged the proposal with criticism and in the end the Cabinet was practically unanimous against proceeding with the measure but left it to the PM to consider what he was to say on Monday and what announcement to make in the meanwhile. The actual announcement made simply dismissed the miners' last proposals and declared that our previous offer remained open for a time.

25 September 1926: . . . to see off the Willingdons, a very cheery send off. I think people who are so delighted with their job will make good all right, and now Mackenzie King is back which is just as well that he should have a Governor General of his own choice [*sic*].

3 October 1926: Worked on a paper on the Crown as a factor of unity in the Empire distinguishing between the monarchy as an institution and the Crown as an embodiment of authority and finished it soon after dinner. After that I went through the draft of the PM's opening speech to the Conference and added a few passages here and there.

4 October 1926: To Claridges and had a short talk with Hertzog but did not open up on any constitutional issues. Found him personally quite agreeable.

5 October 1926: Hurried off to a private view of television, a new invention which shows on a film at the end of either wires or wireless what is seen at the other end of the apparatus. Undoubtedly the invention has solved the principle of the thing but the execution is still technically very imperfect and it was only occasionally that one could really see the face at the other end.

Hertzog, Havengas and Baldwins to dinner. After dinner I gradually got Hertzog on to constitutional issues and he talked away pretty freely, I doing the other half of the talking as I knew the PM preferred the role of listener, interjecting an occasional good humoured observation. Hertzog's line was not really very extreme, his main theme being if only we would show our confidence in S. Africa they would not do anything in the direction of secession which is the last thing they thought of. He also spontaneously expressed the view that the League of Nations ought to understand that our relationship as between ourselves was different from the relationship between other countries in the League. However, Harding tells me he has gathered since from his secretary Steyn that Hertzog's conception is undoubtedly that of a purely personal union and with no real inherent link between the countries of the Empire, and Harding wisely made it clear to him that was not the view which the British Government could possibly accept.

Amery travelled to Scarborough on 6 October for the Conservative Conference.

7 October 1926: Drove into the Conference and sat it out until 5 o'clock with a break for lunch next door. They were evidently full of determination to have Trade Union [Law] all changed and determined that the Government should act. A resolution expressing regret at the Government's apparent inability to do anything was only withdrawn as a result of a very clever and conciliatory little speech by Jacker [F. S. Jackson, Chairman of the Conservative Party Organisation].

8 October 1926: Came up with Leslie Scott [former Solicitor General] and the Duchess of Atholl as far as York . . . Leslie full of the idea that the miners' decision to call out the safety men constituted a criminal conspiracy and concocted a letter to *The Times* to that effect but subsequently changed his mind and telephoned that he would not send it. . . . Talk with Philip Kerr about Canada. His view is that while the constitutional issue had no direct effect on the voter at large it did undoubtedly hearten and enthuse the old Liberal machine. In his view the time for definitely identifying the Governor General with purely sovereign functions and cutting away from all connection with the DO has pretty well come and concurrently with it the creation of a British High Commissioner in the Dominions.

The Imperial Conference of 1926 reshaped the constitution of the Empire, bringing theory into line with practice and removing the 'psychological stumbling blocks' which got in the way of good relations. The Balfour Declaration of 1926 may in reality have changed nothing, as Smuts believed, but 'what it did change was men's hearts, and that was important'.* Amery first set out his part in drafting the Balfour formula in *The Times* (22 March 1930), and when this was privately challenged, Hankey found little to cavil at in Amery's account; indeed he wrote that he 'would not like to deny Amery's claim to have suggested the idea'.†

Amery set out his ideas on the constitution of the Empire when commenting on those put forward by Smuts in 1921 (see p. 273) but the importance of his role has only recently been recognised.‡ It follows that his diary is a key source on the Conference, and on the discussions which preceded it.

Preparations for the Conference began in December 1925 with a Cabinet memorandum from Amery which summarised the issues which had been under discussion with the Dominions since the last Conference in 1923. Detailed preparations were set in motion by the Cabinet's decision on 26 February 1926 to appoint an interdepartmental committee to report on the agenda and organisation of the Conference. Subsequent to its report in March three further interdepartmental committees prepared detailed memoranda on the subjects for the Conference, many of which were circulated to the Dominions. But it was decided not to circulate papers on constitutional issues. Nevertheless a committee jointly composed of representatives from the Foreign and Dominions Offices had prepared ten papers dealing with such subjects as the system of communication and consultation between the Governments of the Empire, the representation of the Empire at international conferences, the diplomatic representation of the Dominions in foreign countries, the procedure for negotiating treaties, and so forth, all of which arrived at recommendations 'designed to give effect to the principle of equality of status, and complete autonomy of the Dominions in foreign affairs, without impairing Com-

*Hankey to Smuts, 25 November 1927 (quoted by Roskill, *Hankey*, II, p. 433).

†Cab. 63/38; Hankey to Harding, 29 March 1930 (cf. Roskill, *Hankey*, II, p. 430).

‡H. Duncan Hall, *The Commonwealth*, pp. 581, 584, 611.

monwealth unity.'* Amery appears to have been the principal architect of these conclusions, and Hall pays tribute to his understanding of the new problems with which the existence of the Commonwealth confronted the Foreign Office. His most important action, however, was to suggest that the political and legal aspects of imperial relations should be referred to a committee composed of the principal delegates, which Balfour was to chair. The idea that he should do so seems to have been Amery's also: Balfour's 'immense personal authority would not only hold the Committee together, but commend its conclusions to the British Cabinet where, I felt, the greatest difficulty might have to be encountered', Amery wrote subsequently (*My Political Life*, II, p. 384). Equally to the point, he had expressed to the House of Lords in July the view that relations within the Empire were necessarily on a basis of equality,† and he was thus clearly in sympathy with Amery's own views on the subject.

In the light of these preparations, there seems to be a good deal of justification for Amery's view that in the constitutional discussions, the Dominions not only found ready understanding for their point of view, but clear and acceptable solutions worked out for their consideration. 'To ascribe, as some authorities have seemed to do, the principal result of the Imperial Conference of 1926 to the forces of Dominion "nationalism" under the determined leadership of Hertzog, Mackenzie King and the Irish is to leave Hamlet out of the play.'‡ Nevertheless Hertzog was important, not least because his insistence on a 'general declaration of constitutional right', such as Smuts had proposed in 1921, led directly to the Balfour formula.

Amery was well aware of Hertzog's views. They had exchanged letters since 1924. One such exchange early in 1925 is revealing. Hertzog had protested at the failure, in negotiations with foreign powers, to insist upon recognition 'of the fundamental fact upon which that system [i.e. of Imperial consultation] is based, viz. that every member of the Commonwealth by itself constitutes a national entity, with equal status'. Amery agreed. It would take time however, before they would remember that 'at international conferences all His Majesty's Governments will be entitled to be presented are each entitled to the individual courtesies due to every sovereign state'.§ In public speeches in April and May 1926 Hertzog claimed that South Africa was 'as free and independent as England itself' and defined a Dominion as 'a free independent state with the right of international recognition by foreign powers, but with a

*Hall, *The Commonwealth*, p. 583.

†Lords Debates, 27 July 1926, col. 286 (cited by D. Judd, *Balfour and the British Empire*, Macmillan, 1968, p. 332).

‡H. Duncan Hall in *Journal of Commonwealth Political Studies*, November 1962, p. 187.

§Quoted in Hall, *The Commonwealth*, p. 615.

common bond between it and Great Britain, residing in the sovereign'. In like words Amery emphasised for his colleagues the organic unity of the Commonwealth, 'bound together not by any rigid constitutional system known to the outside world, but by intangible moral bonds expressed in the traditional form of a common sovereignty'.*

Hertzog wrote to Amery on 26 July to reiterate his belief that an 'authoritative declaration on Dominion status' must be made and published to the world by the Imperial Conference, and Amery at once consulted the Cabinet on the matter. They had already expressed reserve about drafting a constitution for the Empire when discussing and modifying the Interdepartmental Committee's report on 21 July, more particularly the proposal close to Amery's heart that there should be annual conferences,† and they took the view that no specific action was required on Hertzog's letter. The recommendations of the Interdepartmental Committee would go a long way to meet his views, and there was a need for caution because of the possibility of divided opinions within the Cabinet and within the Commonwealth.

Before the Imperial Conference opened, Amery made it his business to talk with each of the Dominion Prime Ministers on their arrival in London. Coates of New Zealand disliked any constitutional or structural change, Bruce was scarcely any more open-minded, and Mackenzie King made clear his dislike for abstract definitions. His clash with Byng had confirmed his long-held belief that the role of the Governor General would need definition, and that he should no longer be regarded as an agent of the British Government. 'I put forward the suggestion that the time had come when there should be a complete separation between the Office of Governor-General as the representative of the Crown and that of representation of the Government being distinct. . . . I suggested that the logical course seemed to be the development within the Empire of an interimperial organisation for diplomatic purposes . . .'‡ King hoped that this proposed definition of the role of the Governor General would be sufficient evidence of autonomy to satisfy everybody.§ Amery welcomed the suggestion, but he had to proceed with caution in the absence of a Cabinet decision on the subject, and Mackenzie King, when he raised the

---

*Memorandum on the Crown as an Element in the Constitutional Evolution of the Empire, circulated before the Conference and referred to in L.S.A.'s RIIA Address, January 1927.

†Hankey to Grigg, 25 May 1926 (Grigg Papers).

‡Mackenzie King's diary for 25 October, cited by H. Blair Neatby, *William Lyon Mackenzie King*, II, *1923–32: The Lonely Heights* (Methuen, 1963), p. 182.

§It is interesting to note that Amery had prompted Hughes to make a similar proposal about Governors General at the Imperial Conference of 1918. He made no headway either then, or with Milner in 1919, nor did Borden and Smuts have any more luck when they tackled Lloyd George on the subject.

idea at the first meeting of the Inter-Imperial Relations Committee, found it pushed on one side by the debate on Hertzog's proposal.

Balfour's opening statement at this first session on 27 October included, it should be noted, most of the ideas and phrases used later in the declaration. Amery, Austen Chamberlain, Hankey and Harding had helped in the drafting. The main thrust of his argument, however, such as it was, would seem to be that equality of status existed despite the differences of function within the Commonwealth (of which Britain's responsibilities in foreign affairs were the most obvious), and that they ought to concentrate on improving the machinery of imperial consultation. Hertzog would have none of this. Despite the assertions of King's biographer, there is no evidence that Hertzog seriously contemplated South Africa seceding from the Commonwealth, and indeed a clear statement to the contrary was made in the discussion on foreign affairs on 25 October. However, he did wish for a 'declaration of rights' which should be published, and he pressed for it with common sense and moderation. Rectification of the constitutional anomalies, which the Irish were pressing and which was probably Amery's own preference, seemed to him not enough.

Hall plays down the initial resistance to the idea, and there is obvious truth in his observation that the British representatives were speaking without benefit of a Cabinet decision. Nevertheless they seem to have been chary of a formal declaration, Amery recounting the history of Smuts's efforts to suggest that a broader-based constitutional conference was really needed for such a step, Chamberlain stressing the dangers of undue rigidity, while Balfour doubted the wisdom of trying to define too closely the exact nature of independence. Hertzog's continual stress on independence and the almost complete absence of any reference to interdependence had, perhaps, alarmed the British delegation.*

If so, Birkenhead's intervention was decisive. He could find nothing in Hertzog's statement to cause him anxiety and he suggested that the South African Prime Minister might put down a draft declaration on paper for their consideration. Bruce promptly supported him and Hertzog agreed to submit a draft. This was circulated the next day (28 October). It was inevitable now that a definition of the Commonwealth would be formulated, but the Irish delegation was not satisfied. They had been with Hertzog to see King on the 27th to persuade him of the need for a declaration, but as the Irish Attorney General, Costello, recalled later, they were 'suspicious of plans making, proceeded on the assumption of co-equality, and demanded its detailed and practical application'.† A

*Neatby, *Mackenzie King*, pp. 183–4; cf. Hall, *The Commonwealth*, pp. 625–6 for a contrasting view.

†J. A. Costello, 'The Long Game', *The Star*, 24 December 1932, quoted by D. W. Harkness, *The Restless Dominion* (Macmillan, 1969), p. 100.

declaration of rights, O'Higgins said, would have little value if the facts contradicted, and he was to complain later to his wife that 'the onus of the "status" push – anomalies and anachronisms' had fallen largely on his own delegation since Hertzog had talked 'a lot and none too clearly' while King since 1923 had 'gone fat and American and self-complacent'.* He might have added that Amery on the British side fully appreciated the need to be rid of constitutional anomalies and had, indeed, suggested that they be referred to a sub-committee, a suggestion which O'Higgins accepted.

Informal discussions on the proposed declaration took place over the next few days. There was agreement that they were not trying for a comprehensive definition of the Commonwealth nor drafting a written constitution for it – Baldwin and Bruce had both warned on 19 October against any attempt to do the latter. King had warned Hertzog on the 27th against too great a stress on independence, which would, so far as North American opinion was concerned, be taken to imply secession. Hertzog was equally wary of anything which smacked of a 'superstate in which duties and obligations were due'.† No minutes were kept of these informal discussions, but it is possible to reconstruct the course of events.

Balfour had immediately drafted an alternative to Hertzog's declaration and it was discussed at an informal meeting that same day with Bruce and Mackenzie King at which Amery made a fourth. King by his own account questioned the emphasis on the ties of Empire, and suggested the inclusion of a phrase from Hertzog's draft, 'entitled to international recognition and freely associated as members of the British Commonwealth of Nations'.‡ King's diary records that he was asked to present the amended draft to Hertzog as his own, but he refused, agreeing only to tell him that he approved of it. He was more amenable to Amery's suggestion that the proposed declaration should be discussed informally at meetings of the Dominion Prime Ministers only.§ Balfour's amended draft was apparently sent to Hertzog, with a covering letter, on 29 October, and was discussed at the first informal meeting later that day. Hertzog, while ready to accept the first paragraph, was quite emphatic that the reference to duties and obligations owed to the Empire and the Crown smacked of the superstate which he had always rejected. Balfour had deliberately left the manner in which they were fulfilled to the individual decision of each country, but this in no way mollified Hertzog, nor

*Quoted by T. DeVere White, *Kevin O'Higgins*, pp. 221–2.
†Quoted from Hertzog's notes by C. M. Van den Heever, *General J. P. M. Hertzog*, p. 214.
‡Cf. Neatby, *Mackenzie King*, pp. 184–5.
§Bruce's claim to have been the author of this suggestion, made many years after the event in an interview with one of the editors of this volume, seems to be incorrect.

was he happy at the way in which the removal of constitutional anomalies was made dependent on common agreement and not conceded as a right. Birkenhead attempted to blend the two drafts, but at the cost of eliminating the word 'Empire', and Amery clearly had to do a good deal of persuasion to convince Hertzog that the word connoted only a complex political structure and had no necessary implications as to its form of government. There was no other word, Amery contended, to embrace a system which included the Dominions, the Indian Empire, colonies, protectorates, mandated territories and naval bases. Amery's diary entry is confirmed and amplified in the account of the meeting sent by Hankey to Baldwin on 29 October, and it is evident therefore that in this respect the account given of the sequence of drafts in Duncan Hall's magisterial history of *The Commonwealth* (which attributes Birkenhead's draft to 1 November) is in error.*

Balfour produced a fresh draft at the outset of the next meeting on 1 November, but it found no favour with Hertzog because it still contained phrases such as 'loyalty to the Empire' and 'the duties of loyalty'. Moreover it omitted both the word 'independence' and the phrases 'freely associated' which, according to his diary, was 'the content of independence'. In the course of a confused discussion Amery produced a draft which he had written over the weekend, and which proved broadly acceptable to Hertzog, apart from its final sentence in which Amery sought to balance the stress on autonomy with an equal stress on 'the obligations of mutual help and co-operation' which sprang from association, and a reference to 'common citizenship of the British Empire'. O'Higgins disliked the reference to 'a common bond of allegiance to the Crown'. According to Hertzog the meeting adjourned 'with a hint to Mr Amery' to omit the last sentence: Amery's diary makes it clear that he had agreed to modify the formula accordingly, and to delete the word allegiance.†
As amended, this was to provide the preamble to any report produced.

It seems clear that Birkenhead's draft was also before the meeting, and that it was this draft to which Coates objected, provoking both Amery and Hankey to write to Balfour. Coates had declared that he could not go home with a statement which contained no reference to the British Empire.‡ Amery's revised draft was evidently acceptable to Coates, but Hertzog at midnight that night was still working on it. 'I could not agree to an Empire possessing a "common citizenship" and including a state unity – I will not', he wrote. Nor did he.

*For the sequence given here, see Van den Heever, *Hertzog*; Hall, *The Commonwealth*, p. 633; Amery, *My Political Life*, II, p. 385.

†Hall is wrong on the point; Amery was clearly ready to use 'common bond of the Crown' although in his revised draft, he actually inserted 'common bond of loyalty to the Crown'.

‡Hankey to Balfour, 1 November 1926 (BM Add. Mss. 49704, ff. 141–5). Roskill, *Hankey*, II, p. 428 is misleading in its suggestion that Coates' objection had no effect.

It was not until 9 November that the Inter-Imperial Relations Committee discussed constitutional status in the light of the informal agreements already reached between the Prime Ministers. The problem of 'common nationality' was the last remaining stumbling block, and it was in the end left in limbo, while a phrase was added to Amery's formula to indicate that the Commonwealth was enclosed 'within the British Empire'. Hertzog was satisfied, but Balfour, in the words of his niece, 'perceived that [the paragraph] needed a setting which would bring out its full importance. It must be introduced, it must be expanded, it must be made the central point in the Committee's Report.'* In doing so he also redrafted Amery's formula, as finally amended by the Committee on 9 November, although the only change of substance he made was to restore from Hertzog's original draft the phrase 'united by a common bond of allegiance to the Crown', to which O'Higgins had so vigorously objected. There is no record of any subsequent Irish protest.

Balfour's setting was designed to offset the somewhat negative character of the formula. It was apparently completed on 12 November and cleared by Hankey with the individual Prime Ministers over the weekend. The Committee approved a very slightly amended version on 15 November, and the Cabinet which saw it on 17 November seems to have approved the paragraphs without alteration. To Amery's chagrin, however, the agreed formula appeared in the final version of the report in italics, and thus a printer's error to some extent undid the effect of Balfour's splendid draft. Amery refers in his memoirs to criticism from the Cabinet (*My Political Life*, II, p. 392) but this concerned not the opening section of the report, but the right of the British Government under the 1865 Colonial Laws Validity Act to 'disallow' such Dominions legislation as conflicted with that of Britain.

Governors General not only had the right to withhold their consent to Dominions legislation but to 'reserve' this consent for the monarch. These were not the only restrictions on the powers of the Dominions to legislate. They could not make laws repugnant to the laws of Britain nor with extra-territorial effect. Nor was the interpretation of the law ultimately in the hands of Dominions law courts since there was a right of appeal to the Judicial Committee of the Privy Council. Indeed the Judicial Committee had recently declared invalid a Canadian law forbidding such appeals in criminal cases in the course of deciding a smuggling case. It was these and like constitutional anomalies which troubled the Irish, and to some extent the Canadian government rather more than the issue Hertzog had raised. In particular the issue of reservation and disallowance divided the British Cabinet on 17 November, with the Lord Chancellor

*B. E. C. Dugdale, *Arthur James Balfour* (National Book Association, 1939), II, p. 279.

leading the attack on Amery's highly realistic view that the powers were quite inconsistent with the present position of the Dominions, and were in effect in abeyance. In this Amery had support from Balfour and from Birkenhead, but he was in the end compelled to secure modifications to the report of the Inter-Imperial Relations Committee. They were not, however, substantial.

The Irish Government had raised these and other issues in a powerful memorandum on 'Existing Anomalies in the British Commonwealth', dated 2 November 1926.* They dealt with the need to establish the legislative autonomy of the Dominions, their plenipotential and consular rights in international affairs, the need for a separate identity of the representatives of the Crown and the British Government in each Dominion, and the need to change the Royal title in order to reflect the Irish Government's view that the Commonwealth would endure only as a free association linked by a common King (although not a common Crown). Amery's diary deals with a number of these issues, some of which the Conference fully resolved, while others were at his instance held over for more detailed examination by an expert Committee on the Operation of Dominions Legislation.

The work of this committee was to lead directly to the Statute of Westminster in 1931. Even on these highly technical subjects, however, the Committee felt bound to place on record the right of each Dominion to advise the Crown in all matters relating to its own affairs, and was clearly looking to establish the legislative competence of the members of the Commonwealth. The most obviously inflammatory subject so far as the Irish were concerned (that of appeals to the Privy Council) found them fighting a lame battle, since in the other Dominions the allocation of powers within the Federation and the rights of minorities like the French Canadians, made their Governments loath to open the issue. In the end Birkenhead and Hogg persuaded the Irish over breakfast not to act immediately, but to leave it for a subsequent conference. In return the Conference resolved that it was no part of the British Government's policy 'that questions affecting judicial appeals should be determined otherwise than in accordance with the wishes of the part of the Empire primarily affected'. The course of events was, however, to undermine that resolution almost immediately (see pp. 530-1). The question of treaty procedures was more satisfactorily resolved. There could be no question of separate Dominion signatures since this would impair the unity of the Empire, but Canada, prompted perhaps by the Dominions Office, came up with the ideal solution whereby the treaty would be signed in the name of the King 'as the symbol of the special relationship between the different

*E (113/26)3 in the Conference documents, printed by Harkness, *The Restless Dominion*, pp. 101-4.

parts of the Empire', with each Dominion involved adhering to the treaty by virtue of the signature of its plenipotentiary.

There can be no doubt that much of the simplification and strengthening of the Commonwealth structures which the Conference accomplished was the direct product of Amery's thinking, even when as in the case of Governors General and High Commissioners, the initiative appeared to come from elsewhere. No longer were Governors General to have the dual role of representing both the Crown and the British Government in each Dominion. Communication between Governments was in future to be direct by means of a network of High Commissioners, which would supplement the already existing system of telegrams between Prime Ministers and the circulation of the Foreign Office Confidential Print. In his first speech to the Commons as Secretary of State for the Dominions, Amery had suggested use of the Dominions' High Commissioners in London as a means of confidential consultation with the British Government, and he had earlier (on 19 November 1924) inaugurated a series of regular weekly meetings with them to brief them on the British Government's thinking. The Cabinet's Interdepartmental Committee on the system of communication and consultation within the Empire had, in its report of 22 June 1926, endorsed the extension of the High Commissioner system. The readiness with which the Dominions accepted the idea is explicable in terms of their own interests. Bruce, for example, saw it as a natural if not wholly necessary extension of Australia's own scheme for a liaison officer in the Cabinet Office, which had been working well since the end of 1924. King, as we have seen, saw it as the necessary outcome both of the need to define the powers of the Governor General following his dispute with Byng, and of Dominions autonomy in foreign affairs. There was some opposition, however, from New Zealand, from the Governors General themselves, and some hostility in the Cabinet led by Carr. In the end, however, the change went through with the sole proviso that the Governor General should be kept as fully informed as the monarch himself.

There was more difficulty over the position of the Crown, where Amery was anxious to establish that it was both unitary and indivisible as the ultimate safeguard of Empire. O'Higgins held that the Crown was several, but he was anxious also to use the 'Kingdom of Ireland' as a bridge to unification. The issue was linked also to that of the royal signature on treaties concluded on behalf of the Dominions. In the end a compromise was reached. Ireland ceased to press for each individual Dominion to be named, but pressed her own case. At first the British Government would agree only to the phrase 'Great Britain *and* Ireland', but eventually they conceded what became known as the 'O'Higgins comma', and the 1927 Royal and Parliamentary Titles Act agreed that

George V was 'by the Grace of God, of Great Britain, Ireland and of the British Dominions beyond the Seas, King, Defender of the Faith, Emperor of India'. There was alarm in Ulster, which Baldwin personally had to still, but also the proud claim 'Defender of the Faith' to reassure them, and to irritate their southern neighbours.

It is wrong to think of Amery as a romantic optimist making the best of Britain's surrender to Hertzog, Mackenzie King and the Irish. The Dominions may have refused to adhere to the Locarno Pact, nor would they respond to Bruce's plea that they bear their share of the Empire defence. But it was not inevitable that the Commonwealth should become 'akin to old Holy Roman Empire', more of a strategic liability than an asset to Britain.* There is too much hindsight here. Amery was well aware that the Conference left open the way to dissolution, but it was a risk he had to take. Without its work he knew there would have been no chance at all of that closer unity which, be believed, could still be achieved by making of the Empire an economic unit. That was now his major goal.

Diary

10 October 1926 (France): Off to Delville [Wood] soon after 9. . . . The monument itself is very fine and so is the equestrian statue on top of it. . . . Hertzog['s speech] quite good except that he did not mention the existence of the British Empire at all. Mrs Botha then pulled the cord which released two great Union Jacks which constituted the unveiling. A curious commentary on Hertzog's schemes for abolishing the Union Jack in S. Africa.

11 October 1926: Had a long talk with Hertzog about accepting the invitation of the City to confer their Freedom on him. He tried to run out of it but I put it to him that while he could clear up misunderstandings with his own people, it would be impossible for him to remove the suspicion and resentment that might be felt by the British section in S. Africa, apart from any feeling here, if he refused. I also indicated the difficulty about the City's presenting him with Kruger's wagon if he refused their Freedom. I did not press him for a decision at the moment but he promised to ring up in the afternoon and I subsequently got a message to say that he had decided to accept. . . .

Saw the King at Buckingham Palace. He talked to me at some length about Hertzog whom he had seen that morning, and the flag question on which he feels very strongly. I deprecated it coming up at the Con-

*C. Barnett, *The Collapse of British Power* (Eyre Methuen, 1972), pp. 11, 202–7.

ference but suggested that it was better that the different Prime Ministers might speak privately. . . . In the morning Hertzog had asked whether there was any chance of inducing the King to go out to S. Africa and I raised this with him. He answered as I expected that he felt he could only do it if he did the other Dominions as well and that at his age it would mean too much bucketing about.

13 October 1926: Across to see PM for a few minutes about Conferenec arrangements. Apparently Winston is to be included among those summoned to the first meeting and presumably therefore to other main meetings of the Conference. I only hope he will not talk too much or say things that will upset the Dominions.

15 October 1926: Saw PM with Hankey and Harding about Conference arrangements, more particularly seating and we decided to stick to the recent arrangement under which all the British Ministers are on one side of the table and the Dominions opposite and at the end. Presently Cave, F.E. and Austen came in with various departmental experts and we discussed the question of a change in the King's title pressed for by the Free State. We decided to press in the first instance for my suggestion of King of Great Britain and Ireland, and of the Dominions, etc. and to fall back if necessary on the departmental proposal of King of Great Britain, of Ireland, and of . . . etc. My further suggestion that the title should be enlarged to include the greater Dominions by name met with no favour but we may come to it yet.* Afterwards some general discussion on trade union legislation which Stanley does not want to introduce till next year. . . .

Back to have a talk with Byng who was most friendly and grateful for all my support. His summary of Mackenzie King is that while he has a great belief in himself and great ambition, and a general belief in God, he has no political convictions or sincerities of any sort whatever and simply says what he thinks may pay at the moment. Back to Downing Street to discuss Governors of Queensland and the possibility of getting Lovat here in Clarendon's place [as Under Secretary for Dominions]. Stanley liked the idea and promised to see Lovat shortly.

18 October 1926: Cabinet. Long discussion of coal situation which looked anxious, but decided to do nothing drastic unless Cook's campaign

*L.S.A. note: '1937', an obvious reference to the change in the Coronation Oath agreed by the Dominions and used for the Coronation of George VI whereby each of the Dominions was mentioned by name so as to indicate that the King was equally King of Great Britain, Ireland, Canada, Australia, New Zealand, and of the Union of South Africa.

to call out the Midlands miners should really succeed.* Also ran through Conference agenda, and passed subject to minor adjustment with Treasury, Winston as usual protesting against my not screwing things up tighter, my new rubber proposals. Had a late tea and long talk with Mackenzie King, much of it occupied with his version of the late constitutional crisis, but got in some talk on Conference issues, and got him well seized, I think, of the idea that he is in a strong mediating position between Hertzog and Bruce. He is all against any formal resolutions on status. His general tone altogether most satisfactory.

19 October 1926: J. H. Thomas to breakfast. Rather worried about the labour situation, but vowing the railwaymen would only lay an embargo on coal over his dead body. He was keenly interested in the Empire Marketing Board and disposed to accept my invitation to come on himself. . . . To Westminster Abbey for the unveiling by the P[rince] of W[ales] of the tablet to the Empire's million dead. The PM, F.E., Worthy and myself were to walk up the aisle with the Prince and stand on each side of him during the ceremony. F.E. having failed to turn up I seized Burdwan on the way, hauling him out of his seat – a better representative really. We all walked across after the short but deeply impressive ceremony, myself with Hertzog and Kevin O'Higgins. Cosgrave sent O'Higgins in his place feeling that he as a 1916 Dublin rebel might be resented by some and put his views in a letter which I persuaded him to publish as likely to heal wounds. We then opened the Imperial Conference, the first which I have attended as a full member though I have taken a considerable part one way and another in every Conference or Imperial Cabinet since 1917 and a pretty close interest in both 1907 and 1911. S.B.'s speech went down very well. M. King struck a very good note and by anticipation largely disarmed Hertzog who was very mild and tactful in language but had to put in his old tag about the danger to the Empire of misunderstanding as to the real status of its parts. Bruce, Coates much as expected. Monroe came out with a most satisfactory spontaneous declaration of his intention to establish preference in Newfoundland. Burdwan spoke well for India. F.E. never turned up – apparently he forgot all about the Conference and was golfing. My statement was well received and has evoked no comment since.

Off to BBC place at Savoy Hill, and there spoke sitting across a baize

*On 15 October the Miners' Federation by a district vote of 460,150 to 284,336 resolved to continue and intensify the strike. Particularly in Nottinghamshire, however, large numbers were already back at work. Despite the temporary success of Cook's speeches, the drift back to work continued; by the end of September there were over 81,000 men working, 34,000 in the Midlands and 16,000 in Nottinghamshire, and by the second week in November not less than 237,000 and perhaps as many as 303,000 men were working.

table to a little hanging box about three inches away, with a red light to show the world was hearing, and a notice to warn me that a sneeze might shatter the nerves of millions. I told them the ABC of the Conference's history and meaning, using notes but talking and not reading, and I was told afterwards that it was very clear and just what they needed.

20 October 1926: Austen gave his full dress survey of foreign affairs all the morning and a good part of the afternoon. It was good, but a little too flat in perspective and too much Europe – Mackenzie King noted how Curzon had in 1923 worked from the periphery back to Europe, while Austen had gone the other way. Also it suffered from the inevitable dullness of being read and read in haste to get through it. The most significant event in European affairs, the meeting of the first Pan Europe Congress in Vienna a few days before, he never referred to.

21 October 1926: When we opened Philip told us his economic survey would only last an hour or so; could I fill up the morning with a full survey of work of Imperial Economic Committee and Empire Marketing Board? I got some papers across while Philip was speaking and refreshed my memory with the history of things, and gave them about an hour, stating the case very persuasively for the IEC's continuance and waxing enthusiastic over EMB. Got away at one and had a couple of hours subject only to tea and biscuit lunch to think out the general lines of my Colonial survey. Back to Conference and gave them about three quarters of an hour of general argument why they should all be interested in the Colonial Empire as an immense economic asset and as a field of trusteeship, and an hour and a quarter survey. They were I think genuinely interested in spite of the length of it all and I was very glad I had not troubled to over prepare or have it all typed out.

Devised plan for a PMs' committee under Balfour, in lieu of S.B., to go into all the constitutional, foreign policy and status questions and get to some sort of settled wording for a report (avoiding a resolution if possible) before we had a general talk in full Conference with the extremes on both sides tilting at each other. [Later L.S.A. note: 'I was particularly anxious to keep Winston out of it, as he would have made things very difficult for Hertzog and O'Higgins.']

22 October 1926: General economic discussion. M.K. helpful and quite prepared to let IEC go on, Bruce full and interesting, not pressing preference directly, and laying great stress on research, etc., Havenga very lucid, well arranged and well disposed, rest also quite good. Mackinder on IEC rather pedantic and not too tactful. Philip summed up quite

473

effectively. In between we had lunch at 112. . . . Horne very keen on something being done in the tariff way. Little conference with S.B., Austen and Balfour over tea at which, after Austen had finished telling us all about Locarno, we agreed the general lines of the arrangements devised by Harding and myself [on Treaty]. Also took opportunity of speaking to S.B. about his amazing indiscretion in giving Byng a viscountcy without consulting me, which had put me in some difficulty with M.K. who was inclined to take it as a slap in the face, and with Harry Foster who is deeply aggrieved that he hasn't been given one! S.B. very apologetic, had acted without thinking after the King had expressed a wish in the matter.

24 October 1926: Short walk in afternoon, polished off papers, wrote an Athanasian creed for the British Empire.

25 October 1926: Conference. Discussed Conference policy. Mackenzie King gave a short account of what Canada had done in her relations with the US. Bruce not quite so direct as Hughes with A.J.B. in 1918, asked what Austen's policy really was as regards Egypt, etc. Evidently Lloyd both impressed and a little frightened them. The whole discussion to the point and friendly but lacking the interest of a real issue for decision such as confronted the Conference in 1921. Took Thomson, the New Zealand Hankey, home for lunch and did what I could to get into his head the importance of really using their High Commissioner as a means of communication.

26 October 1926: [Writing his diary a week later Amery forgot what the discussion in Conference was on the 26th, remembering only the New Hebrides Sub-Committee and] After that Hankey, Austen, Harding and Balfour to dinner for a real good talk on the future work of the 'Prime Ministers' Committee' on inter-Imperial relations which has been set up at my instigation with Balfour in the chair and myself and Austen as his two helpers. We talked till nearly midnight, incidentally helping Balfour with a sort of opening statement he was to make next day.

27 October 1926: Meeting of the British Cabinet. At three o'clock the new PMs' Committee opened in the old Cabinet room at the FO but as Bruce remarked it seemed to be just the Conference over again as everybody had brought one or two colleagues and the room was full of experts and secretaries sitting behind. Balfour's opening was a prepared paper which also made the thing formal. The whole idea had been to start away with a discussion of the best method of conducting foreign affairs but Balfour's paper was so general and he himself gave so little that the next person who spoke, viz. Mackenzie King, raised the subject of channels of communication, in other words assimilating the Governor [General]'s position purely to that of the Crown, and was followed by Hertzog with a general disquisition on status. So there we were right in the middle of the status question and after we had discussed it up till 5 o'clock when the Mandates Committee started in the same room I came to the conclusion that the only thing was to suspend the main committee by letting the Attorney Generals and other legal experts go into the question of the form of treaties while we somehow discussed the status question informally.

28 October 1926: Met Bruce and King informally at Balfour's to discuss what was to be done about Hertzog's proposed declaration of independent status to which Balfour had drafted an alternative. We had a good talk and decided to carry the subject further by simply asking the Prime Ministers and no one else to Balfour's room. Afterwards King came over and had a long talk with me on various points. He is quite keen to carry the change in the position of Governor General further to the point of having a British High Commissioner in Canada.

29 October 1926: . . . to our first purely PMs' meeting at the Privy Council. Hertzog on the whole not unreasonable. Mackenzie King had made him realise that the word 'independent' had a signification at any rate in Canada which made it quite impossible for him to accept and he practically meant to accept the great part of Balfour's alternative draft. F.E. rushed in rather precipitately with a blend of Hertzog and Balfour which only used the phrase 'Commonwealth of nations' and left out any reference to the British Empire. I could see New Zealand getting very restive and chipped in in order to point out that while Commonwealth was an excellent phrase there were some who disliked it as much as others disliked Empire and it was desirable to get in both especially as Empire was the only word which covered the whole of the territories under the Crown. It was a very interesting talk and I think we all got reasonably close together, both Bruce and Mackenzie King very helpful.

1 November 1926: Lunched at the Goldsmiths' Hall. I proposed the guests and intimated that Empire development with Imperial preference left out was like *Hamlet* minus the Prince of Denmark, adding that the part was not wholly omitted at present but that in England at any rate Hamlet's lines were very drastically cut, that in fact we were still limiting him to the question 'To be or not to be'. . . . Then to the PM's inner committee at the Privy Council. Balfour had meanwhile produced a new draft which I had not seen before and which I confess I did not very much like. Discussion rambled on this and we got more at sixes and sevens. Eventually I produced something which I had drafted myself over the weekend bringing in both Empire and Commonwealth of nations and on this with the last sentence left out and with the substitution 'common bond of the Crown' for the 'common bond of allegiance to the Crown' to help O'Higgins this was provisionally accepted as a suitable preamble to whatever report we should subsequently make on matters of detail. At the end of it all I think Hertzog felt that he was getting very little result for all the effort he has been making. Anyhow the document as it stands is fairly innocuous except for one phrase 'freely associated' which I think can be altered.

That day Amery wrote twice to Balfour, on the first occasion telling him that Coates and Monroe were 'anything but happy' and that they 'must be careful not to alienate the people who really matter' for the sake 'of the extreme section of South Africa or of the Irish', and on the latter suggesting that 'associated in equal freedom' would be an acceptable substitute to a phrase which Balfour had disliked.

Diary

2 November 1926: Saw the PM after lunch and discussed with him Mackenzie King's suggestion both about short circuiting the Governor General and establishing a British High Commissioner in each Dominion and found him quite receptive to the idea. . . . Long sitting of PMs' Committee at FO on the issue of Privy Council's appeal resolving itself mainly into a debate between the Irish led by O'Higgins and Cave and F.E. I am afraid Cave by accepting that not sufficiently important Irish appeal has really prejudiced the situation considerably. However, I hope it may be straightened out and I believe F.E., who goes pretty far to meet the Irish, is having them at breakfast for the purpose. Otherwise a general consensus that the matter of retaining or dropping the appeal was one for each Dominion to settle, though no one in particular wanted to do anything.

3 November 1926: Ordinary Cabinet meeting at which I mentioned Mackenzie King's proposals in order to prepare their minds for further development. They took it fairly well but showed some hesitation and it was decided that we should not commit outselves finally in Conference without bringing the matter back to the Cabinet.* . . . PMs' Committee at

*The page appears to have been cut here. The Cabinet minutes deal with L.S.A.'s statement and with Balfour's statement of Imperial relations, but there is no indication that the deletion relat

FO on merchant shipping where the Irish again rode the status hobby horse with great determination. We had a great deal of interesting discussion to which I contributed a spirited advocacy that the status of an Empire ship should be comparable to the status of a British subject and, while I agreed that the general constitutional position with present arrangements was anomalous, urged immense care and secured the reference of the whole matter to a special Imperial conference on merchant shipping.

4 November 1926: Inter-Imperial Relations Committee at FO. Mackenzie King launched his suggestions both as to cutting out the Governors General as channels of communication and also as to the appointment of British High Commissioners in the Dominions. It was met with general assent except for New Zealand and Newfoundland and on the British side we showed ourselves sympathetic but urged that this was a matter we ought to refer to our colleagues and asked for postponement until after the next Cabinet. I also urged the necessity of at any rate warning the Governors General what was coming so that it should not be sprung on them.

Lunch at 112; Winston, O'Higgins, Lapointe [Canadian Minister of Justice], Havenga and Euan [Wallace]. We had a great talk, Winston and I battling freely *à propos* of Coudenhove Kalergi's book, as to whether this country ought to be included in Europe or not. He is an out and out European and regards the combination of England, France and Germany as the pivot of the world's peace. I strongly upheld the view that we were not European though a useful link between Europe and the new world outside. Back to Inter-Imperial Relations and made considerable further progress in the afternoon.

5 November 1926: Very short meeting of the full Conference to pass the report of various committees. . . . [At dinner in Manchester]. They all referred in kindly terms to old C. P. Scott and that reminded me of my midnight visit to C. P. Scott 30 years ago when he gave me my first cheque for a journalistic venture and sent me off to Macedonia after a 10 minutes' interview. The story pleased the old man greatly and I think most of the company.

6 November 1926: To Chequers where we found Hertzog, the Davidsons, Meriel Talbot and Douglas Hogg. S.B. turned up later having had a long day with the coal people. A settlement is apparently not improbable now but certainly not assured. . . . Davidson was very full of his new job [Chairman of the Conservative Party Organisation] which I think he will do well.

7 November 1926: A perfect day – we strolled about on the quarter deck after breakfast and then all marched off through the woods for a 6 or 7 mile walk coming back via Hampden House. The colour of the woods whether from a distance or in the midst of them quite wonderful. I walked out most of the way with Mimi Davidson and then with Douglas and David and later with Hertzog with whom I had already had a long chat about the classics in the morning. We talked trees and countryside and later on native policy on which he was interesting and persuasive. After lunch Hertzog left and I had a good talk on the quarter deck with Mackenzie King who is prepared to speak to Hertzog quietly about the flag question and see what he can do to dissuade him. Afterwards S.B. with Meriel and Mimi and myself walked up to the Beacon. . . . After tea S.B. and I ran through Hankey's draft resolutions on defence with Mackenzie King. With two very small alterations he accepted the lot straight away – a most delightful contrast to his appalling stickiness on defence questions three years ago.

8 November 1926: At Imperial Relations Committee Bruce raised the question of the High Commissioners here and he, Mackenzie King and Hertzog, and the Irish, all agreed that their High Commissioners should see the confidential papers and should be assisted by a secretary of the Casey type. This is undoubtedly the fruit of all my letters during the last 18 months. The only one who objected was Coates who wished to confine it to liaison officers alone attached to a sort of secretariat. He at any rate got his way to the extent of an agreement on our part to accept members of the Prime Ministers' Offices overseas at the FO or DO and vice versa to send out men to be attached to their Prime Ministers' Offices if desired. After that we discussed the difficult question of invitations and attendances at foreign conferences. On the subject of invitations Mackenzie King hit the nail on the head when he said the point was not the form in which the invitation was issued but in the manner of the acceptance which was after all to our discretion. The thing went off confusedly but not unsatisfactorily in a general decision that we should deal with the problem as it arises.

Lunched with Abe Bailey. . . . He told me that he had suggested to Hertzog a way of getting out of the flag difficulty by entering into consultations with Rhodesia on the matter with a point of view of securing a common flag which would include Rhodesia in future.

9 November 1926: Imperial Relations Committee at 10.30. Douglas Hogg handled the Compulsory Arbitration question skilfully and we got that agreed very quickly on the basis that we should none of us accept compulsory arbitration [in international disputes] for the present or do so later on without full consultation. Then followed an hour of general discussion on the constitutional status formula. King did not like 'Citizen-ship of the Empire' and liked still less 'common nationality of the Empire' which Hertzog suggested. We then suggested 'membership of the Empire', really quite another idea getting away from the point of our common individual relationship and does involve a certain transforming of the whole formula. In the end we left it in a semi final form for further consideration. After that all except PMs or senior delegates left and we discussed the question of the King's title. The Dominions have no leaning towards the Free State suggestion that each should be mentioned in the title so it reduced itself to a long discussion between O'Higgins and myself as to whether it should be 'Great Britain and Ireland' or 'Great Britain, Ireland'. In the end I provisionally accepted the latter subject to consultation with the Home Office as to whether it would cause trouble in Northern Ireland. Lastly we disposed of the Dominions' suggestion that they should pay their own hotel bills here.

10 November 1926: British Cabinet at which we spent the greater part of the time discussing Mackenzie King's suggestion of a new channel of communication and a British High Commissioner in the Dominions. The former went through without any discussion but the latter provoked a very long debate. I had not introduced the subject at any length as I had already dealt with it the week before and had not realised how entirely unfamiliar most of the members of the Cabinet would be with the idea and how naturally behind hand they are with the developments of Empire relations. They all felt, strengthened by some of the telegrams from Governors General, that the new High Commissioner would entirely upset the Governor General's position. In the discussion, Austen, as sometimes happens, having seized an idea from me, was prepared to push it further than I was and to press for the thing in its extreme form. In the end it was decided that Baldwin plus Cave as a representative of the doubters should have a chat with Mackenzie King. Turning it over in my own mind afterwards, I rather came to the conclusion that what we need in the first instance at any rate is not one High Commissioner combining a very wide range of functions and a considerable staff under his exalted title, but an Agent General on the business side and a Liaison Officer on the Empire policy side, the two quite separate and neither of them so big as to be obtrusive.

11 November 1926: Cenotaph service. . . . F.E. was in a state of great indignation because he was standing in his Cabinet place below me and not graded as a Prime Minister in view of India's 3 hundred million. To add to his annoyance his wreath blew down.

Meeting of the Committee of Imperial Defence at Whitehall Gardens, a useful revival of a practice which was dropped at the last Conference, and we discussed such matters as poison gas and the principle on which the Empire quotas should be assessed in its disarmament scheme. Hertzog produced a suggestion which I in fact used before, namely that there should be one Empire quota for the Navy based on previous establishment of separate quotas for each Dominion. This found considerable favour until one or two of them began to realise that it would definitely mark out what the various Dominion duties in defence might be and so lead to pressure for their doing it, and the thing then rather fizzled out.... Inter-Imperial Relations Committee at FO where we made really good progress with the Free State paper [Eire's memorandum on Existing Anomalies in the British Commonwealth of Nations] and eliminated a good many difficulties. The most thorny question being left at my suggestion to a committee of lawyers and I was instructed to take the chair at a Drafting Committee which would draft the reference to them.

15 November 1926: Imperial Conference at which we discussed defence, Mackenzie King saying nothing while Bruce gave a very interesting survey of what Australia is doing with a pretty clear hint at the end that others ought to bear their corresponding share of the burden. . . . As I feared, Mackenzie King on further looking through the defence resolutions has taken alarm at some of them and suggested amendments though Hankey tells me that except as regards Singapore they are not serious.

Great lunch both in number of guests and bulk and quantity of viands at the Carlton by Burdwan from which I fled with S.B. in time for questions. Then to our Drafting Committee where considerable confusion reigned firstly owing to a number of new passages that Costello wanted to introduce on behalf of the I[rish] F[ree] S[tate], while old Bill let himself go on the subject of the announcement of equal status. I stayed there for more than [*sic*] 20 minutes late for the main Prime Ministers' Committee at the Privy Council and tried what I could to knock their heads together finally leaving it to Harding to make a single draft out of our confused discussion. Main Committee went on well* and I was left at the end with instructions to draft something about the proposed channel of personal communication at the Dominions end.

Dined at home and afterwards had 3 hours of Harding going through his draft report for our Committee, a really admirable document, and in

---

*L.S.A. noted when preparing his memoirs: 'It was this afternoon that we accepted, with only one small amendment (Hankey says Mackenzie King made one or two at Hever over the weekend) Balfour's memorable setting passage. I remember it so vividly, but it is typical of the hurried dictation of these diaries of mine, often a week after the event, that I never mention it here. It is just possible that it was accepted by the main Committee when I was still at the Drafting Committee and only heard that it had gone through by general consent.'

particular rewriting the passage dealing with personal contact at both ends.

16 November 1926: . . . went on with the inner circle of the Inter-Imperial Relations Committee and got through most outstanding matters so that it was possible now to produce the whole of our conclusions in the form of a report.

17 November 1926: Cabinet in the morning. I thought I might have trouble with Austen and the PM over the appallingly sloppy and weak-kneed telegram which had been sent off without consulting me or any of my office on the subject of proposed punitive measures against Chinese pirates who had just tried to burn a British ship near Hong Kong and abducted two European women. I managed to put my case for re-consideration on the basis of a misunderstanding and insufficient infor-mation and was happily able to get a much better telegram sent. However, in the end it turned out that no landing was required because all the parties were killed or otherwise accounted for before they got ashore. The Balfour Report threatened to make some trouble and after a little desultory conversation it was decided to have an extra Cabinet in the evening . . . at which the old centralised view of opposition to equal status and Dominion autonomy was defended by Cave who is a tremendous old Tory, as well as by Winston who is really a jingo of the late 19th century and has no sympathy with the idea of Imperial unity by free co-operation. Balfour and I waxed eloquent at some length in defence of the modern conception of Empire and were usefully helped by F.E. In the end the Balfour Report was agreed to subject to an effort being made to alter certain passages, more particularly those dealing with reservation and disallowance. . . .

18 November 1926: Inter-Imperial Relations Committee and proceeded paragraph by paragraph through the report continuing again in the afternoon. We had a tremendous hammer and tongs discussion on the passage in the report of my drafting committee on reservation and disallowance. We eventually knocked out both the paragraph which by an oversight practically laid down the wholly irrelevant assertion that no Governor-General could ever refuse assent to any measure favoured by his ministers and also the quite innocuous general paragraph that the powers of reservation and disallowance had fallen into disuse, at which Cave had so strongly objected. And in the end reduced the whole thing to a much shorter form, F.E. at my suggestion having put forward a form of words saying that it was the exclusive privilege of Dominion ministers to give advice on Dominion affairs. After the meeting was over Harding and Davis realised that the thing had got into a form which would have practically forbidden ministers here [in Britain] taking any part in giving advice with regard to the appointment of Governor-General or with regard to the point of many minor matters on which advice is given as regards petitions, etc. Harding was sent round to see the PMs individually and find some amended formula. . . . Somewhere about six we had a short meeting of the Antarctic Committee and practically agreed our report. The process of incorporating the Antarctic in the British Empire which I started pushing when I was Under Secretary in 1919 is now going to make a substantial further stride and I hope I may be justified some day by the discovery of some value in that continent even if only it should be for the purpose of all round winter sports.

19 November 1926: The actual Conference did not last long and we had time after that to deal with the crisis over the passage in the Balfour Report. Two or three suggestions were put up and at first it looked as if O'Higgins wanted to insist on the use of the word 'exclusive', but finally a slight rearrangement by Harding produced a phrase which all could accept and which does not deny to British ministers the right in sharing in advice about the Governor-General. . . .

To the Conference where the Balfour Report was adopted* and it was decided to send it to the press next day so as to give the Monday leader writers plenty of time to read it up. . . . B. and I dined at Claridges with Hertzog who had got a very pleasant little gathering. . . . We all parted on the most affectionate terms. Havenga, I think, has been very genuinely touched by the friendliness of his reception as has Hertzog. I believe our little dinner to them to meet Baldwin when they first arrived did a great deal to set them at their ease and made it possible for me to persuade Hertzog a few days later not to refuse the Freedom of the City. Altogether I think I can take credit for having done a great deal with Hertzog since I first began to correspond with him on my appointment.

22 November 1926: My 53rd birthday and encouraged by the almost unanimous chorus of approval given to the Balfour Report in every quarter. I think I can look on the passage of that report as the completion of at any rate one of the big things I have worked for most of my life. But

*L.S.A. added later, probably when writing his memoirs: 'After I had tried to eliminate the italics from the Key definition. This had been in the roneo copies to show where it fitted in. When I pointed out to Hankey that it was never intended to be so emphasised away from the context he said a last minute change would create some sort of suspicion in Hertzog or O'Higgins' mind and urged me to let it stand.'

only the completion of a stage, and a stage which if neglected means dissolution. It all makes the need for an Imperial economic policy more urgent than ever and I must make my tour round the Empire next year the starting point for that.

23 November 1926: O'Higgins came to see me. . . . He gave me a most interesting account of a talk he had had with Carson the evening before in which he put before Carson his suggestion that Ulster should come in with its present powers under the United Kingdom of Ireland. Carson had listened most sympathetically and had urged no other objection except the possibility that it was premature but that he had better discuss the matter with Craig. I told O'Higgins the obvious thing was to talk to Craig and if Craig thought it premature to hold his hands for the present. I said that it would no doubt make a good deal of difference whether they were ready to put the King's head on stamps and coins and restore the Union Jack in some form. O'Higgins replied that he thought there would be no difficulty whatever about the King's head and no sentiment about dropping the tricolour but that there would be grave difficulty about a flag containing the Union Jack. What he suggested was a harp and a crown on blue background. I thought that might do if he further adopted Hertzog's idea that the Jack should be flown together with the national flag on occasions which brought in the Imperial connection. He also told me that he had told Carson that he would be quite willing to accept someone like Lord Londonderry as first Viceroy on reunion. There is no doubt that the Conference has made a deep impression on O'Higgins in more senses than one. I think he a little bit resents the position of an almost junior Dominion and hopes by reviving a United Kingdom of Ireland to come back at the top of the list. . . .

At the final session of the Conference there were a series of little speeches all expressive of immense satisfaction at the success of the Conference. Looking back on my anxieties as to what we could discuss with any profit and without quarrelling and I am indeed glad that I insisted so strongly on our holding the Conference this year. It really has been a great clearing up of outstanding points on a basis which eliminates friction and leaves the way clear for future co-operation. It is true that it leaves the way equally clear to dissolution. That is a risk we have got to run and if the will to unity is there we shall overcome it. After all the best proof of the new spirit seems to be the fact that while the main committee of Prime Ministers was framing the new status policy all the various sub committees were hard at work, and not unsuccessfully, on detailed projects of closer co-operation, making up in sum total a far more effective series of bonds of Empire than the formal ones we may have dropped. Besides the main Balfour Report itself is much more than a purely negative document. The position of the Crown and the implications derived from it are stated sufficiently clearly I think to avoid any danger of the personal union theory being revived. What is essential now is to get really into people's minds the meaning of the single Crown and all its implications. As for my own part in the Conference it was certainly not a publicly conspicuous one like Chamberlain's in the old days. No one indeed stood out individually. We all were contributing our share except, perhaps, old Balfour whose introductory setting to the status formula was a stroke of genius. On the other hand I think my two years' work both coaching the Cabinet and the office in the right point of view and getting into personal touch with the various Prime Ministers overseas made all the difference and I am particularly pleased with the way in which I managed to nurse Hertzog.

24 November 1926: Cabinet at which I had to raise the Asiatic Labour in the New Hebrides. Otherwise attempted to fall asleep after many late nights while Neville was expounding the virtues of his proposed Poor Law Reform.

25 November 1926: Longish meeting of the CID on S.W. Arabia, China, etc. On the first subject we made some progress at any rate to the extent of strengthening the Air Force there and I got a chance of insisting emphatically that we should never get things right until the administration of Aden was settled. On this Worthy, F.E. and I reached agreement at the beginning of the year. We have had India's assent since. Now the Treasury suddenly take an entirely new point of view and want to go back to the old system of handing the whole thing over to India with a subsidy from us. They are really rather tiresome.

26 November 1926: Mackenzie King came in for a farewell talk. He is leaving very happy and I made him happier by telling him what a helpful part he had played in looking after the left wing and keeping us all together. . . . E[mpire] P[arliamentary] A[ssociation] Dinner in the Royal Gallery – a rather chilly affair. . . . Stanley spoke quite well and confessed that he had wanted to cry off the Conference but had been kept to it by me. . . . Monroe not as amusing as usual. He told the story of how my New Year's telegram to him as an old Harrovian expressing the hope that I might see him again nearly 40 years on had agitated his officials who could not understand why the Secretary of State should be unwilling to see the Prime Minister of Newfoundland for another 40 years. . . . That closed the Conference functions. All's well that ends well.

29 November 1926: Small conference with Worthy, Evans, and Fass of the Treasury, etc. about Aden and decided to push on with our memorandum and bring the thing to an issue in the Cabinet.

1 December 1926: Cabinet at which Austen held forth at length on the China situation and as I had heard it at the Committee the day before and had been up late I found myself going to sleep most of the time.

7 December 1926: First resumed meeting with the High Commissioners, at least Cook, Smit and Gordon [representing New Zealand, South Africa and Australia]. I had previously had a letter from Larkin to say that Mackenzie King was afraid of these meetings being misinterpreted in Canada and so that he had thought he had better not come. I was really very annoyed at this sillinesss and discourtesy but have not yet answered him or Mackenzie King, or quite decided what to do about it. . . .

Had some talk with Stanley both reminding him again about Lovat and more particularly on the long letter to Winston about the gold standard position and preference of which I had sent him a copy. I am very anxious to make him understand that one way or another the question of more effective preference will have to be faced before the next election but that I am only too anxious to find a way of doing it without breaking with Winston.

8 December 1926: Cabinet most of which was taken up with the discussion of the Trades Union Bill. . . . Vote of Censure debate. Listened to Winston. . . . His mastery of the House is really wonderful now.

10 December 1926: Long talk with Fletcher, the Colonial Secretary of Ceylon . . . partly on Ceylon affairs but still more about China, as to which he spoke with great vigour and convincingly. Our policy has been to disregard the actual facts in China throughout but to treat any faction which happened to be in momentary control of Pekin as the government of all China, and at any rate when Curzon was there to treat everyone else as rebels. I gather that it was Curzon's way of handling the situation up to '23 that really finally set the Cantonese against us. His view is that they are anything but bolshevist by nature and really inclined to side with us. They had wanted to train their forces with the help of Indian officers which Curzon had vetoed and it was only after this that they called in the Russians who had immensely improved their efficiency. Kevin O'Higgins to lunch and had a long further talk about his proposals for a Kingdom of Ireland in which he disclosed that he is really after a Dual Monarchy on the Austro-Hungarian pattern and not merely the enhancement of the dignity of Ireland by the title of Kingdom. Took him round to see the PM for a moment before the latter left for Cambridge.

14 December 1926: Long Cabinet discussion on House of Lords Reform where I found myself with Guinness, Peel, Bob Cecil, and Douglas Hogg in rather a minority supporting the Cave Committee's Report for a really definite reconstruction of the Lords as well as some restoration of power. The rest, led off by Sam Hoare, were in favour of doing so little that I doubt if it would be worth doing at all. Douglas came back to lunch with me and we had a good talk on this and on Trade Union legislation.

15 December 1926: Cabinet. . . . Austen held forth at considerable length on the happenings at Geneva on which scribbled a line to F.E.: 'Very interesting for the family archives but is it essential to Cabinet?' The main subject of the afternoon, namely Trade Union Law, had so little time left for it that it was finally decided to have the draft bill further vetted departmentally and reconsider the matter after Christmas.

16 December 1926: CID at Whitehall Gardens on a variety of subjects including piracy in Bias Bay on which at last the FO have come round in their view and sanctioned prompt action in case of the next offence. . . . Cabinet at which at last after nearly 5 years' controversy we got a decision on Aden. Winston fought passionately against the solution recommended by F.E., Worthy and myself and tried to sow dissensions among us by raising the hare of great economies to be achieved by substituting air defence for infantry battalions. We firmly retorted that this might be admirable but was irrelevant to the question of who should be the controlling authority at Aden, and when Worthy instead of protesting took the view that he was quite willing to let the Chief of Staff go into the question of air defence, Winston's case was bust. However, he made a gallant attempt to evade a decision again by asking for postponement until the Lord Chancellor should arbitrate upon a side issue connected with transport charges, but F.E. and I insisted on a decision and the PM gave it our way, Winston making a last solemn protest. Immediately after came Neville's new Poor Law proposals involving an expenditure of 4 millions and something more, possibly a great deal more in order to pacify local authorities and Winston warmly commended the whole scheme. I fear he is always ready to spend millions on domestic purposes whether to find favour or buy off opposition but hates spending thousands on Imperial purposes. Before the Cabinet I had attended a meeting of the Irish Treaty sub-committee at which we agreed to send a fishing letter to the Free State and generally postpone action until we knew the answer.

17 December 1926: Discussed with [Larkin] Mackenzie King's reasons for telling him not to come to my weekly High Commissioners' meetings. Poor man rather embarrassed about it all and I think really feeling that King's attitude was childish and not too civil.

21 December 1926: Discussed with [Baldwin] my plans for next year as to which he said he thought he ought to ask the King before agreeing to my being away for as long as six months.

25 December 1926: This ends the working year – for me a comparatively uneventful one. It opened with the successful carrying through in Parliament of the Iraq Treaty, my final justification coming with the Angora Treaty in July. It ended with the success of the Imperial Conference. . . . But for [the division of the Offices in 1924–5] we should probably have had long discussions on abolishing the CO as a channel of communication and putting everything under the PM. On the economic side, of course, we didn't achieve much, but I was able earlier in the year to persuade Winston to stabilise existing preferences for ten years and have got him generally more amenable to the idea of doing something further if he has to raise new customs revenue. My chief effort on that side was getting the EMB started and thanks to the keenness of the team that I was lucky enough to get together that ought to do real good work. Minor matters were putting through the E. Africa and Palestine Loan Bill and getting Aden transferred. For the rest I suppose I played my part generally as a member of the Cabinet, though I was, happily, not one of the chief actors in either the General Strike or Coal Committee business, and more than my part in the way of speeches all over the place, spade-working away at the idea of Empire Trade which is making real progress. By 1928 things will be ready for me to take the field on a definite policy, with or without my colleagues. Altogether I have a feeling that in domestic and Imperial affairs 1926 has been a turning point year in the national outlook and that the tide will begin to set definitely in the right direction next year and be running strong enough by 1929 to enable us – if only we can mobilise our own faint hearts and reactionaries – to carry things through a General Election. [Later L.S.A. holograph note: 'Alas for my hopes. I did not resign and we went to the country on Safety First.']

14

The Shanghai Crisis and Dominions Tour 1927

Amery's diary for 1927, and particularly the entries for the earlier months, has a great deal to do with the crisis over the British settlements in China, about which he was rather hawkish. In this he was at one with the Governor of Hong Kong, Sir Cecil Clementi.

At the Washington Conference in 1921, Britain, together with the United States, Japan and France, had promised to work for the political and economic emancipation of China. But there was no immediate release for China from foreign supervision of her taxation system or from the rights of extra-territoriality enjoyed by the foreign settlements. The Chinese intelligentsia were outraged; Sun Yat-sen, the leader of the Kuomintang, the Chinese Nationalist movement, put himself at the head of this wave of nationalist feeling to accomplish a revolution in China, which was exploited by the Bolsheviks. The Kuomintang quickly won control of southern China from the Peking Government and organised their rule from Canton. Most of the remainder of the country was prey to warring factions.

Austen Chamberlain, the Foreign Secretary, although sharing much fear of Bolshevik influence, was prepared to try a more conciliatory approach and in December 1926, with the Cabinet's backing, he offered the prospect of treaty revision. What made the situation difficult was the decision by Chiang Kai-shek, Sun Yat-sen's effective successor, to strike north for the Yangtse. Along this river lay several British settlements. In October 1926 one of the towns in which there was such a settlement, Hankow, fell to the Nationalists. The Admiralty reinforced the China station and consideration was given to the despatch of troops in December. Early in January rioters threatened the British concession in Hankow and the decision was taken to abandon it.

The Chiefs of Staff discussed the situation on 11 January and recommended prompt reinforcement of Shanghai and co-operation with Japan, France and the United States. The Cabinet at first held their options open but eventually on 17 January agreed to despatch three infantry brigades to Shanghai, which was to be held. One was to come from India, one from the Mediterranean and the third from Britain. Co-operation from Japan, which had at first seemed likely, was by the time of the special Cabinet on 19 January unlikely. Effectively therefore a Cabinet which had been called to deal with the defence of the Shameen turned into a general discussion of policy as a result of which it was agreed that Chamberlain should sound the Japanese further, and that troop movements should be postponed, largely in order not to deter the Japanese from offering their help, although it was of assistance also in not prejudicing the negotiations with the Cantonese Foreign Minister, Eugene Chen, over Hankow.

By 21 January it was clear that Japan would send no troops, and the British Government despatched the Shanghai Defence Force in the full realisation that it would be two months before it could be assembled in Shanghai. But the Cabinet also agreed at the beginning of February that if Chiang Kai-shek did not attack Shanghai, there could be negotiations over Hankow, and the troops would be held at either Singapore or Hong Kong. The British Ambassador, Sir Miles Lampson (whom Amery was later to encounter as High Commissioner in Egypt in 1940 and as a candidate for the Indian Vice-Royalty in 1943), thought this last decision disastrous, and the Cabinet on 10 February left it to the man on the spot, Admiral Tyrwhitt, who decided that the troops should go to Shanghai.

In fact Chen and the British Consul at Hankow, O'Malley, reached an agreement over Hankow and Kinkiang (a similar threatened settlement), on the strength of which the British Government held back all but one brigade from Shanghai. On the pretext of a bellicose speech by Austen Chamberlain, however, the Cantonese Government refused to honour the agreement. Chiang Kai-shek made public his intention not to use force against Shanghai but to rely on strikes and boycotts, and to negotiate once it had been evacuated.

The defeat of the Pekingese forces by Chiang Kai-shek forced a reconsideration of the position on 17 February, although the Cabinet was still, it made plain, prepared to ratify the agreement already reached in return for an undertaking not to attack Shanghai. However, the Cantonese were by now firm in their demand for the abolition of extra-territorial rights and would not exclude Shanghai from their demands. Clementi went so far as to propose a blockade of Canton on 22 February, but Amery told him that this would be premature in the absence of support from the other powers and Lampson advised that it could only alienate the moderates in the Kuomintang, few of whom were anti-British. The Foreign

Office were clearly hopeful of a break between the moderates and extremists but it was to be May before their hopes were realised: the pro-Communist elements in the Kuomintang at first persuaded the Government to suspend Chiang Kai-shek from command in the middle of March. On 24 March there was severe rioting in Nanking and the British and American cruisers there were forced to open fire.

Tyrwhitt argued for the exaction of reparations and the Chiefs of Staff showed that by control of the river, the British could enforce both this and a peaceful settlement at Shanghai. The Cabinet was evidently hesitant about unilateral action, even when Beatty reported that the Chinese were trying to close the river by the use of batteries and mines. On 30 March Chamberlain was asked to press Washington and Tokyo into co-operative action, and the Cabinet would not respond the following day to warnings from Beatty and Trenchard that any delay would increase the difficulty of carrying out the proposed sanctions. With Tyrwhitt also sounding a cautious note, the Cabinet on 1 April contented itself with approving Chamberlain's appeal to the Americans and Japanese.

The situation was now complicated by the success of a Northern counter-attack, which the Chiefs of Staff were reluctant to prejudice, and by Chiang Kai-shek's final break with his masters. He had taken action against the Communists in Shanghai and on 15 April, two days before his dismissal as Commander-in-Chief, he set up a rival Kuomintang Government at Nanking. There was marked hesitation about any action which would damage his chances of success. On 12 April the more ambitious sanctions plans were dropped in the face of Chamberlain's warning that the Japanese could not endorse them and on the 13th the Cabinet substituted the capture of Hankow as Chamberlain proposed. The Chiefs of Staff poured cold water on this idea, preferring the seizure of the Cantonese Customs and Cantonese fleet. The Consul General at Canton argued, however, that it was wrong to take action at a different place from where the original outrage had taken place.

Chamberlain, Lampson and Tyrwhitt remained convinced that Hankow should be the target of any operation, and the Chiefs of Staff were equally clear that any prolonged reoccupation was not feasible. The Cabinet agreed to the reoccupation in principle, but by now British commercial interests were beginning to get cold feet and the evident hesitations of the Chief of Staff about the reoccupation communicated themselves to the Cabinet on 2 May. Two days later, however, further inquiry was authorised into both the Hankow operation and a proposal by Lampson that discretion should be given for immediate retaliation. Beatty drafted instructions to Tyrwhitt along these lines.

In effect Chiang's success had led to a drastic reappraisal of policy, and this is reflected in Amery's diary by the absence of any report of later developments: Austen Chamberlain's decision to suspend the withdrawal of representatives from Hankow, reported to the Cabinet on 11 May; the Cabinet decision on 19 May to remain neutral between the various Chinese factions; the ratification of the Chen–O'Malley agreement; and the gradual withdrawal of British forces when Chiang Kai-shek's success gave good prospect of a friendly regime in China with whom successful negotiations for treaty revision could be conducted.

An important factor in the Cabinet's approach to the crisis had been its knowledge of Soviet activities in China, which produced a sharp argument in Cabinet between those who wished for a break in diplomatic relations with Russia of whom Birkenhead, Amery and Churchill were the most prominent, and the Foreign Secretary, who seemed determined to avoid a rupture. In the end a compromise was reached, and a stiff note was handed to the Soviet *chargé d'affaires* on 23 February. In the end a break was made inevitable by the activities of the Home Secretary, Joynson-Hicks. On 12 May the premises of the Soviet trading company Arcos and the Soviet Trade Delegation were searched vainly for a missing Government document, but the evidence which came to light documenting the Soviet Union's espionage and provocative activities seemed a clear justification for putting an end to the trade agreement and to diplomatic relations with Russia. Baldwin and Austen Chamberlain had been reluctant to authorise the raid, and while on 23 May they agreed to the break, Baldwin made it clear that legitimate trade would continue. No doubt the tension felt over Soviet activities in China was reflected also in the concern for the defence of India on which Amery records several discussions, mostly about the position and defence of Afghanistan.

The Government had an ambitious programme of legislation in 1927, but on advice from the Chief Whip, Eyres Monsell, about the parliamentary timetable both Neville Chamberlain's reform of the Poor Law and the very controversial Factories Bill put forward by the Home Office were postponed in favour of constitutional reform. Among these measures was the extension of the franchise to women aged twenty-one (hitherto it had been limited to those over thirty), to which Churchill and Birkenhead were so opposed that reference to a Cabinet Committee was necessary before the Bill could be announced on 13 April. Another was reform of the House of Lords, which was discussed at length on 14 December 1926 but on which so little agreement was possible that when the subsequent Cabinet Committee's proposals were sketched out in response to three motions for reform in the House of Lords, neither the Chief Whip nor the Chairman of the Party had been consulted nor was the Cabinet really committed to them. Baldwin met the subsequent vote of censure in the House of Commons head on, but very willingly let Conservative criticisms of the proposals from John Buchan and others kill the whole idea of

reform. (Despite later efforts by Cave and in the early 1930s from Salisbury, Baldwin never let it revive.) Lastly, the Trades Disputes Bill, which
Baldwin had kept in Cabinet Committee throughout 1926, was in the end
strictly limited, with none of the proposals for altering the legal status of
trade unions finding favour. General strikes were declared illegal, the
law on picketing amended, and that on the political levy altered so as to
make trade unionists contract to pay it rather than force them to contract
out from an automatic payment. Neville Chamberlain, backed by Cunliffe
Lister, had favoured bringing into the Bill a compulsory hearing before
an industrial tribunal before a strike was allowed to begin, in effect a
conciliation pause closely modelled on the provisions of the Lemieux Act
which operated in Canada. The Ministry of Labour was deeply suspicious
of anything which looked like compulsory arbitration, but the Cabinet at
first supported the suggestion on 15 March. The Cabinet Committee which
discussed the proposal in detail came down against it, and after a further
reference to the Cabinet on 23 May the proposal was eliminated from the
Bill by eleven votes to seven largely because Baldwin sided with its opponents on the ground that it had not been properly discussed with industry.

Amery's departmental concerns in this period centred on the Colonial
Conference which opened on 10 May and which was intended to draw the
Colonial Service together, his proposed tour of the Empire, which began
on 22 July, and above all the moves towards a Federation in East Africa,
the diary entries on which are self-explanatory.

Much more complex is the story of the American attempt to extend the
limitations agreed at the Washington Naval Conference in 1921 to
cruisers and destroyers and in which Amery as a former First Lord took
a great interest. The Admiralty's requirements were dictated by the need
to protect the extensive trade routes of Empire and were put at seventy
cruisers. The British would, however, have been prepared to reduce the
maximum tonnage of a cruiser from 10,000 to 7500 tons and the size of
their guns from 8-inch to 6-inch, and they actually proposed to the Conference the establishment of two classes of cruisers with the numbers of
each type limited specifically. The Americans were seeking parity with
Britain and a ratio of 5:3 with Japan and proposed also a maximum limit on
tonnage with no restriction on the size of armament or the ships involved.

With the Conference deadlocked, Bridgeman, the First Lord, made it
clear to the press that Britain had no wish to deny the United States the
right to build an equivalent strength in cruisers, but this was queried by
his First Sea Lord, who, backed by Churchill, argued that if this in turn
led to an increased building programme by Japan, Britain would have to
respond. The Cabinet adhered to Bridgeman's statement and asked the
British Ambassador to Washington, Sir Esmé Howard, to communicate
it to the United States Government. The concession won no dividends.

The American delegation adhered to a tonnage limit, which Bridgeman thought outrageous, and would not contemplate the small cruiser. There seemed some chance of progress when the British and Japanese agreed to a compromise but Churchill and Beatty persuaded the Cabinet to summon the British delegation home for consultation. The Cabinet Committee at first approved this Japanese scheme, but after Baldwin's departure for Canada there were further discussions as a result of which the Government decided that they must stand by both Bridgeman's words about parity and the 6-inch gun cruiser. No agreement was possible, and the Conference broke up without any result. Lord Robert Cecil, who with Bridgeman had been a member of the British delegation, as a result resigned from the Cabinet.

Amery was not in England for the later part of this controversy. Instead, at the start of his Dominions tour, he was dealing with almost equally sensitive matters, the amalgamation of the Rhodesias, the question of the South African Flag, and above all the possible Federation of East Africa.*

Diary

19 January 1927: Talk with Ormsby-Gore and Wilson about China and about my projects for a Colonial Conference in May. Then to a small gathering of Ministers on China at No. 10, the PM, Austen, Worthy, the three Chiefs of Staff and Tyrrell. I made no attempt to raise the general issue of our [China] policy which seems to me to have been rather weak and timid but confined myself to backing up Worthy in stiffening the telegram Austen proposed to send to Japan about co-operation and in preventing the Indian Brigade being delayed.

20 January 1927: Saw Casey and discussed with him the situation in China both generally and in regard to the possibility of developments which might make it desirable for Australia to mark solidarity by sending some unit. We also discussed his own future, my advice to him being strongly that if he is thinking of politics he ought to go in for Australian politics and not be tempted by the idea of getting into the House here.

21 January 1927: Discussion with O[rmsby-]G[ore] and Wilson about the proposed Colonial Office Conference at which we decided definitely to go ahead with it. Lunched at home and walked back to No. 10 for a short

*For a separate introductory passage to the entries concerned with East Africa and the 1927 White Paper, see pp. 507–11.

notice Cabinet, not very strongly attended, on China. The general upshot was that the Indian Brigade is to go ahead and every preparation to be made with the Mediterranean Brigade, but the calling out of Reserve 'A' for the Home Brigade is to stand over for a few days.

26 January 1927: And so to Cabinet where we chiefly discussed China. I cannot help feeling that our policy, while it makes the maximum show of conciliation, may not [*sic*] land us in real trouble eventually. So many who know China are convinced that the only way to preserve peace is to take a high and drastic line with them.

29 January 1927 (Birmingham): Austen fired off a long speech on China.... Given the wisdom of the whole policy of concession it was a good speech and has been well received since.

31 January 1927: Conference with Trenchard and Shuckburgh about Iraq Air Estimates which the Treasury are trying to cut down by another three hundred thousands after we have already reduced them nearly a million. Decided that all we could do was to suggest the Indian Battalion going away next September saving thirty thousand or so. Trenchard very keen on the establishment of a permanent mobile Middle Eastern Air Force, its distribution left entirely to strategical considerations. This would keep 4 or 5 squadrons always in Iraq and getting them off the Middle Eastern Vote would finally end controversy.

1 February 1927: Longish talk with Austen about China. Clementi pressed in a strong telegram for immediate action on the last piracy, but Austen, as I thought he would, deprecated all action pending the delicate negotiations with Chen. I am afraid now that Chen has broken off the negotiations he will deprecate action lest it should be thought that we have taken it in a spirit of revenge.

2 February 1927: Cabinet at which we discussed China, if I remember rightly, at some length, and then found we had not left enough time for our decisions as to the King's Speech and what we were to get into the session, and accordingly had another Cabinet at 3 at the end of which F.E., Hogg, Salisbury and myself were deputed to revise and as far as might be required to redraft the draft King's Speech.

4 February 1927: Up in time for a Cabinet at which we polished off the King's Speech and the programme for the session. In view of Bobby's [Eyres Monsell, the Chief Whip] account of the time available we decided to jettison both Neville's Poor Law Bill and the Factory Bill but to introduce them both in a new session beginning late in November. We then started on China but had to break up at 1.45. . . . Had time for a short stroll round the Park before the afternoon Cabinet. To my horror Austen proposed that, Chen having told us that he would not continue negotiating unless we diverted our troops from Shanghai, we should tell him that if he signed the Hankow agreement we would agree not to land the troops. I at once pointed out all the dangers of a proposal which inevitably implied our giving way to Chen's threat and showed that it was entirely inconsistent with the attitude recommended by O'Malley at Hankow, and Lampson at Pekin. I also took the opportunity of reading a scathing personal telegram from Clementi about the whole policy of scuttle and surrender as he considers it, not identifying myself with his criticism but pointing out that that was the view that an able and responsible person inevitably took from the Hong Kong angle, and suggesting that we really could not go indefinitely in that direction without creating a reaction here. I think I was carrying the majority of the Cabinet with me, both against Austen's original proposal and against a modification of it which Baldwin suggested, viz. that we should put it to Lampson merely as an inquiry and not as a direct instruction to make an offer to Chen. Unfortunately Balfour intervened with the ingenious suggestion that we should stop the troops, not on the strength of any discussion with Chen but by asking the Japanese whether they would not prefer us to stop them in view of certain things they have recently said to us.

This was eagerly jumped at by various members of the Cabinet, but F.E. and I and Worthy and several others proposed that this was all right after letting the first Brigade land. In the end after interminable discussion we voted. Balfour's proposal was carried against my amendment that the first Brigade should land anyhow, by the PM's casting vote. A division on Balfour versus Austen's original proposal as amended by Baldwin was carried in favour of Balfour by one. I suggested a direct vote on the issue whether the troops should go on or not but we decided very weakly that both proposals should be submitted to Lampson for his opinion, and for any other suggestions he cared to make.

7 February 1927: Cabinet at noon and just had time before it to see all the latest telegrams showing clearly that Lampson, O'Malley, Barton and Tyrwhitt at Shanghai, were all against any wobbling and wanted the troops at Hong Kong. Judge of the general surprise when Austen opened by reading out a draft telegram concocted by the FO telling Lampson that we were stopping the first Brigade at Hong Kong to please the Japanese. I led off the opposition, which was pretty general, and it was clear that this time Austen would be definitely turned down by a substantial majority of the Cabinet. We resumed after lunch and Winston stepped in with a suggestion that we should leave the decision to Tyrwhitt at first in the form that Tyrwhitt should tell us, to order the ships along from Hong Kong. This secured a majority though some of us opposed on the ground that we ought not to abdicate our responsibility. The original FO proposal was never further discussed. Austen took it all with good grace and everything that has happened since has confirmed the wisdom of the decision, but it fills me with fear as to what the FO may wish to do next.

8 February 1927: Meeting of Ministers, Bob Cecil, Philip, Eustace Percy, Steel-Maitland, to discuss co-partnership, etc. and got as far as deciding that S.M. should detach a man for special investigation of the whole problem of better industrial relations. It is interesting to find myself and Bob [Cecil] protagonists together for once.

10 February 1927: Cabinet. Tyrwhitt having definitely ordered the first Brigade on to Shanghai and Lampson strongly urging the same, that issue was settled. Meanwhile influenced in the right direction by the approach of the troops Chen seems to have been more reasonable and the Hankow local agreement is by way of being signed. All this enabled Austen to make a very good speech in his defence in the afternoon in reply to a very weak attack.

15 February 1927: CID meeting at which *à propos* of stationing an air squadron at Khartoum I got the whole idea of a Middle East Air Reserve greatly advanced and prepared the position for the retention of our air squadrons in Iraq after 1928. . . .

Long conference in the PM's room with Austen, Bridgeman, Winston, Balfour and Bob Cecil about the line to be taken over President Coolidge's proposal for an extension of the Washington [Naval Treaty] scheme. The problem was how to show sufficient enthusiasm in accepting and yet safeguard our own particular position as well as the susceptibilities of the French and others who are already committed to the League of Nations scheme. In the end a blend of Winston's and my drafting was agreed to.

16 February 1927: Cabinet at which we first disposed of the Coolidge reply and then embarked on the problem of whether we could break with Russia. Austen very much opposed, drawing a most gloomy picture of the bad effect that would be produced everywhere, more particularly on Germany and Japan. Philip, who had put in a bulky memorandum showing the disadvantages of a breach from the trade point of view, gave strong evidence of the general dissatisfaction in the Party and came round on the whole in favour of breaking. The case for breaking was put at

length and with much eloquence by F.E. I followed agreeing in considerable measure and suggesting that if we did not actually break diplomatic-
ally we might at any rate meet them with their own weapons in China,
Russia and elsewhere, quoting Queen Elizabeth and Drake as examples,
but I do not think the Cabinet took the suggestion very seriously. Winston
just before we separated produced the suggestion that we should launch a
document of protest threatening to turn them out if any bloodshed
occurred in China as a result of their mischief making.

17 February 1927: A Cabinet at six on China, during the first part of
which while I was there we agreed to let O'Malley sign the arrangement
about Hankow with Chen on terms which I fancy are not likely to be
accepted by Chen, viz. our declaring afterwards that we regard ourselves
free to negotiate with any officials in China. The unlikelihood was increased by the decision taken by the Cabinet afterwards to reverse a
previous suspension of Tyrwhitt's orders to the second Brigade to come
on to Shanghai in view of the immediate fall of Hangchow which was
taken after I left. It really is a mercy that we overrode Austen about landing the first Brigade at Hong Kong; we should have been in an awful
position both at Shanghai and *vis à vis* Parliament.

18 February 1927: Cabinet down at the House where we went further
into the Russian question, deciding eventually to send a protest winding
up with a warning that we might feel obliged to break off if they did not
mend their manners. This codicil drafted by Neville was generally accepted
as an improvement to the original weak ending of the FO of linking up
our future action entirely with the eventuality of bloodshed in China.

After that we got on to the War Graves Commission, the final stage of
the long Treasury vendetta against Fabian Ware for having tried to maintain the inter-Imperial character of his organisation independent of the
Treasury. Winston gave way reluctantly on the question of Ware's salary
in view of the strong opposition of Worthy and myself and the attitude
of the PM, but advanced the claim that Ministers should be agreed or
else get Cabinet decision in future and not to have Ministers on the
Commission taking a line which the Treasury disagreed with. I expressed
my general concurrence, but subject to an equally strong insistence that
the Treasury should not be allowed to write letters calculated to cause
trouble to the Commission without previous consultation with my
Department. The matter is not quite settled yet as neither Winston nor
myself have agreed on the wording of the minutes. . . .

Godfrey [Locker Lampson] rather poured out his soul to me about the
FO. He is apparently allowed to do nothing except see papers after
decisions have been taken and is never invited by Austen to any of the

conferences on policy. He has been throughout in favour of the kind of policy that Clementi has urged, explicit recognition of the Cantonese at a much earlier date coupled with firm dealing when they misbehaved and he had had no sympathy with the FO attempt to back out of landing troops at Shanghai. On Russia, too, he had had definite views, but on this and all other matters his memoranda would seem to have been dismissed without much consideration. All this is a pity. Austen as a born bureaucrat would be much better off if he got a political opinion as well as the purely official opinion. I certainly never feel happy on a difficult question unless I have had Billy [Ormsby-Gore]'s opinion as well as that of the office.

19 February 1927: The Turkish Ambassador and his wife came to tea.... As they were going away Ferid drew me into a corner and told me he had heard rumours that in the Cabinet we were exercised in mind as to what view Turkey would take of our breaking with Russia. He assured me that it was a matter of entire indifference what we did with Russia and it certainly would not affect the friendship now so securely established between us.

21 February 1927: Down to the House where I met Winston, very truculent about the War Graves Commission about which I had a further talk with Worthy. On the other hand he has given way to my insistence on letting the Jerusalem School of Archaeology have its widow's mite of £500.

23 February 1927: Cabinet. Austen announced that Rosengolz [the Soviet *chargé d'affaires*] was going to see him in the afternoon and he wished to anticipate any argument or possible counter charges by him by anything [*sic*] in our protest at once. I demurred, pointing out that I had explained at the last Cabinet that we ought to consult the Dominions, or at any rate inform them as to its general terms, before handing in a document which was in fact the penultimate stage in the possible breaking off of relations. Austen greatly excited and protested that it was impossible to carry on any policy on these lines, that he had been unable to give an answer for nearly a week on naval disarmament so that we, the leading naval nation in the world, were hanging back while everybody else had taken their line. Salisbury, just back from Australia, was almost the only member of the Cabinet who seemed to realise that our foreign policy has got to become leisurely in its methods and accept the limitations of the new Imperial system. In the end I accepted the position and got a telegram sent off to the Dominions explaining that the necessity for anticipating a possible counter-stroke by Rosengolz made it necessary for us to act at once.

25 February 1927: CID where we discussed the future of Iraq defences. Winston, having I think been talked at a good bit by Trenchard, and beginning to realise that Iraq so far from a military embarrassment might become of great military advantage in the event of trouble with Russia, announced quite firmly that he thought that a certain number of squadrons ought always to be kept there on our charges, as part of the Imperial reserve, Iraq eventually contributing the difference between the cost of keeping them there and keeping them at home. For the rest Iraq has to pay entirely for her own defence subject to some compromised adjustment over the first few years. It is very amusing to see how Winston has gradually come round over all this. Sam Hoare backed up well having only just been in Baghdad, and so a great issue on which I expected to have to make a serious fight has gone through without any and all that remains for me is to bargain with Winston for a reasonable subsidy for the first two or three years after 1928.

28 February 1927: Went in to have a talk with the PM about my own Empire tour. . . . As regards myself I was very much bored to find that the King had received the idea very stuffily and had objected to his Ministers travelling at all.

3 March 1927: Cabinet, more talk about Russia and in particular about a recent document the authenticity of which we decided to let Douglas Hogg investigate before we took further action, but which if genuine is decidedly worse than any of the ones we quoted in our official protest.

4 March 1927: Talk with Bob Cecil and Willie [Bridgeman] in my room at the House about the naval disarmament conversations, and were quite clear that no Admiralty proposals should be trotted out until there was a full conference to consider them. Bob of course very anxious to make the whole thing as much as possible a part of the Geneva disarmament conference, Willie on the other hand anxious to get away from it and suggesting its transfer to London.

Then CID at which Austen held up his hands in horror at the thought of transferring the naval discussion from Geneva and we discussed the draft Disarmament Convention at length, very few of us really liking it though in the end we sanctioned the draft with some minor changes but with some hope that nothing would come of it all.

8 March 1927: Some talk with the PM who has now decided that he does not want to send anyone to Australia for Canberra and is still a little sticky about my own tour later, at any rate as regards to the length of time I am to take away.

We also discussed the enlargement of the Franchise and I took the opportunity of telling him that the essential thing for us was not to try and capture Liberal votes, which we had got already, but to prevent our working men drifting off to Labour. . . .

Farewell dinner to Jackie [F. S. Jackson, appointed Governor of Bengal] at which S.B. made a charming speech to which Jackie replied in very good taste and with sound thought behind it. In response to appeals Winston got up to propose the PM's health and referred to his relations of strict submission and obedience to Jackie when they were at Harrow together. S.B. in replying briefly remarked that as long as Winston's relations to him continued to be the same as they had been to Jackie in old days all would be well.

13 March 1927: Kept rather late over remnants of my box, including the problem of the defence of Afghanistan on which the General Staff India and CIGS have put up papers dealing with the matter purely locally and ignoring Persia and Iraq. Among the papers produced were Balfour's long memoranda of 1903 in connexion with the railway to Seistan and its development, reminding me of the long talk I had with him on that subject just about that time, the first occasion when I had ever met him at any rate intimately. That was the occasion when he asked me to lunch and a servant told him in a whisper there was nothing in the house except one poached egg for himself and a small sole they were frying for Lord Lansdowne who had been asked, it being August holidays and Downing St shut up except for one servant, whereupon I went out and had my own poached egg at the ABC by Westminster Bridge.

15 March 1927: Cabinet to decide our policy on the Trade Union Bill and agreed to accept Neville's ingenious proposal to graft the principle of the Lemieux Act on the clauses prohibiting the general strike. Accepted these clauses as well as those dealing with intimidation, dropped the clauses with regard to separation of funds, etc. which might be considered as interference with the internal organisation of the Trade Unions and after considerable discussion decided to include political levy, on which Winston and I were both eloquent, for once in the same direction.

16 March 1927: Cabinet with a small agenda which has so often ended in a long debate on things outside. We began with Hogg's report on the Russian documents which he had no doubt were genuine though it could no more be proved than the Zinoviev letter. He was against publication now and breaking off with Russia and so were most of the Cabinet though Winston and F.E. were in favour and I rather mildly with them. After that discussion on India's financial liability under certain headings arising out of the war, as well as the question of whether she should make an actual profit out of her troops going to Shanghai. Winston pressed very vehemently on the former point for arbitration on both, F.E. took up an absolutely *non possumus* line on the ground that India simply would not do what was wanted. I am a little afraid that these financial questions with India are going to involve us in continual trouble in the next 20 years. The position is really not unlike that between ourselves and the American colonies after 1763. I am not sure that the final solution will not be the creation of a new frontier empire with Afghanistan, Persia, etc. leaving India behind as a dominion contributing increasingly less both in money and men to a defence which will have advanced beyond her.

17 March 1927: CID on the Afghan question. The Government of India's contention that we need not stand out for the integrity of Afghan territory against Russia either on military or political grounds but confine ourselves to the Hindu Kush line was defended with considerable ability by Denys Bray whom I had not seen since Oxford days. But it seems to me throughout that there was a mixing up of a political frontier which we were obliged to keep inviolate, in virtue of our former protectorate, and of a frontier which from the point of view of military and political integrity was worth preserving under the present conditions. Trenchard alone put up any sort of military case for the present frontier on the ground that it pushed back the starting point of their aeroplanes a long way. Eventually it was agreed that a committee, including myself, should study the whole question and I got it clear from S.B. that the terms of reference would enable us to discuss Persia and the Middle Eastern situation generally which none of the staff papers had taken into account at all.

21 March 1927: Afghanistan Sub-Committee where we decided at Winston's instance to consider the military situation first proceeding on the assumption that we regarded the crossing of the Afghan frontier as a *casus belli*. I am not sure that that is the best way of proceeding. The rest of the morning was mainly taken up with heckling Bray. I hope I can get them to realise gradually that it is as much a Persian question as an Afghan one and that it would be better to sacrifice Afghanistan north of the Hindu Kush than to let Persia fall under Russian control. . . . Met Stanley [Baldwin] who told me he had had a talk with the King and that all was clear for my Empire Tour though not until the end of the session. I must now come to a definite conclusion as to whether I go with him [Baldwin] via Canada first or out by S. Africa coming back through Canada at Christmas.

22 March 1927: Saw Austen at the FO about Clementi's intimation that unless he got word to the contrary at once he would start an expedition against Bias Bay on the last piracy. Agreed to send him a telegram that he must not act without Lampson's concurrence trusting that Lampson would have given it. So far I really do not know whether the expedition has taken place or not but Lampson seems to have asked Barton at Shanghai what he thought about it instead of answering directly.

23 March 1927:   Cabinet at which we decided to drop Neville's addition to Clause (1) of the Trade Union Bill, viz. the one introducing the principle of the Lemieux Act. S.B. was strongly against it influenced by Steel-Maitland. In loyalty to Neville I expressed my regret at the idea of dropping the clause but confessed I felt rather doubtful.

28 March 1927:   Cabinet at which I raised Clementi's suggestion that we should threaten serious action against Canton if they start a campaign of assassination in Hong Kong (of which he has evidence as directed at himself and other senior officials). Austen sticky but Winston intervened eloquently on my side. In the end the matter was left to be included in whatever action we are to take about the outrages at Nanking. We then discussed leasehold enfranchisement and by a sort of understanding between Salisbury, Hogg and the PM allowed the Bill to be still further emasculated. Most of us as a matter of fact very doubtful about the wisdom of this but too ignorant about the law to uplift our voices.

Winston, Sam, Philip Lister and myself then met again at Philip Sassoon's plus F.E., who had not turned up at the Cabinet pretending that he had not known it was fixed for that morning. Winston in very good form and rather amusing on the subject of Austen's triumphs, which have been mainly forced upon him as against the policy of a purely defensive treaty with France, and Shanghai when F.E. and I had to fight for our lives to prevent the FO stopping the troops at Hong Kong.

30 March 1927:   A visit from ... Athlone['s former private secretary] to convey to me privately a suggestion made by Tielman Roes and certain other Nationalists, that Athlone should be proclaimed king of S. Africa. Cabinet at which we reversed our previous decision on the Leasehold Bill and stiffened it considerably much to Salisbury's sorrow. As for China events at Nanking have considerably gingered up Austen and we had before us an admirable report from the three Chiefs of Staff written by Hankey suggesting effective coercion of the South by holding the Yangtse against them, confiscating their fleet and if necessary also action at Canton, leaving it to Japan to do her share of the business in the North.

31 March 1927:   Then to Imperial Affairs Committee and heard the first part of Grigg's very effective statement in favour of increase of political power to the settlers in Kenya; Conference in Willie [Bridgeman]'s room about the naval disarmament question and decided to wire to the United States to say that we assumed that the conversations which are to commence in June are in fact to be a regular conference. Then a Cabinet with the usual China prelude followed by discussion of House of Lords Reform. I joined in early giving an Australian example to show the dangers ahead and insisting very strongly that the key to the problem is far-reaching reform which will make the House reasonably impartial, and that this is even more important than a restoration of powers. [L.S.A. later noted: 'It was the attempt to restore the latter that wrecked the proposals.']

1 April 1927: Cabinet at 4 on China. The C-in-C out there does not like our Chiefs of Staff proposals and they do not like his so more telegrams of inquiry as to reasons are going backwards and forwards.

6 April 1927: Cabinet at which we finally decided the House of Lords business on the basis of not much change in the Parliament Act but considerable change in the House of Lords, omitting, however, the elective proposals of Cave's Committee. My remarks at the previous Cabinet followed up by a memo written over the weekend have made them realise that the danger of the swamping of the House under constitutional references was more serious than the more use of the Parliament Act.

7 April 1927: Cabinet to which Winston unfolded his budget, a footling affair of makeshifts and windfalls with no realization of the magnitude of the financial or of the political problem before us. I gently intimated something of the sort at the end but everybody is so terrified of the fiscal question that they all said 'Hush, hush' in unison.

11 April 1927 (Windsor): After dinner the King took Worthy and myself through to a further room where we stood for nearly an hour discussing the Budget and the Trade Union Bill, with regard to which the King was very anxious that we should all speak in our constituencies before a barrage of general misrepresentation had made things impossible for us. I gather he himself does not like the Bill much, more particularly the [political] levy side of it. Later we went back into the main ante-room but the King continued talking to me about Imperial things. He has a great dislike and contempt for Mackenzie King whom he thinks a miserable creature considerably worse than Hertzog. He appears to have freely expressed the same views about him to B. at dinner.

12 April 1927: Had to go off early with Worthy for a Cabinet. . . . On the way up Worthy and I planned a very good scheme for the recasting of the House of Lords, viz. 150 selected from peers including life peers and the other 150 nominated by the Government and the opposition in proportion to their respective strengths at the last election. At the Cabinet Stanley opened with a short resumé of the position with regard to our pledges on the women's vote concluding that the only thing we could do was to give it all round at 21. Winston led the opposition with great vehemence and our opinions were then taken all the way round. I took the view with many others that 25 for both sexes would be preferable but did not think we should see it through and therefore favoured 21 and without a conference beforehand. I did not think that we should lose particularly from the party point of view and added that I thought all this strengthened very much the case for reforming the House of Lords. As for an increase in the actual size of constituencies I suggested that broadcasting would presently largely supersede ordinary platform speaking and incidentally help the party of moderation and steadiness a good deal. In the end 21 without a conference prevailed by a considerable majority. Winston very unhappy as indeed were also F.E. and several others.

13 April 1927: The Round Table dinner at Chatham House to discuss the future of East Africa. I took the view that white settlement and control could no more be stopped at the present boundaries of South Africa than they could be stopped at the Fish River and Orange River a century ago and that we have got to accept the situation that the dual system will extend from the Cape to Abyssinia.

26 April 1927: Defence of India Sub-Committee at which Milne brought forward his proposals for an Afghan campaign. The interesting thing in them was the suggestion of a really mobile small force highly mechanised and with strong air support and even air transport, to push on at once to Farah. During the discussion I strongly urged that this principle should not be applied merely at the opening stage but right through and that if it was, conscription at home would not be necessary. I also pressed strongly that on the whole northern and eastern section the one thing that mattered was having enough officers with real mountaineering knowledge to lead small forces of Afghans or Afridis and that a hundred such officers with a few thousand men could stop any Russian Army in the world crossing the Hindu Kush.

27 April 1927: Cabinet at which we agreed to give Austen and Chiefs of Staff a free hand to re-occupy Hankow. I have always felt that once we had got troops and ships at Shanghai we should be bound to come round from the policy of pure scuttle which we were following at the end of the year.

2 May 1927: Cabinet to consider the Hankow project. Lampson wants to destroy Hanchiang arsenal and not re-occupy the concession. The Admiral wants to re-occupy the concession plus British properties outside and take up 4 battalions [up the Yangtse]. The Chiefs of Staff here only want a rest[r]icted portion of two battalions and are doubtful of staying the winter. Among ourselves some of us wanted to do it as the sanction for Nanking, others entirely divorced from Nanking but on the strength of the breach of its provisions. I urged the limited operation justified by the breach of Chen's pledges of which Nanking was not the least signal instance. In the end in view of the variety of opinions we decided to do nothing by a narrow majority. No doubt we shall reconsider this a few days later.

3 May 1927: Defence of India Committee at which we discussed the problem of Afghanistan up and down. The CIGS was in favour of pushing well ahead with a highly mechanised force, Winston rather for letting the Russian tortoise stretch its head out to where we could conveniently cut it off. Winston rather left out the alternative of the Russians sitting at Herat and proceeding very slowly. We cannot afford to let them consolidate and the more highly mechanised and 'aerated' our force is the further it can afford to work from its railhead. I could not get either side to realise the full importance of effective control with small forces of all the mountain country.

4 May 1927: Saw Mont[agu] Barlow [former Conservative Minister of Labour] just back from a great tour through all the East African colonies and the Congo and back up the Nile. Very insistent on the importance of early federation but also on the difficulty of having it bossed by Kenya.... Sandeman Allen subsequently spoke to me in the House to tell me how strong the feeling was in East Africa generally for some form of federation to reassure men's minds as to Tanganyika really being integrally British.

5 May 1927: CID meeting at which we discussed Aden at some length. I offered to be responsible for the whole defence and at much less cost if they would agree to let me do it with air advice as in Iraq and Palestine. War Office horrified but I may get my way presently. In this at any rate I have a strong ally in Winston.

10 May 1927: Opening of the first Colonial Conference and addressed them on the general theme of closer co-operation and getting away from watertight compartments. The only topics I dealt with at all individually were the constitutional problem and the possibility of creating a pool for the financing of a research service. This last idea, which has been the object of calling the Conference together in my own mind, was warmly responded to by all the representatives in the subsequent remarks and has been pushed in the Press since.

11 May 1927: At the afternoon Conference Donald Cameron launched out with the bold suggestion of a single Colonial Service with common entry and rate of increments. There was some endorsement to this but the majority felt that the scheme was too ambitious and that it would be sufficient if the unified service were confined to the higher grade of research specialists and a committee was appointed to go into the whole question. The keenness at this was very satisfactory.

15 May 1927 (All Souls College, Oxford): Walked round Quad with Lionel [Curtis] discussing both the E. African problem, as regards which he thought Ned was in too great a hurry and the thing might be to send out a commission of one . . . to inquire and frame a scheme on the spot.

17 May 1927: Conference morning and afternoon. I think it was at this meeting that I gave them a general disquisition on the unsatisfactory position into which we were drifting everywhere constitutionally by following the line of least resistance, i.e. introducing elected members into a council in a minority and then conceding a majority, without really thinking out whether that involved a training in responsibility or a training in factiousness. I gave them a good deal of history on the unsatisfactory character of representative government generally as contrasted with responsible government.

19 May 1927: Cabinet. Jix had prepared a very careful and rather colourless statement about the Arcos finds. Austen thereupon produced a much more effective one by C. [Admiral Sir Mansfield Cumming, Head of the Secret Service] bringing out the salient points more clearly. We preferred this but immediately realised that its publication would there and then commit us to breaking off relations with Russia. Salisbury strongly demurred to our doing so without having a little time for discussion of the decision in all its bearings, a view which others were inclined to agree, while I had to point out that we could not take so vital a decision without at any rate notifying the Dominions a few days beforehand and giving them time to put objections if they had any. In the end we decided to make Jix defer his answer until next Tuesday giving me time to warn the Dominions of what is likely to happen and allowing upon another Cabinet meeting as well as for more careful drafting of the reply.

20 May 1927: CID discussion on our policy at the Naval Disarmament Conference. My feeling is that Beatty and Willie [Bridgeman] are prepared to go almost dangerously far in contemplating the possibility of agreeing to some fixed number in cruisers and smaller craft.

23 May 1927: Cabinet at which we decided definitely to get rid of both Arcos and Chesham House and settled the general form of the statement that Stanley was to make.

When Amery had been Milner's Under Secretary at the Colonial Office, he had tried hard to secure the unification of the three East African territories of Kenya, Uganda, and Tanganyika, but all that Milner would permit was a clause in the mandate for Tanganyika expressly providing for the possibility of federation. 'The problem', as Amery recalled in his memoirs, 'was not altogether simple.' Uganda had a relatively advanced native civilisation, with what could almost be described as a feudal parliament, Kenya a more primitive one, while the paramountcy of native interests had been written into the Tanganyika mandate. In Kenya there was a small but vigorous white settler population, vocal in defence of its right and duty to rule the Africans, and jealous of the possibility that any other settler, be he Jew or Indian, could make a similar claim. The Colonial Office had waged a rearguard action against the pretensions of the white settler, but, step by step, they had established a degree of 'elective representation' and effective segregation in land terms. Their prejudices had been confirmed by successive Governors, who, in defiance of the Colonial Office's view, had told the settlers that East Africa was primarily for European development. That view had dominated the report of the post-war Economic Commission issued in March 1919, and Milner had been driven to condemn publicly its references to the Asian community. It could not, however, prevent the transfer of African land to new settlers.

White settler policy provoked opposition from both the missionaries, who spoke for nascent African opinion, and the Government of India, who sought equality of rights for the Indian settlers in East Africa. Milner did not halt Indian immigration, although he continued to endorse the reservation of land ownership in the Highlands for the European settler. Nor did he exclude the Indian from representation on the legislative council. His successor, Churchill, pointed to a future for East Africa as 'a characteristically and distinctively British Colony' looking to ultimate self-government, but anyone who took this to mean that white interests should be dominant clearly failed to note that he reiterated Rhodes's principle 'equal rights for all civilised men'. The Colonial and Indian Offices reached an accord that there would be no ban on Asian immigration and that there would be a common electoral roll. The white settlers made preparations to resist.

It fell to Churchill's successor, the Duke of Devonshire, Colonial Secretary in Baldwin's first administration, to summon both the representatives of the Europeans and the Indians to London in July 1923 and to impose terms which pleased neither. There was to be no ban on immigration, and segregation in the townships was to come to an end. On the other hand the Highlands would stay 'white'. The common electoral roll was withdrawn and the Indians confined to five elected representatives only. Responsible government was, however, ruled out for the immediate future. Most striking of all was the Duke's rediscovery of the African population and his assertion that not only must their interests be paramount, but that Whitehall was their only trustee. The exact relationship of the interests of the other communities with the African remained to be worked out.

The white settlers refused to accept their defeat, and they sought to exploit the idea of 'Closer Union' to their own end. The idea had come to the fore in the House of Commons in April 1924, and the settlers' immediate suspicions of a Labour Government initiative were converted by their leader, Lord Delamere, into a constructive attempt to influence the report of the Commission set up by the Colonial Secretary, J. H. Thomas, and chaired by Ormsby-Gore. The Commission echoed the European settlers' view that they were the proper trustees for the Africans, but recommended also a Native Lands Trust Board to safeguard African interests. All this they set in the framework of closer co-operation between the three colonies to be achieved by regular Governors' Conferences.

This was the position Amery inherited, and when the Governor of Kenya died in February 1925 he appointed a close personal friend, Sir Edward Grigg, as his successor with a specific remit to bring about Federation in the interests of economic development. An early practical step was Cabinet approval at the beginning of 1926 for the unification of the railways, harbours and steamships of Kenya and Uganda under Grigg's control: he had been appointed High Commissioner of Transport for both countries with a view to separating the finances of the railways from those of Kenya. In practice there remained considerable suspicion of Grigg's dual role, which was quite unfair. He was conscious himself also of the difficulty inherent in his role as chairman of the Governors' Conference, which met for the first time in January 1926, and at which the idea of a central executive for the three territories came under discussion. Gowes, the Governor of Uganda, favoured such an idea. Cameron, the Governor of Tanganyika, because of his concern for the interests of the African and the need to complete the Tabora–Mwanza railway, to which his fellow Governors were opposed, was deeply sceptical about the whole idea. Grigg himself was at this stage looking for something short of federal union, and thought a central executive the road forward.

So far as Kenya was concerned, Grigg found that he had to act with the consent of the European settlers. The official majority on the Legislative Council lacked cohesion, many of its members siding by training and instinct with the settlers. Grigg therefore suggested to Amery in September 1926 the introduction of an unofficial majority, with a reserve power left to the Governor. Amery was not, however, prepared to weaken Britain's 'control over a difficult situation'.* In their election manifesto in December the Europeans took up the demand, encouraged by Grigg's overt sympathy for their cause.

Delamere had made an elected majority on Kenya's legislative council the key to federation, which he was now prepared to further by calling a series of conferences of the settler leaders as a prelude and parallel to the meetings of the East African Governors. Grigg for his part was ready to move on from European control in the economic field, which the Governors' Conference had endorsed in January 1926, to 'the complementary development of native and non-native communities' in the political field. He persuaded the Secretary of the International Missionary Council, J. H. Oldham, that the influence of the settlers in Kenya was now such that the idea of an Imperial trusteeship for the native races, which could neither be delegated nor shared, was quite impracticable. It had, in his view, already been surrendered, and he sought formally to associate the white colonists more closely in the trust. He remained unsympathetic to Indian aspirations, however, and by 1928 was being charged in the sub-continent with being 'the Arch Anti-Indian of Kenya'.†

Grigg made representations to Amery late in 1926 and early in 1927 about the difficulties and ambiguities of his position. In London in March he submitted a memorandum on the East African scene which embodied his recommendation that there should be an unofficial majority on the legislative council, which would include nominees for native interests, and which would lead to a shared trusteeship for the African population. Amery decided to take the idea of closer union forward by means of a small commission which would visit East Africa and advise on how it could be brought about. In his memoirs he notes that 'it became clear that to secure Cabinet consent to actual Federation I should have to produce some authoritative backing independent of the view of the Colonial Office' (*My Political Life*, II, p. 361), but he accompanied his recommen-

---

*Grigg to L.S.A., 21 September 1926; L.S.A. to Grigg, 22 September. Cf. G. Bennett, *Kenya: A Political History* (Oxford University Press, 1963), p. 59.

†R. E. Gregory, *India and East Africa* (Oxford University Press, 1971), p. 294.

dation of the Commission to the Cabinet with a draft 'declaration of policy by His Majesty's Government in favour of closer union between the territories of Central and Eastern Africa, more particularly in regard to the development of transport and communications, Customs tariffs and Customs administration, scientific research and defence'. He was immediately under pressure from Birkenhead on Indian interests, and was compelled also to delete from his proposed White Paper on 'Future Policy in Regard to Eastern Africa'* his suggestion that elected representatives in Kenya should be associated with the executive functions of government. Hankey thought the proposal would have gone through from sheer boredom had it not been for Joynson-Hicks who 'took fright . . . and said that we were laying the foundations of a new Dominion and that a Cabinet Committee ought to look into it'.† In committee Amery had to give further ground in response to the argument that the Government ought to reserve 'a certain amount of liberty of action'.‡ There was clearly some feeling that he was trying to rush a decision.

Even so the White Paper indicated that closer union appeared desirable to the Government and announced a special commission to recommend 'as to whether, either by federation or some other form of closer union, more effective co-operation between the difficult Governments in Central and Eastern Africa may be secured', to consider which territories could be brought within such a closer union, and to recommend on the consequent changes in the power and composition of the various legislative councils as a result of the establishment of a common authority. Two other aims were mentioned under this last heading, the association of the immigrant communities with the responsibilities and trusteeship of government, and the more direct representation of native interests. More sinister in the view of many was the proposal that the Commission should also suggest how the complementary development of native and non-native communities could best be applied in the political as well as the economic sphere. In the face of strong criticism in the Commons, Amery denied that there was any attempt to reverse the Devonshire policy, and indeed he had specifically made clear the Government's commitment to the underlying principles of the White Paper of 1923. Nevertheless it is clear that the White Paper of 1927 did envisage the European community sharing in the trusteeship and implied a speedy move towards self-government, and that in these respects existing policy was modified. Nor, with the stress now placed on the complementary development of the communities, did it seem that paramountcy had quite the force it did in

*Published as Cmd. 2904.
†Thomas Jones, *Whitehall Diary*, II, p. 105.
‡Cab. 23/55, f. 128 (Cabinet of 6 July 1927).

1923. There appeared to have been a revolution in policy and suspicions were aroused. More to the point, in the event, was Indian suspicion of the Commission and of Grigg's 'unholy alliance with Lord Delamere and his henchmen'.* That was to be the rock on which Amery's dreams of one African federation foundered.

Diary

30 May 1927: Talk with Henn about East Africa generally, as to which his recommendation is that a commission or commissioner should spend some months on the spot to frame a definite scheme both of federation and if necessary of constitutional change in Kenya.

31 May 1927: We managed by 6.30 to agree our [Conference] report. Thus ended a most successful experiment. The Colonial Office Conference has come to stay and meanwhile it has already achieved, I think, the one thing I had particularly in my mind in summoning it, namely the acceptance of the principle of a joint fund and a joint service.

1 June 1927: Cabinet, where we discussed many things, more particularly at the end the implementing of the Blanesburgh Committee Report [reforming the unemployment insurance system] on which I supported Steel-Maitland against Winston both as to the need of carrying out the Report and as to the financial unsoundness of the employers' contribution. We left the matter unsettled, and I walked down to the House with Stanley for lunch. We discussed the Athlone question and I put to him the only possible objection that occurred to me, namely that if Labour came in and Hertzog together they might weakly accept the idea of a local Governor-General. S.B. thought the contingency remote and that if it did occur Thomas could be trusted to hold his own. Balfour had expressed to me some anxieties about my going to South Africa while the flag question was so critical, but I told him that I could trust myself not to put my foot into it in public and believed I might help to a possible compromise in private. . . . [Talk] with Austen as to telling Iraq that we would definitely support her over the League of Nations in 1932 on which he was prepared a little reluctantly to support me.†

---

*Presidential Address to Seventh East African Indian National Congress (quoted by Bennett, *Kenya*, p. 62).

†It was proposed that the mandate should be terminated at that date and Iraq seek membership of the League as an independent sovereign power. The decision was made public in September 1929 and Iraq admitted to the League in 1932.

8 June 1927: 3 hours' conference at the office with the E. African govern-ors and secretaries on the problem of federation and made quite satisfactory progress, Grigg and Cameron only sparring occasionally.

9 June 1927: More E. African conference at which we came to the general conclusion that a commission ought to be sent out and that the British Government should make an announcement to that effect indicating definitely that federation was in view and that it would involve constitu-tional changes, also that we meant to develop the dual policy politically as well as economically. Threw on Billy the job of producing a suitable Cabinet memorandum as well as a short statement for the public while I went off to the Clyde.

13 June 1927: East African conference for which Billy had prepared a really admirable paper with conclusions which we straightened out satisfactorily by lunch time. Ned [Grigg] rather disappointed that he has not got things all his own way as he had hoped but still not ill content to have got a move on; myself quite satisfied to have got so much move on in the time and to have got them all in agreement.

15 June 1927: Cabinet on House of Lords and other matters. I cannot get them to see that the key to the whole question is thorough going reform both to prevent future swamping and also to justify in the public eye any subsequent increase of powers. They all seem to think as if objections on the part of the Lords themselves would kill the proposal whereas I am convinced that if it were put to them with real conviction it would be accepted and certainly accepted if we put it through the House of Com-mons and showed we meant business.

16 June 1927: Walter Elliot and Billy came to see me about the attack on the EMB which the Treasury are launching and offered to resign at once if they got their way. I assured them that there was no danger, but that I would not hesitate to use them as a card if I had to make the same threat myself. Short meeting of China Committee after which I told Stanley that I hoped he would not allow a lot of wasted time and ill feeling to take place over this EMB business as I wished him to understand from the outset that I was not going to make any concessions. The only thing he could say was 'wait till you see the actual letter'.

22 June 1927: A few minutes with Grigg very anxious to have his report published even with excisions.

25 June 1927: Lunched with Lady Lavery to meet O'Higgins. There were a good many others there and during lunch I sat between her and Mrs Ronnie Greville, but afterwards I had a long talk with O'Higgins who is very tired but quite prepared to go ahead and confident of his ability to carry things through though anxious about finance and a little credulous at public ingratitude.* I told him he must not worry about the latter and that P[roportional] R[epresentation] had no doubt helped the process of disintegration among his supporters though it would later on perhaps prevent their ever being snowed under completely.

27 June 1927: Meeting of Civil Research Committee on unemployment in mines at the PM's room which gave me an opportunity of raising the possibility of training the younger miners for oversea settlement. Advertising Association's dinner to Sir W. Crawford at which I supported McCurdy who was in the Chair in praise of the guest. McCurdy said that Crawford like so many others who had risen to fame had started from that wonderful springboard Scotland. I retorted that this was unjust to Scotsmen who needed no springboard but like fleas owed their progress in the world entirely to their own healthy appetites and innate powers of propulsion.

28 June 1927: Looked in at the National Unionist gathering to see what they thought about the House of Lords question. This was moved by Marriott and presently a mildly hostile amendment was introduced by Shirley Benn which practically amounted to telling the Government that their scheme was a bad one and that they ought not to have introduced it without previous submission to some sort of party caucus in the Commons. Selborne dealt with this very moderately and sensibly but was followed by Duff Cooper who delivered a vehement and wholly unfair attack. I thought I was the only member of the Government present so I jumped up in order to counteract the obvious effect his eloquent denunciation was producing and swung the whole meeting round by explaining what the real principles were on which we were working and that we should of course do a good deal in the way of discussion and consultation before we actually produced a scheme in black and white. The original motion was accordingly carried. . . . We then adjourned and I found that Jix and Walter Guinness had also been on the platform. All the same I think I did well to intervene.

29 June 1927: Cabinet at which I had 4 items on the agenda two of

---

*The general election which had just taken place in Eire had seen the strength of the Government Party, Cumann na nGaedheal, reduced from sixty-three seats to forty-six in a legislative of 153 deputies. Fifty-one of the deputies, however, were Republicans who would not take the oath.

which, Iraq and Aden, were dropped at the outset, at Austen's request until he should return. Next came E. Africa which I had hoped to get through without discussion but Jix was frightened about the powers that might be given to the white settler and he and Salisbury ran off the rails on an *obiter dictum* about unofficials* on the Executive being responsible for particular departments and scented diarchy. In the end I had to agree to an emergency committee to look into the thing. I feared even worse over the New Hebrides where the mere mention of sending 400 Chinese labourers paralysed the whole Cabinet, thoroughly frightened by the House of Lords situation, into unreasoning refusal, Stanley himself saying that every Chinaman would lose us a seat. This with 200,000 Chinamen going annually to Singapore! The only idea they had to offer was that we should throw our share of the New Hebrides at Australia's head, but I do not think that Austen will like the friction that probably will result from this. This is a poor outcome after sending a special commission by three Governments to consider the situation.

30 June 1927: Conference with Grigg, Wilson, Billy and Strachey on the proposed Kenya native land trusts and straightened things out on the basis that the trusts should control the use and disposal of the land but actual ownership still being vested in the Crown and that the trusts should be composed of two officials, one in the chair, and two or three non officials appointed for a longish term of years. I also got Ned to agree that it was better not to publish his report, and so he went off on the whole reasonably satisfied with his expedition here.

4 July 1927: Cabinet Committee on East Africa which I squared up in three quarters of an hour with a slight modification of one or two words in the terms of reference. Cabinet at which I got through my views about Iraq and the League of Nations again by consenting to trifling modification of words in the instructions to Dobbs. On the other hand I found the general sense of the Cabinet against me over the proposed answer to be given to the Imam of Yemen to his offer to come and negotiate and had to promise to circulate a milder reply for the next meeting. We discussed briefly the answer to be given in the House on the 6th to the Labour vote of censure on the House of Lords and then we got on to the difficult question of Geneva and the American claim to parity. Winston and Beatty both wanted to water down or explain away Willie [Bridgeman]'s latest announcement in such a sense as to mean that if the Americans built as many cruisers as we did we should feel obliged to build more. That may be true for the ultimate strategic needs but would be a fatal

*'Unofficials' were representatives of white settlers, elected or otherwise selected.

thing to say now, would break up the Conference and provoke a general competition in armaments. In the end we decided to tell Howard [British Ambassador in Washington] to repeat Willie's statement making it clear that we must be free to build what we need in the way of cruisers, but have no objection to America building as many if she thinks she needs them. The difficulty I see is that if Japan asks for three-fifths of any total which we may possibly consent to in cruisers, or even a lesser proportion, America will feel bound to build level with us.

6 July 1927: Cabinet at which I got through the E. African business. Had my proposed telegram to Yemen further toned down and at which we discussed at length the difficult situation arising at Geneva from the American demands. . . .

10 July 1927: Home just before dinner to be rung up with the news of Kevin O'Higgins' assassination. Poor fellow, he had many attractive personal qualities as well as real courage and patriotism. What a curse hangs over Ireland. To unravel it would be like the tale of Atreidae, but I fear the starting point is a fault in the blood, some element of ape-like savagery which has survived every successive flood of settlers.

11 July 1927: Lunched alone with the Duke and Duchess of York at their new Piccadilly house to talk over his Australian tour and found him much easier and more interesting on the subject with her to stimulate him than he had been when he first called on me. He is keen to keep in touch with Dominion affairs and I suggested that I would send him occasional papers and also encouraged him to do some entertaining. Princess Elizabeth was sent in afterwards for my inspection and greeted me with great enthusiasm. . . .

Longish talk with Creswell about S. African affairs including the Flag business. The best case he makes for Hertzog is that the latter is trying to get rid of secession entirely and feared that if the two Malans and another minister went over the Flag Bill that would create an active secessionist party and capture many of the Boers, and that by giving way to them on the Flag and keeping them in the Government he would really be holding them for the Empire! . . .

Civil Research Committee on coal unemployment in the PM's room. Lovat was there and stated the case for doing something by way of Oversea Settlement. The PM took me over to lunch and drink Burgundy at St Stephens Club and we had a useful talk on a number of points; among others I referred to the question of the EMB and told him that my letter of a fortnight or so ago was my last word and that I could not possibly concur in what I regarded as a breach of faith to the Dominions. I added that it was not fair that Government pledges should be regarded as departmental expenditure of my own for which I alone had to put up the fight and that it was his task rather than mine to sit upon Winston in this matter. He seemed to concur and said he would speak to Winston, but I am still afraid of trouble when I am gone; certainly Winston referred to the matter in his most aggressive mood at the CID this morning (July 14th).

13 July 1927: Memorial Service to O'Higgins. These RC services strike me as curiously barbaric and in the direct line of descent from ancient Egypt. Short Cabinet at which we discussed the further developments at Geneva. What it comes to is that a conference convened by the Americans for the reduction of expenditure on naval armaments is becoming a conference for increasing naval armaments in order to satisfy America's claim to be equal with us in every class of vessel. The unscrupulousness of the American Press at Geneva has gone beyond all limits. It all confirms me in my own conviction that disarmament conferences are fundamentally wrong and that the only real way to bring about disarmament is peaceful policy.

14 July 1927: CID at which we chiefly discussed Geneva and decided to ask Bridgeman to come home and discuss things with us before he irrevocably committed us to an overhead total. . . . A long Conference with Dobbs, Billy, Sammy and Shuckburgh on Iraq, our general conclusion being in favour of negotiating for a new Treaty which should both satisfy the League of Nations now as fulfilling our mandatory obligations and yet not require to be dropped and replaced when Iraq enters the League.

16 July 1927: George Lloyd and Blanche came to lunch and I had a long talk with George afterwards about Egyptian affairs. He is still terribly upset over what he considered the readiness of the FO to let him down during the last crisis and not yet recovered from the nervous strain of practically disobeying instructions. He was very anxious for plenty of Government support for what he thinks may be a decisive crisis in the winter and badly wants to address the Cabinet again.

18 July 1927: Questions and subsequently Civil Research Committee in the PM's room on the coal situation and with Lovat's help got sanction to go ahead with a scheme for harvesters to Canada, as well as a move on with some of our other training ideas.

20 July 1927: Conference with Trenchard, Dobbs, and our people on the line to be taken with regard to [King] Feisal [of Iraq] and his demand for a revision of the Treaty, and modified the proposed telegram to Iraq to meet Air Ministry fears that we were going too far without Cabinet sanction. Cabinet at which I successfully got through the remission of the Cyprus tribute* largely on the strength of the convincing eloquence of an old memorandum of Winston's which I had exhumed and which Dawe incorporated very skilfully in his memorandum. Most of the Cabinet were already convinced of the iniquity of the tribute before I spoke and Stanley had had a letter from Stamfordham to say that the King was very keen we should drop it. So after a short show of fight Winston surrendered. Thus ends an old injustice and incidentally Storrs will really be given a chance to make something of the Island. We also got through the recommendations as to representation [by High Commissioners] in the Dominions, Winston reserving to himself the right to object to any expenditure exceeding £10,000. After that came the really critical thing for me, namely the proposal to annex the whole unexpended balance of the EMB asking the Dominions for their consent. I had had no notice until that morning that the question was to be raised at all and from what S.B. had said thought he had told Winston to drop it. I was taken at some disadvantage and had no figures with me or indeed a clear idea what it was that was asked for except generally to reverse the whole principle on which the EMB had gone. Winston weighed in very sarcastically and took the line that it was no business of mine to object to the PM sending a telegram to the Dominions as the Dominions Secretary was only a post office in these matters and the real responsibility rested with the PM. I replied vigorously on merits and finished up by saying that after all the responsibility at the last resort might be the PM's but a colleague could not necessarily be bound to associate himself with it. This was taken as a direct threat of resignation and to some extent as a veto on the discussion and considerably flustered and agitated the Cabinet, who knowing nothing of the merits of the case and having never seen any papers were inclined to think me unreasonable. The discussion went on for some time and I was able to gather that what Winston wanted for the moment was this year's money only and not a general abandonment of the principle of carry forward, a proposal to which I was quite willing to agree if the money were eventually brought back. We finally broke up in some little agitation, myself particularly annoyed with S.B. for definitely siding against me when I had certainly got the impression at dinner with him a week before that he agreed with the arguments in my long letter to him of nearly a month ago which had never been answered. . . . [After lunch saw] Billy Gore, Walter Elliot and Lovat all very agitated about the EMB situation and prepared to resign and make a row. . . . Neville came in and earnestly appealed to

*Tribute was payable by the Government of Cyprus under the Treaty of Berlin, 1878.

me not to push things too far. I was able to convince him that really my case was reasonable and he agreed he would support me on the lines that I should insist on eventual restitution of the money as and when required, not naming however a fixed date or scheme of re-payment. I got over Tallents and his financial man from the EMB and worked out to my satisfaction that I could certainly do without the money for the next two or three years. Saw S.B. again and convinced him that I had gone the furthest length I could and that if we could not agree on that I would go and my team with me. When the Cabinet met we first of all discussed the appointment of the Indian Commission* on which F.E. made a second reading speech lasting exactly an hour which could have been done equally well in 20 minutes. After we had agreed to F.E.'s proposals for the Parliamentary Commission and no Indians but to meet an Indian delegation afterwards, Philip brought up the appeal of the Iron and Steel industry [for protection] and practically suggested that we should tell them we could do nothing for them in this Parliament. In other circumstances I should have made a fight over this though I think I should have been practically alone, the Cabinet only thinking of the inconvenience of raising the issue and not thinking at all of the real seriousness of the problem, though S.B. remarked quietly that he thought the whole problem of safeguarding would be the one we should have to face before the next election. Walter Guinness in his fear of being asked to protect agriculture has become an almost fanatical Free Trader, and as for Philip he is hopeless. However, I had immediate diplomatic work to do and held my peace. Next came EMB and I opened up with an explanation of the way in which I had been treated over the matter, a proposal sprung on me by the Economic Committee to which I had never been summoned and before which I had never been asked to present a case, a long reasoned reply from myself never having been seen in the Economic Committee or anybody and a month of silence at the end of which I had some reason for assuming that things were all right; if I had unintentionally in my annoyance created the impression that I wished to veto the ordinary give and take of argument in Cabinet by threatening the embarrassment of resignation at the outset of the discussion I unreservedly apologised to my colleagues; I then stated my terms as reasonably as I could saying that I was quite prepared to urge the Dominions to agree in the six hundred thousand being short issued on the understanding that they would be available

---

*The Statutory Commission of Inquiry, which was to be chaired by Sir John Simon, into the reforms made by the Government of India Act of 1919, which had established partial self-government in the provinces. This Act had provided for a decennial review, but at Birkenhead's prompting the Government advanced the date of the inquiry and decided that the Commission should be composed entirely of parliamentarians. Indian opinion was outraged and at the prompting of both the chairman designate and Ramsay MacDonald, it was agreed that the Commission should consult with a committee selected by the Indian legislature.

again, after the end of the present Parliament as and when required by the growth of the EMB. The reference to the present Parliament satisfied Winston, to whom Neville had also spoken helpfully in the interval, and my proposal was accepted together with a definite proviso that this was to be no precedent for asking for a reduction of the million next year or in future years or for any change in the principle of the carry forward. Net result [was] that I have secured in the Cabinet resolution a considerable protection against Treasury designs on the whole principle of the EMB in the future at the cost of having to ask the Dominions to agree to a variation as regards this year's finance, and having to beg separately for the money back in the next Parliament if we are still in office. At any rate my lads will be reasonably safe during my absence though Warren Fisher is out definitely to smash the EMB and has said so. . . . Afterwards I had a long talk with Winston about reminiscences of old days and altogether very friendly. He is convinced that this Empire tour can be made a big thing and I think rather envies me the opportunity. He also talked a bit about Geneva on which he is all out for defying the Yanks and saying that we will not allow anyone to build up a parity with us in small cruisers. I do not see how we can say this after what we have made Willie say already, nor can I understand the consistency between this and Winston's attempt to cut down the Navy Estimates. The only argument I gather is that he thinks that if we tell the Yanks sharply to mind their own business and not to presume to compete with us at sea they will take it lying down and we can then afford not to build more than a minimum ourselves.

21 July 1927: To the Admiralty and had a short talk with Willie, afterwards writing to Stanley to say that he could not ask Willie to eat his words and that anyway our only chance is to accept parity hoping that the Americans will not build or that the Senate will throw out the agreement anyway. Back to Buckingham Palace for a farewell audience with HM who was most friendly, keen on the whole object and anxious to get occasional personal letters from me. He was anxious to know whether the vote for the expense had been criticised and still very excited at Kirkwood's having criticised the expenses for the Duke of York's tour vowing he would never again expose any member of his family to such insults.

The Amerys reached Cape Town on 8th August. In *My Political Life* (II, pp. 402–73) Amery has provided a very full account of his Empire tour. No attempt, therefore, will be made to repeat all the topographical and tourist detail of Amery's diaries in the entries which follow.

Diary

10 August 1927 (Pretoria) : Had a general preliminary talk with Hertzog about our future subjects of discussion, . . . had a long talk with Smuts who is anxious about affairs but confident about the outcome of things in the long run. He looks thin and rather older but in great condition. His supporters are all confident that they will win the referendum but he is by no means sure of the result. . . .

15 August 1927 (Salisbury) : An hour and a half with Ministers: our first item was the land report on which I agreed entirely with their desire to have things put through as quickly as possible but had a long argument on the disposal of the 17 million acres of unallotted land as to which I wished them to give a guarantee that at least 50% would ultimately go to the natives, an easy guarantee to give really as most of it is the low lying land unsuited to European farming. Both Chancellor and Sir H. Taylor, the Native Commissioner, favoured this. The Ministers were rather sticky though I think they may agree in the end.*

Their next topic was the possibility of Northern Rhodesia being amalgamated with them on which I discussed all the various possible solutions indicating that if there were any question of their joining with Northern Rhodesia that would only apply to the western part, the eastern going with Nyasaland. I refused to give any definite lead beyond saying that no door was finally closed in any direction. This subject was very much to the fore in every section of public opinion in Southern Rhodesia. They feel so determined to have nothing to do with the Union in view of the present attitude over the flag that they wish to build up Rhodesia as a big buffer state, a dominion of its own, thoroughly British in character, and their general economic success in the last 2 or 3 years makes them feel that they can stand the burden of bringing Northern Rhodesia up to their general level and presently secure the profits of Northern Rhodesian mineral developments. The more ambitious would like to incorporate not only the whole of the north but also Nyasaland and form a single big block.† My own view is that while a separate South central state may be

---

*The Southern Rhodesia Lands Commission appointed in 1926 had revealed that the alienable land outside the native reserves created in 1915 was rapidly passing into European ownership while the reserves could not hold the growing population for long. There seemed a clear need to secure to the African enough land to contain the growing population, and this was eventually done by the creation of the Native Purchase Area under the Land Apportionment Act of 1931.

†Amalgamation became the cause of Godfrey Huggins and his Reform Party, and became the subject of the Bledisloe Commission, which reported in 1939. After the war the idea of federation eventually superseded that of amalgamation and the three territories were federated in 1953. The Federation of Rhodesia and Nyasaland finally broke up ten years later.

desirable for a time Rhodesia's ultimate destiny still is with the Union and may help to keep the Union straight. Consequently an enlarged Rhodesia ought not to be carried further than we are prepared to see the Union ultimately extend.

18 August 1927 (Bulawayo): An hour and a half of *indaba*. The Matabele are very different from the Mashona. For one thing lighter coloured many of them with distinctly Semitic or almost European features, much quicker witted politically and more prepared to hold their own. They spoke standing and with a good deal of gesture and eloquence. The first chief, a heavy solid old boy with wise face, who had fought against us in '96, simply asked for more education. The next Mbutu, very smart in khaki and leather gaiters, made a long and eloquent speech on the need for land, and the rest of the speeches were on that theme or on the iniquities of being asked to dip their cattle and pay for doing so. . . . At last I got my chance for a reply and told them the land question would soon be definitely settled, pointed out from my own knowledge of the state of affairs in 1902 what a terrible disaster cattle disease could be and said that bitter medicine was better than dying. They took my speech very well but at the end old Mbutu got up with one more grievance namely his not being allowed to brew as much Kaffir beer as he wished, illustrating with delightful pantomime and provoking immense merriment and a gleam of white teeth transforming all the dusky faces. The announcement of a distribution of cattle and beer disposed of this argument and so to lunch. The *indaba* impressed me very much both with the virility and the intelligence of the Matabele and also with the fact that they were sitting round me at the very spot where some of them sat before Lobengalu himself.

20 August 1927 (Livingstone, Northern Rhodesia): After tea I had some talk with two Natal members, Nicholls and O'Brien, who wished to consult me about what they could do about the flag business. I urged them very earnestly to give no countenance to any talk of secession or any illegal action, reminding them of the unfortunate consequences in our own experience of our attitude with regard to Ulster. Their business was to confine themselves to organising real effective opposition on constitutional lines. I also had a long talk with [Leopold] Moore who was rather disappointed that I could not let him announce categorically that I would veto any idea of union with Southern Rhodesia. I told him my mind was in no way made up as to any of the possible alternative solutions but assuring him that at any rate nothing would be done before I considered the report of the Hilton Young Commission. I encouraged him to think that if they got out of Treasury control they might make

N[orthern] R[hodesia] a colony and put it in the way of raising loans on
good terms. I had some talk with Goode [the acting Administrator of
Northern Rhodesia] afterwards on N.R. affairs generally. I gather the
officials are all for joining northwards [East Africa] and eastwards
[Nyasaland] to keep under the Colonial Office with its good pay, etc.
The settlers mostly are for union with S.R.

6 September 1927: Arrived at Pretoria about 10 o'clock and drove
straight to Government House and had some talk both on the Protectorate
situation and on the Union political situation with Athlone before lunch. . . .
At three o'clock I had my first business talk with Hertzog. We began with
the Protectorates and I told him very definitely that I had come to the
conclusion that any question of a transfer of Swaziland or of the European
blocks in Bechuanaland was out of the question for some time to come. I
had expected some difficulty but the whole thing went through most
amicably.

7 September 1927: Spent the whole morning with Hertzog dealing with
every kind of problem of representation at both ends. . . . [At a Government dinner] I think I must have made some impression upon him
[Hertzog] at any rate for he immediately began opening up to me on the
flag question which I had carefully avoided discussing with him up till
then. We had quite a good half hour's talk and we left it with an invitation
from him that we should continue to discuss it further. After dinner
Duncan came back to Government House and we had a good hour's talk
mainly on the flag question. Duncan strikes me as a little weak on the
subject and inclined to accept almost everything that would include a
small Union Jack somewhere. He thought my suggestion of the Union
Jack flown permanently as South Africa's Imperial flag, coupled with the
re-arrangement of the present flag proposal so as to bring the stars outside
and all the flags into the shield, with a further option of a combination
flag, far better than they could possibly hope for.

9 September 1927: I had got up early in the morning and written a long
letter to Hertzog about the flag question and before dinner wrote out a
memorandum containing a suggested scheme for the flag difficulty.

10 September 1927: Conference with H.E. [Athlone] and Hertzog . . . on
the proper communication of information to the G[overnor] G[eneral].
Hertzog was most reasonable on this and I think we have laid down lines
which ought to secure the position in the future and which every Government will no doubt concur in. Lunched at Government House and afterwards went for a drive of an hour and a half with Hertzog. . . . He was

anxious to discuss the European situation and is very much afraid of the French. Coming back I opened again on the flag question. I had previously discussed this with Athlone and Clifford and decided first of all not to send my letter but to use it as the substance of my talk and secondly also not to use my memorandum but to leave it (with the reference to the combination flag taken out) for Athlone to use later on. Our talk was on the whole useful. Hertzog was much impressed by the line I took about the Union Jack being flown regularly as South Africa's own Imperial flag. He made a lot of to do about the threat of his colleagues to resign if he dropped the original Bill. I pointed out that it was quite different, only expanding one of the provisions of that Bill to give the Union Jack its regular place alongside the National flag. I laid great stress on the real power he had in the country if he would only lead. I believe he is really taken with the idea of solving the difficulty in this way. . . . Anyhow he thanked me warmly for having spoken and for the whole line I had taken throughout my visit.

18 September 1927 (Stellenbosch): I reminded [Sir Thomas] Smartt of the first occasion I had met him, at dinner at Rhodes' a month or so before the South African War, when I stood up against Rhodes and all his political satellites in declaring that the Boers would fight and when Smartt had been the only person to support me. On that occasion Rhodes had bet Smartt 3–1 in £50 that there would be no war and the day they came away after the siege of Kimberley Rhodes suddenly remembered and gave Smartt £150 worth of diamonds which he set in a star and produced as confirmation of our story. [Amery left South Africa by sea on 24 September, reaching W. Australia on 10 October.]

14 October 1927 (Western Australia): Went back to Government House with Collier [Prime Minister of Western Australia] . . . for an hour and a half's detailed discussion on . . . suggestion that we should tackle under the migration agreement the whole of the block 20 miles by 200 miles between the present limit of settlement south of the main line and the railway from Southern Cross to Esperance. The scheme appeals to me strongly as a possibility of doing something tangible and making sure that we do get in extra settlers and find work for them from the start instead of frittering our money away on subsidising the ordinary activities of the State Governments.

On 22 October Amery opened the new bridge over the Murray in the course of touring the development there, and on 25 October he reached Melbourne. He left next day for Tasmania, where he discussed the economic position of the island with its premier, Lyons. He returned to Melbourne on 30 October. Paterson, the Minister of Markets, had accompanied him to Tasmania, and as a result of their talks Amery thought (as noted in his diary entry for 30 October) there was 'no doubt real trend in favour of getting away from the present exaggerated protectionism' in Australia's economic policy.

Diary

31 October 1927: Two and a half hours' talk with Ministers chiefly on migration; all of them fairly sticky and one old boy, Prendergast, convinced that all migrants were criminals or paupers. His extreme views I think helped a good deal to make the others realise the absurdity of the position.

1 November 1927: At 10.30 Bruce came in and he and Johnny [Stonehaven] and myself had a good talk about routine arrangements for keeping the G[overnor] G[eneral] informed. Bruce was most helpful and reasonable on all this and it is a good thing to have got two Dominions straightened out on this question.

3 November 1927: Arrived at Canberra in time for breakfast with the Bruces at their very nice little new Prime Minister's residence, more tasteful than the ordinary Australian house with good panelling but with no room large enough for any reception. . . . To Bruce's Cabinet room where we had a two hours' conference with the Migration Commission on the principles on which we were to work the agreement. A few minutes at home to think of something for my evening speech and then back to the House for the Government dinner in the Members' dining room. I sat between Bruce and Earle Page the Treasurer, who struck me as rather odd in his manner of thinking. . . . The speeches were broadcasted and were I am told heard well all over Australia. We got through all this before nine o'clock and then we adjourned to the House of Commons where there was an informal secret sitting which I addressed for one and a half hours on Locarno, Egypt, Iraq, China, Naval Disarmament Conference, South Africa, India, Colonial Empire and the British policy towards Empire development. They all listened with the greatest interest putting a few questions afterwards which I did the best I could to answer. The whole proceedings stopped about eleven. Bruce told me afterwards that this alone made my whole Empire tour worth while and that I did more good than he as an Australian would have done in five years.

4 November 1927: Had some talks in private with Latham about the

Imperial sub conference on legislation* and with Pratten on tariff matters and finally a wind up sitting with the Commission settling up migration points. The main basis of our agreement was that the Commissioners should produce for us a programme over a period of years so that we could know where we stood financially:

Amery left Canberra for Sydney on 6 November. Two days later he was in Brisbane. He spent another week in Australia, finally leaving for New Zealand on the 17th. On 19 November, while on his way to New Zealand, he summed up the value of his visit for Baldwin:

I have been immensely impressed by the usefulness of such a visit as mine has been. At an Imperial Conference the British public and Government learn something of two or three Australian Ministers and they of us. But the rest of Australia learns nothing. Whereas on a journey like this I have taken part at the meetings of seven different Cabinets, got to know more or less intimately most of the Ministers in all those Cabinets, and addressed many thousands of people directly and tens of thousands, if not hundreds of thousands, over the wireless. To a great part of Australia at any rate the idea of the British Government is now not something purely abstract about which they occasionally read short cables, but something living and concrete represented by somebody they have seen or heard, or whose speeches they have read more or less in full.

Amery reached Auckland early on 21 November and celebrated his birthday there the following day. He was to spend a little over a month there, but a week of it was spent climbing. He has described this week in vivid detail in his book *In the Rain and the Sun*, the failure through blizzard to climb Mount Cook, and a successful traverse over the Minarets and down the Franz Josef Glacier to Waiho. His autobiography is equally full on the visits and speeches he made. Only one or two entries, therefore, from his New Zealand visit are printed here.

Diary

24 November 1927: We were held up at Waitara by the Mayor and a few others who sent 13 down to a Rose show and took the rest of us up a steep path to an old Maori Pah, the trenches of which were still very visible while its defence at the back was a perpendicular cliff overhanging the Waitara river. Placing his heels on the extreme edge of the cliff the Mayor suddenly started delivering a civic welcome at me and I had the greatest difficulty in resisting the temptation to butt him on the tummy

*The Committee on the operation of Dominions legislation was to apply the principles of the Balfour Declaration. It met in 1929 and virtually drafted the Statute of Westminster which translated that Declaration into legal form.

and see him go over. However, I refrained and placed myself in the same position on the cliff edge to reply.

28 November 1927: To the House of Commons where I addressed a private session. This was a more formal affair than Canberra in so far as it was a real session of the Lower House. . . . I sat next to Coates . . . and addressed them for an hour and three quarters on much the same lines as at Canberra, followed by half an hour of questions. Holland, the Labour leader of the Opposition, who was rather annoyed because Coates would not agree to the representative of a Labour paper not already in the Press Gallery to come in, in thanking me said that I had said nothing which he did not know before and could not just as well have been said in public. As a matter of fact I had spoken very freely indeed about France, Russia, and the United States and my speech would have created no little trouble if it had been delivered in public.

29 November 1927: Talked with Holland in his room at the House and found him very pleasant and genuine but curiously ignorant on some matters. He actually thought that we received more alien immigrants in a year than we sent out of our own people to the Dominions and was astonished when I told him the actual figure was probably not over 500. Apparently he had been looking at the figures of tourists and other visitors.

On 20 December Amery left New Zealand for Canada. He travelled by way of Suva in Fiji, and while *en voyage* penned this valediction on the year.

31 December 1927: Looking back over 1927 it doesn't seem as if I had achieved very much. Still the Colonial Conference and the Dominions tour are two important new experiments which have both succeeded and are not likely to be discontinued. At the former I hope I have succeeded in starting a co-ordinated agricultural research service for the Colonies as the nucleus of closer organisation in many other directions. In the course of the latter I think I can claim the chief credit for the solution of the Flag question in South Africa: at any rate the principle of the double flag was my suggestion, and my speeches and presence did much to create the atmosphere in which this compromise was accepted. The launching of the East African Commission, freeing Cyprus of the tribute, resisting attempts to wreck the EMB may also be included as minor achievements. In Parliament I had practically no opportunity for opening my mouth and made no work. On the other hand I have had plenty of opportunity for speech making in the Dominions and have enormously widened my constituency. Altogether a year of organisation and preparation which may bear fruit later. Next year will see the battle on policy in the Cabinet and decide whether I can convince my colleagues on the economic and Imperial issue or whether I shall have to go out as Joe [Chamberlain] did. I still hope it may be the former, but all will depend on the workings of S.B.'s inscrutable mind. The rest, except for Neville and Willie Bridgeman, are timid folk and easily frightened by Winston. My only card may well be the threat of making even worse trouble if I don't have my way. I shall know better how the land lies in six weeks' time. Meanwhile there is still Canada to be done, the most difficult of all the Dominions.

From Victoria, where they arrived on 6 January, Amery travelled to Vancouver, to Banff, where he skied up Squaw Mountain, and to Edmonton on the 13th.

Diary
13 January 1928: After breakfast we went down to the fine Government building and Parliament House and I spent a couple of hours with ministers discussing migration and to some extent EMB. Hoadley quite keen on enlarging their boy training scheme and generally all for strengthening the British element. This is stronger anyhow in Alberta than in Saskatchewan but Edmonton itself is largely surrounded by Ruthenians and Hoadley is afraid that the Peace River, which seems to me a really wonderful country with at least ten million acres of first class arable land, should similarly get into foreign hands. I think I must take up with Forke the possibility of a large scale settlement scheme for the Peace River.

From Edmonton, they travelled on to Calgary, Regina, Winnipeg and Toronto, and from there to Whitby where Mrs Amery visited her parents' grave and the much altered remains of Spencer House. Toronto and Hamilton completed the stops on the way to Ottawa which was reached on the 22nd. At Toronto Amery heard from Mrs Ferguson about Bennett's election to the Conservative leadership.

Diary

20 January 1928: Apparently Meighen had made a last minute attempt to recover his place though professing not to want it and his eloquence had rather swept the Convention off its feet when Ferguson restored the situation by what I gather must have been a blunt and truculent little speech. I also gathered that if the decision could have been postponed for another year or so Ferguson might have liked the leadership himself.

23 January 1928: The whole morning with Mackenzie King chiefly discussing the new British representative at Ottawa. His idea now is if possible to get Harding and I told him that though I had not thought of it before I would do so seriously and see if I could possibly spare him. Drove out with Mackenzie King to Bennett's lunch at the Country Club. I seem to have come at a rather useful moment on the eve of the session to bring the new leader of the Opposition into friendly touch with the PM for they had to meet two or three times in this way. As a matter of fact Bennett, who can do a bit of generalising himself, is not consumed by the same passionate hatred of M.K.'s squishiness as Meighen was. After lunch Bennett made a nice little speech about me and I got up and talked about the romance of what I had seen. M.K. very delighted and indeed with every speech I made and every talk we had his nervous fear of me diminished and he became in fact quite enthusiastic. Filled in the afternoon with talks with some of the Ministers, more particularly a long set to with Forke and Egan on migration. Forke would repeat mildly from time to time that the only thing that mattered was land settlement but Egan brushed him aside firmly by stating that the only thing that mattered was cheap transportation. I found Egan's attitude all that I had expected and more thoroughly negative and only inclined to do anything even on a small scale if the British Government found all the money. Finally when he suggested that we should find all the contribution to any housing scheme on the ground that it helped our unemployed I exploded and gave him a vigorous dressing down which rather startled him and made old Forke most friendly and apologetic whenever I met him afterwards.

24 January 1928: Short talk with Ralston, the Minister for Defence, who is vigorous and shrewd and very popular with the Forces. I think he means to get something done presently and at any rate has begun by ordering two destroyers. Then some more talk with Mackenzie King and disposed of one of two minor questions before going on to the Canadian Club lunch at the Château Laurier. . . . In the evening we dined with Mackenzie King at Laurier House, a pleasant party including Phillips, the very charming and adroit American Minister. Afterwards Mackenzie King showed us all round the house and library, much of it very pleasing, and also specially displayed his wonderful bound collections not only of every menu card of every function he attended at Imperial Conferences but of every invitation even that he had not been able to accept. His love for collecting little oddments and everything concerned with functions and every little civility is amazing.

26 January 1928: Further talk with M.K. joined a little later by Willingdon who opened the theme of migration on which M.K. was thoroughly fluffy and evasive. On the question of communication to the G[overnor] G[eneral] we had not much to say as everything is going well. On the other hand M.K. launched out into a real tirade of passionate indignation on the subject of *The Times* having appointed Stevenson as its Ottawa correspondent and not only hinted that *The Times* could hardly expect any Canadian Government advertisement in its special supplement but that *The Times'* criticism of himself might disrupt the Empire. It was really a surprising outburst and Willingdon said he had never seen him like that before. . . . M.K. came down from the House to see us off and was in every way charming and affectionate – a quaint creature. Had a good talk on the train with Stevenson, *The Times'* correspondent, and told him that he must be free from bias against M.K.

From Montreal, the Amerys went first to Quebec, where, speaking in French, Amery delighted his hosts, and then to New Brunswick and Newfoundland.

Diary

3 February 1928:   So ends the last lap of the great pilgrimage of Empire. I think I have done good in Canada, more perhaps than anywhere else except possibly South Africa, in quickening the consciousness of Empire and the sense of its possibilities. I have made useful contact here as elsewhere, and I have enormously strengthened my personal equipment, in fact and in public esteem, for tackling the really big job, the conversion of my colleagues and of Great Britain to the idea of economic co-operation and preference. The next six months will see if I can get my way, even partially, without a break. I hardly dare hope so, but I must stick to the hope as long as I can and not go off at half-cock if I can avoid it.

In addition to his discussions with Ministers both at national and state level, Amery had made no less than three hundred speeches on his tour, sixty-one in South Africa, eighty-seven in Australia, eighty-seven in New Zealand, fifty-six in Canada, six in Fiji and three on board ship. The message was constant. He returned to Liverpool in one of the worst gales for years and did not get ashore until 12 February.

15

At Odds with Colleagues
1928-9

Amery returned from his Empire tour to find himself at once plunged
into the difficult question of *ex gratia* compensation for the losses suffered
by the Irish Loyalists after the truce of July 1921 (see page 271). The
question had been remitted to a committee under Sir A. Wood Renton,
but the delay in dealing with individual cases and fears that the report
would be ungenerous had led to an outburst from Conservative back
benches. Amery calmed the storm with an assurance on 23 February
that the Wood Renton recommendations, then estimated to cost £1
million, would be paid in due course. He personally believed that the
payment should be made in full and urged this in the Cabinet in December
1928. Churchill demurred, and his view that the Commission's recommendations totalling £1.4 million could not be met but that the Government
should stick to £1 million, prevailed over Amery's. When, however, this
was put to the House, it was clear that it would not be accepted, and
Baldwin had first to adjourn the debate and then arrange for a humiliating
and unconditional surrender on the point.

In the course of the year Amery was involved also with the pensions
of those Civil Servants who had been transferred to the services of the
Irish Government as a result of the Government of Ireland Act 1920,
but were subsequently dismissed when the Irish Free State was created.
The Irish Treaty had allowed fair compensation. In 1927, contrary to
almost all precedent, two Civil Servants, suing the Irish Government in
respect of a particular payment, had appealed to the Judicial Committee
of the Privy Council. That such a right of appeal still existed was a sore
point with the Irish, but they had been persuaded by Birkenhead at the
Imperial Conference of 1926 temporarily to abandon their claim for its
abolition. The Judicial Committee, presided over by the Lord Chancellor,
Cave, ruled in their favour both in terms of the issue and their right to
sue. He was, it may be added, no friend of the Free State and had stamped
out of the 1926 Conference 'saying he was not going to be a party to the

breaking up of the British Empire'.* The Irish Government refused to accept the decision. Cave for his part believed that they had an 'effective and ingenious' way of circumventing the decision by retrospective legislation making their own view law. Politely Amery's Under Secretary of State for the Dominions told Baldwin that he wondered whether Cave appreciated the undesirability of a unilateral alteration by the Irish Free State of the Irish Treaty.

By March 1928 Cave had come to believe that there was an error in his original judgment and he confessed as much to Baldwin. He continued to urge the Free State's right to legislate to correct the matter, subject only to Britain's right to approve the legislation. In April 1928, after Cave's death, the Lords debated the question, and Carson questioned the justice of the British Government acquiescing in amending legislation. Reading suggested ingeniously that the matter should be referred back to the Judicial Committee for reconsideration, and the Government gratefully accepted the suggestion. In November 1928, despite the error in the original judgment, the Judicial Committee upheld it. The Irish Government were confirmed in their determination to be rid of Appeal to the Privy Council; although at the instance of the British Government they would first consider a substitute tribunal to take its place, the failure of the 1930 Imperial Conference to reach agreement on the subject led directly to the de Valera Government's abolition Bill in 1933. The appellants were paid, perhaps by the British Government,† and a tribunal set up to assess the claim of others.

The overriding issue, which dominates the diary until the resignation of the Conservative Government in June 1929, and which probably bore chief responsibility for their defeat in that general election, was unemployment. Baldwin could point to almost a million new jobs; critics of the Government fastened on to the million out of work, and the problem was the more acute because it was very largely confined to Britain's traditional export industries and to certain areas of the country, the depressed areas. In January 1928 the Industrial Transference Board was established under the chairmanship of Sir Warren Fisher, to facilitate migration from the depressed areas, and, in particular, from the coalfields. Churchill had, however, a more dramatic scheme to combat unemployment which was to be unveiled in his Budget. It had been under discussion by senior Ministers since the previous summer, and was intended wholly to remove the burden of rating from industry and agriculture. The argument for this was straightforward. The burden of unemployment

*R. Cook, 'A Canadian Account of the 1926 Imperial Conference', *Journal of Commonwealth Political Studies*, III, no. 1, pp. 60-1.

†At least so the Irish Minister for External Affairs, Fitzgerald, hints in a letter to his wife, 6 October 1930 (cited in D. W. Harkness, *The Restless Dominion*, p. 207).

through the operation of the Poor Law fell directly on the rates and was reflected also in low assessable values. A vicious cycle was created by which the surviving industries in an already depressed area found increasing rates a threat to their existence. Churchill tied his scheme to Neville Chamberlain's reform of local government finance by which block grants weighted for need would replace proportionate grants-in-aid to local authorities. It was to be financed by taxes on profits and on liquid fuel. There were doubts about the scheme, expressed most notably by Neville Chamberlain, who was concerned about the effect on local government of wholly exempting the main producers from rating. The Cabinet which considered the question on 20 January 1928, with Amery and four other Ministers absent, was on the whole favourable to the idea, however, and by the beginning of February its inclusion in the Government's programme was firmly agreed.

Amery had returned from his Empire tour convinced that every Dominion would respond to new efforts in the direction of practical economic co-operation. He was convinced also that the Treasury's deflationary finance was largely responsible for the depressed state of British industry, and that tariffs would not only restore the fortunes of industries directly protected but, through increasing employment, would generate additional consumption benefiting the entire economy. He found, however, that in his absence both his own position and the attractions of tariff reform to the Government had weakened. He did not really study Churchill's scheme until he had been home a fortnight, but he then concluded that it was intended to bury the question of safeguarding. Its very complexity seemed to offer him the chance of advocating tariffs as an alternative, and he put in a critical Cabinet paper. The diary reveals how little headway he made, the arguments turning rather on the conflict between Churchill and Chamberlain over the retention of partial rating and the question of who should control the rating relief funds. Chamberlain also fought to retain rating of railways, something which Churchill was prepared and found it necessary to concede, but only so long as the relief for industry was total.

When the Cabinet discussed the matter on 2 April, it was evident that the general feeling was with Chamberlain, and the next day the Cabinet decided on the derating of agriculture and the continued rating of railways. At Churchill's suggestion the proposals for industry were made subject to Chamberlain's consent, and that evening the Policy Committee resolved that there should be a fractional rate of a quarter on industry. The Cabinet endorsed the compromise on 4 April.

In the light of this compromise Churchill felt free to raise the question of the railways once again, and, in agreement with Baldwin, he did so when he presented his Budget to the Cabinet on 19 April. A special meeting of the Cabinet followed and Baldwin gave a lead: railways, he explained, had been left out of the scheme because of a majority decision on Churchill's committee to favour the complete derating of industry, and since that decision had been modified, they should reconsider the reinstatement in the derating scheme of the railway companies. This was agreed to by a majority, and Churchill was quick to urge on Baldwin the introduction of the proposals with regard to railways that autumn.

Unemployment was again increasing and the Fisher Committee's report published in July confirmed that Britain faced no transient or cyclical depression. They advocated both internal migration and settlement overseas, in Canada and Australia particularly. Amery welcomed the report but the efforts made further to stimulate emigration had only small result by the time the Government left office.

Temporary work harvesting in Canada, which might lead also to permanent settlement, was seen as capable of absorbing more than the 8500 men selected and despatched in 1928. But land settlement was Amery's main aim and Canada the most obvious field. Lord Lovat was despatched to negotiate with the Provinces and companies like the Canadian Pacific Railway. Despite Churchill's objections an assisted passage scheme was introduced. The Canadian Government would not reserve land, however, and the Treasury would not lend large sums to potential settlers. Total migration rose but only from 39,000 in 1928 to 53,000 in 1929. 'Cheap fares', Professor Drummond concludes, 'were not enough to induce migrants to give up the dole when Canada's own unemployed were numerous and ill protected.'* Nor could the Canadian Government be stirred into more helpful action.

Bruce's Cabinet in Australia had been more forthcoming, but the scheme agreed between Amery and Bruce in March 1925 was scarcely more successful. By the end of 1928 the Australian States had bound themselves only to a total of 86,908 migrants. A grand total of 345,400 assisted emigrants in the years 1922-31 seems a poor return for all Amery's effort, but the export of capital and labour was at least working in the direction of Britain's economic recovery and contributed to the self-sufficient Empire for which Amery hoped. And in human terms the schemes must have done a great deal of good.

Amery had used the Industrial Transference Board's report to reopen the whole question of safeguarding, not just of relatively minor products like enamelled hollow ware, which was agreed in June, but of iron and steel. Churchill was strenuous in his resistance, and Amery's diary chronicles their struggle for the Prime Minister's mind. There was

*I. M. Drummond, *Imperial Economic Policy* (Unwin University Books, 1974), p. 106; cf. I. M. Drummond, *British Economic Policy and the Empire* (George Allen and Unwin, 1972), pp. 83-4.

considerable backbench pressure, but Baldwin's reluctance to raise the issue was patent. Amery drafted a letter for despatch on 12 July reminding Baldwin that the most definite pledge he had given was in his election address of 1924 that he would deal with unemployment *as a primary obligation* and that while he had ruled out a general tariff, he was committed to apply the principle of the Safeguarding Act. 'I maintain that on any reasonable construction of that pledge we are in honour bound to help the iron and steel industry', Amery wrote, nor could he find anything in Baldwin's subsequent pronouncements to rule out action.

Although Baldwin turned down a backbench deputation on iron and steel organised by Page Croft on 23 July, the Government had little or no reply to Labour censure on unemployment and this clearly moved Joynson-Hicks to his strongly protectionist speech at Broadlands on 28 July. Baldwin was seriously annoyed, and rebuked his colleagues in Cabinet on 1 August. However, a declaration of policy was clearly needed, and Baldwin agreed to issue one in the form of a letter to the Chief Whip stating that there would be no introduction of protection nor any tax in food, but that the safeguarding procedure might be modified and no industry would be barred from it. Once again Baldwin's fatal ambiguity moved Amery to thoughts of resignation. Nor, despite Amery's efforts, was Baldwin's speech to the Conservative Annual Conference much clearer; in a letter of 1 October Amery insisted on knowing what was in Baldwin's mind.

In fact Baldwin was moving towards the idea of a permanent tribunal to replace *ad hoc* safeguarding inquiries, which would be free to consider any industry whatsoever, and whose terms of reference were clearly bent in the direction of more protective duties. Agriculture would be barred from it. He remained conscious of the need not to go too far ahead of public opinion, however, fearing to be accused of sharp practice. Thus fresh pressure for a safeguarding inquiry from the iron and steel manufacturers met with a refusal, but a request from the iron and steel workers' trade union had a more favourable reception. The result was the same. Persuaded at first to accept a commission, Baldwin was subsequently persuaded, by Steel-Maitland among others, that a safeguarding inquiry would still be needed, and the whole question was postponed until after the election.

Perhaps inevitably the Government seemed a little too safe and unexciting in the face of Lloyd George's fierce challenge on unemployment. But Lloyd George's own remedies, boldly set out in the pamphlet 'We can conquer unemployment' and endorsed by the economists Keynes and Hubert Henderson, did not carry sufficient conviction to bring him back to Downing Street. The Conservatives polled the largest vote in the 1929 election, but Labour returned the largest number of MPs and formed a minority government. Amery was not too unhappy at the result. Despite a strong socialist tide in Birmingham, he was safely returned to the new House of Commons, and he had long concluded that only defeat would free the Party from that incubus at the Treasury, Winston Churchill.

If unemployment was the leading issue during the last year and a half of Baldwin's government and played a large measure in its election defeat, disarmament and the Government's inability to make progress with it ranks not far behind. 1928 did see the signature of the highly idealistic Kellogg–Briand Pact, which sought to abolish war (and remains in existence, one world war and many minor wars later) but the only effective disarmament was achieved by Churchill, who used both the need to woo the United States from her own cruiser building programme and the technological progress of the Germans to urge successive postponements of cruiser construction on an unwilling Admiralty. He was not without success as Amery's diary shows.

The abortive Anglo-French compromise on disarmament which was the Government's principal effort in the field of naval disarmament will be referred to at an appropriate place later in the year (see page 548), but it would seem appropriate to outline here the history of the proposal to outlaw war. This had its origins in the United States with the American Committee for the Outlawry of War and the Carnegie Endowment for International Peace, and it was the officers of the latter organisation who sold the idea to Briand. In his hands it became a way of restoring Franco-American relations and buttressing France's alliance system. That was why a proposal made in April 1927 lay on the American Secretary of State's table until Congress met in December. Public and congressional opinion backed the idea of a pact of eternal peace, however, and Kellogg had therefore to find a way of divesting it of its French dress. The solution came from Senator Borah who proposed making the pact multilateral. Kellogg embraced the idea, and there was little that Briand could do about it.

Diary

14 February 1928: Walked up to the office with Lovat who told me something about the Irish Loyalists crisis and the need for doing a good deal better than the Government had offered to do in December. Then Ware for a few minutes about yet another attempt to raid the Graves Commission fund. Across to No 10 where the PM and I had it out with Winston and made him realise that he must go a decided step further over the Loyalists. . . . Questions, after which I received a deputation led by

Gretton of the champions of the Loyalists and then met Sir A. Wood Renton and Sir H. Brunyate and Jamieson, the secretary, to get myself further posted on the Irish question. Back to the House and tackled Austen on the question of British representatives in the Dominions being on the Dominions Service Vote. He was obstinate at first, relying on the Cabinet minute last summer, but finally gave way without prejudice to the question of what type of representative should be selected for Canada. After the division B. and I dined alone with Neville and Annie and heard something about what had happened in our absence, Neville giving us a very entertaining account of the Prayer Book debate. Usual wallowing through files and preparation for next day's Cabinet.

15 February 1928: Cabinet at which the Irish business took the greater part of the time. After my statement of the case the only question really remaining was whether we should pay the Wood Renton awards in full or fix a definite limit of one million (Jamieson's estimate of the total likely to be awarded is about £950,000). Winston felt so strongly against what he called a blank cheque that we could not fairly press him further though it makes our acceptance of the position much less gracious.

16 February 1928: Lunched at Buckingham Palace, just B. and myself and Their Majesties. They were both very charming personally but the King more talkative not to say noisy than usual. His main theme is of course dislike of all the new developments in constitutional relations and he is quite incapable of understanding that the Governor General is no longer the British Government's representative. I tried to steer him a little in argument at intervals but without much success and I do not know what he will say when our proposals for a British High Commissioner in Canada actually come before him. From this George III atmosphere I went back to the House to discuss with Stanley and Austen the question of our representation in Canada. Both of them convinced, Stanley especially, that we must have a really good man, at least of 'ambassadorial stamp' said Stanley. I told them the substance of my talks with Mackenzie King and we finally decided that everything depended on the individual whatever Service he came from. Harding, whom Mackenzie King had suggested, did not seem to either of them to have quite enough personality. We also agreed that 'High Commissioner' was the suitable title.

17 February 1928: ... to a further Cabinet [the second of the day] where we had to deal with Winston's onslaughts on the Navy and on matters which concerned me. I surrendered a hundred thousand on the OSO estimate on condition that it was regarded as a shadow cut and then to

Winston's great surprise accepted his reduction of the EMB Vote by five hundred thousand on the clear understanding that I could have the money this year or subsequently whenever I wanted it and that it was clearly put down on the estimates as only a payment on account. In return for this I got him to take off the EMB the twenty-five thousand for advertising the British Industries Fair which they had put on to it in my absence which Bruce had protested against, and I also afterwards got him to promise to deal fairly with me over Swaziland. His attempt to raid the War Graves was firmly rejected by Worthy and myself, and the naval position was eased not only by my surrenders but by the decision, very repugnant to poor Austen, to annex temporarily the balance of the Boxer Indemnity leaving Chinese education, etc., to whistle for better times. I find two critical Cabinets with no time to prepare myself and a speech in the middle distinctly tiring but I think I was wise in being as accommodating as I was. If there is any chance of my winning round Winston on major issues of policy, I must be as reasonable to him on lesser matters as I can and the same holds equally good if I am going to have a stand-up fight.

20 February 1928: After questions I had some talk with Winston first about Swaziland on which he has given me something on account and promised to be reasonable about the rest, and then on the general question of future policy. He told me he had met my views about the sugar refiners by a device which will cost the Exchequer nearly two million. I asked him why he could not have done it by a small additional duty which would have brought in some revenue instead. That let him loose on the whole theme of food taxation and protection. He announced that he meant to stick to his guns even if he had to resign and that there was no chance of our going to the country with any programme that would enable us even to include the safeguarding of iron and steel, adding that Baldwin agreed with him. I think he may be bluffing but we are certainly in for a tussle during the next few months.

23 February 1928: Stayed in my room at the House waiting and preparing for the Supplementary Estimate for the Irish Loyalists which did not come on until 8.30. Made a very conciliatory statement which thoroughly pleased our people and wound up just before eleven in the same spirit and so got the estimate through without a division.

26 February 1928: Began to tackle Winston's great scheme of rating reform. It is a vote catching scheme and too ingenious but I see in it a great opportunity for putting in my own tactics for dealing with the fiscal question as an alternative.

27 February 1928: Lunched with Balfour to meet Winston and Weizemann in order to discuss a League of Nations Loan to the Zionist Commission on which I found Winston surprisingly forthcoming. . . . Interview with Peto and Davidson about the Irish Civil Servants. I foresee we shall have a certain amount of trouble on that.

28 February 1928: Hankey came round to tell me that after all Winston and the PM thought that a Cabinet committee on the Baghdad–Haifa Railway was immediately required. [L.S.A.'s request for this had been postponed at the Cabinet of the 22nd]; naturally I fell in with the proposal at once.

2 March 1928: Walked round to see the Prince of Wales and talked with him for over an hour about my tour. . . . At the end we also briefly discussed the possibility of his going to Kenya next autumn. I asked him to let us have as much notice as possible; his own preference would be to dash off without notice.

4 March 1928: Lazy morning but made a beginning with my memorandum in answer to Winston's new project. It looks as if we may have a real tussle over this for he intends his scheme definitely to bury all questions of safeguarding and preference. I think I have rather riddled his scheme and hope its collapse will pave the way to better things.

5 March 1928: Saw Guggisberg and told him that Fiji was the only thing I had in store for him at this moment, and that subject to satisfactory domestic relations. He answered me they were satisfactory enough for that purpose, that there would be no scandal and that she would even come out if required.

7 March 1928: Cabinet, where we dealt with Akhwan raids, many of them terrified of our getting into trouble, Basle Mission on which India has refused to pay any compensation to anybody, and other matters. Lunched with the Laverys . . . Lady L. tells me that the pushing out of Tim and instating McNeill [as Governor General of the Irish Free State] was done with the idea of making things easier if de Valera should come in, Tim having said that he would never accept him. Meanwhile poor McNeill has had an operation of nearly three hours the other day and is not likely to live long. Baghdad–Haifa [railway] sub-committee in the PM's room where we examined first Cadman and Waley Cohen on the presence of the oil which seems pretty certain, and secondly Stern and Tiarks on their own financial proposals which we all agreed to regard as unacceptable. In the end we appointed a departmental sub-committee to look further into the matter.

13 March 1928: At 4 o'clock went into the lion's den, in other words a gathering of 60 or 70 Members mostly Die-Hards to heckle me on the subject of the Irish Pensions case. I made as good a case as I could but inevitably could not help disclosing the fact that I thought the Privy Council judgment absurd with the result that I had them all attacking me most passionately, some from the Irish point of view, others from the point of view of the scandal of upsetting a judgment of the Privy Council. I wish it had been possible for me to say frankly that unless the Privy Council is drastically reformed in the next two or three years it will cease to function any longer.

20 March 1928: Talked [with Baldwin] of various things including the probability that Cave will retire and Douglas [Hogg] be made Lord Chancellor. We agreed that the dangers attending F.E.'s return to the Chancellorship were too great; besides he wishes in any case to go into Berry's business after this Parliament. We also discussed Chilcott and Austen and Ivy's infatuation for him.

21 March 1928: Cabinet at which we discussed Imperial Wireless and I got my way as far as insuring a reasonable answer in the House and keeping negotiations open with the merger.

22 March 1928: Saw Sir R. Hopkins on the subject of the motor duties and I think impressed him with the folly in adding petrol taxation to the present horsepower taxation [L.S.A. added on 27 April: 'No effect!']. He confessed that the Exchequer had practically come to the end of its resources unless we were prepared to have import duties. Conference with Macnaghten, [Sir Granville] Ram and another on the new Empire Settlement Bill and decided to go as far as 75% in contributions to training schemes. . . . While down at the House I met Page Croft who told me that Philip had a big party meeting upstairs, had ended an otherwise satisfactory statement about safeguarding with the query, 'I assume that we are all unanimous in rejecting the idea of any food duties?' Page Croft had intervened and said that he could not agree as this would mean no extension of preference whatever and the matter then dropped. I scribbled a strong note to Stanley afterwards to tell him that if that was the line to be taken I should have to fight. I fancy things may come to a head in the next few weeks but I shall try throughout to stick to the offensive–defensive, i.e. say things fully justified by S.B.'s declarations ever since 1923, and leave it to those who wish to protest to do so.

25 March 1928: Met General and Lady Duncan just back from Shanghai. . . . Duncan very interesting and very definitely on the side of Nationalist

China against Peking. Thinks Chiang Kai Shek quite a decent patriotic fellow though no genius. Sure we were wrong in truckling to force at Hankow but on the other hand very down on the way in which the white people out in China refuse social intercourse and will not even allow the Chinese into the park at Shanghai.

28 March 1928: Cabinet at which my proposals for amendment of the Empire Settlement Act were postponed pending receipt of Warren Fisher's transference report, almost everybody being against them. I fear the Cabinet has drifted into a hopelessly negative attitude especially on Empire questions but perhaps they may begin to wake up presently to the seriousness of the mining situation. Left rather depressed but a little amused to hear afterwards that it made no difference as the Bill could not go to Standing Committee before Easter anyway.

29 March 1928: Went to CID where we discussed Aden. General Stewart very anxious to make an immediate Treaty with Imam on the basis of his evacuating all our territory. Austen and to some extent Sam very anxious that we should not press him too far about evacuating all and so lose the chance of peace. I tried to meet them by a judiciously worded telegram which still left the Resident a pretty free hand. . . . John [Buchan] told me that the PM was very much carrying the Government in the country and that very few of my other colleagues were much of an asset, some like Winston and F.E. an actual handicap. I was surprised at what he said about Winston who I thought had won a certain amount of popularity but John is definite on the point. We agreed that in spite of his picturesqueness of phrasing he lacks any vision and was really 20 or 30 years behind the times. I did not ask John whether I was also regarded as in the nature of a handicap.

2 April 1928: Cabinet at which I brought up the final most satisfactory settlement with the Basle Mission business. . . . after which we went on to the discussion of the great Winston Plan, most of the morning being taken up by Neville in stating his case for retaining some element of contribution to local finances. . . . More Cabinet at 4.15 in the course of which I came down very strongly on the side of Neville and Jack Gilmour in favour of local contribution and also against derating of railways, the tide flowing pretty definitely in this direction in spite of Philip and Worthy and a majority on Winston's Committee.

3 April 1928: More Cabinet where the tide ran still further with Neville, even F.E. deserting Winston for once.

4 April 1928: Cabinet where I had to raise the question of allowing munitions to go out to Ibn Saud; also the proposed Zionist loan for which Balfour and Winston in their enthusiasm had let me in but which obviously Winston has now ratted on and Austen turned down on FO grounds. However, they were postponed in order to spare poor old Balfour a shock while he is ill.

Amery spent Easter at Neaden farm in Devonshire, walking, climbing and riding, a 'peaceful and much needed Easter holiday', from which he returned on 16 April.

---

12 April 1928: Drove over to Ugbrooke to lunch with Charles Clifford. . . . A rambling old house, the main block in the worst 18th century style, Charles C. just beginning to tidy up and redecorate some of the inside. Some nice old Lelys and interesting papers, including the original of Charles II's secret Treaty of Dover by which he undertook, for money from Louis, to declare himself a Roman Catholic as soon as a convenient opportunity offered itself. When we left Julian shook hands with Clifford and said: 'Thank you very much for letting me see that most interesting historical document' and has been discussing it freely since.

18 April 1928: Campbell Stuart and Baillieu, the Australian representative on the Wireless Conference, came to see me to urge the importance of getting the beam leased to the new merger. This was raised at the Cabinet immediately afterwards but in spite of the efforts of Gilmour and myself it was decided to remit the matter again to the sub-committee which had previously considered it.

19 April 1928: Long Cabinet on the Budget at which Winston unfolded his whole scheme until 1.15, the remaining quarter of an hour being the Cabinet's opportunity for critical suggestion or amendment. I strongly urged some extra preference on sugar but Winston refused though he conceded the point of 99 degrees of polarisation for Queensland sugar. In the afternoon we had a long meeting of the cabinet sub-committee on wireless which I managed to stir in the right direction.

20 April 1928: Further Cabinet to reconsider the rating aspects of Winston's scheme, the PM having been persuaded by Winston to bring the railways in after all. This of course is not really a derating scheme but only an indirect subsidy to certain industries, but on the whole the Cabinet were prepared, in view of the PM's attitude, to reverse their previous decision, though I am glad to say stood to their guns in favour of the rate still left being variable and not a fixed one.

21 April 1928: Discussed [with Horne] his big Albert Hall meeting for the EIA on May 15th and I told him I might offer to come and address it. He thought that would immensely enhance the importance of the meeting itself but was not quite certain how it would affect my permanent influence in the right direction in the Cabinet. I told him that was just what I was considering and was a point on which I could not make up my mind until I had a straight talk with Baldwin.

24 April 1928: The [Budget] was done with Winston's best literary skill and above all with his power of investing the business with importance. He still lives entirely in the 19th Century in his outlook on things. There is no doubt that the first impression was very favourable indeed and our party was delighted and is I think still very happy at the end of the week. My own cue will be throughout to treat it as the first instalment of a policy of helping the producer and to press home later the inadequacy of the instalment.

26 April 1928: Long meeting of the Wireless Committee at which we all agreed, except Mike [Mitchell Thomson] and Jix, in favour of leasing the beam to the merger.

28 April 1928: Conference with the Lord Chancellor about the Irish Pensions tangle. As he does not think he can get the Irish draft bill through the House of Lords and is inclined towards a new trial I have written to Blythe to come over with his Attorney General.

2 May 1928: Cabinet on Egypt and American peace proposals. We overrode Lloyd who was for pressing Nahas still further, I being the only member of the Government at all inclined to support him.

4 May 1928: Emergency Cabinet on the American Multi-Lateral Treaty. Austen told us that Kellogg was now dead against any suggestion of meeting of jurists or ministers and wanted direct acceptance of the Treaty as it stood. He recommended, and we were all in agreement pretty well, that the thing is to accept the Treaty accompanying our acceptance by such reference to our position with regard to Locarno and to such commitments and responsibilities as we have analogous to the Monroe doctrine as will prevent the Treaty giving us any serious trouble in Egypt or Afghanistan.

7 May 1928: Had nearly an hour with Baldwin for my long deferred blowing off of steam on the general position. I rehearsed all I had submitted to ever since Bonar broke his pledge to me in 1922 to keep a free hand on the fiscal question, all the difficulties of my position *vis à vis* Winston and the urgency of the industrial situation. I made it clear that I was not prepared to acquiesce either in another 1924 with its consequent paralysis and sterility, or in another 1923 with the big issue brought forward without preparation, and that in one way or another the issue has got to be advanced this summer. I told him he had to choose between Winston and myself, that this could not be done by just talking to Winston, by telling him to be a little more considerate on Empire Questions. It could only be done by either moving Winston or putting me in some place like the Board of Trade where I could make my own safeguarding regulations and he would have to accept what I did. I also told him that I contemplated going to the Albert Hall meeting on the 15th. Stanley was as usual silent, sympathetic and friendly but gave no real indication of what he thought beyond a general suggestion that we ought to make up our minds before the autumn. . . . Gave lunch at the Carlton Club Annexe to Blythe and Costello, the Irish ministers, who have come over on the Pensions Case. . . . Had a good talk with Neville who strongly urged me not to go to the Albert Hall meeting and by irritation definitely throw some of our wobblers the wrong way. His suggestion is that I should draft a full memorandum of policy which I could agree with him, on which both of us could then convert Philip and so with increasing authority bring the thing to the PM and get his approval for Cabinet committee on the scheme as such. Nearly two hours with the Irish in the Lord Chancellor's room. F.E. had been asked to come too in view of his friendship with the Irish and previous experience of handling them. He came in looking more hopelessly sodden than I could have imagined possible, a really awful sight, but no sooner had the discussion begun than he took the whole thing in hand and dealt with it with masterly insight, tact and decision, Douglas and I only occasionally interjecting a sentence or two. In the upshot we came to the conclusion that the best thing was to get a new advisory opinion from the Privy Council, the Irish having given us their clear reasons of a political character to show that a new case would be impossible. Had another talk with Neville and decided with some searching of heart to abandon the Albert Hall meeting. I confess I hate the idea of not testifying on the 25th Anniversary of Joe's great declaration, and I generally regret it when I have been prudent and yielded to the 'wiser' counsel of my friends. [L.S.A. holograph notes: 'I do now!' (1945); 'Even more!' (1951)]. However, we shall see and I may explode before long.

9 May 1928: Cabinet in the PM's room at which we decided the general form of the draft answer to the US [on the Kellogg Pact] to be submitted to the Dominions. Saw Harding afterwards and worked in one or two amendments as well as a final paragraph which made it clear that we were asking the Dominions to concur with us in accepting the principle of the Treaty but not to commit themselves to every sentence of our draft; otherwise we might have been weeks getting the thing through and had some awkward snags to get past.

11 May 1928: Godfrey Thomas about the Prince of Wales's tour. I think he fully understands the foolishness of going through the Upper Nile region at the wrong time of the year involving a fortnight at least of boredom and discomfort not to speak of the prospects of malaria or sleeping sickness. The whole tour would be so much simpler and easier if the Prince would only start at the South African end but he has set his mind on getting down to SA for Christmas with the Athlones and he is not easy to shift [L.S.A. holograph note: 'In the end decided to go from Khartoum to Port Sudan and on by sea']. . . . Gave lunch at the Carlton Annexe to Hilton Young just back from East Africa. He tells me it will not be easy to shepherd his team into any report. They are all very anti-Kenya and got at cross purposes with Grigg. His own idea is a High Commissioner acting for the CO co-ordinating Kenya, Uganda and Tanganyika and residing principally at Mombasa, and another similar High Commissioner for the two Rhodesias and Nyasaland, in this case, however, combined with the Governorship of Southern Rhodesia. There is much to be said for this new division of Africa into three, but the High Commissionership does not look easy to work though of course it is only intended as a transitional stage.

14 May 1928: Conference in Austen's room on the American Note arising from the last Canadian telegram, the main point being that while our reply should not commit the Dominions to anything to which they are not committed we must equally avoid the position of their committing themselves to non participation in any issue which might arise out of such a question as Egypt. Our further discussions concentrated round the question of invitation and were clarified by a bald summary of the Irish reply which came in during the proceedings to the effect that they could not concur in our proposed paragraph about Dominion approval unless they were separately invited. Later on in the evening I saw Whiskard and Harding and agreed drafts both as to the invitation and as to the issue of substance.

17 May 1928: To Pilgrims dinner in honour of Tim Healy, a rather wonderful finale to a wonderful career. As I said in my speech if Tim 40 years ago had been asked to put down the names of all the people who could not possibly attend any banquet to him it would have included

Viceroys, Chief Secretaries, Archbishops of Canterbury, etc. All ex-Chief Secretaries except A.J.B. were there including Gerald Balfour whom I sat next to and found very charming.

22 May 1928: CID at Whitehall Gardens where we got through fairly satisfactorily both on the Ibn Saud and Imam negotiations. . . . Then to a conference between Northern and Southern Ireland on the question of Lough Foyle fishery and navigation, etc., both Irish sides very difficult but both sides anxious to postpone indefinitely the issue of sovereignty and puzzled how to settle the fishery matter unless the sovereignty question were decided. By 1.30 we had come to no conclusions. . . . Back to more Irish and got to the point that we were agreed on everything except the fishery and thought the fishery question could be solved either by the Irish Society taking action in the Free State courts in the hope that these courts or ultimately the Privy Council should sustain their claim, or else the two governments by leasing the fishery in Lough Foyle itself and recouping themselves from the present tenants. . . . Further conference with MacGilligan about the Irish attitude over the Rome copyright conference where they wished to get away from the high contracting parties of conference and make it an ordinary countries one so as to be qualified alphabetically and not need the British Empire umbrella. They are really very tiresome [L.S.A. holograph note: 'I insisted on being firm over this and the Irish getting no support, walked out and so have no copyright'] and from what the telegrams from South Africa report Hertzog is being no less so over the flag business, i.e. always trying to go back in effect upon an agreement and never attempting to honour it in the spirit.

12 June 1928: The King and Stamfordham most affable and grateful for my giving way about the proposed prolongation of de Chair for a year [in the Governorship of New South Wales]. . . . To PM's room where the Industrial Transference Board, viz. Warren Fisher, Cadman and Shackleton, interviewed the PM, Winston, myself and Steel-Maitland just back. Beyond denunciation of the stickiness of the Dominions with regard [to] oversea settlement Fisher and his colleagues had very little to say while Winston who was in a thoroughly naughty mood could only denounce all action and say that the miners had better go out and find some work as things improved.

13 June 1928: A short Cabinet at which Sam and I got authorisation to bomb the Imam if he does not clear out of Dhala by the 20th.

14 June 1928: Lunch at No. 11, Mrs Winston quite recovered and in very good form, Winston pre-occupied with his determination to inter-

T

vene in the Prayer Book debate in order to justify his voting to his constituent. . . . Spent the rest of the day at the House. Jix opened speaking with intense emotion, an odd mixture of fundamentalism and ultra Erastianism, not really effective as it seemed to me. . . . Winston who had been bubbling over with excitement all the afternoon got in about 7.30. The actual argument of his speech was good but whether it was the Winstonian diction or the fact that he rather lost his temper with interrupters, or the general feeling that he was not the person to intervene, made the speech ineffective and indeed damaging to his cause. . . . The PM wound up with a simple expository speech aimed at capturing the 10% of undecided votes. . . . The Opposition parties had made up their minds to treat it as a party question and with few exceptions went solidly into the Lobby again[st] with the result that the Prayer Book was beaten again by 260 to 220.

18 June 1928: Good talk with Lovat about Oversea Settlement. He is now coming round to the idea of a board and I believe there is a good deal to be said for it. Then a long rambling talk with Stern about his Haifa–Baghdad railway, my difficulty being that I had nothing to tell him and his that he had no real alternative to offer to the original proposals which we did not think good enough.

20 June 1928: Cabinet. Balfour brought up the Zionist proposal arguing it very ably and I supported. Austen very definitely opposed chiefly on the line that any international collaboration would strengthen the case for interference by other nations in Palestine and might add to any difficulties with France over the Haifa–Baghdad railway, a line of argument which undoubtedly influenced me as well as all the Cabinet. I suggested that we need not guarantee the loan at all but simply ask the League Financial Committee to approve the loan as a good one if the British Government controlled the expenditure but he did not like that. Winston, who had apparently been seeing Weizmann, to my surprise backed us up at any rate to the extent of being willing to find the money but the PM and most of the Cabinet were definitely against and it was turned down for the time being at any rate. Meanwhile the one thing that did emerge was the need for doing something more for Palestine and for pushing ahead with Baghdad railway business on which Stanhope's report is very half-hearted and dilatory. This took up nearly all the Cabinet but we had a few minutes at the end on Neville's rating scheme.

22 June 1928: Cabinet on disarmament which was not as protracted as I feared because the French had put up a new proposal on the naval side which might also ease things with the Americans.

Next to unemployment, disarmament was probably the most central concern of the electorate before the 1929 General Election. The long lists of casualties which, day after day, filled the newspapers of 1916, 1917 and 1918, left the British people with an overwhelming horror of modern war. In 1928 the publication of Edmund Blunden's *Undertones of War* and the appearance of R. C. Sherriff's play, *Journey's End*, reinforced their image of the Western Front.

Disarmament was called for as the best guarantee against a repetition of such horrors; more sober observers thought it a means to avoid the coming of war itself. Revisionist historians headed by the former Foreign Secretary, Lord Grey, blamed its onset on the armaments race which had preceded it, and even those who did not accept the claim that 'Great Armaments' necessarily led to war saw that diplomacy had been overtaken by railway timetables as the generals mobilised and counter-mobilised. The concept of the League of Nations embodied notions both of collective action and of delay in its onset during which the pressure of world opinion could be brought to bear. The reduction of national armaments to the lowest point consistent with national security was essential to both. Making a virtue of necessity, British governments relied increasingly upon international disarmament both to forward their peace policy and to safeguard in an economic way the country's vital interests. In a curious alliance the Treasury, believing in the need to reduce public expenditure in the face of economic depression, and the Chiefs of Staff, realising that arms limitation might be the only road to parity of strength, ensured that disarmament was taken very seriously indeed. Inevitably, when success proved elusive, this made the Government vulnerable to popular feeling. 'The ratification of an international convention for the reduction and limitation of armaments became, as the abolition of slavery . . . a century before, the outstanding popular issue of British foreign policy.'*

Inside the Cabinet, Bridgeman found the 'most tiresome thing . . . the perpetual efforts to avoid a breakdown of the Disarmament Preparatory Committee at Geneva . . the F(oreign) O(ffice) are obsessed by the notion that if the conference breaks down, we shall be blamed, and something awful will result. . . .† There was continual pressure for the Government to solve the problems which beset the work of the League of Nations Preparatory Commission for the Disarmament Conference. By November 1927 it was clear that the most acute divergences of opinion centred on the extension of arms limitation to the smaller classes of warship, especially cruisers and submarines, and to trained army reserves. France, with her long tradition of conscription, was the principal obstacle to agreement about reserves; Britain, concerned for her trade routes, was an equally

*R. A. Chaput, *Disarmament in British Foreign Policy* (George Allen and Unwin, 1935), p. 44.
†Bridgeman's *Political Notes*, II, December 1928.

formidable obstacle to progress in naval disarmament. In March 1928, shortly before the opening of the fifth session of the Preparatory Commission, Austen Chamberlain intimated to Briand that the British Government would be ready to abandon its attitude on the limitation of trained reserves in exchange for a similar concession from France over Britain's latest naval proposals. In the event no agreement could be reached at Geneva that spring, but when in June Captain Deleuze, one of the French naval representatives on the Preparatory Commission, made an informal approach to Vice-Admiral Kelly with suggestions for a compromise, the Government attributed more importance to the approach than it perhaps deserved.

Subordinate only to the need to secure the Preparatory Commission from shipwreck (and so prevent the Germans from denouncing the provisions in the Treaty of Versailles limiting their armaments) was Britain's desire 'to keep in line with the French without which (as Salisbury argued) we may be isolated on this question in Europe'.* However she had also 'to avoid friction with America',† and these objectives were difficult to reconcile. Anglo-American relations had been poor since the abortive Geneva Naval Conference the year before (see pp. 492–3) and while the Cabinet's decision to adhere to the Kellog–Briand Pact (Diary, 4 May 1928) was calculated to improve them, the rider reserving Britain's position in certain parts of the globe which she regarded as crucial to her security, could not but take away much of the effect. In the United States opinion was finely balanced. The proponents of a strong navy had secured, in the aftermath of the Geneva Conference, the introduction into the House of Representatives in December 1927 of a major building programme. The British Government, at Churchill's prompting, had already cancelled two of the three cruisers that should have been built in 1927 as part of the construction programme agreed two years before, and in January 1928, again under heavy pressure from Churchill, the Admiralty reduced their 1928 programme by one. This conciliatory gesture did strengthen American opposition to their Navy Department's proposals, which were in February withdrawn. The so-called 'Fifteen Cruiser Bill' was substituted and passed with a rider urging President Coolidge to a fresh conference on the limitation of armaments.

There was more than a suspicion in the Foreign Office that at the root of the failure of the Geneva Naval Conference was Britain's attitude towards blockade as an instrument of war. There had been differing interpretations of the law of the sea in Britain and the United States, and the exercise of belligerent rights by the British Navy in the 1914–18 war had on occasion brought the two nations close to conflict. With Germans

---

*C.P. 192(28) of 18 June. Salisbury deputised for Baldwin in CID and chaired the Cabinet Committee on disarmament.

†*Ibid.*

and Irish prominent in America's population, it had by no means been inevitable that she would enter the war on the Allied side. The United States had asserted the right of free passage for all neutral shipping while Britain insisted on the right to search for contraband and to detain should any be found. Subsequently, after America's entry into the war, President Wilson had made absolute freedom of navigation outside territorial waters the second of his Fourteen Points and had excepted only the possibility that the seas might be closed by international action. At Balfour's persuasion, Lloyd George had resisted any attempt to include the point in either the Peace Treaties or the Covenant of the League.

By the autumn of 1927 there was real concern that blockade was not only 'at the root of our differences with the US over naval limitation [but] the one question which might lead to war between us'.* In correspondence with the British Ambassador to the United States, the Permanent Under Secretary to the Foreign Office noted that there were 'forces at work . . . whose aim it is to point to this country as the great enemy and competitor of the United States in every channel, political and commercial. This is all the more serious when one remembers that of the American population the Anglo-Saxon proportion is rapidly decreasing.'† It was not the possibility of direct confrontation with the United States that concerned British diplomats and politicians, but the thought that, should Britain at any time become involved in conflict with another power, the enforcement of a blockade might provoke the United States to use her fleet to break it. 'We should be confronted with the alternatives of either going into a war with the United States . . . or coming to an agreement with that country which would amount to accepting United States dictation.'‡

There was therefore a suggestion of a timely agreement with the United States, involving some abatement of British claims. It was felt too that the United States with a stronger commercial and military marine might advance some way towards the British position. The question was lent urgency by renewed discussions at the League of Nations about linking arbitration with the strengthening of the Covenant: security had long been seen as essential to disarmament and the defeat of the Geneva Protocol had been a check only for those who favoured some form of compulsory arbitration in disputes, not least as a sure means of identifying an aggressor should one party refuse to accept it.

Hankey, bitterly opposed to any abrogation of British rights at sea, secured the remission of the whole question to a CID sub committee. On his return from his Empire tour, Amery was added to its membership.

*Memorandum by the Foreign Secretary 16 October 1927, *Documents on British Foreign Policy*, Series 1A, Volume IV, p. 392.
†Tyrrell to Howard, 26 September 1927. *Ibid.*, p. 373.
‡The British Military Attaché's view, endorsed by the British Ambassador. *Ibid.*, p. 389.

The Committee's deliberations lasted into 1929. While Cushendun remained constant that they must appease the Americans, and in February found an ally in Churchill, Austen Chamberlain was persuaded to modify his view. However, Churchill for all his advocacy of a wholesale concession to the United States on 'the immunity of peaceful commerce at sea' remained adamant in his desire to avoid 'a treaty of mathematical parity with the United States'.* Amery found it difficult to reconcile Churchill's advocacy of a navy 'stronger and better than that of the United States' with his actions over the Naval Estimates, and his successful attempt to put the ten-year time horizon, during which no major war was to be expected, on to a rolling basis. Amery does less than justice in his diary to his fight on this, but neither his own nor Balfour's arguments prevailed, and the Ten-Year Rule in its new form lasted until the spring of 1932, less than ten years before the fall of Singapore brought the British Empire to its lowest ebb.

The two again took different sides over the suggestion made by Captain Deleuze, to which passing reference has already been made and which is the offer mentioned in the Diary for 22 June. The suggestion was that only cruisers mounting guns larger than 6 inch should be subject to limitation, but implicit in it was acceptance of the British view that arms limitation should be by category and not total tonnage. The Admiralty recommended acceptance 'and would also be prepared not to oppose the French thesis in regard to Army trained reserves'.† In other words, a deal was to be done. The possibility of a smaller number of categories, and of some switches in tonnage between them, may have been in Amery's mind when he saw the suggestion as a move also towards the American position, since it is quite clear that he underrated probable American hostility.

The British Ambassador was instructed to approach Briand, but when he did, the French repudiated Deleuze. Disclosures appeared in the French press and American suspicion was aroused. Nevertheless the British Government decided on 25 July to forward the proposal to the governments concerned in the disarmament discussions. While they waited for replies, the American press had a field day.

The United States had good cause for concern. The proposal limited the type of cruiser best suited to Pacific warfare, while leaving the smaller cruiser wholly unfettered. Their hostile reaction was not mollified by the curious origins of the proposal, and suspicions were only partly allayed by the disclosure of the relevant correspondence in a White Paper.‡ Wisely it was decided to leave the discussion of further naval disarmament until the Fifteen Cruiser Bill had been disposed of. Once it had been

*Quoted in Roskill, *Hankey*, II, p. 456.
†Adm. 116/2578, P.D., 03056/28.
‡Cmd 3211. See D. Carlton's article in the *Journal of British Studies* (1969).

signed by the President on 13 February 1929, the British Government announced that a further effort would be made. From the pronouncements of both Baldwin and the American delegate to the Preparatory Commission in April 1929, it was evident that agreement was possible. It was left to the in-coming Labour Government to make the London Naval Treaty, and Amery was very critical of the result.

The British Government had been engaged also in considering a new draft Arbitration treaty between Britain and the United States. Kellogg had forwarded this to the British Government in January, and while in principle the idea gave no difficulty, the question of what the two powers should reserve from its operation lent force to the discussion of belligerent rights. Should they be reserved or not? Further impetus to the discussion came from the introduction into the Senate in February 1928 of the Borah resolution calling for the re-codification of maritime law, and by the conclusion of a Convention on Maritime Neutrality by the twenty-one states of the Pan American Union. Nevertheless since the CID sub committee could not agree, it was decided that any overtures to the United States Government would have to be left until autumn 1929.

Further discussions on belligerent rights took place on 27 July, but there was no disposition to concede the British position. The Admiralty, asked to set out what points might be conceded, told the sub committee that visit, search, detention, seizure and blockade were all essential. Attention again focused on the draft arbitration Treaty with America. Amery's diary shows that by December Austen Chamberlain was again supporting 'Freedom of the Seas'. The Foreign Secretary even raised the matter in Cabinet before the sub committee reported (Diary, 7 December).* In the event no decision was reached, but a month later there was pressure from Downing Street to open negotiations. No doubt in the light of the *rapprochement* with the United States that Baldwin had in mind, Vansittart suggested making a virtue of necessity and opening discussions on Belligerent Rights.† Austen Chamberlain, however, came down against a conference. Although the sub committee, whose final deliberations figure largely in Amery's diary (pp. 582-3, 584-5, 586-7) were divided, the majority and minority reports, as Hankey put it, were 'mutually destructive'. 'The final report,' Hankey noted in his diary some months later, 'reached the conclusion that wrought to maintain Belligerent Rights as high as possible; that we should avoid any international discussions if possible; but that if we could not avoid it we should try to come to terms with the Americans.' In effect the whole question was postponed until after the election.

---

*Cf also Cab 63/40 Hankey to Salisbury, 10 December 1928.
†Vansittart to Hankey, 30 January 1929. Cited in Roskill, *Hankey*, II, p. 457.

23 June 1928: Saw Weizmann and broke to him the Cabinet decision about the proposed Zionist Loan. Also had a short talk with Lovat and received Sir Ofari Atta, the Omanhene of Abuakwin who has been a great support to the Government on the Gold Coast Legislative Council. He came attended by his standard bearer, secretaries, etc., including a little boy who is his soul and without whom he cannot go anywhere. It has been with some difficulty that the Court has been able to waive its rules about the accolade being conferred by the King with nobody present except the recipient, but poor old Sir Ofari was so distressed at the idea of being only knighted in the body with his soul waiting in another room that they have given way to him.

26 June 1928: Akhwan Sub-Committee of the CID at which we heard Clayton and Ellington, the former at first rather havering but [encouraged] by leading questions from both Sam Hoare and myself sufficiently effective to lead to Austen's complete surrender on the question of the fortified posts. So Clayton is to go back and tell Ibn Saud that we have no intention of giving way on that issue though we will be as conciliatory as we can on every other point. . . .

27 June 1928: Cabinet, most of it dull except that we got, for the first time, seriously on to the unemployment question. We decided to postpone any detailed consideration of this pending receipt of the Industrial Transference Board's Report, but I think that the steady increase of unemployment this summer is giving them all furiously to think. Winston to everyone's surprise suddenly exploded on Montagu Norman and deflation. He is right of course about Norman's pedantry, but it is rather late in the day to undo the work of the last eight years and in any case inflation is no effective alternative to safeguarding as a practical policy; it will alienate the City and the Press far more than anything else and will provide no battle cry for our people in the country. . . . During the dinner [given in L.S.A.'s honour by Sir E. Nicholl at the Carlton Club] my *vis à vis* [Hamar Greenwood?] told me that the phrase 'to think Imperially' was one which I had originally supplied to Chamberlain. He remembered Mrs Chamberlain telling him so at the time. I had quite forgotten this though I did undoubtedly supply him with a good many arguments and phrases at the time. The other phrase on the same subject which is also originally mine is 'men, money and markets' which I supplied to Bruce and he launched in 1923.

28 June 1928: Down to Wembley and was phono-filmed in a four and a half minutes' speech on my Empire tour. After being done myself I saw and heard the phono film of Worthy on the theme 'Why I am a Conservative'. I only hope I shall not look quite so horribly wicked as he does. There was a leer in his eye and an unction in his voice when he turned to the young people which made me think of the wicked uncle suggesting to the babes a pleasing picnic in the wood.

1 July 1928: After dinner I started towards ten to write a Cabinet memorandum on the report of the Industrial Transference Board which I had been reading in the morning and finished it by 2.30. Went to bed sleepy but satisfied that I had done something to focus discussion on unemployment and safeguarding for next week.

4 July 1928: At the Cabinet we considered the long delayed report of the Industrial Transference Board. By arrangement with the PM I led off with the idea that we should get migration out of the way and then discuss the broader problem of unemployment at large, including safeguarding. I stated the case fully, Steel-Maitland briefly backing me up, and then Winston ran in sweeping my proposals aside as inadequate and entirely imaginary as to finance (in spite of the fact that they had been worked out with his own people), and then started an entirely new hare suggesting that he should give another four millions a year in a subsidy to the railways to cheapen the cost of carrying coal. How much that is going to contribute to easing either the coal or the iron and steel situation he has not of course the slightest idea, and his whole manner was so wild and erratic that all we could do was to look down our noses and let him blow off. Stanley told me afterwards that he thought Winston was badly overdone and in need of rest if he is not to break down. In the end after much confused discussion it was agreed that all the questions, including migration, should be referred to the original committee which dealt with the rating scheme strengthened by myself, and that this committee might appoint sub-committees to deal with the various aspects. This means a tiresome delay as regards migration but also means that I can get the safeguarding point definitely brought forward in committee. Afterwards Philip, Winston, Guinness and myself lunched with Sassoon, and Winston, Philip and I had a great triangular debate on safeguarding, Winston very excited and trotting out all the worst old Free Trade stuff of the campaign of 20 years ago. Philip took a middle line, effectively disposing of Winston over safeguarding of iron and steel but afraid of anything in the nature of Imperial preference. It is surprising how timid they all are and how little they understand that a big scheme appeals to the public. Curiously enough that evening Winston seems to have made a real success at St Stephens Club dinner by saying that the time was coming for a definite advance in the matter of safeguarding, though I fear the audience who cheered him did not realise that he only means safeguarding in little things and looks at present like fighting to the death against inclusion of iron and steel. Anyhow, the question is once more definitely on the *tapis* and for all Winston's resistance and searches for red herrings we shall shepherd him into a position where he will either have to accept or break with us altogether. [L.S.A. holograph note: 'Alas! S.B. was too weak.']

5 July 1928: CID in the morning at which Winston opened his attack upon Singapore, or rather a plea for indefinite postponement by raising the plea that the ten years' period of peace should be a 'continually revolving credit'. We had a long and rambling discussion on this including a general survey of the foreign situation by Austen and a very silly little speech by Ryrie who said that Japan was the only danger to the Empire and that it was not a danger because the US would step in and protect Australia. I intervened to accept the general principle but to insist that it did not mean that if any particular major defence work was to be spread over a certain number of years that those years should be continually prolonged on the plea of the continuous prolongation of the peace period. Winston very much annoyed at this because the real object is of course to commit the CID to a formula which would enable him to postpone Singapore. In the end we never reached Singapore itself.

9 July 1928: Long talk with Billy. I gather Malaya is as hopeless in agriculture as it is good in preventive medicine while Ceylon is just vice versa, a state of affairs which might have been rectified years ago if only someone from the office had gone round. It is obvious that a great Empire cannot be governed by despatches. I also gather that Clifford is very near the border line, and being aware of it, has been pressing upon all the medical men around him chits certifying his sanity which he wants them to sign for him. One at any rate firmly refused. He is coming home on leave and we shall then have to see whether he is fit to go back. . . . Meeting of the Cabinet Policy Committee with Worthy in the chair, where in the absence of Winston we discussed safeguarding pretty fully. Somewhat to my surprise Philip came out vigorously in favour of dealing with iron and steel straight away and even the timid Guinness supported him on this as preferable to leaving it open until the election. David who attended was obviously impressed, and still more I gather when he went up to the 1922 Committee afterwards and found them clamouring for immediate action on iron and steel. Things are really moving and I think the moment may soon come when I can force the pace.

10 July 1928: Meeting of the Singapore Sub-Committee at No. 10, at which Winston made a determined effort to try and get the tenders for the Singapore Dock rejected and the whole matter postponed a year. It emerged, however, that Jackson's contract was so much cheaper than the others and that any new contract was not likely to be less if tenders were postponed that in the end he had to give way only stipulating that Willie [Bridgeman] should somehow make arrangements with the contractors to postpone both expenditure and advances of money during the next year. . . . Unemployment Policy Committee. Winston in the chair proceeded to lay down that there were certain possible ways of dealing with the question. When he had finished I pointed out that he had overlooked not the least important one which was contained in my paper on safeguarding which was on the agenda for the meeting. He grew very excited and frankly refused to touch the subject as controversial without instructions from the Cabinet. Warren Fisher also intervened quite gratuitously about my disparaging remarks on their report and against introducing a subject that would take five years to settle. I was quite content to leave it for the moment and we went on to a discussion of the other projects in the course of which Philip and Neville left not a shred of Winston's wild suggestion for a subsidy to coal rates and for stopping all boys going into the industry. From that we went on to migration which we discussed to some extent and then decided to set up a separate committee under Worthy's chairmanship to deal with it. Feetham came to dinner and we had a good talk afterwards. He told me the whole story of the Boundary Commission, how McNeill had himself suggested that they should be bound by a majority, had co-operated and agreed to everything up to the last moment and then suddenly taken fright. [See p. 426.]

11 July 1928: Saw the PM just before the Cabinet to say that I wished to ask for a ruling about my paper and the Unemployment Committee. He took the view that there could be no possible question of dealing with iron and steel this side of the next election in view of what he had told the ironmasters only the other day and that therefore he did not think there was any good in my getting the matter discussed on the Committee. So when proceedings opened I said that I wished to raise the matter as it seemed to me definitely within the reference to the Committee but that I was quite willing to withdraw it unless and until the Cabinet gave instructions that it should be considered. This leaves us free on the Worthy Policy Committee to go on considering it. I heard later in the day that the demand in the House for immediate action is growing hourly and I believe Page Croft has got something like 150 signatures for it. Later in the evening I wrote a long letter to the PM asking him to give further consideration to the matter. Meanwhile the Cabinet went on, Austen beginning on Egypt and suggesting that we might have something in the nature of a military agreement with the new Government.* This let loose Winston who protested against anything which might revive the folly of last year from which we had escaped thanks to Egyptian stupidity. This was a little too much for poor Austen who was very nettled and only seemed mollified when Douglas Hogg said that we did not all share the views that Winston and Salisbury had been expressing about the proposed Treaty. Austen then raised the renunciation of war but did not make much progress and the Cabinet was altogether a rather inconclusive affair.

12 July 1928: Saw Harding and Whiskard about certain suggested alterations to the answer to Kellogg on the renunciation of war and consequential telegrams to the Dominions. Cabinet at six when the first part of my proposed alterations were accepted, while the second was turned down. The fact is that on these points of inter-Imperial metaphysics and shades of language it is quite hopeless to make the Cabinet understand.

17 July 1928: Migration Sub-Committee. The afternoon was hot and the difficulty of explaining a complex subject involving the psychology of Dominion governments to a thoroughly ignorant committee rather got on my nerves. However, we made some progress though nothing is going to come out of it that is appreciably going to relieve the unemployment situation this winter. Nothing I suppose will ever teach the Treasury, or even the Cabinet as a whole, that you cannot cure unemployment immediately and there are plenty of things which would be helping the situation today if the Treasury had not vetoed them in the last two or three years.

18 July 1928: Winston is getting very agitated about unemployment which is another 25,000 worse this morning, so he complained that his little brain wave for dealing with the matter at the cost of four millions a year had been brutally turned down by Philip to which Philip retorted that he had only produced the arguments of his own experts which the whole Committee had found overwhelmingly against Winston's scheme. Winston then proceeded to denounce the Fisher Committee as the cause of all the trouble to which Neville gently interjected the trouble lay in the facts of the situation.

20 July 1928: Spent all the morning on the migration sub-committee and agreed a draft report which in substance amounted to very much what I had been advocating before. But the difficulty of making people

---

*i.e. the Sarwat administration. Austen Chamberlain proposed to offer them a fresh agreement despite the breakdown the year before.

understand either Dominion conditions or Dominion mentality has been considerable.

21 July 1928: Down to Birmingham considerably exercised in mind as to whether I should make a direct attack on Winston for his gratuitous Free Trade speech the day before. In the end however I confined myself in my speech to generalities though even these have created a certain amount of sensation. . . . [Thought] over my position in view of the whole attitude of the Cabinet under Winston's influence, and the PM's decision not to do anything for iron and steel in the present Parliament. Went round and had a good talk with Hamar after dinner. His view is that most of our people look to me to stay in the Cabinet and keep our end up; that I count for much more with the party as a whole than Winston does, but that I should reserve myself for a clear and obvious issue, and not weaken my position by going out when it would not be understood why I was doing it. On the whole I think I must carry on. . . . But time goes very rapidly and I am not sure whether I may not be missing the right moment by postponing. [Later L.S.A. note: 'I did.'] Time for educating the public will be very short after the autumn.

23 July 1928: General Unemployment Committee which met in Winston's room, a large mob. I secured the alteration of one passage in the migration report to which I objected, but otherwise did not join much in the conversation, leaving it to Worthy to hit back at Winston when he got rude. In the end, apart from our migration proposals, we are to meet the industrial crisis by anticipating the rating relief to the railways and concentrating it on the relief of the coal and iron industries. It will be interesting to see what the House thinks of this somewhat meagre fare this afternoon. . . . At 5.30 to the Cabinet where our migration report was approved of and all the other proposals, S.B. never even referring to the fact that he had just been meeting our party deputation on iron and steel and turned them down. The whole atmosphere of the Cabinet was of the happiest Olympian sort with no sort of realisation of the trouble brewing outside.

24 July 1928: Labour Vote of Censure on unemployment. MacDonald opened well describing the Fisher Report as a cry of despair, and then drifted off into futility. The PM was dull and very slow in the earlier part which consisted of generalities. Later when he had to deal with the actual things to be done, with regard to which passages had been supplied to him, he read them off hurriedly so that the effect was completely lost. Of my migration notes which were just about right in quantity and bal- ance he only read out the first part and suppressed the rest so that he gave the House no sort of idea of what we were going to do. The part in which he asked employers in the districts where unemployment is not quite so bad to take in miners from the black spots created sheer dismay in the ranks of our own party and even the expected anticipation of the relief to railway rates awakened no enthusiasm. In the end he sat down in absolute silence. . . . We all fled to tea and shaking of heads. The debate drifted on, the first sense of life being contributed by a vigorous platform speech by Page Croft on safeguarding, introducing his amendment which the safeguarding members had compelled the Whips to accept as the price of their not putting down a direct demand for the immediate protection of iron and steel. . . . Winston got up for what was intended to be a great effort over which he had been working in his room most of the afternoon and evening, looking in for a few minutes during the debate and then restlessly going off again. The speech fell increasingly flat and what with the heat of the evening people got restless and fell to talking, not confined to the Opposition side by any means. When he came to migration instead of using the notes I had prepared for Stanley which I had passed on to him he trusted to his own judgment and successfully managed in three or four sentences to say everything that could possibly be said to prejudice our schemes in the eyes of the Dominions. . . . My heart sank in my boots when I thought of all the effort I had spent to impress them with what was our view of migration and then having the whole effect undone by a few minutes of stupidity. [L.S.A. marginal note: 'But apparently no actual harm has been done.'] Having a few minutes to fill in he devoted himself to philosophising, beginning by comparing things with a century ago and then trying to say the Government was not committed to any extreme. In the course of doing so his natural Free Trade leanings came out so vigorously, especially when he declared that there was to be no reversal of the fundamental policy of this country, that our people got very angry and some of them even began to shout 'divide'. When he sat down there was a little mild cheering from some of the Liberals but none from our people. [L.S.A. thought this 'nailing of colours to the mast' must bring matters to a head, and that Baldwin, to whom he spoke his mind in the Lobby, would realise how futile his policy seemed to his followers. 'Alas! no', he added later.]

26 July 1928: Dined at the House with Jos Wedgwoods, the others being Chancellor, Walter Elliot, Mrs Dugdale, Simon *but* also Lady Simon. We had much amusing talk at dinner, and Mrs Dugdale having said that Balfour had chuckled consumedly for some hours after lunching with us the other day, had to tell in full the story of my early wanderings with F.E. Afterwards Jos started a serious discussion on the ultimate future of Palestine which became largely a discussion as to how to find a workable bridge from Crown Colony to responsible government. I answered Jos's question by saying that our ultimate end is clearly to make Palestine the centre of a western influence, using the Jews as we have used the Scots, to carry the English ideal through the Middle East and not merely to make an artificial oriental Hebrew enclave in an oriental country. Secondly that we meant Palestine in some way or other to remain within the framework of the British Empire. Thirdly that on the constitution we must mark time hoping that experience in Ceylon and elsewhere will find us new lines of development to follow later.

27 July 1928: Lovat came in in despair to say that he had had a telephone message that Winston had turned down his proposals for dealing with harvesters to Canada, substituting conditions which made the thing quite impossible. The only thing was to go and see Winston personally but the Treasury reported that he had left the office and gone to his house, to prepare a speech for the following night. So I took Lovat over to No. 11 where after some considerable waiting we were taken up to Winston's bedroom where we found him in bed in pink undies, very cross at being collared like this and vowing that he had not sent a mere message of refusal but had empowered Hopkins and Upcott to settle. After much telephoning Hopkins was discovered shaving somewhere and dressing for dinner within the Treasury and Winston unwilling to give any decision himself asked us to go down to the Treasury Board Room to deal with them and come back if we arrived at a deadlock. So we went down and discussed but after a few minutes Winston joined us in a flowered dressing-gown and we spent half an hour during which he seemed quite incapable of either accepting our proposals or turning them down flat, which he obviously was afraid of doing in view of the strong feeling in the Cabinet in favour of the general scheme. Finally he started leaving but spent another five minutes backwards and forwards between the door and the table trying to make up his mind and complaining bitterly of the ill treatment to which he was subjected. Never in 20 years had he known a Chancellor of the Exchequer so ill used. In the end quite incapable of deciding he told me that I had better do what I pleased and he could then bring his complaint before the Cabinet next Wednesday, and we left it at that.

1 August 1928: Talk with Lovat and Macnaghten about the Harvester scheme. Then to Cabinet where we dealt with a number of current questions; among them was the Harvester scheme which was very much approved of by the Cabinet. After I had dealt with it Winston made his complaint about my having worried him personally and the humiliation this inflicted upon his high officials and accused me of always going behind him. I contented myself at the moment with pointing out the extreme urgency of the Harvester scheme and the fact that I had been told that he personally turned down our proposals, but pointed out that things that I had left for negotiations between officials had not been settled in some cases for three years. A few minutes later an opportunity occurred over a memorandum on Free State currency which he had presented to the Cabinet and which neither I nor any of my Department had seen until that minute though it dealt with a letter from Cosgrave more than three weeks old. So I began solemnly complaining about the humiliation of my high officials and the neglect of the ordinary procedure between departments, laying it on very thick, with the whole Cabinet giggling at the success with which I was pulling Winston's leg. The only person who did not see it was Winston who got very indignant, began by trying to claim that it was not his business to consult me at all on any matter which dealt with finance and finally declaring in an angry tone that I was simply out to pick a quarrel with him. I sent him a little mollifying note across the table afterwards and he realised that I had only been ragging him and sent a charming little note in reply. At the end of proceedings the PM made a sort of general statement about the storm which had suddenly broken out from a clear sky when he thought that everything was going to be all right for the election.* I was not at all happy about his attitude which struck me as very decidedly negative and dictatorial. It sufficed to bring Jix to his knees at once with an apology for having said anything indiscreet if he did and promised to be a good boy in future, while Winston was also explanatory though less apologetic. I refused to be drawn as there was not time enough to express my views adequately. As it turned out the suggestion was made that the PM should issue some sort of announcement before we separated and it was arranged to hold a Cabinet the next morning to settle it.

2 August 1928: Walked to the office with Neville and planned with him that I should if possible get in early and open the case against our in-action in the matter of safeguarding, and that Neville should lie low and steady the position afterwards. As a matter of fact S.B. invited me the moment we sat down to fire off so I had a chance of dealing with the whole position comprehensively. I began by expressing my complete disagreement with his analysis the day before, saying that a crisis was inevitable and unavoidable at that particular moment, for the simple reasons that the unemployment figures were there and that we were within

---

*Churchill's speech on the 24th had provoked Joynson-Hicks to a reply at Broadlands on the 28th, which brought the conflict within the Government into the public arena. For the Opposition, A. V. Alexander tabled a question asking which of the speeches represented the policy of the Government.

the penumbra of the general election. I strongly deprecated too negative a declaration because our policy was bound to be settled by the unemployment figures and urged the Cabinet not to treat Stanley as Canute was treated by his courtiers. As for the election I pointed out that the PM and Winston's statements the week before might have passed muster a year or two earlier, but coming at a moment when every member was thinking already of the election they caused nothing but dismay. The Rating Bill was all very well for set speeches or as an item to mention to the credit of our work, but it could not become the main fighting platform. Cabinet Ministers could discuss it but it was not suitable for the street corner, the pub or the bench. I went on to add that the imminence of the election also made many of us determined to have a clearer definition and not to be misled as we thought we had been over his pledges in 1924. The need, however, was not so much for negative statements as for a positive declaration of what he did mean to do such as would keep the Party together. I said no one was asking for a general tariff or for food taxes and I gave what I thought was the kind of formula that would serve the purpose, viz. no general tariff but a simpler and more effective safeguarding procedure and no efficient industry excluded from consideration, and the maximum possible Imperial preference and Empire development consistent with no addition to our existing food taxation. Winston took up this last point and pressed it strongly against anything involving even the smallest element of transference of food taxes. They were all against me on this and I had to give way for the moment. I have no doubt whatever it could be done if someone else were Chancellor of the Exchequer. My views must have been strong meat for some of them there but they were listened to without interruption and I believe created a considerable impression. Philip followed simply dwelling on the need for a simpler form of safeguarding, with some of the present restrictions removed but on the other hand giving agriculture a chance of lodging its complaint if it wanted to. . . . Then Walter Guinness with his usual nonsense about the protection of steel losing the whole of the country seats because the farmer would be so distressed about his fences. Willy [Bridgeman] as another country Member dismissed this as absurd. . . . [Neville Chamberlain] summed up very skilfully by saying that he thought that any minor differences were transcended by our substantial agreement. Douglas Hogg declared that the whole unemployment was due to Free Trade and could only be cured by protection and then went on to say that the essential thing was to say as little about it as possible and avoid letting protection become an issue at the election. Then came Winston and after a certain amount of palaver justifying his past attitude definitely came into line by accepting the fact that iron and steel could not be excluded from the safeguarding inquiry. He thought it would lose us a great many votes but he did not see how we could get out of it. He proposed still to defend our policy in his own way, as an embroidery to the fundamental principles of Free Trade, and thought that he would do better like that than if he professed himself a convert to my creed. I think the strength of the feeling in the Party and a great preponderance of members has convinced him that he has got to accept the situation, and for the time being at any rate he has abandoned such notions as he may have had for forcing the issue and looking towards a coalition with Lloyd George. After this all was plain sailing except for a queer negative hand by Salisbury and we ended by agreeing that the PM should send a letter to the Chief Whip in which the two negatives of no general tariff and no food taxes should be balanced by the two positives of a simplified safeguarding procedure and no industries excluded. So the crisis is over for the moment. . . . During questions S.B. came to my room and thanked me very warmly for the way I had expressed myself at the Cabinet and had helped to contribute to an agreed solution. He thought all the Cabinet appreciated it too. Evidently they had thought I would be more troublesome or at any rate more aggressive in tone, though I confess I could not have put my case more forcibly than I did. The real fact of course is that the strength of the movement outside has frightened them and they may have thought I had lost my head over it and was indifferent about keeping the Party together. . . . Now for a few weeks of pure air and hard exercise to give me new balance and vigour for the autumn fight.

Looking back in 1951 Amery felt he had made the mistake of his life not resigning on 23 July when his authority would have been at its peak and he would have had the bulk of the Party behind him. Good nature, optimism, tiredness and eagerness to get away, he felt, had led to his not forcing the issue.

5 August 1928: The Sunday papers contained S.B.'s letter to Monsell which was a bad shock to me. Instead of 'no general tariff' he had put in 'no protection', and couched the whole thing in so negative a form that we shall either be justifiably accused of breach of faith if we do anything or, more probably, be once again paralysed for fear of such a charge. The letter looked to me as if it had been drafted for S.B. by Winston before the Cabinet and slightly modified after. [Later L.S.A. marginal note: 'I suspect now it was drafted by Eyres Monsell. No one, not even Neville, was consulted.'] I don't know even now if it is sheer stupidity on S.B.'s part and a failure to realise what words mean, or whether he is definitely hobbled by Winston and committed against any progress. Anyhow I wrote to him at once a very strongly worded letter making it clear that I regarded his letter as not in line with our agreement and holding myself free to raise the question again in the autumn. I also let Neville, Hamar and Higgins know that the letter did not embody my views. We went off at four o'clock and in the train down I was still full of disquiet and anger at the way the situation is being let down, and of plans for a real row when we meet in September. But by the time I was eating a bad French dinner in the train on the other side it all began to seem remote and of minor importance and by next morning I was back in proper holiday mood, as I never would have been had I stayed at home. Horace was quite wrong about *'caelum non animum mutant'*; my mind always changes the moment I cross the Channel, and all my cares remain behind with my London clothes.

Amery's holiday consisted of golf, bathing, walking and above all climbing, from which he returned to England on 18 September. Among his reading had been Ronaldshay's *Life of Curzon*.

13 September 1928: [The *Life of Curzon* was not] so wonderfully well done though I think fairly done. For all his high purpose Curzon was too inclined to be a drudge, and not really able to look far ahead in policy. At the FO it seemed to me he had no policy, only an intense interest in drafting good despatches. And his inability to recognise the difference between idle talk and serious movements in the East is shown even worse in his treatment of the Egyptian trouble at the outset than in the Bengal partition.

21 September 1928: Had some talk with Trenchard about our various problems. The Aden experiment seems clearly to be doing well and a dozen young airmen have pushed the Imam out of Dahla, a thing the WO considered could not be done without several divisions of troops. I have no doubt the air will eventually do what no one in history has done before and that is reduce Arabia under civilised authority.

22 September 1928: Went for a walk in the park after tea much perplexed as to what line to take over the fiscal issue created by Baldwin's letter.

24 September 1928: Saw the PM for a few minutes and after an exchange of holiday memories I tackled him about his letter. He was so naive in his surprise that anybody could think the word 'protection' meant anything else but general tariff that he quite disarmed me. He promised that he would take the opportunity at [the Conservative Party's Annual Conference at] Yarmouth of making his meaning on that point quite clear. In the evening I drafted a passage for his speech containing such a definition and have just sent it along. I only hope he will be wise enough to use it. . . . Cabinet at three o'clock, everybody looking bronzed and cheery but a few absentees including Lord Balfour who has been pretty ill. . . . We discussed a certain amount of foreign affairs chiefly the intolerable attitude of the Americans over the Naval compromise with France, and I notice a very healthy atmosphere of breaking away from Geneva and internationalism generally. . . . After dinner Neville came in and we had a good talk. He, too, had not liked the letter which he thought must have been drafted by Bobby Monsell, who is not a friend on this matter which indeed is true of the whole Whips' Office, but we agreed that no irrevocable harm had been done if the PM expressed himself properly. The great thing is to keep the steam up in the Party and I believe the election will take charge of the question by itself.

27 September 1928: Drove into Yarmouth to the Conference after breakfast. . . . In the afternoon we got first on to rating on which someone raised the issue of dropping the Poor Law Reform side of it. This gave Neville an opportunity to make a very effective little speech explaining the relation between the two parts of the Government's policy. The speech was so exactly what the delegates wanted to know that he got a quite remarkable ovation, shouts of *encore* and singing of 'He's a jolly good fellow'. The incident just came pat and has greatly strengthened his position in the Party. After that we came to safeguarding, the thing that the Conference had been most eagerly waiting for and there was the completest unanimity on Page Croft's resolution. Storry Deans moved an amendment to add the words 'especially iron and steel' which obviously the great majority wished to have added, but one delegate opposed rather vehemently so that there was a division, the majority being I should say 4:1. For some reason or other Philip and David seemed rather fussed by this as embarrassing the PM, but it seems to me that they could quite well read it as only affecting what was to be done after the general election. There can be no doubt about the growing intensity of feeling in the Party and it is bound to grow as the election comes nearer. The one fear is that when it does come we shall be tied by a lot of quite unnecessary negative pledges. . . . [That evening the Leader addressed the Conference]. It was a fine and enthusiastic meeting and Stanley in very good fighting form. When it came to safeguarding, however, instead of using any of the carefully prepared notes I had drafted for him, or clearly explaining exactly the sense in which he had used the word 'protection' he plunged things still further into eventual confusion by saying that there could be no question of protection being introduced, or general tariff, by a back door without a general election. This of course opens the door to every sort of objection by Free Traders outside or inside to any loyal fulfilment of the pledge that no industry will be excluded. I do not suppose anyone else noticed the implications of all this at the time, but bitter experience has made me very alert and I came away from the meeting wondering very much if I were wise in falling into line as much as I have done. After all our position is a singularly futile one. We believe certain things to be urgent, and yet we are not prepared even to alter our safeguarding procedure during the present Parliament. Everybody seemed very happy at supper at the Cators afterwards and I did not communicate my fears even to Neville.

30 September 1928: Wrote a letter to Stanley to try and find out if I can what he really meant about his reservation about general tariff by the side-door.

1 October 1928: Cabinet after lunch as the PM was going to Balmoral. Some discussion of the American Note on the Anglo-French naval compromise* which apparently is not to be answered until after the Presidential election. I wish Austen were back again. The FO is timid enough when he is here but it is quite hopeless with Cushendun. It is queer to find this once sturdy Ulsterman and extreme Die-Hard turned to a very timid 'Genevaist'.

3 October 1928: The Chief Rabbi was announced on a matter of urgency, and Clifford in a rash moment gave way and had to wait for over half an hour while my new visitor poured out to me in a state of immense excitement the woes of Jewry all over the world in connexion with the Wailing Wall of Jerusalem where there has been a slight fracas. He even burst into tears and I had great difficulty in trying to explain to him that there were two separate questions, one the general injustice to the Jews that they have no holy place of their own in Jerusalem but only a place by sufferance of Moslem proprietors, and the other the fact that their Beadle had been trying to poach on the status quo by erecting a screen and had only himself to blame for the trouble.

4 October 1928: A good deal of agitated telephoning to Dublin and Balmoral about the attempt to burn down Lascelles' house at Portmina on the eve of his visit there with Princess Mary [the Princess Royal]. Happily Cosgrave took a sane and cheerful view of the situation and followed it up by an invitation from the Governor General to the Lascelleses to breakfast with them tomorrow and the King, though nervous and hating anything to do with Ireland, yielded to the PM's argument and our

---

*The Americans had asked for clarification of the proposals, but in hostile terms in a letter from Ambassador Houghton to Lord Cushendun dated 28 September 1928 (printed in Cmd. 3211, pp. 34–8).

message that all was well. Lunched with Weizmann and a number of Zionists to meet Chancellor. Sat between Reading and Weizmann, the latter obviously did not take the same hysterical view of the Wailing Wall incident as the Chief Rabbi and was obviously bored by the officiousness of the local Beadle who had caused the trouble.

5 October 1928: Lascelles came in for a few minutes, quite cheery and confident about the reception the Princess and himself would get in Ireland but convinced that the King would be angry with him however well it went off. According to him the King so hates Ireland and anything to do with it that he does not like the idea of any of the Royal Family ever going there.

9 October 1928: Saw S.B. for a few minutes about the formula for Dominion ministers over which I cannot get the FO to see reason, and also about bingeing up the Treasury on migration.

10 October 1928: A few minutes late for the Cabinet where we discussed the Anglo-French Naval compromise and decided to publish some papers. The thing that annoys me is that we have let our case go by default all these weeks, making no attempt to bring out the fact that our proposals did mark an advance towards meeting the American arguments and were not merely an arrangement to square the French. I rubbed this in as strongly as I could but they took the view that they would leave this until our note to America appeared. However, I think I shall say something about it at the Navy League dinner. I also raised the issue of the formula under which Dominion ministers are to be appointed at foreign capitals, Cushendun replying as a Die-Hard for the FO. I think I should have had my way but the PM intervened saying that he thought it would have to be settled on my lines but that it was better to postpone the whole question until Austen came back and that I could fence with Mackenzie King and the Irish until then. Went on to an Army Council luncheon. . . . Sat between Milne and Winston and had a good talk with the former about the folly of the whole L.G. policy towards Turkey and about the Middle East generally. . . . Then I turned to Winston with whom I had a good talk both about the naval question and about safe-guarding. I told him that I had made great concessions in accepting the Cabinet's *concordat* last summer but that I must be quite clear that there would be no question of turning down the conclusions of the Safeguard-ing Committee on political grounds if I was going to run the risk that possibly no important industries might get a recommendation in favour. I must also have the chance of all the leading industries getting a favour-able recommendation within the next Parliament. He agreed with the qualification that in such circumstances an individual Cabinet Minister might have to feel obliged to resign ... Dined at the Canada Club sitting between Mackenzie King and that vain old bore Dandurand. King with rather a cold and very much worried about his speech which he had taken the trouble to write out and was not sure that he could remember. . . . [He] devoted himself for 20 minutes to generalities before touching on his main themes, migration and the appointment of ministers abroad by the Dominions. On the former subject he confined himself to a vigorous repudiation of the charge that his Government was not favourable to British settlers; on the latter he endeavoured to convey the impression that Canadian representation abroad would help and not hinder Imperial unity. But he did it very confusedly and digressing at intervals into British representation in Canada and the Canadian High Commissioner in London. Finally he wound up by repeating his old simile of the star which closer examination by the telescope proves to be a system of separate stars each moving freely in space. I heard it at the Guildhall in 1926 and I think also in Liverpool and I think I also heard it in 1923. He really must discover some new parallel.

11 October 1928: Had a talk about Canadian migration first of all with Plant and Macnaghten, the former telling me all about Lovat's very successful tour through Canada, then reinforced by Warren Fisher and Hopkins from the Treasury. After some preliminary sparring on the general question of settlement as a background, on which Fisher definitely got the worst of it, we got on to very satisfactory lines and I hope we can really get something done this winter. Mackenzie King came to dinner and we collected to meet him, Hailsham, the George Lloyds, the Chancellors, Lady Cromer and Lady Willingdon. I sat between Lady Cromer and Lady Willingdon and beyond getting a little more of Lady W. and a little less of Lady C. than I wanted got on very happily. After dinner I did just touch on one question of business with Mackenzie King, namely the formula for the appointment of Dominion ministers abroad, and to my great satisfaction found that he himself wanted to retain the reference to the diplomatic unity of the Empire. George Lloyd looking well and happy, Sarwat's death has eased things a great deal for him; first Zaghloul and now Sarwat, the Egyptians will soon believe that he gets rid of embarrassing native statesmen by the evil eye.

15 October 1928: To a Persian Gulf Committee where I found everybody in favour of upholding our rights on the Persian Gulf except Cushendun who from an erstwhile Die-Hard has become the most timid of pacifists. I only wish Austen were back for he has at any rate a little courage sometimes.

16 October 1928: Conference with Ormsby-Gore and Bottomley on Grigg's agitated requests for leave. Finally decided that we had better call all three Governors back to discuss the Hilton Young Report.

17 October 1928: Cabinet. At the end of the meeting the PM said a few nice words of farewell to F.E. who replied appropriately. Whether his going is on balance a loss to the Cabinet or not it will be difficult to say. His judgement has often been very valuable and he gave great help both with the General Strike and with the Irish during the Imperial Conference. On the other hand the wide and naturally exaggerated reports of his manner of living have made him a doubtful asset in the country. From my own point of view I regret the dropping out of a friend. Went on to the Government lunch to the E[mpire] P[arliamentary] A[ssociation] where I took the chair *vice* the PM. I wish Stanley would take a little more trouble about things of that sort; it would have been so small an effort to come and shown a real appreciation – perhaps I am to blame for not having bullied him about it.

20 October 1928: Read some of Henry Wilson's biography, finishing the first volume before I left. There is no doubt that Henry's intense energy and determination to pull every string he could had a most disastrous effect on the Dardanelles business. That he should have done it being where he was was inevitable, but it was a tragedy that he was not kept behind as CIGS and enabled to form a comprehensive view of the war as a whole, such as he did later.

24 October 1928: Persian Gulf Committee at which I took a strong line against our submitting anything in that region to the League of Nations any more than we should submit a Suez Canal question to the League.

29 October 1928: To a Cabinet; nothing very interesting but I got a Cabinet Committee set up under my chairmanship on migration. . . . Then a Conference with Cadman . . . about the muddle into which the TPC railway proposition has got. I insisted that we should have to stick to Haifa as the railway terminus and have it in the agreement and that this was no concern of the French shareholders, [and] that we find a formula which left the termination of the pipe line or pipe lines vague. On this Cadman thought he could clear matters.

31 October 1928: Had some talk after dinner . . . with a quaint little woman, Mrs Emerson, otherwise Anita Loos and author of *Gentlemen Prefer Blondes*. I gather she made a fortune writing film stories when she was about fifteen. She told me that she was born on the stage, I gather one parent an actress, the other a playwriter and 'I was practically born with the films' so I said, 'You lisped in numbers and the captions came.'

1 November 1928: Conference with Jix . . . on the question of naturalizing Palestinians in the Government service. Jix's whole attitude on this is both hostile to naturalization generally and based on the assumption that Palestine is only temporarily under our control. I laid great stress on the essential necessity of Palestine always being in the Empire and if self-governing, then on the lines of a British Dominion. In the end we compromised on Jix's being willing to consider all good cases brought forward even where the candidate had only served the Empire in Palestine. . . . To Belligerents Rights Committee which sat for a couple of hours. Salisbury and the Lord Chancellor and myself pulling to pieces Hurst's proposed arbitration treaty.

2 November 1928: Dined with Abe Bailey to meet the Athlones; one of his usual large affairs. As I went in I was given a little card to say that I was to take in Lady Stanley and rejoiced thinking it was my Lady S. from Ceylon. Instead I found a terrible strident young woman, the wife of Lord S. the Whip, known as Portia because she lays down the law, who talked to me aggressively about Lancashire and Free Trade and her love for Beaverbrook most of the dinner until at last I seized a moment and turned to old Lady Rossmore who began by gently saying, 'I gather you have been learning a good deal lately.' Kipling, Lady S.'s other neighbour, liked her even less than I did, so I concluded from his remarks next morning.

5 November 1928: I had an inter-departmental conference on the oil situation in the Middle East and we agreed that we might let Cadman put Haifa as the railway terminus in a letter separate from the main agreement, but stiffened up the letter considerably. Cadman has since written and telephoned confirming this and will force it through with his French colleagues. Lunched at home and Cabinet in the afternoon. In the evening PM's eve of session dinner. I sat between Jack Gilmour and Winston. Winston was more forthcoming on safeguarding than I have known him. He tells me that he does a certain amount of work in bed in the morning, spends only 20 minutes on dressing and keeps two hours free every night for dictating his book. I wish I could ever get as free of office work, or have the energy to dictate for two hours a night if I did.

6 November 1928: Unemployment Sub-Committee at the Treasury and agreed the general line of statement to be made in the debate. Lunched . . . with Gilbert Wills in order to put to them the political reasons why it is so important to help Rhodesia to go ahead. Found them only moderately responsive. Apparently the Rhodesian cigarette has not gone quite as well as they expected and Bradbury vowed the taste of it is one that he himself liked less the more he smoked of them. . . . Short talk with the PM both about [raising] C. T. Davis's salary* and the future of the two offices. I told him they would have to be divided but that my inclination was towards the Dominions Office being combined with the Presidency of the Council. He said something to me about our doing more for Empire development in the next Parliament which gave me a chance of speaking to him very straight about the difficulties I have had to contend with in Winston, adding that I was not prepared to go on in my present capacity unless he could shift Winston somewhere else.

7 November 1928: Talk with Clementi whom I assured that we shall certainly never contemplate giving up the leased territory of Hong Kong, and that I was still pressing to enable him to give 99 years leases. . . . I wrote to Cushendun to try and put a little backbone into him. Cabinet, nothing of consequence as far as I can remember, after which I caught the train to Preston thinking out a couple of speeches en route. . . . It was curious talking to an audience who had all seen me ploughing, climbing, bathing as a film star in fact and not as a speaker. Brass is doing wonders of indirect propaganda for the Party all over the country with the film, and incidentally making me a popular character!

8 November 1928: Arrived a little late for Belligerent Rights Committee at which we discussed the draft Arbitration Treaty with America which I asked for at the last meeting. Most of us were against Hurst's draft which had a separate paragraph excluding belligerent rights, and favoured Hailsham's suggestion of inserting a covering reference by way of exception to justiciable cases. I urged leaving it a matter for the special terms of reference, but didn't get much support, though I think I am right. Saw Gretton in my room about Irish Grants and got him to stave off questions. We shall be well in the soup over this as it will cost £350,000 to £400,000 over the £1,000,000 fixed as the final limit earlier in the year. Worse still I hear the new Privy Council Board on the Irish Pensioners is going to confirm the conclusion of the last, but on different grounds. Only in connexion with Ireland could such a tangle ever have arisen.

9 November 1928: Conference with O[rmsby-]G[ore], Wilson and Grindle as to what we could do in the way of Colonial development to help the industrial situation here, the department having put up a very nega-

---

*Warren Fisher was resisting this; on 2 November L.S.A. had found Fisher 'not only sticky but wholly incapable of understanding the importance of this office'.

tive paper. We decided to submit nothing but a suggestion for trade facilities freed from previous restrictions while I should send in a personal letter to Winston to say that I could do a good deal if I were given my money to play with but could not possibly do anything on existing lines held up all the time.

10 November 1928: Wilson, *The Times* Scientific man, told me after [dinner at the Ritz to meet senior staff at *The Times*] that he thought the scientific work being done by the Colonial Office was the outstanding thing in this Government's record.

11 November 1928: Armistice Service in the morning. We adjourned for hot soup in the Cabinet Room afterwards. I suggested to the PM he might ask in the High Commissioners but he doubted whether there was enough soup suggesting that I should remind him about it for next year.

12 November 1928: Persian Gulf Committee where Denys Bray talked to us very straight about the absurdity of being so nervous of the Persians and so League-ridden. Unfortunately Cushendun was not there to hear. However, Bray bold as he was was not prepared for my line of telling the League the Persian Gulf had nothing to do with them.

14 November 1928: Cabinet at which I had a number of matters up, wireless affecting the West Indies, Dominion legislation as to which they agreed that a telegram should go suggesting the sub Conference next autumn, the alarming new Privy Council decision [about Irish Pensions] confirming the previous one though Douglas privately still thinks them wrong.

15 November 1928: Cabinet Migration Committee which I got the PM to let me set up and which I am beginning to regret. We spent an hour or more in a futile wrangle over a small point regarding migrants assisted by loan. The only value of it may possibly be some education of my colleagues.

18 November 1928 (All Souls College, Oxford): There was quite a large party in College ... [sat] in the Common Room between Holdsworth and Lionel Hichens. Lionel is convinced that with a little financial subvention given in the right way, possibly through the export credits, he could get the leading steel firms in the country to rationalise to such a extent for instance as forgings and this would do more immediate good to the iron and steel industry than a tariff. His great complaint is that there is nobody whom he can get at who will decide to do anything. In Lloyd George's day when there was industrial difficulty he would get half a dozen big employers together, snatch at a plan suggested by one of them and carry it out as he did with the Trade Facilities which Lionel told me was his own suggestion. Now nobody has the courage to do anything except sometimes Winston and he doesn't want to do the right things. Lionel deplored the dropping of Trade Facilities which he thought the most useful measure since the war.

20 November 1928: A small hush Cabinet meeting about the APOC [Anglo-Persian Oil Company] in which the Persian Government is suggesting that they should have shares if the concession is prolonged. Cadman expounded the position and we were generally in favour of his going ahead subject to possible repercussions on the Iraq situation which I promised to investigate.

21 November 1928: Cabinet which we got through pretty quickly as the PM had to leave for Scotland at 12.45. The very thorny question of how to deal with the Privy Council decision on Irish Pensions was reached five minutes before the end, but owing to the haste and to Winston's unexpected tractability I got through my recommendation which is that we should find the money but make the Free State pay it in fulfilment of the decision, and not flout the treaty.

22 November 1928: Saw Cadman about the effect of his APOC's scheme on Iraq and came to the conclusion that there were no serious difficulties involved. . . . Then Persian Gulf Committee at which Trenchard set out his ideas for bringing the Gulf and the Trucial Chiefs more directly under the CO and Air Ministry while Bray put forward the case for Indian Imperialism.

27 November 1928: To the Annual Dinner of the Iron and Steel Exchange and gave them a very definitely protectionist speech about which Winston was decidedly annoyed next morning; though I took good care to make no recommendations but only to survey the situation as I saw it as a student.

28 November 1928: Cabinet. There was considerable fuss over the fact that Stamfy had sent a telegram to several foreign capitals and also to Ottawa in much more alarming language than any of the bulletins yet issued about the King. The first decision was to try and stop these messages, the second and wiser one was to let them go and to get Jix make the doctors issue a further statement during the day more or less on the same lines. This was done and the public so far from being alarmed have taken this statement as a reassuring one. As a matter of fact there is no doubt reason for anxiety and the situation might well get worse if the King's strength does not stand up to the continued strain. I had a preliminary tiff with Winston when I mildly protested against his putting down for discussion the paper of his about an Irish loan being a trustee security which raises big constitutional issues without giving my office any warning or time to prepare their views and got the thing postponed a week. Then came the long deferred attack by Philip and Winston on the EMB in the form of a demand that the £25,000 advertising the British Industries Fair should come on the EMB vote. They were very persistent and many of the Cabinet rather wrong-headed and in spite of my earnest appeals supported by the PM and Neville the debate dragged on for over an hour and was finally left unsettled because Winston wanted to review the whole wider position of whether we were getting our value from Dominion preference. The real trouble is that both of them hate the EMB and want to wreck it. Neither of them and, as far as I can make out, very few of the Cabinet attach any importance to the fact that this money fulfils a pledge to the Dominions.

29 November 1928: Long talk with David [Davidson] and young Rhys about the present position as regards safeguarding. David reports Yorkshire frantically keen about it but some of the iron and steel people are moving away, convinced that the industry needs completely reorganising. I pointed out that the two things ought to go together and that what the President of the Board of Trade ought to be able to get is the banks and the heads of industries together and secure from them a complete scheme of rationalisation, common selling and research as the price of a duty. One of the disadvantages of the safeguarding procedure is that this cannot conveniently be done though it might not be impossible. He also reported that many people were pressing for inquiry to get started before the election. I wish he could rub this idea home on S.B.

30 November 1928: Migration Committee at House of Commons. The Board of Trade people announced that they had made what we all considered a satisfactory scheme with the shipping companies to give us £10 British migrants rate and this is at any rate one substantial thing achieved. We then had Egan in to be questioned about his land settlement scheme. There was a good deal of asking questions and answering rather at cross purposes though I did what I could to help him explain himself clearly. After he left they all waxed indignant about him refusing to realise that the scheme is really from our point of view quite a good one. I am sorry to say that ever since the tiresome Fisher Committee the attitude of many of my colleagues about the whole migration business has been rather unreasonable and very anti Dominion. They cannot put themselves into the position of the other fellow, and persist in treating migration as a scheme for dealing with our unemployment which the Dominions ought to be grateful to help us with. Got quite annoyed at the end and gave them a piece of my mind which won't help things. I think it is high time that somebody else took the Dominions Office and enabled the Cabinet to realise that there are certain things inherent in the situation and that it is not merely my always seeing the Dominions' point of view and not our own.

7 December 1928: Cabinet on Anglo-American relations, interspersed with some discussion of Reform of House of Lords, from 11 to 3.30 with a short break for lunch. Everything left undecided, including long delayed answer to American note, because Austen has to rush off to the League Council at Lugano, while Cushendun was left bleating piteously about what we were to do about the next stage at the Disarmament Commission. I suggested that we should say that we couldn't discuss Naval disarmament till we had settled with US and that they had better settle land and air by themselves. Neither Austen and still less Cushendun are anywhere near realising that it is USA friendship and Empire approval, versus Geneva.

11 December 1928: Lunched at the Carlton. Boothby told me that Winston had said that the only issue at the next election was Bolshevism versus anti-Bolshevism which I told him was sheer rubbish.

12 December 1928: Cabinet at which the difficult question of the Irish Grants Commission came up. Having announced that we should pay practically full award, and that we were not going to pay more than a million we now find, thanks to letting in new applicants, that we cannot pay in full under about £1,400,000. Salisbury and I were all for doing this and all the rest for sticking to the million. I asked for my dissent to be recorded and foresee a certain amount of trouble with our own Party. We also had up the trustee stocks in connexion with the Free State and I found the Cabinet on this and on most things just now very anti Dominion, quite prepared to throw out all Dominion securities from the trustee list. I feel myself daily more and more out of touch with a Cabinet which under the influence of day by day work and above all of Winston (and not realising any of the implications of 1926) is becoming steadily 'little England' and even anti-Imperial as well as hopelessly negative on fiscal policy. Possibly the best thing would be that we should be beaten. I confess I cannot at this moment see any other way of getting that 'old man of the sea' Winston off our shoulders.

13 December 1928: Then CID ranging over a variety of speeches beginning with the state of German armaments. Salisbury was fussy about these and I rather shocked them all by saying that I did not think it mattered very much what they were as Germany was not likely to be a menace to us again. Cabinet Migration Committee. The usual talking at sixes and sevens, some of them like Worthy still having no other idea than that I should go and tell Canada that they jolly well must take as many unemployed as we cared to send them. Talk with Peel afterwards about his suggestion of an Indian agent in Eastern Africa. As a compromise he put forward the idea of an unofficial visit of an eminent Indian and this I was disposed to agree to.

17 December 1928: Melchett to lunch alone and had a good talk. He is a whole-hearted safeguarder now, as well as an ardent Empire developer, and thinks the Government very feeble, and from the point of view of the ordinary man uninteresting and uninspiring. Questions. Dined with David and Mimi – the latter momentarily expecting a young Davidson – and had a good talk. David coming on considerably on the fiscal question.

20 December 1928: Back to House where there was a long Belligerent Rights Committee. Austen rather solemn and much shocked at my suggesting that we should tell the Americans that we had much better wait for the next few wars before deciding what line of policy would suit either or both of us.

31 December 1928: So much for 1928, on the whole a dull and unsatisfactory year. The opening month in Canada was a success, but I don't seem to have done anything really effective since then, and I have felt myself very much estranged from most of my colleagues in the Cabinet. I cannot help feeling that they understand nothing about the Empire, and some of them are acquiring a definitely anti Dominion complex. The real root of the trouble I imagine, however, is that I have done all that it is possible to do from the DO and CO end of things, with Winston at the Exchequer. If there were a chance of his being shifted there is much that I could still do. The only alternative would be to go to the Board of Trade where I could get a move on, and where he couldn't stop me. Anyhow, we shall see, and I must continue to be patient, but it has been a great effort all this year.

Despite his assertion that on his holiday he had 'almost completely forgotten office, politics and all the rest', Amery had read office memoranda ('all hopelessly negative') on the Hilton Young Report. 'It won't be easy to get much done', he wrote in his diary for 13 January, 'but I shall try.' On the train journey home he caught up with 'some of Sammy Wilson's notes on West Africa and Hilton Young Report' and spent the morning of the 18th being brought up to date by Wilson and Batterbee. In the afternoon he had a short chat with Baldwin.

Amery had appointed Hilton Young to chair the Commission appointed 'to make recommendations as to whether, either by federation or some other form of closer union, more effective co-operation between the different governments in eastern and central Africa may be secured'. Young himself had been allowed to choose his fellow commissioners: he chose Dr Oldham, Secretary of the International Missionary Council and an authority on native affairs, Sir George Schuster, the Economic and Financial Adviser to the Colonial Office, and, at the insistence of the Government of India, Sir Reginald Mant, who had served under Young on the Commission on Indian Finance and was a member of the Council of India. Both the Europeans in Kenya and the Indian community were extremely suspicious of the Commission, while in India there was out-right hostility to Grigg's pro-European speeches and the tendencies of the White Paper. The Viceroy, who had been one of the authors of the Wood-Winterton Report in 1922, was naturally indisposed to renege on the views he had then expressed, which were very favourable to the cause of the Indian in East Africa. The Indian Government sent a deputation to help prepare the evidence of the East African Indian National Congress to the Commission, and, although Amery refused them permission to accompany the Commission in its investigations, they were twice seen by the Commission and allowed to be present when Indians were inter-viewed. They were opposed both to the creation of an unofficial majority in the Kenya Legislative Council and to closer union; if a federal govern-ment were to be constituted, however, it should be strong rather than weak. They also pressed the case for Indians to share in the administration of African interests and to be nominated to represent them on the legis-lature. To these points Congress itself added the demand for a common roll franchise.

Grigg had done his best before the Commission arrived to placate Congress, but he had not been able to allay their suspicions, nor was he able to persuade them to take up vacant seats on the Legislative Council. It was not a happy background to the Commission's visit to East Africa in the first months of 1928.

On their return to England in May, it was quickly apparent to Amery that the Commission, despite their chairman, were in danger of thwarting his federal ideas by their stress on the primacy of native policy. Curiously enough it was Oldham, for whose appointment Grigg had pressed and whom the settlers trusted, who drafted the section on native policy. The report was published in January 1929 with a brief dissenting report from the chairman. The majority report was not very favourable to the European community. Not only did it reiterate the 1923 declaration on 'paramountcy' but it went on to assert that the immigrant communities might justly claim 'partnership, not control'. The first requirement, they said, was to define, protect and further African interests, but the Government had an obligation also to do all in its power to help the immigrant communities. 'In as much as the progress of the territory must depend on co-operation between the races, the ideal to be aimed at is a common roll on an equal franchise with no discrimination.' The white settlers' dream of responsible government was brushed to one side. There could only be an unofficial majority in the Legislative Council if the interests of the native races were adequately represented and Imperial control maintained until the natives could take a share of Government equivalent to that of the immigrant communities, something which was not in the foreseeable future.

The Commission in effect agreed to the principle of closer union, but thought that there should be three stages in its implementation. First a High Commissioner should be appointed immediately to inaugurate inquiries on questions of native policy, to promote unified control of services of common interest, and to work out modifications in the constitution of Kenya in preparation for the second stage. The High Commissioner would have no administrative or legislative powers, but would preside over meetings of the Governors and exercise the executive powers wielded by the Secretary of State. At the second stage he would himself become Governor General to exercise the functions of control and supervision which until then had been exercised by the Secretary of State. Finally, at the third stage, the Governor General would become directly responsible, with the aid of a small central legislature drawn from the councils of the three territories, for the legislative and administrative control of common services. There was to be modification at the second stage of the Kenya Legislative Council to substitute unofficial members representing native interests for certain official members, thus creating an unofficial but not an elected majority. To safeguard against the possible abuse of this position the Governor General was to have special powers to enact over the head of the Council any legislation which he regarded as essential to the fulfilment of his responsibilities.

There can be no doubt that Amery was greatly dissatisfied with the report, and would have preferred to have acted upon the minority report put in by Hilton Young, a strong supporter of closer union. However, he had to make the best of the position, planning from an early date to send out his Permanent Under Secretary, Sir Samuel Wilson, to salvage what he could in discussions on the spot, subject to a further report to the Government. In a memorandum for the Cabinet, dated 23 February

1929,* Amery described the enunciation of the general principles of native policy as masterly, but damned the *obiter dicta* on the common roll and on the impossibility of full responsible government before the natives took an equivalent share of responsibility as going beyond their terms of reference and the time horizon of their recommendations. Similarly he found a good deal to cavil at in their suggested three stages, in particular the first. The powers of the High Commissioner went too far in the direction of a uniform native policy. Indeed the existing Governors felt that native policy should very largely be left in their hands, subject to the High Commissioner taking the chair of the Governors' Conference, seeing all reports on native policy, and having the right to advise the Secretary of State. On the other hand the Commission had been too cautious over common services. The Governors and Amery seemed to be in agreement that they could move direct to the legislative and administrative unification of defence, customs, transport, posts and telegraphs, wireless, aviation, central research and the like. Amery therefore proposed to send out Wilson to consult along those lines and return immediately after the election to submit the result of his discussions to the Cabinet. This bold scheme deserved better fortune.

Dissatisfaction with the report was not confined to the Secretary of State. The settlers were aghast. In a cabled protest to Amery they took their stand on Churchill's declaration of 1922 and declared that the communal franchise was an essential part of the 1923 settlement. They threatened 'more vigorous action' to assert their claim to responsible government. In England, however, the Commission's report had widespread support. Lord Lugard joined with the Archbishop of Canterbury, Lords Cecil, Olivier, Reading and Southborough, and C. R. Buxton in a letter to *The Times* stressing the importance of the report and calling for its review by a joint committee of both Houses of Parliament. Privately, through Tom Jones, Professor Coupland urged on the Prime Minister the view that the report was of the same historic value as the Durham Report and that it should be given a fair chance. 'Coupland like Oldham and Lugard fears that Amery will stampede the Cabinet and get a pro Delamere policy adopted,' Jones noted.† Baldwin promised to show Coupland's letter to Amery: 'These academic fellows will listen to one another.' *The Times* took a view similar to Coupland's on 25 February.

The attitude of the Government of India proved to be Amery's greatest problem, as the diary clearly shows. The Kenya Indians in effect accepted the report when they assembled at Mombasa late in January 1929.

*C.P. 47 (29), Cab. 24/201.

†*Whitehall Diary*, II, p. 171, for 13 February 1929.

Opinion in India was more mixed.* An informal conference between the leaders of the Indian legislature and the Standing Emigration Committee agreed eventually that the main principles of the report were fair, and that Sir Samuel Wilson should be empowered to consult and investigate only within the context of the majority report. Two days later, on 19 March, the Viceroy conveyed this view to London,† together with the Government of India's acceptance of the majority report and opposition to the political form of closer union, while accepting the appointment of a High Commissioner.

In London Peel had already checked Amery's attempts to salvage closer union. Shown the draft of Amery's Cabinet Paper over the weekend, he replied with one of his own on 25 February in which he urged the importance of the Indian view on the suggested constitutional changes in Kenya. The majority and minority reports were agreed in getting rid of the official majority in the legislative council, but the majority report would have left the Government representatives in a position to command the decision. Hilton Young by contrast would have put the Europeans in a majority. If the proposal to send Wilson out were accepted, the Cabinet must indicate which of these two recommendations he was to put forward, since he was to negotiate, not merely discuss, and to that extent any agreement arrived at, while provisional in form, would in fact be a *fait accompli*.‡ It appears to have been a combination of Peel's arguments with those of Salisbury which prevented a decision on 26 February. Amery returned to the charge with a fresh Cabinet Paper,§ dated 4 March, in which he tried to separate the issues. Closer union he held to be in no sense controversial, at least in Britain, and raising no issue of political principle. The powers of the High Commissioner/Governor General over native policy, as put forward by the Commission, certainly went further than was desirable in the eyes of both the Colonial Office and the Governor: a co-ordinating influence would be sufficient. That left the question of the Kenya legislature, and Amery argued that they were committed by the 1927 White Paper to some advance. An unofficial majority seemed to him a modest proposal, the more so since members selected from missionaries and others responsive to the native point of view would be unlikely to combine with the nominated European element in the way the Indian Government feared. But the position was safeguarded in any event by the High Commissioner's special powers of veto and of enacting legislation in this field over and above the head of the Legis-

---

*Gregory, *India and East Africa*, pp. 317–21.

†Viceroy to Secretary of State, telegram no. 199–5 (19 March 1929).

‡C.P. 39(29), Cab. 24/202.

§C.P. 66(29), Cab. 24/202.

lative Council, powers which would enable him to give equally effective protection to the Indians as well as the natives. Even so Amery was prepared to compromise by telling Wilson to try to secure either the provisions of the majority report, or at least a solution which did not give the unofficial Europeans a clear majority in Council.

On 6 March the whole matter, despite Amery's efforts, was remitted to a Cabinet committee, and something of the reason may be gauged from the comment of an unnamed Cabinet Minister at lunch that day: 'Why will Leo insist on answering every speaker at Cabinet? Why does someone not pull his coat and stop him?'* Peel had already argued that Amery's proposals were inconsistent with the Commissioners' report so far as the direction of policy in native affairs was concerned when the Cabinet met on 26 February, and he continued to put this point of view when the Cabinet Committee met on 12 March. At a subsequent meeting on 25 March Amery found himself in a clear majority (the Committee was composed of himself in the chair, Salisbury, Peel, Joynson-Hicks, Hoare and Ormsby-Gore) and the draft instructions were agreed. The Cabinet next day approved their instructions, but were less happy about proposed exchanges in the House of Commons. Amery, however, insisted that, if there was to be any prospect of agreement, the points of issue had to be made clear before the discussions in East Africa began. In the end it was agreed that he should 'stonewall' as long as possible, but that if he had not been forced to make the points at issue clear before Wilson landed, the latter should do so.

There was one final brush with Peel. The Viceroy had asked on 10 March that his Government be permitted to send a representative (Sastri) to East Africa to assist local Indians in presenting their views to the proposed High Commissioner. Effectively this revived an earlier proposal that the Indian Government should have an agent in East Africa, which Amery had turned down in December 1928 until he had talked with the Governors of Kenya and Tanganyika. In January 1929 Grigg had made it clear to Peel that the proposal reflected on him and would arouse European suspicion. However both he and Amery agreed to India having a representative on the Executive Council.† 'Your refusal of Grigg's offer puts us back where we were', Peel cabled Irwin in exasperation, 'and I do not know of any argument which I can use with Amery which he has not already considered and rejected.'‡ He suggested Sastri should simply be

*Jones, *Whitehall Diary*, II, p. 175. Hailsham, Cunliffe Lister, Churchill, Neville Chamberlain, Howe and Guinness were the Cabinet Ministers present.

†Secretary of State to Viceroy (18 December 1928) and to Government of India (25 January 1929); Viceroy to Secretary of State (22 February 1929), cited by Gregory, *India and East Africa*, p. 323.

‡Secretary of State to Viceroy (14 March 1929), cited by Gregory, *India and East Africa*, p. 325.

in East Africa when Wilson arrived, and said he would ask Amery to instruct Wilson to make all the use he could of him. Irwin continued to press his point in a telegram of 19 March, but he also put Peel's suggestion to Sastri, who refused to go on these terms. Eventually, as part of the final compromise, Amery allowed Sastri to have official status and let him accompany Wilson throughout his East African tour. He had already made it clear to Peel on 14 February that the common electoral roll was not practical politics, and he repeated this in conversation on 27 March, but in the end he allowed Sastri to press the point if he would say also that the Kenya Indians could only hope to obtain a common roll if they could secure European agreement. Amery had, however, already 'definitely instructed' Wilson against a common roll, and on 31 May the latter made it clear that the subject could not be reopened without the common consent of all the communities. The result was an Indian rejection of all proposals for closer union, and Sastri despaired of Wilson's ability to achieve a compromise.*

Of Wilson's return to England after the election and his report it is here enough to say that the compromise he recommended, although at first it found favour with the Labour Colonial Secretary, Lord Passfield, was eventually rejected by the Labour Government. At least part of the reason may be found in the continued opposition of the Indian Government, and it must be said that Amery's public pronouncements in May and June did little to still their fears. Reuters reported him as claiming that the 'mistake constantly made by people in authority at home was to regard themselves as the only champions of the natives, whereas in fact the actual destiny of the country rested upon the white settler', and he seems further to have repeated with approval to an African Society Dinner in June Churchill's notorious words that Kenya was to become 'a characteristically and distinctively British colony, looking forward in the full of fruition of time to responsible self-government'. To a Labour Government that dream seemed a nightmare and for all Passfield's efforts, the prospect of federation receded, never in practice to be realised.†

Diary

19 January 1929: Conference at the Treasury between Winston and Myself and Blythe and Costello on behalf of the IFS, first of all on Irish pensioners and then on Irish coinage. Winston began very cleverly by

*See Gregory, *India and East Africa*, pp. 328-9.

†For the later history up to but not including the abortive attempt post-independence in 1962-3, see A. J. Hughes, *East Africa: The Search for Unity* (Penguin, 1963).

flattering them about their beautiful new coinage and then drawing their views on the pensions though in ignorance he rather queered the pitch later by dragging in the general position of the P[rivy] C[ouncil]. However, I straightened this out and we very soon arrived at an agreement on the basis of the Free State fulfilling the PC's decision and our making good the cost as regards those already retired or retiring and concurrent legislation being passed affording satisfactory conditions though on Treasury terms for the serving men. As regards coinage we left this after a little preliminary skirmishing to the experts and adjourned to lunch at Kettner's where we all had some good talk under the influence of excellent food and drink. In the afternoon we had no difficulty in squaring up things. Meanwhile to fill in time I read some of Winston's proofs of his latest volume, dealing with the Irish situation after the war and under the generally friendly atmosphere of the successful negotiations and of my helpfulness over the proofs I made Winston find me the money for Bruce's Antarctic expedition which he had so far flatly refused.

21 January 1929: Cabinet at which we had a long discussion on the cruiser question, finally deciding to adjourn a little further the tenders for our two cruisers while the Americans are discussing their Bill. Then we had my proposal to inform the League of Nations that we regarded the Persian Gulf as outside their jurisdiction. This brought Austen out in utter horror reading aloud all the various clauses of the Covenant and generally suggesting that I was subverting the foundations of society. Douglas Hailsham supported him and in view of their attitude I dropped the matter but I think I had a lot of sneaking sympathy in the Cabinet and even Douglas afterwards told me that he really agreed on merits and thought the League a dangerous institution, but did not see how we could at this moment face the country with such a flouting of the League. Personally I think nothing would be more popular with everyone except the people who are against us any way. . . . Had a talk with Cameron whose only idea about the Hilton Young Commission is that its general principles should be formally approved and every Governor instructed to write an annual report showing how far he conformed with them and that an extra under secretary should be appointed here and visit East Africa from time to time and preside over Governors' Conferences. Otherwise he is all against any change. He is obviously going to be a real snag. . . . Belligerent Rights Committee in Austen's room at the FO. This time I rather got my own back on Austen and helped break up the absurd atmosphere of hypothetics under which he and Hurst are always assuming that in every war there will be somebody who has violated the Kellogg Pact or been declared the aggressor by the League of Nations.

Happily we got from this on to more technical and concrete grounds of the actual rules of war at sea and made some progress.

22 January 1929: Had a good talk with Grigg (about East Africa) which we carried further at lunch with Hilton Young at Brooke's, Sammy [Wilson] also being present. The provisional conclusions we got to were that Hilton's method of someone already armed with my executive powers going out and then increasing his powers on the spot was not really feasible and that what was necessary was for myself or a representative of mine to confer with Governors and local people in order to settle all the immediate powers a future High Commissioner should definitely be entrusted with. One solution was that local representatives should come and confer with myself here but in the end we felt that they would come with sealed instructions and nothing would be settled. The other was that someone, preferably perhaps Sammy himself, should go out to East Africa and preside both over Governors' and external Conferences and work out the details of whatever scheme we may have decided on.

23 January 1929: Cabinet at which the deferred attack on the EMB was renewed by Philip in a brief but comparatively mild form. I replied briefly and mildly but I think convincingly and the PM promptly followed endorsing my view. No one else spoke so Winston had to give way with rather a bad grace. He has a real dislike for Bruce and resents his having expressed his views on this matter. The next item was my attempt, renewed after three years, to get some sort of consideration for the unclaimed balances of our native carriers in East Africa during the war. Winston poured contempt on this and nobody except Salisbury was prepared to say a word for me. However, while the discussion was going on Austen seized the occasion to tell Winston he would back him if Winston would agree to the outstanding difference between us over the costs of our representative in South Africa. Winston agreed and so at any rate I snatched something out of the discussion. But it is quite absurd that on the nominal ground of finance, when only a few hundred pounds are involved, the Chancellor of the Exchequer should be able to withhold for months or give in a freakish mood things vital to the conduct of Imperial affairs.

25 January 1929: Held an Office Conference on the East African Report and made clear to them what I wanted to get out of it. In spite of the originally rather negative view of the departmental memoranda I found them all very willing to come along and they are now preparing a draft scheme for a High Commissioner with definite powers which I am to

discuss with the Governors and which Wilson is then to take out to
East Africa to discuss on the spot. . . .

29 January 1929: Had a talk with Hodgson, the Duke of York's P[rivate]
S[ecretary], about the desirability of the PM's having a talk to the Duke
and urging him to prepare himself for the possibility of his becoming a
Governor General before long. He tells me the young couple see nobody
except a few intimate personal friends, none of them interesting in the
political sense, and make no attempt to entertain or to prepare themselves
for more responsible work. I spoke to the PM in the afternoon and he
promised to take an early opportunity of rubbing the point in with the
Duke. . . .

Long talk with Cameron preparing him for the definite scheme of
East African federation which I want to put before the meeting of the
Governors on Thursday. I found him less uncompromisingly hostile
than I expected, and that I was right in assuming that the one part he had
feared most was the idea of a High Commissioner interfering in his native
policy. He went so far indeed as to say at one stage in our talk that as long
as his native policy was left uninterfered with he didn't mind who ran his
railways or fixed his customs. However, I have already had evidence that
he dislikes the scheme a good deal more than he said to me and it will take
a lot of steering to bring him along.

30 January 1929: Cabinet at which nothing of great interest came up
except the PM's proposed answer to the request by Mr Pugh [General
Secretary] of the Iron Workers for a commission of inquiry into the iron
and steel industry. This, worked up by David and Philip, was in fact an
offer of a safeguarding inquiry which could set to work at once. Winston
had already consented, and I was quite happy that this should go through
so smoothly and by universal consent without my having stirred a finger
except discussed the matter with David before Christmas. However,
Salisbury protested most vehemently against having the thing sprung
upon him and in the end a decision was postponed until the next Cabinet.

31 January 1929: Long Conference with Grigg, Cameron and Hollis –
the last a smiling spectator – at which we made very good progress with
the East African proposals. We are all clear that the High Commissioner
should be definitely over certain common services with full powers in
respect of them; he should have no powers of interference in native
policy, etc. except such informal power as he would get by acting as
chairman of the Governors' conference.

1 February 1929: Long Belligerent Rights Committee in Austen's room at the FO on the question of inserting a qualification in the arbitration treaty [with the United States] about Belligerent rights. Douglas explained that he had come round to the view that we should really do better if we signed the treaty without qualification and then tried to codify international law afterwards. The arguments were plausible and, with the one exception of Willie who looked very unhappy, we were all rather persuaded and instructed Salisbury to put it that way into the draft report. Since then I have rather come round again in my own mind and while inclined to favour an arbitration treaty without qualification should like to see it accompanied by a definite reservation of Belligerent rights pending the settlement of the question at a conference.

4 February 1929: Long and strenuous Belligerent Rights Committee. Having on the previous Friday rather favoured Hailsham's suggestion of accepting the unqualified arbitration treaty, disliking as I did the insertion into the treaty itself of a veiled reference to belligerent rights, I had subsequently come round to the view that the treaty itself should be unqualified but that we should accompany it by a reservation to the effect that we could not arbitrate belligerent rights until it had been more definitely settled what they were. This view rallied Willie Peel and Bridgeman and very nearly persuaded Salisbury, so that the Committee is fairly equally divided and we decided to state both views in the report.

5 February 1929: 2½ hours solid hammer and tongs on East Africa, Ned Grigg very strong that the thing could only go through with considerable sweetening, the two chief items being remission of the original Uganda railways debt, without which indeed a railway fusion might not be acceptable under the mandate, and the transfer to the High Commissioner of the Northern Provinces and possibly even of the coast or some of it.

6 February 1929: Cabinet. My proposal to stand firm against the Irish and South Africans on including a reference to diplomatic unity in the formula of an appointment of new Dominion ministers was approved of without discussion. The question of the answer to Pugh about iron and steel was raised again to give Salisbury an opportunity for saying that while he did not like the policy he had now read the document and thought his chief objection had been met. I remarked that there was after all no change of policy whatever, the only justification for starting a safeguarding inquiry now being that it would save two or three months of time, an important matter in an inquiry which might be so prolonged. Someone else suggested that a sentence should be added making clear that effect would not be given to the inquiry until after the election in any case. Thereupon Baldwin intervened with the amazing remark that he had assumed that there would always still be a separate safeguarding inquiry after the inquiry promised in his letter and that he would regard anything else as open to the charge of sharp practice. How he could have thought this in view of the actual terms of the letter passes understanding; hardly less so is the almost fantastic fear complex about being thought not to have interpreted any statement he has ever made on this question in its extremist negative sense. [L.S.A. marginal note: 'This was the spirit that finally lost the election.'] However, we all agreed at once that if that were the case there was no conceivable object in having the inquiry and Philip was told to draft a letter rejecting it. S.B. is really a queer creature. With all his great qualities and considerable shrewdness he sometimes just is not all there. I still think of the answer about Mosul which nearly destroyed our whole case at Geneva, and worse still, the appointment of Winston to the Treasury.

7 February 1929: Emergency Cabinet summoned to get Winston, now that the American Cruiser Bill is through, to find yet another reason for holding up the normal cruiser construction of the year. He quoted some figures of a new German vessel dwelling on all the factors of gunpower, range, etc. but omitting the fact that the speed was only 26 knots and urging this as a reason for postponing a year and building something much more up to date later. Willie replied pretty effectively and I followed up by pointing out that his argument was really too formidable being just as strong every year, and that it might be countered by saying that the later we postponed building, even if we are more up to date at the moment of launching, we should be correspondingly more obsolete at the end of the cruiser's life. The PM intervened with some shrewd observations and Winston was turned down. We also had Philip's new draft reply to Pugh with regard to iron and steel which was equally approved. . . .

Long confab with Grigg, Cameron and [J.H.] Thomas to try and put the latter wise as to the general lines we were proposing to work on and found him ignorant but not unreasonable. After that a long Belligerent Rights Committee at the beginning of which Austen sprung on us a couple of telegrams he was proposing to send to Washington in the hope of shaping Hoover's mind before he commits himself irrevocably to the demand for an early Belligerent Rights Conference. The second of these telegrams was avowedly dependent on the Cabinet's decision as to the policy to be adopted but I had to point out that the first preliminary telegram was no less so and in the end Austen consented to its being recast.

15 February 1929: Cabinet on proposed Arbitration Treaty and Belligerent Rights. Austen gave us a long dissertation but never got near the point of difference between the majority and minority views on the BR Committee, but sprung a new suggestion namely that BR should be arbitrated by a special court consisting of a British and American judge and our Chief Justices alternately. I set forth the case for the minority view and especially for consultation with the Dominions at a Conference. Hailsham followed with a vehement plea for the majority view which impressed the Cabinet much more than it did me. My real doubt is whether the safeguard of reference to Parliament is not a sufficient one. If it is I should be prepared to run the risk of all in arbitration.

. . . home with Philip who is very cross with Winston who has got some new stunt about a separate tax to be devoted to the reduction of railway rates.

19 February 1929: Had about one hour to think out what to say in introducing the supplementary estimate for the Irish Loyalists, not an easy matter as I was convinced that the Government's policy was wrong and indefensible. I got up in a small House chiefly occupied by Labour and our own Irish Die-Hards and stated the case for the Government as clearly and persuasively as I could though I could see that it carried no conviction. Winston complimented me warmly on the speech but I felt sure that the case was not going to be an easy one to sustain. Gretton followed quietly and earnestly and then one after another waxing more and more eloquent with a sympathetic House, mixing up these particular post truce loyalists with every injury suffered by Loyalists during the troubles and with the compensation given to rebels, the Whips growing more and more anxious all the time. I went in once to the PM and told him there was a storm on but that I was not prepared to advise him what to do as he knew already what my views were. Winston on the other hand seems to have gone in more than once and implored him to stand pat whatever the Whips might say and finally came back and delivered himself of a thoroughly intransigent speech, able but only irritating to the audience to which it was addressed. The moment he finished Hugh Cecil jumped up and made an effective but not really quite fair speech about compounding debts of honour at 60% and winding up with a passionate reference to the whole Irish settlement as an act of shame. A vain effort by Jack Hills to put the case for the Government only accentuated the general feeling of the Party and the Whips were running about saying that except actual Ministers we would not get a soul in the Lobby with us. S.B. was summoned, came in, got up almost at once and without arguing the case at all, very wisely, moved to report progress [a way of adjourning the House without a division]. It is curious how entirely Winston fails to understand the psychology of our Party especially on such a matter as Ireland where the fire is still there under the cinders all the time.

20 February 1929:   Cabinet . . . we got on to the happenings of the day before. Winston weighed in with an impassioned harangue on Rehoboam lines, let him state the case against this monstrous ramp to the full and with the Whips on he could carry the House or if not take the bump gloriously. I replied urging that the only course was payment to the full and that with the temper of the House no other would be of any use. I confined myself entirely to the present situation and refrained tactfully from reminding the Cabinet of the vehemence with which I had, almost alone, urged the necessity of this course last December and indeed a year ago. The Cabinet were clearly with me, but there were several attempts to try and find some compromise to ease things for Winston. Jix suggested that past recommendations should be paid in full but that for the future the committee was to be reconstituted on some more judicial lines with the right to the Government to be represented by Council (which as a matter of fact the Treasury has had all the time but refused to exercise). Winston suggested creating a judicial body to which claimants might go for their legal rights if they were not satisfied with the present scale under the Wood Renton Committee and I was surprised to find the Lord Chancellor made a similar proposal apparently not understanding that none of them have any legal rights. . . . As the tide went more against him Winston got very unhappy, delivered himself of another earnest harangue ending with an almost whispered declaration that he would have to consider whether he had not outlived his usefulness, and then sat for some minutes with his mouth very tightly pursed up to hold back his tears, which a good blow of the nose removed afterwards. Austen intervened with some soothing statesmanlike remarks and then the PM with infinite tact suggested that we could not come to a decision until the next Cabinet, that meanwhile he would ask Winston to consider whether there was any feasible alternative to complete giving way in which case he would certainly back him, but intimating very clearly that he himself believed that complete surrender was both the most graceful thing and the one which would leave least trouble behind.

. . . the satisfactory settlement of the Irish Civil Servants question has been completely submerged by the Irish Loyalists Grants over which the House was still buzzing. There was a very strong feeling against Winston in our party, and as regards myself I fancy considerable inkling in some quarters that I had not sympathised with the original Cabinet decision.

21 February 1929:   Winston recounted with glee our first meeting in Ducker and I described his first efforts at journalism subject to my censorship. He was in such good form that from that and his making no reference to the Irish Grants question as we drove down to the House together I conjectured that he had bowed to facts.

21 February 1929: During a division afterwards the PM showed me a draft reply accepting payment in full which I at once guessed Winston had himself written. So ends a critical breeze which has rather shaken Winston's position for the time being.

22 February 1929: To the House where the PM had convened Winston, Philip and myself to consider Worthy's scheme for making an election splash by announcing a great land settlement project on the Peace River. Winston criticised it purely negatively from a Treasury brief. I pointed out the practical difficulties which made it out of the question to treat it as an election matter and then went on to say that any real progress in Empire development or settlement could only be done if the financial machinery were right, i.e. if the matter were taken out of Treasury control and dealt with on EMB lines and I instanced some of the delays which the East African railway schemes have met with. Winston at once boiled up with furious indignation at any challenge to his departmental power and I was not able to carry things much further. He then launched out on a scheme of his for an open and unashamed subsidy of railway rates to help industries and agriculture generally. Philip poured considerable cold water on this and we departed for lunch, as you were, except that Worthy's scheme has evaporated. All the same I think S.B. is beginning to understand my point about the finance of Empire development.

26 February 1929: Office until 5.30 when we had a Cabinet. My East African thing came on and I was rather horrified to find them all somewhat negative and indisposed to doing anything. Peel naturally put the Indian point of view while Salisbury declared himself against federation in any form. However we had not discussed it more than about 20 minutes when the PM said he had to go to an early dinner and wished it adjourned until next Wednesday by which time I hope I may square my various opponents.

27 February 1929: Had three quarters of an hour talk with Neville firstly about East Africa, secondly about my ideas for securing freedom from Treasury control as the first condition of any money allotted to Empire development and lastly about the reconstruction of the Cabinet before the election. He agreed with me that it would be a good thing and created an element of novelty and interest which is very much lacking at present but he doubted whether S.B. would screw himself up to a decision sufficiently to do it. The cardinal point of course was Winston. We both agreed that nothing would help the situation more than if he could be moved; the only question was whether I suggested two possibilities; one the Presidency of the Council with a direct mission to co-ordinate the policy of the fighting services; Winston has hankered after this all his life, regarding it as a filial inheritance, and would be kept happy and busy planning wars in Afghanistan and elsewhere. The other alternative was if Austen's health should preclude his carrying on at the FO he might become President and Winston take his place. Neville thought that the PM would not run such a risk and would dread to find himself waking up at nights with a cold sweat at the thought of Winston's indiscretions. I suggested that Winston was not really in fact so rash as he was picturesque, that there were no really critical situations in foreign policy just now and that a little colour and vivacity would do no harm, and that my experience of Winston as a negotiator with his equals was that he was both skilful and reasonable. I told Neville that I thought public opinion would universally welcome him as Chancellor but he said that he was not himself at all keen on the job though he might have to take it if S.B. insisted. I gather that he would really like most of all my present position if I went elsewhere, and we agreed that I would be perfectly happy to go on where I am if he were Chancellor or he happy to take my place if I were Chancellor. He also asked me what I thought of Philip as a possible Chancellor to which I replied that I did not think he was liked by the House or had really got very great confidence from the business world and that a purely administrative bit of work like the War Office would suit him best. I added that I would sooner go to the Board of Trade myself where there was a good deal of independent work to be done than stay here with Winston at the Treasury and without a guarantee of at any rate five millions a year to spend in my own way. Neville thought that there might possibly be a vacancy at the Home Office as Jix might wish to take a peerage and retire on grounds of health but he thought the PM would wish to keep on Willie [Bridgeman] in the Cabinet.

4 March 1929: Talk with the PM on East Africa, Haifa–Baghdad railway etc. and then on to the theme of a long letter I had sent him to read over the weekend asking for the necessary financial freedom to carry out any policy of Empire development. I then urged the necessity of reconstituting the Cabinet, but not the rest of the Government, before the election. When I told him the thing that would help us most in the country would be shifting Winston from the Exchequer he asked me what my solution of the problem was. I told him that Winston's strongest emotion was respect for his father's memory and desire to complete anything his father put his hand to and that the co-ordination of the fighting services had been the dream of his life. At this moment Winston came in himself and we dropped the subject while Winston told us of his woes in the shape of a heavy fall in beer revenue and a nasty increase in the price of petrol. When he went out S.B. asked me to resume again and I sketched out how Winston might be kept interested and busy as President of the Council, Chief of the Chief of Staffs Committee, and generally active with the CID. As an alternative I suggested that Austen might go to the Presidency and Winston do F O where he would have a rare chance of spreading himself and giving life and picturesqueness to what Austen had made a deadly dull business, without at the same time really doing anything very rash.

5 March 1929: Cabinet at which East Africa was up again. I had had a long talk with Peel the evening before and thought I had really squared him. To my surprise he began with an insistent demand for postponement of any decision, the PM for some reason or other having suggested postponement to him, at least so he says, and I found an atmosphere of timid fear about doing anything, Sam Hoare being the only person who really effectively supported me. Even so I thought at one moment that I had got Winston's journey sanctioned though subject to further consideration of his instructions, but in the end the whole thing was remitted to the East African Committee over which I presided two years ago.

12 March 1929: Long meeting of the East African sub-committee. . . . My instructions to Wilson were generally acceptable but Willie Peel launched out into endless denunciation of my policy for varying the report of the Commission, obviously having been put to it by Mant.

14 March 1929: Had a talk with Sir W. Morris of Morris Cars and quickly got a thousand pounds from him for our Birmingham election funds after which we discussed things in general. He is terribly down on Winston for his incapacity to understand what the removal of the Horse Power Tax might mean for the motor industry. He is also today what he was not twelve months ago, ardently in favour of safeguarding steel, having begun to realise that our various industries must work together.

15 March 1929: Long talk with Warren Fisher about the succession to Lovat [whose retirement had been forced by ill health]. He agrees with me that the best thing would be a separate Ministry of Migration. The difficulty is to find the man. We discussed Betterton and one or two others. I also outlined very tentatively to him my ideas for the finances of Empire development to be administered as on EMB lines and found him unexpectedly sympathetic. He confessed he had been very definitely hostile to the EMB originally but had become a convert. At his suggestion I afterwards got Horace Wilson of the Ministry of Labour to come over to give me his confidential opinion on Betterton, which confirmed what I had thought namely that Betterton has every virtue except actual driving power, and is therefore not the ideal candidate though he might just do with a vigorous pushful Vice-Chairman.

16 March 1929: Read Winston's last volume, very readable and on the whole well-balanced and just in its judgment: it is a pity he should think it necessary to spoil so much good history in order to have the satisfaction of writing it up and vindicating himself afterwards.

20 March 1929: Cabinet at which FO attempt to run away from our whole Haifa [Baghdad] railway project at the first bark of the French poodle was frustrated. Spoke as much as was absolutely necessary but very ready.

21 March 1929: Talk with the PM about Lovat's resignation and concluded the best thing was to carry on provisionally with Plymouth as acting Chairman of the OSC, deciding after the election whether to have a separate Minister for migration, permanent chairman or what.

25 March 1929: E[ast] A[frica] Sub-Committee. I began by pitching very violently into Peel both for the character of the Indian intervention and for his own conduct in trying to get India to act as a stalking horse for changes in my instructions to Wilson really prompted by Mant. Delighted to find that both Jix and Sam Hoare were thoroughly with me and Peel was completely routed. Salisbury with the idea of making things easier for Peel proposed the dropping out of the phrase which I had inserted with that same object with the result that my original instructions have gone through in a somewhat stronger form. After that we spent some time in trying to draft satisfactory answers to possible supplementary questions on the Indian Franchise and ultimate self-government. These we fixed up but I am afraid the Cabinet this morning weakened on them and instructed me to avoid committing myself in any way if I could. Cabinets never realise that postponing difficulties invariably makes them worse.

26 March 1929: Cabinet. Here at Zermatt ten days later I cannot recall what it was about [Later L.S.A. note: 'How stupid of me: I got through my East African answer and S.W.'s instructions though told to avoid saying anything in answer to supplementaries.']

27 March 1929: Down to House . . . presently gave my answer about East Africa to Thomas. A pertinacious couple of supplementaries by Saklatvala [Labour MP for Battersea North] forced my hand about the Indian franchise, which was as well. I also told Peel, who is now clamouring for Sastri to go to E. Africa, that if he goes I must make it quite clear that no change in the basis of the franchise is possible. . . . Back to office and urgently asked to come across by Austen who was very distressed that our people didn't want to leave in French possession the whole detailed text of all our telegrams to Dobbs re TPC and Baghdad Railway. I said I thought it was more than enough to let them have a memorandum on the whole affair and let Tyrrell show Berthelot [of the French Foreign Office] copies of our telegrams. I left Austen almost in tears. [Amery was away in Switzerland until 7 April.]

8 April 1929: Morning at the office chiefly conference with S.W. and W. O.-G. about East Africa and more particularly Sastri. . . . After lunch renewed conference on Sastri with Sir L. Kershaw of the IO and got an agreement both as to the announcement to be made and as to its being accompanied by some press explanation which should incidentally make clear that the franchise is not to be altered except by common agreement.

Budgets are determined by Chancellors in conjunction with their Prime Ministers, and 1929 was no exception. Amery had wanted an increase in the sugar preference to help the sugar colonies and had seen Baldwin on 9 April, finding him 'friendly and elusive as usual'. In the event not only was nothing done on sugar but the tea duty was abolished, putting an end to a significant preference, which, as Amery later observed, upset a good many Empire preference men and probably did not help win a single seat.

Diary

10 April 1929: Cabinet at which Winston unfolded his Budget projects. Nothing very sensational on the positive side and an entire ignoring of the sugar issue about which I had to speak strongly with the result that a Cabinet sub-committee was appointed to look into it.

11 April 1929: Cabinet Sub-Committee under Philip to look into the sugar question met in my room at 10 and I had no difficulty in convincing them that the case of the sugar colonies was critical and urgent and that the extra 1/- preference should be given. On the other hand they were also convinced by a communication from Winston sent along by [P.J.] Grigg that it was too late to re-arrange the sugar schedules or to come to agreement with the refiners before Monday. Consequently sugar cannot figure in this Budget but has to be held over until the second Budget after the election and of course runs the risk of not being helped at all if we should be defeated. It really is outrageous that a case which completely convinced the Cabinet Committee should not have even been looked into by Winston and that his behaviour had prevented its being dealt with in time. I afterwards wrote a very strong letter of complaint to the PM of which I sent a copy to Winston. The matter was brought up at the Cabinet after we had listened to Austen meandering for half an hour or more about the Disarmament Conference, having in fact nothing to tell us. [L.S.A. marginal note: 'I ought really to have insisted on resigning and then they would have done it somehow.']

15 April 1929: Listened to Winston's Budget, a brilliant piece of exposition and chaff. But at heart very sick about the dropping of the preference with the tea duty and the whole of his finance of the last four years when summed up has been entirely mark time and unconstruction.

17 April 1929: Cabinet at which there was a perfunctory five minutes' discussion of the PM's election policy, he pleading that he wished to have time to concoct his speech, after which we dealt with a few more or less routine matters. It is astonishing how little time is ever given to any question of policy by the Cabinet as a whole.

18 April 1929: To the big Party meeting at the Drury Lane Theatre where the PM made his heralded statement reading out a certain amount of stuff from sundry dockets put together without much skill and ending on a more earnest note. In one way a very crude performance and yet not without artifice and striking an effective keynote, that of performance versus promise. On safeguarding he read out the rather lamentable letter to Monsell of last summer though it was the only subject except the mention of Neville's name which raised any real spontaneous cheer. Tea duty I noticed evoked no enthusiasm at the meeting or in Birmingham and I feel increasingly unhappy that I did not die in the last ditch rather than agree to its complete remission. He referred to some future independent committee to provide funds for colonial railways but in such a manner as to suggest nothing had been done at all in the colonies in recent years. I do not know why he did not consult me a little more closely before deciding on his actual wording.

24 April 1929: Cabinet at which the sugar question was postponed until after the election, Winston thoroughly hostile, Philip very helpful. My hope is that after the election I may have Neville and not Winston to deal with as Chancellor. Otherwise we mainly discussed the new American move on naval disarmament which on the face of it looks hopeful.

27 April 1929 (Birmingham): Primrose Day celebration, the big hall crammed full and very enthusiastic. I gave them a talk on Cobden, Marx and Disraeli, the sanguine theorist, the gloomy theorist and the statesman who was both realist and idealist and traced the influence of their thought since and their personification in the three parties today.

1 May 1929: Cabinet. Winston started by expressing the hope that the Wool Committee's report [advocating safeguarding] should be held over the election if possible, or if presented kept dark! He did it in a way which was rather offensive to Philip who replied with considerable asperity telling him that the report had already been received and was in favour of a duty. The decision as to publication was left until the next Cabinet but I cannot conceive our being so insane as not to make the fullest use of it, but it is obvious that Winston still means mischief.

2 May 1929: Hailsham's Committee for drafting the PM's election address. This is the first time for a good many years that I have not drafted the address myself but I am rather glad to be relieved of the task having so little real enthusiasm for the policy pursued.

3 May 1929: Spent the morning with Hailsham's Committee for which I had drafted some paragraphs on the Imperial side of things, Neville having already contributed a very good paragraph on Colonial development which the Treasury has since objected to because he proposed that the Colonial Secretary should be chairman of the Development Fund. . . . [Later] Worthy, Walter Elliot and I tried to reduce the verbose paragraphs on agriculture to something like English.

9 May 1929: Cabinet where we discussed whether the report in favour of the duty on woollens should be made public or not. Winston strongly against, Neville and myself for, Philip beginning for and wobbling afterwards, PM likewise. In the end it was left for the PM to consult the Central Office and they decided against. Very weak.

On the 11th Amery drove to Birmingham for the general election campaign, and clearly wrote up his diary afterwards. He spoke at East Wolverhampton, Salford, Macclesfield, Congleton, Wednesbury, Stonebridge and Bierley Hill in addition to meetings in Birmingham and his own constituency.

Diary

30 May 1929: Polling Day. Went three times round the whole division. All the workers in the Committee Rooms were more than satisfied all day but about seven Yates began to look anxious, the numbers coming out to vote were not as good as they should be and by the time the poll was finished I felt sure that the majority would be considerably less than before. At a guess I expected about 2000.

Large supper at the Queen's and then to the count. The first box or two looked very unpleasant and I began to wonder whether I was going to be in at all, but after the first half hour there could be little doubt. In the end when the piles were separated it was clear that I was fairly easily in and that Duggan was nowhere. Final result 15,800 odd for myself, 12,800 odd for Young, 5,600 for Duggan, my majority 2992. Bad rumours came in during the count of Austen's being beaten, and then of a recount which eventually got him in by 43. The recount at Ladywood left poor Lloyd out by eight. Presently we heard that Duddeston, Yardley and Aston [all Birmingham seats] had also gone badly and that we had re-captured King's Norton. We could see on the screen in front of our window the other results coming in. The last before we went to bed was Steel-Maitland with the news of his defeat.

3 June 1929: To the office where they were all pleased at my personal victory, but apprehensive as to what kind of successor they would get. . . . Cabinet at five o'clock: everyone very cheery and Winston most affectionate and congratulatory on my success. S.B. opened up by saying that after much consideration he had decided that his whole line at the election really pledged him to take the verdict of the democracy straight away and resign. Austen, while accepting the decision, urged that in his view we ought to stay and definitely fasten on the Liberals the odium of turning us out. Jix, Hailsham, Neville took the same view; Winston agreed with the PM more particularly because he did not wish to drive the 5 million Liberal voters into the Socialist camp. I took Austen's view, pointing out that of the 5 million 'Liberal' voters, less than one fifth represented Liberals elected, and most of the rest would leave the Liberal party once it had committed itself to putting the Socialists in office. On the whole opinion was fairly evenly balanced, but we all accepted the verdict without demur. Afterwards Winston took me out into the garden to ask if I thought I had left behind at the Admiralty any of the letters he wrote when as agent for the Shell he was trying to get us to sell the Anglo Persian Shares, a scheme which I defeated. He was in tearing spirits, looking forward to a holiday in Canada and USA. He said that on the

Liberal *cum* Socialist attack on the safeguarding duties he would be all with me. I replied that we should need more than a defensive attitude on this issue. We all parted very happily, voting ourselves the best government there has ever been, and full of genuine affection for S.B. If we can add to this mutual goodwill some real fighting spirit, generated in opposition, all may yet be well. Naturally I did not air any retrospective wisdom for my colleagues' benefit, but I remain convinced that our defeat has been due to our complete failure to have a policy which would create enthusiasts on our side. Winston's hostility to Empire development and safeguarding has paralysed us throughout and, in fact, made us just the type of Coalition Government which I tried to avert by the under secretaries' revolt of 1922. Looking back it is clear to me that Baldwin joined the revolt, not from any clear conception of policy so much as from a moral disapprobation of L.G. and all his works. What decided my action then was Austen's speech about the necessity for a combined anti-Socialist front; Lloyd George's morals worried me very little. Now in opposition I shall have to begin the battle over again to save us from an anti-Socialist coalitionism, and I fear that, except as regards L.G. himself, I shall not be able to count on S.B. as an ally. However, in opposition I shall be much freer to act directly upon the general body of opinion in the Party.

4 June 1929: Tried to get hold of Thomas to find that he was at a conference with his colleagues. Sent him a letter urging him to take the DO and CO as being a real man's job and with much more to do than either the FO or IO. He rung up later in the afternoon to tell me that my letter had determined him and I gather again from him this morning that it had been practically fixed up for him to go to the FO when he got my letter and reverted to what was his original inclination. . . . Derby Eve dinner at the Ambassadors Club. . . . F.E. made the usual amusing speech in which he described how he had been sent for to form a government by Lord Rothermere but that Lord Beaverbrook had insisted on coming round as having equally contributed to the destruction of the Unionist Government.

5 June 1929: Had a talk with Thomas about all the major problems before the office. He is very keen on my idea of the Development Fund and I primed him with my notions as to securing EMB financial control both for the Colonial Development Fund and for the OSO. The latter he talked of bringing into the Dominions Office but I think with no very clear idea of what exactly he meant by it. Anyhow he said he would not act precipitately. I also spoke to him very strongly about the sugar preference. On the general situation he had two interesting things to say, one 'that that [Lloyd George had] his own show and he hoped that

neither of us would help to pick him out of the mud'; the other was that
we had wrecked our chances by Winston's raiding of the Road Fund.
'It is certainly Winston that has killed you' was his final summary, and
one with which I could not but agree.

B. and I dined next door with the Griggs. He is rather depressed about
East Africa remaining unsettled for a new Government. Since then I've
seen Wilson's telegram to say that he has successfully squared everyone
except the Indians in favour of a scheme of closer union more or less on
my lines. That is a great justification both of my judgment of the problem
itself and of sending out so skilful a conciliator as Sammy. I only hope
the new Government won't wreck it. [Later L.S.A. note: 'They did.']
In the afternoon Thomas rang up to say all was off. His colleagues had
insisted on his taking up a new job as superintendent of employment. I
told him that this was a rope round his neck in Snowden's hands. He
said 'that —— Snowden shan't hang me!' But he and circumstances will.

Biographical Index

Where the more significant part of a person's career is covered by volume 2 of the diaries (1929–45), there is no reference in this index to biographical details after 1929, which will be included in the index to volume 2.

It should also be noted that the term 'Unionist' is used to describe MPs and candidates in this index for the years 1886–1918, when this term was generally applied. The term 'Conservative' is used for MPs and candidates active before 1886 and after 1918.

Abdullah, Ibn Hussein (1882–1951). As a reward for his part in the Arab revolt against Turkey, became Emir of Transjordan 1921–46 and then assumed the throne. Assassinated 1951. 402

Addison, Dr Christopher, 1st Viscount (1869–1951). Liberal MP 1910–22, Labour MP 1929–35. Parliamentary Secretary of Board of Education 1914–15 and to the Ministry of Munitions 1915–16, Minister of Munitions 1916–17 and of Reconstruction 1917–19. President of Local Government Board 1919 and Minister of Health 1919–21. 163, 234, 235, 256

Aden, Imam of. 540, 545, 563

Alexander, Major Sir Ulick. British Guards officer, subsequently Keeper of the Privy Purse to King Edward VIII. 205

Allemand, General de L'. French staff officer. 180

Allen, Sir John Sandeman (d. 1935). Conservative MP for Liverpool West Derby. 79, 505

Allenby, Field Marshal Sir Edmund,

1st Viscount (1861–1936). British general, commanded the Third Army 1915–17, and the Egyptian Expeditionary Force 1917–19. Captured Jerusalem, Damascus and Aleppo. High Commissioner for Egypt 1919–25. 179, 186–7, 202, 204, 234, 235–6, 263
in Egypt. 249, 392–3, 408, 432

Allenby, Viscountess. 206

Amery, Brydde (née Greenwood)
birth of sons. 85, 258
brother. 109
during First World War. 109, 112–13, 114–15, 117–18, 119, 123–4, 126, 128–32, 213, 240
Home Rule. 84, 100
letters from L.S.A. 77, 78, 84, 99, 100
life with L.S.A. 137, 252
marriage. 22, 60, 70–1
post-war. 267–8, 273, 275–7
tours. 263, 527
visits to Chequers. 349, 361

Amery, Mrs Elizabeth (L.S.A.'s mother), letters to. 23–7, 29, 32, 33, 37, 43–4, 45–6, 49
death. 59

599

Churchill, Sir Winston Leonard—*cont.*
  Imperial Conference 1926. 471, 472,
    473, 481
  Independent candidate. 372, 373, 374
  India. 16
  Iraq. 427, 428, 499, 505, 517
  Ireland. 278–9, 284, 286, 287, 416,
    428–9, 536
  Kenya. 581
  Palestine. 444–5, 505
  Parliament Bill. 81
  safeguarding. 421, 425, 426, 553, 561,
    564, 592
  Singapore, 549–50
  South Africa. 28, 372
  trade unions and General strike. 434,
    439, 451, 454, 485, 511
  USSR. 491, 500
  War Graves Commission. 496, 497,
    535, 537
  War Office. 251, 263, 269–70
Citrine, Sir Walter, 1st Baron (b. 1887).
  General Secretary of the TUC
  1926–46. 436
Clarendon, 6th Earl of (1877–1955).
  Chief Unionist Whip in the Lords
  1922–5. Under Secretary of State
  for Dominion Affairs and
  Chairman of the Overseas
  Settlement Committee 1925–6.
  Chairman BBC 1927–30.
  Governor General of S. Africa
  1931–7. 412, 471
Clarke, Sir George (1848–1933) 1st
  Baron Sydenham. Secretary CID
  1904–7. 40
Clarry, Sir Reginald (1882–1945).
  Conservative MP 1922–9 and
  1931–45. Managing Director of the
  Duffryn Steel Works, Glamorgan.
  356
Clayton, Brigadier-General Sir Gilbert
  (1875–1929). Adviser to Ministry
  of Interior, Egypt 1919–22 after
  service as Director of Military
  Intelligence, Cairo. Chief Secretary,
  Palestine 1922–5. Negotiated the
  Treaty of Jeddah disposing of
  difference between Britain and the
  Hejaz 1927. 206, 248, 552
Clemenceau, Georges (1841–1929).

French politician and war leader.
  Deputy 1875. Leader of anti-clerical
  Radical Party. Senator 1902.
  Prime Minister 1906–9, 1917–20.
  129, 238, 239, 267
Inter Allied Supreme War Council.
  179, 180–1, 182, 183, 184, 187,
  195, 196, 197, 203, 204, 208, 209,
  210–11, 213, 215, 223, 226
post-war. 254
Western front. 215, 221
Clementi, Sir Cecil (1875–1947).
  Successively Colonial Secretary in
  British Guiana 1913–22 and
  Ceylon 1922–5, he returned to
  Hong Kong, where he had served
  first in 1899 as Governor from
  1925–30. Governor of Straits
  Settlements and High Commissioner
  for Malay States 1930–4. 488, 489,
  494, 495, 498, 501–2, 570
Clerk, Sir George (1874–1951). British
  Diplomat. Ambassador to Turkey
  1926–33, France 1934–7. 188
Clifford of Chudleigh, Charles, 11th
  Baron (b. 1887). Succeeded his
  father 1943. Descendant of the
  signatory to the secret Treaty of
  Dover, 1670. 541
Clifford, Sir Hugh (1866–1941). Malay
  Civil Service and Colonial Service.
  Governor of the Gold Coast
  1912–19, Nigeria 1919–25, Ceylon
  1925–7 and the Straits Settlements
  1927–9. 380, 411, 523
Clyde, James Avon. Liberal MP. Lord
  Advocate 1916–20. 216
Clynes, John Robert (1869–1949).
  Labour MP 1906–31, 1935–45, and
  Chairman of the Parliamentary
  Labour Party 1921–2. Lord Privy
  Seal 1924. Home Secretary 1929–
  31. 364
Coates, Joseph Gordon (1878–1943).
  Prime Minister of New Zealand
  1925–8, subsequently serving in a
  Coalition Government 1931–4 and
  the Dominion War Cabinet
  1940–3. 463, 467, 472, 476, 478, 526
Colebatch. West Australian Agent
  General in London. 397

Creedy, Sir Herbert (1878–1973).
Permanent Under Secretary at the
War Office, 1924–39. 283

Crewe, Robert, Marquess of
(1858–1945). Liberal Cabinet
Minister. Ambassador to France
1922–8. 346

Cripps, Charles A., 1st Baron Parmoor
(1852–1941). Unionist MP, who
was Labour Lord President of the
Council 1924 and 1929–31. Father
of Stafford. 80

Croft, Sir Henry Page, 1st Baron
(1881–1947). Conservative MP
1910–17 and 1922–40, holding his
seat as founder of the strongly
imperial National Party 1917–22.
Under Secretary for War 1940–5.
Created Baron 1940. Strong
advocate of tariff reform. 91, 534,
555, 558, 564

Cromer, Rowland, 2nd Earl of,
(1877–1953). Lord Chamberlain
1922–38. 457

Cromer, Countess of. 457, 567

Cronje Piet. Boer general. 34

Crowe, Sir Eyre (1864–1925). Assistant
Under Secretary of State, Foreign
Office 1912–19, a plenipotentiary
at the Paris Peace Conference 1919,
and Permanent Under Secretary
of State, Foreign Office 1920–5.
345, 384

Cuninghame, Sir T. 49

Cunliffe-Lister, Sir Philip, 1st Earl of
Swinton (1884–1973). Conservative
MP 1918–35. Assumed name
Cunliffe Lister in place of Lloyd-
Greame 1924. Parliamentary
Secretary to the Board of Trade
1920–1, Secretary, Overseas
Trade Department 1921–2,
President of the Board of Trade
1922–4, 1924–9, and 1931.
Secretary of State for the Colonies
1931–5 and for Air 1935–8.
Cabinet Minister Resident in West
Africa 1942–4. Minister for Civil
Aviation 1944–5. Chancellor of the
Duchy of Lancaster and Minister
of Materials 1951–2. Secretary of

State for Commonwealth Relations
1952–5. Viscount 1935. Earl 1955.
198, 294, 295, 299, 302, 308, 311,
329, 345, 380, 400, 419, 421, 425,
441, 444, 449, 492, 496, 497, 502,
543, 587, 593
Board of Trade. 350, 363
Conservative Party. 366, 559
election 1923. 353, 355
EMB, 573, 583
Imperial Economic Conference 1923.
347, 348
Imperial Economic Conference 1926.
473
Naval Air Wing. 322, 323
safeguarding, 339, 413, 548, 549, 579
tariff reform, 341, 349, 351, 360, 376,
518

Cuno, Dr Wilhelm, Chancellor of
Germany 1922–3. 306

Currie, General Sir Arthur (1875–1933).
Commanded the Canadian Corps
1917–19 in Flanders. Subsequently
Principal and Vice-Chancellor
McGill University 1920–33. 223,
250

Curtis, Lionel George (1872–1955).
Member of Milner's Kindergarten.
Town Clerk of Johannesburg
1902–3. Assistant Colonial
Secretary 1903–9. Founder of
Round Table and editor 1909.
Founder of the Royal Institute of
International Affairs. Professor of
Colonial History at Oxford 1912.
Attended Paris Peace Conference
1919. Secretary to the British
Delegation at the Irish Conference
1921 and Colonial Office adviser
on Irish Affairs 1921–4. 11, 67, 253,
376, 390, 506

Curzon, Francis (courtesy title Lord
Curzon) 5th Earl Howe (1884–
1964). Conservative MP 1918–29
and a Junior Lord of the Treasury
1924–9. 337

Curzon, George Nathaniel, 1st
Marquess (1859–1925). Junior
minister 1891 and 1895–8. Viceroy
of India 1899–1905. Lord Privy
Seal 1915–16. President of Air

Hiley, Sir Edward. Town Clerk of
Birmingham, Government official.
143
Hills, Major J. W. (1867–1938).
Conservative MP 1906–22, 1925–38.
Financial Secretary to Treasury
1922–3. 64, 157, 319, 587
Hilton Young, Sir Edward, 1st Baron
Kennet (1879–1960). Liberal MP
1915–26. Conservative MP
1926–35. Financial Secretary to the
Treasury 1921–2. Secretary for
Overseas Trade 1931. Minister of
Health 1931–5. Chairman of the
Commission on Closer Union of the
Dependencies in Eastern and
Central Africa 1927–8. Indian
Commission. 521, 568, 575–6,
577–81, 582, 538
Hindenburg, Field Marshal Paul von
(1847–1934). German Commander-
in-Chief of the General Staff of the
German Armies 1916–19. President
of the German Reich 1925–34. 115,
136, 409
Hirst, Sir Hugo (1863–1943). 1st Baron.
Managing Director 1900–43 and
Chairman 1910–43 of General
Electrical Company. 439
Hitler, Adolf (1889–1945). Chancellor
and Führer of Germany 1933–45.
16
Hoare, Sir Samuel, 1st Viscount
Templewood (1880–1959).
Conservative MP 1910–44.
Assistant Private Secretary to
Rt Hon. A. Lyttelton 1903–5.
Member LCC 1907–10. Secretary
of State for Air 1922–4, 1924–9,
and 1940, for India 1931–5, for
Foreign Affairs 1935 and the Home
Office 1937–9. First Lord of the
Admiralty 1936–7. Lord Privy
Seal and member of the War
Cabinet 1939–40. Ambassador to
Spain 1940–4. 16, 299, 314, 315,
316, 319, 320, 321, 322, 323, 324,
338, 421, 499, 502, 540, 545, 552
Air Ministry. 401–2
East Africa. 580, 591
elections. 388

France, pact with. 383, 384, 399, 418
House of Lords. 486
Iraq. 306, 426, 432, 440, 516
1924 Shadow government. 366,
367–8, 374
1925. 391, 396, 408, 409
reparations. 350
tariff reform. 351
Hobhouse, L. T. (1864–1929). Liberal,
then Labour publicist. First
professor of sociology of London
University 1907–29. 133
Hodges, Frank (1888–1947). Labour
MP 1923–4. Secretary of the
Miners Federation 1918–24 and
of their international federation
1921–9. 439
Hodges, Admiral Sir Michael. 365, 369
Hogarth, D. C. Arabist; friend of T. E.
Lawrence. 330
Hogg, Douglas. See Hailsham
Hogge, J. M. (1873–1928). Liberal MP
1912–24. 215
Holdsworth, Sir William S. (1871–1944).
Vinerian Professor of Law, Oxford
1922–44. 571
Holland, Sidney (1893–1961). New
Zealand National Party MP
1935–57. Leader of Opposition
1940–9. Prime Minister 1949–57.
526
Hood, Sir Alexander F. Acland. 1st
Baron St Audries (1853–1917).
Unionist MP 1892–1911. Whip.
72, 74
Hoover, Herbert. President of the
USA, 1929–33. 586
Hope, J. F. 1st Baron Rankeillour
(1870–1949). Conservative MP
1900–6, 1908–29. Junior Lord of
Treasury 1916–19, other offices
including Chairman of Ways and
Means 1921–4, 1924–9. 63, 86, 161
Hopkins, Sir Richard (1880–1955).
Chairman, Board of Inland
Revenue 1922–7. 58
Horne, Sir Robert, 1st Viscount
(1871–1940). Conservative MP
for the Hillhead Division of
Glasgow 1918–37. Third Civil
Lord of the Admiralty 1918–19,

Jacob, Sir Claud—*cont.*
India 1925–6, Secretary of Military
Department, Government of
India 1926–30. 396
Jameson, Rt Hon. Andrew. Irish Free
State Senator. 428
Jameson, Sir Leader Starr (1858–1917).
President of the British South
African Company. Administrator of
Rhodesia 1891–5. Led raid on
Transvaal 29 December 1895,
captured, tried in London and
imprisoned. Member of Cape
Legislative Assembly. Prime
Minister of Cape Colony 1904–8.
54, 56, 58, 66, 115, 127, 393
Jellicoe, Sir John R., 1st Earl
(1859–1935). Various naval
commands. Second Sea Lord of the
Admiralty 1912–14. Commanded
Grand Fleet 1914–16. First Sea
Lord 1916–17. Governor General
of New Zealand 1920–4. 143, 144,
223, 365
Jutland. 317, 331, 340
War Policy Committee. 157–8, 160, 161
Joffre, Joseph, Marshal of France,
French generalissimo 1911–
December 1916. 199
Jones, Dr Thomas (1870–1955).
Deputy Secretary of the Cabinet
1916–30. 318, 343, 362
diaries. 385, 437, 578
Joubert, General Petrus (1834–1900).
Boer commander in early part of
South African War. 28
Joynson-Hicks. *See* Hicks, Sir W.
Joynson

Kellaway, F. G. (1870–1933). Liberal
MP, 1910–22, Postmaster General
1921–2. 75
Kellogg, Frank B. (1856–1937). US
Secretary of State 1925–9. 542
Pact. 534, 543–4, 553, 556, 582
Kemal, Mustafa (1881–1938). Known
as Ataturk. Turkish Nationalist
leader. First President of the
Turkish Republic 1922–38. 280,
291, 292
Kent, Sir Stephenson (1873–1954). 255

Kerensky, Alexander F. (1881–1968).
Russian Minister of Justice and
then of War 1917. Head of the
Provisional Government after the
March 1917 Revolution. 197
Kerr, Philip. *See* Lothian
Kershaw, Sir L. (1869–1947). Senior
Civil Servant, India Office. 588
Keyes, Admiral of the Fleet Sir Roger
(1872–1945). 1st Baron. Deputy
Chief of Naval Staff 1921–5. 315,
323, 335
Keynes, John Maynard, 1st Baron
(1883–1946). Economist and Civil
Servant. Principal Treasury
representative at the Peace
Conference 1919. Editor of the
Economic Journal 1911–44. 169, 245,
534
Khanum, Surma. Religious leader of the
Assyrian Christians in Iraq. 405
King, Sir Alexander. Chief Secretary of
the Post Office in 1912. 87
King, William Lyon Mackenzie
(1874–1950). Canadian Liberal MP
1908–11, 1919–49. Minister of
Labour 1909–11. Leader of the
Liberal Party 1919–48. Prime
Minister and Minister for External
Affairs 1921–6, 1926–30, 1935–46,
and Prime Minister 1946–8. 54,
282, 294, 348, 354, 382, 446, 448,
452, 454, 459, 462, 463–4, 503,
528–9, 536, 566, 567
Imperial Conference 1926. 465, 470,
471, 472, 473, 484, 475, 476, 477,
478, 479, 480, 484, 485, 487
Kipling, Rudyard (1865–1936). Author
and poet, cousin of Stanley
Baldwin. 34, 35, 48, 171, 361, 415,
569
First World War. 115, 258
Kirkwood, David, 1st Baron
(1872–1955). Labout MP 1922–51.
415, 519
Kitchener of Khartoum, 1st Earl,
Horatio Herbert (1850–1916).
Various military and
administrative posts in Egypt
1882–98. Commanded Khartoum
expedition 1898. Chief of Staff

Lindsay, Sir Ronald—*cont.*
Foreign Office 1928–30. Ambassador to the United States 1930–9. 440, 447, 456

Linlithgow, Victor Alexander John Hope, 2nd Marquess of (1887–1952). Succeeded his father in 1908. Civil Lord of Admiralty 1922–4. Deputy Chairman, Conservative Party Organization 1924–6. Chairman, Royal Commission on Agriculture in India 1926–8. Chairman, Joint Select Committee on Indian Constitutional Reform 1933. Viceroy of India 1936–43. 17, 412, 450

Lister, Philip Cunliffe. *See* Cunliffe-Lister, Sir Philip

Lloyd, Blanche. Daughter of the Hon. F. Lascelles. Married George Lloyd 1911. 516

Lloyd, George, 1st Baron (1879–1941). Conservative MP 1910–18, 1924–5. Attached to Arab Bureau 1916–17. Governor of Bombay 1918–23. High Commissioner in Egypt 1925–9. Created Baron 1925. Secretary of State for the Colonies 1940–1. 92, 374–6, 406, 420, 591
Egypt. 411, 456, 459, 474, 516, 567
First World War. 103, 104, 105, 106, 202
India. 374–5, 394, 398
Kenya. 398, 399, 400–1

Lloyd George, David, 1st Earl (1863–1945). Liberal MP 1890–1945. A leading opponent of the Boer War, he served as President of the Board of Trade 1905–8 and Chancellor of the Exchequer 1908–15 and was the author of the People's Budget 1909. Minister of Munitions 1915–16. Secretary of State for War 1916. Precipitated the ministerial crisis of December 1916 and served as Prime Minister of a Coalition Government 1916–22. His section of the Liberal Party was reunited with Asquith's in 1923, and from 1926 to 1931 he led the Parliamentary Liberal Party, finally breaking with

them over their support for the National Government in 1931. 60, 79, 261, 267, 313, 358, 443
Admiralty. 288, 289
and Amery. 117, 125, 181, 288
Balfour. 221, 222, 247, 285
Budget 1909. 59, 235
career. 57, 71, 75, 127, 131, 190, 196, 219, 288, 343, 344, 377, 567
election 1918. 244, 246–7
election 1922. 272, 302
election 1924. 388–9
election 1929. 597
emigration. 256, 257, 258, 289
Empire Development. 292
First World War. 111, 169, 174–5, 192, 193, 222, 224, 238, 331;
Austria. 155–6; Greece. 147, 148, 162, 165; Imperial War Cabinet. 144, 147–9, 152–4, 220, 226, 228, 229, 232; Inter Allied War Council. 168, 178–9, 181, 182, 183, 184, 187–8, 191, 195, 197, 202–3, 215; manpower report. 198–9; munitions. 115, 118; National Service. 125, 125, 145, 165; Palestine. 159, 169, 196, 201, 204; Peace. 152–3, 239; propaganda. 140, 142, 167; Russia. 164–5; territorial changes. 155–6; Turkey. 165, 182, 566; War Cabinet. 145, 163, 215, 334; War Policy Committee. 158, 159–60, 161, 167, 172; X Committee. 220, 223, 227, 228
governments: War. 127, 132, 135, 137, 163, 164, 165, 166, 207, 215–16, 218–20; 1918–22. 276, 277, 280–1; defeat. 282, 283, 290–1, 292, 294; 1924. 379
and W. M. Hughes. 255
Ireland. 156, 157, 212, 216, 217, 232, 279
Marconi case. 86, 93, 118, 171
and Milner. 240, 241–2, 247, 249–50, 254
Pembroke. 388–9
St Katharine's Dock. 87
strikes and unemployment. 454, 534
tariff reform. 13, 83, 341, 342, 343
Trade Committee. 289, 290, 291
Unionist Party. 284, 288, 366, 562

McCurdy, Charles A. (1870–1941).
Liberal MP and Chief Coalition
Liberal Whip 1921–2, subsequently
chairman of the directors of
Lloyd George's *Daily Chronicle*
1922. 7, 153
Macdonald, Murray. 157
MacDonald, James Ramsay (1866–1937).
Labour MP 1906–18, 1922–31 and
National Labour MP 1931–7.
Secretary of Labour Representation
Committee (subsequently the
Labour Party) 1900–11, Treasurer
1912–24, Chairman of the
Parliamentary Labour Party
1911–14. Leader of the Labour
Party 1922–31. Prime Minister
1924, 1929–35. Lord President of
the Council 1935–7. 15, 106, 371,
452, 454, 557
Campbell case. 360, 379, 387
Labour governments. 307, 358, 359,
363, 364, 397
Macdonogh, Lt Gen. Sir George
(1865–1942). Director of Military
Intelligence 1916–18. Adjutant
General to the Forces 1918–22.
President of the Federation of
British Industries 1933–4. 141, 142,
143, 182, 183, 201
McDougall, F. L. Australian
representative on the Imperial
Economic Committee. 1969–73.
395
MacGilligan, Patrick J. Irish Free State
Minister for Industry and
Commerce 1924–6 and
subsequently Minister for External
Affairs until 1932. 545
McKenna, Reginald (1863–1943).
Liberal MP 1895–1918. President
of the Board of Education 1907–8.
First Lord of the Admiralty
1908–11. Home Secretary 1911–15.
Chancellor of the Exchequer
1915–16. Chairman, Midland Bank
1919–43. 79, 118, 124, 126, 302,
322, 339, 345, 350
Chancellor. 329, 341–2
tariffs. 339, 341–2, 349, 375
McKinder, Sir Halford (1861–1947).

Geographer and politician. First
Reader in Geography at the
University of Oxford 1887–1905,
Principal, University College
Reading 1892–1903. Director of
London School of Economics
1903–8. Unionist MP for Glasgow
Camlachie 1910–22. British High
Commissioner for South Russia
1919–20. Chairman of the
Imperial Shipping Committee
1920–45 and of the Imperial
Economic Committee 1925–31.
11, 49, 56, 65, 86, 300–1, 412, 443,
473
Maclay, Sir Joseph, later 1st Baron
Maclay (1897–1951). Glasgow
ship-owner, Minister of Shipping
1916–21. 139, 182
Maclean, Sir Donald (1864–1932).
Liberal MP 1906–22 and 1929–32.
President of the Board of
Education 1931–2. 375
MacMahon, Sir Henry (1862–1949).
High Commissioner Egypt 1914–16.
249
Macnaghten, (Sir) Terence Charles
(1872–1944). Civil Servant. Vice-
Chairman Overseas Settlement
Committee 1918. Assistant Secretary,
Dominions Office. Administrator of
St Kitts and Nevis 1929–31. 246,
255, 395, 539, 559, 567
McNeill, Ronald. *See* Cushendun
MacNeill, Dr J. G. Swift (1849–1926).
Irish Nationalist MP 1887–1918.
Professor of Constitutional Law,
National University of Ireland
1909–26. 157, 385, 426, 427
Macready, General Sir Nevil (1862–
1946). Adjutant-General, British
Expeditionary Force, France,
1914–16. Adjutant-General to the
Forces 1916–18. Commander-in-
Chief, British forces in Ireland
1920–3. 197, 198, 199
Madden, Admiral of the Fleet Sir
Charles (1862–1935). Chief of Staff
to the Commander-in-Chief Grand
Fleet 1914–16. Second in
Command Grand Fleet 1916–19.

O'Connor, T. P. (1848–1929).
Journalist and Nationalist follower
of Redmond. MP for the Scotland
Division of Liverpool 1885–1929. 56

O'Haggarty, Dermot. Secretary to the
Provisional Government 1922
and Commandant of the Irish Free
State Army 1922–30. 428

O'Higgins, Kevin (1892–1927). MP
(Sinn Fein) 1918–22. Minister of
Home Affairs, Irish Free State
1922–3. Vice-President and
Minister of Justice 1923–7. 424,
465, 467, 470, 472, 476, 477, 479,
482, 483, 485, 512–13
assassination. 515, 516

O'Malley, Sir Owen (1887–1974).
Counsellor at the British Embassy
in China 1925–7, where he
negotiated the Hankow agreement
with Dr Chen. Permitted to resign
from the Foreign Office, after an
enquiry into currency speculation
in 1928, but subsequently
reinstated and had a distinguished
diplomatic career. 489, 491, 495, 497

Oldham, Revd J. H. (1874–1969).
Secretary, International Missionary
Council 1921–38. A member of the
Hilton Young Commission. 509, 576

Oliver, Frederick S. (1864–1934).
Author of *Alexander Hamilton*
1906, *Federalism and Home Rule*
1910, *Ordeal by Battle* 1915, and
The Endless Adventure 1930–5. Also
an extremely successful businessman
with Debenham and Freebody.
57, 60, 61–2, 66, 79, 127, 143, 145,
147, 152, 156, 159, 161, 164, 167,
178, 200, 207, 208, 212, 217
Economic Offensive Commission. 181
Imperial 'moot'. 68–9, 70
letter to Amery. 123
and Lloyd George. 71
'Pacifus' letters. 60, 70

Olivier, Admiral of the Fleet, Sir
Henry (1865–1966). Second Sea
Lord 1920–4 and Commander-in-
Chief Atlantic Fleet 1924–7. 336

Olivier, Sir Sydney, 1st Baron (1859–
1943). Colonial civil servant, who
became Governor of Jamaica.
Secretary of the Fabian Society
1886–9. Secretary of State for India
1924. 578

Orlando, Vittorio. Prime Minister of
Italy 1917–19, described as 'virtually
dictator in Italy'. 183, 201, 202, 226

Page, Sir Earle (1880–1962). Leader of
the Australia Country Party 1919–34.
Commonwealth Treasurer 1923–9.
Deputy Prime Minister 1934–9
and Prime Minister 1939. 524

Painleve, Paul (1863–1933). French
Minister of War 1917, 1925–6.
Prime Minister 1917 and 1925.
Minister of Air 1930–1, 1932–3.
168, 178, 182

Pankhurst, Dame Christabel (d. 1958).
Daughter of Mrs Emmeline
Pankhurst, and a founder and
leader of the women's suffrage
movement. 80, 125–6

Parker, Sir Gilbert (1862–1932).
Traveller, author and Unionist
MP for Gravesend 1900–18.
Chairman of the Imperial South
African Association. 63

Parkin, Sir George (1846–1922).
Canadian educationalist. In 1902
became first organizing secretary of
the Rhodes Trust. 149

Passfield, 1st Baron, Sidney Webb
(1859–1947). Fabian social reformer
and historian. Progressive member
of the LCC 1892–1910. Founder
of the London School of Economics
1895 and of the *New Statesman*
1913. Member of the Labour Party's
National Executive 1915–25 and
Labour MP 1922–9. President of
the Board of Trade 1924. Baron
1929. Secretary of State for the
Dominions and Colonies 1929–30
and for the Colonies 1930–1. 11,
41, 76, 581

Pease, H. Pike, 1st Baron Daryngton
(cr. 1923) (1867–1949).
Conservative MP 1898–1910,
1910–23. Assistant Postmaster
General 1915–22. 290, 294

Thomas, Sir Godfrey (1889–1968).
Private Secretary to Prince of
Wales, subsequently Edward VIII
1919–36. 388, 409, 410, 544

Thomas, James Henry (1874–1949).
President 1905–6, organizing
secretary 1906–10, and assistant
secretary 1910–13 of the
Amalgamated Society of Railway
Servants. Assistant secretary
1913–16 and general secretary
1917–31 of the National Union of
Railwaymen. Labour MP 1910–31
and National Labour MP 1931–6.
Colonial Secretary 1924. Lord
Privy Seal 1929–30. Secretary of
State for the Dominions 1930–5.
Secretary of State for the Colonies
1935–6. 390–1, 435, 451, 472, 508,
586, 592, 597, 598

Thompson, Sir William (Mike)
Mitchell-, 1st Baron Selsdon
(1877–1938). Conservative MP
1906–32. After holding junior
office Post Master General and
Chief Civil Commissioner 1924–9.
296, 542

Trenchard, Sir Hugh, 1st Viscount
(1873–1956). Marshal of the RAF.
Commanded the Royal Flying Corps
in France and became the first
Chief of Air Staff 1918. Resigned
after a dispute with Rothermere,
and took over the command of
long-range bombing forces in
France. Chief of Air Staff 1919–20.
Commissioner of the Metropolitan
Police 1931–5. 263, 314, 320, 322,
422, 443, 494, 499, 501, 563, 572

Troubridge, Admiral (1862–1926).
Commander in Mediterranean
1913–16. Served Serbian government 1916–19. 160

Tyrell, Sir William, 1st Baron (1866–
1947). Principal Private Secretary
to Sir Edward Grey 1907–15.
Assistant Under Secretary at the
Foreign Office 1918–25. Permanent
Under Secretary 1925–8.
Ambassador to France 1928–34. 105,
141, 431, 493, 593

Tryon, G. C., 1st Baron (1871–1940).
Held junior office. Minister of
Pensions 1922–4, 1931–5.
Postmaster General 1935–40. 377

Tyrwhitt, Admiral of the Fleet, Sir
Reginald (1870–1951).
Commander-in-Chief China
1927–9. 489, 490, 495–6

Ullswater, James Lowther, 1st Viscount
(1855–1949). Unionist MP 1883–5,
1886–1921. Speaker of the House
of Commons 1905–21. Chairman
of Royal Commission on
Proportional Representation 1918,
of the Lords and Commons
Committee on electoral reform
1929–30, and of many others. 302,
308

Unden, Dr Osten. Foreign Minister of
Sweden and member of the
Council of the League. 402, 403,
430, 431

Venizelos, Eleutherios (1864–1936).
Cretan and Greek patriot. President
of the Cretan National Assembly,
set up after the rising against the
Turks in 1897. Prime Minister of
Greece 1910–15, 1917–20, 1924,
1928–32 and 1933. 112, 129, 148,
182, 183–4, 293

Wake, Brigadier Sir Hereward. British
staff officer, Supreme War Council.
193, 202, 208, 213, 240

Walker, General Sir F. W. Forestier.
British officer commanding in
South African War. 33

Wallace, Euan (1892–1941).
Conservative MP 1922–3 and
1924–41 who subsequently held
junior and Cabinet office in the
1930s. 370, 390, 477

Walsh, Stephen (1859–1929). Labour
MP 1906–29. Parliamentary
Secretary to Ministry of National
Service 1917 and to Local
Government Board 1917–19.
Secretary of State for War 1924.
128–9

Williams, Sir Herbert G.—*cont.*
director of the Empire Industries
Association. 356
Williams, Rhys. 261, 262
Willingdon, Freeman Freeman-Thomas,
1st Marquess of (1866–1941).
Liberal MP and Whip. Created
Baron 1910. Governor of Bombay
1913–19, Madras 1919–24. Created
Viscount. Governor General of
Canada 1926–31. Created Earl.
Viceroy of India 1931–6. 409, 410,
452, 456, 457, 459, 528–9
Willingdon, Lady. 458, 562
Willoughby de Broke, Richard Verney,
19th Baron (1869–1923). Unionist
MP for Rugby 1895–1900.
Succeeded father 1902. 81, 84, 86,
97, 98
Wills, Gilbert. 564–5
Wilson, Sir Henry, Field Marshal
(1864–1922). Director of Military
Operations at Army Headquarters
1910–14. Assistant Chief of
General Staff to Lord French 1914,
Liaison Officer with the French
1915, Commander Eastern Military
District 1916, British Military
Representative at Versailles 1917,
Chief of the Imperial General Staff
1918. 12, 45, 69, 70, 127, 207, 266
and Amery. 115
murder. 279, 287–8
defence. 94, 97, 102
First World War. 103, 104, 105, 106,
107, 108, 124, 125, 126, 162–3,
165, 190, 192, 215, 222, 224, 230–2,
235, 238, 288; Inter-Allied Supreme
War Council. 167, 176–7, 179,
180–1, 182–3, 184–5, 187, 188, 196,
201, 204, 208, 210–11, 215, 225;
Note 14. 195; X Committee. 212
Ireland. 96, 109, 217, 279
Wilson, Sir Horace J. (1882–1972).
Permanent Secretary, Ministry of
Labour 1921–30. Chief Industrial
Adviser 1930–9. Permanent
Secretary of the Treasury and
Head of the Civil Service 1939–42.
436, 591
Wilson, Col. Sir Leslie (1876–1955).

Conservative MP 1913–23.
Commanded the Hawke Battalion
RND at Gallipoli and in France
1915–16. Parliamentary Assistant
Secretary to the War Cabinet 1918.
Chief Unionist Whip 1921–3.
Governor of Bombay 1923–8 and
Queensland 1932–46. 281, 286, 293,
294, 295, 297, 299, 300
Wilson, Sir Samuel (1873–1950).
Assistant Secretary, Committee of
Imperial Defence and secretary,
Overseas Defence Committee
1911–14, 1918–21. Governor of
Trinidad and Tobago 1921–4, and
Jamaica 1924–5. Permanent Under
Secretary, Colonial Office 1925–33.
394, 411, 414
East Africa. 576, 577, 579, 581, 583,
592, 593, 598
Wilson, Woodrow (1856–1924).
President of the United States
1913–20. Founder of the League of
Nations, which the US Congress
then declined to join. 153, 171,
212, 222, 224, 230, 238, 239, 241,
249, 254, 258
Wimperis, H. E. (1876–1960). Director
of Scientific Research, Air Ministry
1925–37. 256
Wingate, General Sir Reginald (1861–
1953). Egyptian Army from 1883.
Sirdar of the Egyptian Army and
Governor General of Sudan
1899–1916. High Commissioner in
Egypt, replaced by Allenby
following unrest 1919. 249
Winterton, 6th Earl (1883–1962).
Conservative MP for Horsham
1904–51. Under Secretary for
India 1922–4, 1926–9. Cabinet
Minister 1938–9. 86
Wiseman, Sir William (1885–1962).
Businessman and head of British
Intelligence in USA during First
World War. 254
Wolmer, Viscount. Succeeded father as
3rd Earl of Selborne 1942.
Conservative MP 1910–40. Junior
Minister 1922–4, 1924–9. Minister
of Economic Warfare 1942–5. 162

Index of Places

Index of Subjects